DANIEL HERAUD

CARNET DE ROUTE / ROAD REPORT INC.

Legal deposit: 4 th quarter 1999
Bibliothèque nationale du Québec
Bibliothèque nationale du Canada

Print and bounded in Canada

ISBN: 1-895100-05-4

SUMMARY

CARS AROUND THE WORLD

ALL MODELS SOLD IN THE USA
BY CATEGORY IN
18 COMPARATIVE TESTS

Apples and oranges...

For a number of years now, Road Report readers have been asking us to include comparative road tests, like "the others". I was never enamoured with the idea because I felt that it was completely illogical and irrational to choose haphazardly as the focus for each yearly publication a single category from among the 20 or so that compose the automotive market in North America. In and of itself, the formula is interesting, especially from the perspective of a buyer's guide, designed to help consumers compare models that are in direct competition with each other. The performance statistics and characteristics found at the end of each chapter in this publication are a unique way to evaluate various models in a very precise way. However, over time the initial suggestion had an effect, as did reader opinion surveys. So to mark the new millennium, this 15th edition of Road Report is entirely organized by category, even as it continues to feature all of the key elements that have ensured its success throughout North America. The approach is one I used for five years in the New Car Guide published by Auto-Trader, another popular publication. When the title was withdrawn in favour of the Recreational Vehicle Guide, a gap was created and this is the reason why I decided to apply the concept to the New Cars Road Report.

Why opt for such an innovation? Because the present publication will be followed next spring by a Used Cars Road Report, an all-new publication applicable to NAFTA countries: the United States, Canada and Mexico. And like the New Cars edition, it will be available in

Spanish and with metric measurements! Progress is unstoppable. Computer systems are a major step in making technical publications easier to compile and with the exception of the final printing stage, our team is able to handle all aspects of such projects, be it illustrations and photographs or databases updated regularly and consistently as test drives are completed and as models are unveiled. Another indication of the changing world of communications, you can now visit our www.road-report.com Web site free of charge for additional information made available throughout the year or to order additional copies, cassettes, T-shirts, sweatshirts or jackets featuring your favourite guide's emblem.

Thanks to strong distribution in the United States with Barnes & Noble, in Canada with Firefly Books and our relationship with Microsoft's CarPoint and to the loyalty shown by our readers, Road Report occupies an enviable position on the North American publishing market.

Thank you for showing a level of enthusiasm that has brought me my greatest satisfaction as a journalist and automotive expert and has inspired me to devote countless hours to achieve the objectives set 15 years ago!

I look forward to our rendezvous in the next millennium and I trust that we will all travel toward it safely and responsibly.

Daniel Heraud

CREDITS

Cover page: Cadillac EVOQ by R.J.
Author's picture: Jacques Grenier
Credits for photos in these pages: Lyse Paquet, Benoit Charette, Michel Condominas, Gérard Heraud, Daniel Heraud, Jean D'Hugues and from the manufacturer's press services.

Chief Editor:	Daniel Heraud
Coordinator - proofreader:	Lyse Paquet
Technical proofreader:	Jacques Gervais
Layout:	Denis Heraud
Translation:	Brenda O'Brien
Sales figures - prices:	Benoit Charette
Cover design:	Imagidée
	Scan Express Inc. (Michel Beaudoin)
Printing:	Québécor Inc. (Michel Tessier)

INTERNATIONAL COLLABORATORS

Germany:	Helmut Herke
Canada:	Sammy Chang
France:	Michel Condominas
	Gérard Heraud
United-States:	Alan McVicar
Great-Britain:	Nick Bennett
Italy:	Andréa Andali

SPECIAL THANKS

To produce this edition of *Road Report*, we had to count on numerous individuals working in the automotive and publishing fields. To all of those whether close by or far away, who have participated in the creation of this book, a sincere and grateful thank you.

Factual information pertaining to the automobiles listed herein, specifically information under the headings "Engine", "Transmission", "Performance", and "Specifications", has been supplied by the manufacturers of such automobiles and the author, publisher, and distributor of this book can accept no responsibility for the accuracy or completeness of such factual information. The commentary and recommendations contained herein are made to the best of the author's knowledge. Author, publisher and distributor accept no responsibility for any loss or damage caused by the use of any of the materials contained in this book, and they explicitly disclaim any and all guarantees.

INDEX BY CATEGORY

Identification of the make and of the model(s).

Evaluation classified by decreasing order of pros and cons following the vehicle's test drive.

Flag of builder's country of origin.

Manufacturer's logo.

Basis of evaluation for rating all the vehicles according to the chart presented on page 7 and according to manufacturer's data plus all the results of our team's road-tests. Each analysis is divided in specific sections for a better understanding.

Updated modifications for the current model year.

Main equipement available for the leading versions of a model as well as available colors for the exterior body and interior setup.

Main available powertrain, engines, transmissions, as well as their computer-calculated performance recorded during our road-tests.

Historical facts, demographics, sales figures, market share, regular maintenance.

IMPORTANT WARNING

• This book is put together with preliminary information given by the manufacturer's during the summer season preceding the arrival on the vehicles on the market. The difference between our data and those of the official catalog's of the company published in the fall season does not constitute a mistake but simply a change they often make without warning. All the information is accurate at the time of printing.

• The manufacturers hold the responsability to provide us with press material about their current product line. Their cooperation is essential in order for us to complete our road-tests so that we can publish accurate reports.

• The data compiled in this book is gathered from preliminary information made available by manufacturers the summer preceding the car's entry into the market. The discrepencies observed between our figures and those published by the manufacturers in the fall or throughout the year do not necessarily constitute flawed data but simply changes made without prior notice.

Color codes

Europe

Asia

America

The marks are explained as follows:

The insurance premium has been established for a person 35 years of age, married, living in a metropolitan area, without any accidents in the last six years and no driver's license suspension. The base premium for $1 million of property and personal liability, with a $ 250 collision and $50 multiple risks deductibles.

The depreciation risk is calculated based on our "Used car guide" for three years. If the vehicle exists for less than three years, the number of years follows in parenthesis.

The cost per mile is calculated by category. It is based on the use of the vehicle during a three-year period at the rate of 12,000 miles per year and includes the insurance rate, registration costs, interest rate, fuel cost, tire wear, maintenance and repairs, depreciation and parking costs.

Road Report is written simultaneously for Quebec, Canada and the United States. It is therefore possible that some models shown will not exactly conform to those sold locally.

TYPES OF ENGINES

H	Horizontal cylinders
L	In-line cylinders
V	V cylinders

FUEL SUPPLY

EFI	Electronic fuel injection
MPEI	Multiple point electronic injection
MI	Mechanical injection
SFI	Sequential injection (multiple point)
TBI	Throttle body injection
EMI	Electronically controlled mechanical injection
RI	Rotary diesel injection
TR or TBO	Turbocharger
Ti	Turbocharger plus intercooler
S	Supercharger

TRANSMISSIONS

M4;M5;M6	Manual 4-speed; 5-speed; 6-speed
A3;A4 A5	Automatic 3-speed; 4-speed; 5-speed
2WD	2-wheel drive
4WD	4-wheel drive

MODELS

cpe	coupe
sdn	sedan
wgn	station wagon
van	van
p-up	pickup
a-t	all terrain
2dr	2-door
3dr	3-door
4dr	4-door

SIZES

cyl	cylinder
cu.ft	cubic feet
hp	horsepower (SAE)
in	inches
ft	feet
lbs/ft	torque: feet-pounds
L	volume in liter
db	sound level in decibels
mph	miles per hour
mpg	miles per gallon

OTHERS

*	original equipment or standard
#	not available at print time
NA	not available
NR	not recommended (towing)
HD	heavy duty
Cd	air drag coefficient / Compact Disc
dc	disc
dr	drum
ABS	anti-locking brake system
TCS	traction control system

SUSPENSIONS

si	semi-independent
r	rigid rear axle
r&p	rack and pinion
pwr	power assisted
ball	recirculating ball steering
	sector and roller

2000 EVALUATION CHART

Notes in %	0	10	20	30	40	50	60	70	80	90	100
CONCEPT											
Technology:	drag coefficient		platform		powertrain			engine		materials	
Safety: NHTSA	structures		doors	environment		seat-belts	air bags				
Interior space: EPA cu.ft	57	64	70	78	85	88	92	99	106	113	120
Trunk: EPA cu.ft	3.5	5.5	7	9	10.5	12.5	14	16	17.5	19	21
Quality/fit/finish:		appearance			assembly			materials			finish
DRIVING											
Cockpit:		seat		visibility		commands		controls			
Performance: 0/62 in s.	16	15	14	13	12	11	10	9	8	7	5
Handling: lat. G force	0.66	0.68	0.70	0.72	0.74	0.76	0.78	0.80	0.85	0.90	0.95
Steering:	ratio		precision		calibration		assist		return		
Braking: 62 to 0 in ft.	215	200	180	165	150	130	125	120	110	105	100
ORIGINAL EQUIPMENT											
Tires: grip:	dry		wet	winter		comfort		noise			
Headlights:	range		brightness	efficiency		antifog					
Wipers:	coverage		speed		intermittent		kind of blade				
Rear defroster:		area covered			speed						
Radio:	MA/MF		cassette	Cd	sound quality		power		richness		
COMFORT											
Seats:		seat		lateral support		back support			padding		trim
Suspension:		damping		amplitude		roll			pitch		frequency
Sound level: dBA	73	72	71	70	69	68	67	66	65	64	63
Conveniences:											
Air conditioning:		quicknest		distribution		hot		cold	power		commands
BUDGET											
Price: $ US	30,000	27,000	24,000	21,000	18,000	15,000	12,000	10,500	9,000	7,000	6,000
Fuel economy: l./100	20	18	16	15	14	13	12	11	10	8	6
Insurance:% of retail price	16	14	12	10	9	8	7	6	5	4	3
Satisfaction:	5	10	20	30	40	50	60	70	80	90	100
Depreciation: %	100	90	80	70	60	50	40	30	20	10	5

ABS : Initials for anti-locking brake system. This system detects and prevents wheel lockup during hard braking. Sensors at each disc or drum brake detect a sudden speed decrease indicating the beginning of lockup. Fluid pressure to that brake is reduced and reapplied at the rate of several pulsations per second till the wheel regains rotation speed. The sophistication of these systems varies between makes. Some are mechanical, others detect deceleration and lateral G-forces (centrifugal force in a turn) to prevent spinouts or large shifts in direction: always possible with more simplistic devices.

ADJUSTABLE STEERING COLUMN: Changes the angle of the steering wheel or its length, to accommodate the driver.

AIR DAM: A device to deflect air, usually under the front bumper or other locations. It can be fixed or movable.

ALL-WHEEL DRIVE and 4-WD: All wheels, front and rear, provide traction. A differential splits the torque between the front and rear axles.

ALTERNATOR: The belt-driven alternator supplies current for ignition, battery charge, AC and other accessories.

AUTOMATIC TRANSMISSION: Automatic shift change: offering 3, 4 or 5 ratios is also set up for holding the transmission in lower gears for torque or grade retard.

BAGGAGE COVER: Cloth or cover to conceal baggage in coupes, sedans or station wagons.

BODY BELT LINE: Artificial line dividing the sheet metal lower body from the glazed upper body.

BORE/STROKE: Dimensions that allow figuring the cylinder displacement. The bore is the diameter of the piston and the stroke is the distance it travels. Displacement formula is B/2 squared X Pi X S X number of cylinders = volume. Keep consistent measurements, inches or centimeters, to get cubic inches or cc volume. of the engine displacement

CAMBER: Lateral wheel angle, relative to a vertical plane, to compensate for tire roll in the turn.

CAMSHAFT: A steel part with lobes to operate intake and exhaust valves either directly or through rocker arms. It is gear, chain or belt-driven.

CARBURETOR: Meters fuel in proportion to the air needed by the engine and controls the air through one or more throttle blades.

CASTER: Forward or rearward inclination of the steering axis.

Cd: Coefficient of drag of the automobile body, usually measured in a wind tunnel. Multiply the Cd by the frontal area to get a comparison index from car to car. The lower the number, such as .029 , the higher the efficiency.

CLUTCH: Couples or disengages the engine and the transmission.Has one or more discs engaging by friction. Many clutches are used in automatic transmission. The clutch action can be timed for progressive engagement.

COMPRESSION RATIO: When the piston is at the bottom of its stroke, the cylinder and combustion chamber are filled with air. The ratio between that and the combustion chamber volume is the compression ratio. Higher compression ratio improves combustion efficiency. Supercharged or Turbocharged engines may need a lower nominal compression ratio, while a Diesel needs 22:1 compression to initiate ignition.

COMPRESSION STROKE: After intake, the piston moves up to compress the airfuel mixture. More compression improves efficiency: the fuel octane limits the maximum compression that can be used.

CONNECTING ROD: The part which connects the piston to the crank. The rod conveys the alternating piston motion to rotary crank motion and vice versa.

CONTROLLED SHOCKS: The shock settings can be externally changed by an electronic control.

COUPE: 2-volume body with 2 main seats and 2 mini-seats, and a sports look.

CRANKSHAFT: The crankshaft turns on main bearings and has offset journals, just like a bicycle crank, to transform the alternating piston motion to a rotary motion.

CYLINDER HEAD: The part over the block which contains the combustion chambers and intake valves, as well as intake and exhaust ports. It carries the valves and valve train parts.

CYLINDERS: The barrel-shaped part of the block in which the piston forms a moving wall and which is closed off at the top by the combustion chamber. Cylinders can be laid out IN-LINE, in V6 or V8 or horizontally opposed (BOXER) as in VW Beetle or Subaru.

DIESEL: A denser fuel than gasoline. It requires much higher compression ratios to spontaneously ignite. *Cetanes*, not octanes, rate Diesel fuel and is a measure of ignitability under compression, while octanes measure the resistance to ignition due to compression. A direct injection sprays into the cylinder. Glow plugs may be used but not a conventional ignition or fuel injection into the manifold.

DIFFERENTIAL: The gear train which allows the drive wheels to turn at different speeds up when going around a corner. You will find differentials in the front and rear drive trains in the 4WD, while transmitting torque to both wheels, as well as in the transfer case.

DISC BRAKE: The disc turns with the wheel and the caliper with pads applies friction for efficient stopping power. *Ventilated disc:* Fins between the 2 sides of the disc circulate air and cool the disc. Disc brakes work at very high temperatures and cooling is important.

DOHC: One cam operates the intakes, the other the exhausts, which allows timing refinements.

DRIVE RATIO: Determines the final drive ratio between the transmission output and the drive wheel rpm. Numerically higher ratios make the engine turn faster. More wear, but also more power.

DRUM BRAKE: A drum turns with the wheel. Shoes with friction-lining material rub against the drum and retard it during brake application.

ELECTRONIC IGNITION: Electronic ignition replaces points and may also control timing in conjunction with the computer.

ENGINE TORQUE: The turning effort delivered by the engine at any given rpm. Torque is pull on a moment (lever) arm, given in lbs/ft. or in m/kg. 1.0 lb/ft = 0.1382549 m/kg. Pulling on a wrench applies torque to the bolt.

FLOOR PAN: Bottom of the car, which also includes reinforcing and suspension mount members.

FUEL INJECTION: Atomizing the fuel under pressure, as it exits from a nozzle, so it can mix with air.

FULL-TIME 4WD: All 4 wheels always driving.

GAS SHOCK: May use gas pressure to prevent foaming up of the fluid or to produce additional lift. On some shocks, electronic controls adjust damping. In a suspension a spring temporarily stores, then releases energy and the shock absorber dissipates: damps out - energy and converts it to heat.

GRILL: Decorative air inlet to the radiator and engine.

HEAT EXCHANGER: A heat exchanger is used to transfer heat from engine oil or transmission oil or a power steering to the engine coolant or to ambiant air.

HYDRAULIC SHOCK: Uses internal oil forced through orifices by the motion of a piston in a cylinder to generate daming forces.

HYDROPNEUMATIC SUSPENSION: Uses gas pressure to maintain and adjust height, and fluid to control damping.

INDEPENDENT SUSPENSION: Each wheel moves independently of the other.

INDIRECT INJECTION: Used on Diesel engines with a pre-chamber to improve ignitability. *Jets* are calibrated orifices to meter fuel.

KNOCK SENSOR: Detects combustion noise and is used in conjunction with the computer to alter spark or fuel supply. See *Octane*.

LEAF SPRING SUSPENSION: A stack of flat leaf springs of decreasing lengths connects to the axle at a spring pad and pivots on the frame or body. Since the leaf gets longer when it deflects, a swing shackle compensates for the length change.

LIMITED SLIP DIFFERENTIAL: A device which limits the rpm difference between 2 wheels by engaging a clutch or other coupling.

LOCKING DIFFERENTIAL: It can lock the 2 output shafts to each other. *Viscous coupling:* A clutch filled with high viscosity silicon to increase the lockup as the difference in rotation speed increases.

MACPHERSON: Independent suspension with a single lower control arm, connected to a housing with a shock absorber and a coil spring. The upper portion of the shock pivots on the unit body. There are modified MacPhersons with upper and lower control arms, as on the Honda, which maintain better camber control when the car leans in a turn.

MANIFOLDS, INTAKE AND EXHAUST: Castings or tubular assemblies with the passages that connect each cylinder to the intake or exhaust side of the engine. Their shape can have a large affect on performance.

MANOMETER: One way to measure air or fluid pressure.

MANUAL TRANSMISSION: Provides a choice of gear ratios to match car speed with engine speed. The driver selects the gear ratio through cable or rod controls and couples the pair of gears needed to the input and output shafts, while disengaging the clutch to interrupt power flow.

MASTER CYLINDER: Part of the brake system, when the driver applies pedal pressure it provides the pumping action to deliver fluid to the individual wheel cylinders, drum or disc.

MECHANICAL INJECTION: A pump controls the fuel delivery. *EFI*: Electronic fuel injection. *MPI* or *EMPI*: Electronic multiple injection. SFI: sequential fuel injection, each cylinder fed in turn according to firing order.

MODULATION: How well the driver can control the brake or steering, so that the input force results in a proportioned output.

MULTIFUEL ENGINE: Engine capable of utilizing several types of fuel.

MULTIVALVE ENGINE: Engine with 3, 4 or more valves per cylinder.

OCTANE: The fuel's ability to resist detonation (knock) or preignition.

OIL PAN: The section under the engine which holds the oil supply and the oil pump.

OVERDRIVE: In the manual or automatic transmission, a final drive ratio that is higher than 1 to 1. The engine is turning slower than the transmission output shaft. Great economy but no acceleration.

OVERHANG: What extends behind the rear wheels or ahead of the front wheels.

OVERSTEER: The vehicle has a tendency to turn at a tighter radius than steering wheel input and at the limit the rear is kicking out. During oversteer, the driver applies reverse lock to the steering to keep from spinning out.

PANHARD ROD: It provides lateral control by connecting the body to the opposite side of the axle housing. Now the back of the car can't swing out on a turn.

PART-TIME 4WD: A differential or a slip coupling divides the power between the front and rear. Usualy includes a lockup feature.

PUSH ROD ENGINE V6/V8: A cam which runs inside the block operates the valves through lifters, pushrods and rocker arms, in succession.

QUARTER PANELS: Side body panels at the backlight, trunk and rear wheels.

RAILS: Lengthwise sections in the chassis or unit body, U, C or box-shaped. They are generally tied in by cross members.

RIGID SUSPENSION: The 2 wheels are connected by a rigid axle. On a rear-wheel drive car, the rigid axle includes the differential.

RACK-AND-PINION: Two hypoid gears at right angles to each other that transfer power from a drive shaft sitting lengthwise to the differential and the axle shafts of the rear wheels. It also provides a final drive gear ratio. The pinion is powered by the driveshaft and the ring gear drives the differential.

ROTARY ENGINES (WANKEL - MAZDA): A rotor controls intake and exhaust and moves eccentrically within the housing to complete intake compression and exhaust in one turn.

SEDAN: Body with 2 or 3 volumes and 2, 3, 4- or 5 doors offering 4 to 6 seats.

SERVO: Another word for assistance. The driver's input is multiplied by allowing it to control an outside power source.

SHOCK ABSORBER: Controls the amplitude (travel) and speed of suspension and wheel travel due to road undulations and also partially controls body movements such as roll, pitch, loading and unloading. Shock absorbers cannot substitute for larger springs or stabilizer bars.

SHOULDER BELT: Upper part of safety belt harness.

SIDE VALVE ENGINE: Used on antique, in-line and V8 engines with side valves (valves next to the cylinder as in an old Ford).

SKIRT: Air deflector along the side of the car.

SOHC: Single overhead cam located in the cylinder head. It may operate the valves through cup followers or through rocker arms and controls both intakes and exhausts.

STABILIZER BAR: Long torsional bar connecting a pair of wheels and the body to limit roll during the turn. It does not support the car vertically, but stabilizes it by opposing roll.

SUPERCHARGER: A crank-powered belt or chain drives an external pump (supercharger), which feeds air to the engine to increase output, compared to a naturally-aspirated engine (the piston pumps its own air). There are Roots blowers (Ford Thunderbird SC) or spiral blowers (VW Corrado).

SYNCHRONIZATION: During the shift in a manual transmission, a small internal cone clutch equalizes gear and synchro sleeve speeds so engagement can be completed without grinding.

TIMING BELT DRIVE: A toothed timing belt that powers one or more cam shafts: flexible, quiet, doesn't require outside lubrication. When one breaks, you require a new engine.

TIMING CHAIN: A chain of either roller or toothed type that drives one or more cam shafts.

TIRE ASPECT RATIO: Speaks of the ratio of the height to the width of the tire cross section. Example: 185/60 R 14: the 60 says that 60 percent of 185 mm width is the height. Less than 60 percent (low profile) helps handling; larger than 65 percent gains comfort.

TOE-IN: A steering geometry designed to have the wheels tip toward each other.

TOE-OUT: The same, but with the wheels toeing away from each other. It is equally important at the front and as the rear.

TORQUE CONVERTER: A hydraulic coupling used with automatic transmissions to provide slip, as with a manual shift clutch, and to multiply torque.

TORQUE TUBE DRIVE: A tube or an arm extends forward from the drive wheel axle housing to near the center of the body to handle axle windup torque. An antique last seen on Opels, Vegas and early Fords, but very effective.

TORSION BAR SUSPENSION: A torsion bar is a straight coil spring. The bar works in twists: one side fixed in the frame and the other connected to the suspension arm. Most torsion bar suspensions offer initial ride height adjustment.

TRACTION CONTROL: Often combined with ABS to apply braking to the wheel that shows traction loss, which restores torque transfer to the opposite wheel.

TRANSFER CASE: Used on 4WD vehicles to shift into 2WD, N or 4WD in High or Low range.

TRANSMISSION HOUSING: The outer case of the transmission which contains the shafts, gears, clutches (automatic) and the transmission fluid.

TUNNEL: A long, tunnel-shaped section of the floor pan, in the middle of the car, makes room for the drive shaft and sometimes the exhaust.

TURBOCHARGER OR SUPERCHARGER HEAT EXCHANGER: Same concept. Either of the two devices adds heat. By cooling, the temperature of the air delivered to the engine is reduced and efficiency improves.

TURBOCHARGER: A form of supercharger which is driven by the engine's exhaust instead of by a crank-driven belt. It adds power, can add efficiency and is used not only in sports car performance but in big, Diesel trucks.

UNDERSTEER: At the limit, the vehicle is understeering when it tries to go out nose first; during understeering you need to increase the steering wheel angle.

UNIT BODY: The body, floor pan and various reinforcing sections combine into a single, structural shell as opposed to a separate frame and body connected by mounts.

VALVE: Works like a sink stopper, this mushroom-shaped part with a long stem is closed by a spring and opened by a cam shaft. Intake valves admit air, exhaust valves let out burned gases.

VENTURI: Senses air flow. The carburetor is designed to atomize the fuel, mix it with the air so the engine can burn it to make power. The number of throttle plates in the carburetor decides the number of barrels. A 2-barrel has 2 venturis, 2 throttles.

WASTE GATE: A valve controlled by intake manifold pressure which bypasses some of the exhaust to stay within pressure limits tolerated by the engine.

WHEEL RIM: Retains the tire.

Road Report.com

You are cordially invited to visit our brand
new web site on the Internet at:

http://www.road-report.com

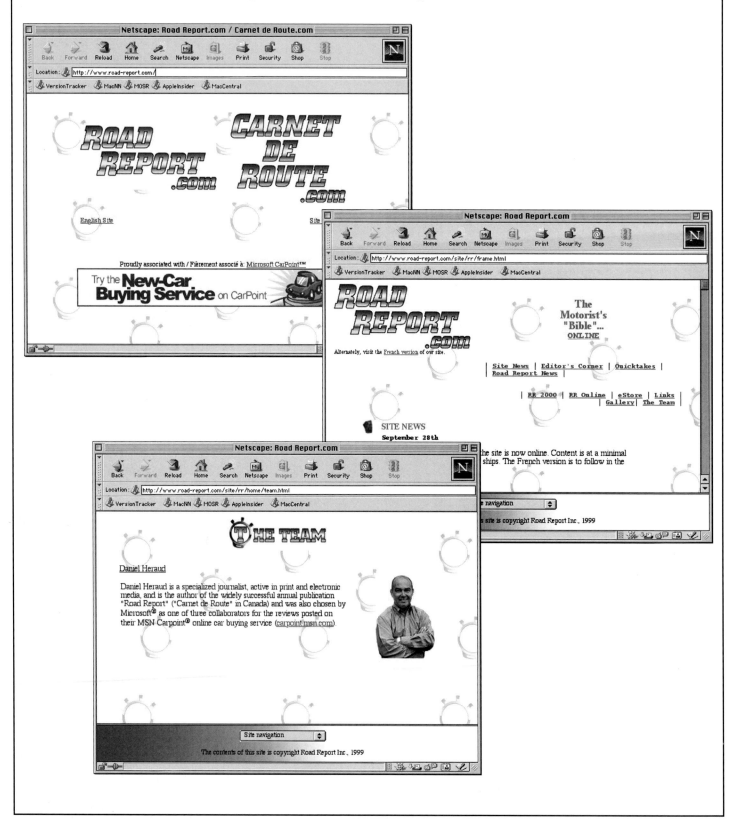

TECHNICAL

HONDA

Honda decided on the Detroit Auto Show to unveil its VV hybrid prototype, billed as the vehicle with the best fuel economy in the world. Scheduled to enter standard production in early 2000, the coupe does 70 mpg and complies with California's ULEV (Ultra Low Emission Vehicle) regulations. Its engine is a 1.0L 3-cylinder equipped with VTEC valves. It recharges a battery that powers an electric engine designed to take over from the gasoline alternative whenever needed. Ignition and fuel supply are managed by an onboard computer that also adjusts rpm levels.

Technical

VOLVO

This Swedish builder has always been a safety pioneer. It recently celebrated the 40th anniversary of three-point seat belts, developed specifically for Volvo in 1958 by engineer Nils Bohlin (pictured above).

Since a high number of traffic accidents result in a cerebral trauma, Volvo engineers developed a system (opposite) designed to prevent head and spine injuries. Known as WHIPS, for Whiplash Protection Study, it uses the seat's inclination to counter injuries to the neck area. The S80 model (below) features no less than 80 microprocessors. To cut down on wiring needs, they are designed to interact via a Multiplex system.

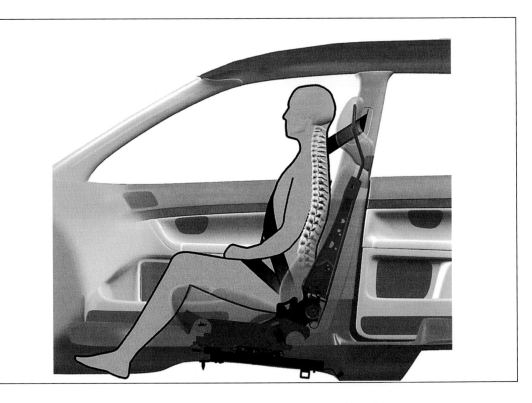

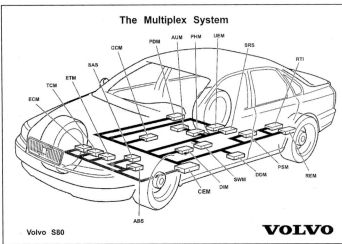

The Multiplex System

Volvo S80

VOLVO

Technical

CADILLAC

Who would have thought that a builder whose models are often designed for conservative consumers would stage a return to the LeMans 24-hour competition some 50 years after its first incursion. True: General Motors' luxury division plans to enter the race in 2000. To achieve its objective, GM Motorsport called upon the renowned Indianapolis design firm of Riley & Scott (R&S). The chassis will be powered by a Northstar 4.0L V8 engine equipped with two turbochargers that should be ready for next June's race. The last time Cadillac was involved in the celebrated race dates back to 1950. At the time, Briggs Cunningham had raced two cars and had finished 11th along with Phil Walters.

Technical

PORSCHE

This manufacturer is the first in the world to develop a ceramic composite disc brake featuring a cooling channel. Composed of carbon fibers assembled at high temperature and under a vacuum, the disc weighs 50% less than a standard disc and resists temperature variations and rust. Elaborate testing seems to indicate that this kind of disc could last throughout the lifetime of any vehicle it is installed on.

TM4

Technologie M4 and the Michelin Group have joined forces to develop the E-Wheelcontrol drive system. It consists of a direct drive electric engine placed inside a Pax system wheel, developed by Michelin. Should a puncture occur, the anchoring system prevents the tire from separating from the wheel. Since the tire can run flat, there is no need for an emergency wheel and as a result, there is room enough for a bigger fuel tank. For optimal vehicle control, a central electronic controller is in constant touch with the engine-wheel assembly.

Technical

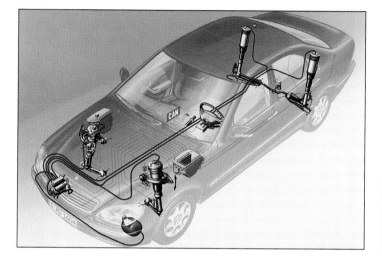

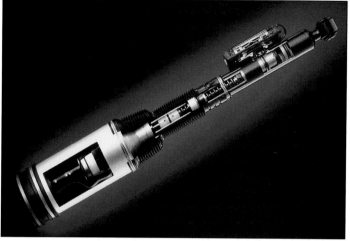

MERCEDES-BENZ

The unveiling of the latest S-Class model was the opportunity for a genuine technological festival for the Stuttgart builder.

Pictured opposite is the dashboard, remarkably simple in design, with a certain number of controls grouped around the navigation system screen.

The AIRmatic system, illustrated above, combines the pneumatic suspension with an adaptive shock absorption system to improve the comfort and safety levels of this sedan by instantly correcting its level.

Positioned in the grille, the Distronic is a system that automatically calculates the distance separating the Mercedes-Benz from other vehicles on the road.

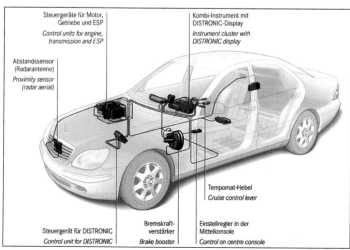

Steuergeräte für Motor, Getriebe und ESP
Control units for engine, transmission and ESP

Abstandssensor (Radarantenne)
Proximity sensor (radar aerial)

Kombi-Instrument mit DISTRONIC-Display
Instrument cluster with DISTRONIC display

Tempomat-Hebel
Cruise control lever

Steuergerät für DISTRONIC
Control unit for DISTRONIC

Bremskraft-verstärker
Brake booster

Einstellregler in der Mittelkonsole
Control on centre console

Technical

SMART

While the industrial adventure launched by the founder of the Swatch watch corporation and Mercedes-Benz is far from an unqualified success (according to rumors the German car-builder may soon bow out of it), at the very least it has generated a number of original ideas.

Designed to feature in-stock models, the vertical showroom concept (opposite) is very attractive while also providing protection against the elements and vandals.

Thanks to removable panelling, it takes only 30 minutes to change a Smart's color.

The exhibit hall (below) and its services are similar to those developed by Saturn to alleviate customer stress and create a friendly and reassuring relationship.

CARS AROUND THE WORLD

PARIS AUTO SHOW

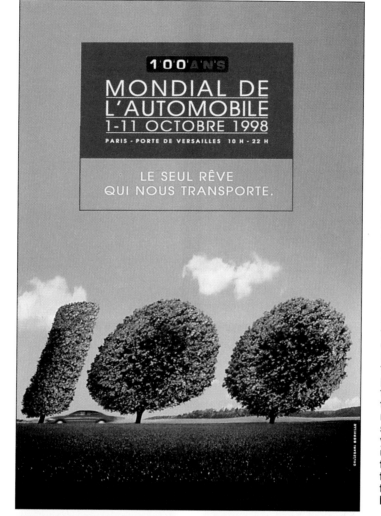

• PARIS

The last Mondial de l'Automobile in Paris, with "The Automobile: the only dream that transports us" as theme, celebrated its hundredth anniversary. In fact, on June 15th 1898, the International Car Show, known as the Exposition Internationale d'Automobiles, opened its doors at the palais des Tuileries and its creator was none other than the Automobile Club de France (that also coordinates the 24-hour Le Mans race...). At the time, 269 exhibitors participated and 140,000 visitors flocked to see the Show, proof that speaks the passion this mode of transportation inspired even then... A hundred years later, the craze hasn't let up an iota, in spite of all the traps and trials that have beset the history of these vehicles that have become indispensable to our way of life.

• ALFA ROMEO

The most recent 166 was one of the eye-catching attractions at the Paris Auto Show. This upper-crust model built by the transalpine manufacturer and designed by Pininfarina had a very tapered, classic look to it and driven by a whole lineup of engines, including a 2.0L 4-cylinder model with two spark plugs per cylinder, a zoomy 3.0L V6 and a 2.4L Turbodiesel.

Paris Auto Show

• AUDI

This was the first public appearance of the mass-produced TT coupe (above), that integrates almost all the elements of the concept car unveiled at the Frankfurt Auto Show in 1995. Named after the famous Tourist Trophy, this uniquely styled vehicle was built on the Audi A4 platform and is driven by the same 1.8L engine, offered in front-wheel or quattro 180 or 225 hp versions.

• BUGATTI

The Volkswagen group bought back all the shares of this illustrious brand and asked Giugiaro, stylist with Ital Design, to hurriedly create an exterior body to dress up this originally engineered vehicle, including a 6.3L W18 engine that boasts 555 hp, the end result of joining up three V6 engine blocks. The interior has a very art deco flair with its doeskin trim.

Paris Auto Show

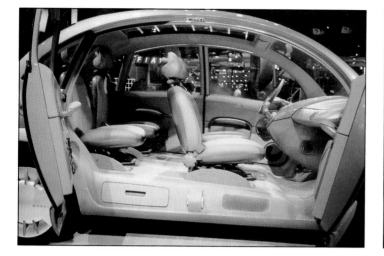

• CITROËN

The concept car christened "Lumière" (above) is a version of what the French 2CV might look like in the future. Apart from its rounded silhouette, its built-in top and shifter set in the middle of the dashboard, this small sedan is in a league of its own with such unique and unconventional doors and the non-existent B pillar that makes for great access. The Xsara Picasso (opposite) is a new unibody compact vehicle in the Renault Scenic class that has won the heart of many Europeans.

• DAIMLER-BENZ

Mercedes has finally updated its S-Class model (below) by putting it on a par with rivals sizewise. Yet the decreased weight has left its sophisticated personality unscathed since this newcomer is loaded with innovative electronic functions.

Paris Auto Show

• FIAT

The Multipla is Fiat's version of a compact minivan. It has a unique front-end profile and dashboard as well as two rows of multiadjustable triple seats. It's powered by a 1.6L 4-cylinder gas engine or a 1.9L Turbodiesel.

• FORD

The Focus (below), that replaces the Escort, has made its first official steps in Europe where it's been sold since late 1998. The lineup includes coupes, sedans and station wagons and the new kid on the block sports a whole new exterior and dashboard that's nowhere like the very traditional treatment on the defunct Escort. Let's hope that more conservative North American buyers won't dislike and dismiss this popular model.

Paris Auto Show

• HEULIEZ

The silhouette of the Pregunta speedster (that means question in Spanish) was inspired by that of a fighter plane. Its technical features are just as avant-garde as its looks, since it's equipped with a Formula 1 dashboard, high-intensity headlights and a 530 hp 5.7L V12 that makes for 0 to 62 mph takeoff in 4 seconds flat.

• HONDA

Three spanking new models were displayed at the Honda exhibit. Opposite, the latest model Legend (the Acura RL in North America), the Logo (below right), a tiny three-door 65 hp 1.3L urban car equipped with a constant variation transmission. The 5-door Accord (below left) is tailored to the European market with its more compact size and less powerful engines and is quite different from the model sold in North America. It also comes as an R sport version.

Paris Auto Show

• ISOTTA FRASCHINI

Italian fanatics are trying to resurrect this famous Italian-brand car that saw the light of day in 1898. The T8 (above) comes in a Fissore-designed coupe or convertible version. It's driven by a 300 hp 4.2L V8 engine. Yet, beneath its aluminum body, features include all-wheel drive and a gearbox driven by a sequential shifter.

• JAGUAR

The XK180 concept roadster, created to celebrate the 50th anniversary of the XK lineup, was built on the XKR coupe platform, but engine zoom has gone from 375 to a whopping 456 hp. No one is really saying that this car will one day be available on the market, but this prototype includes an interesting aluminum body panel treatment and a sequential transmission with controls located on the steering wheel.

Paris Auto Show

• LADA

The Togliati firm, set on showing that Russian automakers are far from unimaginative, exhibited the Rapan (above), an electric vehicle geared to urban travel. Its biodesign style, pushed to the extreme, is quite fetching. It's equipped with the formerly displayed Oka Electro features, namely a nickel cadmium battery.

• MASERATI

Ferrari has taken up the reins of destiny of the Maserati firm and the GT 3200 is the first expression of this "sacred union". It's a 4-passenger minicoupe graced with the ultra-famous Giugiaro touch and the stylist has come up with a classic, tasteful design. The twin turbo 3.2L V8 engine, in keeping with the manufacturer's approach, delivers 370 hp. For now, the only transmission available is a 6-speed manual.

Paris Auto Show

• MICHEL HOMMEL

The Curara (opposite) is a rather conventional convertible model but its classic exterior, inspired by models from the sixties, is quite sensational.

• PEUGEOT

The number two French manufacturer offered two concept vehicles (above) boasting of traits taken from its recent 206 version. On the right, the bold and brassy S16/GTi sports coupe and on the left, the Escapade, a lightweight all-terrain vehicle.

• RENAULT

The Vel Satis, (below) the prototype of a futuristic coupe that really seats four, is fitted with a unique windshield and one-piece glass top as well as huge double-hinged doors. Strangely enough, this model that suggests what the upcoming top-of-the-line Renault cars will look like, is only powered by a lowly 3.0L V6...

Paris Auto Show

• SAAB

The 9⁵ now includes a station wagon model aimed at maximizing its chances of making headway in new market niches. Like the sedan, it can be equipped with a 4-cylinder 2.3L or a 3.0L V6, both Turbo.

• TOYOTA

In order to make more of a splash on the European market, the number one Japanese builder has created the Yaris model to be assembled in a French plant. This minicar is heavily inspired by the famous Twingo, but it comes in a 4-door model that's currently unavailable in the Renault lineup. Its instrument panel setup also borrows from its French rival since it sports digital instruments located in the middle, but it's less far-fetched and trimmer looking. The Yaris is powered by a 68 hp 1.0L 4-cylinder engine linked to the only 5-speed manual transmission available.

Paris Auto Show

• VOLKSWAGEN

The top German auto manufacturer had huge, sprawling exhibits at the most recent Paris Auto Show, thus expressing its intentions of staying in the lead on the European market. It displayed the latest versions of its famous Golf and Jetta lineup known as the Bora in Europe. Modifications are mostly skin-deep, since these cars come equipped with the same mechanical components as before, namely a 1.9L 4-cylinder TDI, a 2.0L conventional gas engine and the 2.8L VR6. The car has a shapelier silhouette that's more like that of the Passat, so family traits are easier to identify.

The Lupo (below) is the most compact model built by Volkswagen. Its Diesel version burns a mere 3 liters per 62 miles.

DETROIT AUTO SHOW

• DETROIT

The Detroit Auto Show may not be the most dramatic, but it does offer the advantage of being the first of the year. It's the stronghold of the North American auto industry and is the mirror image of current trends and of styles flirted with by General Motors, Ford and Chrysler. But you have to visit the Chicago and New York Auto Shows so as to have a complete overview of how the industry will evolve over the current year in North America. It's held in Cobo Hall in the heart of lovely downtown Detroit, a stone's throw from the Renaissance Center; the monumental building complex built by Henry Ford II that today houses headquarters for General Motors...

• BMW

The unveiling of the X5 was indubitably one of the highlights of this show. Built on the 5 Series platform and equipped with the same mechanical features, this vehicle is an awesome rival to the Mercedes-Benz M-Class introduced at the Detroit Auto Show two years ago. Unlike the former model, the X5 has a unitized body, a sure sign of pared down weight. It will also come with standard traction control and four-wheel ABS. Its trim, compact size suggests that the X5 will be agile and easy to handle. It will be driven by 2.8 and 4.4L, 6 and 8-cylinder engines. Like the Z3, the X5 will be built in the United States at the Spartanburg assembly plant in South Carolina.

Detroit Auto Show

• BUICK

Debut for the Buick LeSabre 2000 (above), whose traditional design "is timeless" as purported by its stylists... Its overall treatment is inspired by the Park Avenue and it shares its famous 3.8L V6.

The Cielo, which means sky in Spanish, (opposite and below) is the concept car of a midsize 4-door convertible, aimed at enjoying the freedom of open space without having to compromise when it comes to comfort and safety features. The two longitudinal roll bars make for a more rigid platform and act as guides for the rigid roof panels that can be stored in the trunk.

Electronic features are at center stage on the Cielo, including voice commands or remote controls for some features such as the power door opener.

Detroit Auto Show

• CADILLAC

The Evoq made quite an impression when it was unveiled, for no one dared imagine that the deluxe GM brand would dare break its tradition of conservative luxury... In a few years from now, the Evoq will become the Super Corvette from Cadillac. This exotic convertible coupe, with its relatively compact size and sharp lines, comes with a fold-away hard top and a whole arsenal of electronic wizardry worthy of a US Air Force fighter plane: head-up display, infrared imaging system, lateral rearview cameras, rear bumper radar and a multimedia communication function. It's powered by a Northstar supercharged all-aluminum 4.2L V8 engine that delivers 405 hp and is linked to an automatic transmission with Performance Algorithm Shifting system.

Detroit Auto Show

• CHEVROLET

The Impala (above) is back. After several years' absence, one of the strongest General Motors icons is back in the saddle. The newcomer replaces the Lumina in the midsize model range. It's equipped with 3.4 and 3.8L V6 engines.

The concept vehicle "Nomad" (opposite) is more retro than futuristic, since it borrows from a prototype launched way back in 1953, precursor of the 1954 Motorama. It's a sporty SUV driven by a V8 powerplant. Noteworthy items include the sunroof fitted with Venetian blinds and the two seat benches that can be folded down to form a flat floor area.

The ZR2 Tracker (below) that we got a glimpse of at the SEMA Show in Las Vegas was on display in Detroit. Beneath the hood lurks a 201 hp 3.4L V6 that is a welcome replacement for the original engine...

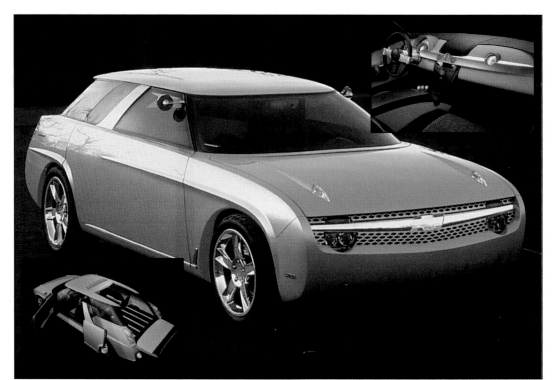

Detroit Auto Show

• CHRYSLER

The new Neon (above as the sporty R/T model) was introduced at Cobo Hall in Detroit. It has the same looks as the former model, as well as its 2.0L engine and outdated 3-speed automatic transmission.

The Citadel prototype (opposite) is representative of a futuristic multi-purpose hybrid vehicle. Here, the rear wheels are powered by a 3.5L V6 engine, while the 70 hp electric engine controls the front wheels. The electric engine gets its juice from a battery located under the floor of the cargo hold.

The PT Cruiser (below) is without a doubt the most disconcerting mass-produced vehicle built over the past few years. Built on the most recent Neon platform, it's a car as well as a compact minivan, equipped with modern features, but wrapped in a retro package...

Detroit Auto Show

• DODGE

Dodge has given new life to its Charger icon (above) with the R/T concept vehicle that, unlike the original, comes fitted with four doors, since nowadays, coupes aren't what the customer wants... It's driven by a turbocharged 4.7L V8 fed by pressurized liquid propane and gas tanks being located under the rear wheels.

The Power Wagon (opposite) illustrates the probable evolution of the current Ram truck. This vehicle has the grille, fenders and running boards found on the legendary Dodge truck way back in 1946. Yet the roundish cab roof, high intensity headlights, four doors, clean-running 250 hp Turbo-diesel L6 engine, as well as the all-wheel drive automatic transmission are state-of-the-art. Some exterior assembly details bring a goldsmith's craftsmanship to mind...

Detroit Auto Show

• FORD

In keeping with Ford's quest towards a world car, they will replace the Escort with the Focus (above) in the fall of 1999. This near clone to the model now available in Europe will be offered in a base model or ZX3 coupe, in LX, SE or ZTS sedan and SE station wagon, driven by two 2.0L engines. The SPI powerplant develops 110 hp and the Zetec musters 130 hp.

The T-Bird is back. It should reappear (opposite) at the dawn of the next millennium, as a car quite similar to this concept model that scrupulously borrows all the attributes that graced the original 1955 model.

In the wake of the SUV craze, the SUT's are now wowing potential buyers. These pickup trucks are ever more traveler-friendly and now come fitted with four real doors and offer twice as much seating capacity. This is the case for the F150 Crew Cab and the Explorer Sport Track (below right).

Detroit Auto Show

• HONDA

The S2000 roadster, introduced in Japan in the fall of '98, has made its first appearance on North American soil, along with the VV hybrid model that could soon be available.

• HYUNDAI

The Santa Fe (opposite) will be the next SUV to be introduced on the North American market. It will be the first of its kind to be built by the Korean firm and will be powered by a V6 engine.

• JAGUAR

The S -TYPE (below), the latest addition to the British builder's lineup, is cousin to the Lincoln LS since it shares its platform and is equipped with many similar technical features. It's offered with either a 3.0L V6 or a 4.0L V8 powerplant.

Detroit Auto Show

• JEEP

The Commander (above) is a concept sport utility vehicle that aims at having the least possible impact on the environment. So it's equipped with a fuel cell that generates electricity via a chemical reaction using methanol.

• LINCOLN

Spurred on by the Navigator's success, Lincoln is toying with the idea of adding a luxury pickup truck to its model range. This concept vehicle, christened Blackwood, (opposite) has a very unique and original cargo box opening.

• LEXUS

Following in Infiniti's footsteps, Lexus is introducing a new entry-level model to its North American lineup. The IS 200 (below) is a rear-wheel drive sedan with a sporty soul that will be offered with the GS 300's engine, namely the 3.0L L6.

Detroit Auto Show

• MAZDA

Mazda's concept vehicle (above) that influenced the MPV's renewal, created quite a buildup to the unveiling of the mass-produced vehicle at the Chicago Auto Show.

• MERCEDES-BENZ

The SLR coupe (opposite and below) grabbed a lot of attention at the first North American Auto Show of 1999. It's the precursor of the next exotic model that the Stuttgart firm will produce and takes up the torch of the legendary 300SL coupes whose current descendants seriously lack panache. This "silver arrow toward the future" has a front-end design reminiscent of a Formula 1 McLaren and it's light as a feather thanks to all its aluminum and carbon fiber components. It's equipped with a supercharged V8 engine that develops 557 hp and with electro-hydraulic brakes fitted with ceramic discs.

Detroit Auto Show

• MERCURY

The "(my)" (above) is a multi-purpose vehicle that can go anywhere and do anything the driver pleases. Its 5 doors make for easy boarding and the glass top gives you a great outdoors feeling without all the hassles.

• MITSUBISHI

The SSU (opposite) suggests the concept of a racecar offering high-level luxury and space to five lucky passengers. Built on the 3000GT VR-4 platform, it's equipped with a twin turbo V6 engine developing 310 hp, a 5-speed automatic gearbox with sequential shifter and 20-inch tires that can run flat.

• NISSAN

North American customers will finally be able to buy a 4-door Frontier pickup truck. This model has been sold in certain developing countries for quite some time, which isn't necessarily good news...

Detroit Auto Show

• NISSAN

The Xterra (above) is a new all-terrain compact built on the Frontier pickup platform and equipped with the same 4 and 6-cylinder engines. It has a really distinctive "Tonka" look to it and its roof rack can be adapted to transport scads of sports equipment such as skis, bicycles or kayaks.

• OLDSMOBILE

The Recon (opposite) is another all-wheel drive SUV concept vehicle whose most original feature is its big sunroof. It's driven by a 3.0L V6 engine and comes fitted with Pax system Michelin tires.

• PANOZ

The Esperante (below) is the first convertible to be produced by the Georgia automaker. Most components are made of aluminum and the car is driven by a 320 hp 4.6L V8 powerplant.

Detroit Auto Show

• PONTIAC

The GTO prototype (above) has a bulky and angular body that's supposed to suggest the muscle power of zoomy models of yesteryear.

The Aztek (opposite) hails in a vehicle that's a cross between an all-terrain vehicle and a station wagon, an ideal companion when it comes to leisure activities. Its 3.4L V6 engine boasts a 3500 lb. trailering capacity.

• TOYOTA

The Echo (below) will replace the Tercel in the fall of '99. It's a variant of the small Yaris built for the European market. It's geared to a young clientele and offers a rather roomy interior and trunk, given its trim size. It will be available with 2 or 4 doors and will come equipped with a 108 hp 1.5L engine. This lightweight car (less than a ton) will be really fuel-efficient.

Detroit Auto Show

• TOYOTA

The XYR (above) indicates that the leading Japanese automaker is back in the light-weight sports coupe race. This California-designed car is inspired by the 1967 model of the 2000-GT and comes equipped with a 180 hp 1.8L engine, yielding a trim overall weight of 2500 lb.

• VOLKSWAGEN

This mean-looking RSi New Beetle has had its mechanical components beefed up with a steroid treatment, since it's equipped with a VR6, all-wheel drive and 18-inch wheels.

CHICAGO AUTO SHOW

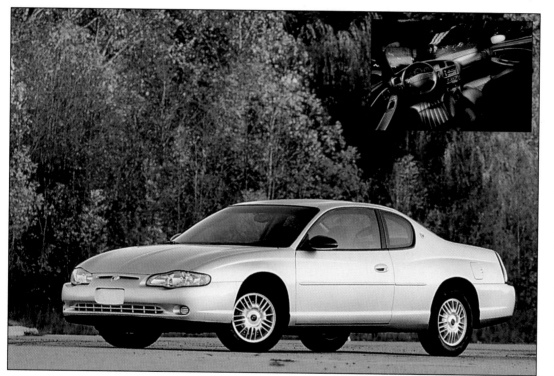

• CADILLAC

The Catera Steinmetz concept car (above) was fashioned to illustrate the potential of the entry-level model in the Cadillac contingent. The turbocharged V6 engine delivers 284 hp, the suspension is of competition design and the wheel diameter is 18 inches.

• CHEVROLET

The Monte Carlo coupe (opposite) has been rejuvenated. The exterior body has more personality than the former model. It's still offered in an LS version driven by a 3.4L engine or an SS powered by a 3.8L.

• DODGE

As seen in Detroit, the Dakota now comes with 4 doors, so it's now in the latest SUT fashion lineup, a trend that's casting out SUV's when it comes to popularity. This model truly seats 5 passengers and climbing aboard is easier than for extended cabin models.

Chicago Auto Show

• GMC

The Jimmy Diamond (above left) is a cosmetic way of celebrating it's 30th anniversary.

• HONDA

The Civic Si coupe is back on the scene (above right) with its 160 hp engine, 5-speed manual transmission, sporty suspension and aluminum 15-inch rims.

• MAZDA

The Miata roadster's 10th anniversary was celebrated in Chicago in a worthy manner with a special, yet recognizable version (opposite) dressed in blue sapphire, chrome rims and two-toned seat trim.

• NISSAN

The latest model Maxima (below) has an overt California look to it, thanks to the efforts of Jerry Hirshberg's team from NDI, located in La Jolla, a suburb of San Diego.

Chicago Auto Show

• NISSAN

The NCS (New Concept Sedan) prototype (above) blends practical station wagon character and handy minivan features. It's like a sedan sizewise, yet its style is more original than elegant.

The notorious Z (above left) will rise from its ashes as a more compact car equipped with technical features borrowed from the 240 SX.

• PONTIAC

The new Bonneville (opposite) does not betray its roots, in spite of its bold and overdone exterior design. It's still powered by 3.8L V6 engines delivering either 205 or 240 hp.

• SATURN

The Tennessee-based builder wants to add zest to its SC2 coupe demeanor, so this prototype is the precursor of a model to be equipped with a zoomier engine and boasting of more dramatic looks.

Chicago Auto Show

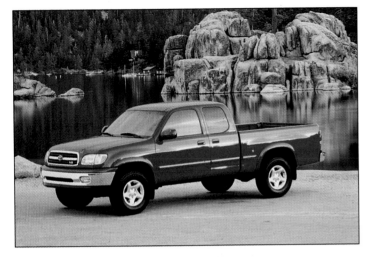

• TOYOTA

The Tundra (above), that replaces the T100, looks quite a bit like its precursor, yet there's a 4.7L V8 under the hood. Will this be enough of an asset to make it a full-fledged rival when compared with what the Big Three in the United States put on the market?

The MR Spider (opposite) could join the Toyota lineup in its race with the Miata. It's driven by a 140 hp 1.8L engine linked to a 5-speed sequential transmission with button controls on the wheel or a conventional shifter, but without a clutch pedal.

Toyota is resurrecting the memory of the first Land Cruiser models with this concept vehicle that has the general appearance of its classic and timeless ancestor. The body is made of aluminum, the frame and technical features are very modern, still the inside sports fine leather seats and terrific climate control.

NEW YORK AUTO SHOW

• NEW YORK

The International New York Auto Show is the last of the major car exhibits in North America. It's held in the heart of Manhattan at the Javis Center, a huge building complex with a skylight that gives you a lovely view of the famous skyscrapers of the American metropolis.

• ASTON MARTIN

The DB7 coupes and convertibles (opposite) will at long last receive an engine worthy of their lineage. The 6.0L V12 delivers 420 hp and can be associated with either a 6-speed short gear ratio manual transmission or a 5-speed automatic, providing the ooze needed to go from 0-62 mph in less than 5 seconds.

New York Auto Show

• CHEVROLET

The Suburban (above) has had a complete overhaul and is built on the Silverado pickup platform, a truck introduced last year. The 1500 version will come equipped with 4.8L, 5.3L and 6.0L V8 Vortec engines. Components have been chosen to lessen pollutant effects on the environment.

• FORD

The number two American automaker has given more conservative stylistic touches to the front end of the Taurus, so as to put a finish to poor sales and give the customer what he wants (opposite). Here's hoping the same fate doesn't await the Focus, whose exterior is also pretty far-out...

• INFINITI

The I30 (below) has evolved, but it's still closely paired with the Maxima platform and mechanical features.

New York Auto Show

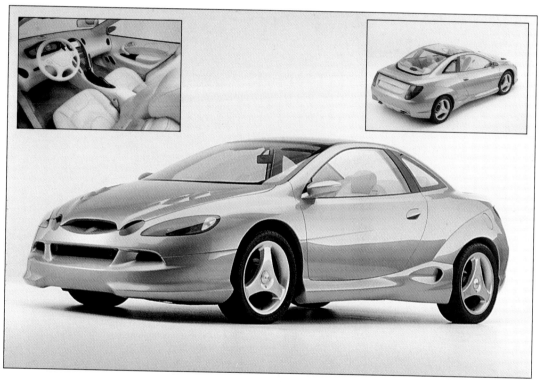

• GMC

Just like the Suburban on the preceding page, the Yukon (above) and its sibling the Tahoe are more in step with current tastes with Silverado-Sierra pickup trucks-based frame and powertrains.

• KIA

The concept car called the KMS-4 (opposite) is that of a sports coupe inspired by "classic Italian sculptures" (?) and has a distinctive glass top fitted with a solar energy collector. Its 2.0L engine develops 151 hp and is linked to a sequential transmission that's controlled by two plates located under the steering wheel, as in Formula 1 racecars.

• MERCEDES-BENZ

The CL coupe shares the S sedan's underframe and 302 hp 5.0L V8 engine, but inaugurates the Active Body Control suspension that gets rid of tiresome ride roll.

New York Auto Show

• MAZDA

This is the official debut of the new MPV (above) built by Mazda. It borrows the front-wheel drive and 2.5L V6 engine of Ford's Contour-Mystique.

• NISSAN

This is a prolific year for Nissan who's on a great roll. The Tino (opposite) is an HUV (High Utility Vehicle) that's half-minivan, half-station wagon, a model that buyers simply love in Europe and Asia.

• OLDSMOBILE

The Aurora (below left) will get a drastic face-lift in 2001, in the form of a very familiar and attractive package, equipped with the same 4.0L V8 engine.

• SATURN

The new LS (below right), based on the Opel Omega and powered by 4-cylinder and V6 engines, will be competing with the Honda Accord and Toyota Camry.

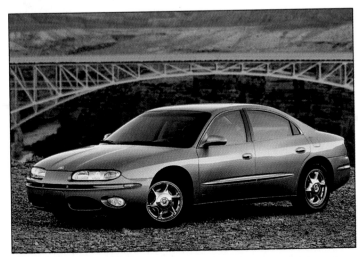

CARS AROUND THE WORLD

GENEVA AUTO SHOW

Le Printemps au
69° **Salon** International
de l'Auto & Accessoires
11 – 21 mars 1999
Genève
Palexpo

• GENEVA

The Geneva Auto Show is a true European showcase, even though Switzerland isn't a member of the European Union per se. It's a prestigious event that nary an automobile expert would want to miss. It's held at the Palexpo, located opposite the airport and along the Lausanne-Paris highway. Each year, about two million visitors take in this show.

• ASTON MARTIN

The Newport Pagnell automaker has revamped its old V8 model by furbishing it with a "Le Mans" engine that develops from 550 to 600 hp, so this car can hit 200 mph, going from 0 to 100 mph, in ten seconds.

• AUDI

This was the first showing of the TT Series convertible. It will be sold in North America next year. It's powered by the same engines that equip the coupe, its top has an electro-hydraulic control and is fitted with a glass window.

Geneva Auto Show

• BENTLEY

The "BY 8.16 Hunaudières" coupe (above) is a move towards rekindling the racecar spirit at this venerable British brand builder that's been taken over by Volkswagen. It's equipped with a 8.0L W16 powerplant that develops a mere 623 hp...

• BERTONE

This coupe is called Bella, which means beautiful in Italian (opposite and below). This car design explores the possibility of maximizing cabin space on a 2+2 architecture. In order to offer roomier rear seats and trunk, the rear seats pivot 90°.

The Bella is equipped with Alfa Romeo power ooze, since it has a 3.0L 6-cylinder engine developing 166 hp.

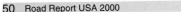

Geneva Auto Show

• BMW

The Bavarian firm took advantage of the Swiss Auto Show to show off its latest 3-Series coupe (above) that comes in 323 and 328 Ci trim levels equipped with 2.5L and 2.8L L6 engines.

• CALLAWAY

The C12 coupes and convertibles (opposite) are inspired by the new and improved Corvette built by this manufacturer, established namely in Germany and in the USA, who has succeeded in extracting 440 hp from the 5.7L V8 engine.

• CITROËN

The French automaker didn't apply the usual imaginative touch when it came up with this concept vehicle called Lignage (below), that's supposed to represent the forthcoming upper-crust model.

Geneva Auto Show

• CONTENDER

This strange-looking all-terrain coupe christened XG (above) is built by the Swiss manufacturer Status & Class, along the same platform as the multi-purpose G vehicle at Mercedes-Benz. It borrows its 211 hp 3.2L L6 engine, 4-speed automatic transmission and three differentials.

• FERRARI

The 360 Modena barchetta (opposite and below), that everyone's been dying to see, replaces the F355. It's a superbly styled car thanks once again to the Pininfarina designers. Its 3.6L V8 powerplant gives 405 hp being transmitted to the rear wheels through a 6-speed transmission fitted with an electro-hydraulic shifter, with control plates under the steering wheel as on F1 racecars.

Geneva Auto Show

• FORD

The Puma ST160 (above) is an attempt to see what the public response will be to a limited edition small sports coupe, equipped with a 160 hp engine, limited slip differential, 17-inch wheels, oversized brakes and a stiff suspension.

• IDEA

The Italian Institute exhibited its version of a V-8 powered luxury sedan (opposite) with aluminum frame, advanced electronic features and innovative accessories aimed at cushy comfort.

• ITAL DESIGN

The Structura (below) is a foretaste of the car of the future. It's spacious, transparent, packed with high-tech accessories and is an unusually traveler-friendly vehicle.

Geneva Auto Show

• LAMBORGHINI

The GT variant of the illustrious Diablo (above) is mean-spirited, as is seen by its unique, big and bold appendages, unusual cabin layout and especially its new 6.0L V12 engine that develops 575 hp, thus providing performances that could make one blush: 210 mph at top speed...

• LOTUS

The 340R roadster is a spin-off of the Élise, so it has an aluminum frame and mechanical features made up of a 170 hp L4 engine linked to a 5-speed gearbox. Jutting wheels transform the car into a kind of modern Super Seven and it's fitted with detachable, synthetic resin body panels. Cabin size is pared down to next to nothing since some motorcycles offer a lot more seating space.

Geneva Auto Show

• MAZDA

This was the Premacy's world premiere (above). It has a new single-volume design, midway between conventional station wagons and minivans. It's fitted with swing doors and can seat five passengers and handle quite a load of luggage. It's equipped with the Protegé's 115 hp 1.8L L4 engine.

• OPEL

GM Europe exhibited the Speedster (opposite) with its bonded aluminum frame and synthetic resin exterior. This car is made for the thrill of the open road, since it's powered by the latest model 2.2L L4 Vectra engine. The Microvan Concept 4 (below) is a prototype of an all-purpose vehicle with modular cabin that can accommodate four passengers or a hefty cargo load.

Geneva Auto Show

• PEUGEOT

The 306HDI concept vehicle may not have flashy looks, but its super high pressure direct fuel injection Turbodiesel engine (1,350 bars) develops 90 hp and has maximum torque at 1,900 rpm.

• RENAULT

The French auto manufacturer got together with Matra to develop this "Coupéspace" called Avantime (opposite and below), a single-volume coupe that borrows the Espace's mechanical features and is aimed at offering the best all-around multi-purpose capabilities. Its exceptional cabin space can hold four full-size seats and the rear hatch reveals a huge cargo hold. The cool, clean interior is a tasteful blend of leather, aluminum and fabric.

Geneva Auto Show

• RINSPEED

The Swiss wizard had kept a lovely surprise under cover, till it was unveiled at the Geneva Auto Show. The M.U.V. X-Dream (above and opposite) is an oversized leisure beast, a kind of truck aimed at transporting "modern man's toys" (motorcycle, Sea-Doo, hovercraft) thanks to a first-of-its-kind loading system. Its 5.5L V8 engine propels this "nightmare" on wheels to a speed of 62 mph in 6.9 seconds and has a 145 mph top speed.

• STRATHCARRON

The newcomer from Great Britain offers a tiny, nicely priced racecar called SC4 (below). Its engine develops 100 hp/L, so racecar thrills are now within everyone's reach.

Geneva Auto Show

• SBARRO

The colleagues of our friend Franco, the maestro at Grandson, concocted several interesting and original concept cars. We took an admiring look at the Millennium Roadster (above) derived from the Golf model equipped with a 150 hp 2.3L VR5 engine. Opposite is the GT1, a trim sedan with a sporty soul and sleek exterior, that's powered by a 7.0L V8 Mercedes-Benz engine that now pumps out a whopping 600 hp, so it can soar to 62 mph in five seconds flat and can go beyond 185 mph.

The Flânerie (below left), a beach vehicle that seats seven and can transport a wheelchair, along with the Clio coupe (below right) were designed by students at Espera, the Sbarro stylists' school located in Pontarlier, France.

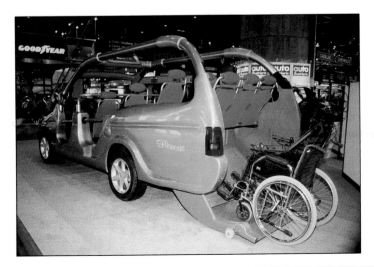

Geneva Auto Show

• SEAT

The Spanish brand that's a member of the Volkswagen family dreamed up a roadster called Formula that will sure add zip and zest to its family-oriented image. The 2.0L L4 Turbo develops 240 hp via a 6-speed transmission with sequential shifter.

• ZONDA

The C12 coupe is the work of Pagani Automobili in Modena, the Italian birthplace for a fanciful flock of dream cars. This exotic coupe was designed to honor the famous Argentinean champion, Juan Manuel Fangio. It was created around a Mercedes-Benz 6.0L V12 engine delivering 394 or 500 hp. With its steel frame and carbon fiber shell, it weighs in at 2,755 lb.

In any automotive journalist's life, there are unforgettable moments. I'll always remember how I made an appointment to meet with EVOQ. As an international star, she was arriving from France and scheduled to leave for Japan to meet other journalists. She agreed to a photo session and a short drive in the Detroit area on a certain Thursday afternoon in the month of August. Take it or leave it. I immediately called my travel agency and reserved an airline ticket to Detroit. Since I'd met her in the uncontested capital of the American automobile industry, I was sure that she'd be an excellent subject for the front cover: she was futuristic, very stylish and terribly exciting.

Weather conditions were precarious and there was a definite threat of rain. I was worried - I knew that I wouldn't get another chance to rendez-vous with this beauty before my book went to press. My guide, Richard James, had arranged all of the details of the meeting and was convinced that everything would go well. The General Motors Design Center is a huge complex and its main function is to house all of the design operations that underlie the make's future products. It's a fortress and all those who enter must show complete goodwill and provide a detailed list of any photographic equipment on hand before entering the forbidden chamber. The endless corridors that lead to the meeting place are decorated with mock-ups of the vehicles scheduled for the very near future: the upcoming Saturn SUV, the next Blazer, etc. No chance to take a closer look; I'm carefully escorted.

At last we reach the huge paved courtyard surrounded by a high brick wall, the better to scrutinize prototypes in broad daylight. She's there, almost minuscule in the large and wide-open space, resplendent and positioned on a revolving platform. As we draw nearer, it's easier to get a better idea of her real size. She's huge and very, very tall. When the photo session comes to an end comes the moment of truth. The engineer in charge of the EVOQ's destiny gives me the go-ahead: "Have fun, but don't break the car!". I can well understand, she's really and truly one-of-a-kind and development costs apart, her bill adds up to a half-million in U.S. funds. The beauty's agent guides me aboard, carefully explains that a prototype isn't necessarily as perfect as a race car or a standard-production model, a fact that becomes obvious as soon as I set out. Quality consistency is questionable and the

doors, trunk and roof panels stored inside it seem to be struggling to go their own separate ways. Engine noise is impressive, but the 405 hp output isn't all there on this particular day. No matter. Luckily the top is down, because the side-view camera's monitors located on the center console cannot be read in strong sunlight.

The driver's seat is so low and the belt line so high, I feel as if I'm in a bathtub. Fortunately the passenger compartment is very well-designed, otherwise claustrophobia would be almost inevitable! After an all too brief time behind the wheel of this fabulous beauty, in a setting no less stunning, I headed back home hoping that my photos would be as crisp and clear as I thought they would be, otherwise I'd put a lot of people to trouble for nothing. Richard James was right: everything went perfectly well!

Frankfurt Auto Show

• AUDI

The A2 (above) is the first compact standard-production model in the world to feature an aluminum body. It weighs 330 pounds (150 kg) less than an equivalent conventional model.

• BUGATTI

The 18/3 "Chiron" (opposite) is a race car with fiber carbon panelling signed by Giugiaro. Its 18-cylinder engine is center-mounted, it has a 6.3L displacement and a 555-hp output, coupled with permanent AWD.

• CITROËN

The Pluriel (below) is an experimental modular car that thanks to its moveable features can serve as a soft-top sedan, a sports convertible or a Spider pickup.

Frankfurt Auto Show

• MAZDA

The "Nextourer" (above) is a prototype blending the advantages of a conventional sedan and a 4X4 vehicle. Roomy, it's equipped with a 3.0L V6 engine and a Toroïdal transmission.

•MERCEDES-BENZ

The Stuttgart master has unveiled the roadster version of the SLR (opposite), introduced earlier this year in Detroit. Its all-aluminum body is complemented by SBS brakes with fiber-reinforced ceramic discs.

• PEUGEOT

The French builder presented its top-of-the-line model, the 607 (below), intended to vie with the most prestigious alternatives on today's market.

Frankfurt Auto Show

Scénic RX4

RENAULT

• RENAULT

The Scenic RX4 (above) is an AWD version of Europe's bestselling small minivan. It's derived from the Megane compact and shares its 2.0L engine.

• SKODA

The Czech make, part of the Volkswagen group, introduced the Fabia (below), derived from the Polo and sharing the same 1.9L TDI.

•VOLKSWAGEN

The D Concept (opposite) is the basis for an upscale model that the Wolfsburg builder will introduce shortly. Under the hood is a 313-hp 5.0L TDI V10 engine, coupled with a five-speed Tiptronic transmission and AWD.

CHEVROLET Metro

DAEWOO Lanos

Comparative Test

MINI-CARS

HYUNDAI Accent

MITSUBISHI Mirage

**See their performance, their specifications, their price
and their classification at the end of this chapter.**

TOYOTA Echo

SUZUKI-CHEVROLET

Swift-Metro

Minimalist

Small car sales are dropping steadily and numbers for the Metro/Swift are the best proof. While it's obvious that utility vehicles are of no interest to buyers who opt for these mini road warriors, their main enemies are models in superior categories, capable of offering more comfort and better safety.

MODEL RANGE

The Chevrolet Metro, Suzuki Swift and Pontiac Firefly (in Canada only) propose a 3-door hatchback and 4-door sedan in one trim only, with 1.0L 3-cylinder (3-door) and 1.3L 4-cylinder (4-door) engines, optional on the coupe. The 5-speed manual transmission is standard on all models and a 3-speed automatic is available as an option. The Swift is now available solely as the 3-door SLX with a 1.3L 4-cylinder engine. The equipment on these vehicles is bare-bones but it does include dual airbags and intermittent windshield wipers. Power steering, air conditioning, the automatic transmission and the radio are optional, as is antilock brakes on the Swift.

TECHNICAL FEATURES

The steel unibody is relatively light and its drag coefficient is reasonable. The fully independent suspension, based on the MacPherson principle is with triangular arms and a stabilizer bar in the front and oblique triangles and cross arms at the back. Braking is mixed and the steering system is a rack-and-pinion. The 3- and 4-cylinder engines are the smallest on the North American market and they also offer the best fuel consumption.

PROS

+ PRICE. It's economical - these cars are among the most inexpensive on the market and they offer the best fuel consumption.

+ HANDLING. Better with the introduction of 13-inch wheels, a significant weight gain and bigger overall size.

+ STYLING. The latest generation's is appealing and fun. Some lines have been redesigned to take away the Matchbox car look, especially on the 4-door model, which manages to look bigger than it really is.

+ PASSENGER ROOM. It's surprising on the 4-door sedan, which can easily accommodate four adults.

+ DRIVEABILITY. These "toy cars" are peppy, easy to handle and their small size makes driving in the city and finding a parking spot as simple as can be.

+ VERSATILITY. The 3-door hatchback's transformable trunk makes it true mini wagon, up to handling just about any task .

CONS

- SAFETY. It can't pretend to be on par with larger vehicles and its fragile structure remains vulnerable to collisions because of its thin cladding, used to reduce the weight.

- BRAKING. It's unreliable in emergency stops because wheels lock too quickly, the ABS system being available solely as an option for the Swift. Because brakes don't bite and fade fast under intense use, stopping distances are long. Lastly, the small wheels tend to react unpredictably during emergency stops under poor road conditions.

- PERFORMANCE. Those offered by the Metro-Firefly's 1.0L or the 1.3L with automatic transmission are particularly anemic. Acceleration and pick-up are sluggish and drivers should beware before attempting to overtake a vehicle.

- STEERING. It's imprecise at center, which complicates driving on poor road surfaces where it is very sensitive to crosswinds or ruts caused by heavy-duty trucks.

- COMFORT. It's not top quality on these small cars. Seats are firmer than on larger subcompacts and so is the suspension, which causes the small-sized wheels to hop. The passenger compartment is narrow and occupants rub elbows; rear access on 3-door models isn't easy.

- INSURANCE. Close to a subcompact's, the premium for these small cars is not proportionate to their size or their price.

- CHOICE. Like sales figures, the number of available choices is dropping and GM and Suzuki now offer only one finish level.

- QUALITY. It remains mediocre and some materials or components, such as tires, leave room for improvement. Finish is utilitarian, particularly on GM versions where plastics and trim fabric used in the interior are definitely down market.

- TRUNK. The hatchback offers minimal volume when the rear seat is occupied; when it isn't, it folds down to provide more cargo space.

CONCLUSION

Perfect for city driving or as an entry-level vehicle for young drivers, the Metro and Swift are losing some of their popularity. Their rudimentary comfort and very basic equipment and above all their vulnerable sizing and structure go a long way in explaining why the buying public is gradually looking elsewhere.

RATING
CHEVROLET Metro - SUZUKI Swift

CONCEPT :		57%
Technology :	75	
Safety :	80	
Interior space :	30	
Trunk volume :	30	
Quality/fit/finish :	70	

DRIVING :		46%
Cockpit :	70	
Performance :	20	
Handling :	45	
Steering :	65	
Braking :	30	

ORIGINAL EQUIPMENT :		66%
Tires :	65	
Headlights :	75	
Wipers :	70	
Rear defroster :	70	
Radio :	50	

COMFORT :		55%
Seats :	60	
Suspension :	50	
Sound level :	40	
Conveniences :	50	
Air conditioning :	75	

BUDGET :		76%
Price :	90	
Fuel economy :	90	
Insurance :	80	
Satisfaction :	70	
Depreciation :	50	

Overall rating :		60.0%

NEW FOR 2000

• Body colours: Dark Blue (Metro sedan) and Metallic Blue (Metro coupe).

Compare Performance, Specifications, Prices, and Classification at the end of this chapter.

EQUIPMENT

CHEVROLET Metro	3dr. base	3dr. LSi	4dr. LSi
Automatic transmission:	-	O	O
Cruise control:	-	-	-
Power steering:	-	-	O
Anti-lock brakes:	-	-	-
Traction control:	-	-	-
Air conditioning:	O	O	O
Leather:	-	-	-
AM/FM/radio-cassette:	O	O	O
Power door locks:	-	-	O
Power windows:	-	-	-
Tilt steering:	-	-	-
Dual adjustable mirrors:	SM	SM	SM
Alloy wheels:	-	-	-
Anti-theft system:	-	-	-

Colors
Exterior: Black, White, Red, Blue, Green, Gold, Silver.

Interior: Grey.

AT A GLANCE...

HISTORIC
Introduced in: 1987, 1995.
Made in: Ingersoll, Ontario, Canada.

DEMOGRAPHICS

Model	Men./Wom.	Age	Married	College	Income $
Metro	53/47 %	36	46 %	28 %	23,000
Swift	39/61 %	37	39 %	30 %	24,000

INDEX

Safety:	70 %	Satisfaction:	82 %
Depreciation:	47 %	Insurance:	$ 500
Cost per mile:	$ 0.35	Number of dealers:	4,466

SALES

		Canada			USA	
Model	1997	1998	Result	1997	1998	Result
Metro	3,515	2,281	- 35.0 %	55,629	28.515	- 48.7 %
Swift	2,572	2,078	- 19.2 %	1,462	2,254	+ 54.2 %

MAINTENANCE REQUIRED BY WARRANTY

First revision:	Frequency:	Diagnostic plug:
3,000 miles	6,000 miles	No

Mini-cars

Surprising

The Lanos is the smallest Daewoo commercialized in North America. It was the first model developed entirely by Daewoo, where it replaced the Nexia, nothing more than a revamped Opel Kadett known here under the name of the Pontiac Le Mans or the Passport Optima. It has a lot of convincing to do in a segment where some of its competitors sales are appreciably high.

MODEL RANGE

The Lanos is sold as a 3- or 4-door sedan in S, SE (USA) or SX versions, all of which are equipped with a 1.6L 4-cylinder engine and a standard 5-speed manual transmission or an optional 4-speed automatic. While the base version's equipment is cursory, the SX's is more elaborate and includes air conditioning, power windows, power door locks and power sideview mirrors, and a radio with CD player.

TECHNICAL FEATURES

The Lanos has a steel unibody and its drag coefficient falls within the average range. The front suspension features elastic struts and the rear is based on a semirigid axle and longitudinal control arms. Coil springs and a stabilizer bar are installed on both the front and rear wheel assembly. The power rack-and-pinion steering system is standard and brakes are mixed, with optional ABS. The E-TEC engine is a recent development. It includes an adapted air intake system and a variable injection system making it possible to optimize power and torque in the lower RPM range.

PROS

+ **VALUE.** Although Daewoo's very attractive asking price is considered to be a special introductory offer in disguise, given the model's equipment level it's bound to make inroads to the detriment of a number of Korean and Japanese competitors.

+ **PRESENTATION.** Anybody who sees a Lanos for the first time finds its styling attractive and its looks racy with flowing lines, aluminum wheels and a grille a lot like BMW's.

+ **DRIVEABILITY.** The Lanos' energetic and modern little engine, precision controls and good road stability are surprising on a car in this price range.

+ **HANDLING.** Despite a smooth suspension the Lanos hugs the road consistently — provided it sports good quality tires. It's stable and predictable on straight-line trajectories and fun on winding roads, where it proves to be very agile.

+ **RIDE.** A well-gauged and smooth suspension and well-designed seats provide good lateral and lumbar support.

+ **BRAKING.** Even without ABS stops are straight, the pedal is easy to gauge and fading is virtually nonexistent.

+ **QUALITY.** It may not be the next wonder of the world, but the Lanos is carefully constructed, its finish is good and the materials used are attractive to the eye and the touch. Certain rivals would be well-advised to sit up and take notice!

+ **TRUNK.** Volume is good thanks to a design that's well proportioned in width and in height. However, the floor is lower than the sill, which complicates the unloading process.

CONS

- **STOPPING DISTANCES.** They're fairly long given current standards but in all fairness they're the product of "borderline" braking, making it possible to stop the vehicle without causing the wheels to lock.

- **PERFORMANCE.** Levels are only average and acceleration and pickup are both laborious when the vehicle is fully loaded, especially with the automatic transmission. Drivers should be careful when overtaking other vehicles — to be safe, the process requires plenty of room.

- **NOISE LEVEL.** The loud engine, road noise on bumpy surfaces and wind leaks around the windshield maintain a high overall noise level due mainly to a serious lack of soundproofing material.

- **SUSPENSION.** Too soft on smooth roads it goes wild on rough surfaces and creates some jumping, though the latter has no noticeable effect on the car's trajectory.

- **REAR SEATS.** Besides being hard to access because of narrow doors and a front seatback that takes up a lot of space, they offer only enough room for two adults and their storage spaces are limited to a single, solitary cupholder.

- **TRANSMISSION.** There's a noticeable gap between second and third gear on the automatic transmission, which has a negative effect on performance capabilities.

- **DRAWBACKS.** The instrument panel doesn't show which gear the car is travelling in with the automatic transmission, wipers create a huge blind spot on the right-hand side of the windshield and there are very few storage spaces in the front and none at all in the back. Lastly, the fabric used to cover the trunk's interior is very lightweight and it isn't glued into place, which tends to be very annoying.

- **RADIO.** Although its reception and sound are both excellent, its controls and digital display are a nightmare and call for all the patience the user can muster.

- **DEALER NETWORK.** Although the number of dealers is increasing each week, it's still smaller than the competition's and this may hinder the new make's sales and maintenance possibilities.

CONCLUSION

While the Lanos still needs a few improvements here and there, it's a good bargain for the asking price and is sure to shake things up in its market niche.

RATING
DAEWOO Lanos

CONCEPT : 66%
Technology :	75
Safety :	75
Interior space :	60
Trunk volume :	40
Quality/fit/finish :	80

DRIVING : 61%
Cockpit :	80
Performance :	35
Handling :	55
Steering :	80
Braking :	55

ORIGINAL EQUIPMENT : 66%
Tires :	75
Headlights :	75
Wipers :	55
Rear defroster :	75
Radio :	50

COMFORT : 60%
Seats :	75
Suspension :	75
Sound level :	40
Conveniences :	40
Air conditioning :	70

BUDGET : 82%
Price :	90
Fuel economy :	90
Insurance :	85
Satisfaction :	75
Depreciation :	70

Overall rating : 67.0%

NEW FOR 2000

- **New entry-level make and model on the Canadian market.**

Compare
Performance,
Specifications, Prices,
and Classification
at the end of this chapter.

EQUIPMENT

DAEWOO Lanos	S	SE	SX
Automatic transmission:	O	O	O
Cruise control:			
Power steering:	S	S	S
Anti-lock brakes:	O	O	O
Traction control:	-	-	-
Air conditioning:	O	O	S
Leather:	-	-	-
AM/FM/radio-cassette:	S	S	SCd
Power door locks:	-	S	S
Power windows:	-	O	S
Tilt steering:	-	-	S
Dual adjustable mirrors:	SM	SM	SE
Alloy wheels:	-	-	-
Anti-theft system:	-	-	-

Colors

Exterior: White, Blue, Red, Green, Grey, Black.

Interior: Grey.

AT A GLANCE...

HISTORIC
Introduced in: 1997.
Made in: Pupyong, South Korea.

DEMOGRAPHICS

Model	Men./Wom.	Age	Married	College	Income $
Lanos	NA				

INDEX

Safety:	75 %	Satisfaction:	75 %
Depreciation:	25 %	Insurance:	$ 520
Cost per mile:	$ 0.32	Number of dealers:	115

SALES

		Canada			USA	
Model	1997	1998	Result	1997	1998	Result
Lanos	NA					

MAINTENANCE REQUIRED BY WARRANTY

First revision:	Frequency:	Diagnostic plug:
4,000 miles	6 months / 8,000 miles	Yes

A Warm Front

The Accent is the model that gave Hyundai a renewed taste for success. The combined effect of a good price and an adequate fit and finish led to a flurry of sales in Canada and the United States. The Accent has been revamped for this year, but it was unveiled too late for a detailed description in this edition. The following comments apply to the 1999 model.

MODEL RANGE

The Accent 3-door hatchback coupe comes in L and GSi versions and the 4-door sedan is sold exclusively in GL trim. The cars are all equipped with the same direct fuel injected 1.5L SOHC 4-cylinder engine paired up with a 5-speed manual gearbox or with an optional 4-speed automatic. The L base model's equipment is pretty minimal, since it doesn't include much besides intermittent wipers, manually adjustable mirrors and radio with tape deck. The GSi/GL versions also receive power steering. The automatic gearbox, antilock braking system, airbags, air conditioning, sunroof and light alloy wheels are all billed as extras.

TECHNICAL FEATURES

The Accent has a steel unibody with a lightly rounded silhouette that procures good aerodynamic yield with a drag coefficient of 0.31. The fully independent suspension consists of MacPherson struts up front and a dual-link at the rear, with a stabilizer bar at both extremities. All models are equipped with disc and drum brakes, but ABS is sold as an extra, as are the two front airbags.

PROS

+ PRICE. It's very competitive, because it doesn't include some vital safety features such as airbags and antilock braking. The base hatchback model gets pretty slim trimmings when it comes to equipment, since it doesn't even come equipped with standard power steering, a feature that the other models benefit from.

+ CABIN SPACE. The cabin is quite modest, but it can accommodate four adults and all their luggage quite nicely, since there's enough breathing room all-round.

+ PERFORMANCES. They're more thrilling with the manual transmission that warrants livelier accelerations and pick-up, whereas the automatic downshifts at the least molehill and siphens off a good part of available juice, not to mention the air conditioning... Here, there isn't an ideal choice.

+ FUEL EFFICIENCY. It's one of the most frugal on the North American market, but not as impressive as that of some Japanese rivals.

+ STYLE. It's upbeat shape and fun-loving roundish mug look pretty sharp in some of the bright shades and when the car's equipped with light alloy rims.

+ DRIVING. It's definitely more fun with the precise, responsive power steering that makes for slick moves due to a short steer angle diameter and trim body size.

+ RIDE COMFORT. It benefits from the super suspension and nicely shaped front seats that provide pretty good support, depending on the occupants' physique.

+ ROADHOLDING. It's quite impressive, but isn't as competent as that of some Japanese rivals. The GSi/GL versions are more reassuring in this respect, thanks to their more generous tires, whereas the lowly L model is equipped with pretty Dinky toy tires.

+ QUALITY. Construction, fit and finish job and the type of trim materials used have really come a long way and the cabin has a livelier, lovelier look than on some rivals, although the Accent can't really hide its lowly origins.

CONS

- STEERING. Manual steering is absolutely awful, it's all over the map and suffers from a poor reduction ratio, so driving the base model is no fun at all.

- PERFORMANCES. They're very middling, for engine strain on accelerations and pick-up, especially with a load.

- FINISH JOB. It could be neater without spending a mint. Some details like the trunk lining are really neglected.

- MANUAL GEARBOX. It's far from perfect, since it's vague and wavering, which makes city driving a bit frustrating, since it often mixes up first and third gears.

- BRAKES. They lack grip and lasting power, so sudden stopping distances stretch out too far for a car of this weight. Car path is rather uncertain without ABS.

- ATTENTION. Road ruts also affect car path for these compact, high-perched vehicles and you really, we mean really, have to watch out for the small tires on the base version that are Soupy shuffle slippery.

-NOISE. It's loud at all times, since the engine roars at the least coaxing, and wind and road noise increase with speed.

- ODOR. Plastic components on the dashboard emit a scent that's really sickening on hot summer days, so you have to leave the windows open to offset it.

CONCLUSION

The advent of the Daewoo Lanos and Toyota Echo may well stir things up in the market segment where the Accent has earned first place in terms of sales. To maintain its positioning, the new model will have to be very clever and competitively priced to boot.

Accent HYUNDAI

RATING
HYUNDAI Accent

CONCEPT : — 61%
Technology :	75
Safety :	50
Interior space :	50
Trunk volume :	60
Quality/fit/finish :	70

DRIVING : — 59%
Cockpit :	75
Performance :	50
Handling :	50
Steering :	70
Braking :	50

ORIGINAL EQUIPMENT : — 70%
Tires :	70
Headlights :	75
Wipers :	70
Rear defroster :	65
Radio :	70

COMFORT : — 59%
Seats :	65
Suspension :	60
Sound level :	40
Conveniences :	60
Air conditioning :	70

BUDGET : — 79%
Price :	85
Fuel economy :	85
Insurance :	80
Satisfaction :	80
Depreciation :	65

Overall rating : 65.6%

NEW FOR 2000

• Model will be entirely renewed in December 1999.

Compare Performance, Specifications, Prices, and Classification at the end of this chapter.

EQUIPMENT

HYUNDAI Accent	L	GL	GSi
Automatic transmission:	-	O	O
Cruise control:	-	-	-
Power steering:	-	S	S
Anti-lock brakes:	-	O	O
Traction control:	-	-	-
Air conditioning:	-	O	O
Leather:	-	-	-
AM/FM/radio-cassette:	S	S	S
Power door locks:	-	-	-
Power windows:	-	-	S
Tilt steering:	-	-	-
Dual adjustable mirrors:	SM	SM	SE
Alloy wheels:	-	-	S
Anti-theft system:	-	-	-

Colors
Exterior: Green, Silver, Plum, Blue, White, Black, Red.

Interior: Grey-Green.

AT A GLANCE...

HISTORIC
Introduced in: 1995.
Made in: Ulsan, South Korea.

DEMOGRAPHICS
Model	Men./Wom.	Age	Married	College	Income $
Accent	45/55 %	38	53 %	32 %	24,000

INDEX
Safety:	50 %	Satisfaction:	80 %
Depreciation:	48 %	Insurance:	$ 520
Cost per mile:	$ 0.35	Number of dealers:	500

SALES
Model	Canada 1997	1998	Result	USA 1997	1998	Result
Accent	9,852	12,585	+ 27.7 %	40,355	30,231	- 25.1 %

MAINTENANCE REQUIRED BY WARRANTY
First revision:	Frequency:	Diagnostic plug:
3,000 miles	6,000 miles	Yes

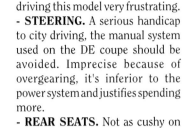

Mini-cars

Timid

Like other Mitsubishi models, the Mirage lives in the shadow of lofty industry leaders such as Honda, Toyota and now, Hyundai and Daewoo as well. It owes most of its sales to it's inexpensive price, which is due in turn to minimum equipment and a stark presentation.

MODEL RANGE

Given its two engine's displacements, the Mirage is on the borderline that separates small cars from minicars models. It's available as a 2-door coupe and a 4-door sedan, in base DE or LS versions. The DE coupes and sedans are equipped with a 1.5L 4-cylinder and the LS models have a 1.8L engine. A 5-speed manual transmission is standard and a 4-speed automatic is optional. The DE version's standard equipment doesn't include all that much except for power steering on the sedan (it's manual on the coupe), dual airbags and a tilt steering column. The LS is enriched with a radio, intermittent windshield wipers and light alloy wheels. This means that besides the automatic transmission, air conditioning, cruise control, power windows, power rearview mirrors, remote keyless entry, a sunroof and ABS brakes are all optional.

TECHNICAL FEATURES

The latest Mirage models have a wider body and the sedan is also longer and higher to provide more passenger room. Steel unibodies are more rounded and aerodynamically efficient, though a bit less so since the Cx has gone from 0.29 to 0.30. They've been made more rigid thanks to bigger siderails and beams, whose extremities are used to support the vehicle's bumpers. The fully independent suspension uses MacPherson struts at the front and a multi-arm configuration at the back. Brakes are mixed, but an antilock system is optional on the LS models. Both engines have been revised to provide higher performance levels and are mounted transversally to minimize the weight put on supports.

PROS

+ PRICE. These models are competitively priced. The DE coupe is a bargain for those looking to pay as little as possible and its 1.5L engine is more economical than the more powerful 1.8L alternative.

+ PASSENGER ROOM. With the Mirage's wider body, there's plenty of room for four good-sized passengers to travel aboard without rubbing elbows.

+ SUSPENSION. More sophisticated than its rivals choices, it's relatively smooth for a car in this category. It provides a clearly comfortable ride and wheel travel is sufficient to swallow road defects effectively.

+ PERFORMANCE. The 1.8L is significantly stronger and provides excellent driveability without exaggerated fuel consumption levels.

+ HANDLING. While it depends heavily on tire size and quality, handling is strong and exciting despite a certain amount of roll when cornering, the result of a smooth suspension that tends to accentuate understeering.

+ INSTRUMENT PANEL. Simple and ergonomic, it's well organized but very dull to look at — maybe using any other color but grey is just too expensive!

+ SEATS. In the front they provide good support and mold well, but the thickness and softness of their upholstery depends on the finish; the rear seat bench is flat and firm.

+ RELIABILITY. Mitsubishi products are usually problem-free, but some owners have complained of minor persistent problems that should have been solved long ago.

+ NOISE LEVEL. It's significantly lower thanks to a more rigid body, engine insulation and a body design that has eliminated a good deal of wind noise. However, during accelerations engines are loud and the reason is a lack of proper soundproofing material.

CONS

- BRAKING. As is the case with most Japanese cars, it's mediocre. Power is well-balanced and easy to gauge under normal use, but front wheels block immediately in emergency situations which increases stopping distances and shifts the car's trajectory on non-ABS versions.

- 1.5L ENGINE. It's fuel economy is not a good enough excuse to choose it; when coupled with the automatic transmission, it makes driving this model very frustrating.

- STEERING. A serious handicap to city driving, the manual system used on the DE coupe should be avoided. Imprecise because of overgearing, it's inferior to the power system and justifies spending more.

- REAR SEATS. Not as cushy on coupes as they are on sedans, their access also calls for acrobatic skills.

- EQUIPMENT. It's minimal on the base model to keep the price as low as it is, which seriously affects ease of use.

- PRACTICALITY. Since this car is billed as mainly utilitarian, the lack of storage spaces in the passenger compartment is especially surprising.

CONCLUSION

From the technical and financial standpoints, the Mirage models compare favorably to their rivals. However, the price to pay is extremely limited equipment and an exaggeratedly utilitarian presentation.

RATING	
MITSUBISHI Mirage	
CONCEPT :	**66%**
Technology :	75
Safety :	90
Interior space :	50
Trunk volume :	40
Quality/fit/finish :	75
DRIVING :	**58%**
Cockpit :	75
Performance :	35
Handling :	55
Steering :	70
Braking :	55
ORIGINAL EQUIPMENT :	**70%**
Tires :	60
Headlights :	75
Wipers :	75
Rear defroster :	70
Radio :	70
COMFORT :	**61%**
Seats :	70
Suspension :	70
Sound level :	50
Conveniences :	40
Air conditioning :	75
BUDGET :	**72%**
Price :	85
Fuel economy :	85
Insurance :	60
Satisfaction :	85
Depreciation :	45
Overall rating :	**65.4%**

NEW FOR 2000

• No details available at press time.

Compare
Performance,
Specifications, Prices,
and Classification
at the end of this chapter.

EQUIPMENT

MITSUBISHI Mirage	DE	LS
Automatic transmission:	O	O
Cruise control:	-	O
Power steering:	S	S
Anti-lock brakes:	-	O
Traction control:	-	-
Air conditioning:	O	O
Leather:	-	-
AM/FM/radio-cassette:	-	-
Power door locks:	O	S
Power windows:	O	O
Tilt steering:	S	S
Dual adjustable mirrors:	-	S
Alloy wheels:	-	S
Anti-theft system:	-	S

Colors

Exterior: Blue, Red, Green, White.

Interior: Grey, Blue.

AT A GLANCE...

HISTORIC

Introduced in: 1979 (rwd), 1997.
Made in: Mizushima/Korashiki, Japan.

DEMOGRAPHICS

Model	Men./Wom.	Age	Married	College	Income $
Mirage	47/53 %	36	51 %	44 %	27,000

INDEX

Safety:	85 %	Satisfaction:	85 %
Depreciation:	NA	Insurance:	$ 475
Cost per mile:	$ 0.28	Number of dealers:	550

SALES

Model	Canada 1997	1998	Result	USA 1997	1998	Result
Mirage	Not on sale in Canada.			31,717	33,072	+ 4.3 %

MAINTENANCE REQUIRED BY WARRANTY

First revision:	Frequency:	Diagnostic plug:
3,500 miles	6 months / 7,000 miles	Yes

TOYOTA

Echo

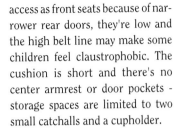

Funnily Economical

When it replaced its low-end model, Toyota took the risk of changing its name even if it was one of the most solidly ensconced on the small car market in North America. The explanation is the No. 1 Japanese builder's desire to attract a younger and broader clientele base at a time when fuel prices have begun to show a tendency to climb ever higher.

MODEL RANGE

The Echo is available in only one version, a 2- or 4-door sedan with a 1.5L 4-cylinder engine coupled with a standard 5-speed manual transmission or an optional 4-speed automatic. Standard equipment includes the bare minimum, namely power steering and a radio and cassette player.

TECHNICAL FEATURES

The Echo has a steel unibody featuring some galvanized parts and a positive drag coefficient of 0.32. With its cab forward design, its style is inspired by the Prius, remarkable for its unusual height. The front suspension features MacPherson struts and the rear uses a torsion axle with coil springs positioned low to minimize their intrusion into the trunk's cargo space. Brakes are mixed and ABS is optional, rack-and-pinion power steering is standard. The engine is a version of the Tercel's and is equipped with a new mechanical-hydraulic valve control system known as the VVT-i, which admits the ideal amount of air into cylinders. The crankshaft is slightly off center to increase piston power

during release and friction has been decreased by 25% in comparison to the previous engine.

PROS

+ STYLING. Inspired by the Prius' lines, the Echo is refreshing, with bold lines and oversized headlights. The two-tone dashboard and door linings and seat fabric patterns give the passenger compartment a young and relaxed look.

+ ROOMINESS. The passenger compartment and trunk are unusually roomy for a model in this category and it can easily take on five passengers and their baggage. Thanks to the body's unusual architecture, the rear offers remarkable legroom and headroom. Good-sized doors that open wide provide excellent access to front seats.

+ DRIVEABILITY. The Echo's good weight-power ratio (9.9 kg/hp or 22 lb/bhp) makes it a lot of fun to drive, even with the automatic transmission and it's remarkably energetic for a model in this category.

+ PERFORMANCE. Like the Tercel it's replacing, the Echo provides good fuel economy considering its performance capabilities.

+ EQUIPMENT. Compared to its predecessor, the Echo offers more quality for the same price for its

equipment is more elaborate.

+ PRACTICALITY. The latest little Toyota has a lot of storage spaces, located mainly in the front, including two adjacent glove boxes, door pockets and two cupholders.

+ COMFORT. It's surprisingly good on a car of this size; the suspensions are smooth but never soft, seats are well upholstered and the noise level is reasonable at cruising speeds.

+ INSTRUMENT PANEL. Resolutely modern, it's distinctive because of its instrument cluster, positioned dead center and at the foot of the windshield, just like on European models. This has the advantage of providing the driver with more room to maneuver and makes it easy to read dials, almost without taking your eyes off the road. But it's too bad that Toyota stopped short and decided to use standard rather than digital displays.

+ REAR WINDOWS. They roll down all the way, much to the joy of kids who like to feel the wind on their faces.

+ BONUS POINTS. Efficient wipers whose rhythm and reach keep the windshield clean even in the heaviest rain.

CONS

- REAR SEATS. Not as easy to

access as front seats because of narrower rear doors, they're low and the high belt line may make some children feel claustrophobic. The cushion is short and there's no center armrest or door pockets - storage spaces are limited to two small catchalls and a cupholder.

- ERGONOMICS. The instrument panel would have earned higher points if designers had switched the radio and air conditioning controls for one another. Sideview mirrors aren't positioned high enough and limit the driver's field of vision.

- TIRES. Optional 14-inch tires provide more road stability than the standard 13-inch alternatives. Our test drive model was equipped with excellent Bridgestone Potenza RE92 tires.

- TRUNK. Its presentation could be better; trim fabric is flimsy and clumsily attached to the rear fold down seat and carpeting tends to "fly".

CONCLUSION

Toyota is convinced that young buyers are those who will revive the small car category. Their financial needs and their unconventional tastes should find their match in this newcomer - it refuses to sacrifice driveability merely for the sake of maximum practicality.

RATING
TOYOTA Echo

CONCEPT :		64%
Technology :	80	
Safety :	75	
Interior space :	50	
Trunk volume :	35	
Quality/fit/finish :	80	

DRIVING :		60%
Cockpit :	80	
Performance :	45	
Handling :	50	
Steering :	70	
Braking :	55	

ORIGINAL EQUIPMENT :		72%
Tires :	75	
Headlights :	75	
Wipers :	65	
Rear defroster :	75	
Radio :	70	

COMFORT :		67%
Seats :	75	
Suspension :	75	
Sound level :	50	
Conveniences :	60	
Air conditioning :	75	

BUDGET :		79%
Price :	80	
Fuel economy :	90	
Insurance :	80	
Satisfaction :	90	
Depreciation :	55	

Overall rating :	68.4%

NEW FOR 2000

• An all-new model derived from the Yaris, developed for the European market, the Echo is powered by an environment-friendly 1.5L 4-cylinder engine.

Compare
Performance,
Specifications, Prices,
and Classification
at the end of this chapter.

EQUIPMENT

TOYOTA Echo	base
Automatic transmission:	O
Cruise control:	O
Power steering:	S
Anti-lock brakes:	O
Traction control:	-
Air conditioning:	O
Leather:	-
AM/FM/radio-cassette:	S
Power door locks:	O
Power windows:	O
Tilt steering:	O
Dual adjustable mirrors:	O
Alloy wheels:	-
Anti-theft system:	O

Colors
Exterior: White, Red, Silver, Black, Blue.

Interior: Grey.

AT A GLANCE...

HISTORIC
Introduced in: 2000
Made in: Takaoka-Toyota City, Japan.

DEMOGRAPHICS

Model	Men./Wom.	Age	Married	College	Income $
Tercel	43/57 %	42	57 %	53 %	30,000

INDEX

Safety:	75 %	Satisfaction:	92 %
Depreciation:	45 %	Insurance:	$ 500
Cost per mile:	$ 0.37	Number of dealers:	1233

SALES

Model	1997	Canada 1998	Result	1997	USA 1998	Result
Tercel	16,465	23,395	+ 42.1 %	31,651	1,743	- 94.5 %

MAINTENANCE REQUIRED BY WARRANTY
First revision:	**Frequency:**	**Diagnostic plug:**
3,500 miles	3,500 miles	Yes

MINI-CARS
PERFORMANCE

Model/ version	Type / timing valve / fuel system	Displacement cu in	Power hp @ rpm	Torque lb-ft @ rpm	Compres. ratio	Driving wheels / transmission	Final ratio	Acceler. 0-60 mph s	Standing 1/4 & 5/8 mile s	Passing 50-75 mph s	Braking 60-0 mph ft	Top speed mph	Lateral acceler. G	Noise level dBA	City	Highway	Fuel type Octane
CHEVROLET Metro																	
2dr.	L3 1.0 SOHC-6-EFI	61	55 @ 5700	58 @ 3300	9.5 :1	front- M5*	4.39	14.3	19.3	37.2	13.5	151	90	0.75	70	43	55	R 87
2/4dr.LSi	L4 1.3 SOHC-16-MPFI	79	79 @ 6000	75 @ 3000	9.5 :1	front- M5*	3.79	13.2	18.8	36.4	11.8	160	100	0.75	68	37	48	R 87
						front- A3	3.61	14.0	19.5	37.5	13.0	157	93	0.75	68	31	38	R 87
DAEWOO Lanos																	
base	L4 1.6 DOHC-16-MPFI	97.5	105 @ 5800	106 @ 3400	9.5 :1	front- M5*	4.176	10.8	17.6	32.8	8.2	144	102	0.77	68	26	36	R 87
						front- A4	3.910	11.8	18.2	34.0	9.7	151	100	0.77	70	23	33	R 87
HYUNDAI Accent																	
base	L4 1.5 SOHC-12-MPFI	91	92 @ 5500	97 @ 4000	10.0 :1	front- M5*	3.842	11.5	17.7	32.8	7.3	148	109	0.76	70	28	36	R 87
						front- A4	3.656	12.8	18.8	34.8	10.2	151	103	0.76	70	27	35	R 87
MITSUBISHI Mirage																	
DE	L4 1.5 SOHC-12-MPFI	90	92 @ 5500	93 @ 3000	9.0 :1	front- M5*	3.71	11.8	18.5	34.7	10.0	144	103	0.78	68	34	43	R 87
						front- A4	3.72	12.9	19.2	35.6	11.5	141	100	0.78	68	30	36	R 87
LS	L4 1.8 SOHC-12-MPFI	112	113 @ 5500	116 @ 4500	9.5 :1	front- M5*	4.02	9.1	16.5	30.0	6.7	135	109	0.82	68	27	37	R 87
						front- A4	4.02	10.0	17.6	31.0	7.2	138	106	0.82	68	27	37	R 87
SUZUKI Swift																	
base	L4 1.3 SOHC-16-MPFI	79	79 @ 6000	75 @ 3000	9.5 :1	front- M5*	3.79	13.2	18.8	36.4	11.8	160	100	0.75	68	37	48	R 87
TOYOTA Echo																	
base	L4 1.5 DOHC-16-MPFI	91	108 @ 6000	105 @ 4000	10.5 :1	front- M5*	3.72	9.6	17.5	32.7	7.2	144	102	0.77	68	32	44	R 87
						front- A4	2.82	11.0	18.5	32.5	8.5	148	100	0.77	68	28	41	R 87

SPECIFICATIONS

Model	Version Trim	Body/ Seats	Cabin volume cu ft	Trunk volume cu ft	Cd	Wheel base in	Lgth x Width x Hght in x inx in	Curb weight lb	Susp. ft/rr	Brake ft/rr	Steering type	Steering ø turns ft number	Fuel tank gal	dimensions	make	model	Standard powertrain	99 Price msrp $
CHEVROLET	General warranty: 3-years / 36,000 miles; perforation corrosion:5-years / unlimited. 24 hrs Roadside assistance.																	
Metro	base	3dr.sdn. 4	85.8	8.4	0.33	93.1	149.4x62.6x54.7	1895	ih/ih	dc/dr	r&p.	31.5 3.7	10.3	155/80R13	Goodyear	Invicta GL	L3/1.0/M5	9,423
Metro	LSi	3dr.sdn. 4	85.8	8.4	0.33	93.1	149.4x62.6x54.7	1895	ih/ih	dc/dr	r&p.	31.5 3.7	10.3	155/80R13	Goodyear	Invicta GL	L3/1.0/M5	10,220
Metro	LSi	4dr.sdn. 4	90.4	10.3	0.34	93.1	164.0x62.6x55.4	1984	ih/ih	dc/dr	r&p.	31.5 3.7	10.3	155/80R13	Goodyear	Invicta GL	L4/1.3/M5	10,832
DAEWOO	General warranty: 3-years / 36,000 miles; powertrain: 5-years / 60,000 miles; corrosion perforation: 5-years / 60,000 miles.																	
Lanos	S	3dr.sdn. 4	94.6	8.8	0.32	99.2	160.4x66.1x56.4	2447	ih/ih	dc/dr	pwr.r&p.	32.0 3.0	12.7	185/60R14	Khumo	Steel Belted	L4/1.6/M5	8,299
Lanos	SE	3dr.sdn. 4	94.6	8.8	0.32	99.2	160.4x66.1x56.4	2447	ih/ih	dc/dr	pwr.r&p.	32.0 3.0	12.7	185/60R14	Khumo	Steel Belted	L4/1.6/M5	10,600
Lanos	SX	3dr.sdn. 4	94.6	8.8	0.32	99.2	160.4x66.1x56.4	2527	ih/ih	dc/dr	pwr.r&p.	32.0 3.0	12.7	185/60R14	Khumo	Steel Belted	L4/1.6/A4	11,699
Lanos	S	4dr.sdn. 4	90.8	11.4	0.32	99.2	166.8x66.1x56.4	2522	ih/ih	dc/dr	pwr.r&p.	32.0 3.0	12.7	185/60R14	Khumo	Steel Belted	L4/1.6/M5	9,699
Lanos	SE	4dr.sdn. 4	90.8	11.4	0.32	99.2	166.8x66.1x56.4	2522	ih/ih	dc/dr	pwr.r&p.	32.0 3.0	12.7	185/60R14	Khumo	Steel Belted	L4/1.6/M5	10,900
Lanos	SX	4dr.sdn. 4	90.8	11.4	0.32	99.2	166.8x66.1x56.4	2595	ih/ih	dc/dr	pwr.r&p.	32.0 3.0	12.7	185/60R14	Khumo	Steel Belted	L4/1.6/A4	11,969
HYUNDAI	General warranty: 3-years / 36,000 miles; powertrain: 5-years / 60,000 miles; corrosion perforation: 5 years / 60,000 miles; antipollution: 5-years / 36,000 miles.																	
Accent	L	3dr.sdn. 4	88.0	16.1	0.31	94.5	161.5x63.8x54.9	2088	ih/ih	dc/dr	r&p.	31.8 3.9	11.9	155/80R13	General	HP 40	L4/1.5/M5	9,184
Accent	GS	3dr.sdn. 4	88.0	16.1	0.31	94.5	161.5x63.8x54.9	2132	ih/ih	dc/dr	r&p.	31.8 3.9	11.9	175/70R14	General	HP 40	L4/1.5/M5	9,934
Accent	GL	4dr.sdn. 4	88.0	10.7	0.31	94.5	162.1x63.8x54.9	2119	ih/ih	dc/dr	r&p.	31.8 3.9	11.9	175/70R14	General	HP 40	L4/1.5/M5	9,934
MITSUBISHI	General warranty: 3-years / 36,000 miles; powetrain: 5-years / 60,000 miles.																	
Mirage	DE	cpe.2 p. 5	85.6	11.5	0.30	95.0	168.1x66.5x51.3	2127	ih/ih	dc/dr	r&p.	32.8 3.6	13.2	175/70R13	-	-	L4/1.5/M5	11,575
Mirage	LS	cpe.2 p. 5	85.6	11.5	0.30	95.0	168.1x66.5x51.3	2260	ih/ih	dc/dr	r&p.	32.8 3.2	13.2	175/70R13	-	-	L4/1.8/M5	15,025
Mirage	DE	sdn.4 p. 5	91.4	11.5	0.30	98.4	173.6x66.5x52.5	2227	ih/ih	dc/dr	pwr.r&p.	33.4 3.2	13.2	175/70R14	-	-	L4/1.5/M5	12,875
Mirage	LS	sdn.4 p. 5	91.4	11.5	0.30	98.4	173.6x66.5x52.5	2348	ih/ih	dc/dr	pwr.r&p.	33.4 3.2	13.2	185/65R14	-	-	L4/1.8/M5	13,825
SUZUKI	General warranty: 3-years / 50,000 miles; corrosion perforation: 5-years / unlimited. 24 hr roadside assistance																	
Swift	DLX	3dr.sdn.4	85.8	8.4	0.33	93.1	149.4x62.6x54.7	1895	ih/ih	dc/dr	r&p.	31.5 3.7	10.3	155/80R13	Goodyear	Invicta GL	L3/1.0/M5	9,479
TOYOTA	General warranty: 3-years / 36,000 miles; powertrain 5-years / 60,000 miles; corrosion, perforation: 5-years / unlimited.																	
Echo	base	2dr.sdn.5	87	13.6	0.32	93.3	163.2x65.4x59.1	2375	ih/ih	dc/dr	pwr.r&p.	- 3.0	10.0	155/80R13	Bridgestone	Potenza RE92	L4/1.5/M5	-
Echo	base	4dr.sdn.5	87	13.6	0.32	93.3	163.2x65.4x59.1	2375	ih/ih	dc/dr	pwr.r&p.	- 3.0	10.0	155/80R13	Bridgestone	Potenza RE92	L4/1.5/M5	-

Notes:
1) Tire makes and models are provided solely as an indication; they are subject to change without prior notice from the automobile manufacturer.
2) See the 2000 price list at the back of this edition.

CLASSIFICATION

OUR CLASSIFICATION

Rank	Models	Concept	Driving	Equipment	Comfort	Budget	Rating
1	**TOYOTA Echo**	64	60	**72**	67	79	**68.4 %**
2	DAEWOO Lanos	**66**	**61**	66	60	**82**	67.0 %
3	HYUNDAI Accent	61	59	70	59	79	65.6 %
4	MITSUBISHI Mirage	**66**	58	70	61	72	65.4 %
5	CHEVROLET Metro & PONTIAC Firefly	57	46	66	55	76	60.0 %

YOUR CLASSIFICATION

Rank	Models	98 Sales
1	**MITSUBISHI Mirage**	33 072
2	HYUNDAI Accent	30 231
3	CHEVROLET Metro	28 515
4	SUZUKI Swift	2 254
5	TOYOTA Tercel-Echo	1 743

Not classified:
DAEWOO Lanos

GM J Series

CHRYSLER Neon

DAEWOO Nubira

FORD Focus

HONDA Civic

HYUNDAI Elantra

KIA Sephia

MAZDA Protegé

NISSAN Sentra

Comparative Test

SMALL CARS

See their performance, their specifications, their price and their classification at the end of this chapter.

VW New Beetle

TOYOTA Corolla

SUZUKI Esteem

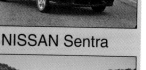

SATURN S

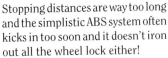

The Cavalier and Sunfire continue to meet with extensive success given a very competitive price, made available in spite of a very adequate equipment level. The Cavalier is three times more popular than its counterpart and ranks in the Top 10 sales hit parade on the North American market.

Attractive

MODEL RANGE

It comes in five versions at Chevrolet and four at Pontiac: a base sedan and coupe RS or SE, an LS sedan furbished with richer equipment, as well as a Z24 or GT coupe and convertible with a more sports feel. The base engine is a 2.2L 4-cylinder model assisted by a 5-speed manual gearbox or a 3-speed automatic. A 2.4L 150-hp double overhead camshaft multivalve engine motivates the Z24 and GT versions and it's listed as an option for the LS sedan. This model also receives a standard 4-speed electronically controlled automatic gearbox with traction control who is optional on the other versions.

TECHNICAL FEATURES

Their steel unibody construction is robust and yields sure and steady roadability, besides assuring enhanced passenger protection. Road noise and vibration are well blotted out as well. But their clean, silhouette hides rather poor aerodynamics, as the drag coefficient of 0.38 to 0.42 attests to. The front suspension consists of MacPherson struts and at the rear, there's a tubular semirigid axle. Front disc brakes and rear drum brakes are linked to standard ABS. Power steering is also part of the original equipment items. The LS sedan gets an optional traction control feature with the 4-speed automatic transmission.

OUTSTANDING

++ DESIGN. To appeal to so many buyers, this car's style is very attractive. The majority of the Cavalier-Sunfire owners are women, who say to be very sensible to the appearance of these vehicles.

PROS

+ VALUE. This car's main drawing card is still its generous standard equipment, offered at an affordable price. But watch out, those sets of optional accessory items tend to inflate the initial price.

+ COMFORT. Long rides are very pleasant when you're travelling in such a roomy cabin, good front seats, with an effective suspension.

+ SIZE. The Cavalier-Sunfire are blessed with a convenient format and cabin space, proportional to vehicle size. The numerous storage areas are handy, particularly the glove compartment which is very roomy and the trunk is accessible and can be extended on all models by lowering the rear seatbench.

+ TRIM FEATURES. The 2000 modifications make these cars looks more spiffy than ever thanks to the youthful trim shades.

+ CHASSIS. On the road, the Cavalier-Sunfire feel solid and their sway is moderate. This really makes the steering accurate on curves and for generally predictable behavior, but of course, road handling depends also on tire quality.

+ ENGINE. The 2.4L multivalve engine pumps out crisper accelerations and pick-up than does the base 2.2L 4-cylinder version. Yet it isn't as smooth as the V6 that graced the former generation. It doesn't develop as much torque either.

CONS

- QUALITY. Some components or finish details give away the reason behind this car's affordability. You get what you pay for and even though reliability has come a long way, there's still room for improvement.

- 2.2L ENGINE. It lacks vim and vigor when paired up with the old 3-speed automatic. It's even more sluggish when you turn on the air conditioning.

- TIRES. The lower end models are equipped with poor-quality tires. On curves, they squeal. On dry roads, they offer little grip and are even more slippery on wet surfaces. We recommend to exchange them for better results and safety.

- STEERING. If its reduction ratio is adequate, it's assistance is too powerful making it too light and fuzzy at the center. In bad weather, you sure have to keep an eye and a grip on things.

- BRAKES. Brakes hold up well, but they're only fair to middling when it comes to effectiveness. The pedal is too spongy, which makes it hard to adjust precisely the effort.

Stopping distances are way too long and the simplistic ABS system often kicks in too soon and it doesn't iron out all the wheel lock either!

- NOISE. Both engines are very generous when it comes to noise and vibrations. It shows that soundproofing isn't really efficient, especially on the base models.

- HOOD. The wide gap between the bumper and the hood lid of the Cavalier is annoying because you get the impression that the hood isn't properly close. A simple rubber sealing strip could correct this stylistic flaw.

- TRANSMISSION. The old 3-speed gearbox puts a strain on the engine and imposes high rpm levels, which translates into hefty gas bills.

CONCLUSION

The Cavalier-Sunfire continues to provide excellent value at a realistic price thanks to intelligent compromises in sizing, appearance, equipment and performance levels, all of which have nothing in common with what you get from Asian-born economical subcompacts.

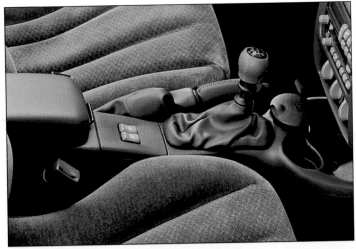

RATING
CHEVROLET Cavalier

CONCEPT :		66%
Technology :	75	
Safety :	75	
Interior space :	55	
Trunk volume :	55	
Quality/fit/finish :	70	

DRIVING :		63%
Cockpit :	75	
Performance :	60	
Handling :	55	
Steering :	70	
Braking :	55	

ORIGINAL EQUIPMENT :		74%
Tires :	70	
Headlights :	80	
Wipers :	80	
Rear defroster :	70	
Radio :	70	

COMFORT :		69%
Seats :	75	
Suspension :	70	
Sound level :	50	
Conveniences :	70	
Air conditioning :	80	

BUDGET :		67%
Price :	70	
Fuel economy :	75	
Insurance :	60	
Satisfaction :	75	
Depreciation :	55	

Overall rating :		67.8%

NEW FOR 2000
- Redesigned front-end, headlights, taillights, wheels and spoiler on the Z24, redesigned dashboard.
- Improved shifter on the 5-speed manual transmission.
- Antitheft alarm included with remote keyless entry.
- Two new colors: Colorado Green and Ultra Metallic Silver.

Compare Performance, Specifications, Prices, and Classification at the end of this chapter.

EQUIPMENT

CHEVROLET Cavalier PONTIAC Sunfire	RS SE cpe	RS SE sed	LS sdn	Z24 GT cpe	Z24 GT cabrio
Automatic transmission:	O	O	S	O	O
Cruise control:	O	-	S	O	S
Power steering:	S	S	S	S	S
Anti-lock brakes:	S	S	S	S	S
Traction control:	O	O	O	O	O
Air conditioning:	S	S	S	S	S
Leather:	-	-	-	-	-
AM/FM/radio-cassette:	O	O	S	-	S
Power door locks:	O	O	O	S	S
Power windows:	O	-	O	S	S
Tilt steering:	O	-	S	S	S
Dual adjustable mirrors:	SM	SM	SE	SE	SE
Alloy wheels:	-	-	O	S	S
Anti-theft system:	S	S	S	S	S

Colors
Exterior: Metallic Green, Bright White, Black, Dark Colorado Metallic Green, Gold Metallic, Metallic Blue, Sandrift Metallic, Red, Ultra Silver, Cayenne.
Interior: Neutral, Graphite, Medium Grey, White (convertible).

AT A GLANCE...

HISTORIC
Introduced in:	1982 -1995.
Made in:	Ramos Arizpe, Mexico, Lordstown, Ohio, Lansing, Michigan, USA.

DEMOGRAPHICS
Model	Men./Wom.	Age	Married	College	Income $
convertible	44/56 %	29	43 %	46 %	31,000
coupe	40/60 %	34	34 %	36 %	33,500
sedan	50/50 %	40	51 %	41 %	32,000

INDEX
Safety:	75 %		
Depreciation:	46 %	Satisfaction:	75 %
Cost per mile:	$ 0.44	Insurance:	$ 555 to 765
		Number of dealers:	4,466

SALES
		Canada			USA	
Model	1997	1998	Result	1997	1998	Result
Cavalier	50,089	43,942	- 12.7 %	302,161	256,099	-15.2 %
Sunfire	44,964	40,797	- 9.3 %	102,160	82,748	-19.0 %

MAINTENANCE REQUIRED BY WARRANTY
First revision:	Frequency:	Diagnostic plug:
3,000 miles	6,000 miles	Yes

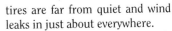

Manual Or Musical

The Neon 2000 made its debut in 1999, at the last Detroit Auto Show. Roomier than the previous generation, it has kept the same architecture and most of the same mechanical components. In a class where competition is hot, Neon has a hard time swaying potential buyers and its sales fail to reach the same levels as its competitors can.

MODEL RANGE

The latest Neon models come solely as a 4-door sedan, sold in the United States in base or SE versions at Dodge and base or LX versions at Plymouth. In Canada, the Neon is made available only by Chrysler, as an LE or an LX. In all instances it's powered by a 132-hp SOHC 2.0L engine with a 5-speed manual transmission and power steering; the old 3-speed automatic and antilock brakes are available as options.

TECHNICAL FEATURES

The Neon body is inspired by the cab forward design. Its steel structure is more sturdily built so as to offer good passenger protection in the event of an accident and to provide more competent handling. Aerodynamics are good, since the drag coefficient is 0.34. The suspension is fully independent on all wheels, using MacPherson struts up front and a Chapman arrangement at the rear. The Neon is equipped with power rack-and-pinion steering and disc and drum brakes on all models.

As modern as it is, the 2.0L engine isn't as refined as its Japanese competitors' engines and the 3-speed automatic transmission is a major handicap even if it has no negative effect on comfort or performance levels.

PROS

+ STYLE. The Neon's front end has rather frog-like traits, due to the headlamp design, but inside the trim palette is fresh and lovely.

+ HANDLING. It's very confident on smooth road surfaces, since sway is under control and shock absorbers do their stuff. But in some circumstances, the suspension may seem to be a bit firm for a family sedan.

+ CABIN & TRUNK SPACE. It's fairly generous with such a relatively wide body, but head and legroom in the rear seat area is less comfortable. The trunk holds quite a bit and it can be extended by lowering the back cushion on the rear seatbench.

+ INSTRUMENT PANEL. With its color-contrast center console its design is appealing; the steering wheel and shifter offer better grip than they did on the previous model.

+ WINDSHIELD WIPERS. They're remarkably efficient with a rhythm of 52 and 80 sweeps per minute — a record for this category. As a bonus, the wipers clean more than 80% of the windshield's surface.

+ QUALITY. It has improved significantly: adjustments are tighter, trims are richer looking, plastics aren't as shiny and design features are more sophisticated.

+ COMFORT. The comfort level is noticeably higher, the suspension is smoother thanks to better shock absorption and front seats are well padded and designed to hug the body.

CONS

- VALUE. If the latest generation Neon is more refined than its previous counterpart, from the marketing standpoint its price and its equipment level isn't as interesting. Standard features include only power steering, an AM/FM radio and cassette player, and power locks and once buyers bring the Neon's equipment in step with the competition, its price is higher than average.

- AUTOMATIC GEARBOX. It's old as the hills with its 3 speeds that sure don't cut down on fuel consumption. But at least it provides braking effect when downshifting. The manual gearbox is smoother, but the shifter is vague.

- ENGINE. It's rough, noisy and it has the shakes, sort of like its rough and ready counterparts at GM and Saturn. Power and torque aren't too impressive, given the displacement.

- BRAKING. Its efficiency is marginal and without the ABS system, it isn't very consistent. The pedal is spongy and makes gauging power difficult. The most reassuring choice: four discs and the antilock system.

- NOISE LEVEL. The Neon is generous when it comes to noise; the engine is loud during acceleration, tires are far from quiet and wind leaks in just about everywhere.

- SUSPENSION. There isn't enough suspension travel at the rear, so you're in for some unpleasant roughing up on poor road surfaces.

- OUTWARD VIEW. It's limited towards the rear due to the high trunk lid and the sharply slanted rear window that darkens at the first sign of rain.

- HEADLIGHTS. As is the case on other Chrysler models, they lack reach and luminosity.

- PRACTICALITY. Storage spaces are miniature in the front and non-existent in the rear; the trunk opening is particularly narrow, which makes loading large objects awkward.

- ERGONOMICS. The center console is still slightly too low and designers should switch the radio and air conditioning controls for one another.

- BENCH SEAT. It's seat is very short to create the illusion of spaciousness and its flat back provides almost no support.

CONCLUSION

The latest Neon shows improvement, but not enough to worry any of the other rivals in its class. While it has gained ground when it comes to presentation and comfort, it wins no points for its sluggish engine, outdated automatic transmission, minimal soundproofing and less than competitive price.

Small

RATING
DODGE-PLYMOUTH Neon

CONCEPT :		70%
Technology :	80	
Safety :	80	
Interior space :	60	
Trunk volume :	55	
Quality/fit/finish :	75	

DRIVING :		63%
Cockpit :	75	
Performance :	60	
Handling :	60	
Steering :	75	
Braking :	45	

ORIGINAL EQUIPMENT :		73%
Tires :	80	
Headlights :	60	
Wipers :	80	
Rear defroster :	70	
Radio :	75	

COMFORT :		61%
Seats :	70	
Suspension :	75	
Sound level :	50	
Conveniences :	40	
Air conditioning :	70	

BUDGET :		72%
Price :	75	
Fuel economy :	85	
Insurance :	75	
Satisfaction :	75	
Depreciation :	50	

| **Overall rating :** | | **67.8%** |

New 2000 Model

NEW FOR 2000

- New model introduced in spring 1999.
- New Patriot Blue body color, different roof and sunroof trims, standard AM-FM radio and cassette player.
- Improved 5-speed manual transmission.
- Child-safety seat in the rear.

Compare
Performance,
Specifications, Prices,
and Classification
at the end of this chapter.

EQUIPMENT

CHRYSLER Neon	LE	LX
Automatic transmission:	O	O
Cruise control:	O	O
Power steering:	S	S
Anti-lock brakes:	O	O
Traction control:	-	-
Air conditioning:	O	S
Leather:	-	-
AM/FM/radio-cassette:	S	S
Power door locks:	S	S
Power windows:	O	O
Tilt steering:	O	O
Dual adjustable mirrors:	SM	SM
Alloy wheels:	O	O
Anti-theft system:	O	O

Colors
Exterior: Green, Patriot Blue, Red, Silver, Cinnamon, Cranberry, Black, White, Amethyst.
Interior: Agate, Taupe.

AT A GLANCE...

HISTORIC
Introduced in: 1995.
Made in: Belvidere, Illinois, USA & Toluca, Mexico.

DEMOGRAPHICS
Model	Men./Wom.	Age	Married	College	Income $
Neon	51/49 %	45	61 %	38.5 %	33,500

INDEX
Safety:	80 %	Satisfaction:	78 %
Depreciation:	48 %	Insurance:	$ 510
Cost per mile:	$ 0.38	Number of dealers:	1,887

SALES
Model	Canada 1997	1998	Result	USA 1997	1998	Result
Neon	18,112	16,612	- 8.3 %	121,854	117,964	- 3.2 %

MAINTENANCE REQUIRED BY WARRANTY
First revision: 5,000 miles
Frequency: 6 months / 5,000 miles
Diagnostic plug: Yes

DAEWOO

Small

The Nubira is the mid-range model marketed by Korean automaker Daewoo. Recently arrived in the United States and Canada, the corporation is known for its highly competitive models and prices specifically intended to take on its compatriot manufacturers, Hyundai and Kia.

MODEL RANGE

The Nubira is available as a 4-door sedan and wagon, in SX and CDX versions powered by a 2.0L 4-cylinder engine and a 5-speed manual or 4-speed automatic transmission. Standard equipment is fairly detailed on all versions, the SX includes power windows, power door locks and power sideview mirrors, a Sony radio and cassette player, and a tachometer. The CDX adds air conditioning, cruise control, an antitheft system, antilock brakes and alloy wheels.

TECHNICAL FEATURES

The two Nubira models have a steel unibody with an average drag coefficient. A MacPherson-type suspension is featured in front and the rear is equipped with a semirigid suspension with two longitudinal arms, two stabilizer bars and helicoidal springs. Engineers have opted for a rack-and-pinion power steering system and the CDX's front disc and rear drum brakes are equipped with ABS. The original Korean-made tires are 185/65R14 models.

PROS

+ PERFORMANCE. The engine is a real workhorse and acceleration and pick-up are both more than satisfactory. However, drivers should be careful when passing: the transmission's gear ratio isn't designed to make overtaking other

Nubira
A Pleasant Surprise

vehicles a smooth process.

+ BRAKING. It's the most efficient in this class; stopping distances are short, power is easy to gauge, wheels have only a very slight tendency to lock and linings are very heat resistant — at least on our test drive models.

+ SIZE. The passenger compartment on these models is roomy enough to accommodate four adults comfortably and space is generous, particularly headroom. Doors open a full 80°, providing easy access to front and rear seats.

+ DESIGN. Although intended as an economical model, the Nubira's passenger compartment is conservatively presented. Controls are ergonomic and materials all look good.

+ EQUIPMENT. While very detailed on CDX versions, it's still very adequate on the SX models, which feature power controls and a good quality radio.

+ DRIVEABILITY. These little cars are fun to drive and they react quickly and consistently. Braking is reassuring and the precise steering system spells good handling ease.

+ RIDE. In spite of only average tires, the Nubira offers good road stability and corners with only moderate roll, showing a definite talent for slalom-type driving. Bumpy roads have no effect on the car's trajectory and the driver feels in control at all times.

+ TRUNK. Cargo space on the wagon is cleverly arranged around the emergency wheel, making it easy to transport smaller items. It includes a baggage cover, an easily accessible floor and the 60/40 split folding seat provides extra space when needed.

CONS

- SUSPENSION. Although its travel and smoothness are within the acceptable average and shock absorption is effective, it's harsh on bad roads, though with no noticeable effect on trajectories.

- NOISE LEVEL. The engine is loud during strong acceleration and road noise is omnipresent, pointing to a serious lack of soundproofing, especially on the wagon.

- STORAGE. It's minimal, with a small glove box and minuscule door pockets in the front and two low and very small spaces in the rear, but no cupholders.

- BENCH SEAT. On the wagon, it's positively rustic; the cushion is short, padding is minimal and the back is almost perfectly vertical.

- RADIO. Its display is maddeningly busy and controls are microscopic and hard to master — luckily it has good reception and its sound is surprisingly good for a vehicle billed as economical.

- RELIABILITY. These new models will have to prove their reliability, as yet undetermined as far as

the North American version goes. Daewoo will have to demonstrate that it's as solid as its products and will have to show a positive attitude towards its new clients. Hyundai's rocky start on our continent should be food for thought.

- DEALERSHIP NETWORK. Currently under development, it doesn't include as many sales and service outlets as the competition has, which may hinder these models' popularity and may complicate maintenance over the long term.

CONCLUSION

If buyers decided to give a newcomer a break and if its price, performance and reliability are satisfactory, like other models from this Korean builder the Nubira will shake up sales in its category, where competition is bitter.

Small

RATING
DAEWOO Nubira

CONCEPT :		67%
Technology :	75	
Safety :	75	
Interior space :	50	
Trunk volume :	55	
Quality/fit/finish :	80	
DRIVING :		64%
Cockpit :	80	
Performance :	50	
Handling :	55	
Steering :	80	
Braking :	55	
ORIGINAL EQUIPMENT :		76%
Tires :	75	
Headlights :	75	
Wipers :	75	
Rear defroster :	80	
Radio :	75	
COMFORT :		69%
Seats :	80	
Suspension :	75	
Sound level :	50	
Conveniences :	60	
Air conditioning :	80	
BUDGET :		75%
Price :	90	
Fuel economy :	85	
Insurance :	75	
Satisfaction :	75	
Depreciation :	50	
Overall rating :		**70.2%**

NEW FOR 2000

• New Korean made and new models introduced recently on the North American market.

Compare
Performance,
Specifications, Prices,
and Classification
at the end of this chapter.

EQUIPMENT

DAEWOO Nubira	SX	CDX
Automatic transmission:	O	O
Cruise control:	-	S
Power steering:	S	S
Anti-lock brakes:	O	S
Traction control:	-	-
Air conditioning:	-	S
Leather:	-	O
AM/FM/radio-cassette:	S	O
Power door locks:	S	S
Power windows:	S	S
Tilt steering:	S	S
Dual adjustable mirrors:	SEH	SEH
Alloy wheels:	-	S
Anti-theft system:	O	S

Colors

Exterior: Silver, Blue, Green, Beige.

Interior: Grey.

AT A GLANCE...

HISTORIC
Introduced in: 1997.
Made in: Kusan, South Korea.

DEMOGRAPHICS

Model	Men./Wom.	Age	Married	College	Income $
Nubira	NA				

INDEX

Safety:	75 %	Satisfaction:	75 %
Depreciation:	30 %	Insurance:	$ 500
Cost per mile:	$ 0.42	Number of dealers:	115

SALES

Model	Canada 1997	1998	Result	USA 1997	1998	Result
Nubira	Not on sale during this period.			NA		

MAINTENANCE REQUIRED BY WARRANTY
First revision: 4,000 miles
Frequency: 6 months / 8,000 miles
Diagnostic plug: Yes

Disturbing

As it replaces the Escort, the Focus will enable Ford to take aim at a new clientele: younger buyers. This explains both the "New Edge" styling adopted for the front-end and the new model's psychedelic dashboard. More versatile than the previous model, it's also the roomiest in its class, beating even the Mazda Protegé, the former titleholder in this area.

MODEL RANGE

The Focus family includes the ZX3 3-door sedan, the LX, SE and ZTS 4-door sedans and the SE wagon. All are equipped with a SOHC 2.0L 4-cylinder engine (LX, SE) or a DOHC Zetec (ZX3, ZTS), teamed with a 5-speed manual or 4-speed automatic transmission.

TECHNICAL FEATURES

The Focus models have a steel unibody and zinc-clad panels. Their drag coefficient ranges from 0.30 for the wagon to 0.31 for the 4-door sedan and 0.36 for the 3-door sedan. The front suspension features struts and the rear is equipped with multiple longitudinal and transversal arms forming a preassembled self-contained unit installed on side rails. Stabilizer bars and helicoidal springs are used at the front and rear. Brakes are mixed and the ABS system is optional.

PROS

+ PRICE. Like the Escort, the Focus is competitively priced, but to the detriment of its equipment and the fact that a number of practical features haven't been included.
+ SIZE. The body's rounded lines and other styling touches make the Focus look bigger than most of its rivals.
+ BRAKING. Stopping distances are relatively short, power is progressive and easy to gauge and linings are heat resistant. However, during emergency stops front wheels lock quickly and make it hard to keep the car on course.
+ PERFORMANCE. The Zetec engine has more pep thanks to its 20 extra horses — but don't be fooled, it has barely enough power to reach average performance levels. It would take a good dose of added energy to really rip up the asphalt!
+ HANDLING. The Focus is lucky enough to have inherited the road stability and efficiency of the Escort and its revamped rear-end design. It can take all kinds of corners easily, provided standard production models are equipped with tires of the same quality as those featured on the preproduction models made available for our test drives.
+ TRUNK. It can take on a fair amount of baggage thanks to its added width and height, both more generous than its length, which is only average. The rear seat folds down for added space, but a narrow opening makes it hard to load large items. The wagon's hatch opens wider and is more practical.
+ RADIO. The quality of the radio on our test drive models was remarkable, especially when compared to other only mediocre equipment. Its sound was excellent and its controls well-positioned and well-sized.

CONS

- STYLING. Designed in Europe, this newcomer's unusual styling is sure to baffle the Escort's conservative clientele. The "New Edge" approach favored by Claude Lobbo never quite caught on (Mercury Cougar) and it's likely that sooner or later Ford will be forced to tame down this model's lines, just as it did with the Taurus-Sable in an effort to boost slumping sales. With its tortured lines the dashboard is a nightmare to look at and it already looks seriously outmoded.
- QUALITY. It's disappointing to see that for a number of design details, the finish and the quality of materials, fabrics and plastics is exactly the same as it was on the old Escort. The overall look is decidedly inexpensive and the pathetic fake wood inlays on the ZTS model only make matters worse.
- PASSENGER ROOM. Front seats are reasonably roomy but there is limited hip room and headroom in the back; rear seats are hard to get into because of limited space and doors that open only on a 60° angle.
- BASE ENGINE. Acceleration and pick-up are unimpressive, especially with the automatic transmission, whose noise and vibration are equally high.
- SUSPENSION. It's smooth enough to make the ride comfortable, but its poor shock absorption causes front wheels to hop when roads present major defects.
- VISIBILITY. It's not ideal because of thick A and C pillars and small triangular windows are a further drawback.
- NOISE LEVEL. Major road, wind and engine noise points to very poor soundproofing, as evidenced by a noise level ranging from 68 to 74 dBA.
- OVERSIGHTS. A number of practical features are lacking: the driver has no dummy pedal, there is no gear indicator for the automatic transmission, and rear-seat passengers have no headrests and no storage spaces. No wonder the price is so good!

CONCLUSION

Time will tell whether Ford can succeed in attracting younger buyers with the Focus's modern styling — or whether it ends up losing the clientele it attracted with the Escort. To their credit, however, these new models are as competent as they are affordable.

RATING
FORD Focus

CONCEPT :		**71%**
Technology :	80	
Safety :	90	
Interior space :	65	
Trunk volume :	50	
Quality/fit/finish :	70	
DRIVING :		**61%**
Cockpit :	60	
Performance :	45	
Handling :	50	
Steering :	80	
Braking :	70	
ORIGINAL EQUIPMENT :		**73%**
Tires :	75	
Headlights :	75	
Wipers :	70	
Rear defroster :	70	
Radio :	75	
COMFORT :		**65%**
Seats :	70	
Suspension :	70	
Sound level :	50	
Conveniences :	60	
Air conditioning :	75	
BUDGET :		**72%**
Price :	75	
Fuel economy :	85	
Insurance :	70	
Satisfaction :	80	
Depreciation :	50	
Overall rating :		**68.4%**

New 2000 Model

NEW FOR 2000

• All-new models based on the platform inaugurated in Europe in September 1998. The Focus featuring "New Edge" body and dashboard styling, a new 4-speed automatic transmission, a revamped independent rear suspension and optional driver- and passenger-side airbags.

Compare Performance, Specifications, Prices, and Classification at the end of this chapter.

EQUIPMENT

FORD Focus	ZX3 3 dr. sdn	LX 4 dr.sdn	SE	ZTS	SE 4 dr. wgn
Automatic transmission:	O	O	S	O	O
Cruise control:	O	O	S	O	S
Power steering:	S	S	S	S	S
Anti-lock brakes:	O	O	O	O	O
Traction control:	-	-	-	-	-
Air conditioning:	O	O	S	S	S
Leather:	-	-	-	-	-
AM/FM/radio-cassette:	S	S	S	S	S
Power door locks:	O	O	O	O	O
Power windows:	O	O	O	O	O
Tilt steering:	-	-	S	S	S
Dual adjustable mirrors:	-	-	O	O	O
Alloy wheels:	-	-	O	O	S
Anti-theft system:	O	O	O	O	O

Colors
Exterior: Gold, Orange, Red, Blue, Green, Silver, Black, White.

Interior: Graphite, Parchment, Charcoal.

AT A GLANCE...

HISTORIC
Introduced in: 1999.
Made in: Wayne, Michigan, USA & Hermosillo, Mexico.

DEMOGRAPHICS
Model	Men./Wom.	Age	Married	College	Income $
Escort sedan	60/40 %	50	59 %	41 %	31,500
Escort wagon	63/37 %	55	83 %	39 %	32,500

INDEX
Safety:	90 %	Satisfaction:	80 %
Depreciation:	48 %	Insurance:	$ 450-650
Cost per mile:	$ 0.35	Number of dealers:	5,200

SALES
Model	Canada 1997	1998	Result	USA 1997	1998	Result
Escort	34,432	27,185	- 21.0 %	283,898	291,936	+ 2.8 %

MAINTENANCE REQUIRED BY WARRANTY
First revision: 3,000 miles
Frequency: 6 months / 5,000 miles
Diagnostic plug: Yes

Civic

Universal

The success of its big sister, the Accord, tends to make us forget that the Civic is one of the most popular models in North America with close to 350,000 units sold in 1998. As the years have gone by the model has gained weight and today, it's exactly the same size as a 1988 Accord. It attracts a wide range of consumers: the average age of Civic buyers goes from 29 to 42 years old!

MODEL RANGE

The Civic is sold in three guises: a hatchback, a coupe and a sedan. The 3-door hatchback comes in CX or DX versions, the 2-door coupe comes in DX, Si or SiR trims in Canada and in DX, HX, EX and Si trims in the United States, and the 4-door sedan is available as a DX (USA), LX or EX. New for 2000 is the SE trim. Base versions don't have much to offer and in all cases, the automatic transmission, antilock brakes and air conditioning are optional.

TECHNICAL FEATURES

Civic models have a steel monocoque body. It's been seriously rigidified during the last reworking and vehicle dimensions have been extended to increase cabin and trunk space. Cars are heavier as a result and aerodynamics are very conservative. The fully independent suspension is made up of a double wishbone setup and the rear axle is supported by trailing arms. All versions are equipped with rack-and-pinion steering and disc and drum brakes (4 discs on Si,SiR), but ABS is offered as an extra on all models except for both hatchbacks. The Civic's are motivated by three 16-valve 1.6L SOHC engines. The engine under the hood of the CX, DX, LX and EX develops 106 hp, the models that motivate the Si, SiR coupe develops either 127 or 160 hp, thanks to an electronically controlled variable valve timing system, called VTEC. For the last two years, Honda has sold engines with low and ultra low pollution emissions (LEV and ULEV) that meet stringent California emission laws that will go into effect as of next year.

PROS

+ CABIN & TRUNK SPACE. It's now roomier, especially in the rear of the hatchback with the higher interior ceiling clearance and bigger-volume trunk.

+ PERFORMANCE. The 160-hp engine provides gritty acceleration and pick-up and it purrs gratifyingly when it goes beyond the 6,000 RPM level, making drivers feel as if they were behind the wheel of a mini race car.

+HANDLING. It depends essentially on tire quality that's really very poor on base models. The Civic's are fun to drive, because they're compact and quick as bunnies. They're competent and safe, exhibit good roadability and zip in and out of city traffic with great agility.

+ RIDE COMFORT. It's quite good, considering vehicle price and format. The suspension is smooth when tackling road faults and engine and road noise and vibration are well-muffled.

+ DRIVING PLEASURE. It's great with such accurate and silky controls, a manual transmission that's easy to use and super power steering, although it does suffer from a bit of over-assistance.

+ FUEL ECONOMY. For regular runs, the 1.6L engine is amazingly economical, since fuel consumption sits at around 30 mpg, even with the whole performance range it's capable of.

+ QUALITY. It's more obvious in terms of engineering, assembly and finish job, but the bodywork still looks a bit "light".

+BONUS POINTS. Powerful headlights ensure safe driving even in harsh weather. Good quality Michelin XGT-V4 tires are well adapted to the performance capabilities of the Si and SiR coupes.

CONS

- PERFORMANCES. With the beefier body, vehicle weight has been plumped up to more than a ton, thus affecting power to weight ratio, so engine performances and braking suffer. Accelerations and pickup on the sedans have suffered the most due to these modifications.

- BRAKES. They still lack gripping power and emergency stopping distances are too long and car path is very uncertain on models without ABS.

- THE CX HATCHBACK. This vehicle isn't the best choice, due to manual steering that's vague and crippled by a poor reduction ratio, a soft suspension and Spartan equipment items, at a higher price than that of the competition.

- LOOKS. Civic fans find the recent make-over less attractive than past attempts.

- SPACE. It's limited in the coupe and hatchback rear seat area and getting aboard the rear seats is awfully tricky, due to low head clearance and reclining front seats on some models that don't free up enough leg room for tallish passengers.

- SEATS. They're not a perfect example of what a seat should offer in terms of comfort. Upholstery is thin and hard and the seatbench provides less support than do front seats. Not the best choice of vehicle to take on a world tour...

- CABIN DESIGN. It's terribly blah either in light or dark grey trim and some components look very bargain basement.

- QUALITY. It's really not too great when you consider some materials like the plastic door trim, seat fabric or crummy radio that's unworthy of a Japanese product.

- TRUNK. It's smallish on the hatchback when the rear seatbench is occupied, but it can be extended by lowering the seatbench.

CONCLUSION

Like the Accord, in its class the Civic is a car with universal appeal, extremely well suited to the needs of a certain group of consumers who find it absolutely perfect — or almost!

Small

RATING
HONDA Civic

CONCEPT :		67%
Technology :	80	
Safety :	90	
Interior space :	35	
Trunk volume :	50	
Quality/fit/finish :	80	

DRIVING :		64%
Cockpit :	70	
Performance :	60	
Handling :	70	
Steering :	80	
Braking :	40	

ORIGINAL EQUIPMENT :		74%
Tires :	80	
Headlights :	80	
Wipers :	75	
Rear defroster :	70	
Radio :	65	

COMFORT :		65%
Seats :	65	
Suspension :	75	
Sound level :	50	
Conveniences :	60	
Air conditioning :	75	

BUDGET :		73%
Price :	75	
Fuel economy :	70	
Insurance :	75	
Satisfaction :	85	
Depreciation :	60	

Overall rating :		68.6%

NEW FOR 2000

• Introduction of an SE version for each type of body, based on the DX base model recognizable because of its all-over color scheme and the "Special" badge affixed to its rear.

Compare
Performance,
Specifications, Prices,
and Classification
at the end of this chapter.

EQUIPMENT

HONDA Civic Hbk	CX	DX	SE			
HONDA Civic Coupe				EX-Si		
HONDA Civic Sedan					LX	EX
Automatic transmission:	O	O	O	O	O	O
Cruise control:	-	-	-	S	-	S
Power steering:	O	O	S	S	S	S
Anti-lock brakes:	-	-	O	O	O	O
Traction control:	-	-	-	-	-	-
Air conditioning:	O	O	O	O	O	O
Leather:	-	-	-	-	-	S
AM/FM/radio-cassette:	O	O	S	SCd	O	S
Power door locks:	-	-	S	S	S	S
Power windows:	-	-	-	S	-	S
Tilt steering:	O	S	S	S	S	S
Dual adjustable mirrors:	SM	SM	SM	SEH	SM	SEH
Alloy wheels:	-	-	-	S	-	-
Anti-theft system:	-	-	O	O	O	O

Colors

Exterior: *Coupe & Hatchbacks:* Black, Silver, Red, Amethyst.
Sedans: Black, Silver, Green, Red, White, Teal.
Interior: Grey, Dark grey.

AT A GLANCE...

HISTORIC
Introduced in:	1996.
Made in:	Alliston, Ontario, Canada.

DEMOGRAPHICS
Model	Men./Wom.	Age	Married	College	Income $
Hatchback	47/53 %	31	39 %	57 %	33,000
Coupe	50/50 %	29	30 %	56 %	35,000
Sedan	42/58 %	42	60 %	54 %	40,000

INDEX
Safety:	90 %	Satisfaction:	90 %
Depreciation:	42 %	Insurance:	$ 535-575
Cost per mile:	$ 0.34	Number of dealers:	1,000

SALES
Model	Canada 1997	1998	Result	USA 1997	1998	Result
Civic	28,750	28,209	- 1.9 %	315,546	334,562	+ 6.0 %

MAINTENANCE REQUIRED BY WARRANTY
First revision:	Frequency:	Diagnostic plug:
4,000 miles	4,000 miles	Yes

Elantra

Threatening

After the Accent, the Elantra is the second-best in the Hyundai lineup in terms of sales. Design touchups made last year have maintained the demand for this model and its performance levels and quality have both improved steadily over the years, to the point that this model is now a true challenge to the category's long-established leaders.

MODEL RANGE

The Elantra is sold as a 4-door sedan or station wagon in base and GLS versions. Both models are equipped with the 2.0L engine that powers the Tiburon, associated with a standard 5-speed manual transmission or an optional 4-speed automatic that benefits from dual-mode function, namely sport or normal. As is the case for the Orphan Annie Accent base model, the Elantra base version doesn't come with many goodies, since equipment only includes power steering, intermittent wipers, manually adjustable mirrors, tilt steering wheel and radio with tape deck. The GLS versions are more pampered since they receive standard dual front-impact airbags as well as power windows, locks and mirrors. Optional items are: air conditioning, automatic transmission, four-wheel antilock braking (GLS sedan and wagon), light alloy wheels and sunroof (GLS sedan).

TECHNICAL FEATURES

The Elantra's steel unibody benefits from adequate aerodynamic finesse with a drag coefficient varying between 0.32 for the sedan and 0.34 for the station wagon. The four-wheel independent suspension consists of MacPherson struts up front and a dual-link setup at the rear,

with stabilizer bars on both axles. Cars are equipped with standard disc and drum brakes and power steering. The new engine is a derivative of the previous one. It's a modern, front-wheel drive 140-hp 16-valve DOHC engine. It only weighs 300 lbs. with its aluminum block and plastic rocker arm cover. Engine and cabin soundproofing have been beefed up to transmit only minimal noise, vibration and harshness.

PROS

+ PRICE. It's competitive, since it's about 5 to 8% lower than those of Japanese cars of comparable quality and equipment. But many features found on the options list make the Elantra models look less expensive than their rivals, which isn't always necessarily the case.

+ PERFORMANCE. With its 140-hp 2.0L Hyundai engine, the Elantra has better acceleration and pick-up than a lot of more elaborate models in this category and its peppy attitude is refreshing.

+ LOOKS. This is a good-looking car. The body design is clean and has nice plump curves, especially the station wagon, one of the rare such models in this category.

+ QUALITY. These vehicles are well-built, component fit is tight and trim materials look and feel lovely. The over-all look is more attractive, so now the Elantra is more on a par

with the competition.

+ TECHNOLOGY. It's simple and straightforward, yet works like a charm and it owes nothing to former Mitsubishi products. The engine inherited from the Tiburon is friskier and more competent than the one it replaced and the body structure is more rigid, which gives a solid as a rock feeling that helps vehicle control, but doesn't add much to ride comfort.

+ DRIVING. It's pleasurable due to a willing and eager engine that has good power output, accelerations are brisk and steering is smooth, accurate and quick to respond, so there's a great get-up-and-go feeling behind the wheel, although you really can't qualify it as sporty, since tires that equip the base version are undersized and their quality average.

+ HANDLING. It's come a long way compared to the early days, chiefly due to tire quality, but also due to the simple-design four-wheel independent suspension that does the trick and the stiffer, more solid structure.

+ FUEL EFFICIENCY. The Elantra's engine benefits from a favourable power to weight ratio for this category and fuel consumption is frugal at normal speeds.

+ RIDE COMFORT. Travel feel has improved with a more flexible suspension, sculpted seats, lower noise level and fewer shakes and rattles.

+ STATION WAGON. Sales have stagnated, but it's a practical way of putting off buying a more expensive minivan for a few years.

+ EQUIPMENT. The more richly equipped GLS is a better buy and it's a handier car than the base version that's tougher to resell.

CONS

- SAFETY. The safety index for collision tests given by the NHTSA and the owner satisfaction rate are below average for the category.

- BRAKES. The standard braking system is mediocre, since it lacks bite and stability during emergency stops and the optional rear disc brakes with ABS are a must for safety reasons.

- ENGINE. It peaks at high rpm., it's noisy as heck and thirsty when pushed hard.

- SEAT UPHOLSTERY. Seat shape has improved, but cushions still aren't comfy enough to our taste, especially the rear seats that are flat and thinly upholstered.

- AUTOMATIC GEARBOX. It "pumps" lots of the available power and the shifter is very sluggish when downshifting, so you often have to work the gears.

- TRUNK. Volume is decent, but its narrow opening makes for awkward luggage handling.

- TO BE IMPROVED UPON. The quality of some finish details and some design touches that look pretty cheap.

CONCLUSION

As it improves gradually, the Elantra is gaining ground. The sedan is more popular than the wagon and it doesn't need much more to let it rival a number of Japanese models that are showing their age.

Elantra   HYUNDAI

Small cars

RATING HYUNDAI Elantra		
CONCEPT :		**61%**
Technology :	75	
Safety :	50	
Interior space :	50	
Trunk volume :	60	
Quality/fit/finish :	70	
DRIVING :		**59%**
Cockpit :	75	
Performance :	50	
Handling :	50	
Steering :	70	
Braking :	50	
ORIGINAL EQUIPMENT :		**70%**
Tires :	70	
Headlights :	75	
Wipers :	70	
Rear defroster :	65	
Radio :	70	
COMFORT :		**59%**
Seats :	65	
Suspension :	60	
Sound level :	40	
Conveniences :	60	
Air conditioning :	70	
BUDGET :		**79%**
Price :	85	
Fuel economy :	85	
Insurance :	80	
Satisfaction :	80	
Depreciation :	65	
Overall rating :		**65.6%**

NEW FOR 2000

• "Value Edition" including an automatic transmission, air conditioning, cruise control and the VE badge on the back of the vehicle.

Compare
Performance,
Specifications, Prices,
and Classification
at the end of this chapter.

EQUIPMENT

HYUNDAI Elantra	base	GLS
Automatic transmission:	O	O
Cruise control:	O	O
Power steering:	S	S
Anti-lock brakes:	-	O
Traction control:	-	-
Air conditioning:	O	O
Leather:	-	-
AM/FM/radio-cassette:	S	S
Power door locks:	-	S
Power windows:	-	S
Tilt steering:	S	S
Dual adjustable mirrors:	SM	SE
Alloy wheels:	-	O
Anti-theft system:	-	-

Colors

Exterior: Green, Red, White, Black, Sandal, Blue, Grey.

Interior: Dark Grey, Beige.

AT A GLANCE...

HISTORIC

Introduced in:	1991-1995.
Made in:	Ulsan, South Korea.

DEMOGRAPHICS

Model	Men./Wom.	Age	Married	College	Income $
Elantra	57/43 %	42	69 %	42 %	31,500

INDEX

Safety:	70 %	Satisfaction:	68 %
Depreciation:	50 %	Insurance:	$ 535
Cost per mile:	$ 0.44	Number of dealers:	500

SALES

Model	Canada 1997	1998	Result	USA 1997	1998	Result
Elantra	6,388	7,211	+12.9 %	41,303	37,501	- 9.2 %

MAINTENANCE REQUIRED BY WARRANTY

First revision:	Frequency:	Diagnostic plug:
3,000 miles	3 months/ 3,000 miles	Yes

Warmed Over

After investing in the United States, the third-largest South Korean make is setting out to conquer the Canadian market. Absorbed by Hyundai to save it from imminent bankruptcy, Kia markets a sedan known as the Sephia, easily confused with the Corolla, which says a great deal about the newcomer's ultimate goals.

MODEL RANGE

The Sephia is offered as a 4-door sedan in base or LS versions, both of which are powered by a 1.8L engine coupled with a 5-speed manual or 4-speed automatic transmission. The base version is very pared down, to the point that it doesn't even have power steering. The LS does, along with a radio and cassette player and a tilt steering column. The LS+ is the most elaborate Sephia, with equipment ranging from air conditioning to a CD player and power features. Antilock brakes are available solely as an option on the LS and LS+ models.

TECHNICAL FEATURES

This model is derived from the Mazda 323/Protegé and to a point, from Ford's old Escort/Tracer models. Offering a conservative drag coefficient, its steel unibody features a fully independent suspension with elastic struts and transversal triangles, antiroll bars and helicoidal springs in the front and back. Brakes are mixed and the ABS system is optional.

PROS

+ PRICE. Cost is the strongest attraction of all Korean models, especially considering their equipment level. However, the base Sephia has nothing very exciting to offer — except for its unbeatable price. The LS is the true base model, with the LS+ as its luxury version, with a wider range of options.

+ PERFORMANCE. The 1.8L inherited from the Protegé ensures interesting acceleration and pick-up, even with the automatic transmission. In other words, the Sephia is fun to drive.

+ FUEL CONSUMPTION. This model is relatively economical in absolute terms even if fuel consumption is higher than it is on some more recent models featuring comparable engines.

+ QUALITY. The Sephia boasts careful fit and finish, comparable to what buyers can find on a Japanese model. However, the feel and look of some materials, including plastics, are a throwback to another era.

+ SIZE. Comparable to the Corolla, which it resembles very strongly, depending on their size the Sephia can take on two or three rear-seat passengers.

+ INTERIOR. It's conservative and logical, with a well-organized dashboard and a series of storage spaces in the front.

CONS

- DESIGN. Although not completely out of fashion, it does date back some 10 years; the passenger compartment's presentation is questionable, the suspension is mushy and there are better steering systems in today's automotive industry.

- BRAKING. It's mediocre and stopping distances are long, but its biggest drawback is instability and wheels that lock in emergency situations, when trajectories are unpredictable when the vehicle doesn't have an ABS system.

- RELIABILITY. The U.S. experience shows that Kia is the builder that has experienced the highest number of problems per hundred vehicles sold — nothing very encouraging for buyers. More than assembly, the quality of some components is the issue most often cited by consumers.

- EQUIPMENT. The base model is stripped down to ensure a price that is almost equal to the price for a model in the next lowest market segment; the LS offers less than the LS+.

- COMFORT. Like the models it is derived from, the Sephia is far from quiet and entertains passengers and driver with a very loud engine and road noise that results from poor soundproofing. Seats have very thin padding, the suspension is stiff and this car is not made for long-distance driving.

- TRUNK. It's one of the smallest in this category and its floor is 6 inches (15 cm) lower than the bumper, which makes unloading heavy objects a challenge.

- APPEARANCE. Upholstery, plastics used for the dashboard and lining material look decidedly inexpensive and are a blast from the past.

- RESALE VALUE. As is the case with all new economy models, depreciation is higher than average and will remain so as long as the model's reputation has not been clearly established.

- FLAWS. Lack of storage spaces in the rear, very low sideview mirrors, no gear indicator with the automatic transmission.

- DEALERSHIP NETWORK. Embryonic, as expected for a manufacturer newly active on the market, it has to grow quickly to boost the model's popularity and to make maintenance easier.

CONCLUSION

The Sephia will have earned the right to its billing as a good, cost-effective mode of transportation when it proves its reliability and when the efficiency of its Korean manufacturer — still in the process of building its dealership network — is demonstrated beyond doubt. Sales figures for inexpensive vehicles are more a sign of buyers seeking to pay as little as possible than of cars whose value is genuine.

Small cars

RATING
KIA Sephia

CONCEPT : 66%
Technology :	75
Safety :	80
Interior space :	60
Trunk volume :	40
Quality/fit/finish :	75

DRIVING : 57%
Cockpit :	80
Performance :	40
Handling :	60
Steering :	75
Braking :	30

ORIGINAL EQUIPMENT : 70%
Tires :	75
Headlights :	70
Wipers :	65
Rear defroster :	75
Radio :	65

COMFORT : 61%
Seats :	75
Suspension :	70
Sound level :	40
Conveniences :	50
Air conditioning :	70

BUDGET : 73%
Price :	90
Fuel economy :	75
Insurance :	75
Satisfaction :	75
Depreciation :	50

Overall rating : 65.4%

NEW FOR 2000

- New make and new model on the Canadian market.

Compare
Performance,
Specifications, Prices,
and Classification
at the end of this chapter.

EQUIPMENT

KIA Sephia	base	LS	LS+
Automatic transmission:	O	O	O
Cruise control:	-	-	S
Power steering:	O	S	S
Anti-lock brakes:	-	O	O
Traction control:	-	-	-
Air conditioning:	-	O	S
Leather:	-	-	-
AM/FM/radio-cassette:	O	S	SCd
Power door locks:	-	-	S
Power windows:	-	-	S
Tilt steering:	-	S	S
Dual adjustable mirrors:	SM	SM	SE
Alloy wheels:	-	-	-
Anti-theft system:	-	-	-

Colors
Exterior: White, Red, Grey, Green, Blue, Silvert, Black.

Interior: Grey, Beige.

AT A GLANCE...

HISTORIC
Introduced in:	1993.
Made in:	Asan Bay, South Korea.

DEMOGRAPHICS
Model	Men./Wom.	Age	Married	College	Income $
Sephia	NA				

INDEX
Safety:	75 %	Satisfaction:	75 %
Depreciation:	50 %	Insurance:	$ 500
Cost per mile:	$ 0.42	Number of dealers:	115

SALES
	Canada			USA		
Model	1997	1998	Result	1997	1998	Result
Sephia	Not on sale during this period			35,494	54,311	+ 53.0 %

MAINTENANCE REQUIRED BY WARRANTY
First revision:	Frequency:	Diagnostic plug:
5,000 miles	7,500 miles	Yes

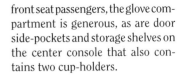

Seductive

The latest Protegé has managed to seduce more consumers than the previous model — nothing surprising considering that its lines have been rejuvenated, its performance levels are higher (even with the 1.6L engine) and its overall value has been enhanced. Given the effort made, Mazda deserves the encouragement it's getting.

MODEL RANGE

The Protegé is still offered as a 4-door sedan that comes in DX and ES (SE) versions with a 1.6L engine delivering 105 hp and in LX with a DOHC 1.8L engine that develops 122 hp. The standard transmission is a 5-speed manual but a 4-speed automatic is available as an extra. Original equipment on the DX includes power steering with tilt and power windows while the ES, LX also receives radio and CD player, cruise control (ES), power locks and mirrors. The ABS device is optional on the SE and LX only.

TECHNICAL FEATURES

The Protegé's monocoque body is made of steel of which 90% of the panels are galvanized. It's more rigid to resist impact from every angle. The silhouette is more angular, but aerodynamics are just as good, since the drag coefficient sits at 0.32. Suspensions are independent, made up of Macpherson struts and double trapezoidal control arms with stabilizer bar both front and rear on all versions that are equipped with disc and drum brakes and standard power steering.

The new 1.6L engine is an extrapolation of the former 1.5 that's been modernized and reinforced. The gearbox is new too, contains 26% fewer parts and weighs 8 lb. less than the former model.

PROS

+ **STYLE.** It's simple and nicely balanced, so it pleases the ladies who represent more than half of this model's buyers. It doesn't have any trait that's out of the ordinary but it's lovely, for it's polished and well-proportioned.

+ **FORMAT.** Neither too big nor too small, the Protegé sits between two categories. Subcompact due to its engines, but it's almost a class 3 compact due to its cabin that can accomodate five passengers quite nicely. Interior space is generous and the trunk is convenient with its good-size opening that lowers to bumper level. The trunk can also be extended by lowering the seatbench back.

+ **HANDLING.** The Protegé has always exhibited good road adherence due to its elaborate suspension. With a suspension including dual anti-roll bars, more precise steering and good-size tires, the most recent Protegé is even easier to control and it behaves in a crisp, predictable way even on poor roads.

+ **FUEL EFFICIENCY.** Both engines meet anti-pollution ULEV (1.6) and LEV (1.8) standards and are super fuel-efficient even with the automatic, since city consumption varies between 26 to 28 mpg.

+ **PERFORMANCES.** The 1.8L engine is smooth and chomping at the bit, so it's fun to drive and you can achieve almost racy moves. The

1.6L isn't as colorful, but it performs better when linked to the manual gearbox.

+ **RIDE COMFORT.** It's surprisingly cushy for a car in this category, the shock system is effective and seats are nicely shaped, more so in the front seats, and cushion upholstery seems less firm than it once was.

+ **CABIN DESIGN.** The cabin interior seems less blah than before and the main trim components have a nice feel. Plastic components look more spiffy and their simili-perforated design on the dashboard is original.

+ **QUALITY.** Construction, finish details and trim components are typical of Japanese products and give the Protegé its very cohesive character.

+ **CONFIDENCE.** The Protegé has always had a great reputation when it comes to dependablity since again last year, 80% of owners were very satisfied.

+ **WARRANTY.** It's more advantageous at Mazda than for some of the competition.

+ **PRICES.** Compared to some rivals, the Protegé prices seem pretty reasonable, but equipment is quite rudimentary, except on the LX version.

+ **CONVENIENCE FEATURES.** The Protegé is an economy car, but it still has enough storage compartments in the cabin, especially for

front seat passengers, the glove compartment is generous, as are door side-pockets and storage shelves on the center console that also contains two cup-holders.

CONS

- **STEERING.** It's gained in precision, but it's over-assisted, so it's light, which takes some getting used to.

- **BRAKES.** All models are equipped with disc and drum brakes, so braking is only fairly effective. Stops take long stretches to achieve in emergency situations, since wheels lock without ABS, so the car tends to swerve. Even with the rather simplistic ABS, some wheel lock still occurs, but it's more of a hassle than a real hazard.

- **THE 1.6L ENGINE.** It's tougher than its predecessor, but its accelerations and pickup are laborious with the automatic transmission, especially if the vehicle is loaded or equipped with air conditioning. In these conditions, passing should be done with caution.

- **TRUNK.** The trunk is slightly smaller and it isn't quite proportional to cabin space, but it can be extended by lowering the rear seatbench, which makes up for this aspect.

- **NOISE.** The small Mazda's have always been noisier than average and the most recent Protegé is no exception. The noisy engines and weak soundproofing are the cause.

CONCLUSION

Buyers out to choose a small car should put the Protegé on the top of their list of potential candidates. Its reliability and its resale value are both increasing and it's a problem-free acquisition that can even be fun to drive on a day-to-day basis.

Small cars

RATING	
MAZDA Protegé	
CONCEPT :	**72%**
Technology :	80
Safety :	80
Interior space :	65
Trunk volume :	55
Quality/fit/finish :	80
DRIVING :	**60%**
Cockpit :	80
Performance :	40
Handling :	55
Steering :	70
Braking :	55
ORIGINAL EQUIPMENT :	**75%**
Tires :	75
Headlights :	80
Wipers :	75
Rear defroster :	70
Radio :	75
COMFORT :	**67%**
Seats :	70
Suspension :	70
Sound level :	50
Conveniences :	70
Air conditioning :	75
BUDGET :	**70%**
Price :	80
Fuel economy :	70
Insurance :	70
Satisfaction :	80
Depreciation :	50
Overall rating :	**68.8%**

NEW FOR 2000

- Reinforced rear bumpers.
- Standard tachometer on the SE version.
- Braking power allocation system (EBD) included with ABS.
- LX Touring package includes ABS, spoiler, sunroof, 15-inch aluminum wheel with 195/55R15 tires.

Compare Performance, Specifications, Prices, and Classification at the end of this chapter.

EQUIPMENT

MAZDA Protegé	DX	LX	ES/SE
Automatic transmission:	O	O	O
Cruise control:	-	-	S
Power steering:	S	S	S
Anti-lock brakes:	-	O	O
Traction control:	-	-	-
Air conditioning:	O	O	S
Leather:	-	-	-
AM/FM/radio-cassette:	O	SCd	SCd
Power door locks:	-	S	S
Power windows:	S	S	S
Tilt steering:	S	S	S
Dual adjustable mirrors:	SM	SM	SE
Alloy wheels:	-	O	O
Anti-theft system:	-	-	-

Colors

Exterior: White, Sand, Green, Black, Red, Sandalwood, Blue, Silver.

Interior: Grey, Beige.

AT A GLANCE...

HISTORIC

Introduced in:	1977 -1995-1999.
Made in:	Hiroshima, Japan.

DEMOGRAPHICS

Model	Men./Wom.	Age	Married	College	Income $
Protegé	44/56 %	36	61 %	67 %	$ 34,000

INDEX

Safety:	80 %	Satisfaction:	82 %
Depreciation:	50 %	Insurance:	$ 535 - 585
Cost per mile:	$ 0.42	Number of dealers:	871

SALES

	Canada			USA		
Model	1997	1998	Result	1997	1998	Result
Protegé	13,764	15,196	+10.4 %	53,930	58,349	+ 8.2 %

MAINTENANCE REQUIRED BY WARRANTY

First revision:	Frequency:	Diagnostic plug:
5,000 miles	6 months / 5,000 miles	Yes

Misunderstood

The Sentra is infinitely less popular in Canada than it is in the United States. How can this disproportionate reaction be explained beyond using cultural or monetary considerations? The main reason is that small economical cars are usually greeted most warmly in eastern marketplaces.

MODEL RANGE

The Sentra is sold in Canada in three versions: XE, GXE and SE to which the United States market adds the base version and GLE. They're equipped with a standard 1.6L engine (SE-2.0L) linked to a 5-speed manual transmission. The base model gets only the most rock-bottom, essential equipment, but the other models are more richly equipped, although antilock braking (except GLE,SE), automatic transmission and sunroof (SE) are sold as extras for each and every model.

TECHNICAL FEATURES

The Sentra has a steel monocoque body that's now more resistant to torsion due to added reinforcements aimed at providing better passenger protection in the event of a collision. The resonance frequency of the chassis sits at 26 Hertz and stifles noise and vibration so that it doesn't assail passengers inside the cabin and the structure has a drag coefficient of 0.33. The front suspension is a MacPherson strut setup and the rear suspension consists of a Scott-Russell multilink design that frees up more cabin and trunk space, while ensuring better than average ride comfort. All models are equipped with standard disc and drum brakes, except the GXE and GLE models with optional rear-wheel disc brakes and antilock braking system, which are both standard on the SE.

PROS

+ STYLE. The Sentra's trim, prim and uncluttered body design makes it look bigger than it actually is, so much so that some people think it's a compact.

+ CABIN SPACE. It's less stingy than for some of its rivals in the small cars category, so much so that a fifth passenger can even be seated in the middle of the rear seatbench, when really necessary.

+ HANDLING. The famous "multi-link" rear axle is the secret ingredient that yields such yummy road holding. This straightforward, simple design ensures more precise vehicle control, so the car is nice and stable on curves and is much more competent than some of the rivals in this department. Tire quality on the various models is also a major factor and the end result varies a lot between the base model's roadability and that of the SE model.

+ PERFORMANCES. They're sprightly even with the base engine since accelerations and pickup are right in keeping with this brave little engine's roar and you feel like you're travelling faster than is actually the case.

+ FUEL ECONOMY. The 1.6L engine is one of the most fuel-efficient in its category since it settles for 28 mpg in the city.

+ STEERING. The power steering system is neat, since it's accurate and benefits from a good reduction ratio, so this little car zips around wherever it pleases in the city.

+ RIDE COMFORT. It's really something for a small car, the suspension is very silky and the nice-design seats procure good hip and shoulder support that isn't spoiled by the rather firm upholstery.

+ QUALITY. These cars are well-built and exhibit careful, trim finish details, in the Japanese tradition, but you can't say the cabin interior is one of the loveliest you've set eyes on.

+ CONVENIENCE FEATURES. Just great with all those roomy storage areas. The trunk is a fairly good size and connects with the cabin via a slot located behind the rear seatbench.

+ ERGONOMICS. The dashboard is handy and logical and the main section curves outwards, so controls are within easy reach. Too bad the radio and climate control dials are reversed.

CONS

- BRAKES. The base, XE and GXE aren't equipped with a really good braking system, not with those incredibly long stops in emergency situations, quite unusual for such a lightweight car. The pedal is a bit spongy so brakes are hard to apply as needed. One good thing: even without ABS, car path stays rectilinear.

-SWAY. It's generated by the overly soft suspension that equips all three models, and it provokes understeer effect that's really more of a bother than a real concern.

- STEERING. It's over-assisted, so it's light and frothy, which complicates things in strong crosswinds.

- TIRES. Those installed on the base model are too small and of mediocre quality. They must be replaced when winter is on its way, no if's, and's or but's, since they're hazardous.

- NOISE LEVEL. It stays at top volume all the livelong day, since the engine roars when coaxed to perform and the body is poorly insulated, so road noise is very pervasive.

- CABIN DESIGN. It's very dreary and seat fabrics and plastic trim components sure don't help liven things up and a bit of color would dress the cabin up a bit...

- EQUIPMENT. The base model is so poorly aequipped that it's a real disgrace for Nissan that dares to put such a lowly car on the market, so as to offer the best bargain around...

CONCLUSION

The new Sentra will be unveiled at the next Detroit Auto Show. Here's hoping it will be more successful than the current model, available until the spring of the year 2000.

Small Cars

RATING		
NISSAN Sentra		
CONCEPT :		63%
Technology :	75	
Safety :	75	
Interior space :	50	
Trunk volume :	40	
Quality/fit/finish :	75	
DRIVING :		59%
Cockpit :	75	
Performance :	50	
Handling :	55	
Steering :	75	
Braking :	40	
ORIGINAL EQUIPMENT :		73%
Tires :	70	
Headlights :	75	
Wipers :	75	
Rear defroster :	70	
Radio :	75	
COMFORT :		69%
Seats :	70	
Suspension :	70	
Sound level :	50	
Conveniences :	80	
Air conditioning :	75	
BUDGET :		80%
Price :	75	
Fuel economy :	85	
Insurance :	90	
Satisfaction :	80	
Depreciation :	70	
Overall rating :		68.8%

NEW FOR 2000

• The Sentra will be replaced by a new model early in 2000.

Compare
Performance,
Specifications, Prices,
and Classification
at the end of this chapter.

EQUIPMENT

NISSAN Sentra	base	XE	GXE	GLE	SE
Automatic transmission:	-	O	O	O	O
Cruise control:	-	-	S	S	S
Power steering:	-	S	S	S	S
Anti-lock brakes:	-	-	O	S	S
Traction control:	-	-	-	-	-
Air conditioning:	-	O	S	S	S
Leather:	-	-	-	-	-
AM/FM/radio-cassette:	-	O	S	S	SCd
Power door locks:	-	-	S	S	S
Power windows:	-	-	S	S	S
Tilt steering:	S	S	S	S	S
Dual adjustable mirrors:	-	-	SE	SE	SE
Alloy wheels:	-	-	-	S	S
Anti-theft system:	-	-	-	-	S

Colors

Exterior: Bronze, Blue, Ebony, Charcoal, Sandstone, White, Green, Beige.

Interior: Grey, Brown, Charcoal.

AT A GLANCE...

HISTORIC

Introduced in:	1981-1995.
Made in:	Aguascalientes, Mexico & Smyrna TE, USA.

DEMOGRAPHICS

Model	Men./Wom.	Age	Married	College	Income $
Sentra	54/46 %	44	71 %	61 %	$ 34,000

INDEX

Safety:	75 %	Satisfaction:	80 %
Depreciation:	47 %	Insurance:	$ 560
Cost per mile:	$ 0.37	Number of dealers:	1,100

SALES

Model	Canada 1997	1998	Result	USA 1997	1998	Result
Sentra	2,979	3,812	+ 28.0 %	122,468	88,363	- 27.8 %

MAINTENANCE REQUIRED BY WARRANTY

First revision:	Frequency:	Diagnostic plug:
7,500 miles	7,500 miles	Yes

Small cars

After selling more than two million vehicles of a single model available in three body types, Saturn's true success is building a new relationship with its buyers by creating friendly and trusting ties based on respect and honesty. This year, the body and passenger compartment of S-Series sedans and wagons sport a revamped style. Next year the coupe's turn will come.

MODEL RANGE

The S family (for small) is available in three different body designs: a 2 or 3-door coupe in SC1 and SC2 trim levels, a four-door sedan in SL, SL1 and SL2 trim and a four-door station wagon in SW1 and SW2 versions. Cars are equipped with a standard 5-speed manual transmission or a 4-speed automatic that's available as an extra. The 100-hp SOHC 1.9L engine equips the 1 versions and its 124-hp DOHC counterpart animates the 2 versions. Original equipment varies, from Spartan simple on the SL sedan to the chromed-up, to fancy-looking versions 2.

TECHNICAL FEATURES

All Saturn's have the same structural design, consisting of a metallic cage mounted on a steel platform (that includes some galvanized panels), on which rests the body that includes steel horizontal panels (engine hood, trunk lid and roof) and thermoformed polymer for vertical panels (fenders, doors and rear hatch on the station wagon). The suspension is fully independent Mac Pherson style on the front end and with tri-link in the back. Disc and drum brakes can benefit from optional ABS on all models, on the versions 2.

Still Refined

PROS

+ STYLE. It's rather lovely, but it isn't terribly original, really. Yet this kind of quiet elegance will virtually always be in style and the car has a distinctive look that's easily identified, not to forget the 3-door coupe.

+ DESIGN CONCEPT. It's quite unique on the North American market since the demise of General Motors minivans based on the same technology. The polymer-clad steel structure is rust-resistant as well as ding-and dent-resistant and Saturn is the only carmaker in the world to still use this technique that isn't cheap by any means.

+ CABIN SPACE. There's higher ceiling clearance, but otherwise it has the same length and width dimensions. Two adults and two children will be comfortably seated aboard, even in the rear seats of the most recent coupe and there's quite a bit of room to breathe even with the low ceiling.

+ RIDE COMFORT. It's improved since the front seats were redesigned and they now provide adequate lateral and lumbar support. And more generous suspension travel handles road bumps with more aplomb and the car doesn't bottom out as much.

+ HANDLING. It's a definite asset on these cars that tend to go into understeer, but they stay nice and neutral, so the average driver isn't in for any unpleasant surprises.

+ BRAKES. They're efficient and the average-length sudden stopping distances prove it. The car stays nice and straight with the optional ABS and linings are pretty tough.

+ PERFORMANCES. They're adequate for both engines, but these brutes are rough and rambunctious.

+ QUALITY. Fit and finish is cleaner and trim materials are spiffier than they once were and the cabin looks pretty good for a car in this price range.

+ NOISE LEVEL. It's significantly lower thanks to a more rigid structure and better soundproofing. Slight changes to the front-end have resulted in a decrease in the wind's impact as it hits the car's body.

+ A GOOD POINT. A very good idea to install a third door for the kids on the coupe...

CONS

- PRICE. It goes up and up, as soon as you start checking out all the options, so you end up paying a lot more than the advertised price.

- STEERING. The manual on the SL is an insult to the intelligence. It's imprecise, suffers from a poor reduction ratio and turns every parking maneuver into a nightmare.

- BRAKES. Without ABS, emergency stops can be pretty awful due to front wheel lock that engenders dangerous swerving that's hard to control when you're caught off guard. The antilock braking system and traction control aren't worth their salt, since accelerations and braking can be pretty rough.

- TRANSMISSION. The automatic shifter is jerky and, like the manual, it provides little braking effect, so you often have to brake to slow down.

- CONVENIENCE FEATURES. Storage spots are skimpy when it comes to size and the cargo hold may be modular, but it isn't too deep or wide due to the big wheel housings.

- REAR SEATS. It isn't easy climbing aboard with those slim doors and the curved roof design. Once you're seated, you aren't too comfy either, because the seat cushion is short and the back is hard and flat.

- TO BE IMPROVED UPON. Power window controls poorly located on the center console and poor-quality original tires.

CONCLUSION

The small Saturn sedans and wagons have been improved considerably once again and they don't need much else to rank among the best buys on the market. Maybe a more competitive price?

RATING
SATURN SC-SL-SW

CONCEPT :   73%
Technology :   80
Safety :   100
Interior space :   60
Trunk volume :   50
Quality/fit/finish :   75

DRIVING :   63%
Cockpit :   80
Performance :   50
Handling :   60
Steering :   75
Braking :   50

ORIGINAL EQUIPMENT :   68%
Tires :   75
Headlights :   70
Wipers :   70
Rear defroster :   60
Radio :   65

COMFORT :   72%
Seats :   75
Suspension :   75
Sound level :   60
Conveniences :   70
Air conditioning :   80

BUDGET :   71%
Price :   70
Fuel economy :   80
Insurance :   70
Satisfaction :   85
Depreciation :   50

Overall rating :   69.4%

NEW FOR 2000

- Lower-body styling.
- Entirely revamped interior, including the dashboard.
- Headlights, running lights and flashers.
- Painted front-end (except SL).
- Wheel cover design and aluminum rims.

Compare
Performance,
Specifications, Prices,
and Classification
at the end of this chapter.

EQUIPMENT

SATURN	SL	SC1-*SL1*-SW1	SC2-*SL2*-SW2
Automatic transmission:	O	O	O
Cruise control:	-	O	O
Power steering:	-	S	S
Anti-lock brakes:	O	O	OCd
Traction control:	O	O	S
Air conditioning:	O	O	S
Leather:	-	-	O
AM/FM/radio-cassette:	O	O	O
Power door locks:	-	O	O
Power windows:	-	O	O
Tilt steering:	S	S	S
Dual adjustable mirrors:	O	SM	SM
Alloy wheels:	-	-	O
Anti-theft system:	-	O	O

Colors

Exterior: White, Navy blue, Wildberry, Silver, Plum, Green,Black, Red, Gold.

Interior: Tan, Grey, Black.

AT A GLANCE...

HISTORIC
Introduced in: 1990-1997.
Made in: Spring Hill, Tennessee, USA.

DEMOGRAPHICS

Model	Men./Wom.	Age	Married	College	Income $
Coupe	30/70 %	36	36 %	53 %	43,000
Sedan, Wagon	57/43 %	40	67 %	56 %	38,500

INDEX

Safety:	100 %	Satisfaction:	90 %
Depreciation:	50 %	Insurance:	$ 525 -565
Cost per mile:	$ 0.37	Number of dealers:	300

SALES

	Canada			USA		
Model	1997	1998	Result	1997	1998	Result
Saturn S	20,989	18,263	- 13.0 %	251,099	231,786	- 7.7 %

MAINTENANCE REQUIRED BY WARRANTY
First revision: **Frequency:**   **Diagnostic plug:**
3,000 miles   6,000 miles   Yes

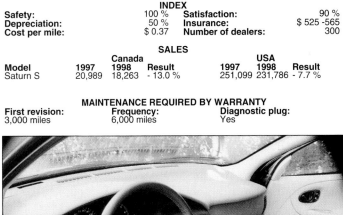

Not As Anonymous

With time, slowly but surely the Esteem has climbed the rungs along the ladder of recognition. And its progress is due much more to its intrinsic qualities than to any efforts its builder has made to promote it. After several years of indifferent treatment, it's one of the most appealing choices in its class.

MODEL RANGE

The Esteem is available as a 4-door sedan or wagon, in GL and GLX versions equipped with 1.6 or 1.8L (standard on wagons) engines and a standard manual or optional automatic transmission (standard on the GLX). The two trims are distinguished solely by their equipment levels. The GL has standard dual airbags, power steering, intermittent windshield wipers, air conditioning and a radio/cassette player. The GLX adds power windows, the 1.8L engine and sideview mirrors.

TECHNICAL FEATURES

The Esteem has a steel unibody, a fully independent MacPherson-type suspension and a front-end stabilizer bar. To insulate the cockpit against vibration from the drivetrain the latter is mounted on an independent frame positioned on rubber insulators.

The 16-valve SOHC 1.6L 4-cylinder engine is the same unit found in the make's Sidekick and Swift models and when the Esteem travels with a full load, its weight-power ratio is barely reasonable. Luckily transmissions feature a good gear ratio and seem to shift more quickly than they actually do.

PROS

+ USEABLE SPACE. It's interesting because of good exterior sizing and occupants travel comfortably. On the wagon the rear seat folds down for more cargo space.

+ PERFORMANCE. Levels are economical as can be and this model's price, fuel economy and maintenance costs are all attractively low.

+ HANDLING. As is always the case, it depends mostly on tire quality. The latest test drive models featured Bridgestone Potenza RE92 tires, which gave the Esteem grip when cornering sharply and otherwise and kept it stable at all times, regardless of the condition of road surfaces.

+ DRIVEABILITY. It's good thanks to smooth controls and reactions that are rarely harsh. The Esteem's excellent handling also makes it ideal for city driving.

+ COMFORT. It's surprising for a car in this class; the suspension is smooth and absorbs road defects effectively. Front seats provide good support and are designed to mold the body.

+ VALUE. The GLX offers better value compared to the competition and it's a better buy than the base version, which is more difficult to resell because of its minimal equipment and inexpensive-looking interior.

+ QUALITY. It's obvious at all levels, assembly is careful, finish is meticulous and — a departure for this category — the materials used in the GLX look very good, especially the seat trims.

+ PRACTICALITY. The trunk and cargo area are modular and easily accessible. Storage spaces are more efficient in the front than in the rear of the vehicle, but door pockets aren't wide enough. In the wagon the space surrounding the spare tire is put to good use.

CONS

- APPEARANCE. In spite of various touchups, styling is dull and makes this model hard to pick out from the pack of competitors.

- STRUCTURE. As is the case with other products of the same make panels are flimsy and give cause for worry in case of a serious collision. Not convinced? Do a test: just close one of the doors a bit harder than usual — you'll see!

- BRAKING. It lacks power in emergency situations and stopping distances are longer than average despite the fact that the vehicle has a reasonable overall weight.

- NOISE LEVEL. It's fairly high at all times and comes from the engine, the road and wind leaking in at various spots around the windshield; poor soundproofing doesn't help matters.

- TIRES. Those mounted on some models are go-kart worthy: small-sized, slippery and ready to squeal at the slightest provocation.

- MANUAL TRANSMISSION. It's slow to react and doesn't like to be pushed. At times it's impossible to shift from 4th to 3rd gear or to go from 1st to 2nd anywhere near quickly. With its stubborn shifting, the automatic transmission isn't much better.

- REAR SEATS. Access isn't easy for hefty passengers, doors are narrow and their opening angle is marginal (50°).

- OVERSIGHTS. The wagon's rear windshield wiper isn't intermittent and with the automatic transmission, the instrument panel includes no gear shift indicator. Windshield wipers are slow on all versions and fail to keep up with heavy rain. There aren't nearly enough cupholders and air conditioning controls are a throwback to the last century.

CONCLUSION

The Esteem is worth a look, more for its practical qualities and cost-effectiveness than for its styling or performance levels — both unexciting. It's too bad that a high noise level makes it unpleasant to ride in this car — from this particular standpoint, it has a lot more to offer than most others in its class.

Esteem SUZUKI

RATING
SUZUKI Esteem

CONCEPT : 66%
Technology :	75
Safety :	75
Interior space :	50
Trunk volume :	50
Quality/fit/finish :	80

DRIVING : 60%
Cockpit :	70
Performance :	40
Handling :	55
Steering :	75
Braking :	60

ORIGINAL EQUIPMENT : 69%
Tires :	70
Headlights :	75
Wipers :	60
Rear defroster :	70
Radio :	70

COMFORT : 66%
Seats :	75
Suspension :	75
Sound level :	40
Conveniences :	65
Air conditioning :	75

BUDGET : 76%
Price :	80
Fuel economy :	85
Insurance :	75
Satisfaction :	85
Depreciation :	55

Overall rating : 67.4%

NEW FOR 2000

- Air conditioning and radio/cassette player standard on the GL .
- ABS brakes standard on the GLX sedan.
- DOHC 1.8L engine standard on all wagons.
- Body colors: Red Pearl and Black Pearl.
- Manual GLX wagon withdrawn.

Compare Performance, Specifications, Prices, and Classification at the end of this chapter.

EQUIPMENT

SUZUKI Esteem	GL	GLX
Automatic transmission:	O	S
Cruise control:	-	-
Power steering:	S	S
Anti-lock brakes:	-	S
Traction control:	-	-
Air conditioning:	S	S
Leather:	-	-
AM/FM/radio-cassette:	-	-
Power door locks:	O /S-w	S
Power windows:	-	S
Tilt steering:	-	S
Dual adjustable mirrors:	-	-
Alloy wheels:	-	SM
Anti-theft system:	S	S

Colors

Exterior: White, Red, Grey, Black, Blue, Green.

Interior: Grey.

AT A GLANCE...

HISTORIC
Introduced in: 1995.
Made in: Kosai, Japon.

DEMOGRAPHICS
Model	Men./Wom.	Age	Married	College	Income $
Esteem	60/40 %	37	65 %	49 %	30,000

INDEX
Safety:	75 %	Satisfaction:	85 %
Depreciation:	47 %	Insurance:	$ 520
Cost per mile:	$ 0.35	Number of dealers:	NA

SALES
Model	1997 Canada	1998	Result	1997 USA	1998	Result
Esteem	2,311	3,033	+ 31.2 %	7,028	13,915	+ 98.0 %

MAINTENANCE REQUIRED BY WARRANTY
First revision:	Frequency:	Diagnostic plug:
3,000 miles	6,000 miles	Yes

Benchmark

In spite of fierce competition, the Corolla (and the Prizm) remains the global benchmark when it comes to subcompacts. Over the years its body and powertrain have become more sophisticated and it has reached maturity while building an enviable reputation. There's no question that's its two strongest points are its long-term reliability and high resale value.

MODEL RANGE

The Corolla like the Prizm is a 4-door sedan that's sold in VE, CE and LE models, powered by a 1.8L DOHC 4-cylinder engine delivering 125 hp. The 5-speed manual transmission is standard equipment on the VE and CE and the 4-speed automatic transmission comes as an extra. The Prizm is available as a base or an LSi model. For 2000 the equipement is more complete than ever, including air conditionning, full wheel covers and AM/FM stereo radio on the base model and power windows, adjustable steering column and larger tires on the LSi version.

TECHNICAL FEATURES

Since the 1998 redesign, the Corolla's steel monocoque body benefits from improved aerodynamic yield, since the drag coefficient has gone from 0.33 to 0.31. Its primary structure is really much more robust. It forms a sort of high-resistance steel cage around the cabin so as to provide passenger protection in the event of a collision and to resist to torsion and flexion on impact. The four-wheel independent suspension is still based on the MacPherson strut design, but now both front and rear suspensions are equipped with a stabilizer bar.
At the rear, the parallel control arm assembly enhances vehicle stability and provides a more neutral demeanor on curves. Power steering and disc and drum brakes are standard on all models, and only the LE version can receive an antilock braking system as an extra. There are some unique technical features, such as the valve in the main exhaust converter that allows for a short cycle at low rpm and a long cycle at high rpm, which reduces pressure and allows for greater exhaust gases circulation.

PROS

+ VALUE. The Corolla maintains an excellent resale value due to its reputation for reliability and never-say-die durability. So used models are rare and cost a pretty bundle. If the car doesn't sell, the car stays in the family, that is, parents pass it on to their children and so on.
+ SAFETY. It's a cut above now that the body is stiffer and now that cars are equipped with airbags. The Corolla has never been as solidly built and feels really secure.
+ STYLE. It's very conservative, but it has a certain appeal and has become a sort of classic, since it has a harmonious, well-balanced design, without any frills that won't go out of style for many a moon.
+ CABIN SPACE. Four adults can be comfortably seated inside and, a rare occurrence, rear seat access is great with the good-sized doors that open wide.

+ DRIVING PLEASURE. Just great with the smooth, velvety controls, neat cockpit, satisfactory all-round visibility and rational dashboard setup.
+ PERFORMANCES. The latest 1.8L engine is pretty lively even with the automatic transmission and accelerations and pickup are very respectable given the efficient fuel yield, since fuel consumption is one of the most frugal around.
+ ROADABILITY. It stays neutral and level in most situations, so anyone can get behind the wheel and drive with assurance, if the car is equipped with good-quality tires, that is.
+ RIDE COMFORT. It's super for a car of this format. The suspension is flexible, but not too much so, soundproofing does its stuff, but the front seats are more nicely contoured and cushioned than the rather flat rear seatbench.
+ CONVENIENCE FEATURES. Storage spots include a generous glove compartment, trim door side-pockets, a compartment located under the air conditioning controls and two storage bins on the center console. The trunk is easy to get to and its size is proportional to that of the cabin and it can be extended by lowering the rear seatbench back.

CONS

- QUALITY. It doesn't seem to be as obvious a trait as was the case on the previous model and the people at Toyota no longer talk about the "hidden quality" concept, that was the in-phrase for so long. Most trim materials are very plain and basic, even on the more well-equipped model.
- PRICE. It's too steep for a small North American-built car and with the "necessary" options that you have to add on, it isn't unusual to pay as much as for a higher-class car...
- PICKUP. They aren't wonderful as soon as the car is loaded at full capacity and in this case, the manual gearbox is more of a boon than the automatic that keeps looking for the best gear.
- TIRES. The Goodyear Integrity tires installed on our test model didn't have the best grab, even on dry pavement and they're noisy and slippery and the base model seems to be equipped with bicycle tires...
- STEERING. It's too light and at times a bit vague due to over-assistance.
- REAR SEATS. The rear seat area isn't as roomy as is the case up front and it's impossible to seat three persons back there, as Toyota purports, for the seatbench isn't too wide, it doesn't offer much lateral support and upholstery is rather hard.

CONCLUSION

Although more expensive than the average, these subcompacts give their owners a unique peace of mind. In fact, they're so reliable year after year that drivers can easily begin to forget their car's age and since they're often passed on to the next generation, they become part of the family.

RATING
TOYOTA Corolla

CONCEPT :   72%
Technology :   80
Safety :   90
Interior space :   60
Trunk volume :   50
Quality/fit/finish :   80

DRIVING :   64%
Cockpit :   80
Performance :   50
Handling :   60
Steering :   75
Braking :   55

ORIGINAL EQUIPMENT :   75%
Tires :   75
Headlights :   80
Wipers :   75
Rear defroster :   75
Radio :   70

COMFORT :   72%
Seats :   75
Suspension :   70
Sound level :   70
Conveniences :   70
Air conditioning :   75

BUDGET :   75%
Price :   70
Fuel economy :   85
Insurance :   70
Satisfaction :   90
Depreciation :   60

Overall rating :   71.6%

NEW FOR 2000
- Standard on all Corolla models: the VVT-i engine, additional carpets, a radio and CD player, child-safety seat braces.
- Pearl Black and Woodland Pearl colors.
- Standard air conditioning and AM/FM radio on the Prizm.
- 185/65R14 tires and new colors on the Prizm LSi.

Compare Performance, Specifications, Prices, and Classification at the end of this chapter.

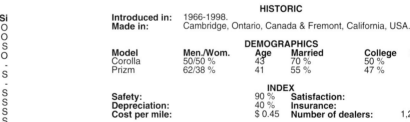

EQUIPMENT

TOYOTA Corolla sedan CHEVROLET Prizm	VE	CE	LE base	LSi
Automatic transmission:	O	O	S	O	O
Cruise control:	-	O	S	-	O
Power steering:	S	S	S	S	S
Anti-lock brakes:	-	-	O	O	O
Traction control:	-	-	-	-	-
Air conditioning:	O	O	S	S	S
Leather:	-	-	-	-	-
AM/FM/radio-cassette:	S	S	S	S	S
Power door locks:	-	-	S	-	S
Power windows:	-	-	S	O	S
Tilt steering:	O	S	S	-	S
Dual adjustable mirrors:	SM	SM	SE	SM	SE
Alloy wheels:	-	O	O	O	O
Anti-theft system:	-	-	-	-	-

Colors
Exterior: White, Black, Iris, Sand, Teal, Emerald, Black Pearl, Woodland Pearl.

Interior: Beige, Grey.

AT A GLANCE...

HISTORIC
Introduced in: 1966-1998.
Made in: Cambridge, Ontario, Canada & Fremont, California, USA.

DEMOGRAPHICS
Model	Men./Wom.	Age	Married	College	Income $
Corolla	50/50 %	43	70 %	50 %	33,000
Prizm	62/38 %	41	55 %	47 %	50,000

INDEX
Safety:	90 %	Satisfaction:	90 %
Depreciation:	40 %	Insurance:	$ 775
Cost per mile:	$ 0.45	Number of dealers:	1,233-4,466

SALES
Model	Canada 1997	1998	Result	USA 1997	1998	Result
Corolla	34,142	40,773	+19.4 %	218,461	250,501	+14.7 %
Prizm	Not sold in Canada			62,992	49,552	- 21.3 %

MAINTENANCE REQUIRED BY WARRANTY
First revision:	Frequency:	Diagnostic plug:
3,000 miles	6,000 miles	Yes

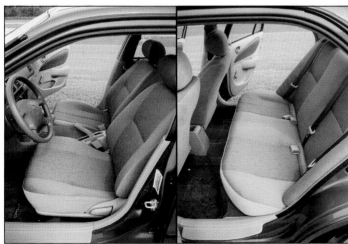

Volkswagen wants to brag that it's succeeded one of the best marketing coups in this end of the century with the reintroduction of its New Beetle. In spite of a very poor practicality rating, this model is selling like hot cakes and continues to grab attention on the roads, where its flashy colors never go unnoticed.

Eye-catching

MODEL RANGE

The New Beetle is sold in a single 2-door trim equipped with a 2.0-liter 4-cylinder gas engine, a 1.9-liter turbodiesel engine or a 1.8-liter 4-cylinder turbo, all with a standard 5-speed manual transmission, or optional 4-speed automatic. Standard equipment includes four airbags (two front-impact and two side-impact), an air conditioner fitted with a pollen and odor filter, a six-speaker stereo with cassette, anti-theft alarm system, and remote-control door locks.

TECHNICAL FEATURES

The New Beetle is built on the newest Golf/Jetta platform. The chassis structure is designed to offer maximum stiffness on impact. Aerodynamics aren't too hot, since the drag coefficient is crippled by all those stylistic curves. Fenders are bolted onto the fully galvanized steel unibody, so the car is built to last, and the 12-year/unlimited-mileage warranty against corrosion proves it. The fully independent suspension includes MacPherson struts up front and a torsion axle at the rear, with anti-roll bars on both ends. The car comes equipped with 4-wheel disc brakes, vented up front, but ABS is only available as an option. Lastly, the car is fitted with 16-inch tires and the teeny spare tire is stored under the trunk floor.

PROS

+ STYLING. Its semicircular roofline and flattened extremities make it simply irresistible and those bright body shades make heads turn.

+ ENGINEERING is very modern, including safety and comfort features that were absent on the original Beetle. The heating and air conditioning systems are efficient in any kind of weather and four airbags protect passengers from road hazards.

+ DRIVING. Safety-wise, it's light years ahead compared with the old model (that's still being assembled in Mexico, by the way). The New Beetle handles well. There isn't much swish and sway, and steering is nice and gradual, which makes for easy control. Brakes are trustworthy in most circumstances and both transmissions are slick and smooth.

+ COMFORT is obviously better up front with easy access, and more than enough room. Seats are well-shaped and padded. The suspension is firm while not being harsh, typically German.

+ THE LOOK is great. All materials (aluminum, plastics and fabrics) are good quality. The finish and construction are finely detailed.

+ THE REAR HATCH is perfectly integrated, and well-crafted. You can tell by the lock hidden under the brand crest. A real work of art!

+ DRIVING. In spite of weak performance, driving is pleasant. The car adequately maneuverable in the city because of precise steering and a reasonable turning radius.

+ TRANSMISSION. The manual gearbox works like a charm. Shifting is precise and smooth, like a true VW.

+ WELL DONE. Instruments all combined into a single module with a mini tachometer and digital screen.

CONS

- IMPRACTICAL. This car may be fun, but it's none too practical. With such a typically rounded roofline, there isn't much cabin or trunk space, at least not according to present-day standards. Car designers didn't even bestow the New Beetle with a decent glove box, door-side pockets or functional cupholders. Rear-seat passengers feel cramped after having bent over backwards to board- those folding front seats aren't any help and the trunk is only really practical with the rear seat folded down.

- PERFORMANCE. The ride isn't that great with either the 2.0-liter gas engine or the 1.9-liter diesel engine on our test models. The New Beetle is heavy and feels a bit lethargic with either the manual or the automatic gearbox. The 1.8-liter turbo will bring more life to this model.

- VISIBILITY. Visibility isn't any better than it was on the original Beetle, not with such a high body belt that sure cuts down on window size. The bulky roof pillars and tiny, high-perched exterior mirrors and slim interior mirrors don't help either. The digital data screen in amongst the other instruments is unreadable by day. Also the right side mirror is ridiculously small, similar to other Volkswagens'.

- NOISE LEVELS. Volkswagens aren't world famous for their quiet ride and the New Beetle is no exception to the rule. The engine emits a loud sound and it shakes a lot. The rearview mirrors hum away at 50 mph and tires are far from unobtrusive.

- DRIVING POSITION. A good position is hard to find, and the windshield (and the outside world) seems far away.

- INSTRUMENT PANEL. The instrument panel is absolutely huge for what it holds, so the interior looks skimpier than it actually is.

- TO BE REVIEWED. A rear wiper would be nice to clear off the water that collects there in poor weather — rear windows can't be opened so you feel claustrophobic — sun visors are too small — headlights aren't bright enough — the clock is inconveniently located on the ceiling — and the cup-holders are hardly practical.

CONCLUSION

The New Beetle is a car you buy more through passion than reason. Its ride and its practicality have been sacrificed for the sake of style and after a while, even its initially strong visual appeal begins to wear off.

RATING VW New Beetle		
CONCEPT :		71%
Technology :	85	
Safety :	100	
Interior space :	40	
Trunk volume :	50	
Quality/fit/finish :	80	
DRIVING :		60%
Cockpit :	75	
Performance :	40	
Handling :	55	
Steering :	80	
Braking :	50	
ORIGINAL EQUIPMENT :		78%
Tires :	80	
Headlights :	75	
Wipers :	80	
Rear defroster :	75	
Radio :	80	
COMFORT :		61%
Seats :	75	
Suspension :	80	
Sound level :	30	
Conveniences :	40	
Air conditioning :	80	
BUDGET :		65%
Price :	50	
Fuel economy :	80	
Insurance :	50	
Satisfaction :	80	
Depreciation :	65	
Overall rating :		**67.0%**

NEW FOR 2000

- Brake wear indicator.
- Improved antitheft system.
- Standard traction control system on GLS and GLX versions.
- "Cold weather" option package with fabric seats on the GLS.

Compare Performance, Specifications, Prices, and Classification at the end of this chapter.

EQUIPMENT

VOLKSWAGEN New Beetle	base	TDI	GLX
Automatic transmission:	O	O	O
Cruise control:	O	O	S
Power steering:	S	S	S
Anti-lock brakes:	O	O	S
Traction control:	-	-	S
Air conditioning:	S	S	S
Leather:	O	O	S
AM/FM/radio-cassette:	S	S	S
Power door locks:	S	S	S
Power windows:	O	O	S
Tilt steering:	S	S	S
Dual adjustable mirrors:	SEH	SEH	SEH
Alloy wheels:	O	O	S
Anti-theft system:	S	S	S

Colors

Exterior: Black, White, Red, Blue, Yellow, Silver, Green.

Interior: Beige.

AT A GLANCE...

HISTORIC

Introduced in: 1998.
Made in: Puebla, Mexico.

DEMOGRAPHICS

Model	Men./Wom.	Age	Married	College	Income $
New Beetle	45/55 %	37	43 %	34 %	25,500

INDEX

Safety:	100 %	Satisfaction:	78 %
Depreciation:	35 %	Insurance:	$ 650
Cost per mile:	$ 0.39	Number of dealers:	650

SALES

Model	Canada 1997	1998	Result	USA 1997	1998	Result
New Beetle	-	9,209		-	55,842	

MAINTENANCE REQUIRED BY WARRANTY

First revision:	Frequency:	Diagnostic plug:
3,000 miles	6 months / 6,000miles	Yes

SMALL CARS
PERFORMANCE

Small

Model/version	Type / timing valve / fuel system	Displacement cu in	Power hp @ rpm	Torque lb-ft @ rpm	Compres. ratio	Driving wheels / transmission	Final ratio	Acceler. 0-60 mph s	Standing 1/4 & 5/8 mile s	Passing 50-75 mph s	Braking 60-0 mph ft	Top speed mph	Lateral acceler. G	Noise level dBA	Fuel economy mpg City	Highway	Fuel type Octane
CHEVROLET Cavalier																	
1)	L4 2.2 OHV-8-SFI	134	115 @ 5000	135 @ 3600	9.0 :1	front - M5*	3.58	9.6	17.6	31.5	7.3	141	103	0.75	68	24	34	R 87
						front - A3-A4	3.18	10.5	18.4	32.7	7.8	144	100	0.75	68	23	31	R 87
2)	L4 2.4 DOHC-16-SFI	146	150 @ 5600	155 @ 4400	9.5 :1	front - M5*	3.94	8.4	16.8	28.5	5.8	144	107	0.78	70	23	33	R 87
						front - A4	3.91	9.2	17.2	30.3	6.3	148	105	0.78	70	22	30	R 87
1) base cpe.& sedans. 2) base Z24 cpe. & con., option sedan LS.																	
CHRYSLER Neon																	
base/ES	L4 2.0 SOHC-16-MPSFI	122	132 @ 5600	130 @ 4600	9.8 :1	front - M5*	3.55	9.6	17.5	31.4	7.7	148	103	0.82	68	28	35	R 87
						front - A3	2.98	11.0	18.3	33.5	8.4	164	100	0.82	70	25	31	R 87
DAEWOO Nubira																	
base	L4 2.0 DOHC-16-MPFI	122	129 @ 5400	136 @ 4400	9.5 :1	front - M5*	3.55	9.2	16.5	31.6	7.8	131	106	0.78	68	22	31	R87
						front - A4	3.91	10.3	17.2	32.5	8.4	135	103	0.78	68	22	30	R87
FORD Focus																	
base	L4 2.0 SOHC-8-SPI	121	110 @ 5000	125 @ 3750	9.35 :1	front - M5*	3.61	10.7	18.2	33.4	8.6	135	106	0.75	68	28	35	R 87
						front - A4	3.69	11.5	18.5	34.0	9.0	138	103	0.75	68	26	33	R 87
ZX3-ZTS	L4 2.0 DOHC-16-EFI	121	130 @ 5300	135 @ 4500	9.6 :1	front- M5*	3.82	9.2	16.8	30.6	7.0	128	112	0.80	65-74	26	33	R 87
						front- A4	3.91	10.0	17.4	31.2	7.4	131	109	0.80	65-74	25	32	R 87
HONDA Civic																	
base	L4 1.6 SOHC-16-MPFI	97	106 @ 6200	103 @ 4600	9.4 :1	front - M5*	3.72	10.7	17.8	32.7	7.8	141	106	0.78	68-74	32	42	R 87
						front - A4	4.35	12.1	18.8	34.8	9.6	160	103	0.78	68-74	30	40	R 87
HX	L4 1.6 SOHC-16-MPFI	97	115 @ 6300	104 @ 5400	9.4 :1	front - M5*	3.72	9.5	17.0	31.2	7.4	145	110	0.80	68-74	30	38	R 87
EX	L4 1.6 SOHC-16-MPFI	97	127 @ 6600	107 @ 5500	9.6 :1	front - M5*	4.25	8.6	16.8	29.8	7.2	151	109	0.80	68-74	28	38	R 87
						front - A4	4.35	10.3	17.6	31.5	7.4	147	106	0.80	68-74	26	35	R 87
Si-SiR	L4 1.6 DOHC-16-MPFI	97	160 @ 7600	110 @ 7000	10.2 :1	front - M5*	4.27	8.2	17.1	30.6	7.0	141	115	0.80	69-73	25	34	R 87
HYUNDAI Elantra																	
Base	L4 2.0 DOHC-16-MPFI	121	140 @ 6000	133 @ 4800	10.3 :1	front - M5*	3.650	9.3	16.8	30.8	6.8	144	109	0.80	67	24	32	R 87
Option	L4 2.0 DOHC-16-MPFI	121	140 @ 6000	133 @ 4800	10.3 :1	front - A4	3.659	10.6	17.8	32.0	7.8	151	106	0.80	67	22	30	R 87
KIA Sephia																	
base	L4 1.8 DOHC-16-MPFI	109	125 @ 6000	108 @ 4500	9.5 :1	front- M5*	4.105	11.0	18.8	32.2	7.6	177	109	0.80	68-72	24	31	R 87
						front- A4	3.833	12.3	19.1	33.8	8.3	180	106	0.80	68-72	23	31	R 87
MAZDA Protegé																	
DX & SE	L4 1.6 DOHC-16-EFI	97	105 @ 5500	107 @ 4000	9.0 :1	front- M5*	3.850	11.0	17.8	32.0	7.6	143	110	0.78	69-72	28	35	R 87
						front- A4	3.904	13.0	19.1	32.6	8.2	145	105	0.78	69-72	26	34	R 87
LX	L4 1.8 DOHC-16-EFI	112	122 @ 6000	120 @ 4000	9.1 :1	front- M5*	4.105	11.0	18.2	31.6	7.1	141	119	0.80	68-72	25	34	R 87
						front- A4	3.904	12.1	18.7	32.2	7.9	144	109	0.80	68-72	23	32	R 87
NISSAN Sentra																	
base	L4 1.6 DOHC-16-MPSFI	97	115 @ 6000	108 @ 4000	9.9 :1	front - M5*	3.789	9.9	17.4	31.6	7.0	157	103	0.78	69	28	41	R 87
						front - A4	3.827	11.0	18.3	32.7	8.1	170	100	0.78	69	26	38	R 87
SE	L4 2.0 DOHC-16-MPSFI	122	140 @ 6400	132 @ 4800	9.5 :1	front - M5*	4.176	8.7	16.1	29.5	6.5	157	112	0.80	70	23	31	R 87
						front - A4	3.822	NA										
PONTIAC Sunfire																	
1)	L4* 2.2 SOHC-8-SFI	134	115 @ 5000	135 @ 3600	9.0 :1	front - M5*	3.58	9.6	17.2	31.0	6.9	154	103	0.76	68	23	34	R 87
						front - A3-A4	3.91	10.7	17.4	31.2	7.0	157	100	0.76	68	23	30	R 87
2)	L4* 2.4 DOHC-16-SFI	146	150 @ 5600	155 @ 4400	9.5 :1	front - M5*	3.94	8.6	16.8	30.5	6.6	148	112	0.78	70	19	28	R 87
						front - A4	3.91	9.4	17.4	30.8	6.4	154	109	0.78	70	22	32	R 87
1) base SE 2) base GT coupe & convertible, option on all SE models.																	
SATURN S																	
1)	L4 1.9 SOHC-8-MPSFI	116	100 @ 5000	114 @ 2400	9.3 :1	front - M5*	4.06	10.5	18.0	32.4	7.8	134	103	0.75	70	28	38	R 87
						front - A4	4.06	11.7	18.5	33.2	10.0	144	100	0.75	70	27	35	R 87
2)	L4 1.9 DOHC-16-MPSFI	116	124 @ 5600	122 @ 4800	9.5 :1	front - M5*	4.06	9.7	16.7	30.6	6.7	138	115	0.78	70	27	36	R 87
						front - A4	4.06	10.8	17.9	31.7	7.2	144	112	0.78	70	23	34	R 87
1) SL,SL1,SC1 2) SC2, SL2																	
SUZUKI Esteem																	
sedan.	L4* 1.6 SOHC-16-MPFI	97	98 @ 6000	94 @ 3200	9.5 :1	front - M5*	3.789	10.8	17.8	32.8	7.8	151	106	0.77	68	29	39	R 87
	L4* 1.6 SOHC-16-MPFI	97	98 @ 6000	94 @ 3200	9.5 :1	front - A4*	3.850	11.8	18.5	33.4	8.2	148	102	0.77	68	28	38	R 87
wagon	L4 1.8 DOHC-16-MPFI	112	121 @ 6200	114 @ 3400	9.8 :1	front - M5*	3.72	-										
						front - A4*	3.85	-										
TOYOTA Corolla																	
1)	L4 1.8 DOHC-16-MPSFI	109	125 @ 5600	122 @ 4400	10.5 :1	front - M5*	3.722	9.1	16.6	30.8	6.9	134	115	0.78	65	30	38	R 87
2)						front - A4*	2.655	10.8	17.8	32.2	7.8	137	112	0.78	67	27	37	R 87
1) base 2) standard LE, option VE, CE.																	
VOLKSWAGEN New Beetle																	
base	L4* 2.0 SOHC-8-MPSFI	121	115 @ 5200	122 @ 2600	10.0 :1	front - M5*	4.24	10.2	17.4	31.6	7.3	128	112	0.76	68-72	24	34	R 87
						front - A4	4.53	11.3	18.0	33.3	9.0	144	110	0.76	68-72	22	31	R 87
TDI	L4T* 1.9 SOHC-8-DI	116	90 @ 4000	149 @ 1900	19.5 :1	front - M5*	3.39	12.5	19.2	33.4	10.6	148	106	0.76	69-74	42	54	D
						front - A4	3.71	13.6	19.8	34.0	11.2	151	102	0.76	69-74	35	50	D
GLX	L4T* 1.8 DOHC-20-EFI	109	150 @ 5700	155 @ 1750	9.5 :1	front - M5*	NA	7.7	15.8	27.5	6.0	161	130	0.78	68-72	23	35	R 87

SMALL CARS

SPECIFICATIONS

Model	Version Trim	Body/ Seats	Cabin volume cu ft	Trunk volume cu ft	Cd	Wheel base in	Lgth x Width x Hght in x in x in	Curb weight lb	Susp. ft/rr	Brake ft/rr	Steering type	Steering ø ft	Steering turns number	Fuel tank gal	Standard tires dimensions	Standard tires make	Standard tires model	Standard powertrain	99 Price msrp $
CHEVROLET		General warranty: 3 years / 36,000 miles; antipollution: 5 years / 50,000 miles; perforation corrosion: 6 years / 100,000 miles. Roadside assistance.																	
Cavalier	RS	2dr.cpe.4	87.3	13.2	0.39	104.1	180.7x68.7x53.0	2626	ih/sihdc/dr/ABS		pwr.r&p.	35.7	2.6	15.0	195/65R15	BF Goodrich	Touring T/A	L4/2.2/M5	12,381
Cavalier	Z24	2dr.cpe.4	87.3	13.2	0.39	104.1	180.7x68.7x53.0	2749	ih/sihdc/dr/ABS		pwr.r&p.	35.7	2.8	15.0	205/55R16	Goodyear	Eagle RS-A	L4/2.4/M5	16,481
Cavalier	Z24	2dr.con.4	83.0	10.5	0.42	104.1	180.7x68.7x54.1	2838	ih/sihdc/dr/ABS		pwr.r&p.	35.7	2.6	15.0	195/65R15	Goodyear	Eagle RS-A	L4/2.4/M5	20,081
Cavalier	RS	4dr.sdn.5	91.7	13.6	0.38	104.1	180.7x67.9x54.7	2676	ih/sihdc/dr/ABS		pwr.r&p.	35.7	2.6	15.0	195/70R14	BF Goodrich	Touring T/A	L4/2.2/M5	12,481
Cavalier	LS	4dr.sdn.5	91.7	13.6	0.38	104.1	180.7x67.9x54.7	2722	ih/sihdc/dr/ABS		pwr.r&p.	35.7	2.6	15.0	195/65R15	BF Goodrich	Touring T/A	L4/2.2/A4	14,921
CHRYSLER		General warranty: 3 years / 36,000 miles; surface rust: 3 years ; perforation: 7 years / 100,000 miles; roadside assistance: 3 years / 36,000 miles.																	
Neon	base	4dr.sdn. 5	90.3	13.1	0.34	105.0	174.4x67.4x56.0	2559	ih/ih	dc/dr	pwr.r&p.	35.5	3.0	12.5	185/65R14	Goodyear	Eagle GA	L4/2.0/M5	12,460
Neon	SE	4dr.sdn. 5	90.3	13.1	0.34	105.0	174.4x67.4x56.0	2559	ih/ih	dc/dr	pwr.r&p.	35.5	3.0	12.5	185/65R14	Goodyear	Eagle GA	L4/2.0/M5	-
DAEWOO		General warranty: 3 years / 36,000 miles; powertrain & corrosion: 5 years / 60,000 miles; antipollution: 6 years / illimited milleage.																	
Nubira	SX	4dr.sdn. 5	89.3	13.1	0.33	101.2	175.4x66.9x56.1	2566	ih/sindc/dr/ABS		pwr.r&p.	34.8	3.0	13.7	185/65R14	Hankook	Radial H406	L4/2.0/M5	12,250
Nubira	SX	5dr.sdn. 5	91.1	11.3	0.33	101.2	175.4x66.9x56.1	2546	ih/sindc/dr/ABS		pwr.r&p.	34.8	3.0	13.7	185/65R14	Hankook	Radial H406	L4/2.0/M5	12,250
Nubira	SX	4dr.wgn. 5	89.3	19.4	0.32	101.2	175.4x66.9x56.1	2694	ih/sindc/dr/ABS		pwr.r&p.	34.8	3.0	13.7	185/65R14	Hankook	Radial H406	L4/2.0/M5	13,650
Nubira	CDX	4dr.sdn. 5	89.3	13.1	0.33	101.2	175.4x66.9x56.1	2566	ih/sindc/dr/ABS		pwr.r&p.	34.8	3.0	13.7	185/65R14	Hankook	Radial H406	L4/2.0/M5	13,560
Nubira	CDX	5dr.sdn. 5	91.1	11.3	0.33	101.2	175.4x66.9x56.1	2546	ih/sindc/dr/ABS		pwr.r&p.	34.8	3.0	13.7	185/65R14	Hankook	Radial H406	L4/2.0/M5	13,560
Nubira	CDX	4dr.wgn. 5	89.3	19.4	0.32	101.2	175.4x66.9x56.1	2694	ih/sindc/dr/ABS		pwr.r&p.	34.8	3.0	13.7	185/65R14	Hankook	Radial H406	L4/2.0/M5	14,960
FORD		General warranty, antipollution & battery: 3 years / 36,000 miles; corrosion perforation: 5 years / unlimited.																	
Focus	ZX3	3dr.sed. 5	93.8	18.5	0.36	103.1	168.1x66.9x56.3	2551	ih/ih	dc/dr	pwr.r&p.	35.7	3.0	13.2	175/70R14	Goodyear	Eagle RS-A	L4/2.0/M5	-
Focus	LX	4dr.sed. 5	94.1	12.9	0.31	103.1	174.9x66.9x56.3	2564	ih/ih	dc/dr	pwr.r&p.	35.7	3.0	13.2	185/65R14	Goodyear	Eagle GA	L4/2.0/M5	-
Focus	SE	4dr.sed. 5	94.1	12.9	0.31	103.1	174.9x66.9x56.3	-	ih/ih	dc/dr	pwr.r&p.	35.7	3.0	13.2	195/60R15	Goodyear	Eagle GA	L4/2.0/M5	-
Focus	ZTS	4dr.sed. 5	94.1	12.9	0.31	103.1	174.9x66.9x56.3	-	ih/ih	dc/dr	pwr.r&p.	35.7	3.0	13.2	195/60R15	Goodyear	Eagle RS-A	L4/2.0/M5	-
Focus	SE	4dr.wgn. 5	93.8	37.5	0.30	103.1	178.2x66.9x57.0	2717	ih/ih	dc/dr	pwr.r&p.	35.7	3.0	13.2	195/60R15	Goodyear	Eagle GA	L4/2.0/M5	-
HONDA		General warranty: 3 years / 36,000 miles; powertrain: 5 years / 60,000 miles.																	
Civic	CX	3dr.hbk. 4	86.1	13.4	0.31	103.2	164.2x67.1x54.1	2359	ih/ih	dc/dr	r&p.	32.8	3.6	11.9	185/65R14	Firestone	FR-680	L4/1.6/M5	11,065
Civic	DX	3dr.hbk. 4	86.1	13.4	0.31	103.2	164.2x67.1x54.1	2288	ih/ih	dc/dr	r&p.	32.8	3.6	11.9	185/65R14	Firestone	FR-680	L4/1.6/M5	12,515
Civic	DX	2dr.cpe. 4	85.2	11.9	0.31	103.2	175.1x67.1x54.1	2359	ih/ih	dc/dr	pwr.r&p.	32.8	3.6	11.9	185/65R14	Firestone	FR-680	L4/1.6/M5	12,995
Civic	HX	2dr.cpe. 4	82.6	11.9	0.31	103.2	175.1x67.1x54.1	2370	ih/ih	dc/dr	pwr.r&p.	32.8	3.6	11.9	185/65R14	Firestone	FR-680	L4/1.6/M5	13,815
Civic	EX	2dr.cpe. 4	82.6	11.9	0.31	103.2	175.1x67.1x54.1	2515	ih/ih	dc/dr	pwr.r&p.	32.8	3.6	11.9	185/65R14	Firestone	FR-680	L4/1.6/M5	15,865
Civic	Si	2dr.cpe. 4	73.2	11.9	0.31	103.2	175.1x67.1x54.1	2480	ih/ih	dc	pwr.r&p.	32.8	3.6	11.9	195/60R15	Michelin	XGT-V4	L4/1.6/M5	17,860
Civic	DX	4dr.sdn. 5	89.8	11.9	0.32	103.2	175.1x67.1x54.7	2339	ih/ih	dc/dr	pwr.r&p.	32.8	3.6	11.9	185/65R14	Firestone	FR-680	L4/1.6/M5	13,200
Civic	EX	4dr.sdn. 5	86.5	11.9	0.32	103.2	175.1x67.1x54.7	2513	ih/ih	dc/dr	pwr.r&p.	32.8	3.6	11.9	185/65R14	Firestone	FR-680	L4/1.6/M5	17,145
HYUNDAI		General warranty: 3 years / 36,000 miles; powertrain: 5 years / 60,000 miles; corrosion perforation: 5 years / 60,000 miles; antipollution: 5 years / 36,000 miles.																	
Elantra	base	4dr.sdn. 5	93.6	11.4	0.32	100.4	174.0x66.9x54.9	2522	ih/ih	dc/dr	pwr.r&p.	32.5	3.02	14.5	175/65R14	Kumho	SBR	L4/2.0/M5	12,234
Elantra	base	4dr.wgn. 5	94.6	32.3	0.34	100.4	175.2x66.9x58.8	2619	ih/ih	dc/dr	pwr.r&p.	32.5	3.02	14.5	175/65R14	Hankook	880A	L4/2.0/M5	13,134
Elantra	GLS	4dr.sdn. 5	93.6	11.4	0.32	100.4	174.0x66.9x54.9	2586	ih/ih	dc/dr	pwr.r&p.	32.5	3.02	14.5	195/60R14	Michelin	XGT+4	L4/2.0/M5	-
Elantra	GLS	4dr.wgn. 5	94.6	32.3	0.34	100.4	175.2x66.9x58.8	2685	ih/ih	dc/dr	pwr.r&p.	32.5	3.02	14.5	195/60R14	Michelin	XGT+4	L4/2.0/M5	-
KIA		General warranty: 3 years / 36,000 miles; powertrain & corrosion: 5 years / 60,000 miles.																	
Sephia	RS	4dr.sdn. 5	94.1	10.4	0.34	100.8	174.4x66.9x55.5	2478	ih/ih	dc/dr	pwr.r&p.	32.1	3.9	13.2	185/65R14	Hankook	Radial H406	L4/1.8/M5	10,445
Sephia	LS	4dr.sdn. 5	94.1	10.4	0.34	100.8	174.4x66.9x55.5	2478	ih/ih	dc/dr	pwr.r&p.	32.1	3.9	13.2	185/65R14	Hankook	Radial H406	L4/1.8/M5	11,445
MAZDA		General warranty: 3 years / 50,000 miles; powertrain: 5 years / 100,000 miles; corrosion: 5 years / unlimited.																	
Protegé	DX	4dr.sdn. 5	92.6	12.9	0.32	102.8	174.8x67.3x55.9	2385	ih/ih	dc/dr	pwr.r&p.	34.1	2.7	13.2	185/65R14	Firestone	FR 680	L4/1.6/M5	12,420
Protegé	LX	4dr.sdn. 5	92.6	12.9	0.32	102.8	174.8x67.3x55.9	2385	ih/ih	dc/dr	pwr.r&p.	34.1	2.7	13.2	185/65R14	Firestone	FR 680	L4/1.6/M5	13,680
Protegé	ES	4dr.sdn. 5	92.6	12.9	0.32	102.8	174.8x67.3x55.9	2573	ih/ih	dc/dr	pwr.r&p.	34.1	2.7	13.2	185/65R14	Bridgestone	Potenza RE92	L4/1.8/M5	15,475
NISSAN		General warranty: 3 years / 50,000 miles; powertrain: 6 years / 60,000 miles; perforation corrosion & antipollution: 6 years / unlimited.																	
Sentra	XE	4dr.sdn.5	87.2	10.7	0.33	99.8	171.0x66.6x54.5	2381	ih/sih	dc/dr	pwr.r&p.	34.1	3.01	13.2	175/70R13	General	Ameri 45	L4/1.6/M5	12,319
Sentra	GXE	4dr.sdn.5	87.2	10.7	0.33	99.8	171.0x66.6x54.5	2429	ih/sih	dc/dr	pwr.r&p.	34.1	3.01	13.2	175/65R14	General	Ameri 45	L4/1.6/M5	14,719
PONTIAC		General warranty: 3 years / 36,000 miles; antipollution: 5 years / 50,000 miles; perforation corrosion: 6 years / 100,000 miles. Roadside assistance.																	
Sunfire	SE	2dr.cpe. 4	87.2	12.4	0.39	104.1	181.9x68.4x53.0	2606	ih/sih	dc/dr/ABS	pwr.r&p.	35.6	2.66	14.3	195/70R14	Goodyear	Conquest	L4/2.2/M5	13,255
Sunfire	SE	4dr.sdn. 5	91.6	13.1	0.38	104.1	181.8x67.9x54.7	2644	ih/sih	dc/dr/ABS	pwr.r&p.	35.6	2.66	14.3	195/70R14	Goodyear	Conquest	L4/2.2/M5	13,255
Sunfire	GT	2dr.cpe. 4	87.2	12.4	0.39	104.1	181.9x68.4x53.0	2771	ih/sih	dc/dr/ABS	pwr.r&p.	35.6	2.83	14.3	205/55R16	BFGoodrich	Touring T/A	L4/2.4/M5	16,255
Sunfire	GT	2dr.con. 4	83.4	9.9	0.42	104.1	182.9x68.4x54.1	2906	ih/sih	dc/dr/ABS	pwr.r&p.	35.6	2.66	14.3	195/65R15	BFGoodrich	Touring T/A	L4/2.4/A4	21,655
SATURN		General warranty: 3 years / 36,000 miles; antipollution: 5 years / 50,000 miles; perforation corrosion: 6 years / 100,000 miles. Roadside assistance.																	
SC1		2dr.cpe. 4	84.1	11.4	0.33	102.4	180.0x67.3x53.0	2320	ih/ih	dc/dr	pwr.r&p.	37.1	3.0	12.1	175/70R14	Firestone	Affinity	L4/1.9/M5	12,885
SC2		2dr.cpe. 4	84.1	11.4	0.33	102.4	180.0x67.3x53.0	2390	ih/ih	dc/dr	pwr.r&p.	37.1	2.6	12.1	195/60R15	Firestone	GTA	L4/1.9/M5	15,445
SL		4dr.sdn. 5	91.0	12.1	0.31	102.4	176.9x66.7x55.0	2326	ih/ih	dc/dr	r&p.	37.1	4.0	12.1	175/70R14	Firestone	Affinity	L4/1.9/M5	11,035
SL1		4dr.sdn. 5	91.0	12.1	0.31	102.4	176.9x66.7x55.0	2326	ih/ih	dc/dr	pwr.r&p.	37.1	3.0	12.1	175/70R14	Firestone	Affinity	L4/1.9/M5	11,735
SL2		4dr.sdn. 5	91.0	12.1	0.31	102.4	176.9x66.7x55.0	2388	ih/ih	dc/dr	pwr.r&p.	37.1	2.6	12.1	185/65R15	Firestone	Affinity	L4/1.9/M5	13,195
SW1		4dr.wgn. 5	91.8	24.9	0.36	102.4	176.9x66.7x55.6	2391	ih/ih	dc/dr	pwr.r&p.	37.1	3.0	12.1	175/70R14	Firestone	Affinity	L4/1.9/M5	12,735
SW2		4dr.wgn. 5	91.8	24.9	0.36	102.4	176.9x66.7x55.6	2448	ih/ih	dc/dr	pwr.r&p.	37.1	2.6	12.1	185/65R15	Firestone	Affinity	L4/1.9/M5	14,695
SUZUKI		General warranty: 3 years / 50,000 miles; perforation: 5 years / unlimited. 24hr roadside assistance.																	
Esteem	GL	4dr.sdn. 5	85.9	12.0	0.34	97.6	166.3x66.1x53.9	2282	ih/ih	dc/dr	pwr.r&p.	32.1	3.0	13.5	175/70R13	-	-	L 4/1.6/M5	12,629
Esteem	GL	4dr.wgn. 5	86.3	24.0	0.32	97.6	172.2x66.5x55.9	2359	ih/ih	dc/dr	pwr.r&p.	32.1	3.0	13.5	185/60R14	-	-	L 4/1.8/M5	13,129
Esteem	GLX	4dr.sdn. 5	85.9	12.0	0.34	97.6	166.3x66.1x53.9	2282	ih/ih	dc/dr	pwr.r&p.	32.1	3.0	13.5	175/70R13	Bridgestone	Potenza RE92	L 4/1.6/A4	13,729
Esteem	GLX	4dr.wgn. 5	86.3	24.0	0.32	97.6	172.2x66.5x55.9	2359	ih/ih	dc/dr	pwr.r&p.	32.1	3.0	13.5	185/60R14	Bridgestone	Potenza RE92	L 4/1.8/A4	14,229
TOYOTA		General warranty: 3 years / 36,000 miles; powertrain 5 years / 60,000 miles; corrosion, perforation: 5 years / unlimited.																	
Corolla	VE	4dr.sdn.4/5	92.1	12.1	0.31	97.0	174.0x66.7x54.5	2414	ih/ih	dc/dr	pwr.r&p.	32.1	3.2	13.2	175/65R14	Michelin	MXV4	L4/1.8/M5	12,678
Corolla	CE	4dr.sdn.4/5	92.1	12.1	0.31	97.0	174.0x66.7x54.5	2447	ih/ih	dc/dr	pwr.r&p.	32.1	3.2	13.2	175/65R14	Michelin	MXV4	L4/1.8/M5	13,368
Corolla	LE	4dr.sdn.4/5	92.1	12.1	0.31	97.0	174.0x66.7x54.5	2524	ih/ih	dc/dr	pwr.r&p.	32.1	3.2	13.2	185/65R14	Michelin	MXV4	L4/1.8/A4	15,328
VOLKSWAGEN		General warranty: 2 years / 24,000 miles; powertrain: 10 years / 100,000 miles; antipollution: 6 years/ 50,000 miles; corrosion perforation: 6 years / unlimited.																	
New Beetle	2.0	2dr.sdn.4	84.3	12.0	0.38	98.9	161.1x67.9x59.5	2712	ih/sih	dc/dc	pwr.r&p.	35.4	3.2	14.5	205/55R16	Goodyear	Eagle RS-A	L4/2.0/M5	16,425
New Beetle	TDI GLS	2dr.sdn.4	84.3	12.0	0.38	98.9	161.1x67.9x59.5	2769	ih/sih	dc/dc	pwr.r&p.	35.4	3.2	14.5	205/55R16	Goodyear	Eagle RS-A	L4TD/1.9/M5	18,425
New Beetle	1.8T GLX	2dr.sdn.4	84.3	12.0	0.38	98.9	161.1x67.9x59.5	2778	ih/sih	dc/dc	pwr.r&p.	35.4	3.2	14.5	205/55R16	Michelin	MXV4	L4T/1.8/M5	21,425

SMALL CARS
CLASSIFICATION

Small

OUR CLASSIFICATION

Rank	Models	Concept	Driving	Equipment	Comfort	Budget	Ratings
1	**TOYOTA Corolla**	72	**64**	75	**72**	75	**71.6 %**
2	DAEWOO Nubira	67	**64**	76	69	75	70.2 %
3	SATURN SL-SW	**73**	63	68	**72**	71	69.4 %
4	MAZDA Protegé	72	60	75	67	70	68.8 %
4	NISSAN Sentra	63	59	73	69	**80**	68.8 %
5	HONDA Civic	67	**64**	74	65	73	68.6 %
6	FORD Focus	71	61	73	65	72	68.4 %
7	CHEVROLET Cavalier &						
7	PONTIAC Sunfire	66	63	74	69	67	67.8 %
7	CHRYSLER Neon	70	63	73	61	72	67.8 %
8	SUZUKI Esteem	66	60	69	66	76	67.4 %
9	VW New Beetle	71	60	**78**	61	65	67.0 %
10	HYUNDAI Elantra	61	59	70	59	79	65.6 %
11	KIA Sephia	66	57	70	61	73	65.4 %

YOUR CLASSIFICATION

Rank	Models	98 Sales
1	**HONDA Civic**	**334 562**
2	FORD Escort/Focus	291 936
3	CHEVROLET Cavalier	256 099
4	TOYOTA Corolla	250 501
5	SATURN SL-SW	231 786
6	CHRYSLER Neon	117 964
7	NISSAN Sentra	88 363
8	PONTIAC Sunfire	82 748
9	MAZDA Protegé	58 349
10	VW New Beetle	55 842
11	KIA Sephia	54 311
12	HYUNDAI Elantra	37 501
13	SUZUKI Esteem	13 915

Not classified:
DAEWOO Nubira

NOTES

CHEVROLET Malibu

CHRYSLER JA Series

DAEWOO Leganza

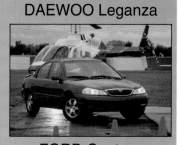

FORD Contour

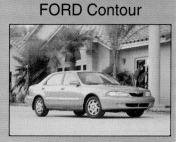

MAZDA 626

MITSUBISHI Galant

NISSAN Altima

Comparative Test

COMPACT CARS

**See their performance, their specifications, their price
and their classification at the end of this chapter.**

VOLKSWAGEN Golf-Jetta

PONTIAC Grand Am

OLDSMOBILE Alero

Compact

Intelligently designed and marketed, the Malibu continues to climb to higher sales levels, selling 250,000 units in North America in 1998. It rivals directly with some Japanese models that don't belong to its own class — such as the Accord and the Camry — with the advantage of a standard V6 engine and particularly elaborate equipment.

Rebirth

MODEL RANGE

The Malibu is a four-door sedan that comes in two versions: the base and LS. The 3.1L V6 engine with an output of 170 horses is standard on both versions. A four-speed electronically controlled automatic transmission rounds out this car's technical portrait. The base model has loads of equipment items, including 15-in. wheels, manually controlled climate control, adjustable steering column and ABS. The LS gets added fog lamps, remote-control door locks, cruise control, adjustable power mirrors, power windows, six-way adjustable driver's seat, alloy rims, front bucket seats and a 60/40 split-folding rear seatbench.

TECHNICAL FEATURES

The Malibu is built on the new "P90" platform that it shares with the new GM N-Series models, the Grand Am and Alero. The Malibu's exterior size is about the same as the Toyota Camry's and cabin space sits between that of the Ford Taurus and Camry. Yet the Malibu isn't a big compact car, but a midsize model! Its monocoque body is fitted with dual-side galvanized steel panels and built is really very solid. But even with those clean sweeping lines, the drag coefficient is only an average 0.32. The suspension is fully independent. Up front, it benefits from MacPherson struts and at the rear, three trailing arms do the job. There are anti-roll bars both front and rear. The disc and drum brake system is linked to fourth-generation ABS on both versions.

Power and torque of the one and only available V6 engine for year 2000 has been increased through revisions made to comply with low emission vehicle standards.

PROS

+ VALUE. The Malibu offers lots of niceties for the going price, so it's very competitive with Asian cars that are often less well-equipped and cost more. But equipment items are unique and chosen to demonstrate that this car is different from other models on the market.

+ LOOKS. This sedan has a distinguished and modern body design that compares favorably with Japanese and North American rival counterparts.

+ CABIN AND TRUNK SPACE. The spacious cabin can easily accomodate up to five passengers who'll be more than comfy inside. Besides, the big convertible trunk can really gobble up the luggage.

+ PERFORMANCE. The V6 engine provides strong acceleration and pick-up thanks to a substantial increase in its power and torque. The Malibu's equipment has a decided advantage over most models in this category, most of which only have a 4-cylinder engine.

+ RIDE COMFORT. The suspension really irons out road wrinkles, and the seats provide good support. The noise level at cruising speed is fine as well. Who could ask for anything more?

+ HANDLING. The Malibu enjoys predictable roadability in spite of its mid-quality tires. It takes curves without leaning into them and can handle sudden emergency moves with ease.

+ CONVENIENCE FEATURES. Contrary to the Lumina, the Malibu has scads of storage spots up front: a generous glove compartment, door side-pockets, a center console compartment and cup-holders, including one to the left of the steering wheel.

+ FINISH DETAILS. They're meticulous and trim materials are very attractive for the most part, especially in comparison with other same-brand products. Chevrolet obviously wanted to put together a car that could compete on an even footing with well-crafted rivals.

CONS

- NOISE. Sound dampening could be more refined, since there's an audible roar from the old-design engine on accelerations and suspension component makes noise when driving over poor-quality pavement.

- FUEL CONSUMPTION. The Malibu doesn't have the same fuel economy as some of its competitors, but this disadvantage will be a major one only if fuel prices climb sharply.

- BRAKES. They're gutsy and easy to gauge, but stopping distances are much longer than average for this category. Poor-quality brake pads seem to be behind this crummy performance, since they wear out quickly.

- TRANSMISSION. The automatic transmission is sometimes jumpy while changing gears. It seems to hesitate between gears, so you're in for some unpleasant jolts.

- STORAGE SPACE. They're sadly lacking in the rear; rear seat passengers have two meagre cup-holders at their disposal.

- TO BE IMPROVED UPON. The plastic trim on door panels and the imitation wood on the dashboard that jar with the ritzy quality of other cabin trim materials. There are no assist grips on the roof and no foot-rest for the driver, which comes across as being a bit cheap.

CONCLUSION

The Malibu's sales figures — like those for other GM models based on the same philosophy — prove that success in the automotive industry is based first and foremost on product enhancement. Quality has to be obvious, from both the design and vehicle performance standpoints. Unfortunately, this is a lesson that America's leading car manufacturer has learned the hard way.

RATING		
CHEVROLET Malibu		
CONCEPT :		74%
Technology :	75	
Safety :	80	
Interior space :	70	
Trunk volume :	70	
Quality/fit/finish :	75	
DRIVING :		60%
Cockpit :	80	
Performance :	50	
Handling :	50	
Steering :	80	
Braking :	40	
ORIGINAL EQUIPMENT :		79%
Tires :	75	
Headlights :	80	
Wipers :	80	
Rear defroster :	80	
Radio :	80	
COMFORT :		70%
Seats :	75	
Suspension :	75	
Sound level :	50	
Conveniences :	65	
Air conditioning :	85	
BUDGET :		65%
Price :	55	
Fuel economy :	70	
Insurance :	70	
Satisfaction :	80	
Depreciation :	50	
Overall rating :		69.6%

NEW FOR 2000
- Higher torque and power levels for the standard 3.1L V6 engine.
- Redesigned aluminum wheels and hub caps on the base model.
- SolarRay tinted front and rear windshields.
- Optional OnStar system available.
- Two new exterior colors, Navy Blue and Dark Bronze, and a new interior color, Ebony.

Compare Performance, Specifications, Prices, and Classification at the end of this chapter.

EQUIPMENT

CHEVROLET Malibu	base	LS
Automatic transmission:	S	S
Cruise control:	O	S
Power steering:	S	S
Anti-lock brakes:	S	S
Traction control:	-	-
Air conditioning:	SM	SM
Leather:	-	O
AM/FM/radio-cassette:	O	S
Power door locks:	O	S
Power windows:	O	S
Tilt steering:	S	S
Dual adjustable mirrors:	SM	SE
Alloy wheels:	O	S
Anti-theft system:	S	S

Colors

Exterior: White, Metallic Silver, Navy Blue, Black, Cherry, Sand, Jade, Bronze.

Interior: Neutral, Oak, Medium Grey, Light Grey, Ebony.

AT A GLANCE...

HISTORIC

Introduced in: 1997.
Made in: Wilmington, Delaware & Oklahoma City, Oklahoma, USA.

DEMOGRAPHICS

Model	Men./Wom.	Age	Married	College	Income $
Malibu	45/55 %	47	78 %	41 %	50,000

INDEX

Safety:	80 %	Satisfaction:	80 %
Depreciation:	50 %	Insurance:	$ 550
Cost per mile:	$ 0.45	Number of dealers:	4,466

SALES

	Canada			USA		
Model	1997	1998	Result	1997	1998	Result
Malibu	13,762	24,685	+ 79.4 %	164,654	223,703	+ 35.9 %

MAINTENANCE REQUIRED BY WARRANTY

First revision:	Frequency:	Diagnostic plug:
3,000 miles	6,000 miles	Yes

On Hold

Daimler's influence on Chrysler's marketing philosophy is obvious. While the old school was always reluctant to slash into model ranges and divisions, the Teutonic firm seems to be much more free-wheeling as it tests its sweeping approach on the Canadian market before applying it in the United States next year. Only time will tell if a tremendous fiasco is in the offing.

MODEL RANGE

While in Canada Chrysler has decided to withdraw the Stratus and Breeze models, the model lineup for the United States remains unchanged.

The Chrysler Cirrus is sold in a single LXi model equipped with a standard 2.5L V6 engine and 4-speed automatic transmission. The Dodge Stratus is offered in a base or ES version with the 2.0L Neon engine and a 5-speed manual gearbox. The Plymouth Breeze gets similar equipment to that of the Stratus and it's only available in a unique base model. The Stratus can receive as an extra either the 2.4L 4-cylinder engine or the 2.5L V6 as well as a 4-speed automatic transmission.

TECHNICAL FEATURES

These compact cars have a steel unibody. It offers an excellent degree of rigidity, be it torsion or flexion resistance and aerodynamic finesse is great thanks to a favorable 0.31 drag coefficient. The four-wheel independent suspension uses MacPherson struts up front with unequal-length arms whose joints isolate the frame from wheel vibration and shake. At the rear, there are unequal-length adjusting control arms with induced directional effect. Anti-roll bars are mounted on front and rear suspensions and cars are equipped with variable assist steering. Brakes are disc and drum, except for the Cirrus animated by a V6, which is easy to understand given the plump weight of these vehicles.

PROS

+ PRICE. Chrysler manages to offer a well-equipped model at a very competitive price thanks to a lower cost price than elsewhere.

+ ESTHETICS. After being on the market for five years, these cars still look fresh and lovely. They're blessed with original, yet classic looks. The cab forward principle gives them a familiar look, since they resemble other Chrysler family members and this design has a unique, swish appearance.

+ HANDLING. It's very effective. These cars handle like European imports, they provide good roadability, but without sacrificing comfort. The car behaves predictably and stays right on track and shock absorbers perform their magic.

+ FUEL ECONOMY. The 2.4L 4-cylinder engine performs almost as well as the V6 and it's just as smooth, but it's more fuel-efficient and thus more economical.

+ RIDE COMFORT. The ride is super due to the flexible, but not too much, suspension, nicely sculpted and cushioned front seats that provide good hip and back support. Besides, road noise is well muffled without having to revert to costly independent cradles to support both vehicle extremities.

+ CABIN & TRUNK SPACE. It's chiefly rear seat passengers that have more toe and head room than is the case for rival models. The trunk is huge and nicely shaped and it can be extended by lowering the seatbench back.

+ BRAKES. Sudden stops are achieved over a shorter distance, at a little more than 130 ft, especially with the Cirrus that really needed rear disc brakes and it's the only model equipped with standard ABS.

CONS

- BRAKES. Without ABS or rear disc brakes, the Stratus and Breeze brake pads and linings can't take the heat. The brake pedal is too soft and hard to adjust just right.

- SAFETY. It's surprising to see the mediocre scores achieved by the structure of these modern cars according to American N.H.T.S.A. collision tests.

- AUTOMATIC GEARBOX. It's one of the worst designs Chrysler has come up with over the last few years. It's horrible to use with its poorly spaced gears, downshifting is as slow as molasses and there's no braking effect at all when you downshift manually.

- PERFORMANCES. The V6 engine isn't wonderful and it lacks enthusiasm compared to its Mazda 626 counterpart of the same displacement, that's a joy to drive with its muscular powerplant. The 2.0L Stratus-Breeze base model engine may be fuel-frugal but it's timid, besides being noisy and shaky as hell.

- OUTWARD VIEW. As is the case for all Chrysler products, visibility is hampered by the high trunk lid and the narrow rear window, so parking maneuvers are tricky.

- STORAGE COMPARTMENTS. There aren't enough of them, for the glove compartment and door side-pockets don't hold much at all.

- FRONT SUSPENSION. When the car is loaded at full capacity, the flexible front suspension pays its dues and takes one nosedive after another on less than perfect surfaces.

- SEATBENCH. It isn't as comfy as the front seats, since it's flat and the uneven upholstery job is somewhat botched. Could it be that there are two classes of travellers?

- QUALITY. Some trim components on the instrument panel and inner door panels are far from ritzy.

- TO BE IMPROVED UPON. The system that holds the trunk open doesn't work too well and terribly insufficient headlight brilliance.

CONCLUSION

Compact models don't seem to sell as well as they could, mainly because they are positioned between small and mid-sized cars, both of which grab the lion's share of the market. Chrysler's JA models seem to be the exception to this rule and their revamping, scheduled for next year, is sure to give them a boost — at least until Ford replaces its Contour-Mystique.

RATING
CHRYSLER JA

CONCEPT : — 71%
Technology :	80
Safety :	60
Interior space :	65
Trunk volume :	75
Quality/fit/finish :	75

DRIVING : — 62%
Cockpit :	75
Performance :	45
Handling :	60
Steering :	75
Braking :	55

ORIGINAL EQUIPMENT : — 70%
Tires :	75
Headlights :	60
Wipers :	60
Rear defroster :	75
Radio :	80

COMFORT : — 64%
Seats :	75
Suspension :	75
Sound level :	55
Conveniences :	50
Air conditioning :	65

BUDGET : — 69%
Price :	60
Fuel economy :	70
Insurance :	75
Satisfaction :	80
Depreciation :	60

Overall rating : — 67.2%

NEW FOR 2000
- New exterior colors: Bright Platinum, Alpine Green, Deep Slate and Black.
- Standard child-safety seat anchors and alloy wheels.
- A 2.4L engine at no extra charge and new interior trims on the Stratus SE.

Compare
Performance,
Specifications, Prices,
and Classification
at the end of this chapter.

EQUIPMENT

CHRYSLER Cirrus DODGE Stratus PLYMOUTH Breeze	LXi	base	ES	base
Automatic transmission:	S	O	S	O
Cruise control:	S	O	S	O
Power steering:	S	S	S	S
Anti-lock brakes:	S	O	O	O
Traction control:	-	-	-	-
Air conditioning:	S	S	S	S
Leather:	O	-	O	-
AM/FM/radio-cassette:	S	S	S	O
Power door locks:	S	O	S	O
Power windows:	S	O	S	O
Tilt steering:	S	S	S	S
Dual adjustable mirrors:	SEH	SM	SEH	SE
Alloy wheels:	O	-	S	-
Anti-theft system:	O	-	O	O

Colors
Exterior: White, Red, Blue, Alpine Green, Amethyst, Cranberry, Platinum, Champagne, Slate, Bright Silver, Taupe Frost, Black Metallic.
Interior: Pebble, Beige, Silver.

AT A GLANCE...

HISTORIC
Introduced in:	1995, 1996 for Breeze.
Made in:	Sterling Heights, MI, USA.

DEMOGRAPHICS
Model	Men./Wom.	Age	Married	College	Income $
Cirrus	70/30 %	54	72 %	44 %	43,000
Stratus	64/36 %	51	74 %	36 %	34,000
Breeze	62/38 %	52	73 %	34 %	33,000

INDEX
Safety:	50 %	Satisfaction:	80 %
Depreciation:	45 %	Insurance:	$ 520-565
Cost per mile:	$ 0.45	Number of dealers:	1,822

SALES
	Canada			USA		
Model	1997	1998	Result	1997	1998	Result
Cirrus	3,598	2,904	- 19.3 %	31,549	38,504	+ 22.0 %
Stratus	9,331	9,713	+ 4.1 %	99,040	106,434	+ 7.5 %
Breeze	7,577	8,045	+ 6.2 %	72,499	59,543	- 17.9 %

MAINTENANCE REQUIRED BY WARRANTY
First revision	Frequency:	Diagnostic plug:
5,000 miles	6 months / 6,000 miles	Yes

DAEWOO

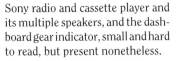

A Species Of It's Own

Leganza

Compact

Korean builders are here in full force. The very bad financial status of these companies, heavily into debt in their native country, goes a long way in explaining their feverish efforts to conquer foreign markets, especially those capable of absorbing small economy cars. In North America, the Leganza is Daewoo's luxury model.

MODEL RANGE

The Leganza is a 4-door sedan available in SE, SX or CDX versions equipped with the same powertrain, a 2.2L 4-cylinder engine and a 5-speed manual transmission standard on the SE or a 4-speed automatic on the SX and CDX.

The SX's standard equipment is relatively detailed and lacks only leather trims, an ABS braking system and alloy wheels, compared to the CDX version which also comes with fake wood inlays.

TECHNICAL FEATURES

The Leganza was designed by Giugiaro of Ital Design, who also had a lot to do with the other Korean builder's models. Its name is a contraction of the Italian words "elegante" and "forza", which mean "elegance" and "strength". Its steel unibody has a conservative drag coefficient of 0.33.

Front and rear suspensions feature MacPherson struts with transversal arms and a double ring in the rear. Antisway bars and helicoidal springs complete the assembly. To minimize transmission noise and vibration, rubber components have been included in wheel wells and the chassis. Four disc brakes are standard, but only the CDX has a standard ABS system. Power rack-and-pinion steering is standard on all models.

PROS

+ PRESENTATION. As its name suggests, the Leganza's lines are elegant and reserved. Its Italian designers have done a very good job — rarely can a vehicle of this size offer both good looks and reasonable roominess. Inside, leather and tasteful fake wood inlays set the tone and the dashboard has just the right amount of originality, with controls positioned logically.

+ VALUE. Available at a reasonable price, the CDX version features all of the equipment typical of a luxury car. Leather trims, automatic air conditioning, antilock brakes, fake wood inlays — all it takes to rival with the Infiniti G20, sold at $23,000 US ($34,000 CDN)!

+ DRIVEABILITY. The Leganza is fun to drive because of its precise steering system that spells excellent handling, and good braking power that's easy to gauge under all circumstances. Visibility is satisfactory and ergonomics are impeccable — even unconventional controls are within easy reach and simple to use.

+ PERFORMANCE. Levels are comparable to the Infiniti G20's and acceleration and pick-up are strong enough to ensure safe driving.

+ HANDLING. In spite of the use of Kumho tires that failed to convince us that they had enough grip, even on dry roads, the Leganza has good road stability, with a lateral acceleration coefficient that approached an enviable 0.80 during our test drives.

+ USEABLE SPACE. Despite its body's modest sizing, the Leganza can accommodate 4 passengers — maybe even 5 depending on their size — and they travel comfortably in an interior that provides plenty of room in every direction. The same goes for the trunk, with a good-sized opening and extra cargo space provided by a rear seat that folds down.

+ ACCESS. Not very many rear seats are as easy to get into as those on this Daewoo. Doors open wide, at an 80° angle, and windows roll all the way down.

+ COMFORT. Several design details combine to provide a very decent comfort level for a car of this size. In spite of only average travel, the suspension counters road defects efficiently and front seats provide good support. The noise level is reasonable at cruising speed, where it's on a par with the level found in some very luxurious sedans.

+ QUALITY. Although lightweight, panels are assembled carefully and the finish is impeccable, with several features unusual for a car sold at this price. From this viewpoint, the Leganza compares well with some of its Japanese rivals, sold at higher prices.

+ BONUS POINTS. Kudos for the full-size spare wheel, the quality Sony radio and cassette player and its multiple speakers, and the dashboard gear indicator, small and hard to read, but present nonetheless.

CONS

- SEATS. Padding is uncomfortable and front seat adjustments are very strange. Users need a lot of patience to find the ideal driving position and the flat bench seat fails to provide enough lateral support.

- TIRES. A weak point in the Leganza's equipment, Korean tires have a way to go before they can equal certain Goodyear or Michelin alternatives that could provide better grip and a quieter ride when negotiating sharp curves.

- STORAGE SPACES. Although generous in the front, they are few and far between in the rear, where they are limited to a few spaces built into the bench seat's back; there's not a single cupholder in sight.

- OVERSIGHTS. At a rhythm of 48 to 68 sweeps per minute, windshield wipers have a hard time handling heavy rain. In spite of average brightness, headlights aren't strong enough to provide excellent night visibility.

CONCLUSION

This is the first Korean-made model that manages not to look cheap, unlike several Hyundai and Kia models. By making the Leganza a small economy car wrapped in luxury-like packaging, Daewoo has innovated. If product reliability and service quality are part of the bargain, the manufacturer deserves the every bit of success it will have earned.

Compact Cars

RATING		
DAEWOO Leganza		
CONCEPT :		**71%**
Technology :	75	
Safety :	80	
Interior space :	60	
Trunk volume :	60	
Quality/fit/finish :	80	
DRIVING :		**65%**
Cockpit :	80	
Performance :	35	
Handling :	60	
Steering :	80	
Braking :	70	
ORIGINAL EQUIPMENT :		**74%**
Tires :	70	
Headlights :	75	
Wipers :	65	
Rear defroster :	80	
Radio :	80	
COMFORT :		**73%**
Seats :	70	
Suspension :	75	
Sound level :	70	
Conveniences :	70	
Air conditioning :	80	
BUDGET :		**64%**
Price :	60	
Fuel economy :	80	
Insurance :	70	
Satisfaction :	80	
Depreciation :	30	
Overall rating :		**69.4%**

NEW FOR 2000
• No details available at press time.

Compare
Performance,
Specifications, Prices,
and Classification
at the end of this chapter.

EQUIPMENT

DAEWOO Leganza	SE	SX	CDX
Automatic transmission:	O	S	S
Cruise control:	O	S	S
Power steering:	S	S	S
Anti-lock brakes:	-	-	S
Traction control:	-	-	-
Air conditioning:	SM	SM	SA
Leather:	-	-	S
AM/FM/radio-cassette:	S	S	S
Power door locks:	-	S	S
Power windows:	-	S	S
Tilt steering:	S	S	S
Dual adjustable mirrors:	S	S	S
Alloy wheels:	-	-	S
Anti-theft system:	S	S	S

Colors
Exterior: White, Blue, Black, Red, Silver, Beige.

Interior: Grey, Beige.

AT A GLANCE...

HISTORIC

Introduced in:	1996.
Made in:	Pupyong, South Korea.

DEMOGRAPHICS

Model	Men./Wom.	Age	Married	College	Income $
Leganza	NA				

INDEX

Safety:	80 %	Satisfaction:	78 %
Depreciation:	30 %	Insurance:	$ 550
Cost per mile:	$ 0.42	Number of dealers:	115

SALES

Model	1997	Canada 1998	Result	1997	USA 1998	Result
Leganza	NA					

MAINTENANCE REQUIRED BY WARRANTY

First revision:	Frequency:	Diagnostic plug:
4,000 miles	6 months / 8,000 miles	Yes

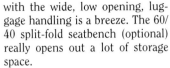
A Fiasco

The sad story of the Contour-Mystique illustrates just how high a risk is involved in wanting to get a step ahead of the latest trends. Ford was one of the first builders to favor model globalization and in the case of these two models, the formula just didn't work. Sharing the same platform and basic mechanical components is one thing, sharing the same body is another. What's good for Europe or Japan doesn't necessarily go over very big in North America. The reason is simple: consumers are human beings with a very wide variety of body types and lifestyles.

MODEL RANGE

The Ford Contour and Mercury Mystique have slightly different stylistic touches (grille and rear end design) and cabin layout. These four-door sedans are offered in two trim levels: LX and SE at Ford and GS and LS at Mercury. The Contour GL and base model Mystique are no longer sold. Both brand cars are equipped with a standard 2.0L Zetec 4-cylinder engine, associated with a 5-speed manual gearbox. A 4-speed automatic transmission is sold as an extra for all versions. On the other hand, the optional 2.5L Duratec V6 engine can only equip the Contour SE and Mystique LS versions. The Ford lineup also includes a high-performance model called the Contour SVT that's powered by a V6 that now develops 200 hp (5 more than last year).

TECHNICAL FEATURES

The Contour-Mystique duo was developed at the same time as the Ford Mondeo that's built and sold across Europe, thus they're called "world cars". The steel monocoque body is very sleek, as the 0.31 drag coefficient indicates. The four-wheel independent suspension uses MacPherson struts up front and a multi-link directional effect setup at the rear. There are anti-roll bars both front and rear. The more sporty versions, the V6-powered Contour SE, Mystique LS and Contour SVT, are equipped with stiffer shocks and bigger-diameter stabilizer bars. These models also benefit from rear disc brakes rather than drum brakes. All models are equipped with power steering, but SE, SVT and LS models have super-quick steering to match their slick moves. Ford states that its engines are at the cutting edge of current technology and will require no major maintenance for 100,000 miles, except for oil and filter changes!

PROS

+ THE SVT MODEL. This unique car performs like a champion and with a lot of flair and the engine sure roars beautifully!

+ STYLE. New touches rendered in 1998 added a lot of character to these sedans. The grille design is simply gorgeous, especially the Mystique's classy, upper-crust grille.

+ TECHNICAL FEATURES. Ford designed these models on the European Mondeo platform, in other words, it pulled out all the stops, technically speaking, so cars have a very robust build and are equipped with a well-honed suspension and modern Zetec and Duratec engines.

+ TEMPERAMENT. The Contour SVT has more gusto and handles beautifully, much more so than the SE/LS models.

+ QUALITY. Assembly and finish details exhibit great craftsmanship. There's no interference heard even on poor roads and trim materials and accessories are spiffy.

+ BRAKES. Brakes on the SE/LS and SVT have a lot of brawn, given the car category. They bite the tarmac, they grip like champions, apply power gradually and in a nice, balanced way with ABS.

+ PERFORMANCES. The 4-cylinder engine puts out more impressive power than the V6 that equips the SE/LS. Acceleration and pickup response time are very close for both engines, which is disappointing. But the SVT benefits from a more brilliant powerplant, so accelerations and pickup are achieved in a second less.

+ RIDE COMFORT. The Contour/Mystique's are blessed with a cushy suspension that eliminates road surface irregularities and seats are thick and nicely designed. Noise level is low, even on the SVT that zips along without being impolite to passengers.

+ HANDLING. On the highway, these sedans are neutral and steering is straight-on predictable. On curved stretches, the SE/LS are more fun to drive since there's less sway, but not as much fun as being at the wheel of the SVT equipped with a still firmer suspension and high-performance tires that really grab the gravel.

+ TRUNK. It's absolutely huge and with the wide, low opening, luggage handling is a breeze. The 60/40 split-fold seatbench (optional) really opens out a lot of storage space.

+ NICE FEATURES. Touches like illuminated inner door handles (at night), a control to lower the seatbench back located in the trunk and the pollen filter climate control system.

CONS

- PASSENGER PROTECTION. In the event of a collision, passenger protection isn't as effective as for the driver who benefits from optimum protection.

- STEERING. The SVT steering is over assisted, so it's light on acceleration and precision suffers from pronounced torque fallout.

- INTERIOR DESIGN. Rear seat leg room is snug even with the new-design seating and so tall passengers will feel cramped.

- V6 ENGINE. Performance scores are too close to those of the 4-cylinder engine, that's definitely more frugal. It just doesn't make any sense!

- MANUAL GEARBOX. Except on the SVT, the shifter is wishy washy and gears take forever to get their act together.

- MANEUVERABILITY. The V6-powered versions suffer from a bigger steer angle diameter than the 4-cylinder versions.

CONCLUSION

In spite of the quality inherent in these models, in a class that remains popular with consumers they've failed to build a major following. On the other hand Ford has made no particular effort to promote them properly. Could the reason be the communications crisis the second-largest carbuilder in the U.S. has been plunged into with the arrival of Jack Nasser at its head?

RATING
FORD-MERCURY Contour-Mystique

CONCEPT : 69%
Technology :	80
Safety :	75
Interior space :	50
Trunk volume :	60
Quality/fit/finish :	80

DRIVING : 66%
Cockpit :	80
Performance :	50
Handling :	60
Steering :	75
Braking :	65

ORIGINAL EQUIPMENT : 76%
Tires :	75
Headlights :	80
Wipers :	80
Rear defroster :	70
Radio :	75

COMFORT : 66%
Seats :	75
Suspension :	75
Sound level :	50
Conveniences :	50
Air conditioning :	80

BUDGET : 72%
Price :	60
Fuel economy :	75
Insurance :	65
Satisfaction :	85
Depreciation :	75

Overall rating : 69.8%

NEW FOR 2000

• At press time, no reliable information on this model was available.

Compare Performance, Specifications, Prices, and Classification at the end of this chapter.

EQUIPMENT

FORD Contour MERCURY Mystique	LX	SE	SVT	GS	LS
Automatic transmission:	O	O	-	O	O
Cruise control:	O	S	S	S	S
Power steering:	S	S	S	S	S
Anti-lock brakes:	O	O	S	O	O
Traction control:	-	-	-	-	-
Air conditioning:	SM	SM	SM	SM	SM
Leather:	-	O	S	-	O
AM/FM/radio-cassette:	O	S	S	S	S
Power door locks:	O	S	S	S	S
Power windows:	-	S	S	S	S
Tilt steering:	S	S	S	S	S
Dual adjustable mirrors:	SE	SE	SE	SE	SE
Alloy wheels:	-	O	S	O	S
Anti-theft system:	S	S	S	S	S

Colors
Exterior: Blue, Brown, Red, Green, Silver, Black, White.

Interior: Blue, Brown, Silk.

AT A GLANCE...

HISTORIC
Introduced in:	1995.
Made in:	Kansas City, Michigan, USA & Cuautitlan, Mexico.

DEMOGRAPHICS
Model	Men./Wom.	Age	Married	College	Income $
Contour	60/40 %	50	69 %	44 %	40,000
Mystique	64/36 %	54	73 %	43 %	41,000

INDEX
Safety:	75 %	Satisfaction:	85 %
Depreciation:	27 %	Insurance:	$ 535 -625
Cost per mile:	$ 0.40	Number of dealers:	5,200

SALES
Model	Canada 1997	1998	Result	USA 1997	1998	Result
Contour	14,563	9,676	- 33.6 %	151,060	139,838	- 7.4 %
Mystique	8,820	6,295	- 28.6 %	41,038	38,274	- 6.7 %

MAINTENANCE REQUIRED BY WARRANTY
First revision:	Frequency:	Diagnostic plug:
5,000 miles	6 months/ 7,500 miles	Yes

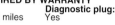

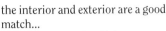

Identity Crisis

Since its introduction, the 626 has continued to search for its true identity. Mazda has modified it continuously in an effort to give it a distinctive personality and a more exciting image than the one Tom Matano has been able to create so far. Maybe the manufacturer should begin to look elsewhere: the world is full of talented designers in search of a challenge. This model's only truly positive point is its V6 engine, which results in extraordinary driveability and should inspire a correspondingly attractive design concept.

MODEL RANGE

The 626 is a 4-door front-wheel drive sedan available in LX version equipped with a 2.0L 4-cylinder engine and ES animated by a 2.5L V6. The original transmission is a 5-speed manual, whereas the 4-speed automatic is sold as an extra, but antilock braking and traction control are only standard on the upper end ES version.

TECHNICAL FEATURES

During its last make-over, the 626's structure was reinforced. The steel unibody includes two cradles supporting the suspension and power trains, so most of the wheel and power train noise and vibration are eliminated. The MacPherson strut suspension is fully independent and is completed by two trapezoidal control arms at the rear axle and an anti-roll bar both front and rear. The LX is equipped with disc and drum brakes, the LX-V6 and ES benefit from disc brakes, whereas ABS is standard on the ES, optional on the LX-V6 and not proposed on the other models. Engines and transmissions are those that equipped the former model.

PROS

+ BODY DESIGN. It's very simple and straightforward, but it's quite harmonious and resembles the Millenia. It doesn't have much personality, but at least it has the advantage of being discreet, so it won't go out of style too quickly.

+ SIZE. The 626 has a spacious interior given its reasonable size and weight, for the cabin and trunk can accomodate four adults and their effects.

+ PERFORMANCES. The V6 is perky, either with the automatic transmission or the manual that procures a more sporty demeanor and that emits very thrilling revs and exhaust noise.

+ HANDLING. It's neutral most of the time, but does tend to go into understeer when pushed to the edge and even with the flexible suspension that equips it, the 626 is ready and able to take on a whole series of curves.

+ RIDE COMFORT. It derives from the roomy interior, supple suspension, neat-design seats that support well and soundproofing that keeps the noise level down to a whisper at cruising speed, even with the 4-cylinder engine.

+ STEERING. It's silky and accurate and assistance is better than in the past. It benefits from a good reduction ratio and steer angle, so it's easy to maneuver and torque wallop that was typical of its predecessor on hard accelerations is almost unnoticeable, at least on dry surfaces.

+ BRAKES. Disc brakes are more effective and easier to apply smoothly than the disc and drum duo that equips the LX, for sudden stopping distances are normal, but it's too bad ABS isn't offered as an option on the LX.

+ QUALITY. Assembly and finish details are nicer than in the past, components have a tighter, cleaner fit and materials used are more pleasing to the eye, such as the leather trim on the ES versions that looks quite elegant.

+ NICE FEATURES. The air vents that pivot automatically and serve as a fan, that Mazda had the ingenuity of adding to the current models. Passengers who find the pivoting movement annoying can turn off this function. Storage compartments are generous up front, since the glove compartment and door side-pockets are nice and roomy.

CONS

- LOOKS. It's awfully anonymous and looks too much like its predecessor or like the many rivals that are look-alike identical twins...

- CABIN DESIGN. The humdrum is lord and master inside the 626 models. These cars are affordable but also terribly run of the mill. Designers could have put a little more effort into livening up the cabin that is bereft of even an ounce of imagination. At least for once, the interior and exterior are a good match...

- BRAKING. It lacks efficiency, stopping distances are long and the antilock system needs improving. However, power is easy to gauge and reliability is acceptable.

- PERFORMANCES. The gutsier 4-cylinder engine and the automatic transmission don't have much vitality when the vehicle is at full load capacity, accelerations and pickup take forever and the transmission is constantly trying to make up its mind as to which gear to use.

- UPHOLSTERY. Seats are terribly firm, especially the thinly clad seatbench and it doesn't have a center console as is the case on some models.

- STORAGE COMPARTMENTS. There aren't any in the rear seat area and door side-pockets and cupholders or armrest are nowhere in sight.

- VISIBILITY. It would be better if the visor on the instrument panel were lower, if the side mirrors were higher and the C pillar less thick at its base.

- DEPRECIATION. It's higher than for most rivals and the V6 model sells more briskly than the 4-cylinder model.

CONCLUSION

The Protegé points the way for other Mazda models. With a decent powertrain, a reasonable price and an appealing look, there's every reason to believe that the 626's sales could increase dramatically. All it needs to hoist itself a few places higher on the sales ladder is an ingenious styling tactic. Who has the magic wand it needs?

RATING
MAZDA 626

CONCEPT :		75%
Technology :	80	
Safety :	90	
Interior space :	65	
Trunk volume :	60	
Quality/fit/finish :	80	

DRIVING :		65%
Cockpit :	80	
Performance :	50	
Handling :	60	
Steering :	80	
Braking :	55	

ORIGINAL EQUIPMENT :		73%
Tires :	80	
Headlights :	80	
Wipers :	60	
Rear defroster :	70	
Radio :	75	

COMFORT :		71%
Seats :	80	
Suspension :	70	
Sound level :	65	
Conveniences :	60	
Air conditioning :	80	

BUDGET :		61%
Price :	50	
Fuel economy :	75	
Insurance :	50	
Satisfaction :	80	
Depreciation :	50	

Overall rating :		69.0%

NEW FOR 2000
- **DX version withdrawn.**
- **Improved power and torque for the 4-cylinder engine.**
- **Redesigned front-end and dashboard.**
- **A long series of improvements: interior trims, tires, center console and CD player.**

Compare Performance, Specifications, Prices, and Classification at the end of this chapter.

EQUIPMENT

MAZDA 626	LX	ES
Automatic transmission:	O	O
Cruise control:	S	S
Power steering:	S	S
Anti-lock brakes:	-	S
Traction control:	-	S
Air conditioning:	SM	SM
Leather:	-	S
AM/FM/radio-cassette:	SCd	SCd
Power door locks:	S	S
Power windows:	S	S
Tilt steering:	S	S
Dual adjustable mirrors:	SE	SE
Alloy wheels:	-	S
Anti-theft system:	-	-

Colors
Exterior: White, Black, Green, Red, Blue, Beige, Driftwood.

Interior: Grey, Beige.

AT A GLANCE...

HISTORIC

Introduced in:	1979-1998.
Made in:	Flat Rock, Michigan, USA.

DEMOGRAPHICS

Model	Men./Wom.	Age	Married	College	Income $
626	74/26 %	48	81 %	60 %	51,000

INDEX

Safety:	90 %	Satisfaction:	85 %
Depreciation:	48 %	Insurance:	$ 540-735
Cost per mile:	$ 0.46	Number of dealers:	871

SALES

Model	Canada 1997	1998	Result	USA 1997	1998	Result
626	6,368	5,906	- 7.3 %	75,800	91,147	+ 20.0 %

MAINTENANCE REQUIRED BY WARRANTY

First revision:	Frequency:	Diagnostic plug:
5,000 miles	5,000 miles	Yes

MITSUBISHI

Galant

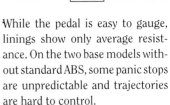

The Galant is to Mitsubishi what the Accord is to Honda and the Camry is to Toyota. Unfortunately, its sales are nowhere near the other two models' — in the United States the Galant is five times less popular than the Accord or Camry. This can be explained by the fact that the Japanese manufacturer is less solidly ensconced than its competitors, which limits the availability of its products.

MODEL RANGE

The Galant is a 4-door sedan available in DE, ES, ES V6, LS and GTZ versions. The first two are equipped with a SOHC 2.4L 4-cylinder engine and the three others feature a 3.0L V6 introduced last year. The 4-speed automatic transmission is standard on all V6 models, a 5-speed manual is standard on 4-cylinder model, as is power steering, air conditioning, power locks, a radio and CD player, and an antitheft system. Only the LS and GTZ come with standard leather trims, a traction control system, side airbags and alloy wheels with 205/55R16 tires.

TECHNICAL FEATURES

The Galant has excellent aerodynamics, with a drag coefficient of 0.29. The fully independent suspension is based on a multi-arm configuration: two stabilizing bars and an anti-dive design in the front and an anti-lift design in the rear. Brakes are mixed and feature ABS. With two lateral balancing shafts designed to eliminate vibration, the 2.4L 4-cylinder engine now has an output of 145 horses. The 3.0L V6 is a less powerful version of the Diamante's engine.

Dull

PROS

+ QUALITY. Assembly and materials are very satisfactory and in some instances, finish shows more care than some competitors offer. In terms of quality, Mitsubishi falls somewhere between Honda and Nissan and its satisfaction rate in the United States stands at 85%.

+ VALUE. Although not in the same class as the Accord or the Camry in terms of sizing, the Galant is on the same footing with marketplace stars when it comes to powertrains. Under the circumstances, it offers a better price-content ratio.

+ PERFORMANCE. The levels reached by the 4-cylinder are surprisingly energetic and acceleration and pick-up are similar to those provided by the more torquey V6 engine, although to its credit the latter is smoother and quieter.

+ HANDLING. The independent suspension ensures good cornering and understeering is obvious only in the case of unskilled or intentionally bad driving. Roll is less noticeable on the sporty GTZ, whose more rigid suspension lets the car take curves flat out.

+ COCKPIT. It's modern, though not particularly original. The driver is comfortable and controls are positioned within easy reach.

+ DRIVEABILITY. Although billed as lean and mean, the Galant is fun to drive. The body feels sturdy, controls operate smoothly and the steering system and suspension provide the responsiveness typical of more sophisticated models.

+ COMFORT. It's ensured by a smooth suspension, good wheel travel and reliable shock absorption that swallows road defects effectively. Front and rear seats are well-designed, mold well and provide good support. The noise level is low thanks to a sturdy body, efficient soundproofing and an engine that generates minimal vibration.

+ PASSENGER ROOM. Comparable to a Mazda 626, the Galant is spacious, particularly when it comes to headroom (even if you decide on a sunroof). Four tall adults can travel comfortably, but a fifth passenger is a good idea over for short outings.

+ TRUNK. It has a lot of volume and its opening is wide and offers easy access. With the exception of the base DE version, the 60/40 split seat folds down to provide extra cargo space.

+ PRACTICALITY. Storage spaces are well sized, though more common in the front of the vehicle.

CONS

- BRAKING. It's only mediocre on models without discs on rear wheels.

While the pedal is easy to gauge, linings show only average resistance. On the two base models without standard ABS, some panic stops are unpredictable and trajectories are hard to control.

- STEERING. The assistance was a bit too much on our test drive vehicle, which made driving precarious and worrisome and resulted in imprecision at center.

- SUSPENSION. The GTZ's is sportier and firmer than it is on the other Galant models. As a result it's fairly stiff and the ride is uncomfortable on poor road surfaces where tires and wheels provide just too much feedback on defects.

- VISIBILITY. Impeccable toward the front and sides, 3/4 and rear visibility are hindered by the body design and high-tail styling.

- REAR SEAT ACCESS. Rear doors are narrow and entry/exit is difficult, particularly for larger passengers.

- PRESENTATION. It's fairly dull inside and falls far from creating a luxurious look, even on the LS and the GTZ, the only versions that come with leather upholstery.

- DEPRECIATION. It's higher than average because the Galant models are less popular than their main rivals.

CONCLUSION

The Galant has never been as competitive from the performance and comfort viewpoints. It's too bad Mitsubishi refuses to invest more in this model's presentation, not as appealing as the Accord's or the Camry's, both of which serve as benchmarks in this regard.

RATING		
MITSUBISHI Galant		
CONCEPT :		**73%**
Technology :	80	
Safety :	90	
Interior space :	65	
Trunk volume :	50	
Quality/fit/finish :	80	
DRIVING :		**68%**
Cockpit :	80	
Performance :	60	
Handling :	70	
Steering :	80	
Braking :	50	
ORIGINAL EQUIPMENT :		**74%**
Tires :	75	
Headlights :	80	
Wipers :	65	
Rear defroster :	70	
Radio :	80	
COMFORT :		**79%**
Seats :	80	
Suspension :	75	
Sound level :	80	
Conveniences :	80	
Air conditioning :	80	
BUDGET :		**65%**
Price :	50	
Fuel economy :	80	
Insurance :	50	
Satisfaction :	85	
Depreciation :	60	
Overall rating :		**71.8%**

Compact Cars

NEW FOR 2000

- No details available at press time.

Compare
Performance,
Specifications, Prices,
and Classification
at the end of this chapter.

EQUIPMENT

MITSUBISHI Galant	DE	ES	ES V6	LS	GTZ
Automatic transmission:	O	O	S	S	S
Cruise control:	-	S	S	S	S
Power steering:	S	S	S	S	S
Anti-lock brakes:	O	O	S	S	S
Traction control:	-	-	-	S	S
Air conditioning:	S	S	S	S	S
Leather:	-	-	-	S	S
AM/FM/radio-cassette:	SCd	SCd	SCd	SCd	SCd
Power door locks:	S	S	S	S	S
Power windows:	O	S	S	S	S
Tilt steering:	S	S	S	S	S
Dual adjustable mirrors:	SM	SE	SEH	SEH	SEH
Alloy wheels:	-	O	O	S	S
Anti-theft system:	S	S	S	S	S

Colors

Exterior: Black, Blue, Silver, White.

Interior: Grey.

AT A GLANCE...

HISTORIC

Introduced in:	1983-1996.
Made in:	Normal, IL, USA.

DEMOGRAPHICS

Model	Men./Wom.	Age	Married	College	Income $
Galant	70/30 %	45	70 %	50 %	45, 000

INDEX

Safety:	80 %	Satisfaction:	88 %
Depreciation:	30 %	Insurance:	$ 550
Cost per mile:	$ 0.44	Number of dealers:	480

SALES

	Canada			USA		
Model	1997	1998	Result	1997	1998	Result
Galant	Not on sale in Canada			42,590	44,201	+ 3.8 %

MAINTENANCE REQUIRED BY WARRANTY

First revision:	Frequency:	Diagnostic plug:
3,500 miles	6 months / 7,000 miles	Yes

NISSAN

Altima

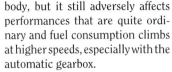

A Leader

The Altima is the bestselling Nissan model on the North American market, where its strategic positioning is unique since unlike most of its competitors, it has no V6 engine and lets the Maxima fight it out in the superior categories, taking on the Camry and Accord without offering a 4-cylinder engine. Until now this approach has been a winning one and the two models have met with unqualified success, untainted by trickery or treachery.

MODEL RANGE

This compact 4-door sedan comes in XE, GXE, SE and GLE trim, all equipped with the same mechanical features consisting of a 2.4L 4-cylinder engine and standard manual transmission or an optional automatic on the XE, GXE and SE, but the automatic is included in the original equipment on the richer GLE version. These cars are pretty much the same, essentially, except for a few variant design details, whereas equipment items for all models include: power steering, tilt steering wheel, adjustable exterior mirrors and intermittent wiper function. The SE also gets light alloy wheels and the luxo-sedan GLE receives leather seat trim. In all cases, the antilock braking system and sunroof are billed as extra items.

TECHNICAL FEATURES

The last Altima derived from the former model's platform. The steel monocoque body is sleeker and has gained in aerodynamic finesse since its drag coefficient went from 0.35 to 0.32. The four-wheel independent suspension is based on the MacPherson strut principle and includes a stabilizer bar for each axle. Disc and drum brakes equip the XE/

GXE/GLE and the sportiest SE benefits from standard four-wheel disc brakes with a variable grip system for the rear axle, that sure improves road adherence. The engine under the hood is the same as for the 1999 model, it has lighter-weight pistons and more generous air filter and it's more lightweight. Displacement is a bit bigger than average and it develops 155 hp yielding an adequate power to weight ratio. In fact, this engine's displacement is equivalent to that of the V6 that animates some rivals, so Nissan was able to avoid offering a second engine model, yet the Altima still takes a bite out of Maxima sales, both models now being on a par in this department.

PROS

+ LOOKS. It's cool and sensible-looking, less curved and more refined, in keeping with the current "Edge Design". It isn't terribly original, but it does get admiring glances, especially the SE and GLE that have luxury car touches comparable to what you get on much more expensive cars.

+ PRICE. It's more affordable than for some of the competition, given that the only engine available is a 4-cylinder.

+ CABIN SPACE. It's roomier with the added length and width that has freed up more elbow and leg room, but ceiling height is the same. Four

adults will enjoy comfortable seating and even a fifth, for short trips.

+ DRIVING PLEASURE. The 2.4L engine has enough juice to muster good accelerations and pickup thanks to wider band torque at low rpm. Steering is responsive and brakes are easy to gauge in normal situations.

+ HANDLING. It derives from the more rigid structure and supple suspension that generates just a bit of sway and doesn't bottom out as it once did on major road faults. The SE is more at ease taking one curve after another because it's equipped with firmer springs and shocks so it stays nice and level on curves.

+ RIDE COMFORT. It's super due to the smooth suspension, nicely shaped and cushy front seats and good soundproofing that keeps noise at a reasonable level at cruising speed and stifles noise and vibration coming from the engine and powertrains.

+ CABIN DESIGN. It provides a pleasant driving environment, for the instrument panel is attractive and logical, now free of that rather flashy imitation wood trim.

+ BONUS POINTS. For the standard CD player and the windshield-mounted antenna.

CONS

- VEHICLE WEIGHT. It's still quite high even with the trimming down. This is due to the beefier, more rigid

body, but it still adversely affects performances that are quite ordinary and fuel consumption climbs at higher speeds, especially with the automatic gearbox.

- MANUAL GEARBOX. It's not as smooth as the automatic, since shifting gears is a bit tricky and gears are poorly spaced. There's a terrible gap between first and second gear and the top gear is too long.

- TRUNK. It's stingy compared to the generous cabin size and given the Altima's dimensions, since it isn't too high at all and the opening is narrow. It now connects with the cabin, but you can't get much stuff through the tiny slot provided.

- BRAKES. Brakes are normally quite effective when first applied and car path is predictable on stops, but linings fade with intensive use.

- SEATS. Leather-clad seats aren't as well-contoured as fabric-covered seats and their upholstery is more firm. And rear seat travellers on the more richly equipped models don't have headrests.

-ACCESS. It's tricky climbing aboard into the rear seats with the arched door design and you have to duck, otherwise you could knock your head against the roof.

- TO BE IMPROVED UPON. Climate control dials where sound system dials should be and vice versa, located back there behind the speed shifter...

CONCLUSION

Nissan is doing all it can to keep its star model in the spotlight. The revisions introduced this year should keep it in first place in its class and on the sales hit parade of Japan's second-largest car builder, which would dearly love a few more similar success stories to restore it to full bloom.

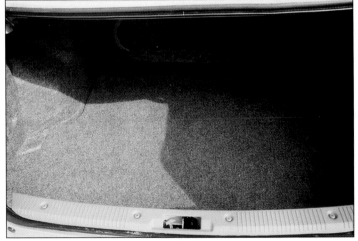

RATING
NISSAN Altima

CONCEPT :		**76%**
Technology :	80	
Safety :	80	
Interior space :	80	
Trunk volume :	60	
Quality/fit/finish :	80	
DRIVING :		**74%**
Cockpit :	80	
Performance :	65	
Handling :	65	
Steering :	80	
Braking :	80	
ORIGINAL EQUIPMENT :		**76%**
Tires :	75	
Headlights :	80	
Wipers :	70	
Rear defroster :	75	
Radio :	80	
COMFORT :		**75%**
Seats :	75	
Suspension :	75	
Sound level :	75	
Conveniences :	70	
Air conditioning :	80	
BUDGET :		**66%**
Price :	50	
Fuel economy :	75	
Insurance :	70	
Satisfaction :	85	
Depreciation :	50	
Overall rating :		**73.4%**

NEW FOR 2000

- Revised front and rear fascias.
- 70 improved features making the Altima faster, smoother and quieter.
- Shock absorption designed for sporty handling and a very comfortable ride.

Compare Performance, Specifications, Prices, and Classification at the end of this chapter.

EQUIPMENT

NISSAN Altima	XE	GXE	SE	GLE
Automatic transmission:	O	O	O	S
Cruise control:	S	S	S	S
Power steering:	S	S	S	S
Anti-lock brakes:	-	O	S	S
Traction control:	-	-	-	-
Air conditioning:	-	SM	SM	SM
Leather:	-	-	O	S
AM/FM/radio-cassette:	SCd	SCd	SCd	SCd
Power door locks:	-	S	S	S
Power windows:	S	S	S	S
Tilt steering:	S	S	S	S
Dual adjustable mirrors:	SE	SE	SE	SE
Alloy wheels:	-	-	S	S
Anti-theft system:	-	O	S	S

Colors

Exterior: Wildberry, Blue, Green, Ebony, Platinum, Grey, White, Pewter, Champagne.

Interior: Dawn, Blonde, Olive.

AT A GLANCE...

HISTORIC

Introduced in:	1993-1998.
Made in:	Smyrna, Tennesee, USA.

DEMOGRAPHICS

Model	Men./Wom.	Age	Married	College	Income $
Altima	69/31 %	46	80 %	62 %	46,000

INDEX

Safety:	80 %	Satisfaction:	88 %
Depreciation:	48 %	Insurance:	$ 550
Cost per mile:	$ 0.45	Number of dealers:	1,100

SALES

Model	Canada 1997	1998	Result	USA 1997	1998	Result
Altima	8,122	8,746	+ 7.7 %	144,483	144,451	0.0%

MAINTENANCE REQUIRED BY WARRANTY

First revision:	Frequency:	Diagnostic plug:
7,500 miles	6 months/ 7,500 miles	Yes

Solid

The Alero did a very nice job of replacing the Achieva, a model which never sold very well. Mainly because of its dull styling, but especially because of its lack of quality and minimal equipment. The newcomer is much like the Aurora and the Intrigue — it has the same design approach and the same consistency, making it an attractive product that's solid from just about every standpoint.

MODEL RANGE

The Alero shares its platform and a number of mechanical features and finish details with the Pontiac Grand Am. It's offered as a 2-door coupe or 4-door sedan in GX, GL or GLS versions equipped with an original 2.4L Twin Cam 4-cylinder engine on the GX and GL or the 3400 overhead valve V6 on the GLS. A 5-speed manual gearbox is now standard on all 4-cylinder cars. The 4-speed automatic is standard on V6 models and optional on 4-cylinder models. The Alero comes equipped with a very extensive list of standard items, even on the least expensive model. Besides ABS-traction control, there's climate control, power door locks, tilt steering wheel, theft-deterrent system and a tire pressure control device.

TECHNICAL FEATURES

The steel unibody has an average aerodynamic efficiency, a tad better than that of the Achieva, with a drag coefficient of 0.32. But its resistance to impact during collision tests has improved since it earned top marks from the NHTSA. It includes an independent cradle up front that supports the powertrain and suspension elements and at the rear end, these elements are mounted on a bolted crossmember. The sus-

pension is now fully independent. There's a MacPherson strut design up front and the rear suspension is new and highly sophisticated, since axles are supported by a three-link arrangement on each side. There are anti-roll bars both front and rear. All three versions share the same springs and shocks, with both engines. Only the GLS can receive the optional FE3 sporty suspension. Cars are equipped with standard disc brakes paired up with the now inseparable duo: ABS-traction control. Steering is variable assist.

PROS

+ STYLE. This newcomer's a real winner and its body design is sensational, blotting out any memory of the lackluster former Achieva. It's inspired by the Aurora's curves, but it's different from the Intrigue and so the Alero has a winsome and solid as a rock character. Inside, there are lots of those GM round shapes, but after all, you do inherit some family traits, and everything exhibits a neat "soft touch" approach.

+ ENGINEERING. For once GM pulled out all the stops and spent the cash needed to build this worthy Alero model. The body, suspension, brake system and V6 engine attest to this determination to do things right, which in the long run does beef up the price higher than for previous models that anyhow did not sell.

+ HANDLING. What strikes you right off once you're behind the wheel is the one-of-a-piece Alero design, a real first, like the feeling you got on the hot-off-the-press Aurora and Intrigue. Roadability is clean and competent and depending on the tires used, there's a nice cohesive directional flow and the car takes really tight curves with amazing assurance. Compared to the previous generation's wishy washy demeanor, this type of crisp handling is a really pleasant surprise. Quality pays.

+ PERFORMANCES. Result stats indicate that they're quite acceptable, especially with the more torquey V6. Accelerations are sprightly and pickup is peppy, so passing on the highway is very safe.

+ DRIVING. It's great with the relatively comfy cockpit and adequate visibility (more so on the sedan than the coupe) but the simple, straightforward dashboard layout is a real treat, and the steering wheel and speed shifter are just where you want them. The driver even has a footrest on the left...

+ NICE FEATURES. Handy storage compartments throughout the cabin, more nicely contoured seats and speed shifter position indicator on the instrument panel.

CONS

- TORQUE STEER. We shouldn't have to mention this phenomenon on such a recent car, but it's due to

the unequal-length drive shafts. But it's only a problem on really slick roads.

- ENGINES. They're fairly new, but they're far from being as smooth and refined as their Japanese homologues that equip the Accord and Camry-Solara. The 4-cylinder is really rough around the edges and you'd think it had farm tractor genes in its blood and the V6 isn't as silky as its rivals.

- CABIN SPACE. Rear seats are wider and higher, but there isn't much leg room if the front seats are pushed back too far.

- MANUAL GEARBOX. The automatic's okay for the sedan, but the coupe should be able to be equipped with an optional manual gearbox with both engines, since statistically the latter doesn't sell as well. This is now the case for the 4-cylinder, but not for the V6.

- PRICE. Quality pays, but you have to pay for quality. The Alero is a better car than the Achieva, but it also costs more and its price is dangerously close to that of the Intrigue that offers more generous space and performances, for just a few extra dollars. This same phenomenon is affecting the Cirrus-Stratus-Breeze compared with the Concorde-Intrepid. Sales will be shared depending on age bracket and market segment.

CONCLUSION

As a result of the impetus created by the Aurora and Intrigue, the Alero has been upgraded to the point of attracting buyers who previously would never have imagined themselves driving a GM. A very nice turn of events for a make that not so long ago seemed to be dying by inches!

RATING	
OLDSMOBILE Alero	
CONCEPT :	**75%**
Technology :	80
Safety :	90
Interior space :	60
Trunk volume :	70
Quality/fit/finish :	75
DRIVING :	**68%**
Cockpit :	80
Performance :	55
Handling :	65
Steering :	80
Braking :	60
ORIGINAL EQUIPMENT :	**76%**
Tires :	75
Headlights :	80
Wipers :	75
Rear defroster :	75
Radio :	75
COMFORT :	**73%**
Seats :	75
Suspension :	75
Sound level :	60
Conveniences :	75
Air conditioning :	80
BUDGET :	**66%**
Price :	60
Fuel economy :	75
Insurance :	55
Satisfaction :	75
Depreciation :	65
Overall rating :	**71.6%**

NEW FOR 2000

- Standard 5-speed manual transmission with the 4-cylinder engine.
- Standard child-safety seat anchors.
- Interior color: Pewter.
- Four metallic body colors: Ruby Red, Prairie Green, Midnight Blue, Electric Blue.

Compare Performance, Specifications, Prices, and Classification at the end of this chapter.

EQUIPMENT

OLDSMOBILE Alero	GX	GL	GLS
Automatic transmission:	O	O	S
Cruise control:	O	S	S
Power steering:	S	S	S
Anti-lock brakes:	S	S	S
Traction control:	S	S	S
Air conditioning:	S	S	S
Leather:	-	O	S
AM/FM/radio-cassette:	O	S	SCd
Power door locks:	S	S	S
Power windows:	-	S	S
Tilt steering:	S	S	S
Dual adjustable mirrors:	SM	SE	SE
Alloy wheels:	-	S	S
Anti-theft system:	S	S	S

Colors

Exterior: Silver, White, Blue, Black, Green, Red, Grey, Jade, Sand, Orchid.

Interior: Grey, Beige, Red, Blue, Taupe, Lime, Graphite, Jade, Pewter.

AT A GLANCE...

HISTORIC

Introduced in:	1999.
Made in:	Lansing, Michigan, USA.

DEMOGRAPHICS

Model	Men./Wom.	Age	Married	College	Income $
Alero/Achieva	72/28 %	52	72 %	31 %	32,000

INDEX

Safety:	90 %	Satisfaction:	75 %
Depreciation:	30 %	Insurance:	$ 560
Cost per mile:	$ 0.45	Number of dealers:	3100

SALES

Model	Canada 1997	1998	Result	USA 1997	1998	Result
Alero/Achieva	2,245	2,537	+13.0 %	63,196	28,134	- 55.5 %

MAINTENANCE REQUIRED BY WARRANTY

First revision:	Frequency:	Diagnostic plug:
3,000 miles	6,000 miles	Yes

The success of the Grand Am is unshakable. Generation after generation, it continues to fascinate a very considerable number of consumers. Its musclebound and unusual lines are impressive and they lead to wild dreams of power and speed levels beyond compare. While it's true that it's most fun to drive with the more powerful V6 engine, the 4-cylinder is very good at bursting any driver's bubble of high-performance pretensions.

MODEL RANGE

The Grand Am comes in a 4-door sedan and 2-door coupe in SE and GT trim. The SE is equipped with the same 2.4L 4-cylinder engine that powered the previous model, but a new 3.4L overhead valve V6 now equips the GT version. Each model can receive the other engine, on request. The standard transmission is a 5-speed manual with the 4-cylinder and 4-speed automatic with the V6. Original items include air conditioning, power steering, traction control and antilock braking, remote control trunk release and lock as well as intermittent wipers.

TECHNICAL FEATURES

The unibody is more rigid than on the previous model. It's made up of galvanized (on both sides) steel panels and yields a drag coefficient of 0.34, which is simply out to lunch for a 2000 car. Wheelbase and wheel tracks have been widened, cabin and trunk space are 20% more generous and a hydroformed cradle supports the front powertrain and suspension. The Grand Am now benefits from a fully independent suspension, with MacPherson struts and aluminum lower control arms up front and a three-link arrange-

A Fantasy

ment at the rear. There's an anti-roll bar at both extremities. The SE models are equipped with disc and drum brakes and GT models benefit from disc brakes availability. But ABS and traction control are original equipment items for both versions. Cars animated by a V6 are equipped with variable assist power rack-and-pinion steering.

PROS

+ STYLE. This new design still smacks of the exuberant and showy looks typical of the Grand Am, thanks to various stylistic accents, including, among other things, those humungous fog floodlights set on the base of the front bumper.

+ GT VERSION. It's a good bargain. For a reasonable sum, you get a zippy V6 powerplant, silky automatic transmission and traction control, features not all rivals come equipped with.

+ V6 ENGINE. The new V6 has a lot of vim and vitality to put the 4-cylinder in its lowly place, with its high torque achieved at lower rpm. The 2.4L is less willing when car is at full load capacity or going uphill and it roars and shakes a heck of a lot.

+ HANDLING. The GT exhibits better road adherence thanks to the firmer suspension and wider, more ruthless tires.

+ CABIN SPACE. The coupe is just as roomy as the sedan, but it's easier to board the sedan, with those nice and wide rear doors.

+ SEATS. Bucket seats are quite comfy with their wrap-around design and they have higher seat backs.

+ TRUNK. It's fairly roomy, but on the GT versions, the split-folding rear seat (optional on the SE versions) makes it modular, but the opening is really tapered and it has a high threshold.

+ STEERING. It's accurate and responsive, so it makes for relaxed driving, especially the vari-rate power steering on the V6-powered models.

+ DEPENDABILITY. The previous model boasted of 80% reliability, so this should help sales for the new model that looks really well-built.

+ HEADLIGHTS. At long last, here's a car that features powerful headlights with a wide beam and satisfactory and reassuring brightness.

CONS

- HANDLING. The SE models suffer from quite a bit of sway due to their overly soft suspension. The new 15-inch tires help offset this tendency, along with the more robust frame. But the GT versions are generally more stable.

- PERFORMANCES. The 4-cylinder is not very exciting and it's still noisy and shaky under heavy accelerations.

- NOISE LEVEL. Compared to the previous model, soundproofing has improved, but there's still wind interference and the GT's exhaust roars away, so it wears you down after a while.

- DRIVING POSITION. The ideal position is hard to find because controls are unusual in design and drivers have to fiddle with them on a daily basis.

- INSTRUMENT PANEL. Like other design features on this model, its styling is exaggerated and just plain tiresome.

- FIT AND FINISH. It's better than it was, but there's still room for improvement because some components still look pretty chintzy.

- BRAKES. They're still not a match for the performances these models can muster. It takes forever to come to a full stop and the spongy pedal makes it hard to apply brakes as required. And ABS doesn't always help keep the car right on track.

- ACCESS. Even with the new body, it's still tough getting to the rear seats, especially on the coupes.

- STORAGE SPOTS. They're somewhat skimpy. Door side-pockets are ridiculously small but the glove compartment is a bit roomier.

- OVERSIGHTS. The parking brake lever is oddly designed. There's no dashboard gear indicator for the automatic transmission. Lastly, windshield wipers are very slow and even at their fastest, they can't keep up in heavy rain.

CONCLUSION

The theme and image car par excellence, the Grand Am lets its owners fantasize about models they can't possibly afford — not too shabby an advantage all things considered!

Compact Cars

RATING
PONTIAC Grand Am

CONCEPT :   69%
Technology :	75
Safety :	95
Interior space :	50
Trunk volume :	50
Quality/fit/finish :	75

DRIVING :   66%
Cockpit :	75
Performance :	65
Handling :	60
Steering :	75
Braking :	55

ORIGINAL EQUIPMENT :   73%
Tires :	75
Headlights :	75
Wipers :	70
Rear defroster :	70
Radio :	75

COMFORT :   65%
Seats :	75
Suspension :	70
Sound level :	50
Conveniences :	50
Air conditioning :	80

BUDGET :   66%
Price :	60
Fuel economy :	70
Insurance :	55
Satisfaction :	80
Depreciation :	65

Overall rating :   67.8%

NEW FOR 2000

- **Manual transmission available with the 4-cylinder engine.**
- **Three new exterior colors: Medium Gulf Blue Metallic, Medium Green-Blue Metallic, Auburn Mist Metallic.**

Compare Performance, Specifications, Prices, and Classification at the end of this chapter.

EQUIPMENT

PONTIAC Grand Am	SE	GT
Automatic transmission:	O	S
Cruise control:	O	S
Power steering:	S	S
Anti-lock brakes:	S	S
Traction control:	S	S
Air conditioning:	SM	SM
Leather:	-	O
AM/FM/radio-cassette:	S	SCd
Power door locks:	S	S
Power windows:	S	S
Tilt steering:	S	S
Dual adjustable mirrors:	SM	SE
Alloy wheels:	O	S
Anti-theft system:	S	S

Colors
Exterior: White, Blue, Black, Green, Red, Grey, Jade, Sand, Orchid, Auburn.

Interior: Grey, Beige, Red, Blue, Taupe, Lime, Graphite, Jade.

AT A GLANCE...

HISTORIC
Introduced in: 1994.
Made in: Lansing, Michigan, USA.

DEMOGRAPHICS
Model	Men./Wom.	Age	Married	College	Income $
Grand Am	58/42 %	47	73 %	39 %	38,500

INDEX
Safety:	95 %	Satisfaction:	83 %
Depreciation:	35 %	Insurance:	$ 650
Cost per mile:	$ 0.45	Number of dealers:	2953

SALES
Model	Canada 1997	1998	Result	USA 1997	1998	Result
Grand Am	23,391	15,865	- 32.2 %	204,078	180,428	- 11.6 %

MAINTENANCE REQUIRED BY WARRANTY
First revision:	Frequency:	Diagnostic plug:
3,000 miles	6,000 miles	Yes

Overblown

The Golf and Jetta continue to meet with a certain degree of success in North America, where close to 140,000 units found buyers last year. They were revamped for the European market in 1998, though the new models reached our continent only in 99. While their styling is still perfectly recognizable, they are larger and even more obviously wider.

MODEL RANGE

Golf models come in 3- and 5-door (hatchback) sedans or 2-door convertibles available in four finishes: GL, GL TDI, GLS, GLS TDI, GTI GLS and GLX and convertible. The Jetta is a 4-door sedan available as a GL, GL TDI, GLS, GLS TDI and GLX. The base GL, GLS and convertible have a 2.0L engine and GLX models have a 2.8L V6. The TDI versions' turbo diesel engines are the latest of the their kind and Volkswagen is the only builder that sells this type of engine in this class on the North American market.

TECHNICAL FEATURES

The steel unibody has a very reasonable drag coefficient: 0.32. It has also been reinforced to provide more sturdiness. The front MacPherson-type suspension is independent, with automatic stabilization and negative offset.

The rear features a torsion axle, with a track that varies to compensate for understeering and to provide an induced torque effect. Brakes are mixed on the Golf GL, GLS and TDI and the GLX and all Jetta models feature four discs. ABS systems are standard on all models. Engines are the same that were used to power older models and the turbo diesel is still noted for its low fuel consumption.

PROS

+ **RIGIDITY.** The structure has been reinforced significantly to improve handling, comfort and safety and this car feels really solid.

+ **PERFORMANCE.** The GLX's VR6 is the most exciting and it provides the kind of acceleration and pick-up that makes you hate the sluggish 2.0L on the pretentious GTI GLS. However, with these models' weight gain, statistics aren't as impressive as they used to be.

+ **HANDLING.** It's very stable and predictable thanks to efficient and sophisticated suspensions that result in precision driving. Although they tend to understeer, these cars are easy to control and are ideal for sporty drivers.

+ **STEERING.** The system is precise and responsive, assistance is just right and it makes driving on winding roads a very pleasant and exciting experience.

+ **FUEL ECONOMY.** The Diesel engine's is more noteworthy than levels recorded for the less economical gasoline engines.

+ **PRESENTATION.** It's not as severe now that materials come in colors other than grey and black. Plastics and fabrics look significantly better than they did on previous models.

+ **ANTITHEFT SYSTEM.** Far from a luxury, it's now part of standard equipment and will no doubt serve to decrease the number of thefts that once reached virtually epidemic levels.

+ **CONVERTIBLE.** The only one of its kind, with four seats, a roll bar and a lined top including a glass rear windshield featuring a defroster, a definite asset for problem-free winter driving. Too bad it isn't available with the VR6 engine.

+ **BONUS POINTS.** High praise for the diesel models' touring range and automatic windshield wipers that spring into action as soon as it begins to rain.

CONS

- **PRICE.** The Golf and Jetta are expensive compared to some of their less problematic Japanese competitors. This is all the more surprising for the Jetta that is built in North America. And the phenomenon is even more true in the case of GLX versions, whose dull design does nothing to justify their asking price.

- **REAR SEATS.** Although they are considerably wider they still aren't long enough and only smaller passengers will feel comfortable when travelling in the back seats of these models. Although doors open wide, they're too narrow to provide good access for rear-seat passengers.

- **RELIABILITY.** A few exasperating problems continue to plague Golf and Jetta owners. Once you get past the product's good looks, you soon see that some manufacturing details could use improvement.

- **PERFORMANCE.** The 2.0L engine is mediocre and acceleration and pick-up are both unenthusiastic.

- **COMFORT.** Travelling in these cars is no picnic; they're noisy, the engine and drivetrains vibrate, the suspension is very firm in spite of recent improvements and seats are unbelievably hard - all of which jars with the attractive design concept.

- **FRONT SEATS.** The dashboard wastes a lot of space and is a hazard for kneecaps.

- **SHIFTING.** Strange for a Volkswagen, the manual transmission takes a long time to warm up and as soon as the car reaches a certain speed, the clutch linkage lacks precision.

- **HANDLING.** The Golf and Jetta GLX are a bit more reassuring than previous models, but they remain suspicious because of the simplistic approach applied to adapt them to a more powerful mechanical system. Although not as noticeable, the torque steer effect is still present on slippery roads and the soft suspension doesn't live up to the expectations most drivers have when its comes to allegedly sporty models.

- **MAJOR FLAWS.** Very weak headlights and slow windshield wipers (40/56 sweeps per minute) are inexcusable, especially on the high-performance GLX versions, where they are downright dangerous. Lastly, the Volkswagen warranty is the most minimalist on today's market.

CONCLUSION

Improvements aside, the Golf and Jetta are overvalued. Their reliability has not yet been proven undeniably and their performance levels and warranties fail to justify their asking price.

RATING
VOLKSWAGEN Golf-Jetta

CONCEPT :		73%
Technology :	80	
Safety :	80	
Interior space :	50	
Trunk volume :	80	
Quality/fit/finish :	75	

DRIVING :		70%
Cockpit :	80	
Performance :	50	
Handling :	60	
Steering :	80	
Braking :	80	

ORIGINAL EQUIPMENT :		76%
Tires :	80	
Headlights :	80	
Wipers :	70	
Rear defroster :	75	
Radio :	75	

COMFORT :		68%
Seats :	75	
Suspension :	70	
Sound level :	40	
Conveniences :	80	
Air conditioning :	75	

BUDGET :		65%
Price :	50	
Fuel economy :	85	
Insurance :	45	
Satisfaction :	75	
Depreciation :	70	

| **Overall rating :** | | **70.4%** |

NEW FOR 2000

- Brake wear indicator.
- More elaborate antitheft system.
- Eight-speaker sound system standard on GTI and GLX models and optional on GLS models.
- Optional CD player positioned in the dashboard.

Compare Performance, Specifications, Prices, and Classification at the end of this chapter.

EQUIPMENT

VOLKSWAGEN Golf VOLKSWAGEN Jetta	GL	GLS	GTI GLX	TDI
Automatic transmission:	O	O	O	O
Cruise control:	O	S	S	S
Power steering:	S	S	S	S
Anti-lock brakes:	S	S	S	S
Traction control:	-	-	-	S
Air conditioning:	O	S	S	S
Leather:	-	O	S	O
AM/FM/radio-cassette:	S	S	S	S
Power door locks:	S	S	S	S
Power windows:	O	S	S	S
Tilt steering:	S	S	S	S
Dual adjustable mirrors:	SMH	SEH	SEH	SEH
Alloy wheels:	-	O	S	O
Anti-theft system:	S	S	S	S

Colors

Exterior: White, Grey, Blue, Red, Silver, Black, Green, Suede, Violet, Wildberry.

Interior: Grey, Black, Beige.

AT A GLANCE...

HISTORIC

Introduced in:	1985-1993. Jetta: 1999.
Made in:	Mexico.

DEMOGRAPHICS

Model	Men./Wom.	Age	Married	College	Income $
Golf	53/47 %	30	48 %	69 %	45,000
Jetta	63/37 %	41	70 %	59 %	48,500

INDEX

Safety:	80 %	Satisfaction:	77 %
Depreciation:	30 %	Insurance:	$ 635-800
Cost per mile:	$ 0.35-0.45	Number of dealers:	650

SALES

Model	Canada 1997	1998	Result	USA 1997	1998	Result
Golf	8,501	10,189	+ 19.9 %	20,702	18,282	- 11.7 %
Jetta	12,725	12,938	+ 1.7 %	90,984	89,311	- 1.8 %

MAINTENANCE REQUIRED BY WARRANTY

First revision: 3,000 miles	Frequency: 6,000 miles	Diagnostic plug: Yes

COMPACT CARS
PERFORMANCE

Model/version	Type / timing valve / fuel system	Displacement cu in	Power hp @ rpm	Torque lb-ft @ rpm	Compres. ratio	Driving wheels / transmission	Final ratio	Acceler. 0-60 mph s	Standing 1/4 & 5/8 mile s	Passing 50-75 mph s	Braking 60-0 ft	Top speed mph	Lateral acceler. G	Noise level dBA	City	Highway	Fuel type Octane
CHEVROLET Malibu																	
base	V6 3.1 OHV-12-SFI	191	170 @ 5200	190 @ 4000	9.6 :1	front - A4	3.05	8.7	16.3	30.0	6.5	148	112	0.75	67	20	30	R 87
CHRYSLER Cirrus																	
base	V6 2.5-SOHC-24-MPSFI	152	168 @ 5800	170 @ 4350	9.4 :1	front - A4	3.91	9.7	17.2	30.6	6.7	141	112	0.83	67	19	26	R 87
DAEWOO Leganza																	
base	L4 2.2 DOHC-16-MPFI	134	131 @ 5400	148 @ 4400	9.6 :1	front - M5*	3.720	9.8	17.0	30.8	7.4	135	110	0.80	66-70	20	29	R 87
						front - A4	2.654	11.0	18.2	32.7	8.8	138	108	0.80	66-70	20	28	R 87
DODGE Stratus																	
base	L4 2.0-SOHC-16-MPSFI	122	132 @ 6000	128 @ 5000	9.8 :1	front - M5*	3.94	11.3	17.6	31.8	7.8	151	103	0.80	68	26	39	R 87
						front - A4	4.08	12.0	18.0	32.2	8.1	144	100	0.80	68	22	34	R 87
option	L4 2.4-DOHC-16-MPSFI	148	150 @ 5200	167 @ 4000	9.4 :1	front - A4	3.91	10.4	17.5	31.1	7.1	137	109	0.81	68	21	29	R 87
option	V6 2.5-SOHC-24-MPSFI	152	168 @ 5800	170 @ 4350	9.4 :1	front - A4*	3.91	9.7	17.2	30.6	6.7	141	112	0.83	67	19	26	R 87
FORD Contour																	
base	L4 2.0 DOHC-16-MPSFI	121	125 @ 5500	130 @ 4000	9.6 :1	front - M5*	3.84	10.0	17.2	31.5	6.8	131	109	0.78	67	26	36	R 87
						front - A4	3.92	11.1	17.8	32.2	7.8	137	106	0.78	68	23	35	R 87
option	V6 2.5 DOHC-24-MPSFI	155	170 @ 6250	165 @ 4250	9.7 :1	front - M5*	4.06	8.8	16.7	29.0	6.5	125	112	0.82	67	21	32	R 87
						front - A4	3.77	9.4	17.1	30.6	6.7	128	109	0.82	68	22	32	R 87
SVT	V6 2.5 DOHC-24-MPSFI	155	200 @ 6700	167 @ 5625	10.0 :1	front - M5	4.06	7.7	16.4	28.5	5.0	125	137	0.85	68	20	28	S 91
MAZDA 626																	
DX, LX	L4*2.0 DOHC-16-MPSFI	121	130 @ 5500	130 @ 3000	9.0 :1	front - M5*	4.105	9.6	17.2	31.0	7.0	134	112	0.78	67	25	34	R 87
						front - A4	4.230	11.7	18.4	33.2	9.5	144	109	0.78	67	22	30	R 87
LX-V6, ES	V6*2.5 DOHC-24-MPSFI	152	170 @ 6000	163 @ 5000	9.5 :1	front - M5*	4.105	8.3	16.8	29.5	6.1	151	123	0.80	68	16	26	S 91
						front - A4	4.157	10.0	17.6	31.5	7.2	147	120	0.80	68	18	26	S 91
MERCURY Mystique																	
base	L4 2.0 DOHC-16-MPSFI	121	125 @ 5500	130 @ 4000	9.6 :1	front - M5*	3.84	10.0	17.2	31.5	6.8	131	109	0.78	67	26	36	R 87
						front - A4	3.92	11.1	17.8	32.2	7.8	137	106	0.78	68	23	35	R 87
option	V6 2.5 DOHC-24-MPSFI	155	170 @ 6250	165 @ 4250	9.7 :1	front - M5*	4.06	8.8	16.7	29.0	6.5	125	112	0.82	67	21	32	R 87
						front - A4	3.77	9.4	17.0	30.6	6.7	128	109	0.82	68	22	32	R 87
MITSUBISHI Galant																	
DE,ES	L4 2.4 SOHC-16-IEPM	143	145 @ 5500	155 @ 3000	9.5 :1	front- M5*	4.32	9.0	16.8	30.5	6.6	144	115	0.80	66	24	33	R 87
						front- A4	4.63	10.2	17.6	31.5	7.1	148	112	0.80	65	22	31	R 87
ES,LS,GTZ	V6 3.0 SOHC-24-IEPM	181	195 @ 5500	205 @ 4500	9.0 :1	front- A4*	3.68	8.6	16.5	30.0	6.4	151	118	0.76	65	20	30	R 87
NISSAN Altima																	
1)	L4 2.4 DOHC-16-SFI	145	155 @ 5600	154 @ 4400	9.2 :1	front - M5*	3.650	9.0	16.6	30.1	6.6	125	118	0.80	65	23	32	R 87
2)	L4 2.4 DOHC-16-SFI	145	155 @ 5600	154 @ 4400	9.2 :1	front - A4*	3.619	10.2	17.3	31.2	7.0	131	112	0.80	65	22	32	R 87
1) XE, GXE, SE.	2) GLE, option XE, GXE, SE.																
OLDSMOBILE Alero																	
GX*, GL*	L4 2.4 DOHC-16-MPSFI	146	150 @ 5600	155 @ 4400	9.5 :1	front - M5*	3.42	9.6	16.8	30.4	6.8	144	103	0.82	68-72	21	32	R 87
GLS*, GL	V6 3.4 OHV-12-MPSFI	204	170 @ 4800	200 @ 4000	9.5 :1	front - M5*	3.05	7.9	16.1	29.7	5.9	138	112	0.82	66-72	20	28	R 87
PLYMOUTH Breeze																	
base	L4 2.0-SOHC-16-MPSFI	122	132 @ 6000	128 @ 5000	9.8 :1	front - M5*	3.94	11.3	17.6	31.8	7.8	151	103	0.80	68	26	39	R 87
						front - A4	4.08	12.0	18.0	32.2	8.1	144	100	0.80	68	22	34	R 87
option	L4 2.4-DOHC-16-MPSFI	148	150 @ 5200	167 @ 4000	9.4 :1	front - A4	3.91	10.4	17.5	31.1	7.1	137	109	0.81	68	21	29	R 87
PONTIAC Grand Am																	
base	L4 2.4 DOHC-16-ISP	146	150 @ 5600	155 @ 4400	9.5 :1	front - A4*	3.42	10.0	17.2	30.8	6.9	144	109	0.76	68	21	32	R 87
option	V6 3.4 OHV -12-ISP	204	170 @ 5200	195 @ 4000	9.5 :1	front - A4*	3.05	8.5	16.4	29.5	6.2	131	112	0.80	67	18	27	R 87
GT	V6 3.4 OHV -12-ISP	204	175 @ 5200	205 @ 4000	9.5 :1	front - A4*	3.29	7.7	15.8	29.0	5.5	148	120	0.83	67-70	16	25	R 87
VOLKSWAGEN Golf-Jetta																	
GL,GLS, GTI GLS, Cabrio	L4* 2.0 SOHC-8-SMPFI	121	115 @ 5200	122 @ 2600	10.0 :1	front - M5*	4.24	10.5	17.2	31.5	6.9	131	112	0.80	67-72	24	34	R 87
						front - A4	4.88	11.5	18.6	33.6	9.0	134	109	0.80	67-72	22	32	R 87
GLX, GTI GLS, option GLS	V6* 2.8 DOHC-12-SMPFI	170	174 @ 5800	181 @ 3200	10.0 :1	front - M5*	3.39	7.7	15.8	27.6	5.6	144	130	0.83	65-71	20	29	R 87
						front - A4	4.27	8.4	16.2	29.0	5.5	125	124	0.83	67-72	19	28	R 87
TDI	L4* 1.9 SOHC-8-DI	116	90 @ 3750	155 @ 1900	19.5 :1	front - M5*	3.39	12.5	18.9	33.6	10.9	138	106	0.75	69-74	41	54	D

COMPACT CARS
SPECIFICATIONS

Model	Version Trim	Body/ Seats	Cabin volume cu ft	Trunk volume cu ft	Cd	Wheel base in	Lgth x Width x Hght in x inx in	Curb weight lb	Susp. ft/rr	Brake ft/rr type	Steering ø ft	turns number	Fuel tank gal	dimensions	Standard tires make	model	Standard powertrain	99 Price msrp $
CHEVROLET	General warranty: 3 years / 36,000 miles; antipollution: 5 years / 50,000 miles; perforation corrosion: 6 years / 100,000 miles. Roadside assistance.																	
Malibu	base	4dr.sdn. 5	98.6	17.1	0.32	107.0	190.4x69.4x56.7	3051	ih/ih	dc/dr/ABS	pwr.r&p. 36.3	2.9	15.0	215/60R15	Firestone	Affinity	V6/3.1/A4	16,535
Malibu	LS	4dr.sdn. 5	98.6	17.1	0.32	107.0	190.4x69.4x56.7	3077	ih/ih	dc/dr/ABS	pwr.r&p. 36.3	2.9	15.0	215/60R15	Firestone	Affinity	V6/3.1/A4	19,495
CHRYSLER	General warranty: 3 years / 36,000 miles; surface rust: 3 years; perforation: 7 years / 100,000 miles; roadside assistance: 3 years / 36,000 miles.																	
Cirrus	LXi	4dr.sdn. 5	95.9	15.7	0.31	108.0	187.0x71.7x54.3	3197	ih/ih	dc/ABS	pwr.r&p. 37.0	3.1	16.0	195/65R15	Michelin	MX4	V6/2.5/A4	19,995
DAEWOO	General warranty: 3 years / 36,000 miles; powertrain & corrosion: 5 years / 60 000 miles; antipollution: 6 years illimited mileage.																	
Leganza	SE	4dr.sdn. 5	96.9	14.1	0.33	105.1	183.9x70.0x56.6	3157	ih/ih	dc/dc	pwr.r&p. 36.0	3.0	17.2	205/60R15	Kumho	ECTSA	L4/2.2/A4	14,450
Leganza	SX	4dr.sdn. 5	96.9	14.1	0.33	105.1	183.9x70.0x56.6	3160	ih/ih	dc/dc	pwr.r&p. 36.0	3.0	17.2	205/60R15	Kumho	ECTSA	L4/2.2/A4	16,660
Leganza	CDX	4dr.sdn. 5	96.9	14.1	0.33	105.1	183.9x70.0x56.6	3163	ih/ih	dc/ABS	pwr.r&p. 36.0	3.0	17.2	205/60R15	Kumho	ECTSA	L4/2.2/A4	18,660
DODGE	General warranty: 3 years / 36,000 miles; surface rust: 3 years; perforation: 7 years / 100,000 miles; roadside assistance: 3 years /36,000 miles.																	
Stratus	SE	4dr.sdn. 5	95.5	15.7	0.31	108.0	186.0x71.7x54.2	2940	ih/ih	dc/dr	pwr.r&p. 37.1	3.1	16.0	195/70R14	Michelin	XW4	L4/2.0/M5	15,810
Stratus	ES	4dr.sdn. 5	95.5	15.7	0.31	108.0	186.0x71.7x54.4	3058	ih/ih	dc/dr/ABS	pwr.r&p. 37.1	3.1	16.0	195/65R15	Michelin	MX4	L4/2.4/A4	19,495
FORD	General warranty, antipollution & battery: 3 years / 36,000 miles; corrosion perforation: 5 years / unlimited.																	
Contour	LX	4dr.sdn. 5	90.2	13.9	0.31	106.5	184.6x69.1x54.5	2769	ih/ih	dc/dr	pwr.r&p. 36.5	2.8	15.0	185/70R14	FirestoneFirehawk GTA		L4/2.0/M5	15,095
Contour	SE	4dr.sdn. 5	90.2	13.9	0.31	106.5	184.6x69.1x54.5	2833	ih/ih	dc/dc	pwr.r&p. 37.3	2.7	15.0	185/70R14	FirestoneFirehawk GTA		V6/2.5/M5	16,590
Contour	SVT	4dr.sdn. 5	89.4	13.9	0.31	106.5	183.8x69.1x54.5	3069	ih/ih	dc/ABS	pwr.r&p. 40.0	2.7	15.0	215/50ZR16	BF Goodrich G-Force T/A		V6/2.5/M5	23,200
MAZDA	General warranty: 3 years / 50,000 miles; powertrain: 5 years / 100,000 miles; corrosion: 5 years / unlimited.																	
626	LX	4dr.sdn. 5	97.1	14.2	0.33	105.1	186.8x69.3x55.1	2798	ih/ih	dc/dr	pwr.r&p. 36.1	2.9	16.9	185/70R14	Bridgestone	SF408	L4/2.0/M5	18,265
626	ES	4dr.sdn. 5	97.1	14.2	0.33	105.1	186.8x69.3x55.1	2800	ih/ih	dc/dc	pwr.r&p. 36.1	2.9	16.9	185/70R14	Bridgestone	SF408	L4/2.0/M5	20,145
626	LX-V6	4dr.sdn. 5	97.1	14.2	0.33	105.1	186.8x69.3x55.1	2994	ih/ih	dc/dr	pwr.r&p. 36.1	2.9	16.9	205/60R15	BridgestonePotenza RE92		V6/2.5/M5	19,515
626	ES-V6	4dr.sdn. 5	97.1	14.2	0.33	105.1	186.8x69.3x55.1	3002	ih/ih	dc/ABS	pwr.r&p. 36.1	2.9	16.9	205/60R15	BridgestonePotenza RE92		V6/2.5/M5	22,695
MERCURY	General warranty, antipollution & battery: 3 years / 36,000 miles; corrosion perforation: 5 years / unlimited.																	
Mystique	GS	4dr.sdn. 5	89.6	13.9	0.31	106.5	184.8x69.1x54.4	2808	ih/ih	dc/dr	pwr.r&p. 36.5	2.78	15.0	185/70R14	FirestoneFirehawk GTA		L4/2.0/M5	17,070
Mystique	LS	4dr.sdn. 5	90.2	13.9	0.31	106.5	184.8x69.1x54.4	2808	ih/ih	dc/dc	pwr.r&p. 37.3	2.71	15.0	205/60R15	FirestoneFirehawk GTA		V6/2.5/M5	18,425
MITSUBISHI	General warranty: 3-years / 36,000 miles; powetrain: 5-years / 60,000 miles.																	
Galant	DE	4dr.sdn. 5	-	14.0	0.29	103.7	187.8x68.5x55.7	2800	ih/ih	dc/dr	pwr.r&p.	-	-	16.3				L4/2.4/M5	
NISSAN	General warranty: 3 years / 50,000 miles; powertrain: 6 years / 60,000 miles; perforation corrosion & antipollution: 6 years / unlimited.																	
Altima	XE	4dr. sdn. 5	94.0	13.8	0.32	103.1	183.1x69.1x55.9	2875	ih/ih	dc/dr	pwr.r&p. 37.4	2.9	15.9	195/65R15	General	XP2000	L4/2.4/M5	15,510
Altima	GXE	4dr. sdn. 5	94.0	13.8	0.32	103.1	183.1x69.1x55.9	2919	ih/ih	dc/dr	pwr.r&p. 37.4	2.9	15.9	195/65R15	General	XP2000	L4/2.4/M5	17,710
Altima	SE	4dr. sdn. 5	94.0	13.8	0.32	103.1	183.1x69.1x55.9	2921	ih/ih	dc/dc	pwr.r&p. 37.4	2.9	15.9	205/60R15	Firestone	Affinity	L4/2.4/M5	19,010
Altima	GLE	4dr. sdn. 5	94.0	13.8	0.32	103.1	183.1x69.1x55.9	2943	ih/ih	dc/dr	pwr.r&p. 37.4	2.9	15.9	195/65R15	General	XP2000	L4/2.4/A4	20,510
OLDSMOBILE	General warranty: 3 years / 36,000 miles; antipollution: 5 years / 50,000 miles; perforation corrosion: 6 years / 100 000 miles. Roadside assistance.																	
Alero GX		2dr.cpe. 5	92.6	15.3	0.32	107.0	186.7x70.1x54.5	3024	ih/ih	dc/ABS	pwr.r&p. 35.1	2.6	15.0	215/60R15	BFGoodrich	Touring T/A	L4/2.4/A4	16,880
Alero GX		4dr.sdn. 5	91.0	15.3	0.32	107.0	186.7x70.1x54.5	3034	ih/ih	dc/ABS	pwr.r&p. 35.2	2.6	15.0	225/50R16	BFGoodrich	Touring T/A	L4/2.4/A4	16,880
Alero GL		2dr.cpe. 5	92.6	15.3	0.32	107.0	186.7x70.1x54.5	3050	ih/ih	dc/ABS	pwr.r&p. 35.1	2.6	15.0	215/60R15	BFGoodrich	Touring T/A	L4/2.4/A4	18,910
Alero GL		4dr.sdn. 5	91.0	15.3	0.32	107.0	186.7x70.1x54.5	3057	ih/ih	dc/ABS	pwr.r&p. 35.2	2.6	15.0	225/50R16	BFGoodrich	Touring T/A	L4/2.4/A4	18,910
Alero GLS		2dr.cpe. 5	92.6	15.3	0.32	107.0	186.7x70.1x54.5	3070	ih/ih	dc/ABS	pwr.r&p. 35.1	2.6	15.0	215/60R15	Goodyear	Eagle LS	V6/3.4/A4	21,430
Alero GLS		4dr.sdn. 5	91.0	15.3	0.32	107.0	186.7x70.1x54.5	3085	ih/ih	dc/ABS	pwr.r&p. 35.2	2.6	15.0	225/50R16	Goodyear	Eagle LS	V6/3.4/A4	21,430
PLYMOUTH	General warranty: 3 years / 36,000 miles; surface rust: 3 years; perforation: 7 years / 100,000 miles; roadside assistance: 3 years /36,000 miles.																	
Breeze	base	4dr.sdn. 5	95.9	15.7	0.31	108.0	186.0x71.7x54.3	2945	ih/ih	dc/dr	pwr.r&p. 37.1	3.1	16.0	195/70R14	Michelin	XW4	L4/2.0/M5	15,650
PONTIAC	General warranty: 3 years / 36 000 miles; antipollution: 5 years / 50 000 miles; perforation corrosion: 6 years / 100 000 miles. Roadside assistance.																	
Grand Am SE		2dr. cpe. 5	107.3	14.3	0.34	107.0	186.3x70.4x55.	3066	ih/ih	dc/dr/ABS	pwr.r&p. 37.7	2.5	15.2	215/60R15	Goodyear	Eagle LS	L4/2.4/A4	16,995
Grand Am SE		4dr. sdn. 5	105.4	14.3	0.34	107.0	186.3x70.4x55.	3115	ih/ih	dc/dr/ABS	pwr.r&p. 37.7	2.5	15.2	215/60R15	Goodyear	Eagle LS	L4/2.4/A4	16,995
Grand Am GT		2dr. cpe. 5	107.3	14.3	0.34	107.0	186.3x70.4x55.	3090	ih/ih	dc/dr/ABS	pwr.r&p. 37.7	2.5	15.2	225/50R16	Goodyear	Eagle RS-A	V6/3.4/A4	19,655
Grand Am GT		4dr. sdn. 5	105.4	14.3	0.34	107.0	186.3x70.4x55.	3168	ih/ih	dc/dr/ABS	pwr.r&p. 37.7	2.5	15.2	225/50R16	Goodyear	Eagle RS-A	V6/3.4/A4	20,055
VOLKSWAGEN	General warranty: 2 years / 24,000 miles; powertrain: 10 years / 100,000 miles; antipollution: 6 years/ 50,000 miles; corrosion perforation: 6 years/unlimited.																	
Golf	Convertible	2dr. con. 5	75.6	9.5	0.38	81.1	160.4x66.7x56.0	3082	ih/sih	dc/dr/ABS	pwr.r&p. 32.0	3.2	14.5	195/60HR14	Goodyear	Eagle GA	L4/2.0/M5	18,500
Golf	TDI GL	5dr. sdn. 5	88.0	17.5	0.31	97.4	163.3x68.3x56.6	2875	ih/sih	dc/dr/ABS	pwr.r&p. 35.1	3.2	14.5	195/60R14	Michelin	Energy	L4/1.9D/M5	16,720
Golf	GL	5dr. sdn. 5	88.0	17.5	0.31	97.4	160.4x68.3x56.6	2723	ih/sih	dc/dr/ABS	pwr.r&p. 35.1	3.2	14.5	195/60R14	Michelin	Energy	L4/2.0/M5	15,425
Golf	GLS	5dr. sdn. 5	88.0	17.5	0.31	97.4	160.4x68.3x56.6	2820	ih/sih	dc/dr/ABS	pwr.r&p. 35.1	3.2	14.5	195/60R14	Michelin	Energy	L4/2.0/M5	16,875
Golf	GTI GLS	5dr. sdn. 5	88.0	17.5	0.31	97.4	160.4x68.3x56.6	2762	ih/sih	dc/dr/ABS	pwr.r&p. 35.1	3.2	14.5	195/60R14	Michelin	Energy	L4/2.0/M5	18,025
Golf	GTI VR6	3dr. sdn. 5	88.0	17.5	0.33	97.4	160.4x68.3x56.6	2890	ih/sih	dc/ABS	pwr.r&p. 35.1	3.2	14.5	205/50HR15	Michelin	MXV4	V6/2.8/M5	22 675
Jetta	TDI GL	4dr. sdn. 5	88.0	13.0	0.31	98.9	172.3x68.3x56.9	2890	ih/sih	dc/ABS	pwr.r&p. 35.7	3.0	14.5	195/65R15	Michelin	Energy	L4/1.9D/M5	18,520
Jetta	GL	4dr. sdn .5	88.0	13.0	0.32	98.9	172.3x68.3x56.9	2819	ih/sih	dc/ABS	pwr.r&p. 35.7	3.0	14.5	195/65R15	Michelin	Energy	L4/2.0/M5	17,225
Jetta	GLS	4dr. sdn .5	88.0	13.0	0.32	98.9	172.3x68.3x56.9	2828	ih/sih	dc/ABS	pwr.r&p. 35.7	3.0	14.5	195/65R15	Michelin	Energy	L4/2.0/M5	18,175
Jetta	GLX VR6	4dr. sdn. 5	84.7	13.0	0.33	98.9	172.3x68.3x56.9	3018	ih/sih	dc/ABS	pwr.r&p. 35.7	3.0	14.5	195/65R15	Michelin	Energy	V6/2.8/M5	24,025

Compact Cars

Notes: 1) Tire makes and models are provided solely as an indication; they are subject to change without prior notice from the automobile manufacturer.
2) See the 2000 price list at the back of this edition.

COMPACT CARS
CLASSIFICATION

OUR CLASSIFICATION

Rank	Models	Concept	Driving	Equipment	Comfort	Budget	Ratings
1	**NISSAN Altima**	**76**	**74**	76	75	66	**73.4 %**
2	MITSUBISHI Galant	73	68	74	**79**	65	71.8 %
3	OLDSMOBILE Alero	75	68	76	73	66	71.6 %
4	VW Golf-Jetta	73	70	76	68	65	70.4 %
5	FORD Contour &						
5	MERCURY Mystique	69	66	76	66	**72**	69.8 %
6	CHEVROLET Malibu	74	60	**79**	70	65	69.6 %
7	DAEWOO Leganza	71	65	74	73	64	69.4 %
8	MAZDA 626	75	65	73	71	61	69.0 %
9	PONTIAC Grand Am	69	66	73	65	66	67.8 %
10	CHRYSLER JA	71	62	70	64	69	67.2 %

YOUR CLASSIFICATION

Rank	Models	98 Sales
1	**CHEVROLET Malibu**	**223,703**
2	PONTIAC Grand Am	180,428
3	NISSAN Altima	144,451
4	FORD Contour	139,838
5	VW Golf-Jetta	107,593
6	DODGE Stratus	106,434
7	MAZDA 626	91,147
8	PLYMOUTH Breeze	59,543
9	MITSUBISHI Galant	44,201
10	CHRYSLER Cirrus	38,504
11	MERCURY Mystique	38,274
12	OLDSMOBILE Alero	28,134

Not classified:
DAEWOO Leganza

NOTES

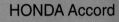
Comparative Test

MEDIUM CARS

See their performance, their specifications, their price and their classification at the end of this chapter.

HONDA Accord

HYUNDAI Sonata

NISSAN Maxima

SATURN L

TOYOTA Camry - Solara

VOLKSWAGEN Passat

Ideal

The Honda Accord is one of the two most popular models on the North American market. The Toyota Camry is its opponent in the fight to see exactly which car is the most widely sold on our continent. Well-sized, comfortable and economical, for many people the Accord is an ideal automobile and some people even claim that its looks are more elegant than its rival's. This sedan is flanked by a coupe with original styling, though it's much less popular.

MODEL RANGE

The Honda Accord is sold as a 2-door coupe in LX, EX and EX V6 trim levels and as a 4-door sedan in DX, LX, EX and EX V6 trim. The DX, LX and EX are driven by an original 135 or 150-hp 2.3L 4-cylinder engine, whereas the EX V6 versions are animated by a 200-hp 3.0L V6. Standard equipment for all models includes torque-sensitive power steering, particulate filter climate control, cruise control, AM/FM radio and tape deck, tilt steering wheel, adjustable exterior mirrors and remote trunk and fuel filler door release.

TECHNICAL FEATURES

Two years ago, the Accord's steel monocoque body got a complete overhaul and gained in resistance to torsion (+ 40%) and flexion (+ 60%). Aerodynamic finesse sits at a comfortable average with a drag coefficient varying between 0.32 and 0.33. Suspensions are mounted on two independent frames so as to isolate the body from powertrain noise and vibration. They consist of a double wishbone design, which includes 5 trailing arms at the rear. The DX and LX versions are equipped with disc and drum brakes,

the EX and EX V6 benefit from four-wheel disc brakes and an antilock braking system comes standard on all models except the base DX sedan. Rack-and-pinion steering is torque-sensitive.

The 2.3L 4-cylinder engine is an enhanced version of the former 2.2L, but the V6 is entirely new. This new-design powerplant has its cylinder rows set at 60° and benefits from VTEC technology that provides for optimum cylinder intake thanks to electronically controlled variable valve timing. A theft-deterrent system that equips all models consists of an ignition key (without battery) that emits a magnetic code activating the microprocessor that controls iginition and engine fuel feed. This coding allows for literally millions of different combinations.

OUTSTANDING

++ VALUE. It's one of the best on the current market, because of the meticulous design, careful assembly and well-known reliability.

++ QUALITY. Construction and fit and finish are simply exquisite, since tolerance points and adjustments are so tight. Trim materials look more noble, especially the plastic components, lovely to look at and to touch.

PROS

+ STYLE. The coupe has a fresh, zippy look and is blessed with a

truly classy, original design. The sedan has a more elegant appearance and has undergone a few minor changes but has remained its graceful, composed self.

+ PERFORMANCES. They're not sensational, since scores obtained are conservative. The V6 is a beautiful specimen blending muscle and silky demeanor and the 4-cylinder engine is lively and responsive even with the automatic gearbox that's nicely calibrated and provides effective braking effect.

+ CABIN & TRUNK SPACE. Honda went out of its way to maximize cabin space so as to really and truly accommodate three average-height rear seat passengers in both coupes and sedans. The good-size trunk can be extended by lowering the rear seatbench cushion.

+ DRIVING PLEASURE. Controls are smooth and precise, for example the brake pedal and steering system, both being well calibrated and benefitting from a good reduction ratio. The suspension is crisp and competent, providing perfect directional flow, so driving one of these beauties is a real treat, with any engine under the hood.

+ RIDE COMFORT. The Accord's suspension is a well-nigh perfect blend between roadhandling and passenger comfort; it's civilized at all times, even when the asphalt goes awry.

+ CONVENIENCE FEATURES.

It's definitely better on the new models, since there are all kinds of generous and convenient spots to stash stuff away.

CONS

- BRAKES. They're stable and tough, but they're rather fair to midling when it comes to making sudden stops, since emergency stopping distances are longer than average.

- SEATS. They could be more comfy, for generally speaking, seat cushions are short, lateral support fair and upholstery is a tad too firm, except for leather-covered seats.

- NOISE LEVEL. Sound dampening could be more effective, since there's engine roar on accelerations and while downshifting and tires thump heavily along over expansion joints.

- ADHERENCE. Wheel grip is far from perfect, especially since no traction control device is included for these models, not even as an extra.

- THE DX VERSION. It isn't a good buy since resale is tough due to minimal equipment that doesn't even include ABS and it's equipped with tiny, crummy-quality tires.

- POOR FEATURES. Inverted sound system and air conditioning controls, light paint shades sensitive to streaking, front center armrest that's awkward with the manual gearbox and too narrow interior rearview mirror.

CONCLUSION

The Accord is one of the best standard production automobiles in the world. It's still a very safe investment, even if the high number of used models available tends to make prices drop.

RATING
HONDA Accord

CONCEPT :		77%
Technology :	85	
Safety :	90	
Interior space :	65	
Trunk volume :	60	
Quality/fit/finish :	85	

DRIVING :		66%
Cockpit :	80	
Performance :	60	
Handling :	50	
Steering :	80	
Braking :	60	

ORIGINAL EQUIPMENT :		78%
Tires :	80	
Headlights :	80	
Wipers :	75	
Rear defroster :	75	
Radio :	80	

COMFORT :		74%
Seats :	75	
Suspension :	75	
Sound level :	60	
Conveniences :	80	
Air conditioning :	80	

BUDGET :		66%
Price :	50	
Fuel economy :	75	
Insurance :	65	
Satisfaction :	90	
Depreciation :	50	

Overall rating :	72.2%

NEW FOR 2000

- Power mirrors and platinum spark plugs.
- Engine adjustments to comply with environmental standards.
- Standard on the SE: exclusive aluminum wheels, wood appliques, CD player, remote control.
- SRS system.

Compare Performance, Specifications, Prices, and Classification at the end of this chapter.

Medium Cars

EQUIPMENT

HONDA Accord sedan HONDA Accord coupe	DX	LX	SE	LX	EX	EXV6
Automatic transmission:	O	O	S	O	O	S
Cruise control:	S	S	S	S	S	S
Power steering:	S	S	S	S	S	S
Anti-lock brakes:	-	S	S	S	S	S
Traction control:	-	-	-	-	-	-
Air conditioning:	SM	SM	SA	SM	SA	SA
Leather:	-	-	S	-	-	S
AM/FM/radio-cassette:	S	S	SCd	S	S	S Cd
Power door locks:	-	S	S	S	S	S
Power windows:	-	S	S	S	S	S
Tilt steering:	S	S	S	S	S	S
Dual adjustable mirrors:	SM	SE	SE	SE	SE	SE
Alloy wheels:	-	-	S	-	S	S
Anti-theft system:	S	S	S	S	S	S

Colors
Exterior: White, Black, Blue, Emerald, Pink, Silver, Raisin, Blackcurrent.

Interior: Lapis, Grey, Ivory.

AT A GLANCE...

HISTORIC
Introduced in:	1986-1998.
Made in:	Marysville, Ohio, USA.

DEMOGRAPHICS
Model	Men./Wom.	Age	Married	College	Income $
Accord cpe.	61/39 %	42	56 %	62 %	54,500
Accord sdn.	73/27 %	55	82 %	55 %	48,500

INDEX
Safety:	80 %	Satisfaction:	90 %
Depreciation:	42 %	Insurance:	$ 560-650
Cost per mile:	$ 0.46	Number of dealers:	1,000

SALES
		Canada			USA	
Model	1997	1998	Result	1997	1998	Result
Accord	21,312	25,490	+19.6 %	384,609	401,071	+ 4.3 %

MAINTENANCE REQUIRED BY WARRANTY
First revision:	Frequency:	Diagnostic plug:
3,500 miles	7,000 miles	Yes

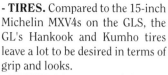

A Worthy Rival

The latest Sonata is in keeping with the international restructuring plan adopted to guild the Hyundai make's image. For too long, the Korean builder's models suffered from the perception that they were merely substandard Japanese products. While the Pony, Stellar and Excel aren't remembered as high-quality automobiles, at least they were biodegradable!

MODEL RANGE

The Sonata is a midsized sedan available in GL and GLS versions. The former is equipped with a 2.4L DOHC in-line 4-cylinder engine and the latter has a "small" 2.5L DOHC V6 (instead of a 3.0L). A 5-speed manual transmission is standard on both models and a 4-speed automatic with overdrive is available, at no extra cost for the GLS. Standard equipment is fairly detailed and among other items, includes power steering, power windows, cruise control, intermittent windshield wipers, air conditioning, a height-adjustable driver's seat and a split folding rear seat.

TECHNICAL FEATURES

The Sonata has a steel unibody mounted on the previous model's platform. Its wheelbase is identical, but its track, length, width and height have increased. The passenger compartment is roomier in all directions. The suspension is fully independent, with two triangular arms in front instead of MacPherson struts and in the rear, the same multi-arm configuration featured on the previous model. Stabilizer bars and helicoidal springs are featured on both assemblies. The GL features four gas shock absorbers, while the GLS's use a nitrogen system. Brakes are mixed on the GL, and the GLS is equipped with four discs. Antilock brakes and traction control are optional only on the GLS.

When it comes to safety, Hyundai offers optional side-impact airbags for front-seat passengers. Standard equipment on both models includes a "passenger detector", a new system that deactivates the passenger-side airbag when the driver is travelling alone. Front seatbelts include pretensioners.

PROS

+ STYLING. The latest Sonata attracts attention with its original rear and front designs and its low trunk line ensures good rear visibility.

+ DRIVEABILITY. Both new engines make driving the Sonata an interesting experience and performance levels are very decent. The 2.4L is powerful and eager, while the V6 is smoother and has more torque. The steering system is progressive and precise, as is braking. Controls feature good ergonomics and handling ease is excellent.

+ COMFORT. The chassis is more rigid, soundproofing is effective and the smooth suspension provides more comfort than the previous Sonata. On the highway at cruising speed, the noise level is similar to the level generated by a Lincoln Town Car and shock absorption provides a velvety smooth ride. It's a shame that seat design is less than ideal.

+ PASSENGER ROOM. While there's a bit less useable space, rear seats are still roomy and passengers can ride in comfort.

+ BRAKING. While distances for panic stops with two or four discs are 148 ft. (45 m) on average, the pedal is progressive and power is obvious enough to give the driver confidence.

+ ACCESS. It's easy thanks to well-sized doors that open at an 80° angle in the front and rear.

+ QUALITY. The level has improved once again, materials look and feel more expensive than they previously did and adjustments show more attention to detail. From the presentation viewpoint, the Sonata GL is similar to the base Camry.

CONS

- SUSPENSION. Its simplistic concept, exaggerated smoothness and poor shock absorption cause hopping on bad roads and depending how far bumpy surfaces extend, it can almost cause seasickness. The GLS's weighted-down front lacks sufficient travel and reactions are harsh.

- TRANSMISSION. The automatic is balky and shifting can be jarring at low speeds. Kickdown is far from instantaneous and drivers have to allow a delay to take advantage of engine breaking or to accelerate.

- TIRES. Compared to the 15-inch Michelin MXV4s on the GLS, the GL's Hankook and Kumho tires leave a lot to be desired in terms of grip and looks.

- TRUNK. It's roomy and the rear seat folds down, but it lacks the height needed for very large items and its sill dips down very low, which complicates loading.

- STORAGE SPACES. There are plenty in the front of the GL, but not a decent one in the rear, not even door pockets or cupholders. The GLS has a center armrest that can accommodate two cups and a box of tissues.

- FLAWS. Headlights and windshield wipers are far from impressive. The former have a decent range, but are not bright enough and the latter have a rhythm of 44/64 sweeps per minute on two continuous settings, well below the average.

- OVERSIGHTS. No alarm warns the driver that headlights have been left on when the vehicle is parked, the positioning of radio and air conditioning controls should be reversed, there is no dummy pedal and no armrest for front-seat passengers and the radio offers inferior sound quality.

CONCLUSION

Thanks to its competitive price/equipment ratio, the Sonata deserves to rank as the second most popular choice in its category, but Hyundai should work hard to improve certain points.

Medium cars

RATING
HYUNDAI Sonata

CONCEPT :   71%
Technology :	75
Safety :	80
Interior space :	70
Trunk volume :	55
Quality/fit/finish :	75

DRIVING :   65%
Cockpit :	80
Performance :	50
Handling :	55
Steering :	80
Braking :	60

ORIGINAL EQUIPMENT :   69%
Tires :	75
Headlights :	75
Wipers :	55
Rear defroster :	70
Radio :	70

COMFORT :   69%
Seats :	75
Suspension :	70
Sound level :	55
Conveniences :	70
Air conditioning :	75

BUDGET :   67%
Price :	60
Fuel economy :	80
Insurance :	70
Satisfaction :	75
Depreciation :	50

Overall rating :   68.2%

NEW FOR 2000

• No major changes.

Compare
Performance,
Specifications, Prices,
and Classification
at the end of this chapter.

EQUIPMENT

HYUNDAI Sonata	GL	GLS
Automatic transmission:	O	O
Cruise control:	S	S
Power steering:	S	S
Anti-lock brakes:	-	O
Traction control:	-	O
Air conditioning:	S	S
Leather:	-	O
AM/FM/radio-cassette:	S	SCd
Power door locks:	S	S
Power windows:	S	S
Tilt steering:	S	S
Dual adjustable mirrors:	SEH	SEH
Alloy wheels:	-	S
Anti-theft system:	-	-

Colors

Exterior: Cherry, Black, Green, Silver, Grey, White.

Interior: Grey-brown.

AT A GLANCE...

HISTORIC
Introduced in:	1989-1994-1999.
Made in:	Asan, South Korea.

DEMOGRAPHICS
Model	Men./Wom.	Age	Married	College	Income $
Sonata	80/20 %	53	79 %	25 %	35,000

INDEX
Safety:	80 %	Satisfaction:	75 %
Depreciation:	52 %	Insurance:	$ 525
Cost per mile:	$ 0.47	Number of dealers:	500

SALES
Model	Canada 1997	1998	Result	USA 1997	1998	Result
Sonata	1,148	1,153	+ 0.4 %	22,128	13,955	- 36.9 %

MAINTENANCE REQUIRED BY WARRANTY
First revision:	Frequency:	Diagnostic plug:
3,000 miles	3 months / 3,000 miles	Yes

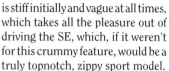
All Done Up

The 2000 Maxima is here. The difference between the new vintage and last year's consists of details that are more cosmetic and practical than truly fundamental - most basic features have remained pretty well unchanged. Styling is in line with the Altima's, at least as far as the front fascia is concerned, and trunk size is now an asset instead of a drawback.

MODEL RANGE

The Maxima is a four-door sedan offered in base GXE, sport SE and luxury GLE that only differ depending on equipment level and design details, for their engine and mechanical components are absolutely identical. All benefit from the fine standard 3.0L V6 linked to a manual or automatic transmission depending on trim level. The base model is quite well-equipped for starters, since equipment includes standard climate control, cruise control, most of the vital power accessories, radio and tape deck, tilt steering wheel, ABS and an antitheft device.

TECHNICAL FEATURES

Its steel unibody has an average aerodynamic efficiency, with a drag coefficient of 0.32. Since it was reworked, build is even sturdier, and it was already one of the most robust before. The front suspension consists of a MacPherson strut design and the rear rigid axle is equipped with the Nissan version of the Scott-Russell multi-link system that allows for constant camber. Cars are equipped with disc brakes, and the ABS system is now standard on all models. The traction control system which consists of a viscous-coupled locking differential is standard with the automatic transmission. The 3.0L DOHC V6 has been

re-engineered and it gains 32 hp. It is assisted by a 5-speed manual transmission on the GXE and SE and a 4-speed automatic on the GLE.

OUTSTANDING

++ V6 ENGINE. It's one of the best in its class; acceleration and pickup are strong and result in very good driveability, especially given the two transmissions' excellent gear ratio. Fuel consumption is reasonable, averaging 22 mpg (11 litres per 100 km).

PROS

+ ROADABILITY. It's pretty impressive thanks to the super rear suspension with differential that keeps these cars solid either on straight stretches or on winding curves. Camber is less obvious on quick lane changes so there's less rear end lift when making emergency stops, and maintains a good stability under all conditions.

+ RIDE COMFORT. The Maxima ride is great on highways where the suspension is super smooth, shock absorbers are ruthless, wheel travel is nice and generous and the noise is kept fairly low.

+ CABIN SPACE. It's adequate for four adults who'll have generous leg, elbow and head room, but a fifth passenger would only be comfortable on short trips.

+ TRUNK. Long undersized, currently it's the roomiest in the cat-

egory and the rear seat folds down for even more cargo room.

+ BONUS POINTS. Air conditioning is efficient and kicks in quickly and windshield wipers are faster.

CONS

- PRICE. The Maxima isn't the bargain it used to be. In fact, it's the most expensive model in its class since it has no economical 4-cylinder engine to offer. While its equipment is more elaborate, some design details have been overlooked, for example storage spaces in the rear of the vehicle.

- PERFORMANCE. Levels are no higher given a major weight gain that results from bigger sizing, something the increase in engine power isn't fully capable of countering.

- STEERING. Slight overassistance makes it light and imprecise at center, leading to a very disturbing driving sensation. Luckily the short turning radius provides very good handling ease.

- BRAKES. They could be better, as those relatively long panic stops indicate and the strange pedal feel is a hassle as well, since it doesn't help to modulate the brake precisely.

- SUSPENSION. It hops on bad roads, but the effect is stronger on passenger comfort than on the car's trajectory.

- MANUAL GEARBOX. The shifter

is stiff initially and vague at all times, which takes all the pleasure out of driving the SE, which, if it weren't for this crummy feature, would be a truly topnotch, zippy sport model.

- STYLING. Based on consumer reaction, the latest Maxima's styling isn't a unanimous success. Some find the front-end too busy and the rear fascia looks an awful lot like a Chrysler Neon's does.

- PRESENTATION. The GXE's has been improved considerably, fabrics look better than they did on the previous model, but plastics used on the dashboard have no place in a model sold at this price level.

- SEATS. Front seats provide better support than the flat rear benchseat, which sports very rounded edges. In both cases, padding is hard and after a while, quite uncomfortable.

- TO BE IMPROVED UPON. Inefficient heating system to tackle really cold weather conditions, the missing shifter indicator among the instrument gauges on the dashboard (unforgivable), the windshield wiper-washer ensemble that never clears the window surface in the wintertime and the rear defroster that takes forever to do its stuff.

CONCLUSION

The latest Maxima is more practical and more comfortable than the previous model, but it's not as much fun to drive. Added weight makes it less peppy and less agile. In its new guise it hopes to attract a new clientele group, which doesn't necessarily mean that it will enjoy the same success it has in previous years.

RATING NISSAN Maxima		
CONCEPT :		**76%**
Technology :	80	
Safety :	80	
Interior space :	70	
Trunk volume :	70	
Quality/fit/finish :	80	
DRIVING :		**71%**
Cockpit :	75	
Performance :	70	
Handling :	60	
Steering :	80	
Braking :	70	
ORIGINAL EQUIPMENT :		**72%**
Tires :	75	
Headlights :	75	
Wipers :	60	
Rear defroster :	75	
Radio :	75	
COMFORT :		**69%**
Seats :	75	
Suspension :	80	
Sound level :	60	
Conveniences :	50	
Air conditioning :	80	
BUDGET :		**59%**
Price :	30	
Fuel economy :	75	
Insurance :	45	
Satisfaction :	90	
Depreciation :	55	
Overall rating :		**69.4%**

New 2000 Model

Medium

NEW FOR 2000

- New model, very close to the previous generation from the mechanical standpoint.

Compare Performance, Specifications, Prices, and Classification at the end of this chapter.

EQUIPMENT

NISSAN Maxima	GXE	SE	GLE
Automatic transmission:	O	O	S
Cruise control:	S	S	S
Power steering:	S	S	S
Anti-lock brakes:	S	S	S
Traction control:	-	-	S
Air conditioning:	SM	SA	SA
Leather:	-	SH	SH
AM/FM/radio-cassette:	S	SCd	SCd
Power door locks:	S	S	S
Power windows:	S	S	S
Tilt steering:	S	S	S
Dual adjustable mirrors:	SEH	SEH	SEH
Alloy wheels:	O	S	S
Anti-theft system:	S	S	S

Colors

Exterior: Mahogany, Olive Green, Sand, Ebony, White, Blue, Silver.

Interior: Grey-Green, Charcoal, Beige.

AT A GLANCE...

HISTORIC

Introduced in:	1981-1995.
Made in:	Oppama & Tochigi, Japan.

DEMOGRAPHICS

Model	Men./Wom.	Age	Married	College	Income $
Maxima	83/17 %	51	83 %	62 %	64,500

INDEX

Safety:	80 %	Satisfaction:	90 %
Depreciation:	47 %	Insurance:	$ 800
Cost per mile:	$ 0.50	Number of dealers:	1,100

SALES

Model	Canada 1997	1998	Result	USA 1997	1998	Result
Maxima	7,194	6,022	- 16.3 %	123,215	113,843	- 7.6 %

MAINTENANCE REQUIRED BY WARRANTY

First revision:	Frequency:	Diagnostic plug:
7,500 miles	7,500 miles	Yes

Medium cars

It took Saturn a while to realize that slowly but surely, the market was shifting from subcompacts to compacts, and then to midsized cars. But the light has finally dawned, and the S now has a big sister: the L. Searching through its worldwide inventory of parts and technical solutions, GM has assembled a model that theoretically has all the qualities needed to grab a few tens of thousands of sales from the Toyota Camry and Honda Accord, maybe even without their knowing it before it's too late!

MODEL RANGE

The Saturn L is available as a 4-door sedan or wagon, in LS, LS1 and LS2 versions for the sedan and as an LW1 or LW2 for the wagon. The LS, LS1 and LW1 have a standard 2.2L 4-cylinder engine and a manual (sedan) or automatic (wagon) transmission. The LS2 and LW2 are entering the fray with a 3.0L V6 and 4-speed automatic transmission. The LS sedan's equipment is limited to power steering, a tilt steering column, air conditioning and manually adjustable sideview mirrors. The "1" versions are more elaborate, adding cruise control, most common power systems and an antitheft system. Alloy wheels and a CD player are featured on "2" versions, but in all cases antilock brakes and traction control are optional.

TECHNICAL FEATURES

Designing the "big" Saturn required the global resources amassed by General Motors and their platform and V6 engine are derived from those found on the Opel Vectra, which like the Saturn L models are front-wheel drives. The 4-cylinder engine is a variation of the 1.9 used on the

An Honest Proposition

Saturn S and the V6 comes from England. The 5-speed manual and automatic transmission coupled with the 2.2L are derived from the Saab 9[3] and Saturn S respectively, and the manual teamed with the V6 comes from the Opel. Their main structure is made of galvanized steel at critical points and is protected by Dupont's Coremax II Plus ELPO coating. Roof, hood and trunk panels are steel and the fenders and doors are covered with plastic paneling. Both body types offer good aerodynamics, with a drag coefficient of approximately 0.31. Suspensions are independent, with MacPherson struts in the front and multi-links in the rear. Both are equipped with stabilizer bars, coil springs and gas shocks absorbers.

PROS

+ STYLING. Though it may not be miraculous, it does have the advantage of making these models immediately identifiable as members of the Saturn family, which is a good beginning. These newcomers' simple and conservative lines will be in style for a good while to come. Interior design is of the same ilk and similar to what you find on the S models. Versions featuring leather trims are particularly appealing, both to the eye and to the touch.

+ DESIGN. By adopting the principle of a structure supporting body panels, including side polymer panels, Saturn has confirmed its technical commitment to build vehicles that keep their good looks over the years.

+ SUSPENSION. It's an excellent compromise between comfort and handling. Smooth but not soft, it's relatively neutral when cornering at average speeds and it provides a comfortable ride.

+ PERFORMANCE. Levels are very respectable with both the 3.0L and 2.2L and manual transmission. Acceleration is strong.

+ BRAKES. Power is reliable, efficient and consistent and on the test drive models equipped with optional ABS, we detected no fading.

+ TRUNK. It's roomy in all directions and the rear seat folds down for extra space. Its opening is average-sized, but the floor dips down to 5 in. (12 cm) below the sill line.

+ QUALITY. This vehicle's careful assembly and nice-looking materials provide a solid feel and look for both the body and the passenger compartment, less utilitarian than those found on some Japanese competitors.

CONS

- NOISE LEVEL. It's strangely high because of engine and tire noise and wind that leaks in around the top of the windshield at speeds of 60 mph.

- EFFICIENCY. When the 4-cylinder engine is teamed with the automatic transmission it's marginal, and performance levels fail to justify its fuel consumption.

- HANDLING. In spite of an average turning radius, the L models offer minimal handling ease and some parking maneuvers are painful.

- WAGON CARGO SPACE. Because its height is limited by the windshield design, it can barely take on as much as the sedan's trunk.

- STORAGE SPACES. They're limited to the minimum; the glove box is not very big, door pockets aren't deep and the console space is narrow and low. In the back, they're limited to two small catchalls and two cupholders.

- TIRES. The Firestone Affinity tires aren't the best choice for these models - they lack grip and generate noise. The V6 engines call for high-performance alternatives.

- OVERSIGHTS. Front seats have no armrests, instrumentation includes no gear indicator for the automatic transmission and no dummy pedal has been included to add to the driver's comfort.

CONCLUSION

Fair is fair: Saturn has introduced a product that is on the same technical level as its competitors, in a sober and tasteful package. The next step is proving these models' reliability and correcting its oversights as soon as possible.

New 2000 Model

RATING
SATURN L

CONCEPT :		79%
Technology :	80	
Safety :	90	
Interior space :	65	
Trunk volume :	80	
Quality/fit/finish :	80	

DRIVING :		65%
Cockpit :	80	
Performance :	50	
Handling :	55	
Steering :	80	
Braking :	60	

ORIGINAL EQUIPMENT :		68%
Tires :	70	
Headlights :	75	
Wipers :	45	
Rear defroster :	70	
Radio :	80	

COMFORT :		63%
Seats :	75	
Suspension :	70	
Sound level :	45	
Conveniences :	50	
Air conditioning :	75	

BUDGET :		65%
Price :	50	
Fuel economy :	80	
Insurance :	50	
Satisfaction :	75	
Depreciation :	70	

Overall rating :		68.0%

NEW FOR 2000

• Saturn's second model will try to capture part of the market for North America's bestselling cars.

Compare Performance, Specifications, Prices, and Classification at the end of this chapter.

EQUIPMENT

SATURN L sedan wagon	LS	LS1	LS2 LW1	LW2
Automatic transmission:	O	O	S S	S
Cruise control:	-	S	S S	S
Power steering:	S	S	S S	S
Anti-lock brakes:	O	O	O O	O
Traction control:	O	O	O O	O
Air conditioning:	S	S	S S	S
Leather:	-	O	O O	O
AM/FM/radio-cassette:	O	S	SCd S	SCd
Power door locks:	-	S	S S	S
Power windows:	-	S	S S	S
Tilt steering:	S	S	S S	S
Dual adjustable mirrors:	SM	SEH	SEH SEH	SEH
Alloy wheels:	-	O	S O	S
Anti-theft system:	-	S	S S	S

Colors

Exterior: White, Gold, Black.

Interior: Grey, Beige.

AT A GLANCE...

HISTORIC
Introduced in: 2000.
Made in: Wilmington, Delaware, USA.

DEMOGRAPHICS

Model	Men./Wom.	Age	Married	College	Income $
SATURN L NA					

INDEX

Safety:	90 %	Satisfaction:	75 %
Depreciation:	70 %	Insurance:	$ 735
Cost per mile:	$ 0.45	Number of dealers:	300

SALES

		Canada			USA	
Model	1997	1998	Result	1997	1998	Result
SATURN L		Not on sale during this period				

MAINTENANCE REQUIRED BY WARRANTY

First revision:	Frequency:	Diagnostic plug:
3,000 miles	6,000 miles	Yes

In The Lead

Overtaking the Ford Taurus and the Honda Accord, the Toyota Camry has taken the lead in automobile sales in North America with more than 450,000 units finding buyers in the United States and Canada alone. Its success is nothing accidental, nor is it the result of clever but deceptive marketing. It's mainly due to this model's intrinsic qualities and its builder's solid reputation, recognized throughout the world and based on its products' reliability and durability.

MODEL RANGE

The Camry is sold as a 4-door sedan in CE, CE V6, LE and XLE V6 trim. The Solara is a two-door, four-passenger coupe sold in SE, SE V6 and SLE. The CE, LE and SE models are equipped with a 2.2L 4-cylinder engine that develops 137 hp, but the other versions receive a 3.0L V6 that develops 194 hp. The 5-speed manual transmission is part of the original equipment with the 4-cylinder, as is the 4-speed automatic with the V6. Standard equipment on the base model only includes power steering, two airbags, tilt steering wheel and intermittent wipers.

TECHNICAL FEATURES

The steel monocoque bodies of these vehicles was really beefed up and reinforced, including items such as floor, steering column, doors and front and rear extremities to absorb impact in the event of a collision. Its aerodynamic finesse was improved without spending megabucks, lowering the drag coefficient from 0.33 to 0.30 so as to reduce wind noise and improve fuel efficiency. The independent suspensions still consist of MacPherson struts, yet they're more sophisticated to provide more accurate steering and crisper wheeltrain precision. Brakes are disc and drum on the 4-cylinder models, while the V6-powered models are equipped with four-wheel disc brakes. ABS is standard on all models except the base CE. Traction control is optional on the SLE coupe and XLE V6. This system can be deactivated by flicking a switch on the instrument panel.

PROS

+ APPEARANCE. The latest remodelled version is more mod-looking and more refined, so the Camry looks like it's smaller than it actually is, and it does bear a resemblance to the Honda Accord.

+ DRIVING PLEASURE. It's due to the smooth blend of various controls: sprightly steering, accurate brakes, performance output for both model engines and especially those of the V6 that can be super silky at cruising speed, but a raging bull on accelerations or pickup.

+ QUALITY. It exudes from every single pore of the Solara. Assembly is tight, over-all design and finish details are flawless and trim materials such as the plastic components and faux-bois accents are attractive.

+ RIDE COMFORT. The cabin space has a lot to do with it, since four or five passengers can be more than comfortably accommodated, without feeling cramped. Ride comfort derives from the neat-design, thickly upholstered seats, more velvety suspension with the more generous wheel travel, that really takes care of road faults. Noise level has been turned down so low that wind and road noise seems louder than it really is.

+ ROADHOLDING. The car stays neutral forever, in spite of moderate sway generated by the flexible suspension and car path is predictable in most situations at regular speeds.

+ DEPENDABILITY. It's the number one asset of this Japanese brand that has developed a quality control approach over the years that sparked people's imagination. Being equipped with such durable components earns the Camry high owner satisfaction rates.

+ CONVENIENCE FEATURES. This aspect is obvious with all the storage spots scattered around the front seats and the roomy trunk that connects with the cabin by lowering the split-folding rear seatbench.

CONS

- DESIGN. It's pretty plain both inside and out of the Camry. Some instrument panel components don't seem to have as tight a fit as before and some plastic trim of the same shade is slightly different in color on some models, confirming that the Camry isn't a luxury car, in spite of its price tag. This sort of universal, generic style doesn't generate any emotion, but it will stay in style for years.

- STEERING. It's over-assisted, so it's light and sensitive to the slightest breeze, which can be a worry on slippery surfaces or when you're swerving to avoid a mishap.

- MANUAL GEARBOX. Synchronization is sluggish and even if it gives the V6 a certain temperament, it doesn't seem to be the kind of option that the targeted clientele will choose. Besides, gears are spaced too far apart, the clutch control is sometimes brutal and pedal travel is too short.

- TIRES. The original tires are very slippery on damp roads and it would be a darn good idea to exchange them for better-quality tires the first chance you get.

- SUSPENSION. It goes haywire even on the tiniest bump, so the front end often takes a nosedive and wheels really lose their adherence.

- TO BE IMPROVED UPON. No adjustable air vents for rear seat passengers and full-size spare tire that's hard to get to since the rug and cover aren't easy to remove. We'd also like to see a better-quality sound system more in keeping with the retail price.

CONCLUSION

While the Camry continues to shatter sales records in this category, much like its Honda counterpart, the Solara coupe doesn't fare nearly as well. What can more can be said: the Camry is the perfect stereotype of the ideal end-of-the-century car.

RATING
TOYOTA Camry-Solara

CONCEPT :   75%
- Technology : 80
- Safety : 80
- Interior space : 70
- Trunk volume : 65
- Quality/fit/finish : 80

DRIVING :   68%
- Cockpit : 80
- Performance : 60
- Handling : 60
- Steering : 80
- Braking : 60

ORIGINAL EQUIPMENT :   75%
- Tires : 80
- Headlights : 80
- Wipers : 55
- Rear defroster : 80
- Radio : 80

COMFORT :   78%
- Seats : 80
- Suspension : 80
- Sound level : 70
- Conveniences : 80
- Air conditioning : 80

BUDGET :   65%
- Price : 50
- Fuel economy : 70
- Insurance : 60
- Satisfaction : 90
- Depreciation : 55

Overall rating :   72.2%

NEW FOR 2000
- 4-lamp headlights in a redesigned grille.
- Redesigned taillights and bumpers.
- 16-inch tires on alloy wheels on the XLE.
- Standard on all models: hood struts, carpets and mudguards.

Compare Performance, Specifications, Prices, and Classification at the end of this chapter.

EQUIPMENT

TOYOTA Camry	CE	CE V6	LE	XLE			
TOYOTA Solara					SE	SE V6	SLE
Automatic transmission:	O	S	S	S	S	O	S
Cruise control:	S	S	S	S	S	S	S
Power steering:	S	S	S	S	S	S	S
Anti-lock brakes:	-	S	S	S	O	S	S
Traction control:	-	-	-	O	-	-	O
Air conditioning:	S	S	S	S	S	S	S
Leather:	-	-	-	O	O	O	O
AM/FM/radio-cassette:	SCd	SCd	SCd	SCd	SCd	SCd	SCd
Power door locks:	S	S	S	S	S	S	S
Power windows:	S	S	S	S	S	S	S
Tilt steering:	S	S	S	S	S	S	S
Dual adjustable mirrors:	SE	SE	SEH	SEH	SE	SEH	SEH
Alloy wheels:	-	-	-	S	O	O	S
Anti-theft system:	-	-	-	S	O	O	S

Colors
Exterior: White, Sage, Black, Wood, Champagne, Red, Sand.

Interior: Grey, Oak, Sage.

AT A GLANCE...

HISTORIC
Introduced in: 1983-1997.
Made in: Camry: Georgetown, KY, USA, Solara: Cambridge, ON, Canada

DEMOGRAPHICS

Model	Men./Wom.	Age	Married	College	Income $
Camry	66/34 %	53	83 %	52 %	45,000
Solara	NA				

INDEX
Safety: 80 %   Satisfaction: 95 %
Depreciation: 45 %   Insurance: $ 565 -665
Cost per mile: $ 0.47   Number of dealers: 1,233

SALES

Model	Canada 1997	1998	Result	USA 1997	1998	Result
Camry	24,270	22,827	- 5.9 %	397,156	429,575	+ 8.2 %
Solara		Not on sale during this period.				

MAINTENANCE REQUIRED BY WARRANTY
First revision: 3,500 miles   Frequency: 3,500 miles   Diagnostic plug: Yes

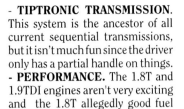

A Prodigal Son

Since its was revamped on the same platform as the Audi A4, the Passat has seen its sales increase dramatically. Previous figures were virtually nonexistent — the public had become very wary of the last generation's capabilities. Less utilitarian than it used to be, its latest presentation and equipment packages give the Passat a luxury connotation, something sorely lacking in the past, especially on a model sold at this price.

MODEL RANGE
The Passat comes in 4-door sedans and station wagons in GLS trim, equipped with a turbocharged 1.8L 4-cylinder or 1.9 TDI engines and in GLX trim, animated by a 2.8L V6. The five-speed manual transmission is standard and the Tiptronic automatic is optional (standard equipment on the GLX) with gas engines only. Original items on the GLS include power steering, cruise control, manual climate control, dual airbags, radio and tape deck, power locks, windows, an antilock braking system, mirrors and a theft-deterrent system. The GLX receives all of the above, as well as alloy wheels, sunroof and leather trim.

TECHNICAL FEATURES
The Passat's steel unibody benefits from topnotch aerodynamics, yielding a drag coefficient of 0.27. In keeping with current trends, the much more rigid body is more resistant to flexion and torsion. The new front suspension, derived from that of the A4, includes four pivoting control arms located so as to eliminate torque transmission to the steering system during strong accelerations. The semi-independent rear wheels are affixed to a torsion axle that's mounted on self-leveling components capable of a slight turn angle when there's lateral pull, so it helps cornering into curves and procures stable demeanor during quick lane changes.

PROS
+ LOOKS. The last Passat has more flair than the previous one and it has a more energetic character. These stylistic changes have brought the drag coefficient to an amazing 0.27. But one mustn't be fooled, for it's a touched-up Audi A4...

+ CHOICE. Customers can choose between two body styles, three very different engine models and two trim levels, so everyone can find what they're looking for.

+ PERFORMANCES. The V6 is really the only engine that puts the Passat nicely through its paces, for the 1.8T and 1.9TDI achieve far less impressive accelerations and pickup.

+ CABIN SPACE. It's well proportioned to vehicle size and passengers have lots of room all-round, but the trunk is actually a bit smaller than on the previous model.

+ HANDLING. It's taut and neutral at normal speeds on good roads or slightly rough surfaces and understeer is only felt in extreme situations. The new suspension is the master mind behind this improved behavior, along with the precise steering, so you can take wide or tight curves with accuracy.

+ BRAKES. They do their stuff and the below-average emergency stopping distances prove it. Pedal effort is easy to gauge as well.

+ STEERING. It's responsive and accurate, benefitting from a good reduction ratio and power function and the short steer angle diameter allows for slick moves.

+ INSTRUMENT PANEL. It's quite lovely, more so than before, and it's more ergonomic and logical as well.

+ QUALITY. Assembly is robust, fit and finish are carefully executed and posh trim materials are in keeping with the Germanic tradition. Besides, the over-all design is much more attractive and the instrument panel has a lot of class.

+ RIDE COMPORT. The suspension isn't flexible, in the American sense of the term, but it benefits from more generous travel than was the case and seats are more plush. Noise heard inside the cabin varies with the engine model.

+ CONVENIENCE FEATURES. The nice and square trunk holds lots of luggage, but inside the cabin, there are just the required number of storage compartments, mostly in the front seat area.

CONS
- STEERING. It's very imprecise and its off-the-wall reaction makes it seem as if the car is floating along. This is due in part to a soft front suspension that hops on bad road surfaces. A long turning radius (the longest in this class) has a negative effect on handling.

- TIRES. The Continental Contact tires on our test car are to be avoided like the plague. They provide only poor grip and they're noisy as heck.

- TIPTRONIC TRANSMISSION. This system is the ancestor of all current sequential transmissions, but it isn't much fun since the driver only has a partial handle on things.

- PERFORMANCE. The 1.8T and 1.9TDI engines aren't very exciting and the 1.8T allegedly good fuel economy is questionable.

- VISIBILITY. It's average, since the bulky headrests and thick C pillar get in the way.

- NOISE LEVEL. It's high with all the wind whistling around the windshield (strange with such a good Cx) and road noise is transmitted via the wheel housings and the 4-cylinder engines roars on accelerations.

- PRESENTATION. The interior is very stark, especially the dashboard, a black monolithic structure that is virtually flat and that jars with the passenger compartment's other design features.

- TO BE IMPROVED UPON. The cockpit is adequate, but it takes a while to get comfy behind the wheel. The digital screen is absolutely illegible in bright sunlight, the orange-colored instruments are tough to decipher and the radio dials are located below the air conditioning controls.

CONCLUSION
The renewed confidence buyers are showing towards Volkswagen products in general and the Passat in particular tends to prove that the leading European car builder's designers have done their homework. It remains to be seen if reliability will be satisfactory and if service outlets will succeed in making owners feel secure.

RATING
VOLKSWAGEN Passat

CONCEPT :		75%
Technology :	80	
Safety :	80	
Interior space :	65	
Trunk volume :	70	
Quality/fit/finish :	80	

DRIVING :		72%
Cockpit :	80	
Performance :	60	
Handling :	65	
Steering :	80	
Braking :	75	

ORIGINAL EQUIPMENT :		73%
Tires :	75	
Headlights :	80	
Wipers :	60	
Rear defroster :	75	
Radio :	75	

COMFORT :		75%
Seats :	80	
Suspension :	75	
Sound level :	60	
Conveniences :	80	
Air conditioning :	80	

BUDGET :		55%
Price :	40	
Fuel economy :	60	
Insurance :	45	
Satisfaction :	80	
Depreciation :	50	

Overall rating :		70.0%

NEW FOR 2000

• Brake wear indicator and improved antitheft system.
• Remote fuel-door release mounted on the door.
• "Cold weather" options package, already standard on the GLX, now optional on the GLS.

Compare
Performance,
Specifications, Prices,
and Classification
at the end of this chapter.

EQUIPMENT

VOLKSWAGEN Passat	GLS 4dr.sdn.	GLS V6 4dr.sdn.	GLX 4dr.sdn.	GLS 4dr.wgn.	GLX 4dr.wgn.
Automatic transmission:	O	O	S	O	S
Cruise control:	S	S	S	S	S
Power steering:	S	S	S	S	S
Anti-lock brakes:	S	S	S	S	S
Traction control:	O	-	S	O	S
Air conditioning:	SM	SM	SA	SM	SA
Leather:	O	O	S	O	S
AM/FM/radio-cassette:	S	S	S	S	S
Power door locks:	S	S	S	S	S
Power windows:	S	S	S	S	S
Tilt steering:	S	S	S	S	S
Dual adjustable mirrors:	SE	SE	SE	SE	SE
Alloy wheels:	O	O	S	O	S
Anti-theft system:	S	S	S	S	S

Colors

Exterior: White, Red, Blue, Green, Grey, Black, Purple, Silver.

Interior: Grey, Black, Blue, Beige.

AT A GLANCE...

HISTORIC
Introduced in:	1973-1998.
Made in:	Emden, Germany.

DEMOGRAPHICS
Model	Men./Wom.	Age	Married	College	Income $
Passat	72/28 %	44	70 %	60 %	$ 40,000

INDEX
Safety:	80 %	Satisfaction:	75 %
Depreciation:	50 %	Insurance:	$ 1,135
Cost per mile:	$ 0.46	Number of dealers:	650

SALES
Model	Canada 1997	1998	Result	USA 1997	1998	Result
Passat	19,850	14,868	- 25.1 %	14,868	39,272	+164.1 %

MAINTENANCE REQUIRED BY WARRANTY
First revision: 3,000 miles	Frequency: 6 months/6,000miles	Diagnostic plug: Yes

MEDIUM CARS
PERFORMANCE

Model/ version	Type / timing valve / fuel system	Displacement cu in	Power hp @ rpm	Torque lb-ft @ rpm	Compres. ratio	Driving wheels / transmission	Final ratio	Acceler. 0-60 mph s	Standing 1/4 & 5/8 mile s	Passing 50-75 mph s	Braking 60-0 ft	Top speed mph	Lateral acceler. G	Noise level dBA	Fuel economy City	mpg Highway	Fuel type Octane
HONDA Accord																	
DX	L4* 2.3 SOHC-16-MPFI	137	135 @ 5400	145 @ 4700	8.8 :1	front - M5*	4.062	9.4	17.2	30.6	6.5	151	109	0.75	67-75	24	33	R 87
						front - A4	4.466	10.2	17.5	31.5	7.8	157	106	0.75	67-74	22	32	R 87
LX-EX	L4* 2.3 SOHC-16-MPFI	137	150 @ 5700	152 @ 4900	9.3 :1	front - M5	4.062	9.0	16.8	30.6	6.4	141	112	0.75	68-76	24	34	R 87
						front - A4*	4.466	9.6	17.2	31.2	7.5	157	109	0.75	66-74	22	31	R 87
SE-EXV6	V6* 3.0 SOHC-24-MPFI	187	200 @ 5500	195 @ 4700	9.4 :1	front - A4	4.200	7.8	15.7	28.8	5.2	138	124	0.77	65-72	20	29	R 87
HYUNDAI Sonata																	
GL	L4 2.4 DOHC-16-MPFI	143	149 @ 5500	156 @ 3000	10.0 :1	front - M5*	3.88	NA										
						front - A4	3.77	10.6	18.0	32.0	7.5	148	109	0.78	65-70	21	31	R 87
GLS	V6 2.5 DOHC-24-MPFI	152	170 @ 6000	166 @ 4000	10.0 :1	front - M5	3.88	NA										
						front - A4*	3.77	9.1	17.0	29.8	6.5	151	124	0.78	65-68	20	29	R 87
NISSAN Maxima																	
GXE,SE	V6* 3.0 DOHC-24-MPSFI	182	222 @ 5600	217 @ 4000	10.0 :1	front - M5*	3.823	8.0	15.7	27.9	5.5	138	137	0.80	66-70	21	27	S 91
GLE						front - A4*	3.789	8.5	16.3	29.2	6.0	147	130	0.80	66-70	20	29	S 91
SATURN L																	
LS,LS1, SW1	L4 2.2 DOHC-16-SPFI	134	137 @ 5800	147 @ 4400	9.5 :1	front - M5*	4.45	9.6	17.3	31.0	6.9	141	109	0.78	67-71	24	32	R 87
						front - A4*	3.91	10.1	17.7	31.6	7.2	144	106	0.78	66-71	23	32	R 87
LS2,LW2	V6 3.0 DOHC-24-SPFI	183	182 @ 5600	190 @ 3600	10.0:1	front - A4*	3.68	8.5	16.6	29.8	6.3	151	112	0.78	65-70	20	26	R 87
TOYOTA Camry - Solara																	
CE	L4* 2.2 DOHC-16-MPSFI	132	136 @ 5200	147 @ 4400	9.5 :1	front - M5*	3.944	10.0	17.7	31.4	7.2	131	112	0.80	67	22	33	R 87
CE, LE						front - A4	3.944	11.3	18.6	32.8	8.6	131	109	0.78	67	21	31	R 87
CE V6,XLE	V6* 3.0 DOHC-24-MPSFI	183	194 @ 5200	209 @ 4400	10.5 :1	front - A4	3.933	8.4	16.5	29.6	6.2	125	131	0.78	66	18	28	R 87
VOLKSWAGEN Passat																	
GLS	L4T* 1.8 DOHC-20-EFI	109	150 @ 5700	155 @ 1750	9.5 :1	front - M5*	3.70	9.0	16.8	29.8	6.4	125	137	0.80	67	23	32	R 87
						front - A5	3.70	10.5	17.2	31.2	6.8	131	131	0.80	67	NA		R 87
GLX	V6* 2.8 DOHC-30-SFI	170	190 @ 6000	206 @ 3200	10.6 :1	front - M5	3.39	8.0	15.6	27.0	5.7	128	141	0.83	66	20	29	R 87
						front - A5*	3.39	9.3	16.7	30.2	6.5	131	137	0.83	66	18	29	M 89
TDI	L4*T1.9 SOHC-8-DI	116	90 @ 3750	149 @ 1900	19.5 :1	front - M5*	3.16	14.5	19.0	37.5	11.5	131	109	0.80	70	31	44	D

SPECIFICATIONS

Model	Version Trim	Body/ Seats	Cabin volume cu ft	Trunk volume cu ft	Cd	Wheel base in	Lgth x Width x Hght in x in x in	Curb weight lb	Susp. ft/rr	Brake ft/rr	Steering type	ø turns ft number	Fuel tank gal	dimensions	Standard tires make	model	Standard powertrain	99 Price msrp $
HONDA		**General warranty: 3 years / 36 000 miles; powertrain: 5 years / 60 000 miles.**																
Accord	LX	2dr.cpe. 5	92.7	13.6	0.32	105.1	186.8x70.3x55.0	2965	ih/ih	dc/ABS	pwr.r&p.	36.1 3.1	17.1		195/65HR15 Bridgestone	Turanza	L4/2.3/M5	18,805
Accord	EX	2dr.cpe. 5	92.7	13.6	0.32	105.1	186.8x70.3x55.0	3009	ih/ih	dc/ABS	pwr.r&p.	36.1 3.1	17.1		195/65HR15 Bridgestone	Potenza E241	L4/2.3/M5	21,135
Accord	EX-V6	2dr.cpe. 5	92.7	13.6	0.32	105.1	186.8x70.3x55.0	3263	ih/ih	dc/ABS	pwr.r&p.	36.1 3.0	17.1		205/60VR16 Michelin	MXV4	V6/3.0/A4	25,715
Accord	DX	4dr.sdn. 5	101.7	14.1	0.33	106.9	188.8x70.3x56.9	2877	ih/ih	dc/dr	pwr.r&p.	36.4 3.1	17.1		195/70SR14 Dunlop	SP40	L4/2.3/M5	15,615
Accord	LX	4dr.sdn. 5	101.7	14.1	0.33	106.9	188.8x70.3x56.9	2976	ih/ih	dc/ABS	pwr.r&p.	36.4 3.1	17.1		195/65HR15 Michelin	MXV4	L4/2.3/M5	18,805
Accord	EX	4dr.sdn. 5	101.7	14.1	0.33	106.9	188.8x70.3x56.9	2877	ih/ih	dc/ABS	pwr.r&p.	36.4 3.1	17.1		195/65HR15 Michelin	MXV4	L4/2.3/M5	21,315
Accord	EX-V6	4dr.sdn. 5	101.7	14.1	0.33	106.9	188.8x70.3x53.3	3285	ih/ih	dc/ABS	pwr.r&p.	36.4 3.0	17.1		205/60VR16 Michelin	MXV4	V6/3.0/A4	24,715
HYUNDAI		**General warranty: 3 years / 36 000 miles; powertrain: 5 years / 60 000 miles; corrosion perforation: 5 years / 60 000 miles; antipollution: 5 years / 36 000 miles.**																
Sonata	GL	4dr.sdn. 5	-	13.2	0.34	106.3	185.4x71.6x55.5	3128	ih/ih	dc/dr	pwr.r&p.	34.5 2.9	17.2		195/70R14 Kumho	SBR 722	L4/2.4/A4	15,434
Sonata	GLS	4dr.sdn. 5	-	13.2	0.34	106.3	185.4x71.6x55.5	3128	ih/ih	dc	pwr.r&p.	34.5 2.9	17.2		205/60R15 Michelin	MXV4	V6/2.5/A4	17,434
NISSAN		**General warranty: 3 years / 50 000 miles; powertrain: 6 years / 60 000 miles; perforation corrosion & antipollution: 6 years / unlimited.**																
Maxima	GXE	4dr.sdn. 5	102.0	15.7	0.32	108.3	190.5x70.3x56.5	3198	ih/ih	dc/ABS	pwr.r&p.	35.4 2.9	18.5		205/65R15 Goodyear	Eagle GA	V6/3.0/M5	22,019
Maxima	SE	4dr.sdn. 5	102.0	15.7	0.32	108.3	190.5x70.3x56.5	3192	ih/ih	dc/ABS	pwr.r&p.	35.4 2.9	18.5		215/55R16 Goodyear	Eagle GA	V6/3.0/A4	24,019
Maxima	GLE	4dr.sdn. 5	102.0	15.7	0.32	108.3	190.5x70.3x56.5	3298	ih/ih	dc/ABS	pwr.r&p.	35.4 2.9	18.5		205/65R15 Goodyear	Eagle GA	V6/3.0/A4	27,419
SATURN		**General warranty: 3 years / 36,000 miles; antipollution: 5 years / 50,000 miles; perforation corrosion: 6 years / 100,000 miles. Roadside assistance.**																
L	S	4dr.sdn. 5	96.9	17.5	0.31	106.5	190.4x69.0x56.4	2910	ih/ih	dc/dr	pwr.r&p.	36.6 2.9	13.1		195/65R15 Firestone	Affinity HP	L4/2.2/M5	-
L	S1	4dr.sdn. 5	96.9	17.5	0.31	106.5	190.4x69.0x56.4	2943	ih/ih	dc/dr	pwr.r&p.	36.6 2.9	13.1		195/65R15 Firestone	Affinity HP	L4/2.2/A4	-
L	S2	4dr.sdn. 5	96.9	17.5	0.31	106.5	190.4x69.0x56.4	3153	ih/ih	dc	pwr.r&p.	36.6 2.9	13.1		205/65R15 Firestone	Affinity HP	V6/3.0/A4	-
L	W1	4dr.wgn. 5	98.7	29.4	0.32	106.5	190.4x69.0x57.3	3075	ih/ih	dc/dr	pwr.r&p.	36.6 2.9	13.1		195/65R15 Firestone	Affinity HP	L4/2.2/A4	-
L	W2	4dr.wgn. 5	98.7	29.4	0.32	106.5	190.4x69.0x57.3	3230	ih/ih	dc	pwr.r&p.	36.6 2.9	13.1		205/65R15 Firestone	Affinity HP	V6/3.0/A4	-
TOYOTA		**General warranty: 3 years / 36 000 miles; powertrain 5 years / 60 000 miles; corrosion, perforation: 5 years / unlimited.**																
Camry	CE	4dr.sdn. 5	96.9	14.1	0.30	105.2	188.5x70.1x55.7	2996	ih/ih	dc/dr	pwr.r&p.	35.4 3.06	18.5		195/70R14 Michelin	MX4	L4/2.2/M5	17,518
Camry	LE	4dr.sdn. 5	96.9	14.1	0.30	105.2	188.5x70.1x55.7	3119	ih/ih	dc/dr	pwr.r&p.	35.4 3.06	18.5		195/70R14 Michelin	MX4	L4/2.2/A4	20,278
Camry	LE V6	4dr.sdn. 5	96.9	14.1	0.30	105.2	188.5x70.1x55.7	3119	ih/ih	dc/dr/ABS	pwr.r&p.	35.4 3.06	18.5		195/70R14 Dunlop	Sport 4000	V6/3.0/A4	22,368
Camry	XLE V6	4dr.sdn. 5	96.9	14.1	0.30	105.2	188.5x70.1x55.9	3247	ih/ih	dc/dr/ABS	pwr.r&p.	36.7 3.06	18.5		205/65R15 Michelin	MX4	L4/2.2/A4	23,238
Camry	XLE V6	4dr.sdn. 5	96.9	14.1	0.30	105.2	188.5x70.1x55.9	3252	ih/ih	dc/dr/ABS	pwr.r&p.	36.7 3.06	18.5		205/65R15 Dunlop	Sport 4000	V6/3.0/A4	25,478
Solara	SE	2dr.cpe. 5	92.1	14.1	0.31	105.1	190.0x71.1x55.1	3120	ih/ih	dc/dr/ABS	pwr.r&p.	38.1 2.88	18.5		205/65R15 Bridgestone	Potenza RE92	L4/2.2/M5	19,118
Solara	SE V6	2dr.cpe. 5	92.1	14.1	0.31	105.1	190.0x71.1x55.1	3263	ih/ih	dc/dr/ABS	pwr.r&p.	38.1 2.88	18.5		205/60R16 Michelin	XW4	V6/3.0/A4	21,668
Solara	SLE	2dr.cpe. 5	92.1	14.1	0.31	105.1	190.0x71.1x55.1	3291	ih/ih	dc/dr/ABS	pwr.r&p.	38.1 2.88	18.5		205/60R16 Michelin	XW4	V6/3.0/A4	25,468
VOLKSWAGEN		**General warranty: 2 years / 25 000 miles; powertrain: 5 years / 50 000 miles; antipollution: 6 years/ 50 000 miles; corrosion perforation: 6 years.**																
Passat	GLS	4dr.sdn. 5	95.3	15.0	0.27	106.3	184.0x68.5x57.5	3122	ih/sih	dc/ABS	pwr.r&p.	37.4 2.8	18.5		195/65R15 Continental	Touring	L4T/1.8/M5	21,725
Passat	GLS V6	4dr.sdn. 5	95.3	15.0	0.27	106.3	184.0x68.5x57.5	3375	ih/sih	dc/ABS	pwr.r&p.	37.4 2.8	18.5		195/65R15 -	-	V6/2.8/A5	24,325
Passat	GLX V6 awd	4dr.sdn. 5	95.3	15.0	0.27	106.6	184.0x68.5x57.5	3580	ih/sih	dc/ABS	pwr.r&p.	37.4 2.8	18.5		195/65R15 -	-	V6/2.8/A5	28,675
Passat	GLS	4dr.wgn. 5	95.3	38.8	0.30	106.3	183.8x68.5x59.0	3201	ih/sih	dc/ABS	pwr.r&p.	37.4 2.8	18.5		195/65R15 -	-	L4T/1.8/M5	22,275
Passat	GLS V6 awd	4dr.wgn. 5	95.3	38.8	0.30	106.6	183.8x68.5x59.0	3653	ih/sih	dc/ABS	pwr.r&p.	37.4 2.8	18.5		195/65R15 -	-	V6/2.8/A5	-

Notes: 1) Tire makes and models are provided solely as an indication; they are subject to change without prior notice from the automobile manufacturers.
2) See the 2000 price list at the back of this edition.

CLASSIFICATION

OUR CLASSIFICATION

Rank	Models	Concept	Driving	Equipment	Comfort	Budget	Ratings
1	**TOYOTA Camry - Solara**	75	68	75	**78**	65	**72.2 %**
1	**HONDA Accord**	77	66	**78**	74	66	**72.2 %**
2	VW Passat	75	**72**	73	75	55	70.0 %
3	NISSAN Maxima	76	71	72	69	59	69.4 %
4	HYUNDAI Sonata	71	65	69	69	**67**	68.2 %
5	SATURN L	**79**	65	68	63	63	68.0 %

YOUR CLASSIFICATION

Rank	Models	98 Sales
1	TOYOTA Camry	429,575
2	HONDA Accord	401,071
3	NISSAN Maxima	113,843
4	VW Passat	39,272
5	HYUNDAI Sonata	13,955

Not classified:
SATURN L

Medium

Comparative Test

MID-SIZE CARS

See their performance, their specifications, their price
and their classification at the end of this chapter.

BUICK Century-Regal

FORD Taurus-Sable

OLDSMOBILE Intrigue

PONTIAC Grand Prix

TOYOTA Avalon

Problem-free

The Buick Century and Regal were among the very first models to benefit from the new quality policy adopted by General Motors. To check the erosion of its market share, the world's leading automobile manufacturer had no other choice but to fall into step with its Japanese competitors, all of whom had long since adopted quality and durability as their watchwords. Reaching beyond finish quality and component design, the quality approach also touches on the detailed study and perfecting of the individual model in question.

MODEL RANGE

The Century has really become the lower end model in the Buick line since the demise of the Skylark, but it's especially suited to the fleet car and car rental market niche. The Regal is more geared to scoring against the Camry and Accord, its more obviously targeted rivals. These four-door sedans are offered in Custom or Limited trim for the Century and in LS or GS for the Regal. The first two models are equipped with a 175 hp 3.1L V6 engine, while the third model gets the umpteenth version of the legendary 3.8L atmospheric gas engine delivering 200 hp or the supercharged version that pumps out 240 hp. Standard equipment on these cars is quite lush, even on the low end version, since it includes automatic transmission, power steering, ABS, traction control, climate control, power windows and locks, tilt steering wheel and theft deterrent system.

TECHNICAL FEATURES

The Century-Regal models are built on the latest revamped W platform and are equipped with the same steel unibody fitted with numerous panels galvanized on both sides except for the roof panel. These cars are sleek, but aerodynamics aren't record-shattering by any means, not with a drag coefficient of 0.32. The fully independent suspension is made up of a MacPherson strut setup up front and struts at the rear with a stabilizer bar on both axels. The Century is equipped with disc/drum brakes, whereas the Regal comes with four-wheel disc brakes; yet ABS linked to traction control is standard on both models. The front wheel drive feature has been around for many years. Yet it's the 3.8L engine that's the outstanding element because of its well-reputed reliability and sheer muscle, in either atmospheric or supercharged format. Climate control includes a dust and pollen filter system, the battery has an anti-discharge control switch, a device prevents the starter from working when the engine is running and variable assist steering comes standard on the Regal but as an extra on the Century Limited.

PROS

+ VALUE. The fact that so much equipment comes at such an affordable price makes even the most basic car very appealing indeed and explains why the car manages to maintain an above-average resale value.

+ STYLE. The Century and Regal are elegant and very much in keeping with a classic approach, with no added frills, so they shouldn't go out of style for many a moon.

+ RIDE COMFORT. The roomy cabin comfortably seats five passengers. Seats are nicely shaped and upholstered and the noise level is decent, since discreet.

+ FUEL ECONOMY. These engines have been around for quite a while, yet fuel intake is frugal considering engine performance range. The zippy 3.8L supercharged engine accelerates better than several so-called sporty cars and gives it the few precious seconds' edge, yet this powerplant is known for its pristine reliability.

+ QUALITY. Although some progress could be made in terms of presentation and the texture of the materials used, these models have made serious inroads in meeting the standards that Japanese products have set for assembly quality and component reliability. They also offer thicker panels that are more rust-resistant over the long term.

+ ROADHANDLING. Thanks to firmer suspensions and good-quality shocks, the Regal handles well in most circumstances.

+ BRAKES. The Regal, equipped with four-wheel disc brakes, stops in a reassuring way, since panic stops at 60 mph are achieved on average in slightly more than 135ft. The brake pedal is clean and gradual, so brake control is easy to manage.

+ CONVENIENCE FEATURES. This is a great car for practical, everyday use. There are loads of storage compartments and the trunk is really roomy and easy to get to with the nice and wide trunk lid.

+ NICE FEATURES. For once it's a pleasure to point out that headlights really cut it either on low or high beam, that rather quick and slick windshield wipers clean most of the window surface and that climate control is quick on the draw in providing heat or cold, although the blower is a bit weak.

CONS

- SUSPENSION. The suspension that equips the Century is so spongy that it reminds you of those dreamboats of yore. The ride is smooth on the ribbon of highway, but elsewhere you're in for a rough trip, since there's a whole lot of swaying going on, which ends up affecting handling and comfort level on curved roads or rough surfaces. Seasickness guaranteed.

- BRAKES. Rear drum brakes on the Century don't provide for really effective stops compared to those achieved by the four-wheel disc brakes on the Regal. Emergency stops stretch out and linings just don't hold up to intensive use.

- TIRES. The original General tires that equip the Century aren't the perfect fit for this car, since grip gets pretty wishy washy on slippery surfaces.

- TO BE IMPROVED UPON. The Century's hohum cabin interior, air vents, multi-control shifter that's so complicated it's a real pain to use, stubby speed shifter, no center armrest in the rear seat nor a convertible trunk on the Century.

CONCLUSION

The Century and Regal offer several permutations and combinations of a car designed for Joe or Jane Average, ranging from the soulless lease model to the sleek and sporty sedan. They are a serious alternative to the Japanese divas, often more expensive and less inspired. And into the bargain, they can boast problem-free reliability and durability.

RATING
BUICK Century - Regal

CONCEPT :		77%
Technology :	75	
Safety :	80	
Interior space :	75	
Trunk volume :	75	
Quality/fit/finish :	80	

DRIVING :		69%
Cockpit :	80	
Performance :	70	
Handling :	55	
Steering :	80	
Braking :	60	

ORIGINAL EQUIPMENT :		77%
Tires :	75	
Headlights :	85	
Wipers :	70	
Rear defroster :	75	
Radio :	80	

COMFORT :		74%
Seats :	75	
Suspension :	80	
Sound level :	60	
Conveniences :	75	
Air conditioning :	80	

BUDGET :		61%
Price :	45	
Fuel economy :	65	
Insurance :	65	
Satisfaction :	80	
Depreciation :	50	

Overall rating :	71.6%

NEW FOR 2000

- More power and torque for the 3.1L V6 engine.
- New electronic automatic transmission.
- Mixed antilock brakes on the Century.
- A 3.8L engine that complies with California standards.
- 4 antilock disc brakes on the Regal GS.

Compare
Performance,
Specifications, Prices,
and Classification
at the end of this chapter.

Mid-Size Cars

EQUIPMENT

BUICK Century BUICK Regal	Custom	Ltd LS	GS
Automatic transmission:	S	S	S	S
Cruise control:	S	S	S	S
Power steering:	S	S	S	S
Anti-lock brakes:	S	S	S	S
Traction control:	S	S	S	S
Air conditioning:	SM	SM	S	S
Leather:	-	O	O	S
AM/FM/radio-cassette:	S	S	SCd	SCd
Power door locks:	S	S	S	S
Power windows:	S	S	S	S
Tilt steering:	S	S	S	S
Dual adjustable mirrors:	SE	SEH	SEH	SEH
Alloy wheels:	O	O	O	S
Anti-theft system:	S	S	S	S

Colors

Exterior: White, Blue, Black, Red, Green, Sand, Silver, Gold.

Interior: Grey, Blue, Red, Taupe.

AT A GLANCE...

HISTORIC
Introduced in: Century: 1981   Regal: 1987; renewed in 1997.
Made in: Oshawa, Ontario, Canada.

DEMOGRAPHICS

Model	Men./Wom.	Age	Married	College	Income $
Century	75/25 %	66	80 %	26 %	34,500
Regal	80/20 %	61	77 %	33 %	42,500

INDEX
Safety:	80 %	Satisfaction:	77 %
Depreciation:	50 %	Insurance:	$ 560-650
Cost per mile:	$ 0.54	Number of dealers:	3,000

SALES

Model	Canada 1997	1998	Result	USA 1997	1998	Result
Century	6,436	9,451	+ 48.2 %	91,232	126,220	+ 38.4 %
Regal	3,204	4,815	+ 50.3 %	50,691	65,979	+ 30.2 %

MAINTENANCE REQUIRED BY WARRANTY
First revision:	Frequency:	Diagnostic plug:
3,000 miles	6,000 miles	Yes

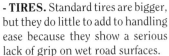
A Second Chance

Things are in a turmoil at Ford, which has realized that it sells more trucks than it does cars. It's about time! After letting its designers stray more and more into New Edge styling for too long — a look that has never been super popular — America's second-largest automobile manufacturer has had to face facts and come back to the drawing board. In the meantime, the Taurus and Sable, former favorites of American car buyers, have seen their sales crumble and have passed on the title of bestselling cars to their Japanese rivals.

MODEL RANGE

Sedans are available in two versions: LX and SE. As for the wagon, it comes only in an SE version. Mercury proposes its sedans and wagons in two finishes: GS and LS. The 3.0L Vulcan V6 is the base engine and the more powerful DOHC Duratec 3.0L V6 is available as an option. All versions have a standard 4-speed automatic transmission, power steering, air conditioning, power windows and power sideview mirrors.

TECHNICAL FEATURES

These new cars feature streamlined styling, but their drag coefficient remains conservative. While the sedans have a number of different design details to differentiate them, the wagons are more similar to one another.

Their steel unibody is one of the most rigid in this market segment and this approach was a top priority in the recent revamping process. The suspension is fully independent, with MacPherson struts. The front-end assembly has been designed to maximize stability and driveability and to counter noise and vibration. The Taurus LX/SE and Sable GS/LS sedans have mixed brakes, while wagons have four disc brakes. In all instances, the ABS system is optional.

PROS

+ STYLING. There's no accounting for taste, but let's just say that because of its more conventional lines, the new look sported by the Taurus-Sable will appeal to a broader range of potential buyers.

+ PRESENTATION. Interior and exterior assembly shows attention to detail. Adjustments are more careful and higher quality materials have been used throughout.

+ PASSENGER ROOM. Wider than before, these models are roomier than their predecessors and they can easily take on five passengers comfortably.

+ BRAKING. While its efficiency is only average during emergency stops, in normal circumstances its power is easy to gauge and slowdowns are progressive and precise.

+ TRUNK. It has more volume and its access is easier thanks to a wider opening. Anchoring systems ensure that baggage isn't jostled around.

+ COMFORT. Although very firm, the suspension is good at swallowing road defects. Seats provide very good support and soundproofing.

+ ORIGINAL FEATURE. Power pedal adjustment makes it easy to find the ideal driving position. A similar feature is found on race cars, whose seats are fixed into place.

+ CLEVER FEATURE. Ford is the first to provide an emergency lid release positioned inside the trunk, designed for use should someone be locked inside accidentally.

+ BONUS POINTS. Compliments go to the new center console that doubles as an armrest and a storage bin. The new models also have more storage spaces, with pockets on each door. Lights are more powerful — by 25% for turn signals and by 34% for high beams.

+ THE "PIZZA". The oval instrument cluster who looks like a pizza and sits in the middle of the dash of the former model, regrouping the sound system and air conditioning controls has finally disappears. It was too confusing and it is replaced par a new organisation, less original perhaps but more practical, more logical and ergonomical and it's a plus for the new model who looks cleaner.

CONS

- DURATEC V6. It's disappointing — the venerable Vulcan can provide very similar performance levels. However, these automobiles have a high weight and this taxes the engine, especially when they travel loaded to capacity.

- TIRES. Standard tires are bigger, but they do little to add to handling ease because they show a serious lack of grip on wet road surfaces.

- BRAKING. It leaves a lot of room for improvement, stopping distances are very long and you have to wonder what Ford is waiting for to equip its sedans with rear discs and a standard antilock system.

- HANDLING. Ford models often have a harder time turning than most of their competitors and the Taurus-Sable cars are no exception to the rule. Worse again, these models have an even longer turning radius than those they're replacing.

- FLAWS. Because of the rear windshield design, 3/4 rear visibility is limited. Windshield wipers aren't fast enough to handle heavy rain. In extreme temperatures, the air conditioning isn't strong enough to cool the passenger compartment efficiently.

CONCLUSION

By keeping what buyers liked and by getting rid of what hindered these two models, Ford is giving them a second chance to regain lost ground. There's a risk to being ahead of your time and there's a price to pay when the gamble doesn't pay off. Time will tell if the public — which always has the last word — will accept the corporation's attempt to make amends.

New 2000 Model

RATING
FORD Taurus - MERCURY Sable

CONCEPT :		80%
Technology :	80	
Safety :	100	
Interior space :	75	
Trunk volume :	70	
Quality/fit/finish :	75	

DRIVING :		63%
Cockpit :	70	
Performance :	60	
Handling :	55	
Steering :	70	
Braking :	60	

ORIGINAL EQUIPMENT :		71%
Tires :	75	
Headlights :	75	
Wipers :	60	
Rear defroster :	70	
Radio :	75	

COMFORT :		68%
Seats :	70	
Suspension :	75	
Sound level :	65	
Conveniences :	50	
Air conditioning :	80	

BUDGET :		54%
Price :	35	
Fuel economy :	60	
Insurance :	50	
Satisfaction :	75	
Depreciation :	50	

Overall rating :		67.2%

NEW FOR 2000

- All-new front and rear styling.
- More horsepower and torque for the base Vulcan V6 engine.
- Larger standard wheels and tires.
- Power adjustable accelerator and brake pedals.
- Additional power point and cup holders.

Compare
Performance,
Specifications, Prices,
and Classification
at the end of this chapter.

EQUIPMENT

FORD Taurus MERCURY Sable	LX 4dr.sdn.	SE 4dr.wgn.	SE 4dr.sdn.	SHO 4dr.sdn.	GS 4dr.sdn.	LS 4dr.sdn.
Automatic transmission:	S	S	S	S	S	S
Cruise control:	O	S	S	S	S	S
Power steering:	S	S	S	S	S	S
Anti-lock brakes:	O	O	O	S	O	O
Traction control:	-	O	O	S	O	O
Air conditioning:	SM	SM	SM	SA	SM	SM
Leather:	-	-	-	S	-	-
AM/FM/radio-cassette:	O	S	S	S	S	S
Power door locks:	O	S	S	S	S	S
Power windows:	S	S	S	S	S	S
Tilt steering:	S	S	S	S	S	S
Dual adjustable mirrors:	SE	SE	SE	SEH	SE	SE
Alloy wheels:	O	O	O	S	O	S
Anti-theft system:	S	S	S	S	S	S

Colors
Exterior: Gold, Red, Green, Blue, Silver, Black, White.

Interior: Medium graphite, Brown, Blue.

AT A GLANCE...

HISTORIC
Introduced in:	1986, 1996.
Made in:	Atlanta, Georgia & Chicago, Illinois, USA.

DEMOGRAPHICS
Model	Men./Wom.	Age	Married	College	Income $
Taurus	73/27 %	62	82 %	40 %	35,000
Sable	75/25 %	61	85 %	46 %	40,500

INDEX
Safety:	100 %	Satisfaction:	73 %
Depreciation:	52 %	Insurance:	$ 585 -785
Cost per mile:	$ 0.48-0.57	Number of dealers:	5,200

SALES
	Canada			USA		
Model	1997	1998	Result	1997	1998	Result
Taurus	23,250	23,547	+ 1.3 %	357,162	371,074	+ 3.9 %
Sable	10,838	11,268	+ 4.0 %	112,400	100,367	- 10.7 %

MAINTENANCE REQUIRED BY WARRANTY
First revision:	Frequency:	Diagnostic plug:
5,000 miles	6 months / 5,000 miles	Yes

Magic Potion

After the Aurora, the Intrigue is the model that has contributed the most to Oldsmobile's rebirth. Although not revolutionary, it has been carefully designed and is styled and equipped to convince the public that General Motors is once again capable of manufacturing quality cars. While it shares a number of mechanical components with other models in the W family, the Intrigue has a charm all its own and it's reflected in its sales figures, aided and abetted by a more than intriguing advertising campaign.

MODEL RANGE

The Intrigue is available in the form of a 4-door sedan, with three finish levels: GX, GL and GLS. This year, all are equipped with the recently introduced 3.5L V6 engine and an electronic 4-speed automatic transmission. Another innovation, this year the three versions are available with an "Autobahn" options package including tires with an "H" speed rating and more powerful brakes (12-inch front discs and a different brake booster system). The base GX's standard equipment is very detailed. It includes four disc brakes, an ABS system, air conditioning, and alloy wheels; the GL adds a power adjustable bucket seat for the driver, a 60/40 folding rear eat, antifog lights and heated sideview mirrors; the GLS offers leather upholstery, a power adjustable passenger bucket seat, fake wood inlays, a sound system with AM/FM cassette and CD players and an automatic day/night rearview mirror.

TECHNICAL FEATURES

The Intrigue has a steel unibody. All panels are galvanized on both sides, except the roof. With a drag coefficient of 0.32, aerodynamics are in the average range. The four-wheel independent suspension consists of MacPherson struts up front and a three-link setup at the rear. There are coil springs and an anti-roll bar at each extremity. Disc brakes, an antilock braking system and traction control are standard features, as is the latest Magnasteer II, a progressive, variable assist system.

PROS

+ STYLE. Inspired as well by the Aurora, the Intrigue is elegant and its distinctive looks attract passersby, especially when clad in dark shades that really add class.

+ PERFORMANCES. The new 3.5L DOHC V6 bestows on the Intrigue a trait that was really lacking: an engine worthy of its chassis and sophisticated suspensions. With 215 hp, accelerations and pickup are akin to those of the Regal supercharged model. The newcomer lets you really let loose at the wheel, without adversely affecting fuel economy, since fuel consumption sat at around 19 mpg during our road test.

+ RIDE COMFORT. On the highway the Intrigue behaves like an import. The suspension is perfectly adjusted and disguises road faults like magic. And the thickly upholstered seats provide lots of support, which adds to travel pleasure.

+ HANDLING. The Intrigue takes curves with superb assurance, thanks to the effective suspension and tires that have excellent grip on wet or dry surfaces.

+ EQUIPMENT. It's one of the most detailed in the industry, even on the base model. GM has come a long way in this regard — not long ago its models were sold stripped to the bone and buyers had to pick and choose among options, with disastrous effects on pricing.

+ QUALITY. The Intrigue is a superior quality model, very near to the Aurora. Adjustment tolerances are stringent and components are chosen carefully (tires, lights, windshield wipers, etc.). The only fly in the ointment is the trunk, with cheap lining and exposed cabling — not very attractive.

+ BONUS POINTS. Mounted on the steering column, headlight, turn signal and windshield wiper switches are well-designed and easy to use. Visibility is good from all angles thanks in part to large sideview mirrors. Wipers are fast and clean a very large area and headlamps are extremely powerful on high beam.

CONS

- TRANSMISSION. The shifter has gears set too far apart; and you have to know how to adjust the accelerator pedal pressure in just the "right" way to shift into overdrive or to downshift at the right moment. And there isn't much braking effect in 3rd gear.

- STEERING. It's precise and very direct, with only 2.5 turns lock-to-lock. Yet the Magnasteer system is crippled by over-assistance, so it gets light and sensitive in strong winds or when driving over poor pavement.

- MATERIALS. Some of the plastic used inside the cabin affects the look of other items (especially the leather trim), because of its lackluster shade (grey) and shiny texture.

- COCKPIT SETUP. The center console is too low, more so than on the Buick Century-Regal and Pontiac Grand Prix. And the shifter is smack in front of the climate control dials.

- NOISE. It's strange that such a sleek body generates so much wind noise, unless its stay in the wind tunnel was a bit too short for its own good...

- SEATS. When covered in leather their padding is very firm, in keeping with the style typical of German- or Japanese-built cars, a bit surprising on an American model.

CONCLUSION

GM has found the magic potion recipe it seemed to have lost for a while and Oldsmobile has applied it well since the Intrigue is selling like hot cakes. However, the corporation would be wise to remember to correct a few oversights that keep it from being perfect.

RATING
OLDSMOBILE Intrigue

CONCEPT :   76%
Technology :	80
Safety :	80
Interior space :	70
Trunk volume :	70
Quality/fit/finish :	80

DRIVING :   68%
Cockpit :	80
Performance :	70
Handling :	55
Steering :	75
Braking :	60

ORIGINAL EQUIPMENT :   79%
Tires :	80
Headlights :	85
Wipers :	70
Rear defroster :	80
Radio :	80

COMFORT :   73%
Seats :	80
Suspension :	75
Sound level :	60
Conveniences :	70
Air conditioning :	80

BUDGET :   65%
Price :	45
Fuel economy :	75
Insurance :	65
Satisfaction :	80
Depreciation :	60

Overall rating :   72.2%

NEW FOR 2000

- Standard DOHC 3.5L V6 engine on all models.
- Optional Precision Control System, heated front seats and gold-trim package.
- Redesigned wheels on the GL and GLS.
- Two exterior colors: Inferno Red and Navy Blue.

Compare Performance, Specifications, Prices, and Classification at the end of this chapter.

EQUIPMENT

OLDSMOBILE Intrigue	GX	GL	GLS
Automatic transmission:	S	S	S
Cruise control:	S	S	S
Power steering:	S	S	S
Anti-lock brakes:	S	S	S
Traction control:	S	S	S
Air conditioning:	SM	SA	SA
Leather:	-	O	S
AM/FM/radio-cassette:	S	S	SCd
Power door locks:	S	S	S
Power windows:	S	S	S
Tilt steering:	S	S	S
Dual adjustable mirrors:	SE	SEH	SEH
Alloy wheels:	S	S	S
Anti-theft system:	S	S	S

Colors

Exterior: White, Silver, Blue, Green, Black, Grey, Red, Gold, Plum.

Interior: Cloth : Grey, Beige. Leather : Grey, Beige, Oak.

AT A GLANCE...

HISTORIC

Introduced in:	1998.
Made in:	Fairfax, Kansas, USA.

DEMOGRAPHICS

Model	Men./Wom.	Age	Married	College	Income $
Intrigue	76/24 %	57	80 %	47 %	45,000

INDEX

Safety:	80 %	Satisfaction:	78 %
Depreciation:	37 %	Insurance:	$ 565
Cost per mile:	$ 0.48	Number of dealers:	3,100

SALES

Model	1997	Canada 1998	Result	1997	USA 1998	Result
Intrigue	4,541	7,201	+ 58.6 %	23,460	90,563	+ 286.0 %

MAINTENANCE REQUIRED BY WARRANTY

First revision:	Frequency:	Diagnostic plug:
3,000 miles	6,000 miles	Yes

Mid-Size Cars

The Grand Prix continues to fascinate a large number of motorists because of its powerful styling, a strong hint of the high performance levels its turbo engine is capable of reaching. The fantasy continues once they get inside, where the dashboard is so impressive, it looks like something out of an F-18. This being said, the Grand Prix's sales have dropped in the United States and Canada alike, no doubt confirming that buyers are turning away from sporty models in favor of more utilitarian vehicles.

MODEL RANGE

The Pontiac Grand Prix is available as a 4-door sedan and 2-door coupe. The sedan is offered in three trim levels: SE, GT and GTP, whereas the coupe is sold in two trim levels: GT and GTP. The SE sedan receives the 3.1L 3100 V6, the GT versions are animated by the 3.8L 3800 Series II V6 and the GTP's are powered by a 3800 SC Series V6, a supercharged version of the same engine. Standard equipment on these cars is quite generous, since it includes an automatic transmission, traction control and antilock braking, main power accessories, manual climate control and theft-deterrent system.

TECHNICAL FEATURES

The Grand Prix's W platform has a long wheelbase and very wide wheel tracks. The main structure is of monocoque design with steel panels that are galvanized on both sides (except the roof panel). The body yields average aerodynamics, with a 0.32 drag coefficient for the sedan and 0.34 for the coupe. A subframe supports the powertrain and the suspension is fully independent, based on MacPherson struts up front and a three-link system at the rear.

Flashy

Front and rear are equipped with coil springs and an anti-roll bar. Four-whxeel disc brakes are associated with a Bosch antilock braking system and traction control, both hooked up to the same sensors. The SE version is equipped with conventional power rack-and-pinion steering, but the GT and GTP versions receive a variable assist MagnaSteer system developed for Cadillac.

OUTSTANDING

++ ESTHETICS. The Grand Prix has a beautiful body. Its nicely curved form exudes feline pounce power. And the GT and GTP, with their bright-colored exterior, always catch people's attention. Such bold and brassy traits inspire a sense of pride for the lucky guy or gal at the wheel, who tends to make the exhaust system roar like blazes!

PROS

+ CABIN DESIGN. The GT is blessed with a neat interior design. This model is a good buy with its rich equipment, loaded instrument panel and very elaborate seats.
+ HANDLING. The new Grand Prix is much more road-competent. The really wide wheel tracks sure help keep things on an even keel.
+ SEATS. The bucket seats follow the contours of your body and provide lots of hip and lower back support, even though upholstery is a bit thin and quite firm.

+ DRIVING PLEASURE. The GT is more fun to zip around in. Steering is quick on the draw and accurate and the suspension is simply super, providing good vehicle control. Sportscar fans will love it!
+ PERFORMANCES. The 200-hp 3.8L V6 is a gutsy engine and the Roots supercharger enhances output by letting another 40 hp loose to do their stuff. Accelerations and pickup are almost akin to those achieved by an exotic car!
+ INSTRUMENT PANEL. It's loaded with controls and gauges that are legible and within easy reach. There are several controls on the steering wheel as well, which does take some getting used to.
+ NICE FEATURES: Assist grips and Head-Up display system that lets you keep track of what's happening by checking the reading on the inner windshield, without having to look down at the instrument panel.

CONS

- SUSPENSION. The suspension on the GT is brutal and really shakes up occupants to its cruel heart's content on rough road surfaces. And the exhaust racket gets on your nerves pretty quick.
- VISIBILITY. The restyled body cuts down on lateral visibility and the view at rear quarterback. The body belt is high, roof supports are wide and the rear window is really slanted, so all these factors add up

to poor visibility all-round.
- FIT AND FINISH. Some materials don't look too spiffy and there isn't the same craftsmanship as you get on an Oldsmobile Intrigue, for example.
- STRUCTURAL RIGIDITY. The structure on our test vehicle wasn't super-solid, since we heard lots of interference on rough surfaces and the suspension often bottomed out.
- ACCESS. Getting into the rear seats is a chore, both on the sedan and the coupe, due to the really strongly arched roof design.
- TIRES. The SE and GT models are equipped with undersized tires and only the GTP's tires are well suited to the car's capabilities.
- PRICE. The GTP price tag looks pretty steep compared to that of the GT that can brag about pretty good performances!
- CONVENIENCE FEATURES. Car dimensions are quite generous, but this aspect seems to have been overlooked. There aren't too many storage spots and the ones you have at your disposal don't hold too much. The trunk isn't high enough, it isn't modular and luggage handling is no picnic with the narrow opening and high trunk threshold.
- TO BE IMPROVED UPON. Front armrest that's too wide and you have to fold it up to drive comfortably.

CONCLUSION

In keeping with Pontiac's philosophy of offering models with a decidedly sporty bent, the Grand Prix can travel far and fast, but no more so than an Intrigue or a Regal, with the difference that there's no chance that it will go unnoticed — a quality and a fault at one and the same time.

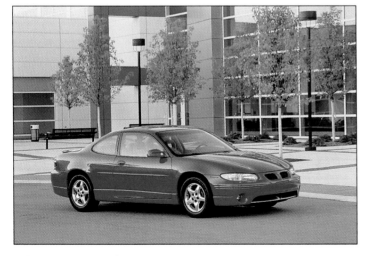

RATING
PONTIAC Grand Prix

CONCEPT :		**77%**
Technology :	80	
Safety :	90	
Interior space :	70	
Trunk volume :	70	
Quality/fit/finish :	75	
DRIVING :		**70%**
Cockpit :	80	
Performance :	65	
Handling :	55	
Steering :	80	
Braking :	70	
ORIGINAL EQUIPMENT :		**77%**
Tires :	75	
Headlights :	80	
Wipers :	70	
Rear defroster :	80	
Radio :	80	
COMFORT :		**69%**
Seats :	75	
Suspension :	65	
Sound level :	55	
Conveniences :	70	
Air conditioning :	80	
BUDGET :		**58%**
Price :	45	
Fuel economy :	70	
Insurance :	50	
Satisfaction :	75	
Depreciation :	50	
Overall rating :		**70.2%**

NEW FOR 2000
- **More power for the 3.1L V6 engine: 175 hp output.**
- **All engines comply with California environmental standards.**
- **Redfire color, Cyclone fabric and silver-toned wheels.**
- **Limited edition replica of the Daytona Pace Car.**
- **Revamped: engine supports, grille and child-safety anchors.**

Compare Performance, Specifications, Prices, and Classification at the end of this chapter.

Mid-Size Cars

EQUIPMENT

PONTIAC Grand Prix	SE sdn.	GT cpe.	GT sdn.
Automatic transmission:	S	S	S
Cruise control:	O	S	S
Power steering:	S	S	S
Anti-lock brakes:	S	S	S
Traction control:	S	S	S
Air conditioning:	SM	SA	SA
Leather:	O	O	O
AM/FM/radio-cassette:	O	O	S
Power door locks:	S	S	S
Power windows:	S	S	S
Tilt steering:	S	S	S
Dual adjustable mirrors:	SE	SE	SE
Alloy wheels:	O	S	S
Anti-theft system:	S	S	S

Colors

Exterior: White, Blue, Black, Green, Red, Bronze.

Interior: Blue, Grey, Taupe, Black.

AT A GLANCE...

HISTORIC

Introduced in:	1997.
Made in:	Fairfax-Kansas City, Kansas, USA.

DEMOGRAPHICS

Model	Men./Wom.	Age	Married	College	Income $
Grand Prix	73/27 %	45	82 %	52 %	55,000

INDEX

Safety:	90 %	Satisfaction:	75 %
Depreciation:	52 %	Insurance:	$ 735-775
Cost per mile:	$ 0.49	Number of dealers:	2,953

SALES

Model	Canada 1997	1998	Result	USA 1997	1998	Result
Grand Prix	11,542	11,215	- 2.8 %	142,018	122,915	-13.5 %

MAINTENANCE REQUIRED BY WARRANTY

First revision:	Frequency:	Diagnostic plug:
3,000 miles	6,000 miles	Yes

Persistance

The Toyota Avalon was created mainly to satisfy the needs of consumers in the United States. At the time, it competed directly with the Oldsmobile 88, which it resembled strongly and strangely. It accomplished its mission admirably and today its rival has disappeared while it continues to sell close to 80,000 units. In Canada the formula hasn't been so magical and only 1,200 units were sold last year. It has been completely revamped for the next millennium and now the question is which market does it intend to take on in full force.

MODEL RANGE

The Avalon is a 4-door sedan that can accommodate 5 passengers and it's available in base XL or luxury XLS versions which share the same mechanical system: a 3.0L V6 engine and a 4-speed automatic transmission. On the base model, equipment includes cruise control, antilock brakes, a stereo radio-cassette player, air conditioning, power windows, power locks and power sideview mirrors. This year alloy wheels, an antitheft system and a radio-CD player are included on the XL, while the XLS adds leather trims, traction control and a CD changer.

TECHNICAL FEATURES

The Avalon is built on the Camry platform and it shares the same main mechanical components. The wheelbase and width have been increased for more useable space. The unibody is made of steel panels, the most exposed of which are galvanized. The front- and rear-end assemblies are independent, insulating the cockpit from noise and vibration from the drivetrains. The

fully independent suspension features MacPherson struts and transversal triangular arms in the front and longitudinal and transversal arms in the rear. Stabilizing bars are featured on both assemblies. Four disc brakes and ABS are standard, but only the XLS has traction control. The Camry's 3.0L V6 has been revised to provide an output of 210 hp, letting it cope with the added weight.

PROS

+ **STYLING.** Not as dull as the previous model, the new Avalon has a stronger personality.

+ **PERFORMANCE.** Levels are surprising for this type of car; acceleration and pick-up are strong and power is sufficient to face just about any situation. The transmission features an excellent gear ratio and shifts very smoothly.

+ **HANDLING.** In spite of slight roll, the Avalon is very competent and corners well, to the point that drivers often find themselves using full power to achieve a sporty driving style.

+ **PASSENGER ROOM.** It's remarkable given the vehicle's reasonable sizing, barely bigger than the Camry. Front and rear seats provide plenty of room in all directions and good-sized doors ensure easy exit/entry.

+ **BRAKING.** Efficient, stable and reliable, it's also fairly easy to gauge

in spite of a spongy pedal.

+ **COMFORT.** It benefits from a smooth suspension, effective support, generous seat padding, and soundproofing that could put many a higher priced model to shame.

+ **QUALITY.** Toyota's reputation is based on meticulous assembly, careful finish and the use of materials of impeccable quality. Plastics and fake wood inlays on the instrument panel are similar to those featured on Lexus models.

+ **COCKPIT.** It's well organized and main controls are within easy reach and are simple to understand and use — visibility is satisfactory from all angles.

+ **PRACTICALITY.** It adds to the luxury of a roomy interior; storage spaces are well positioned and sufficient in number both in the front and the rear. Small catchall spaces have been included in front armrests and in the bench seat's center armrest.

+ **TRUNK.** It's as long as it is wide and its low sill provides easy access. The rear seat doesn't fold down, but it has a pass-through that can accommodate long items such as skis.

+ **EQUIPMENT.** The XLS's is so detailed and its presentation so luxurious, this Avalon may well eat into the smaller Lexus ES 300's sales.

+ **BONUS POINTS.** For digital instrumentation that is clear and detailed but not distracting for the driver.

CONS

- **DASHBOARD.** Stretched out, it looks like those you find on some General Motors models. Motorists can expect more from a product that's more sophisticated from most other standpoints.

- **STEERING.** It's overassisted and as a result, light and imprecise and calls for added attention when winds are strong. A long turning radius hinders handling ease.

- **OVERSIGHTS.** The pedal parking brake isn't practical and should be replaced with a lever positioned on the center console. Windshield wipers are too slow to handle heavy rain.

CONCLUSION

When it comes to comfort, presentation, manufacturing quality, performance or driveability, the Avalon is a superb automobile, midway between Toyota and Lexus models and too often ignored by consumers.

RATING		
TOYOTA Avalon		
CONCEPT :		85%
Technology :	90	
Safety :	100	
Interior space :	80	
Trunk volume :	70	
Quality/fit/finish :	85	
DRIVING :		71%
Cockpit :	80	
Performance :	65	
Handling :	60	
Steering :	70	
Braking :	80	
ORIGINAL EQUIPMENT :		75%
Tires :	80	
Headlights :	80	
Wipers :	55	
Rear defroster :	80	
Radio :	80	
COMFORT :		78%
Seats :	80	
Suspension :	80	
Sound level :	80	
Conveniences :	70	
Air conditioning :	80	
BUDGET :		62%
Price :	25	
Fuel economy :	80	
Insurance :	60	
Satisfaction :	90	
Depreciation :	55	
Overall rating :		**74.2%**

New 2000 Model

NEW FOR 2000

• New model based on the same platform and mechanical components used for the previous model.

Compare
Performance,
Specifications, Prices,
and Classification
at the end of this chapter.

EQUIPMENT

TOYOTA Avalon	XL	XLS
Automatic transmission:	S	S
Cruise control:	S	S
Power steering:	S	S
Anti-lock brakes:	S	S
Traction control:	-	S
Air conditioning:	SM	SA
Leather:	-	SH
AM/FM/radio-cassette:	SCd	SCd
Power door locks:	S	S
Power windows:	S	S
Tilt steering:	S	S
Dual adjustable mirrors:	SEH	SEH
Alloy wheels:	S	S
Anti-theft system:	S	S

Colors

Exterior: White, Black, Pink, Titanium, Sand, Spruce.

Interior: Black, Ivory, Quartz.

AT A GLANCE...

HISTORIC
Introduced in: 1995.
Made in: Georgetown, Kentucky, USA.

DEMOGRAPHICS

Model	Men./Wom.	Age	Married	College	Income $
Avalon	78/22 %	59	87 %	48 %	80,500

INDEX

Safety:	100 %	Satisfaction:	92 %
Depreciation:	45 %	Insurance:	$ 585
Cost per mile:	$ 0.60	Number of dealers:	1,233

SALES

Model	Canada 1997	1998	Result	USA 1997	1998	Result
Avalon	1,744	1,289	- 26.60%	71,309	77,752	+ 9.0 %

MAINTENANCE REQUIRED BY WARRANTY

First revision:	Frequency:	Diagnostic plug:
4,000 miles	4,000 miles	Yes

MID-SIZE CARS
PERFORMANCE

Model/ version	Type / timing valve / fuel system	ENGINES Displacement cu in	Power hp @ rpm	Torque lb-ft @ rpm	Compres. ratio	TRANSMISSIONS Driving wheels / transmission	Final ratio	PERFORMANCE Acceler. 0-60 mph s	Standing 1/4 & 5/8 mile s		Passing 50-75 mph s	Braking 60-0 mph ft	Top speed mph	Lateral acceler. G	Noise level dBA	Fuel economy mpg City	Highway	Fuel type Octane
BUICK Century-Regal																		
Century	V6 3.1 OHV-12-SFI	191	175 @ 5200	195 @ 4000	9.6:1	front - A4	3.05	9.4	17.6	32.0	7.7	167	106	0.75	66-69	20	30	R 87
Regal LS	V6 3.8 OHV-12-SFI	231	200 @ 5200	225 @ 4000	9.4:1	front - A4	3.05	8.0	16.2	29.4	5.9	151	109	0.77	64-68	20	29	R 87
Regal GS	V6C 3.8 OHV-12-SFI	231	240 @ 5200	280 @ 3600	8.5:1	front - A4	2.93	7.5	15.7	28.5	5.3	138	115	0.78	64-67	18	27	S 91
FORD Taurus- MERCURY Sable																		
LX/SE/GS	V6 3.0 OHV-12-MPSFI	182	155 @ 5000	185 @ 4000	9.3 :1	front - A4	3.77	10.6	18.0	31.8	7.2	144	103	0.78	68-72	18	29	R 87
SE/LS	V6 3.0 DOHC-24-MPSFI	181	200 @ 5750	200 @ 4500	10.0 :1	front - A4	3.98	9.4	16.7	30.4	6.7	157	109	0.78	66-72	18	27	R 87
OLDSMOBILE Intrigue																		
G-/X/L/LS	V6 3.5 DOHC-24-SFI	212	215 @ 5600	230 @ 4400	9.3 :1	front - A4*	3.29	8.5	16.4	29.6	6.2	146	120	0.78	67	19	29	R 87
PONTIAC Grand Prix																		
1)	V6 3.1 OHV-12-SPFI	191	175 @ 5200	195 @ 4000	9.6 :1	front - A4*	3.05	9.6	17.2	31.0	6.8	138	109	0.78	67	20	29	R 87
2)	V6 3.8 OHV-12-SPFI	231	200 @ 5200	225 @ 4000	9.4 :1	front - A4*	3.29	8.2	16.5	29.7	6.4	134	115	0.78	67	19	30	R 87
3)	V6C 3.8 OHV-12-SPFI	231	240 @ 5200	280 @ 3200	8.5 :1	front - A4*	2.93	7.0	15.3	28.5	4.6	134	124	0.78	68	18	28	S 92

1) base SE sedan   2) base GT, option SE   3) base GTP, option GT

Model	Type / timing valve / fuel system	Displacement cu in	Power hp @ rpm	Torque lb-ft @ rpm	Compres. ratio	Driving wheels / transmission	Final ratio	Acceler. 0-60 mph s	Standing 1/4 & 5/8 mile s		Passing 50-75 mph s	Braking 60-0 mph ft	Top speed mph	Lateral acceler. G	Noise level dBA	Fuel economy City	Highway	Fuel type Octane
TOYOTA Avalon																		
Avalon	V6 3.0 DOHC-24-MPSFI	183	210 @ 5800	220 @ 4400	10.5 :1	front - A4	3.625	8.2	16.4	29.0	6.1	125	124	0.80	64	18.0	25	R 87

SPECIFICATIONS

Model	Version Trim	Body/ Seats	Cabin volume cu ft	Trunk volume cu ft	Cd	Wheel base in	Lgth x Width x Hght in x inx in	Curb weight lb	Susp. ft/rr	Brake ft/rr type	Steering ø ft	turns number	Fuel tank gal	dimensions	Standard tires make	model	Standard powertrain	99 Price msrp $
BUICK		General warranty: 3 years / 40 000 miles; antipollution: 5 years / 50 000 miles; perforation corrosion: 6 years / 100 000 miles. Road assistance.																
Century	Custom	4dr.sdn. 6	101.8	16.7	0.32	109.0	194.6x72.7x56.6	3368	ih/ih	dc/dr/ABS	pwr.r&p. 37.5	3.0	17.5	205/70R15	General	Ameri G4S	V6/3.1/A4	19,335
Century	Limited	4dr.sdn. 6	101.8	16.7	0.32	109.0	194.6x72.7x56.6	3371	ih/ih	dc/dr/ABS	pwr.r&p. 37.5	3.0	17.5	205/70R15	General	Ameri G4S	V6/3.1/A4	20,705
Regal	LS	4dr.sdn. 5	101.8	16.7	0.33	109.0	196.2x72.7x56.6	3439	ih/ih	dc/ABS	pwr.r&p. 37.5	2.4	17.5	215/70R15	Goodyear	Eagle LS	V6/3.8/A4	22,255
Regal	GS	4dr.sdn. 5	101.8	16.7	0.33	109.0	196.2x72.7x56.6	3543	ih/ih	dc/ABS	pwr.r&p. 37.5	2.4	17.5	225/60R16	Goodyear	Eagle LS	V6C/3.8/A4	24,955
FORD		General warranty, antipollution & battery: 3 years / 36 000 miles; corrosion perforation: 5 years / unlimited.																
Taurus	LX	4dr.sdn.5	104.7	17.0	0.32	108.5	197.6x73.0x56.1	3368	ih/ih	dc/dr	pwr.r&p. 39.8	2.9	16.0	215/60R16	General	Ameri G45	V6/3.0/A4	18,045
Taurus	SE	4dr.sdn.5	104.7	17.0	0.32	108.5	197.6x73.0x56.1	3328	ih/ih	dc/dr	pwr.r&p. 39.8	2.9	16.0	215/60R16	Goodyear	Eagle GS-C	V6/3.0/A4	20,045
Taurus	SE	4dr.wgn.5	104.0	38.8	0.34	108.5	199.6x73.0x57.6	3532	ih/ih	dc/dc	pwr.r&p. 39.8	2.9	16.0	215/60R16	General	Ameri G45	V6/3.0/A4	19,045
MERCURY		General warranty, antipollution & battery: 3 years / 36 000 miles; corrosion perforation: 5 years / unlimited.																
Sable	GS	4dr.sdn.5	104.7	16.0	0.32	108.5	199.8x73.0x56.1	3379	ih/ih	dc/dr	pwr.r&p. 39.8	2.8	16.0	215/60R16	General	Ameri G45	V6/3.0/A4	19,090
Sable	LS	4dr.sdn.5	104.7	16.0	0.32	108.5	199.8x73.0x56.1	3325	ih/ih	dc/dr	pwr.r&p. 39.8	2.8	16.0	215/60R16	General	Ameri G45	V6/3.0/A4	20,190
Sable	LS	4dr.wgn.5	104.0	38.8	0.34	108.5	197.8x73.0x58.0	3473	ih/ih	dc/dc	pwr.r&p. 39.8	2.8	16.0	215/60R16	General	Ameri G45	V6/3.0/A4	21,290
OLDSMOBILE		General warranty: 3 years / 36 000 miles; antipollution: 5 years / 50 000 miles; perforation corrosion: 6 years / 100 000 miles. Roadside assistance.																
Intrigue	GX	4dr.sdn.5	102.2	16.3	0.32	109.0	195.9x73.6x56.6	3428	ih/ih	dc/ABS	pwr.r&p. 36.6	2.5	18.0	225/60SR16	Goodyear	Eagle LS	V6/3.5/A4	21,735
Intrigue	GL	4dr.sdn.5	102.2	16.3	0.32	109.0	195.9x73.6x56.6	3455	ih/ih	dc/ABS	pwr.r&p. 36.6	2.5	18.0	225/60SR16	Goodyear	Eagle LS	V6/3.5/A4	23,135
Intrigue	GLS	4dr.sdn 5	102.2	16.3	0.32	109.0	195.9x73.6x56.6	3467	ih/ih	dc/ABS	pwr.r&p. 36.6	2.5	18.0	225/60SR16	Goodyear	Eagle LS	V6/3.5/A4	25,505
PONTIAC		General warranty: 3 years / 36 000 miles; antipollution: 5 years / 50 000 miles; perforation corrosion: 6 years / 100 000 miles. Roadside assistance.																
Grand Prix	sedan SE	4dr.sdn.5	99.0	16.0	0.32	110.5	196.5x72.7x54.7	3415	ih/ih	dc/ABS	pwr.r&p. 36.9	2.3	18.0	205/70R15	Goodyear	Eagle LS	V6/3.1/A4	20,050
Grand Prix	coupe GT	2dr.cpe.5	99.0	16.0	0.34	110.5	196.5x72.7x54.7	3396	ih/ih	dc/ABS	pwr.r&p. 36.9	2.3	18.0	225/60R16	Goodyear	Eagle RS-A	V6/3.8/A4	21,630
Grand Prix	sedan GT	4dr.sdn.5	99.0	16.0	0.32	110.5	196.5x72.7x54.7	3415	ih/ih	dc/ABS	pwr.r&p. 36.9	2.3	18.0	225/60R16	Goodyear	Eagle RS-A	V6/3.8/A4	21,780
TOYOTA		General warranty: 3 years / 36 000 miles; powertrain 5 years / 60 000 miles; corrosion, perforation: 5 years / unlimited.																
Avalon	XL	4dr.sdn. 5	105.5	15.9	0.28	107.1	191.9x71.7x57.7	3439	ih/ih	dc/ABS	pwr.r&p. 37.6	2.7	18.5	205/65R15	Michelin	MXV4	V6/3.0/A4	25,118
Avalon	XLS	4dr.sdn. 5	105.5	15.9	0.28	107.1	191.9x71.7x57.7	3461	ih/ih	dc/ABS	pwr.r&p. 37.6	2.7	18.5	205/60R16	Michelin	MXV4	V6/3.0/A4	29,128

Notes:
1) Tire makes and models are provided solely as an indication; they are subject to change without prior notice from the automobile manufacturers.
2) See the 2000 price list at the back of this edition.

CLASSIFICATION

OUR CLASSIFICATION

Rank	Models	Concept	Driving	Equipment	Comfort	Budget	Ratings
1	**TOYOTA Avalon**	**85**	**71**	75	**78**	62	**74.2 %**
2	OLDSMOBILE Intrigue	76	68	**79**	73	**65**	72.2 %
3	BUICK Regal-Century	77	69	77	74	61	71.6 %
4	PONTIAC Grand Prix	77	70	77	69	58	70.2 %
5	FORD Taurus &						
5	MERCURY Sable	80	63	71	68	54	67.2 %

YOUR CLASSIFICATION

Rank	Models	98 Sales
1	FORD Taurus	371,074
2	BUICK Century	126,220
3	PONTIAC Grand Prix	122,915
4	MERCURY Sable	100,367
5	OLDS Intrigue	90,563
6	TOYOTA Avalon	77,752
7	BUICK Regal	65,979

Mid-Size Cars

Comparative Test

FULL-SIZE CARS

**See their performance, their specifications, their price
and their classification at the end of this chapter.**

BUICK LeSabre

CHEVROLET Impala

CHRYSLER Concorde-Intrepid

FORD Crown Victoria

PONTIAC Bonneville

Disappointing

In recent years GM has consistently improved its new models, so when we tested the latest Buick LeSabre we were a bit disappointed. The gap between its contemporary lines and its outdated suspension baffled us. And the excuse that this particular car is intended for a very specific clientele group isn't enough to turn attention away from major drawbacks when it comes to comfort.

MODEL RANGE

Now in the full-size car category, the LeSabre is a 4-door sedan that comes in Custom and Limited versions, along with the Grand Touring options package with a shorter gear ratio and better acceleration. It is powered by a Series II 3.8L V6, one of the best engines currently available from GM. Standard equipment is detailed and includes almost everything on the Custom, except for traction control, leather trims, a radio/cassette player and alloy wheels.

TECHNICAL FEATURES

The Buick LeSabre shares the Pontiac Bonneville's platform, derived from the W Series, as well as most of its mechanical components and some body and window design features. Its steel unibody includes galvanized panels and its body is more rigid to comply with the latest safety standards, particularly in the area of side impacts. In spite of new lines, its drag coefficient remains average. The independent suspension features a MacPherson strut in the front and a Chapman strut, coil springs and a stabilizing bar in the rear. All models have antilock disc brakes. The traction control system is optional on both models.

PROS

+ STYLING. Although very classic, the LeSabre's lines have a family resemblance that's reassuring for potential buyers. Its rounded shape has a decided charm and the rear fascia offers the added appeal of imitating the Continental's look.

+ FUEL ECONOMY. Given this car's size, weight and engine output, fuel consumption is surprising, dipping to 30 mpg on the highway.

+ USEABLE SPACE. The passenger compartment and trunk are generously sized. However, while theoretically this model can take on six passengers, let's just say that limiting the number to five is a better idea.

+ PERFORMANCE. Levels are pleasantly surprising and acceleration and pick-up are unusually good for a vehicle in this class. This is explained by a good weight/power ratio, worthy of much more exotic models.

+ SUSPENSION. It's genuinely comfortable only on the highway, where its smoothness keeps passengers in cushy comfort.

+ DASHBOARD. In our opinion this is the biggest breakthrough on this model. Well-designed and rounded to recall exterior lines, it's ergonomic and logically laid out.

+ EQUIPMENT. Even on the base model it's extremely detailed, one of the most detailed you'll find, and it includes many features that are usually optional.

+ PRACTICALITY. Front seats get most of the storage spaces included on the Custom model. In addition to a huge glove box and deep door pockets, the LeSabre has a very practical center armrest with a large bin and two cupholders.

+ BONUS POINTS. For the powerful headlights whose reach and power are effective on low and high beam, for handling ease uncommon on a vehicle of this size, and for air conditioning with dual adjustments for front-seat passengers. Praise also for the onboard computer that shows the travelling speed in both miles or kilometers.

CONS

- RIDE. It's from another era due to the soft suspension that generates major roll and makes wheels hop wildly on bumpy road surfaces.

- TIRES. The Firestone Affinity tires on our test drive car weren't the best choice for this model and their grip wasn't ideal, even on dry surfaces. To add to inconvenience, they're noisy as well.

- STEERING. It's overassisted and provides no feedback on road conditions. To make matters worse, it's imprecise at center and requires constant correction.

- BRAKING. Efficiency is only average, stopping distances are long and linings tend to overheat. The simplistic ABS system lets wheels lock early on and the spongy pedal isn't easy to gauge.

- COMFORT. It's unthinkable that in this day and age, a car can be equipped with seats as uncomfortable as those on the Custom — support is minimal, padding is mushy and the cushion is too short. The suspension can't handle bad roads and thin windows let a great deal of noise leak in from the outside.

- QUALITY. Some materials used in the finish leave much to be desired, such as the flashy fake wood inlays and the very cheap lining used in the trunk.

- GEAR SHIFTER. It isn't easy to use because it isn't long enough, it lacks precision and doesn't let the driver shift smoothly, or with fingertip manipulation.

- TOO BAD. It's a shame that the traction control system isn't standard, it could go a long way in making the driver feel more confident on slippery roads or in winter driving conditions.

- OVERSIGHTS. No functional headrests or storage spaces in the rear, which doesn't even have cupholders!

CONCLUSION

In spite of some improvements, the LeSabre still suffers from the inconsistency of its suspension and steering system, both of which have no place in a modern automobile. This has a negative effect on both comfort and ride and it's about time for someone or something to awaken the old guard to the fact that times and tastes have changed.

RATING
BUICK LeSabre

CONCEPT :   79%
Technology :   75
Safety :   80
Interior space :   85
Trunk volume :   80
Quality/fit/finish :   75

DRIVING :   65%
Cockpit :   70
Performance :   70
Handling :   60
Steering :   70
Braking :   55

ORIGINAL EQUIPMENT :   74%
Tires :   70
Headlights :   80
Wipers :   60
Rear defroster :   80
Radio :   80

COMFORT :   69%
Seats :   75
Suspension :   70
Sound level :   70
Conveniences :   50
Air conditioning :   80

BUDGET :   52%
Price :   35
Fuel economy :   50
Insurance :   55
Satisfaction :   80
Depreciation :   40

Overall rating :   67.8%

New 2000 Model

NEW FOR 2000

• New model based on an extrapolation of the W series, equipped with a 3.8L V6 engine and offered in Custom or Limited versions, with a Grand Touring options package.

Compare Performance, Specifications, Prices, and Classification at the end of this chapter.

Full-Size Cars

EQUIPMENT

BUICK LeSabre	Custom	Limited
Automatic transmission:	S	S
Cruise control:	S	S
Power steering:	S	S
Anti-lock brakes:	S	S
Traction control:	O	O
Air conditioning:	SM	SA
Leather:	O	O
AM/FM/radio-cassette:	O	S
Power door locks:	S	S
Power windows:	S	S
Tilt steering:	S	S
Dual adjustable mirrors:	SE	SE
Alloy wheels:	O	S
Anti-theft system:	S	S

Colors

Exterior: Silver, White, Green, Black, Red, Yellow, Blue, Gold.

Interior: Grey, Blue, Red, Taupe.

AT A GLANCE...

HISTORIC
Introduced in: 1969, 1992, 2000.
Made in: Detroit-Hamtramck, Lake Orion, Pontiac, Michigan, USA.

DEMOGRAPHICS

Model	Men./Wom.	Age	Married	College	Income $
LeSabre	80/20 %	66	85 %	25 %	40,500

INDEX

Safety:	80 %	Satisfaction:	80 %
Depreciation:	52 %	Insurance:	$ 650
Cost per mile:	$ 0.60	Number of dealers:	3,000

SALES

Model	Canada 1997	1998	Result	USA 1997	1998	Result
LeSabre	7,125	6,128	- 14.0 %	150,744	136,551	- 9.4 %

MAINTENANCE REQUIRED BY WARRANTY

First revision:	Frequency:	Diagnostic plug:
3,000 miles	6,000 miles	Yes

Typically Yankee

Full-Size Cars

The new devotion consumers have begun to show to particular builders has led some manufacturers to brush off names that have no special hook. Since the Lumina has never been a particularly bright light, Chevrolet has decided to rename its replacement with the venerable moniker of Impala, a model that reached glorious heights in the 1960s. However, it's amusing to see that none of the models that ever featured the supposedly exciting name had any of the grace or speed of the antelope that inspired them.

MODEL RANGE

The Impala is a 4-door sedan available in two versions: base or LS. The first is powered by a 3.4L V6, and the second features the famous 3.8L V6 so instrumental in the success of most automobiles built by GM today. Both are teamed with a 4-speed automatic transmission. As the trend would have it, the base model is relatively well equipped and besides its mechanical system, the LS adds only cruise control, antilock brakes, a radio and cassette player and aluminum wheels.

TECHNICAL FEATURES

The latest Impala is based on the W platform, made longer for the circumstances, as is the case for the Buick LeSabre and Pontiac Bonneville. Its steel unibody is considerably more rigid than the Lumina's.

However, its drag coefficient breaks no records, standing at a mere 0.31. The fully independent suspension features MacPherson struts in the front and rear. Standard equipment includes four disc brakes, but the ABS system is standard only on the LS version.

PROS

+ VALUE. The price/equipment ratio is an advantage for this newcomer, whose quality is superior to what the defunct Lumina could offer.

+ PERFORMANCE. The Impala's performance levels are surprisingly energetic, even with the base engine. There is only a one-second gap between both engines and each offers the advantage of good fuel economy, with an average of 20 mpg (12.0l/100km) under normal driving conditions.

+ HANDLING. Like all other models GM has launched lately, these Chevrolets hug the road. However, the LS has more stability because its Goodyear tires offer better quality and because its suspension produces less roll when cornering.

+ DRIVEABILITY. The Impala is smooth and particularly good in city traffic, attributes that are rare for a car of this type and this origin.

+ PASSENGER ROOM. The Impala is a bigger car than the Lumina was and it can accommodate six passengers. However, the best bet is to travel with only five aboard — the middle passenger in the front seat will likely tolerate only short jaunts.

+ TRUNK. It's very roomy and the rear seat folds down for extra space. Its hinges are positioned outside the cargo area and a hydraulic system makes loading and unloading maneuvers problem-free.

+ COMFORT. The smooth suspension, well-padded seats and good soundproofing make travelling long distances in the LS a pleasant experience and despite the price difference, it remains the best choice.

+ TRANSMISSION. The 4-speed automatic transmission is one of the most efficient on the market. Shifting is smooth and engine breaking is better than what drivers find on Ford and Chrysler rivals.

+ STYLING. The Impala is nothing revolutionary when it comes to design, but it has more personality than the old Lumina. The front end is more interesting than the rear, where the heavy profiling already looks outdated. On the inside, the dashboard is well presented.

+ VISIBILITY. It's good thanks to C-pillars that minimize the blind spot usually found on this part of the vehicle.

+ BONUS POINTS. For instrumentation controls, easy-to-use radio buttons and fingertip adjustable dual air conditioning settings.

CONS

- BRAKING. Its efficiency is only mediocre, panic stops are very long, especially on the base model where tire grip is nothing extraordinary, and the unsophisticated ABS system leads to a number of wheel locks.

- SEATS. The base model's aren't as good as the LS's, and as a result passengers spend a lot of their time searching for the ideal position.

- STEERING. It suffers from chronic overassistance. When the car is travelling in crosswinds, it also calls for a lot of attention from the driver.

- ROLL. When cornering, the base model's suspension tends to show more roll than the more rigid LS model.

- FINISH. This is an area where the economical side of these cars shines through — the trunk lining and dashboard adjustments could use improvement and the same goes for interior trims on the base model.

- NEGATIVE POINTS. Storage spaces are too few in number, the glovebox is small, door pockets that aren't deep enough to be practical. Only the front center armrest has a storage bin and to its credit, cupholders as well. The poor quality tires on the base model slip even on dry road surfaces and are loud.

CONCLUSION

The Impala is the typical example of a car that only American builders are capable of manufacturing and selling at a reasonable price. Its size and equipment level are well adapted to North American demands and its performance levels have become very reasonable and comparable to those offered by models in higher categories.

RATING CHEVROLET Impala		
CONCEPT :		**78%**
Technology :	75	
Safety :	80	
Interior space :	80	
Trunk volume :	80	
Quality/fit/finish :	75	
DRIVING :		**64%**
Cockpit :	80	
Performance :	60	
Handling :	55	
Steering :	75	
Braking :	50	
ORIGINAL EQUIPMENT :		**75%**
Tires :	75	
Headlights :	75	
Wipers :	70	
Rear defroster :	75	
Radio :	80	
COMFORT :		**76%**
Seats :	80	
Suspension :	80	
Sound level :	80	
Conveniences :	60	
Air conditioning :	80	
BUDGET :		**66%**
Price :	45	
Fuel economy :	70	
Insurance :	70	
Satisfaction :	75	
Depreciation :	70	
Overall rating :		**71.8%**

New 2000 Model

NEW FOR 2000

• New model replacing the Lumina and borrowing a name long famous at Chevrolet. Based on the W platform, it shares the previous Lumina model's mechanical components.

Compare Performance, Specifications, Prices, and Classification at the end of this chapter.

Full-Size Cars

EQUIPMENT

CHEVROLET Impala	base	LS
Automatic transmission:	S	S
Cruise control:	O	S
Power steering:	S	S
Anti-lock brakes:	-	S
Traction control:	-	-
Air conditioning:	S	S
Leather:	O	O
AM/FM/radio-cassette:	O	S
Power door locks:	S	S
Power windows:	S	S
Tilt steering:	S	S
Dual adjustable mirrors:	SE	SEH
Alloy wheels:	O	S
Anti-theft system:	S	S

Colors

Exterior: Silver, Green, Blue, Red, White, Black, Driftwood, Auburn.

Interior: Grey, Oak, Blue.

AT A GLANCE...

HISTORIC

Introduced in: 2000.
Made in: Oshawa, Ontario, Canada.

DEMOGRAPHICS

Model	Men./Wom.	Age	Married	College	Income $
Impala	46/54 %	44	79 %	40 %	60,000

INDEX

Safety:	80 %	Satisfaction:	75 %
Depreciation:	30 %	Insurance:	$ 535
Cost per mile:	$ 0.52	Number of dealers:	4,466

SALES

Model	Canada 1997	1998	Result	USA 1997	1998	Result
Impala	Not on sale during this period					

MAINTENANCE REQUIRED BY WARRANTY

First revision:	Frequency:	Diagnostic plug:
3,000 miles	6,000 miles	Yes

Chrysler LH models may not be the bestsellers in their class, but after the famous minivans, they are certainly the most visible. Revamped two years ago, their styling hasn't aged and it remains well ahead of anything its direct competitors have managed to come up with. While the Intrepid is resolutely futuristic, the Concorde relies on a retro look to attract those who are nostalgic and yearn for the dazzling models popular in the 60s.

Striking

MODEL RANGE

The latest model Concorde and Intrepid are still four-door mid-luxury sedans offered in LX and LXi trim levels for the Concorde and base, ES or R/T for the Intrepid. They're powered by two new V6 engines assisted by an automatic transmission: a 2.7L model for the base versions, a 3.2L model for the LXi and ES and a 3.5L for the R/T. Original equipment items include automatic transmission, power steering, climate control, cruise control, radio cassette player, power locks, windows and exterior mirrors and adjustable steering column. Antilock brakes and traction control are now standard on the Concorde LXi and the sporty Intrepid R/T.

TECHNICAL FEATURES

These models are based on the cab forward concept that consists of thrusting the wheels out towards the four corners of the cabin so as to maximize interior space. This car has really spectacular looks but its clean lines yield impressive aerodynamics as well, namely a drag coefficient of 0.29. The chassis has been improved when it comes to structural rigidity, but it's the three new engines that are the most remarkable. These three V6 beauties are at the cutting edge of present-day technology. They're made entirely of aluminum with a cast iron liner and they're 10% more powerful yet they emit 30% less air pollution. They're paired up to the adaptive electronically controlled automatic transmission that equipped the former models, which isn't the best news, at least not for many disgruntled owners. There's a fully independent suspension and four-wheel high-performance disc brakes. The engine and front suspension of MacPherson strut design are installed on an independent cradle built of hydroformed elements. The rear suspension is made up of a multi-link Chapman setup with aluminum crossmember to lighten and rigidify the whole.

PROS

+ **SILHOUETTE.** It's very dynamic especially at the front end. The grille is reminiscent of the one that graced prestigious models in the sixties such as the Aston Martin, Maserati or Ferrari.

+ **CABIN & TRUNK SPACE.** The cabin and trunk are very roomy. Three passengers can be accommodated in the rear seats where they have a lot of leg room.

+ **HANDLING.** Compared to the preceding model, roadholding is more of a sure thing with the more rigid structure that assures crisper directional movement. The shock absorber system really paves the way to a smooth ride while maintaining a straight-ahead course.

+ **MANEUVERABILITY.** It's superb for such a big car, so parking in the city or doing a U-turn on narrow roads is easy to manage. Power steering is super smooth and accurate.

+ **CONVENIENCE FEATURES.** This facet hasn't been forgotten, for most of the storage compartments are generous both up front and in the rear. Rear seat passengers can store things in the seat pocket or inside the huge storage compartment in the centre armrest and there are two cup-holders as well. The trunk is big, but it isn't convertible, yet you have access to it via a ski-sized pass-through.

+ **HEADLAMPS.** They're definitely a cut above what they were before. They're much brighter and reach further into the dark.

CONS

- **NOISE.** It's pretty poor for a such a new model car. You can hear a lot of little noise from engine, road and wind noise, signs that a good drag coefficient isn't everything...

- **QUALITY.** Plastic trim components on the instrument panel are chintzier-looking than on former models. The over-all effect isn't what you'd expect on such a classy car.

- **PERFORMANCES.** Accelerations and pickup mustered by the new V6 engines are nothing out of the ordinary and scores achieved were lower than before.

- **BRAKES.** They're only average, in spite of refinements, since most stops take an average of 165 ft at 60 mph and brakes really don't bite in when applied.

- **SUSPENSION.** It bottoms out when the car is at full load capacity due to low-level travel that cuts down on ride comfort.

- **A FEW MISSING FEATURES.** There aren't any headrests to speak of in the rear seats and the front headrests can't be adjusted. The remote door lock system is sluggish and the control could be more conveniently located.

- **AUTOMATIC GEARBOX.** Just as before, there is no braking effect whatsoever when you downshift manually, so brakes take a beating on long descents with the Concorde. The "AutoStick" shifter on the Intrepid ES solves this glitch but switching gears is sometimes rough as blazes if you want to hit higher speeds.

CONCLUSION

Attractive because of their appearance and some of their technical features, the Concorde-Intrepid models are a disappointment at the same time. Finish is not particularly careful, materials and accessories are of marginal quality and both these factors are unacceptable on such recently redesigned automobiles.

RATING
Crown Victoria-Grand Marquis

CONCEPT :		85%
Technology :	70	
Safety :	100	
Interior space :	90	
Trunk volume :	90	
Quality/fit/finish :	75	

DRIVING :		57%
Cockpit :	60	
Performance :	60	
Handling :	60	
Steering :	75	
Braking :	30	

ORIGINAL EQUIPMENT :		75%
Tires :	75	
Headlights :	80	
Wipers :	65	
Rear defroster :	80	
Radio :	75	

COMFORT :		76%
Seats :	75	
Suspension :	75	
Sound level :	70	
Conveniences :	70	
Air conditioning :	90	

BUDGET :		55%
Price :	30	
Fuel economy :	40	
Insurance :	70	
Satisfaction :	85	
Depreciation :	50	

Overall rating :		**69.6%**

Full-Size Cars

NEW FOR 2000
- **Emergency lid release inside the trunk.**
- **Better child-safety seat anchors.**
- **Chime reminding passengers to fasten seat belts.**
- **ABS system now optional.**
- **In Canada, the Crown Victoria is reserved for commercial fleets and only the Grand Marquis is available to the general public.**

Compare
Performance,
Specifications, Prices,
and Classification
at the end of this chapter.

EQUIPMENT

FORD Crown Victoria MERCURY Grand Marquis	base	LX	GS	LS
Automatic transmission:	S	S	S	S
Cruise control:	S	S	S	S
Power steering:	S	S	S	S
Anti-lock brakes:	O	O	O	O
Traction control:	O	O	O	O
Air conditioning:	SM	SM	SM	SM
Leather:	-	O	O	O
AM/FM/radio-cassette:	S	S	S	S
Power door locks:	S	S	S	S
Power windows:	S	S	S	S
Tilt steering:	S	S	S	S
Dual adjustable mirrors:	SE	SE	SE	SE
Alloy wheels:	O	O	O	O
Anti-theft system:	S	S	S	S

Colors
Exterior: Gold, Red, Green, Blue, Grey, Silver, Black, White.

Interior: Blue, Parchment, Charcoal, Graphite, White-Graphite.

AT A GLANCE...

HISTORIC
Introduced in:	1979.
Made in:	St-Thomas, Ontario, Canada.

DEMOGRAPHICS
Model	Men./Wom.	Age	Married	College	Income $
C. Victoria	90/10 %	68	85 %	20 %	32,500
Gd Marquis	85/15 %	68	87 %	19 %	37,500

INDEX
Safety:	90 %	Satisfaction:	82 %
Depreciation:	50 %	Insurance:	$ 600
Cost per mile:	$ 0.60	Number of dealers:	5,200

SALES
Model	Canada 1997	1998	Result	USA 1997	1998	Result
C.Victoria	4,391	4,479	+ 2.6 %	107,872	111,531	+ 3.4 %
Gd.Marquis	2,772	3,232	+16.6 %	109,539	114,162	+ 4.2 %

MAINTENANCE REQUIRED BY WARRANTY
First revision:	Frequency:	Diagnostic plug:
5,000 miles	6 months / 5,000 miles	Yes

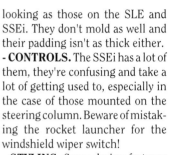

Until now the Bonneville didn't really seem to belong to the Pontiac family — it's rounded lines were just too different. Its revamping was the opportunity to correct this anomaly. It has now adopted the "Batmobile" style so dear to this make, with ribbed panels and an aggressively styled front-end.

Galactic

MODEL RANGE

The latest Bonneville is a 4-door sedan that comes in SE, SLE and SSEi versions. The first two are powered by a normally aspirated 3.8L V6 engine, while the SSEi is equipped with the supercharged version, also installed on the SLE as an option. As to their equipment, it is complete on all versions

TECHNICAL FEATURES

The Bonneville has a steel unibody, with galvanized panels (except for the roof). The current model is more rigid than it's predecessors as it gained 62% in torsional strength and 27% in flexional strength. It still shares the same platform and the same basic mechanical components as the Buick LeSabre, including some body panels and window treatments. The body's sleek lines are deceiving and the drag coefficient has not been provided by the manufacturer. The fully independent suspension features MacPherson struts in the front and Chapman struts in the rear, with a stabilizing bar and variable shock absorbers designed to ensure automatic level control featured in both assemblies. All models have four disc brakes, an ABS system and a Magnasteer power steering system.

PROS

+ LINES. The Bonneville's exterior still turns heads; its powerful styling and pointy front-end create a look that never goes unnoticed. The interior is spectacular as well, with a dashboard and a steering wheel like something from a bomber plane.

+ DRIVEABILITY. The SSEi is fun to drive, and it feels much less like a boat than most models featuring a normally aspirated engine. With a more precise steering system, it produces less roll and seems to be travelling faster than it actually is.

+ PERFORMANCE. The venerable 3.8L V6 still manages well, both versions provide good acceleration and pick-up, shifting is smooth and fuel consumption is very reasonable given their displacement and the vehicles' weights, which have increased once again.

+ USEABLE SPACE. It remains generous in spite of a significant decrease in size affecting both the passenger compartment and the trunk.

+ COMFORT. The SE and SLE versions provide a good ride thanks to their smooth suspension and quiet engine. The SSEi is a bit stiffer and its exhaust system is louder, but it's still very pleasant.

+ TRACTION CONTROL. In spite of a rudimentary design, it keeps the car steady on slippery roads. Too bad it's standard only on the SSEi.

+ CONTROLS. The SSEi's steering wheel is home to a number of controls that are easy to use once you get used to them.

+ EQUIPMENT. Standard equipment is very detailed, especially on the SE version, in our opinion the best value in this range. One of the rare systems of its kind on today's market, the head-up display on the SSEi projects selected instrument readings on to the windshield.

+ TRUNK. It's roomy and easy to load thanks to a wide opening and a lid that opens high. While its length is only average, its width and height more than compensate.

CONS

- HANDLING. The Bonneville SE suffers from extreme understeering, the result of a soft suspension that generates major body movement.

- STEERING. It's overassisted and provides very little feedback on road conditions. In addition, it's overly sensitive and demands a great deal of the driver's attention.

- BRAKING. For a car with a sporty nature, braking could be more efficient. Stopping distances are relatively long and linings show minimal resistance under intense use, quickly producing a foul-smelling smoke. The pedal is hard to gauge and is too firm during emergency stops, when the ABS system fails to prevent all instances of wheel blocking.

- SEATS. The Bonneville SE's seats aren't as comfortable or as good-looking as those on the SLE and SSEi. They don't mold as well and their padding isn't as thick either.

- CONTROLS. The SSEi has a lot of them, they're confusing and take a lot of getting used to, especially in the case of those mounted on the steering column. Beware of mistaking the rocket launcher for the windshield wiper switch!

- STYLING. Some design features on the SSEi's exterior are exaggerated and seem to come straight out of a comic book!

- FINISH. The passenger compartment's finish could use improvement, a case in point being the fake wood inlays, and some plastics used for the dashboard look very downmarket.

- TRANSMISSION. The automatic transmission produces very little engine breaking during manual downshifting. The gear shift, mounted on the steering column (except on the SSEi), is too short and it's balky and imprecise.

- FLAWS. The layout and positioning of some storage spaces, the SSEi's tiresome floor-mounted gear shift, and some oddly placed controls.

CONCLUSION

Not as roomy as it used to be, the Bonneville has become another variation in the large family based on the W platform. At Pontiac it was the last refuge of those who still had simple tastes. What will they buy now?

Full-Size Cars

RATING
PONTIAC Bonneville

CONCEPT :		78%
Technology :	75	
Safety :	80	
Interior space :	75	
Trunk volume :	85	
Quality/fit/finish :	75	

DRIVING :		69%
Cockpit :	80	
Performance :	70	
Handling :	55	
Steering :	75	
Braking :	65	

ORIGINAL EQUIPMENT :		76%
Tires :	75	
Headlights :	80	
Wipers :	65	
Rear defroster :	80	
Radio :	80	

COMFORT :		72%
Seats :	75	
Suspension :	70	
Sound level :	70	
Conveniences :	65	
Air conditioning :	80	

BUDGET :		53%
Price :	35	
Fuel economy :	65	
Insurance :	50	
Satisfaction :	70	
Depreciation :	45	

Overall rating :		69.6%

New 2000 Model

NEW FOR 2000

• Entirely revamped exterior and interior. However, most mechanical components are very close to those found on models in the W family.

Compare Performance, Specifications, Prices, and Classification at the end of this chapter.

Full-Size Cars

EQUIPMENT

PONTIAC Bonneville	SE	SLE	SSEi
Automatic transmission:	S	S	S
Cruise control:	S	S	S
Power steering:	S	S	S
Anti-lock brakes:	S	S	S
Traction control:	O	O	S
Air conditioning:	SM	SA	SA
Leather:	O	O	S
AM/FM/radio-cassette:	S	S	SCd
Power door locks:	S	S	S
Power windows:	S	S	S
Tilt steering:	S	S	S
Dual adjustable mirrors:	SE	SEH	SEH
Alloy wheels:	O	S	S
Anti-theft system:	S	S	S

Colors

Exterior: Grey, Beige, Green, Blue, Bordeaux, Black, White, Silver, Lime, Topaz, Emerald.
Interior: Taupe, Bordeaux, Blue, Grey, Tan.

AT A GLANCE...

HISTORIC
Introduced in: 1992, 2000.
Made in: Lake Orion, Michigan, USA.

DEMOGRAPHICS

Model	Men./Wom.	Age	Married	College	Income $
Bonneville SE	60/40 %	50	86 %	45 %	70,000
Bonneville SSEi	70/30 %	45	75 %	55 %	95,000

INDEX
Safety:	80 %	Satisfaction:	80 %
Depreciation:	52 %	Insurance:	$ 650-785
Cost per mile:	$ 0.60	Number of dealers:	2,953

SALES

Model	Canada 1997	1998	Result	USA 1997	1998	Result
Bonneville	3,749	2,009	- 46.4 %	75,882	59,638	- 21.4 %

MAINTENANCE REQUIRED BY WARRANTY
First revision:	Frequency:	Diagnostic plug:
3,000 miles	6,000 miles	Yes

FULL-SIZE CARS
PERFORMANCE

Model/ version	Type / timing valve / fuel system	ENGINES Displacement cu in	Power hp @ rpm	Torque lb-ft @ rpm	Compres. ratio	TRANSMISSIONS Driving wheels / transmission	Final ratio	PERFORMANCE Acceler. 0-60 mph s	Standing 1/4 & 5/8 mile s	Passing 50-75 mph s	Braking 60-0 mph ft	Top speed mph	Lateral acceler. G	Noise level dBA	Fuel economy mpg City	Highway	Fuel type Octane
BUICK LeSabre																	
base	V6 3.8 OHV-12-SPFI	231	205 @ 5200	230 @ 4000	9.4 :1	front - A4	2.86	8.6	16.5	29.5	6.0	148	115	0.75	66-70	19	30	R 87
G. Touring	V6 3.8 OHV-12-SPFI	231	205 @ 5200	230 @ 4000	9.4 :1	front - A4	3.05	8.2	16.0	29.0	5.8	151	112	0.76	66-70	19	30	R 87
CHEVROLET Impala																	
base	V6 3.4 OHV-12-SFI	205	180 @ 5200	205 @ 4000	9.5 :1	front - A4	2.86	9.2	16.7	29.5	7.0	174	118	0.78	65-70	20	32	R 87
LS	V6 3.8 OHV-12-SFI	231	200 @ 5200	225 @ 4000	9.4 :1	front - A4	3.05	8.1	16.0	28.6	6.0	161	124	0.80	65-70	20	29	R 87
CHRYSLER Concorde-Intrepid																	
1)	V6 2.7 DOHC-24-MPSFI	167	200 @ 5800	190 @ 4850	9.7 :1	front - A4	3.89	10.0	17.2	31.0	7.0	157	112	0.76	66-72	21	30	R 87
2)	V6 2.7 DOHC-24-MPSFI	167	202 @ 5800	195 @ 4200	9.7 :1	front - A4	3.89	10.0	17.2	31.0	7.0	157	112	0.76	66-72	20	29	R 87
3)	V6 3.2 SOHC-24-MPSFI	197	225 @ 6300	225 @ 3800	9.5 :1	front - A4	3.66	8.9	16.7	29.9	6.4	164	118	0.78	66-72	18	28	R 87
4)	V6 3.5 SOHC-24-MPSFI	215	242 @ 6400	250 @ 3950	9.9 :1	front - A4	3.66	NA								18	27	R 87
	1) Concorde LX, Intrepid		2) Intrepid ES		3) Concorde LXi		4) Intrepid R/T											
FORD Crown Victoria & MERCURY Grand Marquis																	
base	V8 4.6 SOHC-16-MPFI	281	200 @ 4250	275 @ 3000	9.0 :1	rear - A4	2.73	8.7	16.5	30.2	6.5	158	109	0.75	65-71	17	26	R 87
dbl.exhaust	V8 4.6 SOHC-16-MPFI	281	215 @ 4500	285 @ 3000	9.0 :1	rear - A4	3.27	8.5	16.2	30.0	6.3	154	109	0.75	65-71	17	26	R 87
NVG	V8 4.6 SOHC-16-MPFI	281	175 @ 4500	235 @ 3500	10.0 :1	rear - A4	3.27	NA										
PONTIAC Bonneville																	
SE,SLE	V6 3.8 OHV-12-SPFI	231	205 @ 5200	230 @ 4000	9.4 :1	front - A4	2.84	8.0	15.7	28.2	5.7	140	115	0.75	66-70	18	30	R 87
SSEi,*SLE	V6C 3.8 OHV-12-SPFI	231	240 @ 5200	280 @ 3600	9.0 :1	front - A4	2.93	7.5	15.8	29.4	6.0	138	124	0.77	66-70	17	27	S 92

SPECIFICATIONS

Model	Version Trim	Body/ Seats	Cabin volume cu ft	Trunk volume cu ft	Cd	Wheel base in	Lgth x Width x Hght in x inx in	Curb weight lb	Susp. ft/rr	Brake ft/rr	type	Steering ø ft	turns number	Fuel tank gal	dimensions	Standard tires make	model	Standard powertrain	99 Price mrsp $
BUICK	General warranty: 3 years / 40 000 miles; antipollution: 5 years / 50 000 miles; perforation corrosion: 6 years / 100 000 miles. Road assistance.																		
LeSabre	Custom	4dr.sdn. 6	107.6	18.0	0.32	112.2	200.0x73.5x57.0	3567	ih/ih	dc/ABS	pwr.r&p.	39.5	2.9	18.5		215/70R15	Goodyear	Eagle GA	V6/3.8/A4	23,505
LeSabre	Limited	4dr.sdn. 6	107.6	18.0	0.32	112.2	200.0x73.5x57.0	3591	ih/ih	dc/ABS	pwr.r&p.	39.5	2.9	18.5		215/70R15	Goodyear	Eagle GA	V6/3.8/A4	27,310
CHEVROLET	General warranty: 3 years / 40 000 miles; antipollution: 5 years / 50 000 miles; perforation corrosion: 6 years / 100 000 miles. Road assistance.																		
Impala	base	4dr.sdn. 5	104.5	17.6	0.31	110.5	200.0x73.0x57.5	3389	ih/ih	dc	pwr.r&p.	38.0	2.9	17.0		225/60R16	Uniroyal	Tiger Paw	V6/3.4/A4	NA
Impala	LS	4dr.sdn. 5	104.5	17.6	0.31	110.5	200.0x73.0x57.5	3466	ih/ih	dc/ABS	pwr.r&p.	38.0	2.9	17.0		225/60R16	Goodyear	Eagle GA	V6/3.4/A4	NA
CHRYSLER	General warranty: 3 years / 36 000 miles; surface rust: 3 years; perforation: 7 years / 100 000 miles; roadside assistance: 3 years /36 000 miles.																		
Concorde	LX	4dr.sdn. 5	107.6	18.7	0.29	113.0	209.1x74.6x55.9	3488	ih/ih	dc	pwr.r&p.	37.6	3.1	16.9		225/60R16	Goodyear	Eagle GA	V6/2.7/A4	21,990
Concorde	LXi	4dr.sdn. 5	107.6	18.7	0.29	113.0	209.1x74.6x55.9	3561	ih/ih	dc/ABS	pwr.r&p.	37.6	3.1	16.9		225/60R16	Goodyear	Eagle GA	V6/3.2/A4	26,235
DODGE	General warranty: 3 years / 36 000 miles; surface rust: 3 years; perforation: 7 years / 100 000 miles; roadside assistance: 3 years /36 000 miles.																		
Intrepid	base	4dr.sdn. 5	104.5	18.4	0.29	113.0	203.7x74.7x55.9	3471	ih/ih	dc	pwr.r&p.	37.6	3.1	17.0		225/60R16	Goodyear	Eagle GA	V6/2.7/A4	20,495
Intrepid	ES	4dr.sdn. 5	104.5	18.4	0.30	113.0	203.7x74.7x55.9	3489	ih/ih	dc	pwr.r&p.	37.6	3.1	17.0		225/60R16	Goodyear	Eagle GA	V6/3.2/A4	23,340
Intrepid	R/T	4dr.sdn. 5	104.5	18.4	0.30	113.0	203.7x74.7x55.9	3511	ih/ih	dc	pwr.r&p.	37.6	3.1	17.0		225/55R17	Goodyear	Eagle LS	V6/3.5/A4	-
FORD	General warranty, antipollution & battery: 3 years / 36 000 miles; corrosion perforation: 5 years / unlimited.																		
Crown Victoria base		4dr.sdn. 6	111.4	20.6	0.37	114.7	212.0x78.2x56.8	3917	ih/ih	dc	pwr.bal.	40.3	3.4	19.0		225/60SR16	Goodyear	Eagle LS	V8/4.6/A4	22,610
Crown Victoria LX		4dr.sdn. 6	111.4	20.6	0.37	114.7	212.0x78.2x56.8	3928	ih/rh	dc	pwr.bal.	40.3	3.4	19.0		225/60SR16	Goodyear	Eagle LS	V8/4.6/A4	24,725
MERCURY	General warranty, antipollution & battery: 3 years / 36 000 miles; corrosion perforation: 5 years / unlimited.																		
Gd Marquis GS		4dr.sdn. 6	109.3	20.6	0.37	114.7	212.0x78.2x56.8	3917	ih/ih	dc	pwr.bal.	40.3	3.4	19.0		225/60SR16	Goodyear	Eagle LS	V8/4.6/A4	23,020
Gd Marquis LS		4dr.sdn. 6	109.3	20.6	0.37	114.7	212.0x78.2x56.8	3949	ih/rh	dc	pwr.bal.	40.3	3.4	19.0		225/60SR16	Goodyear	Eagle LS	V8/4.6/A4	24,920
PONTIAC	General warranty: 3 years / 36 000 miles; antipollution: 5 years / 50 000 miles; perforation corrosion: 6 years / 100 000 miles. Roadside assistance.																		
Bonneville	SE	4dr.sdn. 6	103.8	18.0	NA	112.2	202.6x74.2x56.6	3589	ih/ih	dc/ABS	pwr.r&p.	40.5	3.2	18.5		225/60R16	Firestone	Affinity	V6/3.8/A4	23,625
Bonneville	SLE	4dr.sdn. 5	103.8	18.0	NA	112.2	202.6x74.2x56.6	3736	ih/ih	dc/ABS	pwr.r&p.	40.5	3.2	18.5		235/55R17	Goodyear	Eagle RSA	V6/3.8/A4	-
Bonneville	SSEi	4dr.sdn. 5	103.8	18.0	NA	112.2	202.6x74.2x56.6	3691	ih/ih	dc/ABS	pwr.r&p.	40.5	3.2	18.5		235/55R17	Goodyear	Eagle RSA	V6/3.8/A4	30,625

Notes:
1) Tire makes and models are provided solely as an indication; they are subject to change without prior notice from the automobile manufacturers.
2) See the 2000 price list at the back of this edition.

CLASSIFICATION

OUR CLASSIFICATION

Rank	Models	Concept	Driving	Equipment	Comfort	Budget	Rating
1	**CHRYSLER Concorde &**						
1	**DODGE Intrepid**	83	64	74	**76**	62	**71.8 %**
1	**CHEVROLET Impala**	78	64	75	**76**	66	**71.8 %**
2	PONTIAC Bonneville	78	**69**	**76**	72	53	69.6 %
2	FORD Crown Victoria &						
2	MERCURY Gd Marquis	**85**	57	75	**76**	55	69.6 %
3	BUICK LeSabre	79	65	74	69	52	67.8 %

YOUR CLASSIFICATION

Rank	Models	98 Sales
1	BUICK LeSabre	136,551
2	MERCURY Gd Marquis	114,162
3	FORD C.Victoria	111,531
4	DODGE Intrepid	110,499
5	CHRYSLER Concorde	64,912
6	PONTIAC Bonneville	59,638

Comparative Test

LUXURY CARS
under $ 25,000

**See their performance, their specifications, their price
and their classification at the end of this chapter.**

ACURA EL

INFINITI G20

VOLVO 40 series

ACURA

Ahead Of It's Time

After the Infiniti G20, Acura was the second manufacturer to show any interest in the new market niche for small luxury cars. Sold only in Canada, at least for the moment, in fact it's a Honda Civic presented and equipped more luxuriously and very successful in terms of sales. The imminent introduction of other models in this class will confirm the trend to democratize luxury and to package it in a format formerly believed to be solely reserved for economical models.

MODEL RANGE

The 1.6EL is a four-door sedan offered in base SE, Sport and Premium. The car is driven by a 1.6L engine associated with a 5-speed manual transmission. The base model has standard power steering, cruise control, power windows, locks and exterior mirrors, air conditioning, tilt steering column and a theft-deterrent system. The Sport version gets added antilock braking and light alloy rims. The Premium also receives leather and heated seat covers and sunroof, but in all cases, the 4-speed automatic transmission is sold as an extra.

TECHNICAL FEATURES

The steel monocoque body only benefits from only reasonable aerodynamic efficiency. Its style is quite different from the Civic look, since its front and rear extremities sport unique headlamps and taillamps. The four-wheel independent suspension consists of a double wishbone setup and stabilizer bar on both axles. The suspension has been designed to achieve a nice blend of cushy comfort and clean handling. All models are equipped with disc and drum brakes, but ABS is standard equipment only on the Sport and Premium. The Acura 1.6EL models are driven by a 1.6L SOHC 16-valve engine that delivers 127

hp, thanks to electronic valve timing and lift (VTEC) that also equips the Civic Si sports coupe. All three versions are fitted with the same size and type of tires.

PROS

+ PRICE. The base and Sport versions are attractively priced for the buyer can get a well-reputed small car that's practical, well equipped, all at a reasonable price. The Premium version isn't as affordable.

+ HANDLING. It benefits from the good-quality original tires on the 15-inch tires. Thanks to the two standard stabilizer bars, the 1.6EL models can turn into curves with assurance and they're quite nimble on slalom runs.

+ RIDE COMFORT. The ride is super-smooth for such a trim little car, since the suspension takes care of main road faults in a smooth, imperceptible manner. Engine noise and vibration are well muffled, but the same doesn't apply to the wheels that tend to thump on the least little bump. Thump, bump, thump, bump. Seats provide adequate support, whether they're covered with fabric or leather, but upholstery is quite firm.

+ DRIVING. It's pleasant, even if performances aren't really sporty due to an only average power to weight ratio. As is always the case on VTEC engines, power peaks at high rpm but the manual transmission, with its neat shifter, lets you get better yield than the automatic. Controls are smooth and steering is

well nigh perfect, although it does suffer from a tad poor reduction ratio.

+ EFFICIENCY. The VTEC engine is economical and fuel consumption is reasonable given the performance levels it offers. However, it's brilliant only in the higher rpm range, a tendency growing increasingly common among all car builders.

+ CONVENIENCE FEATURES. The trunk is adequate when the rear seats are occupied, but it can also be extended towards the cabin by folding down the rear seatbench. There are enough storage compartments for front seat passengers, but they're pretty skimpy, size-wise.

+ QUALITY. Assembly and finish job are just as clean and tight as on the Civic. Trim materials are attractive, especially the seat covers. This car has inherited some admirable Civic traits such as ergonomics, instrument panel design, good visibility and the straightforward controls and dials are really neat.

+ CAR DESIGN. It's quite fetching, in spite of the body design that isn't too fresh and new. In some shades, the 1.6EL looks like a little gem and the cabin on the Premium takes on TL airs.

CONS

- DISAPPOINTING. The SE and Sport versions aren't really posh cars and only their richer equipment makes them different from the humble Civic.

- PERFORMANCES. They're only

average, due to heavy vehicle weight due both to a surplus of equipment items and the more rigid body that provides better passenger protection.

- BRAKES. Without ABS, front wheels lock in no time in emergency situations and stops take forever to achieve and car path is less stable than on other models.

- BUILD. The bodywork looks and feels light when you shut the doors, hood and trunk lid and the plastic stuff that decorates the instrument panel is the same, identical plastic you find on the Civic, and after all, this is supposed to be a classy model.

- SILHOUETTE. It's far from ugly, but it's just as blah as that of the Civic with which it's easy to mix up, for its personality hasn't been well enough defined.

- NOISE LEVEL. It's quite uncivilized, for the high-pitched engine song is heard every time your toe touches the accelerator.

- AUTOMATIC GEARBOX. The shifter is jerky at times and it cuts off a bit of the precious horsepower from the small engine, especially when the air conditioning is on.

- TO BE IMPROVED UPON. The instruments are hard to read in the daytime because of the dark orange colors. There's no center armrest or storage compartments in the rear seat area.

CONCLUSION

The Acura 1.6EL deserves to be more different from the Honda Civic and it should have a more original personality. But all in all, the formula is excellent and it lets users ride in a compact and economical car as they enjoy all of the features characteristic of a luxury model.

RATING
ACURA 1.6EL

CONCEPT :		70%
Technology :	80	
Safety :	90	
Interior space :	50	
Trunk volume :	50	
Quality/fit/finish :	80	

DRIVING :		66%
Cockpit :	80	
Performance :	60	
Handling :	60	
Steering :	80	
Braking :	50	

ORIGINAL EQUIPMENT :		75%
Tires :	85	
Headlights :	80	
Wipers :	60	
Rear defroster :	70	
Radio :	80	

COMFORT :		70%
Seats :	75	
Suspension :	75	
Sound level :	50	
Conveniences :	75	
Air conditioning :	75	

BUDGET :		70%
Price :	60	
Fuel economy :	80	
Insurance :	70	
Satisfaction :	85	
Depreciation :	55	

Overall rating :		70.2%

NEW FOR 2000

- **Leather-wrapped steering wheel standard on the SE.**
- **Exterior color: Vintage Plum.**

Compare Performance, Specifications, Prices, and Classification at the end of this chapter.

EQUIPMENT

ACURA 1.6EL	SE	Sport	Premium
Automatic transmission:	O	O	O
Cruise control:	S	S	S
Power steering:	S	S	S
Anti-lock brakes:	-	S	S
Traction control:	-	-	-
Air conditioning:	S	S	S
Leather:	-	-	SH
AM/FM/radio-cassette:	SCd	SCd	SCd
Power door locks:	S	S	S
Power windows:	S	S	S
Tilt steering:	S	S	S
Dual adjustable mirrors:	SEH	SEH	SEH
Alloy wheels:	-	S	S
Anti-theft system:	S	S	S

Colors

Exterior: Silver, Green, Black, Titanium, Red, Plum.

Interior: Charcoal, Grey, Ivory.

AT A GLANCE...

HISTORIC
Introduced in:	1996.
Made in:	Alliston, Ontario, Canada

DEMOGRAPHICS
Model	Men./Wom.	Age	Married	College	Income $
1.6EL	NA				

INDEX
Safety:	80 %	Satisfaction:	87%
Depreciation:	45 %	Insurance:	$ 550
Cost per mile:	$ 0.38	Number of dealers:	290

SALES
Model	Canada 1997	1998	Result	USA 1997	1998	Result
1.6EL	8,587	7,400	- 13.8 %	Not commercialized in USA.		

MAINTENANCE REQUIRED BY WARRANTY
First revision:	Frequency:	Diagnostic plug:
3,000 miles	6,000 miles	Yes

Dreary

During its first attempt at commercialization, the G20 seemed lost on the market, unclassifiable according to the standard's of the day. Even last year, when it was launched for a second time, it wasn't clear just what Nissan's intentions were. Today, with the emergence of new products such as the Volvo 40 series and next year's Lexus IS 200, it's easier to see where this new category fits into the scheme of things in the automotive industry.

MODEL RANGE

This four-door sedan is sold in base model Luxury or "t" for Touring. The latter version benefits from a firmer suspension, rear spoiler, wheels and tires that smack of sportscar traits and demeanor. But both versions are equipped with the same engine, that is a 2.0L 4-cylinder model associated with a 5-speed manual gearbox that's standard on the «t» version as well as a viscous-coupled antilock braking system device. The 4-speed automatic transmission is an extra on the "t" version, but it comes standard on the Luxury, as do leather-clad seats. The G20 is furbished with posh equipment indeed, such as automatic climate control, main power accessories, sunroof, a Bose sound system, front heated seats, all of which bestows a luxury-class status on this car.

TECHNICAL FEATURES

The monocoque body is built of tempered steel called Durasteel and is assembled according to a typical Nissan I.B.A.S. approach ("Intelligent Body Assembly System"), measuring 60 points on the body via a comparator according to a standard model. This stringent system allows for about 1mm tolerance, so assembly is super solid and precise, side panels being welded together in a single piece. Body stylistics are rather ho-hum, but the car benefits from good aerodynamics, namely a drag coefficient of 0.30. The independent suspension consists of a double wishbone arrangement up front and the famous MultiLink axle, made up of multiple control arms at the rear, with an anti-roll bar for each axle. Disc brakes are aided by a four-wheel ABS device fitted with four sensors. The single engine model is a 2.0L DOHC 4-cylinder that develops 140 hp.

PROS

+ DRIVING PLEASURE. It's great, mainly due to right-on suspension, steering and engine response, so like European cars' demeanor. The driver is comfortably seated behind the wheel and enjoys superb visibility all-round. Handling on the "t" version is a cut above, for its refined suspension allows for more competent, level and precise handling of curves, no matter how wide or how tight.

+ EQUIPMENT. It's very rich, which explains partially why the price tag is steeper than for most cars of this format.

+ RIDE COMFORT. Rear seat passengers enjoy a bit more space than those seated up front, but the rear seat still only accomodates two passengers. Seats provide good lumbar and lateral support and they're nice and cushy. The base model suspension is more flexible than that on the «t» model and soundproofing is better, so there's less road noise. But you do hear engine roar when gunning it.

+ CONVENIENCE FEATURES. Storage spots and other amenities are more generous up front and the trunk can be extended by lowering the rear seatbench back.

+ CLEAN OVERALL DESIGN. Assembly technique and compact size really exude a feeling of single-minded design and solidity. Models we tested didn't exhibit any squeaks and such, due to fine fit and finish.

+ THE "t" MODEL. It has more dashing, daring looks and is easy to identify with its rear spoiler.

+ SERVICE. Customers like how they're treated and fussed over by their dealer.

CONS

- LOOKS. The base model looks terribly ordinary, so the G20 breezes through traffic without getting so much as a second glance. It sure doesn't look like a luxury sports car.

- PERFORMANCES. They're rather middling, since accelerations and pickup are average, so lots of current, less furbished cars can do better, and they cost less.

- FRONT SUSPENSION. Suspension travel is more limited up front than at the rear, so the car often goes into a nose-dive on poor roads when at full capacity, which affects ride comfort.

- REAR SEATS. The car is bigger, but rear seats are somewhat cramped and rear storage spots are scarce. Only two passengers will be at ease on long trips.

- TOO BAD. The wood appliqués that graced former models are nowhere in sight, so the interior sorely lacks class and warmth.

- DEPRECIATION. Up until now, the G20 hasn't been the best investment, since poor retail sales cut down on resale value that's lower than for rivals.

- TO BE IMPROVED UPON. The poorly designed main armrest on the center console is a hassle. The horsewhip radio antenna is terribly out-of-date on a car in this price range. After all, lowly GM models are equipped with rear window built-in antennas. Are the Japanese still the gadget geniuses and electronic wizards they once were?

- SERVICE NETWORK. There aren't too many Infiniti dealerships out there, which doesn't help sales and can complicate vehicle maintenance.

CONCLUSION

The G20 is finding it hard to take its rightful place because of the unfair competition waged by two models manufactured by Nissan: the luxurious Altima GLE and the powerful Maxima GXE, both of which have capitalized on its lack of identity and punch to cannibalize its potential sales.

RATING
INFINITI G20

CONCEPT :   **72%**
Technology :	80
Safety :	90
Interior space :	50
Trunk volume :	60
Quality/fit/finish :	80

DRIVING :   **69%**
Cockpit :	75
Performance :	60
Handling :	65
Steering :	80
Braking :	65

ORIGINAL EQUIPMENT :   **79%**
Tires :	80
Headlights :	80
Wipers :	80
Rear defroster :	75
Radio :	80

COMFORT :   **72%**
Seats :	80
Suspension :	80
Sound level :	50
Conveniences :	70
Air conditioning :	80

BUDGET :   **64%**
Price :	35
Fuel economy :	80
Insurance :	45
Satisfaction :	90
Depreciation :	70

Overall rating :   **71.2%**

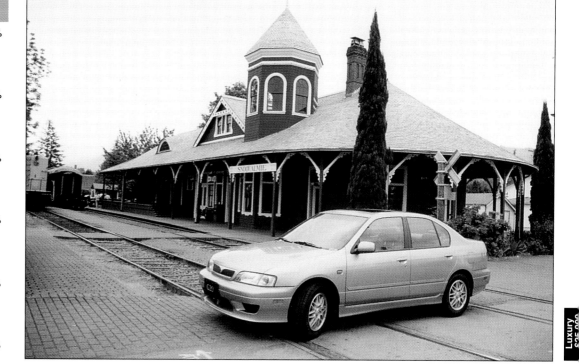

NEW FOR 2000

• Few changes, sportier performance.

Compare Performance, Specifications, Prices, and Classification at the end of this chapter.

Luxury $25,000

EQUIPMENT

INFINITI G20	base	«t»	«t» leather
Automatic transmission:	S	O	O
Cruise control:	S	S	S
Power steering:	S	S	S
Anti-lock brakes:	S	S	S
Traction control:	S	S	S
Air conditioning:	SA	SA	SA
Leather:	SH	O	SH
AM/FM/radio-cassette:	SCd	SCd	SCd
Power door locks:	S	S	S
Power windows:	S	S	S
Tilt steering:	S	S	S
Dual adjustable mirrors:	SEH	SEH	SEH
Alloy wheels:	S	S	S
Anti-theft system:	S	S	S

Colors
Exterior: White, Black, Red, Blue, Green, Beige, Bronze, Titanium.

Interior: Beige, Black.

AT A GLANCE...

HISTORIC
Introduced in:	1991, 1999.
Made in:	Tochigi, Japan.

DEMOGRAPHICS
Model	Men./Wom.	Age	Married	College	Income $
G20	70/30 %	48	72 %	70 %	$ 63,000

INDEX
Safety:	90 %	Satisfaction:	88 %
Depreciation:	35 %	Insurance:	$ 835
Cost per mile:	$ 0.58	Number of dealers:	150

SALES
Model	1997	Canada 1998	Result	1997	USA 1998	Result
G20	35	316	+ 802.9 %	419	7,217	+ 1,622.0 %

MAINTENANCE REQUIRED BY WARRANTY
First revision:	Frequency:	Diagnostic plug:
7,500 miles	6 months / 7,500 miles	Yes

When it revised its product lineup in 1996, Volvo obviously intended to broaden the scope of its sales possibilities and intended to export its 40 series to North America. The mission has been accomplished and the two models in question will be marketed in the United States as of this fall and in Canada one year later. As a result of this decision, we decided to introduce this new class in this year's edition of our publication.

Smooth As Silk

MODEL RANGE

The 40 series is composed of an S sedan and a V wagon powered by the same mechanical system: a turbocharged 1.9L 4-cylinder engine matched with a 4-speed automatic transmission. Equipment is very detailed and main options are limited to leather trims, a sunroof and traction control, with the latter included in one of the three "Cold Weather" packages. The other trims are the Sport-Plus and the Touring.

TECHNICAL FEATURES

The Volvo 40 models are manufactured in Belgium in cooperation with Mitsubishi. The steel unibody meets all the safety standards set for the make, in other words it's very rigid and includes a number of reinforcements designed to absorb impact in case of collision. Its aerodynamic rating is average and its drag coefficient ranges between 0.31 and 0.33. The front suspension features MacPherson struts and transversal triangles, and the rear is equipped with longitudinal and transversal arms with auxiliary levers. Both assemblies also include stabilizing bars, coil springs and hydraulic shock absorbers. These models have variable assist steering and disc ABS brakes.

PROS

+ SIZE. Given their compact exterior dimensions, the Volvo 40 models provide very acceptable roominess and can handle five passengers in comfort, depending on their size. Compared to the 70 models, they offer more useable space.

+ PRESENTATION. There is obvious attention to detail both on the exterior, where lines are polished and rounded while integrating design features characteristic of the Swedish make, and in the inside, where everything is clean and functional. Plastics, fabric and leather trims are sober and quality and adjustments are impeccable.

+ COMFORT. It results from the combination of a smooth suspension with sufficient travel to absorb road defects, seats that mold well and provide good lumbar support despite a slightly short cushion, and soundproofing that muffles engine and road noise up to 60 mph, at which point wind noise begins catch attention.

+ DRIVEABILITY. It's good thanks to smooth-operating main controls and the reaction of the steering system, suspension and brakes, which also create a very comforting sense of security. The Volvo 40 models are easy to keep right on course and their compact size makes it fun to drive in the city and makes parking simple.

+ HANDLING. It's very stable under most circumstances since body roll is moderate and delays the onset of understeering. The suspension reacts well to bad roads and trajectories are straight.

+ SAFETY. It's a sentiment particularly easy to feel aboard a Volvo model: the body is sturdy and the driver feels as if the car is a lot heavier than it actually is. Other features include standard airbags, including side airbags designed to protect the heads, chests and hips of front-seat passengers.

+ EQUIPMENT. The fact that it's very complete explains in part why these new models don't come cheap. Some accessories such as the air conditioning system with a pollen filter, the onboard computer and the toolbox, are most often found on cars that cost significantly more.

CONS

- PERFORMANCE. While they're sufficient with two people onboard they drop when these models are loaded to capacity or when they haul weights of 3,000 lb, something Volvo claims they can do. Why not introduce the 200-hp engine right away, shaving 1 second off the acceleration time and putting these models in the sport category?

- REAR-SEAT ACCESS. It isn't easy, doors are narrow and open only at a 70° angle; legroom is limited.

- CONTROLS. Some, such as those for the power windows, are oddly positioned and hard to reach on the center console, hidden away behind the hand brake as they are. Others, such as the radio controls, are too low and pose a hazard since they force drivers to take their eyes off the road at least momentarily.

- VISIBILITY. Large headrests hinder rear visibility, though there are only two in a car that supposedly has a three-place rear bench seat.

- STORAGE SPACES. Since they're limited to two tiny door pockets and two catchalls, Volvo should have considered tucking a bin out of sight inside the center armrest.

- OVERSIGHTS. Wipers are too slow (44-64 sweeps per minute) and don't clean the windshield fast enough in heavy rain; instrumentation doesn't include an indicator showing the selected automatic transmission gear, a flaw that is common on models of this make; the safety wheel is very low-quality for models that belong to this class; the passenger compartment is austere and wood inlays have a hard time to liven up grey and blacks tones.

CONCLUSION

With these compact models, Volvo is extending its reach considerably. The 40 series models are intended for young families who don't want to spend a fortune to enjoy the luxury typical of models that are beyond their budget restrictions.

RATING		
VOLVO 40 series		
CONCEPT :		**71%**
Technology :	85	
Safety :	90	
Interior space :	50	
Trunk volume :	50	
Quality/fit/finish :	80	
DRIVING :		**70%**
Cockpit :	80	
Performance :	60	
Handling :	60	
Steering :	80	
Braking :	70	
ORIGINAL EQUIPMENT :		**76%**
Tires :	80	
Headlights :	80	
Wipers :	60	
Rear defroster :	80	
Radio :	80	
COMFORT :		**74%**
Seats :	85	
Suspension :	80	
Sound level :	60	
Conveniences :	65	
Air conditioning :	80	
BUDGET :		**59%**
Price :	30	
Fuel economy :	75	
Insurance :	50	
Satisfaction :	90	
Depreciation :	50	
Overall rating :		**70.0%**

Luxury - $25,000

NEW FOR 2000

• New model imported to the United States in 2000 and to Canada in 2001. Launched in Europe in 1995 and built in Belgium in partnership with Mitsubishi.

Compare Performance, Specifications, Prices, and Classification at the end of this chapter.

EQUIPMENT

VOLVO 40 series	S40	V40
Automatic transmission:	S	S
Cruise control:	S	S
Power steering:	S	S
Anti-lock brakes:	S	S
Traction control:	O	O
Air conditioning:	SA	SA
Leather:	O	O
AM/FM/radio-cassette:	S	S
Power door locks:	S	S
Power windows:	S	S
Tilt steering:	S	S
Dual adjustable mirrors:	SEH	SEH
Alloy wheels:	S	S
Anti-theft system:	S	S

Colors

Exterior: White, Red, Blackberry, Blue, Silver, Green.

Interior: Grey, Black.

AT A GLANCE...

HISTORIC

Introduced in:	1995 (Europe), 2000 (USA).
Made in:	Belgium.

DEMOGRAPHICS

Model	Men./Wom.	Age	Married	College	Income $
40 series	NA				

INDEX

Safety:	90 %	Satisfaction:	90 %
Depreciation:	25 %	Insurance:	$ 750
Cost per mile:	$ 0.40	Number of dealers:	405

SALES

Model	Canada 1997	1998	Result	USA 1997	1998	Result
40 series	Not on sale during this period.					

MAINTENANCE REQUIRED BY WARRANTY

First revision:	Frequency:	Diagnostic plug:
3,000 miles	6,000 miles	Yes

LUXURY CARS under $ 25,000
PERFORMANCE

Model/ version	Type / timing valve / fuel system	ENGINES Displacement cu in	Power hp @ rpm	Torque lb-ft @ rpm	Compres. ratio	TRANSMISSIONS Driving wheels / transmission	Final ratio	Acceler. 0-60 mph s	Standing 1/4 & 5/8 mile s		Passing 50-75 mph s	Braking 60-0 mph ft	Top speed mph	Lateral acceler. G	Noise level dBA	Fuel economy mpg City	Highway	Fuel type Octane
ACURA 1.6EL	L4 1.6 SOHC-16-PGM-FI	97	127 @ 6600	107 @ 5500	9.6 :1	front - M5*	4.25	8.8	16.2	29.8	6.5	131	128	0.78	67	28	36	R 87
						front - A4	4.36	10.0	17.0	30.6	6.9	138	112	0.78	68	25	34	R 87
INFINITI G20	L4 2.0 DOHC-16-MPSFI	122	140 @ 6400	132 @ 4800	9.5 :1	front - M5*	4.176	9.0	16.8	29.8	6.4	138	127	0.82	66-70	22	30	S 91
						front - A4	4.072	9.6	17.2	30.4	6.7	144	124	0.82	66-70	22	32	S 91
VOLVO S/V40	L4T 1.9 DOHC-16-MPFI	119	160 @ 5100	170 @ 1800	9.0 :1	front - A4	2.76	8.9	16.7	30.2	6.5	138	124	0.80	67-71	20	30	R 87

SPECIFICATIONS

Model	Version Trim	Body/ Seats	Cabin volume cu ft	Trunk volume cu ft	Cd	Wheel base in	Lgth x Width x Hght in x in x in	Curb weight lb	Susp. ft/rr	Brake ft/rr type	Steering ø ft	turns number	Fuel tank gal	dimensions	Standard tires make	model	Standard powertrain	99 Price msrp $
ACURA		Sold only in Canada.																
1.6EL	SE	4dr.sdn.4	89.8	11.9	0.32	103.1	176.3x67.1x54.9	2478	ih/ih	dc/dr	pwr.r&p.	32.8	3.6	11.9	195/55R15	Michelin	XGT-V4	L4/1.6/M5	-
1.6EL	Sport	4dr.sdn.4	89.8	11.9	0.32	103.1	176.3x67.1x54.9	2522	ih/ih	dc/dr/ABS	pwr.r&p.	32.8	3.6	11.9	195/55R15	Michelin	XGT-V4	L4/1.6/M5	-
1.6EL	Premium	4dr.sdn.4	89.8	11.9	0.32	103.1	176.3x67.1x54.9	3812	ih/ih	dc/dr/ABS	pwr.r&p.	32.8	3.6	11.9	195/55R15	Michelin	XGT-V4	L4/1.6/M5	-
INFINITI		General warranty: 4 years / 60 000 miles; powertrain & antipollution: 6 years / 100 000 miles; corrosion perforation: 7 years / unlimited.																
G20	base	4dr.sdn. 4	90.3	14.2	0.30	102.4	177.5x66.7x55.1	2936	ih/ih	dc/ABS	pwr.r&p.	37.4	3.28	15.8	195/65HR15	Bridgestone	Potenza RE92	L4/2.0/M5	21,520
G20	"t"	4dr.sdn. 4	90.3	14.2	0.30	102.4	177.5x66.7x55.1	3002	ih/ih	dc/ABS	pwr.r&p.	37.4	3.28	15.8	195/60HR15	Bridgestone	Potenza RE92	L4/2.0/M5	23,020
VOLVO		General warranty: 4 years / 50 000 miles; corrosion: 8 years / unlimited; antipollution: 5 years / 50 000 miles.																
S40	1.9T	4dr.sdn.4	88.2	13.2	0.32	100.4	176.5x67.7x55.6	2998	ih/ih	dc/ABS	pwr.r&p.	34.8	3.1	15.9	195/60R15	Michelin	MXV4	L4T/1.9/A4	22,900
V40	1.9T	4dr.wgn.4	89.4	30.2	0.33	100.4	176.5x67.6x55.6	3042	ih/ih	dc/ABS	pwr.r&p.	34.8	3.1	15.9	195/60R15	Michelin	MXV4	L4T/1.9/A4	23,900

Notes: 1) Tire makes and models are provided solely as an indication; they are subject to change without prior notice from the automobile manufacturers.
2) See the 2000 price list at the back of this edition.

CLASSIFICATION

OUR CLASSIFICATION

Rank	Models	Concept	Driving	Equipment	Comfort	Budget	Ratings
1	**INFINITI G20**	**72**	69	**79**	72	64	**71.2 %**
2	ACURA 1.6EL	70	66	75	70	**70**	70.2 %
3	VOLVO 40 series	71	**70**	76	**74**	59	70.0 %

YOUR CLASSIFICATION

Rank	Models	98 Sales
1	**ACURA 1.6EL**	2 369
2	INFINITI G20	92

Not classified:
VOLVO 40 series

ACURA 3.2TL

AUDI A4/S4

BMW 3 Series

CADILLAC Catera

CHRYSLER LHS-300M

INFINITI I30

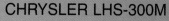

LEXUS ES 300

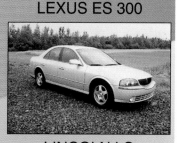

LINCOLN LS

MAZDA Millenia

Comparative Test

LUXURY CARS

under $ 35,000

See their performance, their specifications, their price and their classification at the end of this chapter.

VOLVO 70 series

SAAB 9³

OLDSMOBILE Aurora

MITSUBISHI Diamante

MERCEDES-BENZ C-Class

An Easy Recipe

While previous models failed miserably in their attempt to win over buyers, the latest 3.2TL was perfectly successful in casting its spell and the sales are there to prove that Acura wasn't mistaken.

MODEL RANGE

The Acura 3.2TL is a 4-door sedan offered in a single version equipped with a 3.2L V6 that's completely different from the previous model. The electronically controlled five-speed automatic transmission provides for a semi-manual "Sport-Shift" mode. Thus, the driver can move the speed shifter knob in a particular way so as to change gears manually. As far as equipment goes, Acura didn't leave anything to chance and loaded this car with the works. Only the complete "Aero" options package is offered as well as the optional Gold-plated decoration package that's installed by the dealer. In the United States, the navigation system is also sold as an extra.

TECHNICAL FEATURES

The 3.2TL is based on the last universal Honda platform that was used for the first time when the Accord was redesigned. Its unibody structure is 70% more torsion-resistant and 80% more flexion-resistant, which yields super-solid road competence. Inside, roof supports are filled with foam buffers and wheel housing extensions are fitted with insulation and there are hermetically mounted hydraulic engine supports, all of which cut down on noise interference.

The front suspension uses a double wishbone arrangement with firmer coil springs and recalibrated shocks to take advantage of the more rigid body structure. The rear suspen-sion is a new independent five-link A-arm arrangement that's more effective and much trimmer, so it allows for more cabin and trunk space. The car is equipped with four-wheel vented disc brakes with standard ABS and traction control.

PROS

+ VALUE. Significantly less expensive than the previous model, the 3.2TL is a bargain compared to its main rivals in the same class, such as the Lexus ES 300 and the BMW 3-Series. The fact that they're now manufactured in North America and that they share 45% of their parts with the Honda Accord explains the drop in price. Regardless, its equipment is extremely detailed; Leather upholstery, ABS brakes, traction control, air conditioning, an antitheft system, a power sunroof and heated seats.

+ DRIVEABILITY. It's infinitely good — the steering system is responsive, the power engine makes it seem as if the car is going faster than the speedometer indicates, controls operate smoothly and the cockpit creates a sense of confidence, providing good visibility and letts the driver feel in full control.

+ HANDLING. With a much more rigid body, more power and a better weight allocation, the 3.2TL hugs the road. It stays neutral when cornering thanks to its active rear suspension and quality tires.

+ PASSENGER ROOM. It has increased, especially in the rear, where there's plenty of room along the length and width for three average-size passengers to travel in comfort.

+ COMFORT. Very well calibrated, the suspension is an excellent compromise between sporty handling and a very acceptable comfort level — seats are well padded and support well — efficient soundproofing creates a cushy ambience.

+ PERFORMANCE. Acura has succeeded in giving personality to the 3.2TL, something it sorely lacked. The engine responds well when pushed and never seems to get tired as it climbs higher in the rpm range. The only thing keeping it from being truly superb is a slight lack of power apparent at lower engine rpm.

+ QUALITY. Typically Honda, the construction and finish are exemplary — adjustments are careful and impeccable.

+ TRANSMISSION. The sophisticated transmission includes several interesting functions. One example is the grade logic control that delays shifting when the vehicle climbs a hill to facilitate more energetic pick-up. When travelling downhill, it applies engine breaking with automatic downshifting.

CONS

- BRAKING. It shows a serious lack of power and in emergency situations stopping distances are abnor-mally long for a car in this technological class. We were unable to stop our test model in less than 164 ft and the ABS system failed to stop a number of small wheel locks, a phenomenon bound to have a negative effect.

- SUSPENSION. It begins to hop as soon as it hits a bad patch of road, resulting in some discomfort for passengers.

- PRESENTATION. Although lines are more well-balanced than before, the 3.2TL still lacks the zest it needs to make potential buyers melt at first glance. The passenger compartment is stark and some materials such as wood inlays and the leather trim on seats look too inexpensive to enhance the overall look.

- GEAR SHIFT. Shifting is particularly exasperating and its zigzag pattern inspired by Mercedes-Benz models is both illogical and irritating.

- PRACTICALITY. There's nothing to prevent the manufacturer from making the trunk bigger by adding a fold down rear seat and rear-seat passengers have very few storage spaces to use.

- ODD FEATURES. The leather seats on our test model produced an irritating squeaking noise that we hadn't noticed on previous models.

- OVERSIGHTS. The floor-mounted parking brake on a model this modern and a poorly positioned remote deck lid release.

CONCLUSION

The recipe for success is simple: a price designed to match a model that's appealing, powerful and well equipped. What's to decipher?

RATING ACURA 3.2TL		
CONCEPT :		76%
Technology :	85	
Safety :	90	
Interior space :	65	
Trunk volume :	60	
Quality/fit/finish :	80	
DRIVING :		66%
Cockpit :	80	
Performance :	60	
Handling :	60	
Steering :	80	
Braking :	50	
ORIGINAL EQUIPMENT :		77%
Tires :	80	
Headlights :	80	
Wipers :	60	
Rear defroster :	75	
Radio :	90	
COMFORT :		78%
Seats :	80	
Suspension :	80	
Sound level :	70	
Conveniences :	80	
Air conditioning :	80	
BUDGET :		64%
Price :	30	
Fuel economy :	75	
Insurance :	50	
Satisfaction :	90	
Depreciation :	75	
Overall rating :		**72.2%**

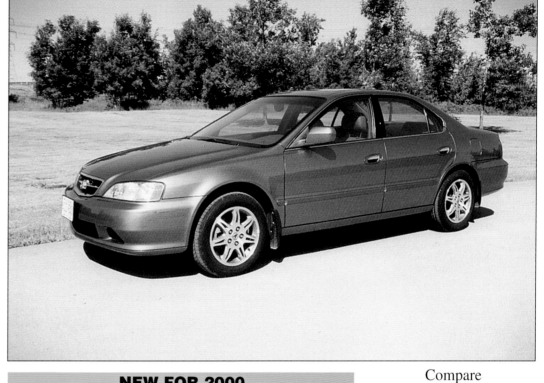

NEW FOR 2000

- The automatic 5-speed transmission with sequential shifting and grade logic control.
- Side airbags for front-seat passengers.
- Front-seat passenger detector deactivating the airbag when a child is onboard.
- Exterior colors: Black, Gold, White, Blue.

Compare
Performance,
Specifications, Prices,
and Classification
at the end of this chapter.

Luxury $25,000

EQUIPMENT

ACURA	3.2TL
Automatic transmission:	S
Cruise control:	S
Power steering:	S
Anti-lock brakes:	S
Traction control:	S
Air conditioning:	SA
Leather:	SH
AM/FM/radio-cassette:	SCd
Power door locks:	S
Power windows:	S
Tilt steering:	S
Dual adjustable mirrors:	SE
Alloy wheels:	S
Anti-theft system:	S

Colors

Exterior: Black, Silver, Lagoon, Emerald, Red, Blue, White, Gold.

Interior: Grey, Beige.

AT A GLANCE...

HISTORIC

Introduced in:	1996, 1999.
Made in:	Marysville, Ohio, USA.

DEMOGRAPHICS

Model	Men/Wom.	Age	Married	College	Income $
3.2TL	74/26 %	46	77 %	56 %	85,000

INDEX

Safety:	90 %	Satisfaction:	90 %
Depreciation:	25 %	Insurance:	$ 765
Cost per mile:	$ 0.67	Number of dealers:	290

SALES

	Canada			USA		
Model	1997	1998	Result	1997	1998	Result
3.2TL	1,504	3,389	+ 125.3 %	1,736	12,949	+ 645.9 %

MAINTENANCE REQUIRED BY WARRANTY

First revision:	Frequency:	Diagnostic plug:
3,000 miles	6,000 miles	Yes

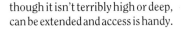
The A4 is the first Audi to enjoy true success in the past few years. More than anything else it owes its popularity to its compact and aggressive styling - the quattro option has always scared off a fair number of potential buyers and the wagon is far from loved. To the A4's credit it has brought traffic into Audi dealerships and with it, the opportunity to discover other models such as the A6, which is sparking increasing interest, and the TT, now an icon in the automotive industry.

Well-sized

MODEL RANGE

The A4 is sold in Canada in a single 4-door sedan model, whereas in the United States, a station wagon is also offered. These front-wheel and all-wheel drive cars are equipped with a 1.8 Turbo 4-cylinder engine or a 2.8L V6 inherited from the A6. The original transmission is a 5-speed manual, but a 5-speed automatic is also available as an extra. The quattro all-wheel drive is optional on all A4's. Original equipment includes climate control, power locks, windows and exterior mirrors, traction control linked to antilock braking, light alloy wheels, heated front seats and a theft-deterrent system that's activated by the remote-control door opener. The 2.8 A4 models can receive leather seat covers, but the sunroof and on-board computer are still optional on all versions. Convenience option packages are listed as well: weather package, audio package or sport package.

TECHNICAL FEATURES

The A4's sleek, attractive body design procures good aerodynamic finesse since the drag coefficient is 0.31. The monocoque body is made entirely of galvanized steel, so Audi can provide one of the best guarantees in the world when it comes to the war against rust. The independent front suspension consists of cross struts and the rear suspension is made up of a semi-rigid axle supported by longitudinal control arms. Quattro models benefit from full-time all-wheel drive that includes a Torsen center differential automatically distributing 66% of power between both powertrains, depending on road adherence. The 1.8L turbocharged engine is a 20-valve DOHC, with 5 valves per cylinder, as is the case for the 2.8L V6, one of the most light and compact engine models in its category. The 5-speed automatic transmission is paired up with an electronic control system that shifts into the gear most suited to driving conditions. The four-wheel disc brakes are teamed up with ABS that doubles as electronic traction control.

PROS

+ **STYLE.** The A4 design is very athletic, one of the best Audi has ever come up with. It makes the car body look trimmer and slimmer than it really is.

+ **ALL-WHEEL DRIVE.** The quattro system really enhances road competence and fuel efficiency and it's super-safe in the wintertime, as long as you've got the right tires.

+ **PERFORMANCES.** They're quite adequate thanks to the 2.8L V6's good power to weight ratio. This engine is perfectly at ease with either the manual or automatic gearbox. Not to forget the S4 performances.

+ **DRIVING.** It's relaxing with the precise, well-assisted steering, though it does exhibit some rather bizarre and bouncy moves. The cockpit provides comfy seating for the driver and the instrument panel is simple and straightforward.

+ **PRICE.** The base version equipped with the 1.8T engine is more affordable and so it's a good buy, given the resale value that's become more and more substantial...

+ **QUALITY.** Audi craftsmanship is one of the best in the world. Cars are solidly built and they do their stuff against rust invasion. The finish job is remarkable due to its utter uniformity and materials used look posh. In this regard, Audi is one up on BMW and Mercedes whose upper-crust models aren't as refined and polished.

+ **RIDE COMFORT.** It's amazing for a car of this size. The flexible suspension is always civilized, front seats are cushy and nicely sculpted and soundproofing takes care of engine and road noise and wind noise is barely perceptible.

+ **CONVENIENCE FEATURES.** It's super with all the generous storage compartments and the trunk, though it isn't terribly high or deep, can be extended and access is handy.

CONS

- **BUDGET.** The 2.8 model is less popular (though it's been readjusted), due to costly insurance premiums and gas bills.

- **ENGINE.** The 1.8T lacks torque at low rpm and the Turbo response time is a bugbear at times. This tendency is more obvious with the automatic since this combination isn't as effective as the V6 when it comes to creamy demeanor.

- **CABIN SPACE.** Rear seat passengers will feel more cramped than those up front, since the seatbench back cushion is too straight, the upholstery is very hard, the seat cushion is stingy and leg room is really snug. The arched door design doesn't help boarding either.

- **CONTROLS.** Most of them are rather unusual for North American drivers, so they're confusing and the digital data screen isn't at all legible in the daytime and it's annoying at night with its eternal amber aura.

- **TO BE IMPROVED UPON.** The twisted wire radio antenna is a bit outdated, since rivals are equipped with antennas built into the window. Rear seat passengers have been overlooked when it comes to storage spots.

CONCLUSION

Slightly bigger than the 3-Series BMW, the Audi A4 also features the extraordinarily efficient quattro AWD transmission and a wagon version (in the United States), giving it an edge on its main rival.

RATING AUDI A4/S4		
CONCEPT :		**76%**
Technology :	90	
Safety :	90	
Interior space :	50	
Trunk volume :	60	
Quality/fit/finish :	90	
DRIVING :		**64%**
Cockpit :	80	
Performance :	50	
Handling :	60	
Steering :	75	
Braking :	55	
ORIGINAL EQUIPMENT :		**80%**
Tires :	85	
Headlights :	80	
Wipers :	75	
Rear defroster :	80	
Radio :	80	
COMFORT :		**73%**
Seats :	75	
Suspension :	75	
Sound level :	65	
Conveniences :	70	
Air conditioning :	80	
BUDGET :		**56%**
Price :	20	
Fuel economy :	75	
Insurance :	45	
Satisfaction :	85	
Depreciation :	55	
Overall rating :		**69.8%**

NEW FOR 2000

- Radio with cassette and CD player.
- Tiptronic automatic transmission with manual gear selection.
- Full-size emergency wheel with alloy rim.
- Navigational system (in the United States only).
- Exterior colors: Light Silver and India Red.

Compare Performance, Specifications, Prices, and Classification at the end of this chapter.

Luxury $ 35,000

EQUIPMENT

AUDI A4/S4	1.8T FWD	1.8T quattro	2.8 FWD	2.8 quattro	Avant FWD	Avant quattro
Automatic transmission:	O	O	O	O	O	NA
Cruise control:	S	S	S	S	S	S
Power steering:	S	S	S	S	S	S
Anti-lock brakes:	S	S	S	S	S	S
Traction control:	S	S	S	S	S	S
Air conditioning:	SA	SA	SA	SA	SA	SA
Leather:	-H	-H	OH	OH	OH	OH
AM/FM/radio-cassette:	SCd	SCd	SCd	SCd	SCd	SCd
Power door locks:	S	S	S	S	S	S
Power windows:	S	S	S	S	S	S
Tilt steering:	S	S	S	S	S	S
Dual adjustable mirrors:	SEH	SEH	SEH	SEH	SEH	SEH
Alloy wheels:	S	S	S	S	S	S
Anti-theft system:	S	S	S	S	S	S

Colors

Exterior: Black, Silver, White, Red, Mica, Titanium, Emerald, Green, Sand, Blue.

Interior: Anthracite, Neutral, Platinum, Titanium, Blue.

AT A GLANCE...

HISTORIC

Introduced in:	1979: 4000; 1982: 90, 1995: A4.
Made in:	Ingolstadt, Germany.

DEMOGRAPHICS

Model	Men/Wom.	Age	Married	College	Income $
A4/S4	74/26 %	40	60 %	78 %	80,000

INDEX

Safety:	95 %	Satisfaction:	86 %
Depreciation:	47 %	Insurance:	$ 1,550
Cost per mile:	$ 0.71	Number of dealers:	290

SALES

	Canada			USA		
Model	1997	1998	Result	1997	1998	Result
A4/S4	2,044	2,335	+ 14.2 %	20,871	26,635	+ 27.6 %

MAINTENANCE REQUIRED BY WARRANTY

First revision:	Frequency:	Diagnostic plug:
7,500 miles	7,500 miles	Yes

Elitist

After presenting a dizzying level of complexity, BMW's small car lineup shows more common sense. Along with last year's revamped sedans, this year consumers can choose from two closely related coupes, different enough to have a personality all their own. Note the disappearance of the 318 ti, which was never really very popular, and the absence of the hot M3.

MODEL RANGE

The 3-Series is available in 323 i and 328 i 4-door sedans and 323Ci and 328Ci 2-door coupes. All models are equipped with an in-line 6-cylinder engines, a 2.5L for the 323 and a 2.8L for the 328. Standard equipment includes most of the usual items associated with this type of automobile, with the exception of an automatic transmission and leather trims.

TECHNICAL FEATURES

The new generation 3-Series have trimmer overhangs, new-design grille and an air scoop on the hood. Dimensions are more generous, both inside and out, for these cars are now 4 cm longer and wider, which has 2 inches extended cabin and trunk space considerably. These models have a different steel monocoque body, of which 60% of the body work is galvanized and that's coated with a rustproof agent. The body design blends the main traditional BMW touches and has an aerodynamic finesse that's starting to show its age, with a coefficient of 0.30. The fully independent suspension consists of a double wishbone construction up front and cross struts at the rear, with a stabilizer bar on both axles. Some of these components are made of lightweight, but robust aluminum. Four-wheel disc brakes, antilock braking, traction and stability control devices are standard on all versions. The automatic transmission, available as an extra for the 323 and 328 models, is a 5-speed adaptive and sequential, that means it adjusts to the driver's style and gears can be shifted manually. Safety-wise, besides the front and side-impact airbags, BMW installs a standard tube-shaped (HPS) airbag that provides head injury protection for front seat passengers. Side-impact airbags located inside the rear doors are also available as an extra. An optional built-in navigation system will also be offered on the new sedans.

PROS

+ DRIVING. It's very creamy due to the chemistry between the rear-wheel drive, engine power ooze and steering that plays a major role in road handling on these models.

+ QUALITY. Finish details are a cut above, notably the lovely instrument panel materials and superb exterior finish job.

+ HANDLING. It's more competent due to the more lightweight suspension components and this checks out on wet roads, since vehicles are more steady and stable, but the reinforced suspension is more sensitive to divergent demeanor exhibited on poor roads. The coupes are even better at gripping the road and taking successive corners on isolated roads in good condition is a sheer pleasure.

+ PERFORMANCES. The 6-cylinder engines are worthy of the sports car label, they're versatile and muscular and adapt well to quiet outings or daredevil moves.

+ TRUNK. It's bigger and can be extended by lowering the rear seat-bench. Its low threshold makes for easy luggage loading and unloading.

+ RIDE COMFORT. The cabin interior has stretched out. Rear seat passengers will be more at ease and the driver and front seat passenger enjoy more hip and leg room. The driver is very comfortably seated behind the wheel.

+ SAFETY. Only the rear side-impact airbags, built into the doors, are optional. The new protection tube that provides head protection in the event of a side-impact collision, HPS, is now standard equipment and is derived from the technology developed for the 5 and 7-Series.

+ BUDGET. So as to persuade reticent customers to enter the BMW fold, maintenance will be free of charge for three years or 36,000 miles. Only regular parts that need to be replaced will be paid for by the owner (clutch disc and brake linings).

+ BRAKES. They're even better yet, for sudden stops are achieved in shorter stretches thanks to the bigger vented discs on all four wheels.

+ VISIBILITY. It's clear except at the rear due to the high trunk design and the small rear window.

+ INSTRUMENT PANEL. It's regained the typical BMW look and looks less busy than was the case on previous generation models.

+ CONVENIENCE FEATURES. Storage compartments are of a more generous size, such as the glove compartment and door side-pockets.

+ NICE FEATURES: The large capacity windshield washer reservoir (1.4 gallon) and the super duper wipers.

CONS

- PRICE. It costs a lot to buy, operate and keep these models in good condition, even with the limited free maintenance offer.

- SAFETY. The index attributed by the NHTSA to the previous generation cars isn't as unfavorable as for the latest models.

- CABIN SPACE. The rear seat may be fitted with three seatbelts, but the 3-Series sedans can at no time really accommodate more than four passengers.

-PERFORMANCES. The 2.5L 6-cylinder engine is a wimp with the automatic transmission and doesn't jive with the idea of a sports car.

CONCLUSION

The 3-Series BMW models are reserved for elite drivers who have the financial resources to show that they're different from most other motorists. As a result, their image is linked with a very special kind of stereotype buyer.

Luxury
$ 25,000

RATING BMW 3 Series		
CONCEPT :		**69%**
Technology :	90	
Safety :	90	
Interior space :	35	
Trunk volume :	50	
Quality/fit/finish :	80	
DRIVING :		**79%**
Cockpit :	85	
Performance :	70	
Handling :	70	
Steering :	90	
Braking :	80	
ORIGINAL EQUIPMENT :		**77%**
Tires :	80	
Headlights :	80	
Wipers :	70	
Rear defroster :	75	
Radio :	80	
COMFORT :		**71%**
Seats :	75	
Suspension :	70	
Sound level :	60	
Conveniences :	70	
Air conditioning :	80	
BUDGET :		**52%**
Price :	10	
Fuel economy :	65	
Insurance :	45	
Satisfaction :	85	
Depreciation :	55	
Overall rating :		**69.6%**

NEW FOR 2000

- 323 and 328 Ci coupes introduced at the last Geneva Auto Show.
- New options: satellite-based navigational system, 5-speed automatic transmission and sequential shifting, power seats, dashboard-mounted CD player, glass sunroof.

Compare Performance, Specifications, Prices, and Classification at the end of this chapter.

Luxury - $35,000

EQUIPMENT

BMW 3 Series	323i	323Ci	328i	328Ci
Automatic transmission:	O	O	O	O
Cruise control:	S	S	S	S
Power steering:	S	S	S	S
Anti-lock brakes:	S	S	S	S
Traction control:	S	S	S	S
Air conditioning:	SA	SA	SA	SA
Leather:	O	O	O	O
AM/FM/radio-cassette:	S	S	S	S
Power door locks:	S	S	S	S
Power windows:	S	S	S	S
Tilt steering:	S	S	S	S
Dual adjustable mirrors:	SEH	SEH	SEH	SEH
Alloy wheels:	S	S	S	S
Anti-theft system:	O	S	O	S

Colors

Exterior: White, Black, Blue, Red, Grey, Silver, Violet, Green.

Interior: Anthracite, Grey, Red, Blue, Turquoise. Leather: Black, Beige, Grey, Yellow.

AT A GLANCE...

HISTORIC

Introduced in:	1982 (320i 2 dr.) 1991, 1999.
Made in:	Dingolfing, (Münich) Germany.

DEMOGRAPHICS

Model	Men/Wom.	Age	Married	College	Income $
3 Series	62/38 %	39	38 %	64 %	62,000

INDEX

Safety:	90 %	Satisfaction:	85 %
Depreciation:	40 %	Insurance:	$ 920 -1,200
Cost per mile:	$ 0.70	Number of dealers:	350

SALES

	Canada			USA		
Model	1997	1998	Result	1997	1998	Result
3 Series	4,753	4,685	- 1.4 %	44,530	48,758	+ 9.5 %

MAINTENANCE REQUIRED BY WARRANTY

First revision:	Frequency:	Diagnostic plug:
15,000 miles	15,000 miles	Yes

Lack Of Style

By adapting an Opel Omega to North American tastes and by including it in the Cadillac lineup, GM has found a product capable of catching the attention of consumers tempted to stray into the showrooms set up by Lexus, Infiniti or Acura, to name only a few of those who have invested in a very lucrative market niche over the past five years. While in the United States it hasn't kept pace with its main rivals, in Canada the Catera has taken the lead, though it still lags far behind the BMW and Volvo superstars.

MODEL RANGE

The Catera is a four-door sedan sold in two version who differs only by their presentation, headlights and the size of their tires. It's powered by a 3.0L V6 engine linked to an automatic transmission, it's equipped with dual-zone climate control, leather power seats, ABS and traction control and a sophisticated theft deterrent system. Main options are aluminum chrome rims, remote garage door opener, glass sunroof and a CD player located in the trunk.

TECHNICAL FEATURES

Built by Opel in Germany, the Catera is inspired by the Omega MV6 and its components hail from the four corners of the globe. The body is built in Germany, the automatic transmission in France, the engine in England and some final trim items in the United States. Its steel unibody is as rigid as it gets. Its architecture is a real classic. The Catera is a rear-wheel drive car. Its main mechanical features are affixed to two independent cradles that support same, away from the main frame. Up front the suspen-

sion is of MacPherson design with some hydraulic links in order to maximize accurate handling and stability on emergency stops — at the rear there's a constant load levelling device. Four-wheel disc brakes are equipped with standard ABS and traction control. The 3.0L V6 engine has its cylinder rows set at 54 degrees. Spark plugs are fitted with triple electrodes, the belt and coolant are made to last, so you can put off your first tuneup to 100,000 miles.

PROS

+ DESIGN. Dignity is what exudes from such a classic and elegant appearance that belies its Cadillac vintage. Inside the cabin, things are quite posh, seats are roomy and the instrument panel is richly equipped.
+ VALUE. The price-package combination is relatively good compared to some of its direct rivals, since you're blessed with leather adjustable seats both up front and in the rear, but it's rather strange that heated seats is an extra.
+ SAFETY FEATURES. This German-built car is loaded with passenger-protection devices and it's as heavy and stalwart as an army tank. Outward view is great any which way, in spite of the rather high body belt. The driver is right at home with the myriad seat adjustments available Night driving is a breeze with such remarkably bright

and powerful headlamps, either on high or low beam.
+ RIDE COMFORT. It's superb with such a voluminous cabin where passengers have all kinds of room to breathe and stretch, such a cushy suspension that filters out road faults, such thickly upholstered seats that provide excellent support and with a low noise level due to very effective soundproofing.
+ HANDLING. On winter roads, the Catera sometimes has serious trouble managing curves even with the sophisticated ABS system, but generally this model holds the road beautifully, yet the rear-wheel drive feature, geared to sporty maneuvers, doesn't really add much, given the rather sluggish engine under the hood.
+ BRAKES. They're powerful and balanced, so you can achieve a whole series of emergency stops without any sign of brake fatigue and the brake pedal is right on.
+ QUALITY. You can sense the German touch right off when you consider the assembly and finish quality and the spiffy trim materials and besides you feel like you're in a solid vehicle that can take on the world.
+ MANEUVERABILITY. Steering benefits from an only average reduction ratio, but it has a really short turn angle diameter so parking is no problem at all. Response is quick on the draw, precise and nicely

calibrated to allow for optimum control in all circumstances.
+ CONVENIENCE FEATURES. Several storage compartments are scattered throughout the cabin and the trunk really holds a lot of luggage and can be extended by lowering the entire or partial rear seatback.

CONS

- LOOKS. You can't really say that the car has much charisma, you can drive by and nobody will even blink. GM designers are usually very innovative, but they missed the boat on this car, since they tried to keep a maximum of the original stylistic features and the look is getting pretty dusty.
- PERFORMANCES. For a car in this price range and class, accelerations and pickup are humdrum, which is an understatement, due to hefty vehicle weight. This sure affects driving pleasure and when the car is loaded, driving is no fun at all.
- INSTRUMENT PANEL. Another side-effect of the old car design, the dashboard is high and massive and really eats up the space surrounding front seat passengers.
- REAR-WHEEL DRIVE. Even with good traction control and tires, you don't have the same assurance as with a front-wheel drive vehicle, especially in winter conditions. You really have to keep an eye on things to stay on track in the snowy season.

CONCLUSION

For the Catera to climb higher in this category's hit parade it needs more panache, from the performance and style standpoints alike.

Luxury - $ 35 000

RATING
CADILLAC Catera

CONCEPT :		78%
Technology :	85	
Safety :	90	
Interior space :	70	
Trunk volume :	60	
Quality/fit/finish :	85	

DRIVING :		67%
Cockpit :	80	
Performance :	60	
Handling :	55	
Steering :	80	
Braking :	60	

ORIGINAL EQUIPMENT :		76%
Tires :	80	
Headlights :	80	
Wipers :	65	
Rear defroster :	75	
Radio :	80	

COMFORT :		79%
Seats :	80	
Suspension :	80	
Sound level :	80	
Conveniences :	75	
Air conditioning :	80	

BUDGET :		52%
Price :	15	
Fuel economy :	60	
Insurance :	45	
Satisfaction :	80	
Depreciation :	60	

Overall rating :		**70.4%**

NEW FOR 2000
• **Front and rear fascias, hood, sideview mirrors, instrument panel and inner door design.**
• **Sport version with high-intensity discharged (HD) Xenon headlights, 17-inch tires, alloy wheels and side airbags.**
• **New exterior colors and interior trims.**

Compare
Performance,
Specifications, Prices,
and Classification
at the end of this chapter.

EQUIPMENT

CADILLAC Catera	base	Sport
Automatic transmission:		
Cruise control:	S	S
Power steering:	S	S
Anti-lock brakes:	S	S
Traction control:	S	S
Air conditioning:	S	S
Leather:	SA	SA
AM/FM/radio-cassette:	S	S
Power door locks:	S	S
Power windows:	S	S
Tilt steering:	S	S
Dual adjustable mirrors:	S	S
Alloy wheels:	SEH	SEH
Anti-theft system:	S	S
	S	S

Colors
Exterior: Ebony, Ivory, Sage, Sand, Cranberry, Platinum, Sapphire, Rainforest.
Sport: Ebony, Ivory, Platinum.
Interior: Neutral, Charcoal, Stone.
Sport: Charcoal.

AT A GLANCE...

HISTORIC
Introduced in: 1997.
Made in: Ruesselsheim, Germany.

DEMOGRAPHICS
Model	Men/Wom.	Age	Married	College	Income $
Catera	78/22 %	56	84 %	59 %	80,000

INDEX
Safety:	90 %	Satisfaction:	78 %
Depreciation:	40 %	Insurance:	$ 880
Cost per mile:	$ 0.65	Number of dealers:	1,600

SALES
	Canada			USA		
Model	1997	1998	Result	1997	1998	Result
Catera	1,560	1,643	+ 5.3 %	25,411	24,635	- 3.0 %

MAINTENANCE REQUIRED BY WARRANTY
First revision:	Frequency:	Diagnostic plug:
3,000 miles	6 months / 6,000 miles	Yes

Chrysler's 300M and LHS twins set themselves apart from their competitors because of their above-average size and their striking style, the key to the success of the third-leading American car manufacturer, led by Tom Gale and his talented team. They are the sports (300M) and luxury (LHS) models in Chrysler's lineup. Their sales have the noted distinction of surpassing those of the Catera, Infiniti, Lexus and other prestigious models, which says a great deal about how highly they are valued by the public.

Generous

MODEL RANGE

The 300M and LHS are four-door luxury sedans offered in a single trim level, but they can be furbished with a "sports handling" package in the case of the 300M. They're powered by the latest 3.5L V6 linked to an electronically controlled automatic transmission with standard "AutoStick" sequential shifter on the 300M. Original equipment includes all the usual luxury items found in this car class, as well as fine leather seats, automatic climate control, CD changer and trip computer.

TECHNICAL FEATURES

The LHS is a spin-off of the Concorde body design, whereas the 300M is inspired by the Intrepid. But they're different from their mentors, since they're equipped with a more rigid front cradle supporting the engine and suspension. This body design in sensational and its aerodynamics are simply super, since the drag coefficient is an impressive 0.31. Structural integrity has been improved by 40% in flexion and by 20% in torsion and an aluminum crossmember solidifies

the rear end. The suspensions are the same as those found on other LH models, but springs and shock absorbers have been carefully re calibrated according to net weight, so as to achieve a creamier ride and more precise handling. Cars are equipped with four-wheel disc brakes with standard ABS and traction control. The V6 engine common to both models is a 3.5L derived from the LH 3.2L powerplant. It's made entirely of aluminum with a cast iron liner and it develops 253 hp and 255 lb.ft. torque. Emissions are 30% cleaner as well. In order to cut down on noise, a second resonator has been added. The transmission is an electronically controlled adaptive automatic. It's the transmission that equipped the old models, which isn't really good news.

PROS

+ LOOKS. The Concorde's 300M-LHS's very dynamic front end is reminiscent of that on legendary cars of the sixties, such as the Aston Martin, Ferrari and such.

+ RIDE COMFORT. The cabin is spacious and the trunk is generous, five passengers and all their luggage can be easily accommodated. The ride is velvety smooth without being soft and syrupy, as is the lot of other classy American cars in this class. The suspension handles road faults like a champion and soundproofing dampens most noise. Com-

pared to the previous LHS, there's far much less wind noise around the windshield and windows.

+ ROADABILITY. It's more solid thanks to the more rigid car architecture and to modifications aimed at making handling as competent as possible. Specially calibrated shock absorbers are flexible but don't cause sway that would affect levelling. This car doesn't tend to buck and nosedive like the Concorde-Intrepid.

+ MANEUVERABILITY. It's great for such substantial cars. City parking or U-turns on narrow roads are no problem at all. Steering is smooth and accurate.

+ CONVENIENCE FEATURES. Most storage spots are roomy both front and rear. In the rear seat, travellers have access to a seat pocket and the center armrest hold a huge storage compartment and two cupholders. The absolutely hug trunk connects to the cabin via a ski slot.

+ HEADLAMPS. Definitely better than before. They have more reach and brilliance so you can drive with confidence.

+ INSTRUMENT PANEL. It's generally a lot like the LH dashboard and the layout is pretty much the same. But it's a lot more spiffy with its lush trim and remarkable instruments, especially inside the 300M with black on white gauges. The look is classy and finish details are exquisite.

CONS

- PERFORMANCES. The 3.5L engine's accelerations and pick-up left us unsatisfied, especially on the 300M, since performances don't match the character that the name evokes. They lack piquant and scores achieved prove it.

- BRAKES. They're only average even with all the elaborate refinements. Most stops were achieved at about 150 ft at 60 mph and they don't bite in when applied.

- AUTOMATIC GEARBOX. It doesn't provide any braking effect when downshifting manually, so brakes get no relief on long descending slopes with the LHS. The «AutoStick» sequential shifter that equips the 300M takes care of this matter, but shifting is sometimes pretty rough and ready if you want to speed up.

- A FEW MISSING FEATURES. There aren't any headrests worthy of the name in the rear seats and up front they can't be adjusted. The remote control for the door locks is slow and the control isn't too handy.

CONCLUSION

The success of the 300M and the LHS combines with that of the Concorde and Intrepid to prove — if any proof is needed — that Chrysler knows a lot more about the market for large North American style cars than it does about subcompacts and compacts, where its sales are languishing. With a little more quality added to interior design details, the ranks of buyers could swell even more.

Luxury - $35,000

RATING
CHRYSLER LHS-300M

CONCEPT :		84%
Technology :	80	
Safety :	90	
Interior space :	80	
Trunk volume :	90	
Quality/fit/finish :	80	

DRIVING :		67%
Cockpit :	80	
Performance :	65	
Handling :	55	
Steering :	80	
Braking :	55	

ORIGINAL EQUIPMENT :		80%
Tires :	80	
Headlights :	80	
Wipers :	70	
Rear defroster :	80	
Radio :	90	

COMFORT :		74%
Seats :	80	
Suspension :	80	
Sound level :	60	
Conveniences :	70	
Air conditioning :	80	

BUDGET :		53%
Price :	20	
Fuel economy :	60	
Insurance :	50	
Satisfaction :	85	
Depreciation :	50	

Overall rating :		71.6%

Luxury - $ 35,000

NEW FOR 2000
- Changes to the rear suspension for reduced NVH.
- Quarter-turn fuel cap design.
- Revised and easier-to-read instrumentation.
- Cupholders in the rear center armrest.
- Exterior colors: Garnet Red, Shale Green, Blue and Silver.

Compare Performance, Specifications, Prices, and Classification at the end of this chapter.

EQUIPMENT

CHRYSLER LH Series	300M	LHS
Automatic transmission:	S	S
Cruise control:	S	S
Power steering:	S	S
Anti-lock brakes:	S	S
Traction control:	S	S
Air conditioning:	SA	SA
Leather:	SH	SH
AM/FM/radio-cassette:	SCd	SCd
Power door locks:	S	S
Power windows:	S	S
Tilt steering:	S	S
Dual adjustable mirrors:	SEH	SEH
Alloy wheels:	S	S
Anti-theft system:	S	S

Colors
Exterior: Platinum, Silver, Garnet Red, Shale Green, Blue, Slate, White.

Interior: Pebble, Beige.

AT A GLANCE...

HISTORIC
Introduced in: 1994-1999.
Made in: Bramalea, Ontario, Canada.

DEMOGRAPHICS

Model	Men/Wom.	Age	Married	College	Income $
300M	60/40 %	50	78 %	41 %	56,500
LHS	90/10 %	60	87 %	37 %	60,000

INDEX

Safety:	90 %	Satisfaction:	78 %
Depreciation:	47 %	Insurance:	$ 765
Cost per mile:	$ 0.58	Number of dealers:	1,822

SALES

	Canada			USA		
Model	1997	1998	Result	1997	1998	Result
300M	-	1,947	-	-	30,765	-
LHS	1,327	1,269	- 4.4 %	30,189	16,753	- 44.5 %

MAINTENANCE REQUIRED BY WARRANTY

First revision:	Frequency:	Diagnostic plug:
5,000 miles	6 months / 6,000 miles	Yes

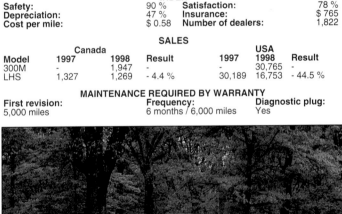

Double Take

The I30 is to Infiniti what the ES 300 is to Lexus. The only difference is that its sales are lower throughout North America. The reason for this shunning no doubt comes from the fact that since its introduction, this make has established no other identity than to act as a mirror image of the Lexus and Acura. Like the ES 300 and the 3.2TL, it is derived from a major standard production model. This leads to a substantial savings on research costs in the area of development and manufacturing since more than 75% of components are shared. The I30 is derived from the Maxima, which was revamped very recently.

MODEL RANGE

The I30 is a 4-door sedan that comes in base or "t" (for "Touring") versions. Their powertrains are identical and are composed of a 3.0L V6 engine and a 4-speed automatic transmission. A glance at the table on the right shows that standard equipment is very detailed and has been enriched with side airbags to protect the heads and torsos of passengers and active safety headrests in the front. Options include traction control, 17- inch alloy wheels, a rear spoiler, a sportier suspension and high-intensity headlights on all models.

TECHNICAL FEATURES

Identical to the Maxima's, the I30's body is distinctive because of its front and rear fascia styling, clearly signed Infiniti. Its steel unibody is very rigid and designed to withstand flexion and torsion. Its aerodynamics has improved and now it has a drag coefficient of 0.30. The I30's front suspension features MacPherson struts mounted on a frame that is independent from the chassis — the rear MultiLink suspension ensures good cornering capabilities. The standard four disc brakes, ABS system and limited-slip differential double as a traction control system.

PROS

+ **STYLING.** It's more successful than the Maxima's, with less controversial and more rounded lines and a smaller though distinctive grille. It has also shed it chromeladen look in favor of a simpler look - though it may be one that some potential buyers may find too stark.
+ **RIDE.** The rigid body and efficient suspensions make for very precise trajectories. The steering system is very responsive and braking is easy to gauge, which makes drivers feel confident. However, the performance levels show no real improvement because the power gain is matched by a gain in weight.
+ **HANDLING.** It's very consistent thanks in large part to the rear suspension which ensures excellent stability on both straight-line trajectories and corners, reducing variations in level control when slalom-type driving is required and at the same time, countering the rear's tendency to lift during emergency stops. The I30 is neutral under most circumstances and is relatively agile on winding roads.

+ **ENGINE.** The 3.0L V6 now offers excellent fuel economy and in spite of its high performance capabilities, its consumption is reasonable.
+ **COMFORT.** Ride is superb on highways, where the I30 capitalizes on its smooth suspension, efficient shock absorption and wheel travel. Thanks to effective soundproofing, the noise level is relatively low.
+ **PASSENGER ROOM.** The passenger compartment shows some improvement and bigger sizing provides easier access to both front and rear seats.
+ **TRUNK.** Its cargo capacity remains average, but the rear seat folds down for added cargo space. It's wide opening makes loading large items a lot easier.
+ **STORAGE SPACES.** They are many and varied. While the glovebox isn't particularly roomy, door pockets are very practical as are cupholders and the spaces positioned above the dashboard and in the center console.
+ **DASHBOARD.** It is remarkably well laid out, with easy-to-read instrumentation and a center console boasting excellent ergonomics and big, clear and easy-to-use radio and air conditioning controls.
+ **PRESENTATION.** It shows more taste than the Maxima's; the dashboard's plastics look good, leather trims are more appealing than before, and discreet wood inlays are very attractive.

CONS

- **SEATS.** They aren't more comfortable than they were on the previous model — the padding is too firm and they don't mold well. They don't provide enough support and are a major drawback on long outings, especially for rear-seat passengers. Given the minimal space between the seat and doors, the controls used to adjust the front-seat position are hard to reach.
- **BRAKING.** Brakes seem less efficient than previously and emergency stopping distances are long. However, stability and endurance are exemplary.
- **STEERING.** Its strong assistance makes it light and very sensitive, which presents some problems when drivers try to keep the car on course in high winds. Handling on the "t" version is questionable because of a turning radius longer than 39 ft. (12 m).
- **OVERSIGHTS.** No dashboard automatic transmission speed indicator, very small sideview mirrors, inefficient windshield wipers and defroster. As is the case with other cars in this class, there are no ventilation outlets in the rear of the car.

CONCLUSION

The I30 has progressed intelligently. More discreet, it offers good qualities including superb reliability - the kind that is likely to create a sense of loyalty among buyers. And should Infiniti ever decide to make an effort to heighten its products' profile, no doubt the number of buyers will increase.

RATING INFINITI I30		
CONCEPT :		**80%**
Technology :	85	
Safety :	90	
Interior space :	75	
Trunk volume :	65	
Quality/fit/finish :	85	
DRIVING :		**68%**
Cockpit :	80	
Performance :	65	
Handling :	60	
Steering :	75	
Braking :	60	
ORIGINAL EQUIPMENT :		**75%**
Tires :	80	
Headlights :	80	
Wipers :	65	
Rear defroster :	70	
Radio :	80	
COMFORT :		**78%**
Seats :	70	
Suspension :	80	
Sound level :	80	
Conveniences :	80	
Air conditioning :	80	
BUDGET :		**52%**
Price :	15	
Fuel economy :	65	
Insurance :	45	
Satisfaction :	90	
Depreciation :	45	
Overall rating :		**70.6%**

New 2000 Model

Luxury – $ 35,000

NEW FOR 2000

• The I30 is based on the Maxima's body and shares some of its mechanical components — the only difference between the two is few design details and equipment features.

Compare Performance, Specifications, Prices, and Classification at the end of this chapter.

EQUIPMENT

INFINITI I30	base	«t»
Automatic transmission:	S	S
Cruise control:	S	S
Power steering:	S	S
Anti-lock brakes:	S	S
Traction control:	S	S
Air conditioning:	SA	SA
Leather:	SH	SH
AM/FM/radio-cassette:	SCd	SCd
Power door locks:	S	S
Power windows:	S	S
Tilt steering:	S	S
Dual adjustable mirrors:	SEH	SEH
Alloy wheels:	S	S
Anti-theft system:	S	S

Colors

Exterior: Beige, Olive Green, White, Black, Chestnut, Blue, Aubergine, Crystal.

Interior: Sage, Beige, Black.

AT A GLANCE...

HISTORIC
Introduced in:	1995.
Made in:	Oppama, Japon.

DEMOGRAPHICS
Model	Men/Wom.	Age	Married	College	Income $
I30	90/10 %	67	81 %	67 %	80,000

INDEX
Safety:	90 %	Satisfaction:	92 %
Depreciation:	35 %	Insurance:	$ 800
Cost per mile:	$ 0.65	Number of dealers:	150

SALES
	Canada			USA		
Model	1997	1998	Result	1997	1998	Result
I30	744	647	- 13.0 %	31,303	26,350	- 15.8 %

MAINTENANCE REQUIRED BY WARRANTY
First revision:	Frequency:	Diagnostic plug:
7,500 miles	6 months / 7,500 miles	Yes

The Lexus ES 300 has often served as the bench-mark for the affordable luxury car. However, over time its price has increased more rapidly than its content level and the result has been a drop in sales on the North American market as a whole. The existence of a Camry that may be less exclusive but that is significantly less expensive has a lot to do with this recent development and so does the arrival of the RX 300, offering AWD and more flexibility for a very similar price.

Dropping

MODEL RANGE

The Lexus ES 300 is sold in a single trim level 4-door sedan equipped with lush standard items including traction control and antilock braking system, memory driver's seat and light alloy rims, not to mention climate control, cruise control, stereo sound system and all the usual power functions, to which can be added options or option packages...

TECHNICAL FEATURES

The ES 300 is derived from the Camry platform, so it's equipped with its mechanical features and bears traces of some similar body and window design details. During the last revision, it received a longer wheelbase and the car is now 2 in. longer from bumper to bumper. Its overall design borrows from the cab forward principle, inaugurated by Chrysler on its LH models, that expands cabin space and provides better visibility. Its very clean body design explains why the drag coefficient sits at 0.29. Most ot the steel unibody's panels are galvanized on both sides. The fully independent suspension uses MacPherson struts and stabilizer bars. The car can also

be equipped with the optional Adaptive Variable Suspension (AVS) that constantly adjusts shock absorber pressure to road conditions and lets you select suspension travel in supple, normal or sport mode, according to 16 different combinations. The front and rear are mounted on independent cradles via rubber components that filter out noise and vibration. The 3.0L V6 engine is just like the one that powered the former model, but a dual exhaust system gives it another 2 hp. The adaptive transmission records the driver's style and anticipates his or her moves.

PROS

+ DESIGN. It's lovely inside and out, graced with delicate, subtle touches. Body design is elegant and the cabin is meticulously rendered.

+ RIDE COMFORT. It's wonderful with the flexible suspension travel, nice cushy seats and very low noise level due to very effective soundproofing. The ride, more American than Japanese or European, which is the reason behind this model's success.

+PERFORMANCES. Accelerations and pickup are brisk due to a favorable power to weight ratio.

+ HANDLING. It's nice and stable in most circumstances, yet the car is quite agile on slalom runs due to reasonable vehicle size and weight (that has increased).

+ BRAKES. They're efficient, well-balanced and tough, but ABS sometimes causes snags as does the traction control that's linked to it.

+ DRIVING PLEASURE. It's the fine result of smooth controls, silky and discreet engine demeanor and the feeling of security when you know you have good control of the vehicle (while braking or accelerating) and you sure get used to all those standard creature comforts in a hurry.

+ INSTRUMENT PANEL. It's slick and looks neat and uncluttered. It's nicely shaped and instrument gauges have cathode-ray tube lighting on which red LED-type needles move, adding a high tech touch to the ensemble.

+ QUALITY. It's obvious in every way: construction is well crafted, fit and finish are meticulously rendered and trim materials are treated to last. It all looks and feels lovely.

+ CONVENIENCE FEATURES. The trunk is very generous and easy to get to and there are more numerous and more convenient storage spots for front seat passengers.

CONS

- VALUE. It's not as obvious as it should be. In spite of its very detailed equipment, the ES 300 is too expensive in this particular class, and when a model's reputation isn't impressive enough to justify the expense, beyond a certain limit, po-

tential buyers simply decide to look elsewhere.

- ADAPTIVE SUSPENSION. Even with the sophisticated AVS system, it isn't perfect for it doesn't really predict the driver's moves and exaggerates suspension response every which way.

- DRIVING. The ES 300 is capable of brilliant performances and is equipped with a high tech suspension, but it isn't really fun to drive, because it has no soul, so to speak. Everything is over-assisted and squeaky clean, like the steering and braking systems that are a bit wishy washy.

- USEFUL SPACE. There's slightly less of it and the cabin can really only comfortably accommodate four adults. The trunk is less roomy than on previous model and it only connects with the cabin via a ski-sized pass-through. But the trunk door is lower to allow for handier luggage handling.

- ERGONOMICS. This aspect of the main section of the dashboard isn't too great, for it isn't angled toward the driver enough and switches located on the left of the steering wheel are nearly invisible.

- TO BE IMPROVED UPON. The rather useless front door side-pockets and lack of storage space for rear seat passengers, hard to adjust brakes and maneuverability that could be better.

CONCLUSION

For many consumers looking for an affordable luxury car, the ES 300 isn't as fascinating as it used to be. The competitive field is too crowded and the attraction of more flexible vehicles is too strong for it to continue monopolizing this market niche for very much longer.

Luxury - $ 35,000

RATING
LEXUS ES 300

CONCEPT :   75%
Technology :   85
Safety :   90
Interior space :   60
Trunk volume :   55
Quality/fit/finish : 85

DRIVING :   70%
Cockpit :   80
Performance :   65
Handling :   60
Steering :   75
Braking :   70

ORIGINAL EQUIPMENT :   77%
Tires :   80
Headlights :   80
Wipers :   65
Rear defroster :   75
Radio :   85

COMFORT :   82%
Seats :   80
Suspension :   85
Sound level :   80
Conveniences :   80
Air conditioning :   85

BUDGET :   53%
Price :   10
Fuel economy :   65
Insurance :   45
Satisfaction :   90
Depreciation :   55

Overall rating :   71.4%

Luxury - $ 35,000

NEW FOR 2000

- **A few minor touch-ups.**
- **A multitude of safety, design and luxury enhancements.**

Compare
Performance,
Specifications, Prices,
and Classification
at the end of this chapter.

EQUIPMENT

LEXUS ES 300   base

Automatic transmission: S
Cruise control: S
Power steering: S
Anti-lock brakes: S
Traction control: S
Air conditioning: SA
Leather: O
AM/FM/radio-cassette: S
Power door locks: S
Power windows: S
Tilt steering: S
Dual adjustable mirrors: SH
Alloy wheels: S
Anti-theft system: S

Colors

Exterior: White, Black, Silver, Ruby, Beige, Pink, Green, Blue.

Interior: Cloth: Black, Taupe. Leather: Black, Ivory, Taupe, Oak.

AT A GLANCE...

HISTORIC

Introduced in: 1992-1997.
Made in: Tahara, Japan.

DEMOGRAPHICS

Model	Men/Wom.	Age	Married	College	Income $
ES 300	73/27 %	54	88 %	66 %	88,000

INDEX

Safety:	90 %	Satisfaction:	90 %
Depreciation:	45 %	Insurance:	$ 875
Cost per mile:	$ 0.68	Number of dealers:	167

SALES

	Canada			USA		
Model	1997	1998	Result	1997	1998	Result
ES 300	1,936	1,435	- 25.9 %	58,430	48,644	- 16.7 %

MAINTENANCE REQUIRED BY WARRANTY

First revision:	Frequency:	Diagnostic plug:
3,750 miles	3,750 miles	Yes

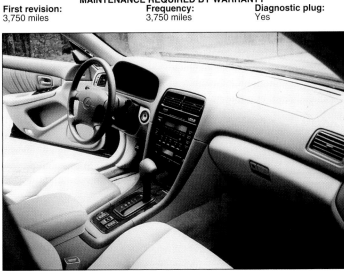

International

After the arrival of the Cadillac Catera, Ford could no longer stay out of the market for luxury cars at "affordable" prices, a niche foreign builders created long ago and where Volvo and BMW clearly dominate in spite of the offensive launched by the Japanese, who still haven't succeeded in dislodging the traditional leaders. When the time came to try to create a small Jaguar, rationalization and globalization gave the second largest car builder the opportunity to create a clone that will double as a down-market Lincoln.

MODEL RANGE

The Lincoln LS is a rear-wheel drive 4-door sedan available in two versions. The LS6 has a Duratec 3.0L V6 borrowed from the Taurus and the Sable and a standard 5-speed automatic transmission and an optional 5-speed Getrag manual transmission. The LS8 is powered by a 3.9L V8 and a SelectShift 5-speed automatic transmission. The latter is derived from the unit that equips the Jaguar S-type and other models of the same British make, including the XK and the XJ. As would be expected on a model in this class, the LS offers fairly detailed equipment.

TECHNICAL FEATURES

The Lincoln LS shares its platform with the Jaguar S-type, introduced a little earlier in the year. Like most European models in this class, it remains loyal to rear-wheel drive — the reason is that unlike Japanese automobiles, it isn't derived from economical models already on the market. To reinforce its sense of belonging to the European automotive heritage, it has been redesigned by an international team led by a German expert. Its arch-like styling capitalizes on the long wheelbase, which spells superior riding comfort. The steel unibody is equipped with galvanized side panels. It also features a subchassis supporting the rear-end assembly, insulated from the cockpit by rubber components. Hoods and fenders are made of aluminum and bumpers are covered with a thermoplastic material. Front and rear suspensions are independent. Both feature long and short arms with coil springs, gas shock absorbers and an anti-roll bar. An electronic power steering system and four disc ABS brakes are standard, only the LS8 has a standard traction control system, effective at all speed levels.

PROS

+ SIZE. On the exterior, it's somewhere between the current Aurora and the Lexus ES 300. However, though it's bulkier than the latter, its useable space is equivalent to what the former offers.

+ COMFORT. Smooth is the only way to describe the combination of a suspension with generous travel and good control and well-padded seats that mold well and provide effective support, even for rear-seat passengers — a rare commodity.

+ PERFORMANCE. Both engines fall into the range that's average for this class. Of course, the V8 is more forthcoming and results in a better weight/power ratio, which in turn leads to quicker acceleration and pick-up. Handling is surprisingly sure and this model is well-balanced and very reassuring. The LS can handle any kind of cornering problem-free and during our test drives, slalom courses proved that these models are agile enough to attract owners who prefer sporty driving.

+ TRUNK. Not many cars in this class have a trunk that's this roomy and the 60/40 fold down seat makes for even more cargo space when needed.

+ BONUS POINTS. For efficient wipers whose high speed ensures efficient cleaning of 80% of the windshield surface, and an automatic setting that adjusts their action to suit rain intensity.

CONS

- PRESENTATION. The body design shows a certain amount of originality, but the Lexus-inspired passenger compartment is deadly dull, with a flat center console. Plastics look down-market and are inferior to those found on much less expensive models. The fake wood inlay above the glovebox is much too loud to be classy. And the same jarring note is repeated in the trunk, where the lining is not something worthy of a car sold at this price.

- SUSPENSION. It reacts badly to poor road surfaces and tends to jostle passengers.

- ACCESS. The doors on our test models didn't open wide enough (75°) to provide easy entry/exit for larger passengers. This phenomenon is more obvious in the rear, where doors aren't as long as they are in the front.

- PRACTICALITY. Designers have forgotten to include the kinds of storage spaces that are so important for people who use the small amenities typical of modern life. The glovebox is ridiculously small and not very practical (basically, it's designed for the owner's manual and not much else), door pockets are useless given the minimal space between doors and seat sides, the center console has a merely symbolic bin, and rear-seat passengers have only two catchalls and two cupholders for their supposed convenience.

- ODD FEATURES. At times the automatic transmission on our test model had a hard time to decide on the best choice between third and fourth gear and shifting was far from smooth. It remains to be seen if this phenomenon is generalized or typical of preproduction units.

- NEGATIVE POINTS. For seats that are almost impossible to adjust when the vehicle is in operation, the reason being the very minimal space between doors and seat sides. For an excessively light steering system that makes some maneuvers harder than they need be.

CONCLUSION

Destined mainly for the North American market, thanks to its international format there's no doubt that the latest LS will be the first Lincoln likely to be sold on a truly worldwide scale.

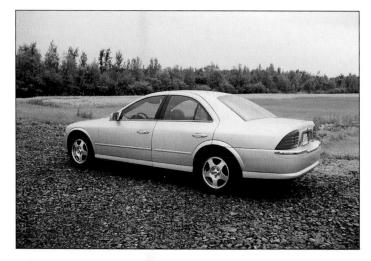

RATING LINCOLN LS		
CONCEPT :		**79%**
Technology :	85	
Safety :	90	
Interior space :	70	
Trunk volume :	70	
Quality/fit/finish :	80	
DRIVING :		**69%**
Cockpit :	80	
Performance :	65	
Handling :	55	
Steering :	75	
Braking :	70	
ORIGINAL EQUIPMENT :		**77%**
Tires :	80	
Headlights :	75	
Wipers :	70	
Rear defroster :	75	
Radio :	85	
COMFORT :		**74%**
Seats :	80	
Suspension :	80	
Sound level :	80	
Conveniences :	50	
Air conditioning :	80	
BUDGET :		**53%**
Price :	10	
Fuel economy :	55	
Insurance :	40	
Satisfaction :	85	
Depreciation :	75	
Overall rating :		**70.4%**

New 2000 Model

Luxury - $ 35,000

NEW FOR 2000

- **The first incarnation of a model that shares with the Jaguar S-TYPE its design concept, platform and some mechanical components, such as the V8 engine.**

Compare
Performance,
Specifications, Prices,
and Classification
at the end of this chapter.

EQUIPMENT

LINCOLN LS	LS6	LS8
Automatic transmission:	S	S
Cruise control:	S	S
Power steering:	S	S
Anti-lock brakes:	S	S
Traction control:	O	S
Air conditioning:	SA	SA
Leather:	S	S
AM/FM/radio-cassette:	SCd	SCd
Power door locks:	S	S
Power windows:	S	S
Tilt steering:	S	S
Dual adjustable mirrors:	SEH	SEH
Alloy wheels:	S	S
Anti-theft system:	S	S

Colors
Exterior: Gold, Green, Cordovan, Ivory, Blue, Wedgewood, Silver, Black, White.

Interior: Graphite, Parchment, Truffle, Charcoal.

AT A GLANCE...

HISTORIC
Introduced in: 2000.
Made in: Wixom, Michigan, USA.

DEMOGRAPHICS

Model	Men/Wom.	Age	Married	College	Income $
LS	NA				

INDEX

Safety:	90 %	Satisfaction:	83 %
Depreciation:	25 %	Insurance:	$ 965
Cost per mile:	$ 0.70	Number of dealers:	5,200

SALES

	Canada			USA		
Model	1997	1998	Result	1997	1998	Result
LS	Not on sale during this period.					

MAINTENANCE REQUIRED BY WARRANTY

First revision:	Frequency:	Diagnostic plug:
6,000 miles	6 months/ 6,000 miles	Yes

Original

There's no question that Mazda is the only company with a model whose name is perfectly timed for the new-millennium fever. For the occasion, the Millenia will be marketed in a special and one-and-only edition. Maybe the new tactic will be the chance to convince more car-lovers to trust it and it might just increase sales, which have always lingered in the lower levels. Proportionately, the Millenia is more popular in the United States than in Canada.

MODEL RANGE

The Millenia is a four-door front-wheel drive sedan. It exists this year only in a millennium special edition based on the S model who receives a 2.3L V6 that benefits from the Miller cycle technology. This version is richly equipped and items include leather-clad seats, front heated seats, traction control associated with an antilock braking device, as well as all the plush power functions that go with this luxury category. For the year 2000, it will also feature 17-inch alloy wheels, an interior design intended to highlight the advent of the year 2000, and a dashboard-mounted CD changer.

TECHNICAL FEATURES

The Millenia has a steel monocoque body blessed with lovely, flowing lines and a 0.29 drag coefficient, proof that aerodynamics are simply great. The fully independent suspension uses shock struts and transverse A-arms with stabilizer bars. Cars are equipped with variable assist steering and disc brakes linked to a standard ABS-traction control system. The S version engine benefits from the Miller cycle which allows for a high expansion rate with a low compression ratio, thanks to well-tailored valve settings and a Lysholm supercharger. Compression time is pared down to create a fifth stroke cycle that optimizes cylinder feed and generates a stronger explosion with equal displacement, the end result being 1.5 more torque and power, yet fuel consumption is cut down by 10 to 15%.

PROS

+ PRICE. By lowering the sales price of year 2000 models, Mazda will make undecided customers think twice and so it'll attract new buyers until the next model hits the market.

+ SILHOUETTE. It's aristocratic elegance has a certain charm, but it doesn't exactly grab your attention.

+ RIDE COMFORT. The millennium model had a cushy suspension rather than being stiff. Seats provide good lateral and lumbar support and low noise interference is the direct result of effective soundproofing.

+ PERFORMANCES. The Miller cycle engine's output equals the sports car kind of power to weight ratio, even with the hefty weight and smaller displacement, performances are above average for this category.

+ HANDLING. It's super, since well-controlled sway lets you negotiate curves with assurance. Responsive steering benefits from a good reduction ratio so directional flow is accurate and the car is agile on snaky runs.

+ EQUIPMENT. This version is very elaborate and its standard heated front seats are sure to be a hit with buyers from northern climats.

+ QUALITY. Assembly has a solid, rugged feel, finish job is clean and trim materials have a nice look and texture.

+ TRUNK. It's unusually deep, so it holds loads of luggage, but it isn't convertible since the rear seatbench is fixed and the CD player cuts down on height.

CONS

- DEPRECIATION. It's dramatic for these models don't have the reputation of the well-loved ES 300 or the panache of the zoomy Infiniti I30.

- AUTOMATIC. It won't turn all sportsy drivers' crank, for it's slow as molasses when upshifting and downshifting and in some cases, you have to force the downshift.

- FUEL CONSUMPTION. The Miller engine isn't as efficient as Mazda states it is, for fuel consumption varies between 17 and 19 mpg, and more if your driving is extreme.

- BRAKES. They aren't the best match for the Millennium version's zippy style, since stopping distances are quite long in emergency situations. But the antilock braking system works beautifully, so stops are straight and brakes hold up well when put through the works.

- SUSPENSION. It's as stiff in the overloaded front as it is in the rear, where wheel travel is limited. This means that it misbehaves on bumpy roads and passenger comfort suffers the consequences.

- INSTRUMENT PANEL. Its stylistic appeal isn't at all like that of the body design and the shape of gauges and layout are distracting, for some controls are a bit weird.

- CABIN SPACE. It's limited for rear seat passengers who have to put up with cramped toe and head room, so much so that a third passenger won't persevere too long. Lastly, the rounded arch design and short rear doors obstruct easy access.

- CONVENIENCE FEATURES. Storage space goes lacking, since the glove compartment has been replaced by the airbag housing and the compartment in the center console, though fairly roomy, can't really replace it.

- FRONT-WHEEL DRIVE. It doesn't do justice to the capabilities of the Miller cycle engine that would be better suited to a rear-wheel car.

CONCLUSION

The Millenia is a little known model, presented in an elegant package and boasting an original and efficient mechanical system. However, it's too bad that a dismal dashboard design and an inferior resale value combine to make this model a financial risk, no matter how much passion it may inspire.

Luxury $ 35,000

RATING
MAZDA Millenia

CONCEPT :   75%
Technology :	80
Safety :	100
Interior space :	60
Trunk volume :	55
Quality/fit/finish :	80

DRIVING :   66%
Cockpit :	70
Performance :	60
Handling :	60
Steering :	80
Braking :	60

ORIGINAL EQUIPMENT :   77%
Tires :	80
Headlights :	80
Wipers :	80
Rear defroster :	70
Radio :	75

COMFORT :   72%
Seats :	80
Suspension :	80
Sound level :	70
Conveniences :	50
Air conditioning :	80

BUDGET :   52%
Price :	20
Fuel economy :	65
Insurance :	45
Satisfaction :	85
Depreciation :	45

Overall rating :   68.4%

NEW FOR 2000

• Only the S version will be marketed in a special version designed to underline the new millennium.

Compare Performance, Specifications, Prices, and Classification at the end of this chapter.

Luxury $ 35,000

EQUIPMENT

MAZDA Millenia	S
Automatic transmission:	S
Cruise control:	S
Power steering:	S
Anti-lock brakes:	S
Traction control:	S
Air conditioning:	SA
Leather:	SH
AM/FM/radio-cassette:	SCd
Power door locks:	S
Power windows:	S
Tilt steering:	S
Dual adjustable mirrors:	SEH
Alloy wheels:	S
Anti-theft system:	S

Colors

Exterior: Red, Silver.

Interior: Charcoal.

AT A GLANCE...

HISTORIC
Introduced in: 1994.
Made in: Hofu, Japan.

DEMOGRAPHICS
Model	Men/Wom.	Age	Married	College	Income $
Millenia	81/19 %	50	87 %	61 %	78,500

INDEX
Safety:	90 %	Satisfaction:	87 %
Depreciation:	53 %	Insurance:	$ 850
Cost per mile:	$ 0.67	Number of dealers:	871

SALES
	Canada			USA		
Model	1997	1998	Result	1997	1998	Result
Millenia	469	501	+ 6.8 %	18,020	16,717	- 7.2 %

MAINTENANCE REQUIRED BY WARRANTY
First revision:	Frequency:	Diagnostic plug:
5,000 miles	5,000 miles	Yes

The entry-level model in the German manufacturer's prestigious lineup has very few changes to offer for 2000 and no doubt it will be revamped sometime during the model-year. The same size as a Jetta, the C-Class models are the least expensive way to own a Mercedes. Small wonder they're the stars of the prestige builder's offerings and the most widely sold throughout the world.

Snobbish

MODEL RANGE

The mini-Mercedes is a 4-door sedan offered in three different versions: the C230K animated by a 2.3L 4-cylinder engine zoomed up by a supercharger (Kompressor), the C280 with 2.8L V6 and the C43, the sportiest of the bunch, that comes equipped with a 4.3L V8 like the one on the CLK's , the E-Class and M-Class. Each of these versions receives a 5-speed automatic transmission including a "Winter" mode that achieves a standing start in 2nd gear and changes speed at low rpm to facilitate certain maneuvers. The antilock braking-traction control combination are standard on all models, while the ASR anti-skid system is standard on the C280 and C43. For year 2000, all models benefit from standard ESP (Electronic Stability Program). Apart from these features, general equipment is lavish, including climate control, cruise control, leather trim and a new Audio 30 sound system with eight speakers.

TECHNICAL FEATURES

The steel monocoque body includes fully galvanized panels but only yields average aerodynamics, since the drag coefficient is a mere 0.32. The structure is very rigid and includes some unusual passenger protection features for the category. The fully independent suspension consists of MacPherson struts and lower A-arms with an anti-dive device and negative roll camber. At the rear, Mercedes has once again refined its famous "multi-link" system, including anti-lift and anti-dive devices with hydropneumatic shocks. Cars are equipped with disc brakes assisted by a standard ABS device.

PROS

+ SAFETY FEATURES. These cars are super-solid and offer optimum resistance in all kinds of collisions and are equipped with all the usual passenger protection devices, even if all these high tech elements aren't reflected in the score given by the N.H.T.S.A.

+ QUALITY. This Mercedes is sturdily built, benefits from a meticulous finish job and is furbished with top-notch trim materials, elements that give an exceptional cohesiveness to these vehicles.

+ STYLE. It's more flowing and balanced than before. Over the years, the C-Class has had a lot of face-lifts and they now look less staid and bulky.

+ ROADHOLDING. It's very reassuring with the superb rear suspension that ensures perfect directional flow and the more competent adherence with the sophisticated and effective traction control. These well-honed systems are amazing since the C-Class now benefits from technical features designed for the E and S-Class.

+ PERFORMANCES. The various engines tested achieved accelerations and pickup, each in their own way, that were truly worthy of sports cars. The supercharger on the 4-cylinder brings a welcome boost, even if this approach doesn't seem to make the most sense.

+ BRAKES. They're very effective since they bring things to a halt in a hurry and car path is straight as an arrow in all situations and brakes can really take a beating.

+ STEERING. It's smooth, crisp and nicely powered and benefits from a better reduction ratio than was once the case, but the steering wheel diameter is still wider than average.

+ CABIN SPACE. It finally accomodates four adults comfortably and the trunk is a good size, it's convenient and can be lengthened by folding down the rear split-fold seatbench.

+ DASHBOARD. It's logically and rationally laid out and controls such as the CD storage box and other items are lined up like soldiers. Instrumentation is easy to read, but the steering wheel still seems oversized.

+ NICE FEATURES. The cruise control that's regulated by a control that's well in sight and within easy reach.

CONS

- CABIN DESIGN. The interior is rather plain for such a pricey car.

- VISIBILITY. Rear view at quarterback is obstructed by the thick C pillar, so some parking maneuvers are a bit tricky.

- RIDE COMFORT. It's never been super-cushy for the suspension and seat upholstery are firm and some power train, road and wind noise reach occupants' ears inside the model equipped with the 4-cylinder model.

- SHIFTER. The automatic transmission is afflicted with one of the most annoying shifters around, it zigzags this way and that so you have to keep looking down to check your moves.

- ACCESS. Tall passengers still have a tough time climbing into the rear seats, since the doors are narrow and ceiling clearance is rather snug.

- DRIVING. On really slick and slippery roads, you have to keep your wits about you, even with all the electronic devices such as the ABS, traction control and anti-skid system, for when adherence gets iffy, the rear end swings and swerves abruptly, not giving the driver much latitude, since he or she can't always accelerate as needed to get things under control.

- TO BE IMPROVED UPON. Certain accessories (windshield wipers, climate control, radio) or controls (headlights, parking brake) aren't in keeping with current world standards and you need a serious briefing or practice session to learn to use them adequately.

CONCLUSION

Although they're the second most popular of the family in the USA, in our view the C-Class models aren't the best that Mercedes has to offer. Their size limitations result in a host of compromises and as a result, no one is every really satisfied onboard these cars.

Luxury
- $35 000

RATING
MERCEDES-BENZ C-Class

CONCEPT : — 74%
Technology :	90
Safety :	90
Interior space :	45
Trunk volume :	55
Quality/fit/finish :	90

DRIVING : — 70%
Cockpit :	80
Performance :	60
Handling :	60
Steering :	80
Braking :	70

ORIGINAL EQUIPMENT : — 78%
Tires :	80
Headlights :	80
Wipers :	70
Rear defroster :	80
Radio :	80

COMFORT : — 74%
Seats :	75
Suspension :	75
Sound level :	70
Conveniences :	70
Air conditioning :	80

BUDGET : — 54%
Price :	10
Fuel economy :	75
Insurance :	45
Satisfaction :	85
Depreciation :	55

Overall rating : — 70.0%

NEW FOR 2000
- Standard Touch Shift 5-speed automatic transmission with electronic cruise control and traction control.
- New options: Xenon headlights and Tele Aid safety communications system.
- Standard Electronic Stability Program (ESP).

Compare Performance, Specifications, Prices, and Classification at the end of this chapter.

Luxury - $ 35,000

EQUIPMENT

MERCEDES-BENZ C-Class	C230K	C280
Automatic transmission:	S	S
Cruise control:	S	S
Power steering:	S	S
Anti-lock brakes:	S	S
Traction control:	S	S
Air conditioning:	SM	SA
Leather:	O	S
AM/FM/radio-cassette:	S	S
Power door locks:	S	S
Power windows:	S	S
Tilt steering:	S	S
Dual adjustable mirrors:	SEH	SEH
Alloy wheels:	S	S
Anti-theft system:	S	S

Colors

Exterior: Black, Red, Blue, White, Grey, Green, Silver.

Interior: Black, Blue, Parchment, Ash.

AT A GLANCE...

HISTORIC
Introduced in:	1993 (C).
Made in:	Sindelfingen & Brement, Germany.

DEMOGRAPHICS

Model	Men/Wom.	Age	Married	College	Income $
C-Class	68/32 %	51	77 %	58 %	71,500

INDEX

Safety:	90 %	Satisfaction:	85 %
Depreciation:	45 %	Insurance:	$ 1,135
Cost per mile:	$ 0.72	Number of dealers:	380

SALES

	Canada			USA		
Model	1997	1998	Result	1997	1998	Result
C-Class	2,488	3,101	+ 24.6 5 %	32,543	34,487	+ 6.0 %

MAINTENANCE REQUIRED BY WARRANTY

First revision:	Frequency:	Diagnostic plug:
3,000 miles	7,500 miles	Yes

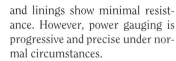
Isolated

When it comes to sales on the North American market, Mitsubishi can't reach the same heights as its main rivals, Toyota and Honda. This is all the stranger given the fact that in other countries, it fares better than Honda, which in Japan is considered to be a secondary power compared to the Mitsubishi empire. The explanation probably lies in this particular builder's market approach and corporate culture, both of which reflect its relationship with the outside world: secretive and baffling!

MODEL RANGE

The Diamante is a 4-door sedan available in a sole version equipped with a SOHC 3.5L V6 engine coupled with a 4-speed automatic transmission. The base's standard equipment includes power steering, cruise control, automatic air conditioning, a radio and cassette player, power windows, power locks and power sideview mirrors, an adjustable steering column and an anti-theft system.

There are three option packages called the "Luxury", "Premium" and "Platinum" which add leather seats, alloy wheels, compact disc, color-keyed moldings, sunroof, fog lights an many-many other convenience items.

TECHNICAL FEATURES

The body is based on the same platform as the previous model's. Its steel unibody has a very low drag coefficient, 0.28, a number that is very impressive for this class. The fully independent suspension features MacPherson struts in the front and multi-arms in the rear, mounted on a subchassis and featuring stabilizing bars. The Diamante is equipped with four disc brakes and ABS.

The latest Diamante doesn't have as many electronic gadgets as the previous model — such as suspension management, four-wheel drive, or traction control.

The latest V6 engine has an output of 210 horses, 38 more than the previous unit, for an increase of 22%. Overall weight has decreased by some 200 pounds (100 kilos), resulting in a power/weight ratio similar to what a sports model can provide.

The sophisticated electronic ATCM transmission is designed to adapt to individual driving styles, matching the gear to road conditions or specific driver parameters.

PROS

+ PERFORMANCE. Levels are significantly higher, to the point of giving this model a completely different personality. While the previous incarnation was sluggish, this one can go from 0 to 60 mph (0 to 100 km/h) in a exactly the same time as it takes a BMW 528i!

+ COMFORT. It's regal given the smooth suspension and completely quiet ride. Seats mold well and provide good support although their firmness is a tad Teutonic.

+ QUALITY. It's as obvious outside, where many features are BMW-like (such as headlamps), as it is on the inside, where leather seats are very nice-looking. Flaws on the previous model (such as ugly fake wood inlays) have been eliminated. Assembly is careful, finish is meticulous and plastics used for the dashboard are appealing to the eye and touch.

+ FUEL ECONOMY. In spite of more engine power, fuel consumption is lower given more streamlined styling and a lower weight.

+ HANDLING. It's more natural and more consistent mainly because it's free of the usual power systems that prevent the driver from getting any real feedback on what's going on between the car and the road surface. The same holds true for the steering system, whose assistance and turning radius ensure driving ease. The only drawback is slight overassistance, which makes the system overly sensitive.

+ PRACTICALITY. Practical features include a large glovebox, a center console bin and spaces for front-seat passengers and a number of similar small spaces for rear-seat occupants.

+ SOUNDPROOFING. The noise level is low, tire and engine noise is well dampened and the model's aerodynamic design minimizes wind noise.

CONS

- BRAKING. Emergency stopping distances are longer than average and linings show minimal resistance. However, power gauging is progressive and precise under normal circumstances.

- TRUNK. It's relatively small for a car of this size, it lacks in length, and rear seats do not fold down. Most of the competition's models offer 1.5 cu. ft. (50 litres) more space and it's about time to add a folddown rear seat to the Diamante.

- DASHBOARD. Far from winning, it's dull and unimaginative and some controls - notably the speed governor positioned below the steering wheel - aren't very practical.

- NOISE LEVEL. When the engine is running all out it's far from quiet and a better exhaust system is in order.

- OVERSIGHTS. Buyers have to pick and choose among options to improve the equipment level, which includes only the minimum number of amenities acceptable in this class. You'd think that this type of approach was a thing of the past, especially since American builders themselves have decided to provide very elaborate standard equipment.

CONCLUSION

The Diamante isn't any worse a car than any of its Asian competitors. However, the corporation's attitude and its marketing policy do nothing to encourage potential consumers to take a risk on this model and as a result, sales have dropped by 25%.

RATING		
MITSUBISHI Diamante		
CONCEPT :		76%
Technology :	80	
Safety :	90	
Interior space :	70	
Trunk volume :	60	
Quality/fit/finish :	80	
DRIVING :		65%
Cockpit :	80	
Performance :	60	
Handling :	50	
Steering :	80	
Braking :	55	
ORIGINAL EQUIPMENT :		76%
Tires :	80	
Headlights :	80	
Wipers :	70	
Rear defroster :	70	
Radio :	80	
COMFORT :		79%
Seats :	80	
Suspension :	80	
Sound level :	80	
Conveniences :	75	
Air conditioning :	80	
BUDGET :		46%
Price :	15	
Fuel economy :	55	
Insurance :	30	
Satisfaction :	85	
Depreciation :	45	
Overall rating :		**68.4%**

NEW FOR 2000
• **No details available at press time.**

Compare
Performance,
Specifications, Prices,
and Classification
at the end of this chapter.

Luxury

EQUIPMENT

MITSUBISHI Diamante	base
Automatic transmission:	S
Cruise control:	S
Power steering:	S
Anti-lock brakes:	S
Traction control:	O
Air conditioning:	SA
Leather:	O
AM/FM/radio-cassette:	S
Power door locks:	S
Power windows:	S
Tilt steering:	S
Dual adjustable mirrors:	SE
Alloy wheels:	O
Anti-theft system:	S

Colors

Exterior: White, Black, Blue, Silver.

Interior: Tan, Black, Blue.

AT A GLANCE...

HISTORIC
Introduced in: 1990-1996.
Made in: Adelaide, Australia.

DEMOGRAPHICS

Model	Men/Wom.	Age	Married	College	Income $
Diamante	55/45 %	51	90 %	56 %	75,000

INDEX

Safety:	90 %	Satisfaction:	85 %
Depreciation:	50 %	Insurance:	$ 900
Cost per mile:	$ 0.68	Number of dealers:	500

SALES

Model	Canada 1997	1998	Result	USA 1997	1998	Result
Diamante	Not sold in Canada			11,402	8,563	- 24.9 %

MAINTENANCE REQUIRED BY WARRANTY

First revision:	Frequency:	Diagnostic plug:
3,000 miles	6 months / 6,000 miles	Yes

The Next Generation

Today, it's evident that the Aurora's development and commercialization marked a true turning point and a major change of mentality at General Motors. From that time on, the concept of quality began to make inroads and the positive reaction from consumers convinced the leading U.S. car builder's executives that whether they liked it or not, they had to continue along the same path, even if it was a departure with a corporate culture that had lasted for decades.

MODEL RANGE

Oldsmobile offers only a single version of the Aurora. This classy four-door sedan benefits from a 4.0L DOHC V8, a spin-off from the Cadillac Northstar. It's paired up with a 4-speed automatic transmission. This car is literally loaded with goodies and the only options available in the catalogue are the Autobahn package (V-rated tires and axle ratio of 3.71), chrome rims, an Acoustimass sound system with seven speakers, a 12-CD changer in the trunk, sunroof, 45/45 bucket seats and gold-plated insignia!

TECHNICAL FEATURES

The Aurora is the upshot of the work of engineers at Cadillac who designed it based on the Riviera platform. The steel body is a unitized structure and in spite of its bold shape, the drag coefficient sits at only an average 0.31. In order to keep vehicle weight down, lightweight materials were used: for example, aluminum for the hood and nylon for the gas tank. A tubular cage provides passenger protection and the chassis has a natural frequency of 25 Hz. The 4.0L V8 engine on this front-wheel drive car

was developed precisely for this model; in fact, 14 patents were registered in the process. This transversely mounted V8 pumps out 250 hp. The fully independent suspension uses MacPherson struts up front and semi-trailing arms with lateral joints at the rear with stabilizer bar at both ends. The disc brakes benefit from standard ABS-traction control.

PROS

+ **CONCEPT.** The Aurora is a beauty, but her appeal is more than skin-deep. The Aurora concept aims at producing a modern, topnotch product at an affordable price. This new approach represents something of a dramatic change at General Motors who don't usually have this attitude.

+ **VALUE.** Compared to rivals, the Aurora is a darn good buy with its sophisticated V8 and lush equipment, offered at a price equivalent to that of V6-animated rivals.

+ **ESTHETICS.** The body design isn't revolutionary, but it's unique and is easily recognizable. Owners like its avant-garde style and the way the cabin interior is rendered.

+ **QUALITY.** Assembly is robust, finish job is more meticulous than usual at GM and most trim materials look spiffy.

+ **CABIN DESIGN.** Inside there's a superb instrument panel with main section curved toward the driver.

+ **HANDLING.** The Aurora is anything but nimble on its feet, for its plump weight is a real handicap. Generally speaking, it stays neutral.

+ **RIDE COMFORT.** The smooth suspension, nicely contoured seats and powerful sound dampening really add to comfort. The cabin is really lovely too and is equipped with details like the rear center armrest that holds a storage compartment and two cup-holders, and the multi-panel sunvisors.

+ **QUALITY.** For a U.S.-built car, overall craftsmanship is outstanding. Tolerance points are tight and clean, trim materials are lovely and the finish job is more nicely executed than usual.

+ **INSTRUMENT PANEL.** The dashboard design is neat and original, including the outcurving center section that offers nicely clustered controls within easy reach.

+ **STORAGE SPACE.** For once, no one can complain that storage spots aren't handy or original!

CONS

- **SAFETY.** The Aurora only earned poor scores in NHTSA tests. This suggests that passengers enjoy only limited protection in the event of an accident, a chronic problem for several GM products, like the Venture, Trans Sport and Silhouette minivans.

- **BRAKES.** Linings lose their

oomph in a hurry when put to the never-say-die test.

- **PERFORMANCES.** Even with the V8 engine, the Aurora's performances aren't startling. Some of the rivals out there do a lot better and they benefit from an equivalent power to weight ratio.

- **FUEL CONSUMPTION.** Hefty weight disadvantages the Aurora when compared to less heavy rivals.

- **STEERING.** The Magnasteer is too light. To make matters worse, the Aurora isn't too competent when faced with maneuvers in the city, due to wide steer angle and poor reduction ratio. At least, steering is more precise on straight runs than it was in 1995.

- **VISIBILITY.** The body belt is very high and seats are too low-slung, so occupants will feel claustrophobic and won't have a clear view of the outside world.

- **CABIN SPACE.** Rear seats aren't too wonderfully welcoming: ceiling clearance is limited and the rear section of the cabin is too narrow to accommodate three passengers really comfortably.

- **TRUNK.** It's fairly roomy, but its tapered opening and high threshold make for awkward luggage handling. At least there's a ski slot connecting to the cabin.

- **TO BE IMPROVED UPON.** This fancy car should be equipped with a shifter position indicator behind the steering wheel. Besides, the front shoulder belts aren't height-adjustable and belt buckles are annoying to use.

CONCLUSION

Dealers will continue to sell the current Aurora until the introduction of the new model, pictured here. To reflect the category's standards more closely, it will be slightly smaller.

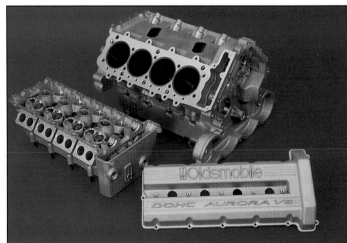

RATING
OLDSMOBILE Aurora

CONCEPT :		74%
Technology :	80	
Safety :	60	
Interior space :	80	
Trunk volume :	70	
Quality/fit/finish :	80	

DRIVING :		68%
Cockpit :	80	
Performance :	60	
Handling :	60	
Steering :	80	
Braking :	60	

ORIGINAL EQUIPMENT :		73%
Tires :	75	
Headlights :	75	
Wipers :	60	
Rear defroster :	75	
Radio :	80	

COMFORT :		78%
Seats :	75	
Suspension :	75	
Sound level :	70	
Conveniences :	80	
Air conditioning :	90	

BUDGET :		46%
Price :	0	
Fuel economy :	50	
Insurance :	45	
Satisfaction :	85	
Depreciation :	50	

Overall rating :		67.8%

NEW FOR 2000

• No major changes. The 2001 model was unveiled at the last New York Auto Show and will be commercialized sometime in 2000.

Compare Performance, Specifications, Prices, and Classification at the end of this chapter.

Luxury

EQUIPMENT

OLDSMOBILE Aurora	base
Automatic transmission:	S
Cruise control:	S
Power steering:	S
Anti-lock brakes:	S
Traction control:	S
Air conditioning:	S
Leather:	S
AM/FM/radio-cassette:	SCd
Power door locks:	S
Power windows:	S
Tilt steering:	S
Dual adjustable mirrors:	S
Alloy wheels:	S
Anti-theft system:	S

Colors
Exterior: Grey, White, Green, Silver, Blue, Black, Red, Cherry, Champagne, Gold, Bronze, Copper.
Interior: Graphite, Blue, Tan.

AT A GLANCE...

HISTORIC
Introduced in: 1995.
Made in: Lake Orion, Michigan, USA.

DEMOGRAPHICS

Model	Men/Wom.	Age	Married	College	Income $
Aurora	83/17 %	57	81 %	41 %	74,500

INDEX

Safety:	60 %	Satisfaction:	85 %
Depreciation:	50 %	Insurance:	$ 950
Cost per mile:	$ 0.65	Number of dealers:	3,100

SALES

	Canada			USA		
Model	1997	1998	Result	1997	1998	Result
Aurora	2,311	1,384	- 40.1 %	25,404	21,374	- 15.9 %

MAINTENANCE REQUIRED BY WARRANTY

First revision:	Frequency:	Diagnostic plug:
3,000 miles	6,000 miles	Yes

Breakdown

General Motors' willingness to acquire all of Saab's capital assets at a time when it owns 50% of the company is a serious indication that the problems facing the Swedish manufacturer are centered more in Sweden than they are in North America. Two-headed management has never been the ideal solution to get a sick company back on its feet. In spite of the arrival of new models and new and dynamic individuals, sales continue to slump to an alarming level and nothing points to an improvement over the short term.

MODEL RANGE

The Saab 9³ comes in a 5-door sedan, a 3-door coupe or a 2-door convertilbe offered in S or SE trim. For Y2K, 3000 Viggen high performance (230hp) versions will also be produced worldwide. The only engines now available are 2.0L 4-cylinder conventional gas engines on the base models and a turbocharged version on the SE models. The 5-speed manual transmission is standard and a 4-speed automatic is sold as an extra. Standard equipment on the 9³ models is very rich, since it includes luxury items such as heated seats and climate control and the only options for the base model are the automatic transmission, leather-trim seats and sunroof.

TECHNICAL FEATURES

The 9³'s steel unibody was derived from the Opel Vectra platform. But it still has the main stylistic attributes that characterized previous models. All the elements are there, car dimensions and shape and the over-all look that make it unmistakably a Saab. The car body is much more robust, especially that of the convertible, that's equipped with a roof, designed and built by ASC, and that's lined and has a power mechanism. Aerodynamics are great, since the drag coefficient is 0.30 for the sedan and 0.36 for the convertible with the roof on. The transversal engines have allowed engineers to trim down the front overhang and improve weight distribution in a 60/40% ratio. The independent front suspension is a MacPherson design with A-arms and struts, while at the rear, there's the semi-independent self-steering axle There's an anti-roll bar at both extremities. Cars are equipped with four-wheel disc brakes linked to a standard ABS system. The automatic transmission (Aisin-Warner) functions according to three settings: normal, sport or winter, the latter allowing the driver to accelerate in 3rd gear at speeds up to 50 mph, for better road adherence. Surprising that traction control isn't included on a car that hails from Sweden...

PROS

+ **LOOKS.** The 9³ has a conservative, classic body design that is in keeping with the carmaker's traditions and was a real asset on previous models.

+ **SAFETY FEATURES.** This meticulously designed, robust car protects occupants in the event of a collision and is equipped with side-impact airbags, still a rather rare feature in this category.

+ **DRIVING PLEASURE.** It's lots more fun with the high output turbocharged engine that achieves above-average performances and gives the 9³ a true blue sport car demeanor. Visibility is good in all directions except at rear quarterback on the convertible, since the top creates big blind spots, but it does include a glass window and electric defroster, a definite bonus in cold weather.

+ **QUALITY.** These cars are solidly built, finish job is clean and tight and trim materials look very sophisticated and creamy, like the superb leather seat coverings.

+ **PRICE.** The 9³'s aren't too expensive when you consider their luxury and sporty attributes as well as their extensive equipment.

+ **BRAKES.** They're gutsy, easy to apply and balanced in all circumstances and lining endurance is better than what it's been up until now.

+ **INSTRUMENT PANEL.** The layout is neat and logical, but it's nothing like an airplane cockpit, as Saab marketing experts purport it to be.

+ **CONVENIENCE FEATURES.** The trunk is very spacious and modular and there are numerous storage areas throughout the cabin.

+ **EQUIPMENT.** It's very rich and extensive, bestowing a luxury status to even the base model, thus justifying its price and putting in a favorable, albeit theoretical, position when compared with rivals.

+ **INSTRUMENTS.** An original feature: you can turn off the instrumentation lighting for night driving, leaving only the speedometer illuminated, to improve concentration. In the event of an emergency, the lighting turns on automatically.

CONS

- **DEPRECIATION.** It's the biggest handicap so these cars aren't a really wise investment.

- **V6 ENGINE.** Its absence puts the Saab 9³ in a disadvantageous position compared to most rivals.

- **RIDE COMFORT.** The suspension isn't the most velvety around and limited suspension travel makes the front end bottom out fairly quickly. On the SE versions, the small tires don't do anyone a favor and noise is always annoyingly loud due to the uncivilized engines and pervasive road noise.

- **TORQUE STEER.** It really affects models equipped with the high output turbocharged engines since there's a lot of wheel slippage on quick accelerations and car path all over the map.

- **CONTROLS.** They're too unusual and take some getting used to, like the ignition key on the main tunnel or the window or interior lighting switches, always hard to find, since they're located in weird places.

- **TO BE IMPROVED UPON.** Narrow cabin space, only average-efficient climate control and limited sales network.

CONCLUSION

When a model doesn't sell well, it's high time to find out why. Anyone who has ever owned a Saab will remember his or her car for a long, long time, as much for its driveability as for the financial burden it eventually brought along. And such things don't stay quiet for long...

RATING SAAB 9³		
CONCEPT :		74%
Technology :	80	
Safety :	90	
Interior space :	50	
Trunk volume :	70	
Quality/fit/finish :	80	
DRIVING :		68%
Cockpit :	80	
Performance :	60	
Handling :	60	
Steering :	80	
Braking :	60	
ORIGINAL EQUIPMENT :		76%
Tires :	80	
Headlights :	80	
Wipers :	65	
Rear defroster :	80	
Radio :	75	
COMFORT :		70%
Seats :	80	
Suspension :	70	
Sound level :	50	
Conveniences :	70	
Air conditioning :	80	
BUDGET :		50%
Price :	25	
Fuel economy :	60	
Insurance :	45	
Satisfaction :	80	
Depreciation :	40	
Overall rating :		67.6%

NEW FOR 2000

- New wheels with 5 or 10 spokes.
- High performance Viggen model with 230hp.
- Several styling enhancements.

Compare
Performance,
Specifications, Prices,
and Classification
at the end of this chapter.

Luxury $ 25,000

EQUIPMENT

SAAB 9³	cpe. S	sdn. S	conv. S	cpe. SE HO	sdn. SE	conv. SE
Automatic transmission:	O	O	O	O	O	O
Cruise control:	S	S	S	S	S	S
Power steering:	S	S	S	S	S	S
Anti-lock brakes:	S	S	S	S	S	S
Traction control:	-	-	-	-	-	-
Air conditioning:	SM	SM	SM	SA	SA	SA
Leather:	OH	OH	SH	SH	SH	SH
AM/FM/radio-cassette:	S	S	S	S	S	S
Power door locks:	S	S	S	S	S	S
Power windows:	S	S	S	S	S	S
Tilt steering:	S	S	S	S	S	S
Dual adjustable mirrors:	SEH	SEH	SEH	SEH	SEH	SEH
Alloy wheels:	S	S	S	S	S	S
Anti-theft system:	S	S	S	S	S	S

Colors

Exterior: White, Black, Blue, Red, Grey, Green, Silver, Violet.

Interior: Grey, Beige, Black, Tan.

AT A GLANCE...

HISTORIC

Introduced in:	1969-1993.
Made in:	Trollhattan, Sweden & Nystad, Finland (convertible).

DEMOGRAPHICS

Model	Men/Wom.	Age	Married	College	Income $
9³	59/41 %	42	91 %	86 %	90,500

INDEX

Safety:	90 %	Satisfaction:	80 %
Depreciation:	60 %	Insurance:	$ 850-1,000
Cost per mile:	$ 0.65	Number of dealers:	365

SALES

	Canada			USA		
Model	1997	1998	Result	1997	1998	Result
9³	1,100	979	- 11.0 %	22,949	12,740	- 44.5 %

MAINTENANCE REQUIRED BY WARRANTY

First revision:	Frequency:	Diagnostic plug:
3,000 miles	6,000 miles	Yes

Truly, Madly, Deeply

Is there any need to say it again: Volvo is doing very, very fine and its models are selling like gangbusters. Since their 1997 restyling and name change, their sales have increased steadily, to a point where the 70 models are in the lead, selling close to twice as strongly as the very popular BMW 3-Series. Now in the Ford fold, it's hard to see what could possibly stop these "flying Swedes", especially since they now offer extraordinary technological potential.

MODEL RANGE

The 70 series includes base sedans and wagons, the GLT, the T-5, and the AWD wagon. The base models come equipped with a 2.4-liter, 20V, 168 bhp engine, while on the GLT, horsepower increases to 190 hp. The T-5's turbo-charged 2.3-liter puts out 236 horses and 261hp on the 2.6L AWD wagon . Depending on the model, a manual 5-speed or a 4 or 5-speed automatic is standard. The base model includes such standard features as cruise control, power steering, ABS brakes, air conditioning, two front and two side airbags, heated front seats, cassette stereo, adjustable steering column and the regular power doors, windows, etc. Options include automatic transmission (standard on the GLT), traction control (standard on the AWD) and alloy rims. Also, the T-5, GLT and AWD all come with a sunroof and antitheft system.

TECHNICAL FEATURES

The 70 series has a steel unibody, with the weight split 60/40. The rounder shape improves the drag coefficient to 0.32. The front suspension is outfitted with MacPherson struts, and the semi-independent rear axle has been christened, «Delta-Link», a Volvo creation to control roll and flexibility. An anti-roll bar is also included. The four-wheel disc brakes are controlled by an anti-lock system and a balancing valve between the front/rear circuits that better distributes braking energy.

OUTSTANDING

++ THE AWD MODEL. The philosophy behind this model opens new horizons, similar to Subaru, but at a higher level of quality and finish. This proves that it is possible to take advantage of all-wheel drive without having to drive a truck.

PROS

+ STYLING. Though rounder, it stills holds true to tradition, and still easily recognizable as a Volvo. The styling continues to exude the same solidity and durability that it has for generations, while at the same time opening up new evolutionary possibilities to the Swedish manufacturer, who seemed enclosed in a world where all lines was straight.

+ PERFORMANCE. The Turbo is superb. Because of very quick acceleration and passing, sporty driving is truly enjoyable. Putting this engine under the hood of a wagon took a certain daring. Performance on the base model isn't as exhilarating, but neither is it anemic, because even with the automatic transmission, there is enough power to make driving fun, thanks to the dual selection transmission.

+ HANDLING has been seriously improved by a more rigid body, but the soft suspension on the base model doesn't make it any sportier, since the roll causes it to understeer (easily controlled). The AWD is remarkable in snow-bound lands, holding the road better than anything else.

+ INTERIOR space easily accommodates five with luggage, and the rear seat folds down for larger loads.

+ COMFORT. The well-designed seats offer good support, the noise level is normal at cruising speeds and climate controls are a breeze to use.

+ INSTRUMENT PANEL. The design is better and more ergonomic, which also breaks from the rugged aspect of previous models.

+ QUALITY. The construction, fit and finish of material is comparable to Japanese models, with complete equipment, though not luxurious.

+ PRACTICALITY. The wagons are remarkably versatile and they have a number of very practical storage spaces.

CONS

- THE PRICE. Its upkeep and fluctuating resale value exacts a lot from the fans of these Swedish beauties.

- BRAKING. Power is easy to gauge and is satisfactory under normal circumstances — but in emergencies, on the AWD wagon stopping distances are longer than average because of the vehicle's high weight and its antilock system.

- THE GEARBOX. The gearbox of the automatic transmission is rougher with the base engine than with the Turbo.

- COMFORT. The hard suspension on the sporty models give you the exact depth of every crack in the road.

- CONTROLS. The unconventional controls require a certain getting used to. Several are placed too low and the steering wheel is still too large.

- OVERSIGHT. Some items are of inferior quality, including the radio, very slow wipers, an anemic air conditioning system and poorly designed armrests. Instrumentation doesn't include an automatic transmission speed indicator.

CONCLUSION

Somewhere between ordinary and luxury cars, given the make's proven reputation for safety and reliability these Volvos are a good compromise between advanced technology and detailed equipment and they're available at a price that remains reasonable.

RATING
VOLVO 70 series

CONCEPT : — 80%
Technology : — 85
Safety : — 100
Interior space : — 65
Trunk volume : — 65
Quality/fit/finish : — 85

DRIVING : — 72%
Cockpit : — 80
Performance : — 65
Handling : — 60
Steering : — 80
Braking : — 75

ORIGINAL EQUIPMENT : — 75%
Tires : — 80
Headlights : — 80
Wipers : — 55
Rear defroster : — 80
Radio : — 80

COMFORT : — 72%
Seats : — 80
Suspension : — 70
Sound level : — 50
Conveniences : — 80
Air conditioning : — 80

BUDGET : — 54%
Price : — 20
Fuel economy : — 70
Insurance : — 40
Satisfaction : — 85
Depreciation : — 55

Overall rating : — 70.6%

NEW FOR 2000
- CVVT system.
- New 5-speed automatic transmission.
- Optional stability and traction control.
- 261-hp engine on the V70 AWD R wagon.
- New exterior/interior colors.

Compare
Performance,
Specifications, Prices,
and Classification
at the end of this chapter.

Luxury

EQUIPMENT

VOLVO 70 series	base	GLT	T-5	AWD
Automatic transmission:	O	S	O	S
Cruise control:	S	S	S	S
Power steering:	S	S	S	S
Anti-lock brakes:	S	S	S	S
Traction control:	O	O	O	S
Air conditioning:	S	S	S	S
Leather:	OH	OH	OH	SH
AM/FM/radio-cassette:	S	S	S	S
Power door locks:	S	S	S	S
Power windows:	S	S	S	S
Tilt steering:	S	S	S	S
Dual adjustable mirrors:	S	S	S	S
Alloy wheels:	O	O	S	S
Anti-theft system:	O	S	S	S

Colors

Exterior: Black, White, Red, Blue, Green, Silver, Graphite, Grey, Sand, Teal.

Interior: Blue, Taupe, Grey.

AT A GLANCE...

HISTORIC
Introduced in: 1992-1997.
Made in: Gand, Belgium: Torslanda, Sweden.

DEMOGRAPHICS

Model	Men/Wom.	Age	Married	College	Income $
70 series	76/24 %	50	82 %	74 %	84,000

INDEX
Safety: 100 % — Satisfaction: 86 %
Depreciation: 45 % — Insurance: $800-1,000
Cost per mile: $ 0.75 — Number of dealers: 405

SALES

	Canada			USA		
Model	1997	1998	Result	1997	1998	Result
70 series	7,334	8,196	+ 11.8 %	51,567	86,101	+ 67.0 %

MAINTENANCE REQUIRED BY WARRANTY
First revision: — Frequency: — Diagnostic plug:
10,000 miles; — 10,000 miles; — Yes
Tbo : 5,000 miles — Tbo : 5,000 miles — Yes

LUXURY CARS under $ 35,000

PERFORMANCE

Model/version	Type / timing valve / fuel system	Displacement cu in	Power hp @ rpm	Torque lb-ft @ rpm	Compres. ratio	Driving wheels / transmission	Final ratio	Acceler. 0-60 mph s	Standing 1/4 mile s	Standing 5/8 mile s	Passing 50-75 mph s	Braking 60-0 ft	Top speed mph	Lateral acceler. G	Noise level dBA	Fuel economy City mpg	Fuel economy Highway mpg	Fuel type Octane
ACURA 3.2TL	V6 3.2 SOHC-24-EFI	196	225 @ 5600	216 @ 4700	9.8 :1	front -A5	4.20	8.6	16.5	28.9	6.0	164	124	0.80	66-72	19	26	S 91
AUDI A4 1.8T	L4T 1.8 DOHC-20-MPSFI	109	150 @ 5700	155 @ 1750	9.5 :1	front - M5*	3.70	8.6	16.3	29.8	6.3	125	130	0.78	67	23	32	R 87
A4 1.8T qt	L4T 1.8 DOHC-20-MPSFI	109	150 @ 5700	155 @ 1750	9.5 :1	all - A5	3.73	9.2	16.8	30.2	7.5	137	124	0.80	67	21	29	R 87
A4 2.8	V6 2.8 DOHC-30-MPSFI	169	190 @ 6000	207 @ 3200	10.3 :1	front - M5*	3.29	8.0	15.7	27.5	5.6	137	130	0.78	67	20	29	R 87
						front - A5	3.29	8.5	16.4	29.6	6.0	141	124	0.78	67	19	29	R 87
A4 2.8 qt	V6 2.8 DOHC-30-MPSFI	169	190 @ 6000	207 @ 3200	10.3 :1	all - M5*	3.89	8.6	16.5	29.8	6.1	144	124	0.78	67	17	27	R 87
						all - A5	3.29	9.0	17.0	31.4	6.5	144	118	0.80	67	17	27	R 87
S4 2.7 ttqt	V6TT 2.7 DOHC-30-ESFI	163	250 @ 5800	258 @ 1850	9.3 :1	all - M6*	4.111	5.9	14.4	NA			143			17	24	S 91
						all - A5	3.511	6.5	14.8	NA			143			-	-	S 91
BMW 3 Series 323	L6 2.5 DOHC-24FI	152	170 @ 5500	181 @ 3500	10.5 :1	rear - M5*	3.07	7.7	16.0	27.0	5.6	131	128	0.78	67	20	31	S 91
						rear - A5	3.46	NA					128			19	30	S 91
328	L6 2.8 DOHC-24-FI	170	193 @ 5500	206 @ 3500	10.2 :1	rear - M5*	2.93	7.3	15.5	26.6	5.4	128	128	0.80	67-71	20	31	S 91
						rear - A5	3.46	7.9	16.2	27.2	5.8	135	128	0.80	67-71	19	30	S 91
CADILLAC Catera	V6 3.0 DOHC-24-MPSFI	181	200 @ 6000	192 @ 3400	10.0 :1	rear - A4	3.90	8.8	16.6	29.8	6.3	131	125	0.78	65-69	18	24	S 91
CHRYSLER LHS-300M	V6 3.5 SOHC-24-MPSFI	215	253 @ 6400	255 @ 3950	9.9 :1	front - A4	3.66	8.2	16.3	29.4	6.1	154	137	0.77	67	18	27	M 89
INFINITI I30	V6 3.0 DOHC-24-MPSFI	182	227 @ 6400	217 @ 4000	10.0 :1	front - A4	3.789	9.0	16.4	30.8	6.6	128	124	0.80	62-68	20	28	S 91
LEXUS ES 300	V6 3.0 DOHC-24-MPSFI	183	210 @ 5800	220 @ 4400	10.5 :1	front - A4	2.64	8.3	16.3	29.3	5.8	138	124	0.80	64-68	19	26	R 87
LINCOLN LS6	V6 3.0 DOHC-24-SFI	181	210 @ 6500	205 @ 4750	10.5 :1	rear - M5	3.31	8.2	16.4	29.5	6.0	142	124	0.78	66-72	19	27	S 91
						rear - A5*	3.58	8.7	16.8	30.0	6.2	144	120	0.78	66-72	18	26	S 91
LS8	V8 3.9 DOHC-32-SFI	241	252 @ 6100	267 @ 4300	10.5 :1	rear - A5	3.58	7.7	16.0	29.2	5.4	141	130	0.78	65-72	17	24	S 91
MAZDA Millenia S	V6C 2.3 DOHC-24-MPFI	138	210 @ 5300	210 @ 3500	10.0: 1	front - A4	3.805	8.2	16.5	29.3	6.2	144	137	0.80	67	19	29	S 91
MERCEDES-BENZ C230K	L4C 2.3 DOHC-16-SFI	140	185 @ 5300	200 @ 2500	8.8 :1	rear - A5	3.27	8.1	16.4	29.3	6.0	116	124	0.80	67-72	22	31	S 91
C280	V6 2.8 SOHC-18-SFI	171	194 @ 5800	195 @ 3000	10.0 :1	rear - A5	3.07	7.8	16.1	28.4	5.8	131	130	0.80	66-71	20	30	S 91
MITSUBISHI Diamante	V6 3.5 SOHC-24-MPSFI	195	210 @ 5000	231 @ 4000	9.0 :1	front - A4	3.50	8.5	16.5	29.6	6.8	148	130	0.75	66	18	24	M 89
OLDSMOBILE Aurora	V8 4.0 DOHC-32-SFI	244	250 @ 5600	260 @ 4400	10.3 :1	front - A4	3.48	9.0	16.7	30.4	6.5	134	134	0.80	66	17	25	S 92
2001 Aurora	V6 3.5 DOHC-24-SFI	212	215 @ 5500	230 @ 4400	9.3 :1	front - A4	3.29	NA								19	27	R 87
Aurora	V8 4.0 DOHC-32-SFI	244	250 @ 5600	260 @ 4400	10.3 :1	front - A4	3.71	NA								17	25	S 92
SAAB 9³ base	L4T 2.0 DOHC-16-EFI	121	185 @ 5500	194 @ 2100	9.2 :1	front - M5*	4.05	9.8	17.4	31.3	7.0	131	127	0.80	68	20	27	S 91
9³ SE	L4T 2.0 DOHC-16-EFI	121	205 @ 5500	209 @ 2300	10.5 :1	front - M5*	4.05	7.3	15.6	27.6	5.5	125	137	0.80	68	19	27	S 91
						front - A4	2.86	10.6	18.0	31.9	7.6	128	124	0.80	68	19	25	S 91
9³ Viggen	L4T 2.0 DOHC-16-EFI	121	230 @ NA															
VOLVO S/V 70	L5 2.4 DOHC-20-MPFI	149	168 @ 6100	170 @ 4800	10.3 :1	front - M5*	4.00	8.9	16.7	29.9	6.5	121	127	0.78	68	20	29	S 91
						front - A5	2.76	9.6	17.0	31.5	7.0	128	124	0.78	68	20	28	S 91
GLT/AWD	L5T 2.4 DOHC-20-MPFI	149	190 @ 5100	199 @ 1600	9.0 :1	front - A4*	2.56	9.0	16.6	30.0	6.4	131	137	0.78	68	19	27	S 91
AWD R	L5T 2.6 DOHC-20-MPFI	159	261 @ 5700	254 @ 2400	8.5 :1	front - A5*	2.56	7.5	15.8	26.8	5.6	134	131	0.80	68	19	25	S 91
T-5	L5T 2.3 DOHC-20-MPFI	142	236 @ 5100	243 @ 2100	8.5 :1	front - M5*	2.54	6.0	14.2	25.5	4.0	134	143	0.80	68	18	25	S 91
						front - A5	2.56	NA										

LUXURY CARS under $ 35,000

SPECIFICATIONS

Model	Version Trim	Body/ Seats	Cabin volume cu ft	Trunk volume cu ft	Cd	Wheel base in	Lgth x Width x Hght in x in x in	Curb weight lb	Susp. ft/rr	Brake ft/rr type	Steering ø ft	turns number	Fuel tank gal	dimensions	Standard tires make	Standard tires model	Standard powertrain	99 Price msrp $
ACURA																		
TL	3.2	4dr.sdn. 5	96.5	14.3	0.32	108.1	192.9x70.3x56.1	3461	ih/ih	dc/ABS	pwr.r&p.. 36.7	3.5	17.2	205/60R16	Michelin	MXV4	V6/3.2/A5	28,405
AUDI		General warranty: 3-years / 50,000 miles; perforation corrosion: 12-years; free maintenance: 3-years / 50 000 miles; roadside assistance: 3-years.																
A4 1.8T	base	4dr.sdn. 4/5	87.9	13.7	0.31	103.0	178.0x68.2x55.8	2998	ih/sih	dc/ABS	pwr.r&p. 36.4	3.1	16.4	205/60HR15	Continental	Supercontact L4T/1.8/M5	24,290
A4 1.8T	quattro	4dr.sdn. 4/5	87.9	13.7	0.31	102.6	178.0x68.2x55.8	3241	ih/ih	dc/ABS	pwr.r&p. 36.4	3.1	16.4	205/60HR15	Continental	Supercontact L4T/1.8/M5	-
A4 1.8T	base	4dr.wgn. 4/5	88.9	31.0	0.31	103.0	176.7x68.2x55.8	3351	ih/sih	dc/ABS	pwr.r&p. 36.4	3.1	15.9	205/60HR15	Continental	Supercontact L4T/1.8/M5	-
A4 2.8	base	4dr.sdn. 4/5	87.9	13.7	0.31	103.0	178.0x68.2x55.8	3164	ih/sih	dc/ABS	pwr.r&p. 36.4	3.1	16.4	205/55HR16	Michelin	Pilot SX V6/2.8/M5	24,940
A4 2.8	quattro	4dr.sdn. 4/5	87.9	13.7	0.31	102.6	178.0x68.2x55.8	3384	ih/ih	dc/ABS	pwr.r&p. 36.4	3.1	16.4	205/55HR16	Michelin	Pilot SX V6/2.8/M5	28,899
A4 2.8	avant	4dr.wgn. 4/5	88.7	31.0	0.31	103.0	176.7x68.2x56.7	3494	ih/ih	dc/ABS	pwr.r&p. 36.4	3.1	16.4	205/55HR16	Michelin	Pilot SX V6/2.8/M5	-
S4 2.7TT	quattro	4dr.sdn. 4/5	87.7	13.7	NA	102.6	176.5x72.8x55.8	3593	ih/ih	dc/ABS	pwr.r&p. 37.4	3.1	16.4	225/45R17	-	- V6T/2.7/M6	31,540
BMW		General warranty : 4-years/ 50,000 miles; corrosion: 6-years / unlimited: antipollution: 8-years / 80 000 miles.																
323	i	4dr.sdn. 4	NA	15.5	0.30	107.3	176.0x68.5x55.7	3152	ih/ih	dc/ABS	pwr.r&p. 34.4	NA	16.6	195/65HR15	Michelin	MXV4 L6/2.5/M5	26,970
323	Ci	2dr.cpe. 4	NA	14.5	0.30	107.3	176.7x69.1x54.6	3152	ih/ih	dc/ABS	pwr.r&p. 34.4	NA	16.6	205/55HR16	Michelin	MXV4 L6/2.5/M5	29,270
328	i	4dr.sdn. 4	NA	15.5	0.31	107.3	176.0x68.5x55.7	3197	ih/ih	dc/ABS	pwr.r&p. 34.4	NA	16.6	205/55HR16	Michelin	MXV4 L6/2.8/M5	33,970
328	Ci	2dr.cpe. 4	NA	14.5	0.30	107.3	176.7x69.1x54.6	3197	ih/ih	dc/ABS	pwr.r&p. 34.4	NA	16.6	205/55HR16	Michelin	MXV4 L6/2.8/M5	33,770
CADILLAC		General warranty: 4-years/ 50,000 miles; antipollution: 5-years / 50,000 miles; perforation corrosion: 6-years / 100,000 miles. Road assistance.																
Catera	base	4dr.sdn. 5	98.2	14.5	0.33	107.5	192.2x70.3x56.4	3770	ih/ih	dc/ABS	pwr.bal. 33.5	3.0	16.0	225/55HR16	Goodyear	Eagle RS-A V6/3.0/A4	
Catera	Sport	4dr.sdn. 5	98.2	14.5	0.33	107.5	192.2x70.3x56.4	3770	ih/ih	dc/ABS	pwr.bal. 33.5	3.0	16.0	235/45R17	Goodyear	Eagle M+S V6/3.0/A4	34,820
CHRYSLER		General warranty: 3-years / 36,000 miles; surface rust: 3-years; perforation: 7-years / 100,000 miles; roadside assistance: 3-years /36,000 miles.																
300M	base	4dr.sdn. 5	105.1	16.8	0.31	113.0	197.8x74.4x56.0	3585	ih/ih	dc/ABS	pwr.r&p. 37.6	3.1	17.0	225/55R17	Goodyear	Eagle LS V6/3.5/A4	29,545
LHS	base	4dr.sdn. 5	107.4	18.7	0.31	113.0	207.7x74.4x56.0	3564	ih/ih	dc/ABS	pwr.r&p. 37.6	3.1	17.0	225/55R17	Goodyear	Eagle LS V6/3.5/A4	29,545
INFINITI		General warranty: 4-years / 60 000 miles; powertrain & antipollution: 6 years / 100 000 miles; corrosion perforation: 7-years / unlimited.																
I30	base	4dr.sdn. 5	102.0	14.9	0.30	108.3	193.7x70.2x56.5	3342	ih/ih	dc/ABS	pwr.r&p. 35.4	2.9	18.5	215/55R16	Bridgestone	Potenza RE92 V6/3.0/A4	29,425
I30	t	4dr.sdn. 5	102.0	14.9	0.30	108.3	193.7x70.2x56.5	3375	ih/ih	dc/ABS	pwr.r&p. 40.0	2.6	18.5	225/50VR17	Toyo	Proxes Ao6 V6/3.0/A4	31,725
LEXUS		General warranty: 4-years / 50,000 miles; powertrain: 6-years / 70,000 miles; corrosion perforation: 6-years / unlimited mileage & roadside assistance.																
ES 300	base	4dr.sdn. 5	92.1	13.0	0.29	105.1	190.2x70.5x54.9	3373	ih/ih	dc/ABS	pwr.r&p. 36.7	3.0	18.5	205/60VR15	Dunlop	SP Sport V6/3.0/A4	31,400
LINCOLN		General warranty: 4-years / 50,000 miles; corrosion perforation antipollution: 4-years / 50,000 miles.																
LS6	M5	4dr.sdn. 5	103.8	13.7	0.32	114.5	193.9x73.2x57.2	3598	ih/ih	dc/ABS	pwr.r&p. 37.7	3.0	18.1	215/60HR16	Continental	- V6/3.0/M5	
LS6	A5	4dr.sdn. 5	103.8	13.7	0.32	114.5	193.9x73.2x57.2	3593	ih/ih	dc/ABS	pwr.r&p. 37.7	3.0	18.1	215/60HR16	Continental	- V6/3.0/M5	
LS8	A5	4dr.sdn. 5	103.8	13.7	0.32	114.5	193.9x73.2x57.2	3692	ih/ih	dc/ABS	pwr.r&p. 37.7	3.0	18.1	215/60VR16	Firestone	Firehawk LH V8/3.9/A5	
MAZDA		General warranty: 3-years / 50,000 miles; powertrain: 5-years / 100,000 miles; corrosion: 5-years / unlimited.																
Millenia	S	4dr.sdn. 5	94.0	13.3	0.29	108.3	189.7x69.7x54.9	3355	ih/ih	dc/ABS	pwr.r&p. 37.4	2.9	18.0	215/50VR17	Dunlop	SP Sport 4000 V6C/2.3/A4	31,695
MERCEDES-BENZ		General warranty: 4-years / 50,000 miles with road assistance.																
C230	K	4dr.sdn. 5	88.0	12.9	0.32	105.9	177.4x67.7x56.1	3250	ih/ih	dc/ABS	pwr.bal. 35.2	3.2	16.4	205/60R15	Michelin	MXV4 L4C/2.3/A5	31,795
C280		4dr.sdn. 5	88.0	12.9	0.32	105.9	177.4x67.7x56.1	3316	ih/ih	dc/ABS	pwr.bal. 35.2	3.2	16.4	205/60R15	Michelin	MXV4 V6/2.8/A5	36,195
MITSUBISHI		General warranty: 3-years / 36,000 miles; corrosion perforation: 7-years/100,000 miles; powertrain: 5-years / 60,000 miles with road assistance.																
Diamante		4dr.sdn. 5	100.9	14.2	0.28	107.1	194.1x70.3x53.9	3440	ih/ih	dc/ABS	pwr.r&p. 36.7	3.2	19.0	205/65R15	Bridgestone	RE92 V6/3.5/A4	27,669
OLDSMOBILE		General warranty: 3-years / 36,000 miles; antipollution: 5-years / 50,000 miles; perforation corrosion: 6-years / 100,000 miles. Roadside assistance.																
Aurora	2000	4dr.sdn. 5	100.5	19.8	0.31	113.8	205.4x74.4x55.4	3967	ih/ih	dc/ABS	pwr.r&p. 41.9	2.5	20.0	235/60R16	Michelin	MXV4 V8/4.0/A4	36,899
Aurora	2001	4dr.sdn. 5	104.4	14.9	0.30	112.2	199.3x72.9x56.7	3627	ih/ih	dc/ABS	pwr.r&p. NA	2.8	18.5	225/60HR16	Goodyear	Eagle LS V6/3.5 A4	
Aurora	2001	4dr.sdn. 5	104.4	14.9	0.30	112.2	199.3x72,9x56.7	3802	ih/ih	dc/ABS	pwr.r&p. NA	2.8	17.5	235/55HR17	Michelin	MXV4 V8/4.0 A4	
SAAB		General warranty: 4-years / 50,000 miles; corrosion, perforation: 6-years / 100,000 miles.																
9³	S	2dr.con. 4	80.0	12.5	0.36	102.6	182.3x67.4x56.0	3140	ih/sih	dc/ABS	pwr.r&p. 34.4	3.4	16.9	195/60VR15	Michelin	MXV4 L4T/2.0/M5	40,025
9³	S	3dr.cpe. 5	89.6	21.7	0.30	102.6	182.3x67.4x56.2	2990	ih/sih	dc/ABS	pwr.r&p. 34.4	3.4	16.9	195/60VR15	Michelin	MXV4 L4T/2.0/M5	26,475
9³	S	5dr.cpe. 5	89.6	21.7	0.30	102.6	182.3x67.4x56.2	3040	ih/sih	dc/ABS	pwr.r&p. 34.4	3.4	16.9	195/60VR15	Michelin	MXV4 L4T/2.0/M5	26,975
9³	SE	2dr.con. 4	80.0	12.5	0.36	102.6	182.3x67.4x56.0	3190	ih/sih	dc/ABS	pwr.r&p. 34.4	3.4	16.9	205/50ZR16	Michelin	Pilot L4T/2.0/M5	32,275
9³	SE	3dr.cpe. 5	89.6	21.7	0.30	102.6	182.3x67.4x56.2	3120	ih/sih	dc/ABS	pwr.r&p. 34.4	3.4	16.9	205/50ZR16	Michelin	Pilot L4T/2.0/M5	43,570
9³	SE	5dr.cpe. 5	89.6	21.7	0.30	102.6	182.3x67.4x56.2	3150	ih/sih	dc/ABS	pwr.r&p. 34.4	3.4	16.9	205/50ZR16	Michelin	Pilot L4T/2.0/M5	44,570
VOLVO		General warranty: 4-years / 50,000 miles; corrosion: 8 years / unlimited; antipollution: 5-years / 50,000 miles.																
S70	base	4dr.sdn. 5	96.4	15.1	0.32	104.9	185.9x69.3x55.2	3152	ih/ih	dc/ABS	pwr.r&p. 33.5	3.2	17.9	195/60VR15	Michelin	MXV4 L5/2.4/M5	27,960
V70	base	5dr.wgn. 5	93.6	37.1	0.32	104.9	185.9x69.3x56.2	3259	ih/ih	dc/ABS	pwr.r&p. 33.5	3.2	17.9	195/60VR15	Michelin	MXV4 L5/2.4/M5	29,260
S70	GLT	4dr.sdn. 5	96.4	15.1	0.32	104.9	185.9x69.3x55.2	3300	ih/ih	dc/ABS	pwr.r&p. 33.5	3.2	17.9	195/60VR15	Michelin	MXV4 L5T/2.4/A5	32,115
V70	GLT	5dr.wgn. 5	93.5	37.2	0.32	104.9	185.9x69.3x56.2	3402	ih/ih	dc/ABS	pwr.r&p. 33.5	3.2	17.9	195/60VR15	Michelin	MXV4 L5T/2.4/A5	33,515
S70	T-5	4dr.sdn. 5	96.4	15.1	0.32	104.9	185.9x69.3x55.2	3272	ih/ih	dc/ABS	pwr.r&p. 34.5	3.2	17.9	205/55ZR16	Michelin	XGTV4 L5T/2.3/M5	33,785
V70	T-5	5dr.wgn. 5	93.6	37.1	0.32	104.9	185.9x69.3x56.2	3371	ih/ih	dc/ABS	pwr.r&p. 34.5	3.2	17.9	205/55ZR16	Michelin	XGTV4 L5T/2.3/M5	35,085
V70	AWD R	5dr.wgn. 5	93.5	37.2	0.32	104.9	185.9x69.3x56.2	3433	ih/ih	dc/ABS	pwr.r&p. 37.7	3.2	17.9	205/65R15	Michelin	XGTV4 L5T/2.6/M5	41,970

Notes: 1) Tire makes and models are provided solely as an indication; they are subject to change without prior notice from the automobile manufacturers.
2) See the 2000 price list at the back of this edition.

LUXURY CARS under $ 35,000
CLASSIFICATION

	OUR CLASSIFICATION								YOUR CLASSIFICATION		
Rank	Models	Concept	Driving	Equipment	Comfort	Budget	Ratings		Rank	Models	98 Sales
1	**ACURA 3.2TL**	76	66	77	78	**64**	**72.2 %**		**1**	**VOLVO 70 series**	**86,101**
2	CHRYSLER 300M-LHS	**84**	67	**80**	74	53	71.6 %		2	BMW 3 Series	48,758
3	LEXUS ES 300	75	70	77	**82**	53	71.4 %		3	LEXUS ES 300	48,644
4	INFINITI I30	80	68	75	78	52	70.6 %		4	MERCEDES C-Class	34,487
4	VOLVO 70 series	80	72	75	72	54	70.6 %		5	CHRYSLER 300M	30,765
5	CADILLAC Catera	78	67	76	79	52	70.4 %		6	AUDI A4	26,635
5	LINCOLN LS	79	69	77	74	53	70.4 %		7	INFINITI I30	26,350
6	MERCEDES C-Class	74	70	78	74	54	70.0 %		8	CADILLAC Catera	24,635
7	AUDI A4	76	64	**80**	73	56	69.8 %		9	OLDSMOBILE Aurora	21,374
8	BMW 3 Series	69	**79**	77	71	52	69.6 %		10	CHRYSLER LHS	16,753
9	MAZDA Millenia	75	66	77	72	52	68.4 %		11	MAZDA Millenia	16,717
9	MITSUBISHI Diamante	76	65	76	79	46	68.4 %		12	ACURA 3.2TL	12,949
10	OLDSMOBILE Aurora	74	68	73	78	46	67.8 %		13	SAAB 9[3]	12,740
11	SAAB 9[3]	74	68	76	70	50	67.6 %		14	MITSUBISHI Diamante	8,563

Not classified:
LINCOLN LS

ACURA 3.5RL

AUDI A6

BMW 5 Series

BUICK Park Avenue

CADILLAC DeVille

CADILLAC Seville

JAGUAR S-TYPE

INFINITI Q45

LEXUS GS

Comparative Test

LUXURY CARS
from 35 to $ 70,000

**See their performance, their specifications, their price
and their classification at the end of this chapter.**

VOLVO S80

SAAB 9⁵

MERCEDES-BENZ E-Class

LINCOLN Town Car

LINCOLN Continental

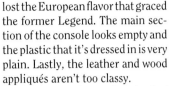

Acura did well in making sure that its 3.5RL isn't in direct competition with Japanese models of the same ilk. With its front-wheel drive, 3.5L V6 engine and special sizing, it inevitably nudges its way between two Lexus or two Infiniti models. Although roomier and more refined than the defunct Legend it replaced, it still has not broken the ice of consumer indifference, mainly because it lacks the prestige a V8 engine could give it.

Outsider

MODEL RANGE

The 3.5RL is a big 4-door sedan equipped with a 3.5L V6 engine and a 5-speed automatic transmission. It's sold in only one version, with very detailed equipment including everything you'd expect to find on a luxury model: the usual power systems, leather trims, heated front seats, a stereo sound system with a CD player and automatic loader, alloy wheels and a theft-deterrent system designed to immobilize the car. Added to this long list is a practical rear-seat trunk pass-through to accommodate oddly shaped items such as skis.

TECHNICAL FEATURES

The steel monocoque body is entirely made of galvanized steel. The car silhouette has only average aerodynamic finesse, yielding a coefficient of 0.32, even with a wind deflector located behind the front bumper that reduces airflow under the car and directs it towards the sides and roof. This car is a heavyweight, tipping the scales at about 2,850 lbs. curb weight, and weight distribution is 60% up front and 40% at the rear. The fully independent suspension consists of a double wishbone arrangement and anti-roll bar both front and rear. The four-wheel disc brakes benefit from a standard antilock braking system associated with a traction control system (TCS) that's linked to brakes and prevents single wheel slippage. The 90-degree 24-valve SOHC V6 is

made of aluminum with cast-iron cylinder sleeves. To maximize power and torque, Acura has developed a 3-stage variable-intake system. To reduce the shakes that go with this type of engine, a balance shaft system is mounted on the side of the engine and driven by the timing belt. The engine is also mounted on an independent cradle via electronically controlled hydraulic supports, thus providing two shock settings, depending on whether the engine is revving above or below 850 rpm.

PROS

+ STYLE. The body design is clean and elegant, but it's too much like that of the previous model and there's nothing eye-catching about it whatsoever.

+ PRICE. It isn't too inflated for it sits exactly between those of the Saab 9⁵ and BMW 528, almost equivalent to what you pay for a GS 300.

+ COMFORT. It's pretty impressive, when it comes to the huge trunk, very tough soundproofing, competent suspension and seats offer nea3.5RLy ideal lateral and lumbar support.

+ PERFORMANCES. They're honorable for such a heavy car. The engine is brawny, spontaneous and discreet, the transmission does its stuff like a wizard, tires are good-quality and just the right size and the traction control helps control

road adherence when things get slick. The engine is also fuel-efficient since gas consumption stays at a reasonable level at all times.

+ HANDLING. It's fine at regular speeds and on silky roads, since the car stays level on straight runs and on curves and it also stays nice and neutral on turns, but the 3.5RL is a big, heavy car, so agility isn't one of its strong suits.

+ SAFETY. After lagging behind its rivals, the 3.5RL has fallen into step by offering multiple airbags and ABS and traction control systems, which all add up to a higher safety level.

+ BRAKES. They're pretty efficient at first go, since they bring the hefty 3.5RL to a complete halt in less than 130 ft. with ABS.

+ COCKPIT. The driver is comfortably seated, enjoys clear visibility and has an ergonomic, neatly organized instrument panel at his or her disposal.

+ QUALITY. Construction is well crafted and fit and finish are carefully rendered, features you're sure to get on a Honda product.

CONS

- SIZE. This «in-between» format chosen by Honda is supposed to be roomier than mid-range Lexus models and it's less costly than V8 model cars, but it really doesn't turn anyone's crank.

- DESIGN. Body stylistics are terribly lackluster and the interior has

lost the European flavor that graced the former Legend. The main section of the console looks empty and the plastic that it's dressed in is very plain. Lastly, the leather and wood appliqués aren't too classy.

- DRIVING. Being at the wheel of the 3.5RL is pretty boring. The engine is frisky and roadability is super, but the car has a squeaky-clean demeanor and lacks definition.

- BRAKES. They're efficient but hard to gauge due to the soft pedal and they only have average lasting power when put to the test.

- STEERING. It's over-assisted, crippled by a poor reduction ratio and it's too light and soft when you're gunning it. You sometimes have the awful feeling that the front wheels have lost their grip.

- SUSPENSION. It's too flexible, so it generates lots of wavering, which affects passenger comfort more than handling per se. We're still wondering why the 3.5RL, an expensive, high-tech car isn't equipped with a dual-mode adjustable suspension, depending on driving style, as well as an automatic setting.

CONCLUSION

The 3.5RL lacks nothing in competence or charm, but it doesn't have the prestige of its closest rivals, the Lexus LS 400 and the Infiniti Q45. What can Honda be waiting on before it introduces a V8 engine capable of withstanding comparison and hoisting the flag a bit higher?

RATING ACURA 3.5RL		
CONCEPT :		**81%**
Technology :	90	
Safety :	90	
Interior space :	80	
Trunk volume :	60	
Quality/fit/finish :	85	
DRIVING :		**72%**
Cockpit :	80	
Performance :	65	
Handling :	60	
Steering :	75	
Braking :	80	
ORIGINAL EQUIPMENT :		**80%**
Tires :	85	
Headlights :	80	
Wipers :	70	
Rear defroster :	75	
Radio :	90	
COMFORT :		**79%**
Seats :	80	
Suspension :	80	
Sound level :	70	
Conveniences :	80	
Air conditioning :	85	
BUDGET :		**50%**
Price :	0	
Fuel economy :	65	
Insurance :	45	
Satisfaction :	90	
Depreciation :	50	
Overall rating :		**72.4%**

NEW FOR 2000

- **The VSA (Vehicle Stability Assist) system replaces the TCS (Traction Control System).**
- **An engine that complies with California ULEV (Ultra Low Emission Vehicle) standards.**
- **Exterior colors: Monterey Blue and Sebring Silver.**

Compare Performance, Specifications, Prices, and Classification at the end of this chapter.

Luxury 35-$70,000

EQUIPMENT

ACURA	3.5RL
Automatic transmission:	S
Cruise control:	S
Power steering:	S
Anti-lock brakes:	S
Traction control:	S
Air conditioning:	SA
Leather:	SH
AM/FM/radio-cassette:	SCd
Power door locks:	S
Power windows:	S
Tilt steering:	S
Dual adjustable mirrors:	SEH
Alloy wheels:	S
Anti-theft system:	S

Colors

Exterior: Black, White, Gold, Green, Blue, Silver.

Interior: Black, Parchment, Quartz.

AT A GLANCE...

HISTORIC

Introduced in: 1996.
Made in: Sayama, Japan.

DEMOGRAPHICS

Model	Men/Wom.	Age	Married	College	Income $
3.5RL	81/19 %	54	90 %	56 %	82,000

INDEX

Safety:	90 %	Satisfaction:	90 %
Depreciation:	50 %	Insurance:	$ 950
Cost per mile:	$ 0.93	Number of dealers:	290

SALES

	Canada			USA	
Model	1997	1998	Result	1997	1998	Result
RL3.5	940	844	- 10.2 %	16,004	15,024	- 6.1 %

MAINTENANCE REQUIRED BY WARRANTY

First revision:	Frequency:	Diagnostic plug:
3,000 miles	6,000 miles	Yes

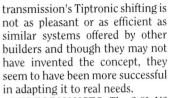

Out To Conquer

Never mind all of its many qualities and its original styling, the A6 has always suffered the consequences of its sluggish engines, leaving buyers who prefer a sportier driving style wishing for a lot more. Under the pressure applied by BMW and Mercedes-Benz, Audi has no other alternative but to follow the wave of multiple-choice and increasingly high-performance powertrains. This year, a twin turbocharged V6 and the V8 borrowed from the A8 give it the ammunition to attract a clientele group different from its usual target market.

MODEL RANGE

The A6 is available as a sedan or wagon, with front-wheel drive or quattro AWD, powered by a 2.8L V6 with a 5-speed Tiptronic automatic transmission. Two high-performance quattro sedans are making their debut this year. One is equipped with a twin turbocharged 250-hp 2.7L V6 engine and the other features a 300-hp 4.2L V8. Standard equipment is very detailed and includes all of the features usually available on automobiles that sell at this price level.

TECHNICAL FEATURES

The latest model Audi A6 is still a completely galvanized steel unibody, with some aluminum and magnesium components, like the hood and some suspension parts. So new models are lighter than their predecessors, even though the body is wider and higher, with a longer wheelbase, but is shorter bumper-to-bumper. Aerodynamics are admirable, since they yield an impressive drag coefficient of 0.28. The fully independent suspension consists of four-link, upper and lower control arms mounted on an auxiliary frame up front and at the rear, there's a multi-link system on the front-wheel drive model and un-

equal-length control arms on the quattro. Both axles are fitted with a stabilizer bar and four-wheel disc brakes are teamed up with ABS that also serves as traction control.

The "adaptive" 5-speed automatic gearbox is fitted with an electronic shifter, inspired by the Tiptronic design developed by Porsche. Gear shifting varies with driving style and road conditions, either automatically or manually. Full-time AWD includes three differentials, one for each axle and a center Torsen differential that distributes torque to the axle and wheel lacking adherence.

OUTSTANDING

++ SAFETY. Both passive and active safety features are incredibly refined, since the A6 comes equipped with dual front-impact airbags and 4 side-impact airbags housed in the seat backs. The A6 body is one of the most rigid in the world and was awarded one of the top marks in NHTSA collision tests and the quattro system gives it a safe traction in all season.

PROS

+ QUALITY. The assembly job and trim materials used are clearly a cut above average. The over-all treatment is simply flawless with its superb finish details far ritzier than those on Mercedes and BMW cars.

+ PERFORMANCE. The twin turbocharged V6 and the V8 give wings to this model - and it needed them. The magic of the quattro sys-

tem ensures strong pick-up even when cornering and road stability is remarkable under all circumstances.

+ CABIN SPACE. Five passengers will be comfy inside and the longer and wider trunk can also be extended by lowering the rear seatbench back, a rare feature in this category.

+ RIDE COMFORT. You're in for a smooth, comfy ride due to the supple suspension, effective seat design and low noise interference at cruising speed, thanks to the stiff body and impressive soundproofing.

+ TECHNOLOGY. Audi's cars are ahead of their time and the competition in this department, due to avant-garde techniques such as the completely galvanized body, light alloy components and quattro all-wheel drive.

+ FUEL EFFICIENCY. It's quite economical on the front-wheel drive version that's frugal due in part to a good power to weight ratio and fine aerodynamics.

+ DEPRECIATION. Over the years, Audi's reputation and image have improved, which has affected resale value that isn't as poor as it was at one time.

CONS

- PRICE. The Audi A6's aren't within the average buyer's means and the fact that repairs are free during warranty isn't much of a consoling thought.

- TRANSMISSION. The automatic

transmission's Tiptronic shifting is not as pleasant or as efficient as similar systems offered by other builders and though they may not have invented the concept, they seem to have been more successful in adapting it to real needs.

- PERFORMANCES. The 2.8L V6 may be more brawny, but it often strains, especially with the quattro system that's heavier and adversely affects the power to weight ratio.

- DIGITAL SCREEN. It's impossible to read in the daytime, even when it isn't too bright and sunny, which is awkward when you use the Tiptronic function, since you can't really see which gear's engaged.

- SUSPENSION. It's overly flexible, so there's sway which is more annoying than a serious drawback when it comes to handling, especially at regular speeds.

- STEERING. It's lighter on the front-wheel drive model than the quattro and you have to really keep an eye on it in slippery conditions.

- CONTROLS. Some of them are unusual and complex, so it takes a while to get used to them, so you really have to concentrate on how they work.

- OVERSIGHTS. Flash to pass headlights aren't bright enough and wipers are slow enough to be maddening and are very poorly suited to a vehicle in this class.

CONCLUSION

All other things being equal, the Audi A6 always has the advantage of its quattro AWD transmission. However, the problem is that not all buyers are convinced that they really need it.

Luxury
25-$70,000

RATING
AUDI A6

CONCEPT :   82%
Technology :   90
Safety :   90
Interior space :   60
Trunk volume :   85
Quality/fit/finish :   85

DRIVING :   70%
Cockpit :   85
Performance :   55
Handling :   65
Steering :   80
Braking :   65

ORIGINAL EQUIPMENT :   80%
Tires :   80
Headlights :   80
Wipers :   80
Rear defroster :   80
Radio :   80

COMFORT :   78%
Seats :   80
Suspension :   80
Sound level :   70
Conveniences :   80
Air conditioning :   80

BUDGET :   48%
Price :   0
Fuel economy :   60
Insurance :   45
Satisfaction :   85
Depreciation :   50

Overall rating :   71.6%

NEW FOR 2000
- 2.7L twin turbocharged V6 or 4.2L V8 engine.
- Optional navigational system.
- Standard full-size emergency tire with alloy wheel.
- Manual 5-speed transmission on quattro 2.7T V6 versions.
- Different gear ratio and torque converter on the automatic transmission.

Compare
Performance,
Specifications, Prices,
and Classification
at the end of this chapter.

Luxury
35-$70,000

EQUIPMENT

AUDI A6	FWD 4dr.sdn.	quattro 4dr.sdn.	quattro 4dr.wgn.
Automatic transmission:	S	S	S
Cruise control:	S	S	S
Power steering:	S	S	S
Anti-lock brakes:	S	S	S
Traction control:	S	S	S
Air conditioning:	SA	SA	SA
Leather:	O	O	O
AM/FM/radio-cassette:	SCd	SCd	SCd
Power door locks:	S	S	S
Power windows:	S	S	S
Tilt steering:	S	S	S
Dual adjustable mirrors:	SEH	SEH	SEH
Alloy wheels:	S	S	S
Anti-theft system:	S	S	S

Colors
Exterior: Black, Silver, White, Mica, Byzance.

Interior: Anthracite, Neutral, Blue, Platinum.

AT A GLANCE...

HISTORIC
Introduced in: 1982 (5000), 1998.
Made in: Neckarsulm, Germany.

DEMOGRAPHICS

Model	Men/Wom.	Age	Married	College	Income $
A6	85/15 %	53	92 %	72 %	130,000

INDEX

Safety:	100 %	Satisfaction:	85 %
Depreciation:	48 %	Insurance:	$ 985-1,100
Cost per mile:	$ 0.95	Number of dealers:	290

SALES

	Canada			USA		
Model	1997	1998	Result	1997	1998	Result
A6	397	1,105	+178.3 %	9,949	18,050	+ 81.5 %

MAINTENANCE REQUIRED BY WARRANTY

First revision:	Frequency:	Diagnostic plug:
7,500 miles	7,500 miles	Yes

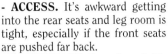
Focused

As models climb higher and higher along the BMW ladder, eligibility criteria are increasingly selective. While almost anyone can acquire a 3 Series model, fewer people can realistically afford a car from the more expensive and more demanding 5 Series. And this is even more true in the case of the latest M5, which is truly and genuinely lean and mean.

MODEL RANGE

The 5 Series is sold as a 4-door sedan and station wagon Touring in 528i trim, equipped with a 2.8L 6-in-line engine developing 193 hp linked to a standard 5-speed manual gearbox or optional 4-speed automatic, or in 540i trim, driven by a 4.4L V8 that delivers 282 hp, paired up with either a 5-speed manual or automatic gearbox at no extra cost, or an optional 5-speed "Steptronic" borrowed from the 7 Series. The M5 is back with its exclusive price and personality and its 400 hp output — a very powerful mix. Enumerating a list of original equipment items here would be too long, but let's say it's very extensive.

TECHNICAL FEATURES

The steel monocoque body is made up mostly of galvanized panels and it's highly resistant to torsion and flexion. The front surface is quite substantial, but aerodynamic finesse is adequate with a drag coefficient varying between 0.30 and 0.31. To eliminate most exterior noise, doors are fitted with double-pane windows, some flat bodywork has been lined with aluminum and hollow components have been injected with expanding foam. The body itself isn't built of aluminum, but this metal has been used for suspension components, so the car now weighs 145 lbs less. The fully independent suspension consists of double-pivot struts and trailing arms up front and the rear axle is supported by cross struts and longitudinal struts and there's a stabilizer bar for front and rear axles. Four-wheel disc brakes benefit from a standard electronic antilock braking system that serves as traction control. These vehicles are equipped with a residual heat accumulator that provides warm air at 104 degrees Farenheit in less than 30 seconds, even if the car stays parked for two days at an icy minus 4 degrees Farenheit and it defrosts windows in no time flat. These cars also come equipped with six airbags, two front-impact and four side-impact airbags located inside the doors. Lastly, cast solid headlights include Xenon gas-discharge high beam lamps that provide excellent visibility without blinding on-coming drivers and they last longer than halogen lamps. The "Steptronic" automatic transmission can be adjusted to function automatically or in manual mode, without having to use a clutch pedal, as is the case for the Porsche's famous "Tiptronic".

PROS

+ LOOKS. This car is a refined thoroughbred that exhibits a perfect and subtle blend of typically BMW attributes and a modern, angular design, with grille integrated into the hood.

+ PERFORMANCES. They're above average for both engines that provide very comfortable accelerations and pickup, reassuring for safe travel. The 528's performances are quite adequate, but the 540 benefits from the V8's strength that's dauntless and raring to go, mostly the M5 which strikes 0-60 mph in 5.3 seconds.

+ RIDE COMFORT. It's definitely come a long way, thanks to the silky suspension, nicely shaped and cushy seats and an almost imperceptible noise level, the direct result of efficient soundproofing.

+ STEERING. It's smooth and nicely powered, so it provides superb maneuverability, in spite of a slightly high reduction ratio that sometimes makes it seem vague.

+ INNOVATIONS. The 5 Series has inherited all kinds of gadgets and accessories from the 7, including heated steering wheel, six airbags, residual heat accumulator, off-center windshield wiper on the passenger side to reduce the blind spot and radar system located on the rear bumper that lets you back up safely.

+ CONVENIENCE FEATURES. The trunk is deep and it's modular as well. Access is super due to its tapered opening, and there are lots of generous-size storage compartments throughout the cabin.

CONS

- BUDGET. It takes a pretty bundle to own one of these beauties. Purchase price, insurance and upkeep are extremely costly and frequent, expensive trips to the dealership are no reason to jump for joy. Besides, these cars depreciate quite a bit, so there again, you lose out, financially speaking.

- ACCESS. It's awkward getting into the rear seats and leg room is tight, especially if the front seats are pushed far back.

- CABIN SPACE. Even though it's more generous than on the former generation, it can't really compare with more modest cars that offer roomier passenger space.

- IN POOR TASTE. The burl walnut wood appliqués look like bizarre imitation wood and they've been discarded by other automakers for precisely this reason.

- TRUNK. It's so deep you have to climb into it to fetch objects that have shifted during transport.

- CENTER CONSOLE. It's very wide and less oriented towards the driver and some controls are almost out of reach.

- REAR MIRRORS. They're very tiny and don't provide good rear visibility.

- CONTROLS. Some of them are rather unusual and complicated, like the radio dials that require a crash course to be able to tune into your favorite station.

- LEGIBILITY. Instruments are hard to read at night, since the fluorescent lighting and the small, close-set numbers require real concentration on the part of the driver.

CONCLUSION

The 5 Series models offer the same powertrains and performance levels as the 7 Series, in a size that is barely bigger than the 3 Series. Concentrated power makes these cars remarkably consistent and gives them a rare charm that is reserved for a financially privileged clientele group.

RATING	
BMW 5 Series	
CONCEPT :	**80%**
Technology :	90
Safety :	90
Interior space :	60
Trunk volume :	70
Quality/fit/finish :	90
DRIVING :	**76%**
Cockpit :	80
Performance :	75
Handling :	65
Steering :	80
Braking :	80
ORIGINAL EQUIPMENT :	**82%**
Tires :	85
Headlights :	80
Wipers :	75
Rear defroster :	80
Radio :	90
COMFORT :	**81%**
Seats :	90
Suspension :	90
Sound level :	60
Conveniences :	80
Air conditioning :	85
BUDGET :	**46%**
Price :	0
Fuel economy :	55
Insurance :	40
Satisfaction :	85
Depreciation :	50
Overall rating :	**73.0%**

NEW FOR 2000

- An M5 version with a 400-hp output.
- Options such as the satellite navigation system, rear airbags, an electronically adjustable suspension, rain detector wiper system, dashboard-mounted CD player.

Compare
Performance,
Specifications, Prices,
and Classification
at the end of this chapter.

**Luxury
35-$70,000**

EQUIPMENT

BMW 5 Series	528i	528iT	540i	540iT	M5
Automatic transmission:	O	O	O	S	NA
Cruise control:	S	S	S	S	S
Power steering:	S	S	S	S	S
Anti-lock brakes:	S	S	S	S	S
Traction control:	S	S	SA	S	S
Air conditioning:	SA	SA	SA	SA	SA
Leather:	OH	OH	SH	SH	SH
AM/FM/radio-cassette:	SCd	SCd	SCd	SCd	SCd
Power door locks:	S	S	S	S	S
Power windows:	S	S	S	S	S
Tilt steering:	S	S	S	S	S
Dual adjustable mirrors:	SH	SH	SH	SH	SH
Alloy wheels:	S	S	S	S	S
Anti-theft system:	S	S	S	S	S

Colors

Exterior: White, Red, Green, Black, Anthracite, Silver, Blue, Grey, Beige.

Interior: Black, Beige, Grey, Stone, Green, Caramel.

AT A GLANCE...

HISTORIC

Introduced in:	1972.
Made in:	Dingolfing,(Münich) Germany.

DEMOGRAPHICS

Model	Men/Wom.	Age	Married	College	Income $
5 Series	80/20 %	50	84 %	67 %	135,000

INDEX

Safety:	90 %	Satisfaction:	87 %
Depreciation:	47 %	Insurance:	$ 1,250
Cost per mile:	$ 1.10	Number of dealers:	350

SALES

	Canada			USA		
Model	1997	1998	Result	1997	1998	Result
5 Series	1,612	2,338	+ 45.0 %	31,347	35,100	+ 12.0 %

MAINTENANCE REQUIRED BY WARRANTY

First revision:	Frequency:	Diagnostic plug:
15,000 miles	15,000 miles	Yes

Traditional

The Park Avenue is the heir to the tradition of big luxury sedans as defined by Buick. Over the years, it has acquired a size and a personality that appeals to those who don't want to be seen aboard a classic Cadillac or an exuberant Aurora. Like all bigger automobiles, it's suffering the slings and arrows of intentionally versatile vehicles that offer more at the same price.

MODEL RANGE

This four-door sedan is offered in a base model driven by a 3.8L V6 atmospheric engine or in the Ultra that's animated by an additional supercharger. Original equipment is quite complete, since it includes automatic transmission, ABS, climate control, cruise control, radio-tape deck, power windows, door locks and mirrors, light alloy wheels and the theft deterrent Pass-Key III keyless entry system. The Ultra is also equipped with traction control, leather trimmed, heated seats and a sportier suspension.

TECHNICAL FEATURES

Built on the same C platform as the Cadillac Seville, Eldorado and Oldsmobile Aurora, the Park Avenue has a monocoque steel body yielding rather ordinary aerodynamics with a drag coefficient of 0.34. Independent chassis cradles support the front and rear powertrains that support the engine and four-wheel independent suspension. Up front, there are MacPherson type struts and double wishbones with cross struts at the rear. The brake system includes four disc brakes linked to state-of-the-art ABS, also enhanced by standard traction control on the Ultra.

Luxury 35-$70,000

PROS

+ **STYLE.** The nicely rounded curves of this model are classic and distinguished looking, touches very

typical of Buick beauties. The car has clean, classic lines but when it comes into your line of vision, you know at once that it's a Buick.

+ **USEFUL SPACE.** The cabin and trunk can easily accommodate five passengers and all their luggage. A sixth passenger would be welcome on board, but only for short jaunts, since space is a bit snug for six passengers.

+ **OVERALL DESIGN.** The design blend is almost perfect with the sturdy body, effective suspension and fairly muscular drivetrain, so the ride is interesting even on the base model.

+ **RIDE COMFORT.** The Park Avenue and the Ultra are real winners with such a velvety suspension, plush seats and soundproofing that cuts noise down to a whisper at highway cruising speed. And the really impressive climate control system can roast your buns in the winter and put frost on your nose in the good old summertime...

+ **EQUIPMENT.** The base model car has lots and lots of accessories and features, since the Ultra only has added leather trim, heated front seats and traction control.

+ **PERFORMANCE.** The supercharged 3.8L V6 gives the Ultra a unique drive feel, as accelerations and pickup are crisper and gutsier than those of the base model Park Avenue, thanks to a more favorable power to weight ratio. Going from 0 to 60 mph in 8.5 seconds is impressive for a middle class car that weighs in at 3,884 pounds... The gearbox

really enhances overall performance, since it's silky smooth, precise and well calibrated.

+ **ROADHOLDING.** The Park Avenue Ultra is less affected by swish and sway than its base model counterpart equipped with softer, more comfort-oriented springs and shock absorbers and less beefy stabilizer bars. The car approaches curves in a more gingerly fashion, but it's nice and dependable in everyday circumstances.

+ **BRAKES.** Rear disc brakes have cut down on stopping distances and have improved resilience to overheating.

+ **FUEL ECONOMY.** Both 3.8L V6 engines deliver a lot of power and torque, but this still doesn't affect the relatively frugal fuel consumption for this type of car, since it sits above 18 mpg.

+ **FIT & FINISH.** Over the years, this car is getting better and better. It boasts of an ever sturdier body build, more careful craftsmanship and lusher trim materials.

+ **CABIN DESIGN.** The interior is neat with its modern instrument panel and very practical main console with scads of storage compartments and convenient armrest.

+ **NICE FEATURES.** The pollen filter climate control and tilt mirrors when in reverse.

CONS

- **HANDLING.** The Park Avenue is sometimes tricky when it comes to maneuvers and parking because of its wide steering diameter.

- **SUSPENSION.** The spongy suspension on the base model really affects body control and provokes a lot of sway, so you have to slow down on serpentine stretches.

- **TRANSMISSION.** Untypical of GM products, the transmission doesn't provide enough braking effect when you downshift manually to slow down.

- **SEATS.** Designed for more mature, elderly folk, they don't provide enough lateral and lumbar support, since they're quite flat and too soft when covered with fabric.

- **OUTWARD VIEW.** Rear view at quarterback is crippled by the thick C pillar that creates a large blind spot.

- **NOISE LEVEL.** The Ultra engine roars at the least acceleration or pickup, which isn't too appropriate for a car that's blessed with such a plush, discreet interior and style.

- **TIRES.** The Goodyear Eagle GA tires on our test car performed quite well on other model cars, but they're less suited to the Park Avenue since they suffer from weight transfer on turns. Bigger-diameter tires would also make for more stable brake performance.

- **TO BE IMPROVED UPON.** The skimpy-sized ashtray, shallow, totally useless door side-pockets and crummy ergonomics on the middle section of the instrument panel.

CONCLUSION

The Park Avenue offers a special kind of ride that has its own special charm, but that may not be as magical when compared to the miracles worked by multi-purpose vehicles.

RATING	
BUICK Park Avenue	
CONCEPT :	**78%**
Technology :	80
Safety :	80
Interior space :	85
Trunk volume :	70
Quality/fit/finish :	75
DRIVING :	**65%**
Cockpit :	80
Performance :	70
Handling :	55
Steering :	70
Braking :	50
ORIGINAL EQUIPMENT :	**75%**
Tires :	75
Headlights :	80
Wipers :	70
Rear defroster :	75
Radio :	75
COMFORT :	**72%**
Seats :	75
Suspension :	80
Sound level :	70
Conveniences :	50
Air conditioning :	85
BUDGET :	**51%**
Price :	20
Fuel economy :	60
Insurance :	50
Satisfaction :	80
Depreciation :	45
Overall rating :	**68.2%**

NEW FOR 2000

- **Standard StabiliTrak system on the Ultra version.**
- **Design-type wheels.**
- **Different interior trims.**
- **Side airbags positioned in front-seat backs.**
- **Three exterior colors and one trim.**

Compare
Performance,
Specifications, Prices,
and Classification
at the end of this chapter.

Luxury 35-$70,000

EQUIPMENT

BUICK Park Avenue	base	Ultra
Automatic transmission:	S	S
Cruise control:	S	S
Power steering:	S	S
Anti-lock brakes:	S	S
Traction control:	O	S
Air conditioning:	SA	SA
Leather:	O	SH
AM/FM/radio-cassette:	S	SCd
Power door locks:	S	S
Power windows:	S	S
Tilt steering:	S	S
Dual adjustable mirrors:	SE	SEH
Alloy wheels:	S	S
Anti-theft system:	S	S

Colors

Exterior: Silver, White, Blue, Green, Black, Bordeaux, Red, Gold, Bronze, Beige.

Interior: Grey, Blue, Red, Taupe.

AT A GLANCE...

HISTORIC
Introduced in: 1971.
Made in: Wentzville, Missouri, USA.

DEMOGRAPHICS

Model	Men/Wom.	Age	Married	College	Income $
Park Ave.	87/13 %	68	88 %	37 %	65,000

INDEX

Safety:	90 %	Satisfaction:	82 %
Depreciation:	55 %	Insurance:	$ 765
Cost per mile:	$ 0.60	Number of dealers:	2,850

SALES

	Canada			USA		
Model	1997	1998	Result	1997	1998	Result
Park Ave.	2,535	1,511	- 40.4 %	68,777	58,187	- 15.4 %

MAINTENANCE REQUIRED BY WARRANTY

First revision:	Frequency:	Diagnostic plug:
3,000 miles	6,000 miles	Yes

Paving The Way

The Cadillac DeVille is one of the most unshakable of North American icons. It has become part of the culture and it symbolizes the social success of the middle classes. General Motors has always relied on Cadillac models to launch its technical innovations, using it as a type of rolling laboratory. Some of its ideas, such as front-wheel drive, the Northstar engine or the StabiliTrak traction control system, were successful. Others, such as the V8-6-4 engine were definite fiascos.

MODEL RANGE

The DeVille is a 4-door sedan that comes in base, DHS (DeVille High Luxury Sedan) or DTS (DeVille Touring Sedan) versions, all equipped with the latest edition of the 4.6L V8 Northstar engine. The DTS has 300 horsepower, the others, 275. Standard equipment is fairly detailed and includes antilock brakes, traction control, alloy wheels and automatic air conditioning.

TECHNICAL FEATURES

Given their wide front-end, this model's steel unibody is remarkably aerodynamic, with a drag coefficient of 0.32. Although its length and width have been reduced by 2 inches (5 cm), the new DeVille has as much useable space as the previous model because its wheelbase has been increased by 1.5 inches (3.8 cm). The fully independent suspension is auto adjustable. The front features MacPherson struts, the rear is equipped with oblique triangles and side arms and both assemblies feature antiroll bars. The four disc brakes are complemented by antilock and traction control systems and steering features the Magnasteer magnetic variable effort system. The latest StabiliTrak 2.0 system now acts directly on the steering system's assistance to limit wheel travel and to ensure the vehicle's stability.

From the safety standpoint the DeVille now features front and side airbags for front-seat passengers, rear parking assist sensors, Night Vision and OnStar satellite emergency navigation systems.

PROS

+ **STYLING.** While keeping a still respectable size, the DeVille has been revised without losing any of its classic, sober and well-balanced nature, characteristic of its appeal. Its less rounded lines moves it closer to the Seville, giving it more international proportions.

+ **PASSENGER ROOM.** It remains generous enough for five passengers to travel comfortably.

+ **TRUNK.** It has enough capacity to accommodate luxury-size baggage without scratching or scraping. It opens wide and its sill is low enough to make loading and unloading easy.

+ **COMFORT.** The DeVille is at its best on the highway. Its suspension and seats are cushy and soundproofing and air conditioning are efficient. From A to Z, this is the American car par excellence.

+ **TECHNOLOGY.** Under its classic appearance, the DeVille is surprisingly modern. Its front-wheel drive system is a marvel in winter and its power system ensures equally good stability, grip, braking and visibility.

+ **ENGINE.** The Northstar is one of the best engines of its generation. On these models, acceleration and pick-up are comparable to those of true sports models.

+ **HANDLING.** The DTS offers surprisingly good handling ease thanks to an electronically controlled suspension that keep body roll under tight control.

+ **QUALITY.** Construction, finish and materials all show improvement, which explains why the number of very satisfied owners totals more than 85%.

+ **BRAKING.** Although powerful and well-balanced, its endurance needs improvement and linings tend to react badly when pushed to limit.

+ **FUEL ECONOMY.** The Northstar engine has been reworked to bring it into line with California's LEV standards and its consumption is comparable to that of some big V6s, at least under normal driving conditions.

+ **VISIBILITY.** It has improved considerably thanks to large windowed surfaces and a smaller C-pillar that provides better 3/4 rear visibility.

+ **BONUS POINTS.** For the rain detector that automatically activates wipers, for the OnStar satellite communication system that offers good safety and tourism information possibilities, the rear sensors that signal nearby objects when backing up and the absolutely original Night Vision system.

CONS

- **STEERING.** In spite of all its technology, it's impossible to gauge its assistance, which is too strong and makes it light and overly sensitive, eliminating any feedback on road conditions. Drivers need a good bit of experience to keep the DeVille on course in strong crosswinds.

- **HANDLING.** Although it's slightly smaller, the DeVille is still imposing and hard to drive along city streets that are narrow.

- **SUSPENSION.** The soft suspension on the base and DHS leads to major body sway on poor road surfaces and complicates matters on tight corners, where this kind of car definitely shows its lack of agility.

- **SEATS.** Front seats provide better molding and support than the rear bench seat.

- **DRIVING POSITION.** It would be better if the steering column were shorter and if the steering wheel were positioned closer to the dashboard.

CONCLUSION

The Cadillac DeVille is in keeping with the flavor of the day when it comes to size and design concept, but with its safety and high-tech features, it points the way for the entire automotive industry and more importantly, for its rivals!

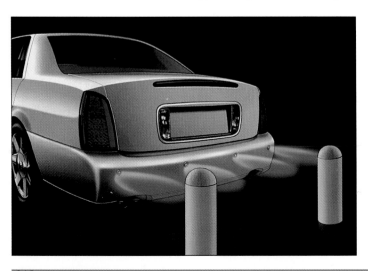

RATING — CADILLAC DeVille

CONCEPT: 87%
- Technology: 90
- Safety: 90
- Interior space: 90
- Trunk volume: 85
- Quality/fit/finish: 80

DRIVING: 70%
- Cockpit: 85
- Performance: 70
- Handling: 65
- Steering: 80
- Braking: 50

ORIGINAL EQUIPMENT: 77%
- Tires: 80
- Headlights: 80
- Wipers: 70
- Rear defroster: 75
- Radio: 80

COMFORT: 80%
- Seats: 80
- Suspension: 80
- Sound level: 80
- Conveniences: 70
- Air conditioning: 90

BUDGET: 46%
- Price: 0
- Fuel economy: 50
- Insurance: 45
- Satisfaction: 85
- Depreciation: 50

Overall rating: 72.0%

New 2000 Model

NEW FOR 2000

- Revamped model, now available in base, DHS and DTS versions with a revised 4.6L Northstar engine meeting California LEV standards.
- Technical innovations: Night Vision, Ultrasonic Rear Parking Assist sensors, navigational system, OnStar emergency system.

Compare Performance, Specifications, Prices, and Classification at the end of this chapter.

Luxury 35-$70,000

EQUIPMENT

CADILLAC DeVille	base	DHS	DTS
Automatic transmission:	S	S	S
Cruise control:	S	S	S
Power steering:	S	S	S
Anti-lock brakes:	S	S	S
Traction control:	S	S	S
Air conditioning:	SA	SA	SA
Leather:	O	S	S
AM/FM/radio-cassette:	SCd	SCd	SCd
Power door locks:	S	S	S
Power windows:	S	S	S
Tilt steering:	S	S	S
Dual adjustable mirrors:	SEH	SEH	SEH
Alloy wheels:	S	S	S
Anti-theft system:	S	S	S

Colors
Exterior: Green, White, Black, Beige, Garnett Red, Mocha, Amethyst, Blue, Argyle, Sand, Carmin.
Interior: Black, Red, Blue, Beige.

AT A GLANCE...

HISTORIC
Introduced in: 1956, 1965, 1971, 1977, 1994, 2000.
Made in: Hamtramck-Detroit, Michigan, USA.

DEMOGRAPHICS

Model	Men/Wom.	Age	Married	College	Income $
DeVille	85/15 %	67	85 %	30 %	67,500

INDEX
- Safety: 90 %
- Depreciation: 52 %
- Cost per mile: $ 0.78
- Satisfaction: 85 %
- Insurance: $ 950
- Number of dealers: 1,600

SALES

Model	Canada 1997	1998	Result	USA 1997	1998	Result
DeVille	3,268	2,329	- 28.7 %	104,743	99,779	- 4.7 %

MAINTENANCE REQUIRED BY WARRANTY
- First revision: 3,000 miles
- Frequency: 6,000 miles
- Diagnostic plug: Yes

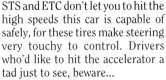

An Ambassador

If the DeVille sets its sights on the classic Cadillac customer, the Seville is intended for those who eyes stray to the magnetic foreign offerings from Germany and England. A shorter version destined for exporting is the ambassador for General Motors' know-how when it comes to luxury cars. As for the Eldorado, which is in fact a two-door version of the Seville, it remains one of the rare coupes to survive the onslaught of more versatile vehicles.

MODEL RANGE

The Seville is a four-door deluxe sedan offered in two models: the luxurious SLS and the sporty STS. The Eldorado coupe is available in two similar models, namely the base and ETC versions. All models are powered by a 4.6L V8 Northstar engine linked to an electronically controlled 4-speed automatic transmission. The engine delivers 275 hp on the SLS and Eldorado and 300 hp on the STS and ETC versions. Standard equipment includes leather seats, a sophisticated sound system, front seats equipped with side-impact air bags and built-in safety belts, a theft deterrent system and anti-skid device called StabiliTrak 2.0. But the OnStar communication and assistance system via satellite is only offered as an extra as well as heated seats.

TECHNICAL FEATURES

The Seville and Eldorado share the Oldsmobile Aurora G platform. The structure has undergone umpteen improvements. In comparison with the previous model, it's 58% more rigid in regard to flexion and 53% more torsion-resistant. We'd like to point out that the Seville models exported to Europe and Asia are slightly shorter than those sold on our North American market. In these countries where space is a rare commodity, laws favor vehi-

cles less than 16.5 ft in length, which explains the trimmer export model size. These precious inches were nibbled at on the front and rear bumper stone deflectors. The unibody is built of galvanized steel and includes two subframes, both front and rear. Hydroformed reinforcing tubes create a safety cage to assure high resistance in the event of a collision. The front suspension made up of MacPherson struts is similar to that on the former model, but the rear suspension now includes a dual wishbone linkage of forged aluminum supported by adjustable cross-struts, stabilizer bar and air suspension levelling control.

Four-wheel disc brakes are fitted with a four-channel system and ABS-anti-skid control. Magnetically controlled rack-and-pinion variable assist steering is identical to that on the Aurora. The Seville is literally loaded with electronic gadgetry; a Multiplex system oversees the transmission of data for all control systems. A noteworthy detail: the on-board computer can deliver information in five languages, making a distinction between standard French and French Canadian. A subtle touch!

PROS

+ RIDE COMFORT. The suspension provides a cushy ride, even on the STS. Wheel travel has been increased by 20% in comparison with the suspension on the former Seville. Adaptive and heated seats are listed among the options; they automatically adjust to fit the occupants' body shape and offer superb support. Effective sound dampening muffles any noise coming from the engine or chassis.

+ PERFORMANCES. The 4.6L V8 Northstar engine yields pretty amazing accelerations and pickup, which ensures really safe driving in emergency situations.

+ STYLE. This car has cool, clean looks both inside and out for an American car. Besides, there's a lovely leather scent, a pleasure you don't experience too often in this antiseptic, squeaky-clean age!

+ HANDLING. On the highway, the Seville exhibits smooth, predictable behavior, whether the driver is relaxed or raring to go. In difficult maneuvers, this is pretty reassuring. Besides, the StabiliTrak 2.0 system, designed to control vehicle attitude, is really appealing since it's more adaptable than on Seville rivals. It never prevents the driver from accelerating when he or she decides to do so.

+ CONVENIENCE FEATURE. That sliding drawer, albeit optional, that you can install in the trunk and that facilitates unloading parcels, especially those stored at the trunk bottom. Lincoln already came up with the idea for the Continental...

CONS

- TIRES. The Z-rated tires included in the "Autobahn" option package are well adapted to the vehicle, but the regular LS tires that equip the STS and ETC don't let you to hit the high speeds this car is capable of safely, for these tires make steering very touchy to control. Drivers who'd like to hit the accelerator a tad just to see, beware...

- FUEL ECONOMY. The STS and ETC engines are gas-thirsty, since it's commonplace to see the on-board computer indicating 12 mpg when high speeds are maintained.

- MANEUVERABILITY. The STS is clumsy in the city and on curved roads and on slalom runs, wheel lock sometimes occurs. Not surprising with a body that weighs slightly more than 2 tons...

- SOME CONTROLS. The new instrument panel is elegant and relatively well organized, but the cruise control is inconveniently located, since it's outside the driver's line of vision. It's a good idea to try it out before setting out on a trek!

- NOISE. Sound dampening is effective when dealing with road or engine noise, so much so that wind whistling around the windshield roars away as soon as you hit 50 mph.

- TO BE IMPROVED UPON. Some finish and equipment details are disappointing, like the exterior weatherproofing around the doors, that tends to buckle — the flat pancake spare tire, the old-design seatbelts up front and the trunk lining that's of Cavalier vintage...

CONCLUSION

The sales for these two models are stagnating. It's easy to understand in the Eldorado's case, since coupes are less popular, but it's harder to understand when it comes to the Seville, which was revamped recently but still can't stand up to the war waged by its overseas competitors.

RATING
CADILLAC Seville-Eldorado

CONCEPT :		82%
Technology :	90	
Safety :	90	
Interior space :	80	
Trunk volume :	70	
Quality/fit/finish :	80	

DRIVING :		68%
Cockpit :	80	
Performance :	75	
Handling :	50	
Steering :	80	
Braking :	55	

ORIGINAL EQUIPMENT :		79%
Tires :	80	
Headlights :	80	
Wipers :	70	
Rear defroster :	75	
Radio :	90	

COMFORT :		82%
Seats :	80	
Suspension :	80	
Sound level :	80	
Conveniences :	80	
Air conditioning :	90	

BUDGET :		45%
Price :	0	
Fuel economy :	40	
Insurance :	45	
Satisfaction :	90	
Depreciation :	50	

Overall rating :		71.2%

NEW FOR 2000
- **Improved Northstar engine.**
- **Upgraded StabiliTrak 2.0 traction control system.**
- **Airbag deactivation system.**
- **Rear parking radar and optional navigational system on the STS and SLS.**
- **Two exterior colors: Midnight Blue and Bronze.**

Compare Performance, Specifications, Prices, and Classification at the end of this chapter.

Luxury 35-$70,000

EQUIPMENT

CADILLAC Seville CADILLAC Eldorado	SLS base	STS ETC
Automatic transmission:	S	S
Cruise control:	S	S
Power steering:	S	S
Anti-lock brakes:	S	S
Traction control:	S	S
Air conditioning:	SA	SA
Leather:	S	S
AM/FM/radio-cassette:	SCd	SCd
Power door locks:	S	S
Power windows:	S	S
Tilt steering:	S	S
Dual adjustable mirrors:	SEH	SEH
Alloy wheels:	S	S
Anti-theft system:	S	S

Colors
Exterior: Green, White, Black, Beige, Garnet Red, Bronze, Blue, Clay, Sand, Carmine.

Interior: Black, Cappuccino, Dark Cherry, Dark Blue, Beige.

AT A GLANCE...

HISTORIC
Introduced in:	1976, 1998.
Made in:	Hamtramck-Detroit, Michigan, USA.

DEMOGRAPHICS
Model	Men/Wom.	Age	Married	College	Income $
Seville	92/8 %	58	84 %	42 %	145,000

INDEX
Safety:	100 %	Satisfaction:	92 %
Depreciation:	50 %	Insurance:	$ 1,100
Cost per mile:	$ 0.88	Number of dealers:	1,600

SALES
Model	Canada 1997	1998	Result	USA 1997	1998	Result
Seville	2,471	2,419	- 2.1 %	29,837	38,888	+ 30.3 %
Eldorado	359	218	- 39.3 %	20,609	15,598	- 24.3 %

MAINTENANCE REQUIRED BY WARRANTY
First revision:	Frequency:	Diagnostic plug:
3,000 miles	6,000 miles	Yes

Ignored

Fate is as unfair for automobiles as it is for humans and the Q45's is all the more cruel given that its lines, described as outdated, were copied in part by Cadillac for its latest DeVille model. In spite of a whole load of qualities - the main one being its remarkable value - the Q45 has not been successful and its sales remain very minimal. Its days are numbered and next year a model with a more striking style will take its place.

MODEL RANGE

The Q45 is a four-door sedan offered in either base or "t" for touring models. The "t" model has a firmer suspension with bulkier anti-roll bar at the rear, rear spoiler and forged aluminum rims. Both versions are equipped with a 4.1L V8 linked to a 4-speed automatic gearbox. Equipment is very generous and includes all the amenities you'd look for in a car in this price range, such as front heated seats.

TECHNICAL FEATURES

The Q45 is derived from the Cima, a Nissan-built car sold in Japan, with new front and rear end stylistic accents, thanks to NDI, the Infiniti stylistics bureau located in California, so as to better tickle North American tastes. The body is more angular, but more lackluster than was the former Q45. There's no real hint as to where these design details come from, they're sort of generic and generally typical of what you see on cars in this category, such as the classic grille and chrome details. The steel monocoque body is fitted with four-wheel independent suspensions consisting of MacPherson struts up front and rear independant with multiple link control arms. The four-wheel disc brakes are linked to a standard ultra-modern ABS system. The aluminum 4.1L V8 engine is at the cutting edge of technology, delivering 266 hp, a very impressive amount of power since it's in the same league as the GM Northstar or Ford Intech engines, with half a liter less of displacement. The automatic transmission doesn't include a manual setting, but it's equipped with viscous-coupled locking differential and standard antilock braking system. The latter reduces engine power when it detects the first sign of wheel slippage.

PROS

+ DESIGN. First off, the Q45 makes a good impression. From the outside, it looks lush and solid, yet has a discreet appearance. Inside, the cabin is more obviously luxurious with the posh leather-clad seats and faux-bois trim. The many chrome accents add a touch of class and the steering wheel is inviting with its attractive punched leather rim.

+ PRICE. Less expensive than the previous model, without any compromise as to quality, equipment or performances, the Q45 is a good buy.

+ RIDE COMFORT. The spacious cabin seats five passengers. Seats and suspension are as comfy as it gets, even on the "t" version equipped with a more flexible suspension than before and sound-proofing does the silence trick.

+ ENGINE. It's silky and powerful, delivering excellent performances thanks to a remarkable power to weight ratio. Accelerations and pickup are lively and the transmission is right on the ball. Gas mileage is a nice surprise, since the engine settles for 20 mpg on average for normal driving, which corresponds to the normal petrol appetite of a V6.

+ ROADHOLDING. It's generally neutral and very stable at high speeds. This car is amazingly agile on serpentine stretches, especially the "t" version that exhibits more crisp moves due to a less flexible suspension design.

+ BRAKES. Always easy to apply just as needed and brawny, providing straight stops in 130 ft, no mean feat considering the vehicle weight.

+ MANEUVERABILITY. It's better than before, due to a shorter steer angle diameter and variable assist steering, so parking is a breeze.

+ EQUIPMENT. It's lavish, including all the power and luxury accessories that come with luxury car territory and convenience features haven't been overlooked either, since there are many storage compartments scattered throughout the cabin.

+ QUALITY. It's evident everywhere you look. Assembly, fit and finish and trim materials are dramatically better than they once were. Dependability is a definite asset as well, since 95% of owners are very happy with their Q45 and are proud to own such a car.

CONS

- STYLE. You could never say that the Q45 is oozing with charm, since it was built for the Japanese market and acts as a sort of American surrogate...

- BUDGET. The Q45 sells for less then before, but not everyone can afford to buy one and upkeep and insurance premiums aren't cheap, yet resale value isn't at all a sure thing.

- TRUNK. It's fairly tiny for such a big car, since it can hold as much as a...Sentra! But it has a nice, regular shape and tapered lid, so it can be used to full advantage.

- CONTROLS. Radio and climate control dials are in reverse order, so you have to dodge the shifter if you want to change radio stations.

- TO BE IMPROVED UPON. No rear stabilizer bar on the base model, so there's a soft, squishy feel and wishy washy demeanor that will only thrill American car fanatics...

CONCLUSION

Because of the reputation and daring design of its competitors, which make it look pretty dull, the Q45 doesn't enjoy anything near the kind of success it deserves. Yet it's very fun to use, easy to maintain and its reliability and fuel economy are far from taxing on the budget.

RATING		
INFINITI Q45		
CONCEPT :		74%
Technology :	85	
Safety :	90	
Interior space :	70	
Trunk volume :	40	
Quality/fit/finish :	85	
DRIVING :		72%
Cockpit :	85	
Performance :	65	
Handling :	70	
Steering :	80	
Braking :	60	
ORIGINAL EQUIPMENT :		82%
Tires :	85	
Headlights :	85	
Wipers :	70	
Rear defroster :	80	
Radio :	90	
COMFORT :		82%
Seats :	85	
Suspension :	80	
Sound level :	80	
Conveniences :	80	
Air conditioning :	85	
BUDGET :		48%
Price :	0	
Fuel economy :	60	
Insurance :	40	
Satisfaction :	90	
Depreciation :	50	
Overall rating :		**71.6%**

NEW FOR 2000

• **No changes for model year 2000.**
• **Touring version exclusively in Canada.**

Compare
Performance,
Specifications, Prices,
and Classification
at the end of this chapter.

Luxury
35-$70,000

EQUIPMENT

INFINITI Q45	base	"t"
Automatic transmission:	S	S
Cruise control:	S	S
Power steering:	S	S
Anti-lock brakes:	S	S
Traction control:	S	S
Air conditioning:	SA	SA
Leather:	SH	SH
AM/FM/radio-cassette:	SCd	SCd
Power door locks:	S	S
Power windows:	S	S
Tilt steering:	S	S
Dual adjustable mirrors:	SEH	SEH
Alloy wheels:	S	S
Anti-theft system:	S	S

Colors

Exterior: Green, Black, Titanium, Pewter, White.

Interior: Beige, Pebble, Black.

AT A GLANCE...

HISTORIC
Introduced in: 1990-1997.
Made in: Tochigi, Japan.

DEMOGRAPHICS

Model	Men/Wom.	Age	Married	College	Income $
Q45	100/0 %	49	100 %	50 %	100,000

INDEX

Safety:	90 %	Satisfaction:	90 %
Depreciation:	55 %	Insurance:	$ 1,250
Cost per mile:	$ 1.00	Number of dealers:	150

SALES

	Canada			USA		
Model	1997	1998	Result	1997	1998	Result
Q45	163	110	- 32.5 %	10,443	8,244	- 21.1%

MAINTENANCE REQUIRED BY WARRANTY

First revision:	Frequency:	Diagnostic plug:
7,500 miles	6 months / 7,500 miles	Yes

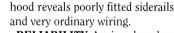
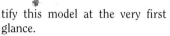

Messiah

Jaguar waited a long time on a mid-priced car capable of letting it rival its German competitors, Mercedes-Benz and BMW, both of whom have built their empire on models whose sales have achieved astronomical heights. Lack of financial means and corporate spirit delayed the project time and time again, until Ford took over the ownership of the Coventry make. And thanks to the American giant's enormous technical and financial resources, the S-TYPE finally saw the light of day, at the same time as its American twin, the Lincoln LS, which shares the same platform and mechanical components.

MODEL RANGE

The Jaguar S-TYPE is available in two versions, the AJ-V6, equipped with a 3.0L Ford Duratec V6 (already used on the Taurus-Sable), and the AJ-V8, powered by the 4.0L V8 that Jaguar developed for its XK and also uses on the XJ. The standard transmission is a 5-speed automatic with manual shifting on a J-shaped grid gate. Equipment includes a large number of technical and comfort-related features commonly found on cars that sell at this price level. From this standpoint both versions are almost identical, but some items available on the U.S. market are not included in Canada, and vice versa, for example the satellite navigation system. Three options packages, known as Memory Assistance, Weather or Sport, let buyers leave the showroom with a car tailor-made to suit their needs and priorities.

TECHNICAL FEATURES

Like its direct rivals, the BMW 5 Series and the Mercedes-Benz E-Class, the S-TYPE is a rear-wheel drive. Its steel unibody has good aerodynamics, with a drag coefficient of 0.32. It features galvanized side panels and two cradles insulated from the main body and designed to support the suspensions and mechanical system. Weight distribution between the front and rear is ideal, providing optimal resistance to flexion or torsion. The fully independent suspension is based on a combination of long and short arms in the front and double triangular arms in the rear, with an anti-roll bar used on both ends. This Jaguar offers adjustable shock absorbers that are controlled electronically, a Dynamic Stability Control anti-skid system and power steering and power brakes. The rack-and-pinion power steering system receives assistance that varies to match speed levels and four disc brakes and ABS and traction control systems are standard on both versions. Both also feature excellent Pirelli P Zero tires.

PROS

+ STYLING. It's extremely good and will prove to be the best bet to encourage sales. Its powerful lines are an inevitable reminder of the Mark II and S-TYPE from the 1960s. While the rear fascia is very "Jaguar", the front is extremely well designed and lets onlookers identify this model at the very first glance.

+ TECHNOLOGY. Compared to the traditional models that the British make has been marketing for lightyears, the S-TYPE is ultra-sophisticated, with voice-activated systems, Dynamic Stability Control, and an adjustable suspension.

+ PERFORMANCE. There is a considerable gap between the levels reached by the V6 and the V8. Never a rocket, the Ford engine has a less favorable weight/power ratio than its British counterpart, which ranks ahead in terms of acceleration, pick-up and, alas, fuel consumption.

+ PRESENTATION. Only British designers are capable of making such beautiful use of the wood inlays and leather typical of luxury cars, setting S-TYPE models far apart from their rivals when it comes to creating a warm ambience for the passenger compartment.

+ COMFORT. Although the seats don't have the same ergonomics found on a Volvo, they are well-padded and the suspension is smooth enough to prevent fatigue on long outings.

CONS

- QUALITY. It's questionable in some instances; a better ashtray and cover can be found on a Honda Civic and overall assembly isn't as refined as it is on this car's German competitors. A quick look under the hood reveals poorly fitted siderails and very ordinary wiring.

- RELIABILITY. A minus based on our team's experience. The first S-TYPE we were loaned couldn't be test driven because of a battery failure: the battery is located in the trunk, which opens using a battery-controlled power system instead of a good old reliable key!

- PASSENGER ROOM. The S-TYPE's passenger compartment isn't the roomiest when front seats are positioned all the way back and rear-seat passengers had best be shorter than average.

- TRUNK. It lacks height and its space is limited given the fact that it also houses a full-size emergency tire and a large battery.

- FUEL CONSUMPTION. The V8 engine is far from economical; it isn't unusual to go beyond 13 mpg (18.0 l/100 km) when driving at faster speeds and the level rarely drops lower than 15 mpg (16 l/100 km) under normal conditions.

- PRACTICALITY. On this count designers failed to match the talents shown by stylists: the glovebox is big enough to hold the owner's manual and not much else when it houses the CD loader, door pockets aren't deep enough, and rear-seat passengers have to get along with minimal amenities.

CONCLUSION

The arrival of the S-TYPE will have the effect of doubling sales (and profits) for the venerable British make and for Ford, which will finally begin to see a return on its investment. While on the whole the product is satisfactory, it needs a few revisions to make it totally competitive.

Luxury
35-$70,000

RATING JAGUAR S-TYPE		
CONCEPT :		**74%**
Technology :	90	
Safety :	90	
Interior space :	55	
Trunk volume :	55	
Quality/fit/finish :	80	
DRIVING :		**71%**
Cockpit :	80	
Performance :	70	
Handling :	65	
Steering :	80	
Braking :	60	
ORIGINAL EQUIPMENT :		**77%**
Tires :	90	
Headlights :	80	
Wipers :	65	
Rear defroster :	70	
Radio :	80	
COMFORT :		**73%**
Seats :	80	
Suspension :	75	
Sound level :	65	
Conveniences :	65	
Air conditioning :	80	
BUDGET :		**43%**
Price :	0	
Fuel economy :	30	
Insurance :	35	
Satisfaction :	80	
Depreciation :	70	
Overall rating :		**67.6 %**

New 2000 Model

NEW FOR 2000

- **All new vehicle sharing the same platform and mechanical components as the Lincoln LS.**

Compare Performance, Specifications, Prices, and Classification at the end of this chapter.

Luxury 35-$70,000

EQUIPMENT

JAGUAR S-TYPE	AJ-V6	AJ-V8
Automatic transmission:	S	S
Cruise control:	S	S
Power steering:	S	S
Anti-lock brakes:	S	S
Traction control:	S	S
Air conditioning:	S	S
Leather:	S	S
AM/FM/radio-cassette:	SCd	SCd
Power door locks:	S	S
Power windows:	S	S
Tilt steering:	S	S
Dual adjustable mirrors:	S	S
Alloy wheels:	S	S
Anti-theft system:	S	S

Colors
Exterior: White, Anthracite, Green, Red, Silver, Blue.

Interior: Ivory, Charcoal, Cashmere, Almond.

AT A GLANCE...

HISTORIC
Introduced in: 2000.
Made in: Castle Bromwich, Birmingham, England.

DEMOGRAPHICS

Model	Men/Wom.	Age	Married	College	Income $
S-TYPE	60/40 %	45	78 %	75 %	100,000

INDEX

Safety:	90 %	Satisfaction:	78 %
Depreciation:	30 %	Insurance:	$ 1,850
Cost per mile:	$ 1.00	Number of dealers:	-

SALES

Model	Canada			USA		
	1997	1998	Result	1997	1998	Result
S-TYPE	Not on sale during this period.					

MAINTENANCE REQUIRED BY WARRANTY

First revision:	Frequency:	Diagnostic plug:
5,000 miles	10,000 miles	Yes

LEXUS

GS

After a successful rejuvenation effort, the Lexus GS models saw their sales increase substantially - particularly the GS 300, which met with truly extraordinary success in the U.S., ranking just below the BMW 5 Series. Things are different in Canada and the beautiful Bavarian ranks fourth after the Cadillac DeVille and Seville and the Buick Park Avenue. How eclectic can you get?

Eclectic

MODEL RANGE
Sitting between the ES 300 and the LS 400, the GS 300 and 400 now offer an added luxury and performance level to the Lexus model range. This 4-door sedan is available in the GS 300 version, animated by the same 3.0L in-line 6 engine as last year or in the GS 400 version powered by the 4.0L V8 borrowed from the LS 400. These cars are equipped with a standard 5-speed automatic transmission but other items such as leather trim is offered as an extra on the 300, while heated seats, sunroof, xenon headlamps, navigation system, CD changer, chrome wheels and bigger tires are available as options on both versions.

TECHNICAL FEATURES
The latest Lexus GS models have a completely new architecture and are built on a brand new platform. It's a steel monocoque structure with front-engine and rear-wheel drive. These cars' silhouette yields effective aerodynamics, since the drag coefficient drops to 0.29. The suspension, mounted on independent cradles isolating it from the body, is fully independent, consisting of a double wishbone design with stabilizer bar both front and rear. Cars are equipped with disc brakes, a standard ABS/traction control device as well as variable assist

steering. Both versions benefit from a standard anti-skid system that helps the driver keep control of the vehicle in the event of skidding or slipping.

PROS
+ STYLE. The distinctively tight, taut stylistics add a lot more personality than before.

+ PERFORMANCES. The GS 400 driven by the V8 puts out very zoomy accelerations and pickup, due to a favorable power to weight ratio. The GS 300 has more zip than before, but it doesn't hold a candle to the 400 that has a lot more panache.

+ HANDLING. It's very safe and competent, in spite of the pronounced roll and this is the case even on wet roads, since the ABS, traction control and anti-skid systems blend their magic potion to assure optimal stability and a nice neutral demeanor that's easy to maintain with the accelerator. But the anti-skid system doesn't always let the driver step on the gas at the right moment.

+ RIDE COMFORT. It's all-round cushy, since seats are nicely shaped and offer good support even for rear seat travellers, the well-honed suspension filters out road faults and superb sound dampening keeps the noise level nice and low.

+ PRICES. They're fairly reasonable, since the GS 400 price tag compares very favorably with that of the BMW 540i. Whether the tran-

quil Nipponese approach or Bavarian prestige comes out as number one in the race, remains to be seen...

+ QUALITY. Construction, finish details and trim materials are beyond reproach and the high customer satisfaction rate as well as one of the top standings in J.D. Power's hit parade confirm Lexus' enviable reputation. The leather seat covers are velvety smooth and the wood appliqués are elegant and very posh.

+ DRIVING PLEASURE. It's simply super due to compact size that makes it easy to maneuver these cars, also due to straight as an arrow steering that works wonders on really tight curves, but the GS 400 is more agile than the 300 in this case, and being at the wheel is a joy with such gutsy engines and competent roadholding.

+ NICE FEATURES. Efficient wipers that sweep 90% of the windshield and powerful xenon headlamps that unfortunately are billed as extras...

CONS
- SUSPENSION. As is the case for the ES 300, it isn't too versatile, even though it's pretty high tech. Its excessive flexibility provokes rear end slipping and sliding, so it's tough staying right on track at high speeds.

- CABIN SPACE. It only seats four passengers, even with the fifth rear seat headrest, as the cabin is quite narrow, especially towards the rear.

- SEQUENTIAL SHIFTER. It

doesn't add much oomph to performances or overall competence, since the touch buttons installed on the steering wheel that control speed changes require a lot of tending to on snaky roads.

- INSTRUMENT PANEL. It's cluttered with all those deep honeycomb shapes and the lighting system is pervasive and distracting. Ergonomics aren't perfect either, since some controls are poorly located.

- VISIBILITY. The rearward view is far from perfect due to the narrow rear window, high-perched headrests and at rear quarterback the thick base C pillar gets in the way.

- TRUNK. It can't be used to maximum because it's weirdly shaped, the floor isn't perfectly flat and it doesn't hold enough because it's short and can't be extended towards the cabin. Rear seat passengers don't have much storage space because the main armrest only includes two cup-holders.

- POOR MARKS. For the deadly slow windshield wipers, definitely not suited to heavy summer rain. The fastest pace (56 sweeps/minute) is the slowest found on some other vehicles.

CONCLUSION
The GS models are taking a run at anything that moves in this category. They're ready to take on the biggest Americans and their most elegant of German counterparts. In all instances they have strong arguments in their favor: quality assembly, convincing performance levels and reasonable fuel economy and a very healthy financial potential.

RATING		
LEXUS GS 300-400		
CONCEPT :		78%
Technology :	85	
Safety :	90	
Interior space :	70	
Trunk volume :	60	
Quality/fit/finish :	85	
DRIVING :		73%
Cockpit :	80	
Performance :	75	
Handling :	70	
Steering :	80	
Braking :	60	
ORIGINAL EQUIPMENT :		82%
Tires :	85	
Headlights :	80	
Wipers :	85	
Rear defroster :	75	
Radio :	85	
COMFORT :		75%
Seats :	80	
Suspension :	70	
Sound level :	70	
Conveniences :	70	
Air conditioning :	85	
BUDGET :		50%
Price :	0	
Fuel economy :	60	
Insurance :	45	
Satisfaction :	90	
Depreciation :	55	
Overall rating :		**71.6%**

NEW FOR 2000

- **New exterior colors: Crystal White, Millennium Silver metallic.**
- **New Brake Assist, safety system as standard equipment.**

Compare
Performance,
Specifications, Prices,
and Classification
at the end of this chapter.

Luxury 35-$70,000

EQUIPMENT

LEXUS	GS 300	GS 400
Automatic transmission:	S	S
Cruise control:	S	S
Power steering:	S	S
Anti-lock brakes:	S	S
Traction control:	S	S
Air conditioning:	SA	SA
Leather:	O	S
AM/FM/radio-cassette:	S	S
Power door locks:	S	S
Power windows:	S	S
Tilt steering:	S	S
Dual adjustable mirrors:	SEH	SEH
Alloy wheels:	S	S
Anti-theft system:	S	S

Colors

Exterior: White, Silver, Bronze, Black Onyx, Gold, Ruby, Jade, Blue.

Interior: Cloth: Grey. Leather: Charcoal, Ivory, Black.

AT A GLANCE...

HISTORIC

Introduced in:	1993-1998.
Made in:	Tahara, Japan.

DEMOGRAPHICS

Model	Men/Wom.	Age	Married	College	Income $
GS 300	77/23 %	54	83 %	60 %	100,000
GS 400	92/8 %	50	64 %	64 %	185,000

INDEX

Safety:	90 %	Satisfaction:	90 %
Depreciation:	45 %	Insurance:	$ 1,000
Cost per mile:	$ 0.87	Number of dealers:	170

SALES

	Canada			USA		
Model	1997	1998	Result	1997	1998	Result
GS 300	117	295	+ 152.1 %	3,825	20,696	+ 441.1 %
GS 400	158	368	+ 132.9 %	3,893	9,926	+ 155.0 %

MAINTENANCE REQUIRED BY WARRANTY

First revision:	Frequency:	Diagnostic plug:
3,500 miles	3,500 miles	Yes

In Jeopardy

Now that the small LS has come along, the Continental is no longer the baby in the Lincoln lineup. Although their prices are about the same, they aren't intended for the same kind of buyer. Or at least that's what the people at Lincoln are trying to tell themselves, but nothing could be less sure.

MODEL RANGE

This big four-door, front-wheel drive sedan is sold in a single trim model driven by the 4.6L V6 "Intech" engine developing 275 hp, coupled to a 4-speed automatic transmission. Its already extensive equipment no longer includes the custom driver style system that lets you drive "à la carte", the most unique feature on the original model. The idea was no doubt too advanced for potential buyers and for the rest of the industry...

TECHNICAL FEATURES

The Continental is the only front-wheel drive Lincoln. Its steel monocoque architecture offers average aerodynamic finesse with a drag coefficient of 0.32. The fully independent suspension is based on the MacPherson strut principle up front and a multi-link system at the rear with a stabilizer bar both front and rear. Air springs keep the rear extremity on an even keel and shock absorbers are hydraulic. Four-wheel disc brakes benefit from an antilock braking device linked to standard traction control. Rack-and-pinion steering is variable assist and can also be adjusted according to 3 settings. All the electronic data is controlled by a Multiplex communication system. The Continental's V8 is exactly the same that equips the Town Car. This "Intech" engine is now on a par with the Cadillac

Northstar engine, but when it comes to prestige, it doesn't hold a candle to its rival the Cadillac Seville, a car with much more international ambitions.

PROS

+ STYLE. The body exterior and cabin design have a neat, new look that reflects the fact that Ford now also owns Jaguar. This trait is more noticeable towards the rear, due to taillights that look a lot like those on the XJ8 and that God-awful chrome bar is gone forever.

+ PERFORMANCES. They're quite remarkable, since this very heavy car achieves accelerations and pickup nowhere near being laughable. The "Intech" engine really does its stuff and is very efficient as well, a pleasant surprise, since fuel consumption is very low when travelling on the highway at cruising speed, so much so that it's comparable to a V6's yield...

+ HANDLING. It's generally neutral for normal driving, but goes into understeer when on sports mode due to the overly elastic suspension that isn't adjustable, not even as an option. At any rate, traction control and ABS provide nice, straight directional flow in all kinds of weather.

+ RIDE COMFORT. Travelling in a Continental is literally like being on cloud nine. The cushy suspension takes care of road nonsense,

seats are thick and plush and sound-proofing takes the starch out of engine and road noise. The body doesn't generate much wind whistle either.

+ TRUNK. It can hold lots of luggage, even when the (optional) storage box, that can be removed and slides in like a drawer, is installed. This accessory is such a clever concept that GM borrowed the idea and equipped the Seville and Bravada with it. This storage box is really handy, since it's divided into sections, so small objects don't roll around or get knocked over. When loading larger pieces of luggage, it slides to the back or can be removed.

CONS

- PRICE. Now that high tech items are listed among the options, it should drop significantly. The Continental doesn't have the prestige that is the Seville's lucky lot, even though its engine is now just as impressive as the shining Northstar...

- MANEUVERABILITY. It's hampered by the big body and wide turning radius.

- DRIVING. The "à la carte" driving feature is now sold as an extra because it's so darn costly. It lets you adjust suspension and steering firmness as well as the seat, mirror and radio station position memory according to three different drivers.

One day, all cars will be equipped with this feature that lets you tailor the same model to satisfy umpteen pilots' wishes.

- CABIN SPACE. It isn't anywhere near what it should be for such a generous-size car and it's downright nasty even thinking of seating a fifth passenger in the middle of the rear seatbench, even for a five-minute errand.

- SEATS. They look super plush but they aren't too comfy. They're well upholstered but the seat cushion is short and the back is flat, so they don't offer good hip and shoulder support.

- STORAGE COMPARTMENTS. They're few and far between inside the cabin and the glove compartment and door side-pockets are stingy as heck. The center console is stuffed with the CD changer or the cellular phone. Rear seat passengers only have access to seat pockets and stylists didn't even think of adding a compartment and cup holders in the center armrest, as is more and more the custom...

- DASHBOARD. Its utilitarian design is very odd on a vehicle sold at this price level.

CONCLUSION

The arrival of the LS relegates the Continental to a makeshift role in the very middle of the Lincoln model range, with a single, solitary original touch: front-wheel drive. Over the years it has lost all of its substance and its streamlined styling is a very small consolation.

RATING		
LINCOLN Continental		
CONCEPT :		82%
Technology :	90	
Safety :	90	
Interior space :	70	
Trunk volume :	80	
Quality/fit/finish :	80	
DRIVING :		72%
Cockpit :	80	
Performance :	65	
Handling :	65	
Steering :	80	
Braking :	70	
ORIGINAL EQUIPMENT :		79%
Tires :	80	
Headlights :	80	
Wipers :	80	
Rear defroster :	75	
Radio :	80	
COMFORT :		73%
Seats :	70	
Suspension :	80	
Sound level :	70	
Conveniences :	60	
Air conditioning :	85	
BUDGET :		43%
Price :	0	
Fuel economy :	50	
Insurance :	40	
Satisfaction :	85	
Depreciation :	40	
Overall rating :		69.8%

NEW FOR 2000

- **Remote deck lid release positioned inside the trunk.**
- **Child-safety seat anchoring system.**
- **Side airbags for front-seat passengers.**
- **Exterior colors: Transparent Green and Autumn Red.**

Compare
Performance,
Specifications, Prices,
and Classification
at the end of this chapter.

Luxury 35-$70,000

EQUIPMENT

LINCOLN	Continental
Automatic transmission:	S
Cruise control:	S
Power steering:	S
Anti-lock brakes:	S
Traction control:	S
Air conditioning:	SA
Leather:	S
AM/FM/radio-cassette:	S
Power door locks:	S
Power windows:	S
Tilt steering:	S
Dual adjustable mirrors:	SEH
Alloy wheels:	S
Anti-theft system:	S

Colors

Exterior: Gold, Ivory, Red, Blue, Green, Grey, Silver, Black, White.

Interior: Parchment, Graphite, Charcoal.

AT A GLANCE...

HISTORIC

Introduced in:	1988, 1995.
Made in:	Wixom, MI, USA.

DEMOGRAPHICS

Model	Men/Wom.	Age	Married	College	Income $
Continental	87/13 %	66	84 %	34 %	72,000

INDEX

Safety:	90 %	Satisfaction:	87 %
Depreciation:	55 %	Insurance:	$ 1,000
Cost per mile:	$ 0.70	Number of dealers:	5,200

SALES

	Canada			USA		
Model	1997	1998	Result	1997	1998	Result
Continental	1,099	894	- 18.7 %	31,220	35,210	+ 12.8 %

MAINTENANCE REQUIRED BY WARRANTY

First revision:	Frequency:	Diagnostic plug:
5,000 miles	6 months / 6,000 miles	Yes

Outdated

The Town Car is an intimate part of the lives of North Americans. Be it for VIP airport shuttle services or as a base for luxury limousines - from high school graduation, to marriage, to funeral corteges, it is witness to the major events in the personal history of those who live on this continent. Its last revamping didn't meet with unanimous approval from the styling and sizing standpoints, but as time goes by it will blend into the everyday landscape and all will be forgiven.

MODEL RANGE

The Lincoln Town Car is a large 4-door sedan available in 4 different versions: Executive, Signature, Signature TS and Cartier. All versions are equipped with the same mechanical features, namely a V8 "Intech" engine coupled with a 4-speed automatic transmission. An antilock braking system is part of the original equipment on all models, along with traction control.

TECHNICAL FEATURES

The Town Car consists of a surrounding chassis made of steel on which is mounted the monocoque body that's made up of mostly galvanized panels. Aerodynamics aren't too hot since the unofficial drag coefficient is 0.34. The front suspension still uses unequal-length control arms with coil springs and stabilizer bar, while the rear suspension consists of a Watt setup with air springs, gas-filled shocks and stabilizer bar with an automatic load-levelling device. Electronic sway and swerve control no longer equips this car, but roadholding is now achieved by the Watt suspension geometry. Disc brakes are beefier up front and the ABS-traction control system comes as origi-

nal equipment. Steering is still a recirculating ball system but it's no longer variable assist on demand as was once the case. The 4.6L V8 has undergone major modifications in regard to cylinder head and pistons and it's protected from seizure in the event of a coolant leak. Radiator vents are electric and the coil ignition system now includes one coil per ignition plug, thus eliminating wiring between plugs and the center-load coil and loss of power in damp weather.

PROS

+ DRIVING PLEASURE. It feels less like a "boat" than before thanks to the more elaborate rear axle design (that could still have benefitted from an independent suspension setup), more accurate steering, more competent suspensions and a stronger structure that has greater torsion and flexion resistance.

+ RIDE COMFORT. It's pretty impressive with such a generous cabin that comfortably seats five (but head room is a bit snug in the rear seats), cool and collected suspension (even with the rigid rear axle) and plush seats that could, however, offer more lateral support. Noise is kept to a civilized minimum.

+ HANDLING. The body exhibits more solid, structural integrity so there's less rattling and much less pronounced roll and rear end directional flow is cleaner, which

all amounts to a longer neutrality on curves and a less noticeable oversteer effect.

+ ENGINE. It's quite competent for this car category, more geared to comfort than to breaking records, since accelerations and pickup are quick and allow for safe passing on the highway. And not to mention that it's pretty efficient since gas consumption sits at around 19 mpg at normal speeds.

+ NICE FEATURES. Some handy items like the rear seat adjustable air vents, and the sound system and climate control remote power switches located on the steering wheel spokes.

CONS

- STYLE. It'll take a while for this model to be accepted because it borrows too heavily from well known models such as the Chrysler LHS (rear window design) or the Jaguar (trunk extremity look) to have a clean, single-minded style. The Town Car traded in its official status tuxedo for a spectacular "patchwork" look that's far from being classic.

- REAR AXLE. Depending on road quality, handling and ride comfort are very up and down. A cheap solution that's unworthy of such an upper-crust car.

- BRAKING. Stopping a massive weight of over two tons when fully loaded isn't exactly a picnic. Brake linings are mediocre, the pedal is

spongy and the ABS system fails to counter a slight tendency towards wheel lock.

- TRUNK. It has a funny shape, so it's hard to use it to full advantage, even if theoretically it's supposed to hold a lot, and the spare tire thrown smack in the middle doesn't help one iota. A problem Lincoln will have to take a serious look at.

- CONVENIENCE FEATURES. They're awfully stingy, since there isn't even a door side-pocket for the front passenger and rear seat passengers have a center armrest, but it doesn't contain any storage space. Front seat passengers don't have a real center storage console either.

- INSTRUMENT PANEL. Its plain Jane instruments and design jar with the Cartier clock and climate control dials are too low to be really within reach.

- VISIBILITY. It's obstructed by the thick roof supports, especially at rear quarterback and the narrow rear window doesn't help.

- TO BE IMPROVED UPON. Poor-quality headlamps that are out of keeping with such lap of luxury equipment, the texture and look of some plastic components that really jar with the Jag leather and wood trim. The Anglo-American blend could have been smoother. There is no footrest for the driver and rear headrests are pretty simplistic since they aren't even adjustable.

CONCLUSION

In spite of its attempt at modernization, the Lincoln Town Car remains an outdated automobile. A symbol of wealth, under its pretentious exterior it hides underpinnings that are unworthy of Ford's legendary ingenuity, much touted in commercials.

RATING
LINCOLN Town Car

CONCEPT : 86%
Technology :	80
Safety :	90
Interior space :	90
Trunk volume :	90
Quality/fit/finish :	80

DRIVING : 62%
Cockpit :	70
Performance :	50
Handling :	60
Steering :	80
Braking :	50

ORIGINAL EQUIPMENT : 75%
Tires :	80
Headlights :	70
Wipers :	70
Rear defroster :	75
Radio :	80

COMFORT : 73%
Seats :	75
Suspension :	80
Sound level :	70
Conveniences :	50
Air conditioning :	90

BUDGET : 45%
Price :	0
Fuel economy :	50
Insurance :	45
Satisfaction :	85
Depreciation :	45

Overall rating : 68.2%

NEW FOR 2000
- Remote deck lid release positioned inside the trunk.
- Child-safety anchoring system.
- Side airbags for front-seat passengers.
- Seatbelt reminder system.

Compare
Performance,
Specifications, Prices,
and Classification
at the end of this chapter.

Luxury 35-$70,000

EQUIPMENT

LINCOLN Town Car	Executive	Signature/TS	Cartier
Automatic transmission:	S	S	S
Cruise control:	S	S	S
Power steering:	S	S	S
Anti-lock brakes:	S	S	S
Traction control:	S	S	S
Air conditioning:	SA	SA	SA
Leather:	S	S	S
AM/FM/radio-cassette:	S	S	S
Power door locks:	S	S	S
Power windows:	S	S	S
Tilt steering:	S	S	S
Dual adjustable mirrors:	SEH	SEH	SEH
Alloy wheels:	S	S	S
Anti-theft system:	S	S	S

Colors
Exterior: Parchment, Gold, Red, Blue, Green, Grey, Silver, Black, White.

Interior: Graphite, Parchment, Blue, Charcoal, White.

AT A GLANCE...

HISTORIC
Introduced in:	1980, 1998.
Made in:	Wixon, MI, USA.

DEMOGRAPHICS
Model	Men/Wom.	Age	Married	College	Income $
Town Car	91/9 %	68	84 %	23 %	52,000

INDEX
Safety:	90 %	Satisfaction:	87 %
Depreciation:	55 %	Insurance:	$ 975
Cost per mile:	$ 1.00	Number of dealers:	5,200

SALES
	Canada			USA		
Model	1997	1998	Result	1997	1998	Result
Town Car	1,960	2,264	+ 15.5 %	92,297	97,547	+ 5.7 %

MAINTENANCE REQUIRED BY WARRANTY
First revision:	Frequency:	Diagnostic plug:
5,000 miles	6 months/ 6,000 miles	Yes

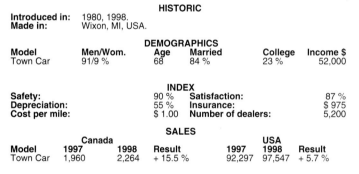

Perfection

The Mercedes E-Class is one of the most accomplished standard production cars in the world. When you take a close look at it, from every conceivable angle, even if your criteria are arbitrary, this is the ideal car. Not too big, not too small, powerful and sophisticated, but at a cost reasonable given its content, it can be either discreet and comfortable or sporty and exciting. In short, this is the automobile par excellence.

MODEL RANGE

The E-Class includes a 4-door sedan, the E300 that's equipped with a 3.0L Turbo Diesel 6-cylinder, a E320 sedan and station wagon equipped with the new 3.2L V6 and that can receive all-wheel drive as well as the E430 that's powered by a 4.3L V8. Lastly, the E55 AMG, the ultra-performance sedan. All models benefit from a 5-speed automatic transmission, antilock braking (ABS) and traction control (ASR) to which can be added the (ESP) anti-skid system. Equipment is lush and includes all the amenities that are typical of this car category.

TECHNICAL FEATURES

The E-Class models have a steel monocoque body that's been rigidified, but that's also been pared down weight-wise. It benefits from good aerodynamics since the drag coefficient is 0.29. The front suspension consists of a double wishbone setup, while at the rear, the «five-lever» assembly is now more lightweight. Cars are equipped with power rack-and-pinion steering and four disc brakes with ABS linked to an ASR 5 traction control system and an anti-skid system. This system, called ESP,

detects the least instability, lateral slippage, over-steer, skidding or swerve and uses the ABS and ASR to control car path and keep the car level. Passive safety devices include two front-impact airbags, but Mercedes has also installed side-impact airbags located in the front and back doors and curtains which protect the head and chest of the passengers, all activated by separate sensors. Front seat belts are fitted with electronic tension retractors and emergency-locking retractors designed to reduce chest injuries. Nice features: the intermittent wiper speed controlled by diodes that measure rain intensity on the windshield and rear bumper radar that detects if children or objects are in the way when parking.

OUTSTANDING

++ CLEAN DESIGN. It's superb, for this model exudes an unusual solid and safe character.

++ FUEL EFFICIENCY. All engines that equip the E-Class are very zoomy and perform like race car counterparts, yet do so with a reasonable fuel consumption.

PROS

+ STYLE. It's less angular than it once was and yields better aerodynamics and those oval headlamps really add class and panache.

+ QUALITY. It's absolutely exquisite

right down to the finest details, when it comes to engineering, construction, finish job, materials and equipment.

+ SAFETY FEATURES. Passive safety benefits from the latest advances in architectural solidity since this car is highly resistant to all kinds of collisions and active devices include front and side-impact airbags and air curtains protecting passengers from head and chest injuries.

+ HANDLING. It's much better in regard to precision, agility and safety thanks to the driving aids (ABS-ASR-ESP) that let the driver regain control of the vehicle after skidding. E-Class models are the summum of competence and they stay superbly neutral in winter driving situations.

+ PERFORMANCES. The gas engines put out racecar-caliber performances, especially the ones that equip the E430 or the E55 AMG that looks like any other car, but can sure zoom along like some so-called exotic models.

+ RIDE COMFORT. It's remarkable for the cabin is roomy enough to seat five passengers more than comfortably. The tough suspension takes care of major road flaws, yet it's civilized and the seats, though still awfully firm, are shaped better, so they're cushier than they once were.

+ MANEUVERABILITY. It's super for a car of this format, due to a

reasonable steer angle, which no doubt explains why in Europe, it's the choice of many cab drivers.

+ CONVENIENCE FEATURES. Increased North American sales have encouraged Mercedes to pay more attention to details such as storage spots, cup-holders and coat hangers, items considered useless at one time.

CONS

- DIESEL ENGINE. North-American buyers will be really frustrated by this engine, since they're more used to creamy conventional V8's and frugal fuel consumption isn't enough of an incentive to have to put up with more sluggish output, noise, vibration and undesirable smoke.

- HEADLAMPS. The xenon headlights work wonderfully well at night, yet they don't blind oncoming drivers. It's really too bad that they aren't included as standard items for this vehicle, because they'd sure make for safer driving.

- VISIBILITY. It's obstructed at rear quarterback by the thick, slanting B pillars and when it rains, the one and only wiper isn't brisk enough to handle hard rain.

- TO BE IMPROVED UPON. The trunk size that's out of whack with the generous cabin space — cumbersome knee bolsters, especially on the driver's side and the annoying shifter travel.

CONCLUSION

Why buy 20 pairs of shoes that cost $100 when one pair sold at $1,000 can go just as far with a lot more style and comfort. It all depends on your life philosophy and the personal choices you're prepared to make.

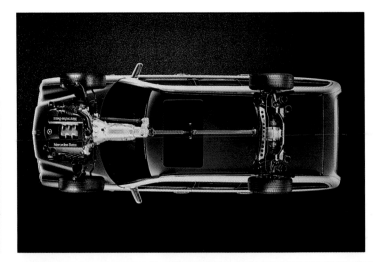

RATING
MERCEDES-BENZ E-Class

CONCEPT :		83%
Technology :	90	
Safety :	100	
Interior space :	65	
Trunk volume :	70	
Quality/fit/finish :	90	
DRIVING :		71%
Cockpit :	80	
Performance :	70	
Handling :	65	
Steering :	80	
Braking :	60	
ORIGINAL EQUIPMENT :		78%
Tires :	80	
Headlights :	80	
Wipers :	75	
Rear defroster :	75	
Radio :	80	
COMFORT :		75%
Seats :	80	
Suspension :	80	
Sound level :	70	
Conveniences :	65	
Air conditioning :	80	
BUDGET :		51%
Price :	0	
Fuel economy :	70	
Insurance :	40	
Satisfaction :	90	
Depreciation :	55	
Overall rating :		71.6%

NEW FOR 2000
- Cosmetic changes to the front and rear aprons.
- Sporty E55 AMG version and E430 4MATIC sedan.
- Side airbags in rear doors and curtain-type head-protection in sedans and wagons.
- Automatic 5-speed transmission with cruise control.
- Standard ESP traction control on all models.

Compare
Performance,
Specifications, Prices,
and Classification
at the end of this chapter.

EQUIPMENT

MERCEDES-BENZ

	E300TD	E320	E430	E55 AMG
Automatic transmission:	S	S	S	S
Cruise control:	S	S	S	S
Power steering:	S	S	S	S
Anti-lock brakes:	S	S	S	S
Traction control:	S	S	S	S
Air conditioning:	SA	SA	SA	SA
Leather:	O	S	S	S
AM/FM/radio-cassette:	SCd	SCd	SCd	SCd
Power door locks:	S	S	S	S
Power windows:	S	S	S	S
Tilt steering:	S	S	S	S
Dual adjustable mirrors:	SEH	SEH	SEH	SEH
Alloy wheels:	S	S	S	S
Anti-theft system:	S	S	S	S

Colors
Exterior: Black, White, Turquoise, Blue, Bordeaux, Silver, Green.

Interior: Black, Blue, Ash, Parchment.

AT A GLANCE...

HISTORIC

Introduced in:	1996.
Made in:	Sindelfingen, (Stuttgart) Germany.

DEMOGRAPHICS

Model	Men/Wom.	Age	Married	College	Income $
E Class	81/19%	52	87 %	70 %	120,000

INDEX

Safety:	100 %	Satisfaction:	92 %
Depreciation:	45 %	Insurance:	$ 1,300
Cost per mile:	$ 1.15	Number of dealers:	380

SALES

	Canada			USA		
Model	1997	1998	Result	1997	1998	Result
E Class	2,034	1,876	- 7.8 %	42,883	47,523	+ 10.9 %

MAINTENANCE REQUIRED BY WARRANTY

First revision:	Frequency:	Diagnostic plug:
3,000 miles	10,000 miles	Yes

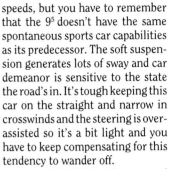
Of the two models offered by this Swedish builder, the 9⁵ performed best during the past year. Very recently revamped, it now comes in a wagon and Aero version and benefits from a more dynamic marketing approach.

A Spark

MODEL RANGE

The 9⁵ comes as a four-door sedan or wagon in base, SE and Aero sedan animated by a standard 2.3L turbocharged 4-cylinder engine developing 170 hp (230 hp-Aero) or equipped with an optional 3.0L turbocharged V6 that develops 200 hp. A 5-speed manual transmission is standard with the 2.3L, but the V6 is only available with an automatic. Original equipment items are very extensive and luxurious since they include such things as climate control, heated seats, antilock braking system, traction control and radio-tape deck and CD player. The most important options are the automatic transmission (on 4-cyl), leather seats (on base), sunroof (on wagons).

TECHNICAL FEATURES

The 9000's successor is inspired by the Opel Vectra platform, a GM product designed and built in Europe. The galvanized steel unibody benefits from super-efficient aerodynamics since the drag coefficient is only 0.29. It's extremely robust so as to provide maximum passenger protection in the event of a collision. The front independent suspension consists of a MacPherson strut design, whereas at the rear, the axle is supported by several control arms and both suspensions include an anti-roll bar. The disc brake system is paired up with an antilock braking device that shares its sensors with the traction control system, both being standard items. The 2.3L 4-cylinder engine, equipped

with two balance shafts to reduce vibrations, is highly efficient, thanks to the 16-valve DOHC distribution and a Saab-designed distributorless ignition system. The V6 develops 200 hp with the help of a Garrett T3 compressor with air interchanger that reduces pollutant emissions, but doesn't produce sheer, brute power that's rather average for an engine of this displacement.

PROS

+ CONCEPTION. The 9⁵ is a big, sturdy, safe car whose sophisticated trends earns them high marks to that end.

+ SAFETY. The 9⁵'s body has been beefed up to effectively protect occupants in the event of an accident. So much so that at Auto Shows, Saab exhibits a model that's undergone a collision test and has come out unscathed.

+ SILHOUETTE. The 9⁵ is a gorgeous car. Its clean, discreet design has an unmistakable resemblance to the previous model, preserving typical Saab traits.

+ PERFORMANCES. The V6 engine is more muscular than the 4-cylinder, since it benefits from a better power to weight ratio on accelerations and pickup, that are average in this category and aren't really noteworthy.

+ DRIVING PLEASURE. The cockpit is super, visibility is only slightly obstructed at rear quarterback, the neatly organized instrument panel is loaded with gauges and such.

+ RIDE COMFORT. Things have really improved in this department, since the rear axle profits from more generous suspension travel and both suspensions are smoother and handle road faults like champions. Seats are just as comfy as before, providing effective lateral and lumbar support.

+ USEFUL SPACE. The 9⁵'s cabin is even more spacious than on the 9000. Five passengers will be right at home and the trunk gobbles up all their luggage with no problem at all. It's also convertible, so you can store heaps of stuff when the seatbench is folded down.

+ QUALITY. This car has a very robust feel, the finish job is beautifully executed and trim materials are of superb quality and of course, there are all kinds of amenities.

+ BONUS POINTS. For remarkably efficient headlamps that are strong and reach wide and far and for a convex left-hand sideview mirror designed to eliminate the blind spot.

CONS

- PERFORMANCES. The 170 hp 4-cylinder engine isn't up to much and only musters run-of-the-mill accelerations and pickup and lots of less expensive cars do a heck of a lot better. The turbocharged engine's response time is rather slow and you have to get used to this gap, otherwise you'll be forever frustrated.

- HANDLING. It's fine at normal speeds, but you have to remember that the 9⁵ doesn't have the same spontaneous sports car capabilities as its predecessor. The soft suspension generates lots of sway and car demeanor is sensitive to the state the road's in. It's tough keeping this car on the straight and narrow in crosswinds and the steering is over-assisted so it's a bit light and you have to keep compensating for this tendency to wander off.

- TRANSMISSION. The manual isn't too zippy and quick on the draw for gears are slow to kick in. You often get the impression that the engine's stalling in first gear, due to very sluggish turbocharger response time.

- BRAKES. They weren't great on our two test cars. Sudden stops were achieved at an average 165 ft. Brakes are nice and gradual, but ABS doesn't get rid of all wheel lock, so car path isn't a sure, straight-ahead thing.

- BUDGET. Saab's aren't great buys. They're fun to drive, but they're pricey and upkeep is costly and then there's the poor resale value to consider. Such an expensive venture is ridiculous, unless of course, you're a dyed-in-the-wool car buff.

- STORAGE SPACE. The glove compartment is of reasonable size, but other storage spots are skimpy, such as the slim door side-pockets. Cup-holders aren't terribly convenient.

- TO BE IMPROVED UPON. The flat pancake spare tire that doesn't jive with such and expensive car.

CONCLUSION

This model is highly developed, potential buyers are ready to give it a try, so what's missing to create the spark that starts the fire? Maybe rethinking the distribution network or deciding to sell it differently?

RATING
SAAB 9⁵

CONCEPT :		87%
Technology :	85	
Safety :	100	
Interior space :	80	
Trunk volume :	90	
Quality/fit/finish :	80	

DRIVING :		63%
Cockpit :	85	
Performance :	50	
Handling :	60	
Steering :	75	
Braking :	45	

ORIGINAL EQUIPMENT :		75%
Tires :	80	
Headlights :	85	
Wipers :	55	
Rear defroster :	75	
Radio :	80	

COMFORT :		69%
Seats :	80	
Suspension :	75	
Sound level :	50	
Conveniences :	60	
Air conditioning :	80	

BUDGET :		44%
Price :	0	
Fuel economy :	65	
Insurance :	30	
Satisfaction :	80	
Depreciation :	45	

Overall rating :		67.6%

NEW FOR 2000
- Side airbags for head and torso protection.
- Aero version featuring a 230 hp HO turbo engine complemented by sporty exterior and interior styling.
- Sunroof as standard equipment on all sedans.
- Traction Control System (TCS) standard on all models.

Compare Performance, Specifications, Prices, and Classification at the end of this chapter.

EQUIPMENT

SAAB 9⁵	base	SE
Automatic transmission:	O	O
Cruise control:	S	S
Power steering:	S	S
Anti-lock brakes:	S	S
Traction control:	S	S
Air conditioning:	SA	SA
Leather:	OH	SH
AM/FM/radio-cassette:	SCd	SCd
Power door locks:	S	S
Power windows:	S	S
Tilt steering:	S	S
Dual adjustable mirrors:	SEH	SEH
Alloy wheels:	S	S
Anti-theft system:	S	S

Colors
Exterior: White, Black, Blue, Red, Grey, Silver, Night blue.

Interior: Grey, Beige, Black, Tan.

AT A GLANCE...

HISTORIC
Introduced in:	1984-1999.
Made in:	Trollhattan, Sweden.

DEMOGRAPHICS
Model	Men/Wom.	Age	Married	College	Income $
9⁵	70/30 %	49	92 %	80 %	90,000

INDEX
Safety:	100 %	Satisfaction:	85 %
Depreciation:	55 %	Insurance:	$ 1,085
Cost per mile:	$ 0.85	Number of dealers:	365

SALES
	Canada			USA		
Model	1997	1998	Result	1997	1998	Result
9⁵	241	400	+ 66.0 %	4,696	7,774	+ 65.5 %

MAINTENANCE REQUIRED BY WARRANTY
First revision:	Frequency:	Diagnostic plug:
3,000 miles	6,000 miles	Yes

With the advent of the now defunct 850, Volvo entered a new era marked by success. The 70 series models followed the trend and now it's the S80's turn to shatter the sales records set by previous models.

Americanized

MODEL RANGE

The S80 is a luxury sedan available in two trims, the base and the T6. The S80 emphasizes the luxury side with a 2.9-liter, inline, 6-cylinder DOHC engine, while the T6 goes for performance with a 2.8-liter inline-6 bi-turbo. The front power seats are fully-adjustable. Both models have leather upholstery but not the same quality, and the T6 has real walnut trim, while you'll have to make do with faux wood on the base model. The steering wheel is fully adjustable. Standard equipment includes dual zone climate control and a 60/40 folding rear seat. The T6 adds foglights and an auto-dimming rearview mirror. A sunroof is optional for both.

TECHNICAL FEATURES

The aerodynamics of the steel unibody are outstanding, with a drag coefficient of 0.28. Both the front hood and rear trunk are made of aluminum. The fully independent suspension has MacPherson struts on the front, while the rear has a multi-arm system mounted on the undercarriage, attached to the chassis with rubber bushings. Both front and rear incorporate anti-roll bars. Brakes are all discs with a three-channel anti-lock system and an electronic brake distribution system (EBD). Standard equipment also includes traction control. Finally, the power steering adapts to vehicle speed. The S80 sets itself apart because of the transverse-mounted inline 6 engine and the compact automatic transmission. Both versions offer more interior space and a larger crumple zone to better protect passengers in a collision. Both engines include a variable valve timing system. The T6 bi-turbo is mated to a Geartronic sequential automatic transmission, allowing you to change gears like a manual, but without the clutch. This model also includes a differential viscocoupler. In addition to the front-impact and side-impact airbags, passenger safety is heightened with an inflatable curtain in the front, and the bucket seats are equipped with a whiplash protection system.

PROS

+ **STYLING.** The styling differs greatly from previous models that have been around for generations. With a more sculptured shape, the S80 is very similar to the 1992 ECC prototype.

+ **SEATS.** The bucket seats in the S80, as in all Volvos, demonstrate what comfort should be. The high back and well-shaped seat provide excellent support. And they're heated.

+ **TRUNK.** Because of the 60/40 rear folding seat, storage space can nearly double. The trunk is very deep and flat.

+ **PERFORMANCE.** Accelerating and passing in the bi-turbo is inspiring. Too bad Volvo didn't put switches on the steering wheel like Porsche did with their Tiptronic.

+ **HANDLING.** It is very smooth. The suspension dampens any roll and minimizes bumps.

+ **INTERIOR SPACE.** The rear bench is very comfortable. There's enough room for heads, shoulders and legs. Headrests are adjustable, which improves rear window visibility slightly, so long as no one is sitting there.

+ **BONUS POINTS.** For detailed equipment, a logically laid out dashboard and powerful headlamps whose brightness and reach are both excellent.

CONS

- **MANEUVERABILITY.** Volvos are well-known to be maneuverable, except for the S80. The transverse-mounted engine increases the width, resulting in a greater turning radius than on the S90.

- **BRAKING.** Although easy to gauge and consistent even on hard to negotiate mountain roads, its efficiency is disappointing and emergency stopping distances are longer than average for this category.

- **VISIBILITY.** In a car that puts so much emphasis on passive and active protection systems, rear window visibility is seriously limited. The high trunk makes backing up an uneasy undertaking in this large car.

- **STEERING.** On both the 2.9 and the T6, it's overassisted and quickly becomes light and imprecise at center, no doubt to please the typical North American driver.

- **PERFORMANCE** of the base S80 is uninspiring since both acceleration and passing are mediocre at best.

- **TIRES.** In spite of the superior performance available on the T6, Volvo has simply installed the same touring tires equipping the S80.

- **OVERSIGHTS.** Wipers too slow to keep up with heavy rain. A flat emergency tire that has no place in a car sold at this price.

CONCLUSION

This model may well have some fine qualities, but it needs a few major revisions before it can claim to be a consistently good automobile. The Americanization of some of its driving parameters just isn't a good enough excuse.

RATING VOLVO S80		
CONCEPT :		**80%**
Technology :	80	
Safety :	100	
Interior space :	70	
Trunk volume :	70	
Quality/fit/finish :	80	
DRIVING :		**74%**
Cockpit :	80	
Performance :	70	
Handling :	60	
Steering :	75	
Braking :	85	
ORIGINAL EQUIPMENT :		**81%**
Tires :	80	
Headlights :	80	
Wipers :	85	
Rear defroster :	80	
Radio :	80	
COMFORT :		**78%**
Seats :	80	
Suspension :	80	
Sound level :	70	
Conveniences :	80	
Air conditioning :	80	
BUDGET :		**46%**
Price :	0	
Fuel economy :	60	
Insurance :	30	
Satisfaction :	90	
Depreciation :	50	
Overall rating :		**71.8%**

NEW FOR 2000

- PremAir catalyzer system built into the radiator to reduce ozone responsible for smog.
- Exterior colors and interior trims.
- Optional warm weather package.

Compare Performance, Specifications, Prices, and Classification at the end of this chapter.

Luxury 35-$70,000

EQUIPMENT

VOLVO S80	2.9	T6
Automatic transmission:	S	S
Cruise control:	S	S
Power steering:	S	S
Anti-lock brakes:	S	S
Traction control:	S	S
Air conditioning:	SE	SE
Leather:	SH	SH
AM/FM/radio-cassette:	SCd	SCd
Power door locks:	S	S
Power windows:	S	S
Tilt steering:	S	S
Dual adjustable mirrors:	SEH	SEH
Alloy wheels:	S	S
Anti-theft system:	S	S

Colors

Exterior: Black, White, Blue, Silver, Java, Turquoise, Grey, Emerald.

Interior: Taupe, Graphite, Granite.

AT A GLANCE...

HISTORIC

Introduced in: 1999.
Made in: Torslanda, Sweden .

DEMOGRAPHICS

Model	Men/Wom.	Age	Married	College	Income $
S80	78/22 %	55	80 %	52 %	70,000

INDEX

Safety:	100 %	Satisfaction:		88 %
Depreciation:	50 %	Insurance:		$ 985
Cost per mile:	$ 0.72	Number of dealers:		405

SALES

	Canada				USA	
Model	1997	1998	Result	1997	1998	Result
S80	-	587	-	-	6,037	-

MAINTENANCE REQUIRED BY WARRANTY

First revision:	Frequency:	Diagnostic plug:
3,000 miles	6,000 miles	Yes

LUXURY CARS from 35 to $ 70,000

PERFORMANCE

Model/ version	Type / timing valve / fuel system	Displacement cu in	Power hp @ rpm	Torque lb-ft @ rpm	Compres. ratio	Driving wheels / transmission	Final ratio	Acceler. 0-60 mph s	Standing 1/4 mile s	Standing 5/8 mile s	Passing 50-75 mph s	Braking 60-0 ft	Top speed mph	Lateral acceler. G	Noise level dBA	City mpg	Highway mpg	Fuel type Octane
ACURA 3.5RL																		
base	V6 3.5 SOHC-24-PFI	212	210 @ 5200	224 @ 2800	9.6 :1	front - A5	4.18	8.2	16.4	29.3	5.7	128	124	0.78	66	19	25	S 91
AUDI A6																		
A6 fwd 2.8	V6 2.8 DOHC-30-MPSFI	169	200 @ 6000	207 @ 3200	10.3 :1	front - A5*	3.409	9.6	16.6	29.5	6.8	138	130	0.80	66	17	27	S 91
A6 qtro 2.8	V6 2.8 DOHC-30-MPSFI	169	200 @ 6000	207 @ 3200	10.3 :1	four - A5*	3.409	11.0	17.8	32.2	7.8	138	130	0.81	66	17	26	S 91
A6 qtro 2.7t	V6 2.7 DOHC-30-MPSFI	163	250 @ 5800	258 @ 1850	9.3 :1	four - M6*	4.111	6.0	14.7				130					S 91
						four - A5	3.511	6.6	15.1				130					S 91
A6 qtro 4.2	V8 4.2 DOHC-40-MPSFI	255	300 @ 6200	295 @ 3000	18.8 :1	four - A5*	2.727											S 91
BMW 5 Series																		
528i - iT	L6 2.8 DOHC-24-EFI	170	193 @ 5500	206 @ 3500	10.2 :1	rear - M5*	2.93	8.0	16.0	28.5	5.8	108	128	0.80	66-72	20	31	S 91
528iA	L6 2.8 DOHC-24-EFI	170	193 @ 5500	206 @ 3500	10.2 :1	rear - A4	4.10	8.3	16.3	29.0	6.0	118	128	0.80	66-72	19	28	S 91
540i - iT	V8 4.4 DOHC-32-EFI	268	282 @ 5400	324 @ 3600	10.0 :1	rear - M6*	2.81	6.7	14.8	26.6	4.8	108	155	0.81	64-70	15	25	S 91
540iA	V8 4.4 DOHC-32-EFI	268	282 @ 5400	324 @ 3600	10.0 :1	rear - A5	2.81	7.0	15.2	27.2	5.2	128	128	0.81	64-70	18	26	S 91
540M5	V8 5.0 DOHC-32-MSFI	302	400 @ 6600	369 @ 3800	11.0 :1	rear - M6	3.15	5.3	13.4	24.1	4.8		155			11	24	S 92
BUICK Park Avenue																		
Park Ave.	V6 3.8 OHV-12-MPSFI	231	205 @ 5200	230 @ 4000	9.4 :1	front - A4	3.05	9.5	16.7	30.5	6.7	151	112	0.75	65-68	19	28	R 87
Ultra	V6 C 3.8 OHV-12-MPSFI	231	240 @ 5200	280 @ 3600	8.5 :1	front - A4	2.93	8.5	16.4	29.5	6.2	144	124	0.77	65-68	18	27	
CADILLAC DeVille																		
Base, DHS	V8 4.6 DOHC-32-MPSFI	279	275 @ 5600	300 @ 4000	10.0 :1	front - A4	3.11	8.8	16.3	30.0	4.8	148	124	0.78	64-70	17	26	S 91
DTS	V8 4.6 DOHC-32-MPSFI	279	300 @ 6000	295 @ 4400	10.0 :1	front - A4	3.71	8.0	15.8	28.6	4.5	138	137	0.80	65-70	17	26	S 91
CADILLAC Seville-Eldorado																		
SLS-Eldo	V8 4.6 DOHC-32-MPSFI	279	275 @ 5600	300 @ 4000	10.0 :1	front - A4	3.11	7.8	15.8	29.0	5.0	135	112	0.77	65-70	17	26	S 91
STS-ETC	V8 4.6 DOHC-32-MPSFI	279	300 @ 6000	295 @ 4400	10.0 :1	front - A4	3.71	7.5	15.5	28.5	4.5	138	150	0.79	65-71	17	26	S 91
INFINITI Q45																		
base	V8 4.1 DOHC-32-MPSFI	252	266 @ 5600	278 @ 4000	10.5 :1	rear - A4	3.692	8.0	16.0	27.5	4.9	131	143	0.75	62-66	17	25	S 91
JAGUAR S-TYPE																		
AJ-V6	V6 3.0 DOHC-24-PSEFI	181	240 @ 6800	221 @ 4500	10.5 :1	rear-A5	3.331	8.0	16.2	29.4	5.8	147	137	0.82	66-70	20	27	S 91
AJ-V8	V8 4.0 DOHC-32-PSEFI	244	281 @ 6100	287 @ 4300	10.8 :1	rear-A5	3.331	7.0	15.0	26.5	5.0	141	149	0.82	66-70	17	26	S 91
LEXUS GS																		
GS 300	L6 3.0 DOHC-24-EFI	183	220 @ 5800	220 @ 3800	10.5 :1	rear - A5	3.916	8.0	15.8	27.8	5.2	121	144	0.85	65-68	19	25	S 91
GS 400	V8 4.0 DOHC-32-EFI	242	300 @ 6000	310 @ 4000	10.5 :1	rear - A5	3.266	6.8	14.6	26.5	4.2	125	149	0.85	64-68	17	24	S 91
LINCOLN Continental																		
base	V8 4.6 DOHC-32-MPSFI	281	275 @ 5750	275 @ 4750	9.85 :1	front - A4	3.56	8.3	15.9	28.6	5.7	138	124	0.82	66	16	24	S 91
LINCOLN Town Car																		
1)	V8 4.6-SOHC-16-MPSFI	281	205 @ 4250	280 @ 3000	9.0 :1	rear - A4	3.08	10.0	18.0	32.0	7.7	148	109	0.78	65-70	16	26	R 87
2)	V8 4.6-SOHC-16-MPSFI	281	220 @ 4500	290 @ 3500	9.0 :1	rear - A4	3.08	9.5	17.6	31.4	7.2	154	112	0.78	65-70	16	26	R 87

1) Executive & Signature. 2) SignatureTouring Sedan & Cartier.

Model/ version	Type / timing valve / fuel system	Displacement cu in	Power hp @ rpm	Torque lb-ft @ rpm	Compres. ratio	Driving wheels / transmission	Final ratio	Acceler. 0-60 mph s	Standing 1/4 mile s	Standing 5/8 mile s	Passing 50-75 mph s	Braking 60-0 ft	Top speed mph	Lateral acceler. G	Noise level dBA	City mpg	Highway mpg	Fuel type Octane
MERCEDES-BENZ C-Class																		
E300	L6TD 3.0 DOHC-24-MFI	183	174 @ 5000	244 @ 1600	22.0 :1	rear - A5	3.46	9.0	16.9	30.3	6.8	131	130	0.82	67	26	36	D
E320	V6 3.2 SOHC-18-SFI	195	221 @ 5500	232 @ 3000	10.0 :1	rear - A5	3.07	7.5	15.6	26.8	5.4	128	130	0.82	65	21	30	S 91
E320 AWD	V6 3.2 SOHC-18-SFI	195	221 @ 5500	232 @ 3000	10.0 :1	rear/4 - A5	3.07	7.8	16.0	27.0	5.7	128	130	0.82	65	20	28	S 91
E430	V8 4.3 SOHC-24-SFI	260	275 @ 5750	295 @ 3000	10.0 :1	rear - A5	2.82	6.5	14.5	26.0	4.5	134	130	0.82	65	19	26	S 91
E55 AMG	V8 5.5 SOHC-24-SFI	332	349 @ 5500	391 @ 3000	10.5 :1	rear - A5	2.82	5.4	NA				155			16	23	S 91
SAAB 9⁵																		
base/SE	L4T* 2.3 DOHC-16-EFI	140	170 @ 5500	207 @ 1800	9.3 :1	front - M5*	4.05	10.6	17.2	29.5	6.4	157	137	0.80	65-72	21	30	S 91
						front - A4	2.56	11.7	17.7	31.2	7.5	167	130	0.80	65-72	19	27	S 91
option	V6T 3.0 DOHC-24-EFI	181	200 @ 5000	229 @ 2500	9.5 :1	front - A4*	2.56	NA								18	26	S 91
Aero	L4T* 2.3 DOHC-16-EFI	140	230 @ 6000	252 @ 2200	NA	front - M5*	NA											S 91
						front - A4	NA											
VOLVO S80																		
2.9	L6 2.9 DOHC-24-EFI	178	197 @ 6000	207 @ 4200	10.7 :1	front - A4	3.73	9.0	16.8	30.0	6.4	121	124	0.78	66-70	17	26	S 91
T6	L6tt 2.8 DOHC-24-EFI	170	268 @ 5400	280 @ 2100	8.7 :1	front - A4	3.29	7.2	15.4	26.6	5.2	125	149	0.78	66-70	16	25	S 91

Luxury 35-$70,000

LUXURY CARS from 35 to $ 70,000
SPECIFICATIONS

Model	Version Trim	Body/ Seats	Cabin volume cu ft	Trunk volume cu ft	Cd	Wheel base in	Lgth x Width x Hght in x in x in	Curb weight lb	Susp. ft/rr	Brake ft/rr type	Steering ø ft	turns number	Fuel tank gal	dimensions	Standard tires make	Standard tires model	Standard powertrain	99 Price msrp $
ACURA		General warranty: 4-years / 50,000 miles; powertrain: 5-years / 60,000 miles; surface rust: 5-years / unlimited.																
3.5RL	3.5	4dr.sdn. 5	110.9	14.8	0.32	114.6	196.6x71.7x56.5	3858	ih/ih	dc/ABS	pwr.r&p. 36.1	3.35	18.0	215/60R16	Michelin	MXV4	V6/3.5/A5	42,355
AUDI		General warranty: 3-years / 50,000 miles; perforation corrosion: 10-years; free maintenance: 3-years / 50,000 miles; roadside assistance: 3-years.																
2.8	FWD 2.8	4dr.sdn. 5	98.3	17.2	0.28	108.7	192.0x71.3x57.2	3560	ih/sih	dc/ABS	pwr.r&p. 38.3	2.81	18.5	205/55R16	Goodyear	Eagle RS-A	V6/2.8/A5	34,250
4.2	quattro 4.2	4dr.sdn. 5	98.3	15.4	0.28	108.6	193.4x71.3x57.1	4024	ih/ih	dc/ABS	pwr.r&p. 38.3	2.81	21.7	235/50HR16	Goodyear	Eagle RS-A	V8/4.2/A5	-
2.8	quattro 2.8	4dr.wgn. 5	99.3	36.4	0.28	108.6	192.0x71.3x58.2	3638	ih/ih	dc/ABS	pwr.r&p. 38.3	2.81	18.5	195/65R15	Goodyear	Eagle RS-A	V6/2.8/A5	37,100
2.7	quattro 2.7tt	4dr.sdn.5	98.3	15.4	0.28	108.7	192.0x71.3x57.2	3759	ih/ih	dc/ABS	pwr.r&p. 38.3	2.81	18.5	215/55R16	Continental	CH95	V6tt/2.7/M6	-
BMW		General warranty : 4-years/ 50,000 miles; corrosion: 6-years / unlimited: antipollution: 8-years / 80,000 miles.																
528i		4dr.sdn. 5	91.0	16.2	0.30	111.4	188.0x70.9x56.5	3450	i/i	dc/ABS	pwr.r&p. 37.1	3.5	18.5	225/60HR15	Michelin	Energy	L6/2.8/M5	39,470
540i		4dr.sdn. 5	91.0	16.2	0.31	111.4	188.0x70.9x55.7	3748	i/i	dc/ABS	pwr.ball. 37.4	3.5	18.5	225/55HR16	Michelin	Energy	V8/4.4/A5	51,670
528iT		4dr.wgn. 5	NA	53.8	0.31	111.4	189.2x70.9x56.7	3725	i/i	dc/ABS	pwr.r&p. 37.1	3.5	18.5	225/60HR15			L6/2.8/M5	41,270
540iT		4dr.wgn. 5	NA	53.8	0.33	111.4	189.2x70.9x56.7	4056	i/i	dc/ABS	pwr.ball. 37.4	3.5	18.5	225/55HR16			V8/4.4/A5	54,050
540M5		4dr.sdn. 5	92.5	16.2	0.31	111.4	188.4x70.9x56.4	3792	i/i	dc/ABS	pwr.r&p. 37.3	3.0	18.5	ft245/40ZR18 rr275/35ZR18			V8/5.0/M6	-
BUICK		General warranty: 3-years / 40,000 miles; antipollution: 5-years / 50,000 miles; perforation corrosion: 6-years / 100,000 miles. Road assistance.																
Park Avenue		4dr.sdn.5/6	112.1	19.1	0.34	113.8	206.8x74.7x57.4	3778	ih/ih	dc/ABS	pwr.r&p.l 39.42.93		18.5	225/60R16	Goodyear	Eagle LS	V6/3.8/A4	31,800
Park Avenue Ultra		4dr.sdn.5/6	112.1	19.1	0.34	113.8	206.8x74.7x57.4	3884	ih/ih	dc/ABS	pwr.r&p.r 40.03.15		18.5	225/60R16	Goodyear	Eagle LS	V6C/3.8/A4	36,695
CADILLAC		General warranty: 4-years / 50,000 miles; antipollution: 5 years / 50 000 miles; perforation corrosion: 6-years / 100,000 miles. Road assistance.																
DeVille	Base	4dr.sdn.6	117	20	0.32	115.3	207.5x74.5x56.0	4012	ih/ih	dc/ABS	pwr.r&p. 41.0	2.65	20.0	225/60R16	Michelin	XW4	V8/4.6/A4	39,900
DeVille	DHS	4dr.sdn. 5	117	20	0.32	115.3	207.5x74.5x56.0	4063	ih/ih	dc/ABS	pwr.r&p. 41.0	2.83	20.0	225/60R16	Goodyear	Eagle RS-A	V8/4.6/A4	-
DeVille	DTS	4dr.sdn.6	117	20	0.32	115.3	207.5x74.5x56.0	4052	ih/ih	dc/ABS	pwr.r&p. 41.0	2.65	20.0	225/60R16	Michelin	XW4	V8/4.6/A4	-
Seville	SLS	4dr.sdn. 5	104.2	15.7	0.31	112.2	201.0x75.0x55.7	3970	ih/ih	dc/ABS	pwr.r&p. 40.5	2.40	18.5	235/60R16	Goodyear	Eagle LS	V8/4.6/A4	44,025
Seville	STS	4dr.sdn. 5	104.2	15.7	0.31	112.2	201.0x75.0x55.7	4001	ih/ih	dc/ABS	pwr.r&p. 40.5	2.40	18.5	235/60R16	Goodyear	Eagle LS	V8/4.6/A4	48,720
Eldorado	base	2dr.cpe. 5	99.5	15.3	0.33	108.0	200.6x75.5x53.6	3843	ih/ih	dc/ABS	pwr.r&p. 40.3	2.65	19.0	225/60R16	Michelin	XW4	V8/4.6/A4	39,905
Eldorado	ETC	2dr.cpe. 5	99.5	15.3	0.33	108.0	200.6x75.5x53.6	3876	ih/ih	dc/ABS	pwr.r&p. 40.3	2.83	19.0	235/60R16	Goodyear	Eagle RS-A	V8/4.6/A4	44,365
INFINITI		General warranty: 4-years / 60,000 miles; powertrain & antipollution: 6-years / 100,000 miles; corrosion perforation: 7-years / unlimited.																
Q45t	«t»	4dr.sdn. 5	97.4	12.6	0.32	111.4	199.6x71.7x56.9	4043	ih/ih	dc/ABS	pwr.r&p. 36.1	3.2	21.4	225/50VR17	Michelin	Energy MXV4	V8/4.1/A4	48,725
JAGUAR		General warranty: 4-years / 50,000 miles; corrosion: 6-years / unlimited mileage.																
S-TYPE	AJ-V6	4dr.sdn. 5	-	13.1	0.32	114.5	191.3x71.6x55.7	3650	ih/ih	dc/ABS	pwr.r&p. 37.7	2.6	18.4	225/55HR16	Pirelli	P-Zero	V6/3.0/A5	42,400
S-TYPE	AJ-V8	4dr.sdn. 5	-	13.1	0.32	114.5	191.3x71.6x55.7	3770	ih/ih	dc/ABS	pwr.r&p. 37.7	2.6	18.4	225/55HR16	Pirelli	P-Zero	V8/4.0/A5	48,000
LEXUS		General warranty: 4-years / 50,000 miles; powertrain: 6 years / 70,000 miles; corrosion perforation: 6-years / unlimited mileage & roadside assistance.																
GS	300	4dr.sdn. 4/5	100.0	14.8	0.29	110.2	189.2x70.9x55.9	3638	ih/ih	dc/ABS	pwr.r&p. 37.1	3.38	19.8	215/60VR16	Bridgestone	Turanza ER30	L6/3.0/A5	37,800
GS	400	4dr.sdn. 4/5	100.0	14.8	0.29	110.2	189.2x70.9x55.9	3693	ih/ih	dc/ABS	pwr.r&p. 37.1	3.38	19.8	225/55VR16 235/45ZR17	Michelin Bridgestone	Pilot HX MXM Potenza RE030	V8/4.0/A5	46,000
LINCOLN		General warranty: 4-years / 50,000 miles; corrosion perforation antipollution: 4-years / 50,000 miles.																
Continental		4dr.sdn.5/6	102.0	18.4	0.32	109.0	208.5x73.6x56.0	3868	ih/ih	dc/ABS	pwr.r&p. 41.1	2.86	20.0	225/60HR16	Michelin	MXV4 ZP	V8/4.6/A4	39,195
LINCOLN		General warranty: 4-years / 50,000 miles; corrosion perforation antipollution: 4-years / 50,000 miles.																
Town Car Executive		4dr.sdn. 6	112.3	20.6	0.34	117.7	215.3x78.2x58.0	3979	ih/rh	dc/ABS	pwr.ball 42.1	3.4	19.0	225/60HR16	Michelin	MXV4	V8/4.6/A	39,195
Town Car Signature		4dr.sdn. 6	112.3	20.6	0.34	117.7	215.3x78.2x58.0	4015	ih/rh	dc/ABS	pwr.ball 42.1	3.4	19.0	225/60HR16	Michelin	MXV4	V8/4.6/A4	41,195
Town Car Cartier		4dr.sdn. 6	112.3	20.6	0.34	117.7	215.3x78.2x58.0	4045	ih/rh	dc/ABS	pwr.ball 42.1	3.4	19.0	235/60HR16	Michelin	Symetry	V8/4.6/A4	43,695
MERCEDES-BENZ		General warranty: 4-years / 50,000 miles; corrosion perforation; 5-years / unlimited; powertrain: 5-years / 75,000 miles																
E300	Diesel	4dr.sdn. 5	95.0	15.3	0.29	111.5	189.4x70.8x56.7	3691	ih/ih	dc/ABS	pwr.r&p. 37.1	3.3	21.1	215/55HR16	Continental	Eco Plus	L6D/3.0/A5	42,995
E320	Gasoline	4dr.sdn. 5	95.0	15.3	0.29	111.5	189.4x70.8x56.7	3525	ih/ih	dc/ABS	pwr.r&p. 37.1	3.3	21.1	215/55HR16	Continental	Eco Plus	V6/3.2/A5	46,795
E320 AWD	Gasoline	4dr.wgn. 7	97.7	43.8	0.34	111.5	190.4x70.8x59.3	3955	ih/ih	dc/ABS	pwr.r&p. 37.1	3.3	18.5	215/55HR16	Continental	Eco Plus	V6/3.2/A5	50,585
E430	Gasoline	4dr.sdn. 5	95.0	15.3	0.29	111.5	189.4x70.8x56.7	3702	ih/ih	dc/ABS	pwr.r&p. 37.1	3.3	21.1	215/55HR16	Continental	Eco Plus	V8/4.3/A5	51,895
E55	Gasoline	4dr.sdn. 5	95.0	15.3	0.29	111.5	189.4x70.8x56.7	3680	ih/ih	dc/ABS	pwr.r&p. 37.1	3.3	21.1ft245/40/ZR/18 rr275/35ZR18	-	-	V8/5.5/A5	-
SAAB		General warranty: 4-years / 50,000 miles; corrosion, perforation: 6-years / 100,000 miles.																
9⁵	base	4dr.sdn. 5	99.0	15.9	0.29	106.4	189.2x70.5x57.0	3285	ih/lh	dc/ABS	pwr.r&p. 35.4	2.9	19.8	215/55VR16	Michelin	MXV4	L4T/2.3/M5	31,600
9⁵	SE	4dr.sdn. 5	99.0	15.9	0.29	106.4	189.2x70.5x57.0	3560	ih/lh	dc/ABS	pwr.r&p. 35.4	2.9	19.8	215/55VR16	Michelin	MXV4	L4T/2.3/M5	34,800
VOLVO		General warranty: 4-years / 50,000 miles; corrosion: 8-years / unlimited; antipollution: 5-years / 50,000 miles.																
S80	2.9	4dr.sdn.5	99.9	15.5	0.28	109.9	189.8x72.1x57.1	3421	ih/ih	dc/ABS	pwr.ball. 35.7	-	21.1	215/55HR16	Michelin	Pilot	L6/2.9/A4	36,395
S80	T6	4dr.sdn.5	99.9	15.5	0.28	109.9	189.8x72.1x57.1	3421	ih/ih	dc/ABS	pwr.ball. 35.7	-	21.1	225/55HR16	Michelin	Pilot	L6T/2.8/A4	40,960

Notes: 1) Tire makes and models are provided solely as an indication; they are subject to change without prior notice from the automobile manufacturers.
2) See the 2000 price list at the back of this edition.

LUXURY CARS from 35 to $ 70,000
CLASSIFICATION

OUR CLASSIFICATION

Rank	Models	Concept	Driving	Equipment	Comfort	Budget	Ratings
1	**BMW 5 Series**	80	**76**	**82**	81	46	**73.0 %**
2	ACURA 3.5RL	81	72	80	79	50	72.4 %
3	CADILLAC DeVille	**87**	70	77	80	46	72.0 %
4	VOLVO S80	80	74	81	78	46	71.8 %
5	INFINITI Q45	74	72	**82**	**82**	48	71.6 %
5	AUDI A6	82	70	80	78	48	71.6 %
5	LEXUS GS	78	73	**82**	75	50	71.6 %
5	MERCEDES E-Class	83	71	78	75	**51**	71.6 %
6	CADILLAC Seville-Eldorado	82	68	79	**82**	45	71.2 %
7	LINCOLN Continental	82	72	79	73	43	69.8 %
8	LINCOLN Town Car	86	62	75	73	45	68.2 %
8	BUICK Park Avenue	78	65	75	72	**51**	68.2 %
9	JAGUAR S-TYPE	74	71	77	73	43	67.6 %
9	SAAB 9⁵	**87**	63	75	69	44	67.6 %

YOUR CLASSIFICATION

Rank	Models	98 Sales
1	**CADILLAC DeVille**	**99,779**
2	LINCOLN Town Car	97,547
3	BUICK Park Avenue	58,187
4	MERCEDES E-Class	47,523
5	CADILLAC Seville	38,888
6	LINCOLN Continental	35,210
7	BMW 5 Series	35,100
8	LEXUS GS 300	20,696
9	AUDI A6	18,050
10	CADILLAC Eldorado	15,598
11	ACURA 3.5RL	15,024
12	LEXUS GS 400	9,926
13	INFINITI Q45	8,244
14	SAAB 9⁵	7,774
15	VOLVO S80	6,037

Not classified:
JAGUAR S-TYPE

Luxury
35 - 70 000

Comparative Test

LUXURY CARS
over $ 70,000

**See their performance, their specifications, their price
and their classification at the end of this chapter.**

AUDI A8

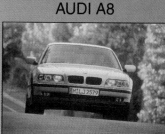

BMW 7 Series

JAGUAR XJ8-XJR

LEXUS LS 400

MERCEDES-BENZ S-Class

The technological effort that Audi deployed for the design of its A8 didn't pay off, and this top-of-the-line model doesn't sell very well at all. Besides styling so timid it goes unnoticed, its quattro technology is virtually invisible and like other models in the same lineup, it has a hard time convincing potential buyers of its true worth. As for the aluminum used to construct the body, its advantages are but an illusion and should owners be unfortunate enough to be involved in a collision, the repair bill is staggering.

Theoretical

MODEL RANGE
The Audi 8 is a four-door sedan offered one version, equipped with 4.2L V8 engine paired up with an automatic transmission and the quattro IV all-wheel drive system. This model is richly equipped. Options consist of a "Cold Weather Package" that includes heated rear seats and steering wheel and a ski bag in the trunk. For those who live in southernly regions, the "Warm Weather Package" includes insulated glass, sunroof with solar panel that's the energy source for fans when the car is parked in the sun and rear panel and rear window shades. Extras also include radio controls on the steering wheel, chrome wheels, high-fidelity Bose sound system, pearly white paint, hands-free cellular phone and CD changer.

TECHNICAL FEATURES
The A8 is the only mass-produced car in the world that has an all-aluminum alloy unibody. Due to the particular properties of this metal, the structure consists of a space frame made of sectional aluminum on which are attached the body panels, resulting in a much more robust body than is the case for an identical steel-built structure. Aerodynamics are outstanding, yielding a drag coefficient of less than 0.30, even with the wide front, beefy tires and generous orifices. There's a four-link, upper and lower control arm front suspension and the rear suspension consists of trapezoidal control arms. Both axles are fitted with a stabilizer bar the quattro system benefits from automatic locking differentials (EDL). The four-wheel disc brakes are associated with an antilock braking device that adjusts to brake pedal effort, so as to provide optimum vehicle stability. Safety features are in keeping with other A8 attributes, since it's one of the few cars to come equipped with six standard airbags (two front and four side-impact airbags).

PROS
+ TECHNOLOGICAL ADVANCES. Audi was a pioneer in all-wheel drive technology and in the use of aluminum as the main building material for car construction. But the rest of the A8 is also at the cutting edge of technical applications, so it's a car that offers top-of-the-heap performances and safety features.
+ SAFETY. It's assured by aluminum's resistance to impact, a metal that's much sturdier than steel, as well as six airbags, pretension seatbelts and electronic driving aids.
+ PERFORMANCES. The engine achieves high-caliber performances, yet not any zoomier than those of rivals. Accelerations and pickup are lively with such a good power to weight ratio, due to the pared down weight of the aluminum body.
+ HANDLING. Sophisticated suspension components and the overall power flow achieved by this vehicle provide a reassuringly stable and neutral behavior in most situations. The load-levelling and anti-skid systems are also definite assets in this department. We were amazed at this big car's nimble negotiating of a whole series of curves.
+ FUEL EFFICIENCY. The favorable power to weight ratio allows for amazingly frugal gas consumption, since it's equivalent to that of a V6.
+ RIDE COMFORT. The posh Pullman seats, velvety suspension and superb soundproofing let you make long, fatigue-free highway trips, making the A8 ideal for long-distance runs.

CONS
- STYLE. It's a shame that such an avant-garde model didn't get blessed with more daring looks in keeping with its innovative character. Audi designers decided to opt for cool anonymity, so the car stays in style for eons.
- BUDGET. You need a hefty cash flow to own this car, for resale value can suffer due to mistrust of all the high tech features. Also, repair jobs to an aluminum structure worry insurance companies and body shop owners.
- DRIVING. The fun at the wheel is really tamed down by this car's squeaky-clean demeanor. This car is maybe too perfect for its own good, that is, it doesn't really get your adrenalin count climbing...
- SUSPENSION. It's stiff on rough roads and some of its reactions don't fit with a car of this supposed standing.
- CABIN DESIGN. The interior is dreary and conventional, a poor reflection of the innovative features that are part of this package. Good old traditional wood trim should have been replaced by carbon fiber components or some other exciting material. There are just too many dull, down-to-earth types at Audi...
- TO BE IMPROVED UPON. Oldish radio antenna design that could have been integrated into the rear window, too many controls (40 switches and 3 buttons) that are complicated and easy to mix up, so you almost have to take a driver's initiation course before you get behind the wheel.

CONCLUSION
Unlike other models in the Audi range, the A8's sales continue to stagnate and consumers will have to wait for its next reincarnation to see if the German builder has learned any lessons from this sorry experience. At a time when designers reign supreme, it costs very little to ensure original and attention-getting lines for a star model.

RATING
AUDI A8

CONCEPT :		88%
Technology :	100	
Safety :	100	
Interior space :	70	
Trunk volume :	80	
Quality/fit/finish :	90	

DRIVING :		73%
Cockpit :	85	
Performance :	75	
Handling :	65	
Steering :	80	
Braking :	60	

ORIGINAL EQUIPMENT :		81%
Tires :	85	
Headlights :	85	
Wipers :	70	
Rear defroster :	80	
Radio :	85	

COMFORT :		83%
Seats :	85	
Suspension :	80	
Sound level :	80	
Conveniences :	80	
Air conditioning :	90	

BUDGET :		44%
Price :	0	
Fuel economy :	50	
Insurance :	30	
Satisfaction :	90	
Depreciation :	50	

Overall rating :	73.8%

NEW FOR 2000

- An extra 10 horses for the engine.
- Navigation system.
- Valcona leather trims.
- Different interior trim colors.
- 16-inch wheels and a full-size emergency tire.

Compare Performance, Specifications, Prices, and Classification at the end of this chapter.

EQUIPMENT

AUDI A8	4.2
Automatic transmission:	S
Cruise control:	S
Power steering:	S
Anti-lock brakes:	S
Traction control:	S
Air conditioning:	S
Leather:	SH
AM/FM/radio-cassette:	S
Power door locks:	S
Power windows:	S
Tilt steering:	S
Dual adjustable mirrors:	SEH
Alloy wheels:	S
Anti-theft system:	S

Colors
Exterior: Aluminum, White, Black, Green, Grey.

Interior: Black, Tan.

AT A GLANCE...

HISTORIC
Introduced in: 1996.
Made in: Ingolstadt, Germany.

DEMOGRAPHICS

Model	Men/Wom.	Age	Married	College	Income $
A8	90/10 %	62	91 %	80 %	165,000

INDEX

Safety:	100 %	Satisfaction:	85 %
Depreciation:	50 %	Insurance:	$ 1,350
Cost per mile:	$ 1.20	Number of dealers:	290

SALES

	Canada				USA	
Model	1997	1998	Result	1997	1998	Result
A8	107	100	- 6.5 %	2,085	2,172	+ 4.2 %

MAINTENANCE REQUIRED BY WARRANTY

First revision	Frequency:	Diagnostic plug:
7 500 miles	7 500 miles	Yes

Royalty

No one should ever take anything for granted - who would have thought that someday BMW could dominate the market for ultra-luxury cars, ranking ahead of Mercedes-Benz. A few errors of judgement and a whole lot of arrogance have stripped the S-Class of its title as "the most sophisticated sedan in the world". As they set out to establish an entirely new standard in the class, BMW's decision-makers in Munich were right on target and the success of the 7 Series has never wavered.

MODEL RANGE

The 7 Series consists of three 4-door sedans. The 740 equipped with a 4.4L V8 is offered in short (i) or long (iL) wheelbase versions, whereas the 750iL animated by a 5.4L V12 is only available in a long wheelbase version. Besides all the electronic driving aids, equipment on these models is as refined and innovative as it gets, since there's a heated steering wheel where radio and telephone controls are located, while 750iL rear seat passengers are protected by a privacy curtain and all doors are fitted with individual footrests. This year a navigation system is added to the list of options for all models.

TECHNICAL FEATURES

The 7 Series' success lies in the magic rendered by BMW stylists who succeeded in trimming down its size while refining its overall body design, yielding good aerodynamics, since the drag coefficient is 0.31 even with the wide front end. The body is very resistant to torsion and flexion, which provides a solid base for both powertrains. The fully independent suspension includes struts up front and a multi-arm axle at the rear, including anti-dive and anti-lift geometry. Four-wheel vented disc brakes are paired up with an ABS-traction control system, to which can be added an optional, highly evolved (DSC) antiskid system that makes the car neutral on curves, in the event of driver error or rough fallout from poor road surfaces. Self-adjusting shock absorbers include a rear load-levelling device. Both engines are linked to a 5-speed "Steptronic" automatic gearbox that includes manual or automatic shifter and so is coined adaptive, since its programming adjusts to road conditions and to the pilot's driving style by anticipating speed shifts.

PROS

+ TECHNICAL COMPONENTS. They're high-brow sophisticated right down to the last detail, be it in regard to high performance, equipment items or safety features. Several safety devices ensure exceptional passenger protection, such as 6 airbags that provide complete front-impact protection, as well as side-impact protection to offset head, chest and hip injuries. Besides, all the driving aid systems provide remarkable stability, whatever the situation.

+ PERFORMANCES. They're comparable to those of a Grand Tourism coupe, yielding rather high acceleration scores, all achieved in cool comfort and style. Putting this competent and well-honed engine through its paces is a real treat, even with the rather hefty vehicle weight and size.

+ HANDLING. The car is really neutral and stable in reasonable circumstances, since all those electronic parameter controls don't amount to much against an idiotic driver out to prove them wrong.

+ SAFETY. It's at an all-time high, including passive and active passenger protection devices, which makes for relaxed, reassuring driving in tough situations, since the driver has complete control of the vehicle.

+ RIDE COMFORT. It's very refined, with a neither too firm nor too flexible suspension, perfectly shaped front seats, adjustable rear seatbench and truly superb-quality sound dampening.

+ REAR SEATS. On longer versions bench seat occupants enjoy plenty of legroom, as much as you find on a limousine. In these models it's easy to get some work done when travelling between the airport and the office - let the chauffeur take care of traffic snags.

+ DUAL PERSONALITY. The 750iL is both a creamy, pearls and tux limo or a zoomy sporty car that takes its weight and size in its stride, so driving one of these babies is a real joy, a rare treat in this car class.

+ CABIN DESIGN. The design is more warm and cozy than inside its rival Mercedes S-Class. Finish touches have flair and feeling and are inspired by Jaguar or Maserati traits, like the lovely folds in the leather seat covers ,wood appliqués and attractive shades used.

+ QUALITY. It's incredibly impressive: construction, fit and finish job and trim materials are absolutely impeccable.

+ CONVENIENCE FEATURES. The 7 Series is loaded with clever storage compartments scattered throughout the cabin and the trunk can swallow up quite a few Vuitton valises...

CONS

- BUDGET. You have to have above-average income or a very understanding bank manager to buy, maintain, insure and pay gas bills for these models.

- COMPLEXITY. It takes a lot of patience and a comfortable I.Q. to quickly know how to master functions and controls on a 7 Series car. Besides, typically European controls do take some getting used to, especially the sound system or climate control that are a bit of a mystery to non-Germanic minds.

CONCLUSION

In spite of the arrival of the new Mercedes S-Class, thanks to very good sizing, technical prowess and most importantly, a more appealing presentation and an astounding V12 engine, the 7 Series is still a good length ahead of its arch rival.

RATING		
BMW 7 Series		
CONCEPT :		**90%**
Technology :	100	
Safety :	100	
Interior space :	80	
Trunk volume :	80	
Quality/fit/finish :	90	
DRIVING :		**79%**
Cockpit :	90	
Performance :	80	
Handling :	65	
Steering :	85	
Braking :	75	
ORIGINAL EQUIPMENT :		**81%**
Tires :	80	
Headlights :	90	
Wipers :	70	
Rear defroster :	80	
Radio :	85	
COMFORT :		**85%**
Seats :	90	
Suspension :	80	
Sound level :	80	
Conveniences :	90	
Air conditioning :	85	
BUDGET :		**38%**
Price :	0	
Fuel economy :	30	
Insurance :	25	
Satisfaction :	85	
Depreciation :	50	
Overall rating :		**74.6%**

NEW FOR 2000

- Steptronic automatic transmission with sequential shifting standard on all models.
- "Intelligent" airbags.
- Fuel supply interruption in case of collision.
- Xenon headlamps.
- Chrome grille.

Compare Performance, Specifications, Prices, and Classification at the end of this chapter.

Luxury + $70,000

EQUIPMENT

BMW 7 Series	740i/iL	750iL
Automatic transmission:	S	S
Cruise control:	S	S
Power steering:	S	S
Anti-lock brakes:	S	S
Traction control:	S	S
Air conditioning:	SA	SA
Leather:	S	S
AM/FM/radio-cassette:	SCd	SCd
Power door locks:	S	S
Power windows:	S	S
Tilt steering:	S	S
Dual adjustable mirrors:	SEH	SEH
Alloy wheels:	S	S
Anti-theft system:	S	S

Colors

Exterior: White, Red, Green, Black, Silver, Blue, Grey, Beige, Crimson.

Interior: Black, Grey, Beige, Marine.

AT A GLANCE...

HISTORIC

Introduced in:	1986-1997.
Made in:	Dingolfing, (Münich) Germany.

DEMOGRAPHICS

Model	Men/Wom.	Age	Married	College	Income $
7 Series	96/4 %	61	96 %	41 %	110,000

INDEX

Safety:	100 %	Satisfaction:	87 %
Depreciation:	50 %	Insurance:	$2 325-3 650
Cost per mile:	$ 1.60	Number of dealers:	350

SALES

	Canada			USA		
Model	1997	1998	Result	1997	1998	Result
7 Series	736	677	- 8.0 %	18,273	18,309	+ 0.2 %

MAINTENANCE REQUIRED BY WARRANTY

First revision:	Frequency:	Diagnostic plug:
15,000 miles	15,000 miles	Yes

As its rivals continue to progress steadily, the Jaguar XJ is beginning to show its increasingly venerable age. Compared to the BMW 7 Series and the Mercedes-Benz S-Class replete with electronic systems and the latest technological and safety features, eventually this aging British model will serve as a relic of a time long gone by. It owes its unhoped for success mainly to its traditional design approach, with the strong appeal of leather and wood used in a way only the British can.

Nostalgia

MODEL RANGE

The XJ family consists of 4-door sedans called XJ8, Vanden Plas and XJR. The 4.0L V8 engine is common to all models, but the first two are animated by a conventional engine, whereas the XJR is powered by a supercharged engine. Two new 5-speed transmissions equip these cars, a ZF with the conventional powerplant and a Mercedes-Benz with the supercharged model. These cars are lavishly equipped and some items only vary according to the degree of decadent luxury they provide.

TECHNICAL FEATURES

XJ sedans were reworked in 1998 so as to integrate the V8 engine borrowed from the XK8 coupes and convertibles. This year, there's a cleaner burning engine offered to meet American emission standards. Their steel monocoque body includes two subframes on which are mounted the four-wheel independent suspensions consisting of double wishbones with anti-dive, anti-lift devices and stabilizer bars. Four-wheel disc brakes benefit from ABS linked to traction control. The V8 conventional engine develops 290

hp, while the model equipped with an Eaton supercharger pumps out 370 hp. Five-speed automatic transmissions provide very efficient dual-mode settings. Cars are equipped with more safety features, since dual side-impact airbags are located in the front doors and front seatbelts are fitted with heat-sensitive tensioners.

OUTSTANDING

++ **STYLE.** Always classy and elegant, with lovely, flowing lines and dressed up with chrome details that put it in a class apart.

++ **DESIGN.** The cabin interior reminds you of an English parlor with its rich Connolly leather and simply exquisite walnut appliqués that have a lovely look and feel. Too bad the leather has lost its aura of perfume...

PROS

+ **DRIVING FEEL.** It's a treat beyond words, with the perfect osmosis between available power and a transmission blessed with the best sequential shifter on the market, responsive steering, strong brakes that are easy to apply and superb roadholding benefitting from the more robust body.

+ **PERFORMANCES.** They're remarkable. The engine can propulse these rather heavy vehicles and hit top speeds in no time flat. The 370-hp engine that motivates the XJR, the most savage of the lot, shouldn't

be handed over to anyone but an experienced driver who knows what he or she is doing.

+ **RIDE COMFORT.** The creamy suspension and ruthless sound-proofing that stifles most unwanted noise create a cozy, typically English ambience.

+ **QUALITY.** Craftsmanship, fit and finish details and trim components keep getting better and reliability is no problem for cars in this price range. Original items such as tires, headlamps and climate control are more effective than before.

+ **INSTRUMENT PANEL.** More logical and ergonomic than before and everything is where you'd expect it to be, typical to the brand dashboard design.

+ **CONVENIENCE FEATURES.** They haven't been disregarded, since there are numerous, roomy storage compartments including even rear, removable picnic shelves in the rear of the Vanden Plas. "Would you have any Grey Poupon?" "But of course..."

+ **VALUE.** It increases according to quality and reliability, so these cars don't lose as much resale value as was once the case...

CONS

- **BUDGET.** These cars are demanding mistresses, for their upkeep is costly and they consume a lot: the XJR supercharged engine can easily go as low as 11 mpg. Luckily, the conventional engine is less greedy,

at least for normal driving.

- **TECHNOLOGY.** Year after year, XJ models are falling further and further behind the pack. Compared to the latest German accomplishments, they're beginning to look antiquated. Their most badly outdated elements are their structure and suspensions, not to mention their lack of power systems and state-of-the-art safety features.

- **HANDLING.** These sedans are heavier and more plump, so they're considered to be rather sedate, that is they prefer gentlemen to wild sporty types.

- **USEFUL SPACE.** The XJ8 cabin isn't as roomy as you'd expect for such a big car and the extended Vanden Plas version is practical by comparison. The same applies to the trunk, for it's ridiculously small with the huge spare tire gobbling up all the available space.

- **SEATS.** They're weirdly shaped and do take some getting used to.

- **MANEUVERABILITY.** The Vanden Plas is handicapped by a wide steer angle diameter.

- **TO BE IMPROVED UPON.** Some unusual controls, limited visibility at rear quarterback and some finish details such as the Taurus/Sable exterior door handles or the illegible instruments sunken into the massive dashboard. During our test run, hubcaps covering wheel bolts came off the rims with disarming ease.

CONCLUSION

The replacements for the current XJ models are on the way and if the Coventry-based make wants to capitalize on new momentum, they can't possibly get here too soon!

Luxury + $70,000

RATING
JAGUAR XJ8-XJR

CONCEPT :		74%
Technology :	85	
Safety :	90	
Interior space :	65	
Trunk volume :	50	
Quality/fit/finish :	80	

DRIVING :		74%
Cockpit :	80	
Performance :	75	
Handling :	60	
Steering :	80	
Braking :	75	

ORIGINAL EQUIPMENT :		78%
Tires :	85	
Headlights :	80	
Wipers :	65	
Rear defroster :	75	
Radio :	85	

COMFORT :		80%
Seats :	80	
Suspension :	80	
Sound level :	80	
Conveniences :	80	
Air conditioning :	80	

BUDGET :		42%
Price :	0	
Fuel economy :	40	
Insurance :	40	
Satisfaction :	80	
Depreciation :	50	

| **Overall rating :** | | **69.6%** |

NEW FOR 2000
- **XJ: improved power brakes and ABS system.**
- **Automatic wipers and child-safety seat anchors.**
- **Theft-deterrent system with coded vehicle immobilizer.**
- **Exterior colors: Platinum and Westminster Blue.**
- **XJR: different wheel and seat designs.**

Compare Performance, Specifications, Prices, and Classification at the end of this chapter.

EQUIPMENT

JAGUAR XJ8 JAGUAR XJR	XJ8	XJ8 L	Vanden Plas	base
Automatic transmission:	S	S	S	S
Cruise control:	S	S	S	S
Power steering:	S	S	S	S
Anti-lock brakes:	S	S	S	S
Traction control:	S	S	S	S
Air conditioning:	SA	SA	SA	SA
Leather:	S	S	S	S
AM/FM/radio-cassette:	S	S	SCd	SCd
Power door locks:	S	S	S	S
Power windows:	S	S	S	S
Tilt steering:	S	S	S	S
Dual adjustable mirrors:	S	S	S	S
Alloy wheels:	S	S	S	S
Anti-theft system:	S	S	S	S

Colors
Exterior: Grey, White, Black, Mistral Blue, Meteorite, Green, Topaz, Anthracite, Cabernet, Titanium, Turquoise, Amaranth & Madeira Red, Sherwood.
Interior: Blue, Charcoal, Oatmeal, Coffee, Nimbus.

AT A GLANCE...

HISTORIC
Introduced in: 1987.
Made in: Browns Lane, Coventry, England.

DEMOGRAPHICS

Model	Men/Wom.	Age	Married	College	Income $
XJ8-XJR	90/10 %	58	90 %	50 %	150,000

INDEX
Safety:	90 %	Satisfaction:	80 %
Depreciation:	48 %	Insurance:	$ 1,350-1,450
Cost per mile:	$ 1.15	Number of dealers:	130

SALES

	Canada			USA		
Model	1997	1998	Result	1997	1998	Result
XJ8-XJR	664	1 001	+ 50.8 %	12,588	16,642	+ 32.2 %

MAINTENANCE REQUIRED BY WARRANTY
First revision:	Frequency:	Diagnostic plug:
4,000 miles	6,000 / 10,000 miles	Yes

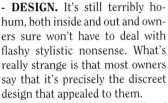

In this well-heeled category, the Lexus LS has the honor of being the bestselling model in North America. Although its status, technology and price aren't exactly the same as those of its rivals, it's still a very interesting phenomenon in the automotive industry. Strangely, its progress is inversely proportional to the reputation it has in J.D. Power surveys, where it's rated the most reliable car in the world.

MODEL RANGE

The LS 400 is a 4-door sedan sold in a unique trim level equiped with a 4.0L V8 engine linked to a 5-speed automatic transmission. Original equipment is very rich and the only options available to buyers are sunroof, self-adjusting air suspension, heated seats and chrome wheels.

TECHNICAL FEATURES

The LS 400 don't seem to change much, but in fact it's constantly being revised and it shares the same identical platform and main mechanical features with the SC coupe, which is now only sold on the US market. The steel monocoque body is galvanized on both sides and benefits from good aerodynamics, with a drag coefficient of 0.28. The four-wheel independent suspension consists of a double wishbone organization with stabilizer bar both front and rear. Vented disc brakes are linked to an ABS, traction control and anti-skid system (VSC), so vehicle behavior is well under control when adherence or car path go askew. The latest 4.0L V8 pumps out 30 more hp and 30 lb.ft. more torque than its predecessor, yet it has the same displacement and main characteristics.

Conservative

PROS

+ **QUALITY.** It's spiffy all-round. Design, craftsmanship, fit and finish job and trim materials are exquisite. Toyota is a genius when it comes to inner door and dashboard design, they look simply superb and really add a touch of class.

+ **RELIABILITY.** You just have to look at the high owner satisfaction rate to know why Lexus has scored among the finest cars sold for some time now.

+ **RIDE COMFORT.** The sedan is cushy with its spacious interior, supple suspension (especially the optional air suspension), nicely designed and cushioned seats and amazing sound dampening that provides impressive quiet at cruising speed.

+ **THE V8 ENGINE.** It really moves these big, heavy cars and is amazingly civilized, since it emits little or no noise or vibration. It provides the power and torque needed to achieve accelerations, pickup and top speed comparable to those of zippy German rivals.

+ **BRAKES.** They aren't the best on the market, but they're quite competent given the weight of the cars they have to bring to a full halt.

+ **FUEL ECONOMY.** The V8 is quite fuel-efficient for an engine of this displacement that animates such a beastly bulk. It does around 18 miles per gallon.

+ **HANDLING.** The car is more neutral than before due to various driving aids such as an anti-skid system and traction control that make for more competent demeanor.

+ **LOOKS.** This elegant and discreet sedan borrows from the great classics in this category and has a definite similarity to the Mercedes silhouette and shape.

+ **INSTRUMENT PANEL.** It's no doubt one of the most straightforward, rational and ergonomic designs on the market. Your hand reaches instinctively for the right controls, such as the most frequently needed big dials that control temperature or radio volume.

+ **RESALE VALUE.** It's quite good compared to that of other equally sophisticated cars.

CONS

- **PRESENTATION.** The Lexus LS 400 has nothing particulary exciting to look at on the inside or outside. Its lack of imagination is flagrant and inexcusable on the part of a major manufacturer such as Toyota, especially at a time when design is at its peak.

- **PRICE.** It's considerably less competitive than it used to be and is dangerously close to the cost of a Mercedes or a BMW model, either of which offers a good deal more refinement. This is very disturbing to buyers who attach a lot of importance to logos and names and the status attached to them.

- **DESIGN.** It's still terribly ho-hum, both inside and out and owners sure won't have to deal with flashy stylistic nonsense. What's really strange is that most owners say that it's precisely the discreet design that appealed to them.

- **STEERING.** It's over-assisted and suffers from a poor reduction ratio, so it's light, sensitive and offers no road feel, so driving is really quite dull.

- **TRUNK.** It's relatively small on this sedan given the vehicle size, but it's nice and square and has a low opening, so luggage handling is convenient.

CONCLUSION

The Lexus LS 400 is attractive to anyone looking for discretion, value and above all else, peace of mind and the knowledge that they have access to a reliable means of transportation. Not particularly interested in the automotive world, their focus is low depreciation levels, a quiet ride, reliability, advanced technology and high performance.

Luxury
+ $70 000

RATING
LEXUS LS 400

CONCEPT : 80%
Technology :	90
Safety :	90
Interior space :	75
Trunk volume :	55
Quality/fit/finish :	90

DRIVING : 75%
Cockpit :	85
Performance :	75
Handling :	60
Steering :	80
Braking :	75

ORIGINAL EQUIPMENT : 77%
Tires :	80
Headlights :	80
Wipers :	65
Rear defroster :	75
Radio :	85

COMFORT : 80%
Seats :	80
Suspension :	80
Sound level :	80
Conveniences :	80
Air conditioning :	80

BUDGET : 49%
Price :	0
Fuel economy :	60
Insurance :	35
Satisfaction :	95
Depreciation :	55

Overall rating : 72.2%

NEW FOR 2000

• No major changes.

Compare Performance, Specifications, Prices, and Classification at the end of this chapter.

EQUIPMENT

LEXUS	LS 400
Automatic transmission:	S
Cruise control:	S
Power steering:	S
Anti-lock brakes:	S
Traction control:	S
Air conditioning:	SA
Leather:	S
AM/FM/radio-cassette:	SCd
Power door locks:	S
Power windows:	S
Tilt steering:	S
Dual adjustable mirrors:	SEH
Alloy wheels:	S
Anti-theft system:	S

Colors

Exterior: White, Silver, Black, Red, Beige, Jade, Mica, Teal, Wildberry.

Interior: Ivory, Grey, Black, Pebble.

AT A GLANCE...

HISTORIC
Introduced in:	1990.
Made in:	Tahara, Japan.

DEMOGRAPHICS
Model	Men/Wom.	Age	Married	College	Income $
LS 400	96/4 %	60	91 %	52 %	145 ,000

INDEX
Safety:	90 %	Satisfaction:	95 %
Depreciation:	46 %	Insurance:	$ 1,150
Cost per mile:	$ 1.05	Number of dealers:	170

SALES
Model	Canada 1997	1998	Result	USA 1997	1998	Result
LS 400	375	302	- 19.5 %	19,618	20,790	+ 6.0 %

MAINTENANCE REQUIRED BY WARRANTY
First revision:	Frequency:	Diagnostic plug:
4,000 miles	4,000 miles	Yes

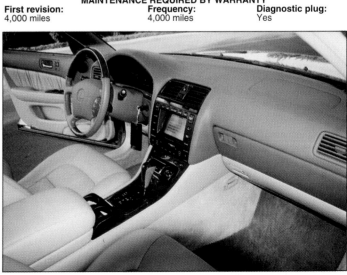

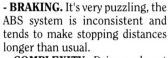
Room For Improvement

Mercedes-Benz finally re-vamped its prestige sedan, making its size more realistic and taking a cue from the BMW 7 Series that stole the spotlight from it. As is its habit, the builder has spared no expense in finding avantgarde technical solutions.

MODEL RANGE

The S-Class includes two 4-door sedans: the S430, available with a short or long wheelbase, and the S500, offered solely with a long wheelbase. The former is equipped with a 4.3L V8, and the latter has a 5.0L V8. For the moment, no V12 is available. The standard transmission is an electronic 5-speed automatic. Given the high asking price, equipment is very detailed and very refined, including eight airbags, dual automatic air conditioning, and highly original power systems.

TECHNICAL FEATURES

The latest S-Class models have a unibody made of steel specially treated for long-term rust-resistance. It has been designed to provide maximum protection for occupants. Its flowing lines provide excellent aerodynamics, with a drag coefficient of 0.27 on the S430 and the S500. The fully independent suspension features four superimposed arms in the front and five in the rear, all mounted on frames that are insolated from the body. Shock absorption is designed to maintain constant levelling regardless of the load and its reactions adjust to road surface quality. The S-Class features rack-and-pinion steering and four disc brakes with standard ABS, traction control and anti-skid systems on all models.

PROS

+ STYLING. It's remarkably more refined; the latest S has very graceful lines that have nothing in common with the military tank look typical of the previous model. The new concept is repeated in the now more imaginative dashboard, which includes all of the accessories considered essential for a modern automobile.

+ HIGH TECHNOLOGY. It is remarkable and these sedans are chock full of leading-edge electronics that ensure road grip regardless of weather conditions thanks to a host of complex systems backed by an army of sensors.

+ SAFETY. It's among the best in the industry thanks to an exceptionally sturdy body with a built-in safety cage, multiple airbags and head protection systems and seat belts that adjust automatically.

+ PERFORMANCE. The S500's better weight/power ratio makes for more spectacular acceleration and pick-up than available on the S430, whose short wheelbase version shows more agility and more energy than the extended wheelbase alternative.

+ HANDLING. It's exceptional given the combined efficiency of the suspension, steering system, brakes, motor functions and road grip and only major weight shifts will have a negative effect when the car is travelling on slippery road surfaces.

+ DRIVEABILITY. This S-Class is more fun to drive than its predecessor; the new model is more responsive and easier to keep on course. A smaller size and a lower weight are responsible, as are smoothly operating power systems designed to make the driver's life easier.

+ QUALITY. It's most obvious at the technical and technological levels and the exterior design is more attractive than it once was.

+ COMFORT. The level is enhanced by a roomy passenger compartment, seats that mold better than they used to, a well-calibrated suspension, and excellent soundproofing. On the extended wheelbase version, rear seats are regally accommodating and there is plenty of room in all directions.

+ GADGETS. Equipment on the latest S-Class models is the most elaborate found anywhere in the automotive world. It includes accessories as unusual as a sensor that deactivates the cruise control system when the vehicle gets too close to another one, front seats with ventilation and a massage function, and headlamp position indicators in the rearview mirror.

+ BONUS POINTS. For the sequential transmission, no doubt the simplest, most logical and most efficient available on today's market. For a number of storage spaces that make this car very practical for both front- and rear-seat passengers. For a nice-looking interior with very attractive wood inlays and leather trims.

CONS

- PRICE. Along with their asking price, these models' insurance, fuel and maintenance costs are proportionate to the financial means their owners are clearly expected to have at their disposal.

- BRAKING. It's very puzzling, the ABS system is inconsistent and tends to make stopping distances longer than usual.

- COMPLEXITY. Drivers almost need a pilot's license and at the very least some serious training to use the instrument cluster on the center console, grouping together the controls for the radio, air conditioning, navigation system and hands-free telephone.

- SIZING. As outrageously oversized the previous model was, as cramped the latest S-Class feels, particularly the shorter S430, where rear-seat access isn't as easy as it is on models with a longer wheelbase. The same goes for the trunk, where there's no space to spare, and as you would expect of a model out to establish its lofty standing, where cargo space doesn't benefit from the decided advantage of a fold down rear seat.

- QUALITY. It leaves an awful lot to be desired on the inside, where details are rather utilitarian and some plastics don't look very good at all. The tires (Continental Contitouring Contact) on our test model were a very poor choice for a car that is this exceptional in all other regards.

- MAJOR FLAWS. Very slow wipers hinder the safety level, the driver has no dummy pedal, wind noise sets in early on and disrupts an otherwise pleasant ride.

CONCLUSION

In spite of obvious progress, the latest S-Class still needs improvement when it comes to certain design details and it has room for improvement.

Luxury S70,000

RATING
MERCEDES-BENZ S-Class

CONCEPT :		87%
Technology :	100	
Safety :	100	
Interior space :	75	
Trunk volume :	70	
Quality/fit/finish :	90	

DRIVING :		75%
Cockpit :	80	
Performance :	80	
Handling :	70	
Steering :	80	
Braking :	65	

ORIGINAL EQUIPMENT :		79%
Tires :	85	
Headlights :	80	
Wipers :	65	
Rear defroster :	80	
Radio :	85	

COMFORT :		82%
Seats :	80	
Suspension :	80	
Sound level :	90	
Conveniences :	80	
Air conditioning :	80	

BUDGET :		40%
Price :	0	
Fuel economy :	30	
Insurance :	25	
Satisfaction :	90	
Depreciation :	55	

Overall rating :		72.6%

New 2000 Model

NEW FOR 2000

• **The S-Class sedans were revamped for 1999. They're smaller, their weight favors better performance levels and for the moment, the simplified lineup doesn't include 6-cylinder or V12 engines.**

Compare
Performance,
Specifications, Prices,
and Classification
at the end of this chapter.

Luxury + $70,000

EQUIPMENT

MERCEDES-BENZ S-Class	S430 SWB	S430 LWB	S500 LWB
Automatic transmission:	S	S	S
Cruise control:	S	S	S
Power steering:	S	S	S
Anti-lock brakes:	S	S	S
Traction control:	S	S	S
Air conditioning:	SA	SA	SA
Leather:	S	S	S
AM/FM/radio-cassette:	SCd	SCd	SCd
Power door locks:	S	S	S
Power windows:	S	S	S
Tilt steering:	S	S	S
Dual adjustable mirrors:	SEH	SEH	SEH
Alloy wheels:	S	S	S
Anti-theft system:	S	S	S

Colors

Exterior: Black, White, Red, Blue, Silver, Indigo. SL: Turquoise, Red, Green.

Interior: Black, Blue, Parchment, Grey. SL: Ash, Java, Shell.

AT A GLANCE...

HISTORIC
Introduced in:	1992 (sedan).
Made in:	Sindelfingen, (Stuttgart) Germany.

DEMOGRAPHICS
Model	Men/Wom.	Age	Married	College	Income $
S-Class	75/25 %	52	87 %	81 %	185,000

INDEX
Safety:	100 %	Satisfaction:	87 %
Depreciation:	45 %	Insurance:	$ 1,900
Cost per mile:	$ 1.25	Number of dealers:	380

SALES
	Canada			USA		
Model	1997	1998	Result	1997	1998	Result
S-Class	761	605	- 20.5 %	16,119	15,010	- 6.9 %

MAINTENANCE REQUIRED BY WARRANTY
First revision:	Frequency:	Diagnostic plug:
3,000 miles	10,000 miles	Yes

LUXURY CARS over $ 70,000

PERFORMANCE

Model/ version	Type / timing valve / fuel system	Displacement cu in	Power hp @ rpm	Torque lb-ft @ rpm	Compres. ratio	Driving wheels / transmission	Final ratio	Acceler. 0-60 mph s	Standing 1/4 & 5/8 mile s		Passing 50-75 mph s	Braking 60-0 mph ft	Top speed mph	Lateral acceler. G	Noise level dBA	Fuel economy mpg City	Highway	Fuel type Octane
AUDI A8																		
A8 4.2	V8 4.2 DOHC-32 MPSFI	255	310 @ 6200	302 @ 3000	10.8: 1	all - A5	2.91	7.2	15.4	27.6	5.4	148	131	0.80	65	17	25	S 91
BMW 7 Series																		
740i/iL	V8 4.4 DOHC-32-MFI	268	282 @ 5700	324 @ 3700	10.0 :1	rear - A5	2.93	7.5	15.8	26.8	5.6	135	128*	0.82	64-70	17	26	S 91
750iL	V12 5.4 SOHC-24-MFI	328	322 @ 5000	361 @ 3900	10.0 :1	rear - A5	2.81	6.5	14.6	26.2	5.0	138	128*	0.81	64-70	15	22	S 91
JAGUAR XJ																		
XJ8	V8 4.0 DOHC-32-EDFI	244	290 @ 6100	290 @ 4250	10.75 :1	rear - ZFA5	3.06	7.3	15.2	26.6	5.4	128	150	0.80	64-66	17	24	S 91
XJ8 L- VdP	V8 4.0 DOHC-32-EDFI	244	290 @ 6100	290 @ 4250	10.75 :1	rear - ZFA5	3.06	7.9	16.4	29.0	5.7	134	150	0.80	64-68	16	24	S 91
XJR	V8C 4.0 DOHC 32-EDFI	244	370 @ 6150	387 @ 3600	9.00 :1	rear - M-B A5	3.06	5.8	14.2	25.7	4.2	144	155	0.80	65-68	14	22	S 91
LEXUS LS																		
LS 400	V8 4.0 DOHC-32-MPSFI	242	290 @ 6000	300 @ 4000	10.5 :1	rear - A5	3.27	6.9	15.2	26.6	5.2	135	149	0.80	65-69	18	25	S 91
MERCEDES-BENZ S-Class																		
S430	V8 4.3 SOHC-24-IES	260	275 @ 5750	295 @ 3000	10.0 :1	rear - A5	2.87	6.7	15.0	26.6	4.8	141	130*	0.77	63-70	17	24	S 91
S500	V8 5.0 SOHC-24-IES	303	302 @ 5600	339 @ 2750	10.1 :1	rear - A5	2.87	6.2	14.5	25.5	4.0	144	130*	0.77	63-70	16	22	S 91

SPECIFICATIONS

Model	Version Trim	Body/ Seats	Cabin volume cu ft	Trunk volume cu ft	Cd	Wheel base in	Lgth x Width x Hght in x inx in	Curb weight lb	Susp. ft/rr	Brake ft/rr type	Steering ø turns ft number	Fuel tank gal	dimensions	Standard tires make model	Standard powertrain	99 Price msrp $
AUDI	General warranty: 3 years / 50 000 miles; perforation corrosion: 10 years; free maintenance: 3 years / 50 000 miles; roadside assistance: 3 years.															
A8 4.2	quattro	4dr.sdn.5	99.8	17.6	0.29	113.4	198.2x74.0x56.6	4068	ih/ih	dc/ABS	pwr.r&p. 40.2 2.7	23.0	225/60HR16	Michelin Pilot SX	V8/4.2/A5	65,500
BMW	General warranty : 4 years/ 50 000 miles; corrosion: 6 years / unlimited: antipollution: 8 years / 80 000 miles.															
740	i	4dr.sdn. 5	99.5	17.6	0.31	115.4	196.2x73.3x56.5	4255	ih/ih	dc/ABS	pwr.ball 38.0 3.5	22.5	235/60HR16	Michelin MXV4 XSE	V8/4.4/A5	62,970
740	iL	4dr.sdn. 5	105.0	17.6	0.31	120.9	201.7x73.3x56.1	4288	ih/ih	dc/ABS	pwr.ball 40.0 3.5	22.5	235/60HR16	Michelin MXV4 XSE	V8/4.4/A5	66,970
750	iL	4dr.sdn. 5	105.0	17.6	0.32	120.9	201.7x73.3x56.1	4697	ih/ih	dc/ABS	pwr.ball 40.0 3.5	25.1	235/60HR16	Michelin MXV4 XSE	V12/5.4/A5	92,670
JAGUAR	Warranty: 4 years / 50 000 miles; corrosion: 6 years / unlimited; antipollution : 4 years / 50 000 miles ; free maintenance: 2 years / 20 000 miles.															
XJ8		4dr.sdn.5	93.0	12.7	0.37	113.0	197.8x70.8x52.7	3997	ih/ih	dc/ABS	pwr.r&p. 39.7 2.8	23.1	225/60ZR16	Pirelli P4000	V8/4.0/A5	55,780
XJ8	L	4dr.sdn.5	NA	12.7	0.37	117.9	202.7x70.8x53.2	4012	ih/ih	dc/ABS	pwr.r&p. 40.7 2.8	23.1	225/60ZR16	Pirelli P4000	V8/4.0/A5	60,830
XJ8	Vanden Plas	4dr.sdn.5	NA	12.7	0.37	117.9	202.7x70.8x53.2	4048	ih/ih	dc/ABS	pwr.r&p. 40.7 2.8	23.1	225/60ZR16	Pirelli P4000	V8/4.0/A5	64,880
XJR		4dr.sdn.5	93.0	12.7	0.39	113.0	197.8x70.8x52.7	4074	ih/ih	dc/ABS	pwr.r&p. 39.7 2.8	23.1	255/40ZR18	Pirelli P Zero	V8C/4.0/A5	69,030
LEXUS	General warranty: 4 years / 50 000 miles; powertrain: 6 years / 70 000 miles; corrosion perforation: 6 years / unlimited mileage & roadside assistance.															
LS	400	4dr.sdn.5	102.0	13.4	0.28	112.2	196.7x72.0x56.5	3890	ih/ih	dc/ABS	pwr.r&p. 34.8 3.5	21.9	225/60VR16	Bridgestone Turanza ER 33	V8/4.0/A5	54 300
MERCEDES-BENZ	General warranty: 4 years / 50 000 miles; corrosion perforation: 5 years / unlimited mileage															
S430	base	4dr.sdn.5	99.6	15.4	0.27	116.7	198.3x73.1x56.8	4089	ih/ih	d/ABS	pwr.r&p. 38.3 2.8	23.2	225/60HR16	Michelin MXV4	V8/4.3/A5	101 900
S430	L	4dr.sdn.5	105.0	15.4	0.27	121.4	203.0x73.1x56.8	4134	ih/ih	d/ABS	pwr.r&p. 39.7 2.8	23.2	225/60HR16	Michelin MXV4	V8/4.3/A5	-
S500	L	4dr.sdn.5	105.0	15.4	0.27	121.4	203.0x73.1x56.8	4134	ih/ih	d/ABS	pwr.r&p. 39.7 2.8	23.2	225/60HR16	Michelin MXV4	V8/5.0/A5	117 900

Notes: 1) Tire makes and models are provided solely as an indication; they are subject to change without prior notice from the automobile manufacturers.
2) See the 2000 price list at the back of this edition.

CLASSIFICATION

OUR CLASSIFICATION

Rank	Models	Concept	Driving	Equipment	Comfort	Budget	Ratings
1	**BMW 7 Series**	**90**	**79**	**81**	**85**	38	**74.6 %**
2	AUDI A8	88	73	**81**	83	44	73.8 %
3	MERCEDES S-Class	87	75	79	82	40	72.6 %
4	LEXUS LS 400	80	75	77	80	**49**	72.2 %
5	JAGUAR XJ8-XJR	74	74	78	80	42	69.6 %

YOUR CLASSIFICATION

Rank	Models	98 Sales
1	LEXUS LS 400	20,790
2	BMW 7 Series	18,309
3	JAGUAR XJ8-XJR	16,642
4	MERCEDES S-Class	15,010
5	AUDI A8	2,172

ACURA Integra

CHRYSLER FG Series

FORD Mustang

GM F Series

HONDA Prelude

HYUNDAI Tiburon

MAZDA Miata

Comparative Test

SPORTS CARS
under $ 35,000

**See their performance, their specifications, their price
and their classification at the end of this chapter.**

TOYOTA Celica

MERCURY Cougar

A Record

If ever the Acura Integra was able to beat a record hands down, there can be no question that it's the record for longevity. Evidence: this model looks exactly the same as it did in 1993. Of course the lineup has experienced some changes, such as the arrival of the sporty GS-R version and ever-changing equipment permutations and combinations that helps sustain interest in any given model as time goes by. Each year experts speculate on the Integra's replacement - in vain. Pundits will have to wait until the next Tokyo Auto Show to see what the next years have in store as far as this popular sport coupe is concerned.

MODEL RANGE

The Integra is a hatchback coupe sold in LS, GS, GS-R and the limited edition Type R models. They're powered by a 1.8L 16-valve DOHC 4-cylinder engine that develops 139 hp on the LS and GS, 170 hp on the GS-R, thanks to a VTEC valve intake control system and 195 hp on the Type R. The original transmission is a 5-speed manual or an optional 4-speed automatic, except for the Type R that can only receive a manual.

Standard equipment on the LS/GS includes air conditioning, power windows, locks and mirrors, light alloy rims, tilt steering column, theft-deterrent system and radio with tape deck and CD player. The GS is also equipped with cruise control and antilock braking. The GS-R has a more muscular engine and different-design light alloy rims. As for the Type R version, its engine develops 25 more hp and it sports a leather-wrapped steering wheel, bucket seats and carbon fiber trim

on the dashboard. In all cases, the automatic transmission, leather seat covers and sunroof are sold as extras.

TECHNICAL FEATURES

Integra models have a steel unibody that yields average aerodynamics, with a drag coefficient of 0.32. The fully independent suspension consists of unequal length A-arms at each corner and stabilizer bars for both front and rear axles. Brakes are four-wheel disc and the LS, GS and GS-R versions are fitted with ABS, while the Type R model benefits from yet a more sophisticated antilock braking system.

The all-aluminum engine that equips the GS-R and Type R versions is unique, since it has a dual-stage intake manifold and a VTEC distribution system, namely an electronic variable valve timing and lift, so the engine doesn't strain as much at high rpm The Type R now has a more robust body, beefier disc brakes, thicker anti-roll bars and a lower center of gravity. Too bad the tires that equip the Type R aren't any bigger than on other models in the lineup.

PROS

+ STYLE. It's quite fetching with the lens-shaped headlamps that really distinguish this car from its main rivals.

+ DRIVING. It's a blast with such slick, spontaneous moves warranted by accurate steering that benefits

from a good reduction ratio, so young drivers really love to get behind the wheel of one of these coupes. The manual speed shifter is quick on the draw and gears are nicely spaced, so you can really milk the engine power. Neat-design seats, clear visibility and good instrument panel layout create a sporty ambience.

+ PERFORMANCES. The VTEC engines really pump out the power beyond 3,000 r.p.m., so accelerations and pickup have quite a surge, but you often have to drive beyond legal speeds to get the best out of these engines.

+ HANDLING. Thanks to the sophisticated suspension, these cars take curves with great aplomb as long as anti-roll bars are thick enough, for there's moderate sway and wavering. The Type R suspension is more competent still, for it benefits from a lower center of gravity and is less sensitive to understeer.

+ QUALITY. Typical to Japanese products, construction and finish details are very rigorous and assembly tolerances are super-tight.

+ CONVENIENCE FEATURES. They haven't been overlooked, since the trunk is convertible and storage compartments are a good size and scattered throughout the cabin.

+ RELIABILITY. The owner satisfaction rate is very high (90%), which explains the good resale value and the scarcity of models on the used car market.

CONS

- SAFETY. The Integra models don't benefit from resistance to impact on a par with more recent models and according to test scores, passengers don't seem to enjoy as much protection as the driver.

- BRAKES. The base model isn't equipped with ABS, so front wheel lock is a common occurrence, which is hard on tires and affects car stability, especially since "threshold" braking is hard to apply with any precision on this model.

- QUALITY. Some construction materials are rather chintzy, bodywork and seat fabrics are thin and the plastic trim on the dashboard looks far from ritzy.

- ENGINES. The multivalve engines develop only low torque below 3,000 rpm, so pickup at low rpm is pretty frustrating, especially with the automatic gearbox that simply strips this car of its sporty side.

- RIDE COMFORT. It's no great shakes with the firm seat upholstery, snug head and leg room in the rear seats, brutal suspension response on poorly maintained roads and loud noise interference that just doesn't let up.

- CABIN DESIGN. It's looking a bit dusty and the instrument panel needs to be spruced up to better reflect this car's character...

- ACCESS. The rear end has been reinforced, so the high trunk threshold complicates luggage loading and unloading.

CONCLUSION

Although time inevitably marches on, the Integra remains a popular model whose appearance and performance are far from outdated. It's still a reference within the industry and it has successfully withstood the war waged by utility vehicles.

RATING ACURA Integra		
CONCEPT :		**64%**
Technology :	80	
Safety :	75	
Interior space :	30	
Trunk volume :	55	
Quality/fit/finish :	80	
DRIVING :		**70%**
Cockpit :	80	
Performance :	65	
Handling :	70	
Steering :	80	
Braking :	55	
ORIGINAL EQUIPMENT :		**74%**
Tires :	75	
Headlights :	80	
Wipers :	65	
Rear defroster :	75	
Radio :	75	
COMFORT :		**71%**
Seats :	75	
Suspension :	75	
Sound level :	55	
Conveniences :	70	
Air conditioning :	80	
BUDGET :		**64%**
Price :	50	
Fuel economy :	80	
Insurance :	45	
Satisfaction :	90	
Depreciation :	55	
Overall rating :		**68.6%**

NEW FOR 2000

- Immobilizing system.
- Exterior colors: Black, Red, Beige.
- Leather trims on the GS-R version.

Compare Performance, Specifications, Prices, and Classification at the end of this chapter.

EQUIPMENT

ACURA Integra	LS	GS	GS-R	Type R
Automatic transmission:	O	O	O	NA
Cruise control:	-	S	S	S
Power steering:	S	S	S	S
Anti-lock brakes:	-	S	S	S
Traction control:	-	-	-	S
Air conditioning:	S	S	S	S
Leather:	O	O	S	-
AM/FM/radio-cassette:	SCd	SCd	SCd	SCd
Power door locks:	S	S	S	S
Power windows:	S	S	S	S
Tilt steering:	S	S	S	S
Dual adjustable mirrors:	SE	SE	SE	SE
Alloy wheels:	S	S	S	S
Anti-theft system:	S	S	S	S

Colors
Exterior: Silver, White, Red, Green, Black.

Interior: Black.

AT A GLANCE...

HISTORIC

Introduced in:	1987-1993.
Made in:	Suzuka, Japan.

DEMOGRAPHICS

Model	Men/Wom.	Age	Married	College	Income $
Integra	66/34 %	32	33 %	66 %	45,000

INDEX

Safety:	75 %	Satisfaction:	90 %
Depreciation:	45 %	Insurance:	$ 765
Cost per mile:	$ 0.44	Number of dealers:	290

SALES

	Canada			USA		
Model	1997	1998	Result	1997	1998	Result
Integra	4,113	3,765	- 8.5 %	38,331	34,904	- 8.9%

MAINTENANCE REQUIRED BY WARRANTY

First revision:	Frequency:	Diagnostic plug:
3,000 miles	6,000 miles	Yes

A Discovery

The Sebring convertible is much more popular than the coupe, whose sales have never taken off since it replaced the old Le Baron model. This trend is due in part to the fact that the coupe has never established a strong image and this kind of vehicle suffers from the assault waged by utility vehicles. On the other hand, although convertibles are aimed at a limited clientele, they are very carefully and specifically targeted.

MODEL RANGE

The Avenger is no longer sold in Canada but is offered in a base or ES coupe at Dodge on the US market. The Sebring is sold as a JX, JXi and JXi Limited convertible, or an LX or LXi coupe at Chrysler. The coupes are equipped with a standard 2.0L L4 and the convertible with the 2.4L 4-cylinder Cirrus-Stratus engine linked to a 4-speed automatic transmission, whereas the 2.5L V6 is available as an option, linked to a 4-speed automatic. Equipment on base models does include power steering, radio cassette player and tilt steering wheel.

TECHNICAL FEATURES.

These two cars don't share the same ancestry. The coupes are look-alike cousins, except for a few cosmetic touches. They were built on the Eagle Talon platform, a model that's just like the Mitsubishi Eclipse...from which they borrow their main mechanical components such as suspensions, engines, transmission as well as the instrument panel design. They're still built by Mitsubishi, as is the optional 2.5L V6 engine. The convertible is built in Mexico. It's directly inspired by the Cirrus-Stratus-Breeze platform and shares these models' features, like some front end design details

and instrument panel. Their silhouette is sweeping, but it only yields very midling aerodynamic efficiency. The steel monocoque body is equipped with four-wheel independent suspensions. They're made up of unequal-length upper and lower control arms on the convertible and double wishbone front and rear on the coupes. All suspensions include coil springs and stabilizer bars. Steering is rack-and-pinion and disc brakes benefit from standard ABS on some versions.

OUTSTANDING

++LOOKS. The Sebring convertible exudes charm with the top up or down. The convertible top is a breeze to manipulate and includes a glass rear window fitted with a defroster. It's one of the most weatherproof designs on the market and it's lined with a canopy to mask the arches. The BMW Z3 doesn't even compete...

PROS

+ STYLE. With all the touch-ups, the coupes finally do have a rather lovely design. The convertible body is more sleek and fluid with its deeply slanted windshield and its rear extremity that is very akin to the Camaro-Firebird rear end design.

+ CABIN SPACE. A rare commodity for this type of vehicle, it's as generous inside the coupes as it is in the convertible. Four adults can be comfortably seated, provided passengers in the rear seats aren't

too chunky or spindly. There's sufficient head and leg room, but the seatbench back slants quite a bit, so even short trips can be tiring.

+ DRIVING PLEASURE. It comes mostly from the right-on steering and well-honed suspension, so handling is competent.

+ PERFORMANCES. The 2.4L engine is better suited to these vehicles, even with the automatic transmission that could be better calibrated.

+ ACCESS. Thanks to those long doors that open wide, getting aboard is easy and natural for both models, both front and rear. Rear seat passengers have good leg room.

+ TRUNK. Coupes have a roomier trunk than does the convertible, since the trunk on the latter model can't be extended and has to hold the car top as well.

+ BRAKES. The brake system is more effective and accurate and the pedal is less mushy, especially on the heavier convertible. Latest-generation ABS really makes a difference.

CONS

- RIGIDITY. It's pretty iffy, since these cars emit a lot of strange noises when driving on less than perfect secondary roads.

- ANONYMITY. The coupes haven't got an ounce of charisma, especially the Avenger that doesn't get any benefit from the aura surrounding the Viper monster sold in the same division.

- PERFORMANCES. The V6 engine is a disappointment. It just doesn't have the punch or pizzazz of its popular counterpart at Mazda.

- FINISH DETAILS. The coupes' interior design is so dull, it's a crying shame and the imitation wood trim inside the Sebring doesn't help one bit. Instrument panels are very lackluster on the coupes and the convertible's dashboard, inherited from the Cirrus, is crippled by a too low-slung center console.

- OUTWARD VIEW. It' just as poor on both types of models. You're seated at rock bottom up front and the trunk lid is so bloody high that rearward view is poor. The thick C pillar on the coupes and the teeny rear window on the convertible top form a big blind spot at quarterback and the inside rearview mirror is minuscule.

- CONVENIENCE FEATURES. Storage space wasn't a priority when the designers drew up plans for these cars. All you get are tiny glove compartments and hard to get at door side-pockets.

- TO BE IMPROVED UPON. The simplistic cabin design and cheap components on some models — weak blower that doesn't cool things down on hot, scorching days — rear windows that don't open on the coupes and the totally unacceptable headlight quality that seems to be the blight of Chrysler brand products. Not too bright...

CONCLUSION

These days, sport coupe sales are dropping in favor of the more versatile sport utility vehicles on the market. Of these two models, the convertible is the more interesting: it's the only automobile in its class to offer an economical 4-cylinder engine and a price that's considerably lower than its competitors'.

RATING
CHRYSLER FG Series

CONCEPT : 71%
Technology :	80
Safety :	90
Interior space :	60
Trunk volume :	50
Quality/fit/finish :	75

DRIVING : 60%
Cockpit :	70
Performance :	40
Handling :	50
Steering :	80
Braking :	60

ORIGINAL EQUIPMENT : 69%
Tires :	75
Headlights :	50
Wipers :	80
Rear defroster :	60
Radio :	80

COMFORT : 68%
Seats :	75
Suspension :	80
Sound level :	50
Conveniences :	60
Air conditioning :	75

BUDGET : 68%
Price :	50
Fuel economy :	75
Insurance :	60
Satisfaction :	80
Depreciation :	75

Overall rating : 67.2%

NEW FOR 2000
- The Dodge Avenger coupe is no longer available in Canada.
- Standard 2.5L V6 engine on the base model.
- More elaborate equipment on all models.
- Exterior color: Silver.
- LX trims replaced by Jaegar & Regina.

Compare Performance, Specifications, Prices, and Classification at the end of this chapter.

EQUIPMENT

CHRYSLER Sebring / DODGE Avenger	JX con.	JXi con.	JXiL con.	LX cpe.	LXi cpe.	base cpe.	ES cpe.
Automatic transmission:	S	S	S	O	S	O	O
Cruise control:	O	S	S	O	S	O	O
Power steering:	S	S	S	S	S	S	S
Anti-lock brakes:	O	S	S	O	S	O	O
Traction control:	-	-	-	-	-	-	-
Air conditioning:	S	S	S	S	S	O	O
Leather:	-	S	S	-	O	-	O
AM/FM/radio-cassette:	SCd	SCd	SCd	S	SCd	S	S
Power door locks:	O	S	S	O	S	O	O
Power windows:	S	S	S	O	S	O	O
Tilt steering:	S	S	S	S	S	S	S
Dual adjustable mirrors:	SM	SE	SE	SM	SE	SM	SM
Alloy wheels:	O	S	S	O	S	O	S
Anti-theft system:	O	S	-	-	-	-	S

Colors
Exterior: White, Amethyst, Champagne, Green, Red, Silver, Blue, Slate, Coffee, Black, Plum, Paprika, Silver.
Interior: Grey, Red, Pebble, Beige, White-Black, Gray-Black, Black-Beige.

AT A GLANCE...

HISTORIC
Introduced in: 1995.
Made in: *coupe:* Normal, Illinois, USA. *convertible:* Toluca, Mexico.

DEMOGRAPHICS
Model	Men/Wom.	Age	Married	College	Income $
coupe	53/47 %	33	41 %	66 %	45,000
convertible	62/38 %	52	85 %	47 %	70,000

INDEX
Safety:	90 %	Satisfaction:	80 %
Depreciation:	47 %	Insurance:	$ 575-665
Cost per mile:	$ 0.50	Number of dealers:	1 887

SALES
	Canada			USA		
Model	1997	1998	Result	1997	1998	Result
coupe	1,692	951	- 43.8 %	35,365	33,584	- 5.0 %
convertible	1,116	1,141	+ 2.2 %	53,054	51,342	- 3.2 %

MAINTENANCE REQUIRED BY WARRANTY
First revision:	Frequency:	Diagnostic plug:
3,000 miles	6 months / 6,000 miles	Yes

Sports cars - $35,000

Mythical

At Ford, the Mustang is a mythical model very closely associated with the make's history. Generation after generation, more or less successfully, designers have tried to perpetuate the spirit typical of the original and the latest attempt introduced last year is particularly successful. With a 320-hp output and an independent rear suspension designed to provide superior handling ease, the Cobra version targets automobile industry enthusiasts and collectors.

MODEL RANGE

The Mustang is available in coupe and convertible versions in three trim levels: base, GT or Cobra. The base model is equipped with a 3.8L V6, the GT is powered by a 4.6L SOHC V8 and the Cobra by its DOHC version. The 5-speed manual gearbox is standard and the 4-speed automatic is sold as an extra on every version but the Cobra. Convertibles are equipped with a power droptop control and can receive an optional polymer hard top. Standard equipment is just about the same, but options include high-performance traction control that's effective at all speeds and that's activated by ABS sensors.

TECHNICAL FEATURES

The last Mustang body is inspired by the 1964 1/2 model. It has a nice folded flowing look similar to that of the original model and there's even the authentic emblem and grille motif to boot. Headlights and taillights sport a new design as do air intakes and rims. The steel unibody is much more rigid and robust on both versions, especially the convertible that thus improves roadholding and resistance to impact. The independent front suspension is made up of MacPherson struts, but at the rear, the rigid axle design, except for the Cobra with its

independant rear suspension (IRS), is as old as the hills! It's suspended by four trailing arms and is fitted with an anti-roll bar.

The V8 models are equipped with bigger-diameter anti-roll bars and the rear axle is fitted with four shock absorbers. All versions benefit from four-wheel disc brakes. Both available engines have a lot more gusto and get-up-and-go. The 3.8L V6 delivers 190 hp, the GT's 4.6L V8 puts out 70 more hp and the Cobra another 60 hp thanks to the DOHC and a number of refinements such as a more balanced crankshaft, reinforced engine blocks and new aluminum bearings.

PROS

+ STYLISTICS. The Mustang has an appearance akin to that of the very first model, which will sure please all those Mustang nostalgia fans out there.

+ SUCCESS. Trim size and competitive price, given the reasonable array of equipment, add up to a successful recipe, so this car remains popular even at a time when this type of vehicle isn't exactly in the limelight.

+ PERFORMANCES. The V6 can boast of 40 more hp, so it's zippier than before. The V8's accelerations and pickup scores were about the same as for the Cobra who is a real beast.

+ HANDLING. With each passing year and with each new generation, the Mustang exhibits more competent handling due to a stiffer chassis

and better-quality tires. In the case of the Cobra the rear independant suspension makes a big difference.

+ DRIVING PLEASURE. It's simply great, especially when it comes to revving the lively 4.6L V8 that's smooth as silk and has power to burn. Steering is quick and benefits from a good reduction ratio, transmissions are well-synchronized and gears are nicely adjusted. You can do what you please inside this car, you can go for a quiet, relaxing drive or you can take this wild horse out for a thrilling run.

+ RIDE COMFORT. It's much better than in the past. The suspension is more civilized, seats are more comfy, noise level is more appropriate, yet this car still boasts of being on the wild side and rear seats, get this, are almost useful!

+ THE SOUND AND THE FURY. The V8's low growl is an absolutely vital part of the Mustang experience. Nonetheless, when at cruising speed, things quiet down, you're in for a generally more comfortable spin!

+ NICE FEATURES: The much more sturdy build, especially noticeable on the convertibles, the lined easy-to-use soft top that's equipped with a glass rear window and defroster, which isn't the case for the snooty BMW Z3...

CONS

- QUALITY. There have been some glitches in regard to build quality and reliability. Owners are supposed to be crazy about their car, but the

owner satisfaction rate is never higher than 77%!

- RIGID AXLE. It's still this car's major flaw, it swings on rough surfaces and generates a lot of annoying jostling about, but luckily it isn't dangerous per se. It looks like Ford just doesn't have the intention to transfer the IRS from the Cobra to the other models.

- BRAKES. Without ABS, they're inaccurate and unstable and this feature would sure make for safer driving if it were included as standard equipment on all models.

- TRACTION. The rear end often slips and slides, especially with the gutsy V8 engines. Once again, too bad Ford can't come up with a better idea and include standard traction control.

- STEERING. It's a bit vague on the convertibles that don't have as rigid a frame and body as the coupes.

- REAR SEATS. They're uncomfortable. Space is snug and the flat seatbench offers no lateral or lumbar support.

- ROAD AUTONOMY. The GT animated by a V8 has very limited road autonomy that isn't more than 215 miles at continuous speeds, so you have to make a lot of stops at the pumps along the way if you're on a long trip.

- SEATS. The base model offers passengers pretty crummy, poor-design seating, while seats on the GT don't offer the support you'd expect in a zoomy sports car!

CONCLUSION

More tempting than ever before, the latest Mustangs are exciting to drive and affordable to buy. No wonder they outclass their rivals!

RATING
FORD Mustang

CONCEPT :		**61%**
Technology :	75	
Safety :	90	
Interior space :	30	
Trunk volume :	35	
Quality/fit/finish :	75	
DRIVING :		**76%**
Cockpit :	80	
Performance :	80	
Handling :	70	
Steering :	80	
Braking :	70	
ORIGINAL EQUIPMENT :		**73%**
Tires :	80	
Headlights :	75	
Wipers :	65	
Rear defroster :	65	
Radio :	80	
COMFORT :		**65%**
Seats :	75	
Suspension :	70	
Sound level :	50	
Conveniences :	50	
Air conditioning :	80	
BUDGET :		**57%**
Price :	50	
Fuel economy :	60	
Insurance :	50	
Satisfaction :	75	
Depreciation :	50	
Overall rating :		**66.4%**

NEW FOR 2000

- **A hood with a composite air intake.**
- **A rear spoiler and fog lights on the GT.**
- **Standard Securilock antitheft system.**

Compare
Performance,
Specifications, Prices,
and Classification
at the end of this chapter.

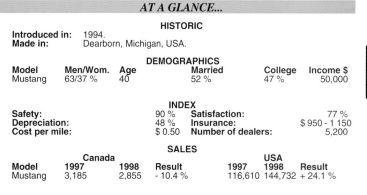

Sport - $35,000

EQUIPMENT

FORD Mustang	base		GT		Cobra	
	cpe.	con.	cpe.	con.	cpe.	con.
Automatic transmission:	O	O	O	O	NA	NA
Cruise control:	O	O	O	O	S	S
Power steering:	S	S	S	S	S	S
Anti-lock brakes:	O	O	S	S	S	S
Traction control:	O	O	O	O	S	S
Air conditioning:	SM	SM	SM	SM	SM	SM
Leather:	O	O	O	O	S	S
AM/FM/radio-cassette:	O	O	S	S	S	S
Power door locks:	S	S	S	S	S	S
Power windows:	O	S	O	S	S	S
Tilt steering:	S	S	S	S	S	S
Dual adjustable mirrors:	SE	SE	SE	SE	SE	SE
Alloy wheels:	O	O	S	S	S	S
Anti-theft system:	S	S	S	S	S	S

Colors

Exterior: Orange, Red, Blue, Green, Black, Silver, White.

Interior: Brown, Medium graphite, Black, Parchment.

AT A GLANCE...

HISTORIC

Introduced in:	1994.
Made in:	Dearborn, Michigan, USA.

DEMOGRAPHICS

Model	Men/Wom.	Age	Married	College	Income $
Mustang	63/37 %	40	52 %	47 %	50,000

INDEX

Safety:	90 %	Satisfaction:	77 %
Depreciation:	48 %	Insurance:	$ 950 - 1 150
Cost per mile:	$ 0.50	Number of dealers:	5,200

SALES

	Canada			USA		
Model	1997	1998	Result	1997	1998	Result
Mustang	3,185	2,855	- 10.4 %	116,610	144,732	+ 24.1 %

MAINTENANCE REQUIRED BY WARRANTY

First revision:	Frequency:	Diagnostic plug:
5,000 miles	6 months / 5,000 miles	Yes

Relics

It's been a long time since the Camaro and Firebird have been competitive in this category and their heyday predates the deluge of versatile vehicles that have all but killed the sport model market for good. With an outdated size and old-fashioned technology, they continue to slide down the sales scale and it's easy to see that their end in near. Regardless, they still embody a certain vision of the American automobile - one that reached its peak in the 60's.

MODEL RANGE
The Camaro and Firebird have different exterior stylistic details, but they're built on the same platform and are equipped with identical mechanical features. The Chevrolet model range is made up of coupes and convertibles that vary according to equipment level: base and Z28. The Pontiac is available in base, Formula and Trans Am models. A 3.8L V6 engine paired up with a 5-speed manual transmission animates the base model. As for the Z28 and Trans Am versions, they borrow the 5.7L LS1 V8 from the Corvette. It's zoomy with its 305 hp (320 hp for the SS and WS6 Ram Air option packages) and is linked to a 4-speed automatic gearbox or an optional 6-speed manual gearbox. Chevrolet sells "performance" sets of options for the V6 (RPO Y87) and the Z28 (RPO 1LE).

TECHNICAL FEATURES
This sleek-looking body yields good aerodynamics, with a drag coefficient of 0.32 for the coupe and 0.36 for the convertible. The body is built of galvanized steel (rear fenders and hood) and composite polymer (door panels, front fenders, roof, trunk lid and rear spoiler). Compared to former models that it replaced in 1993, this Camaro benefits from a more rigid structure due to reinforcements and longitudinal beams running under the doors. The front suspension consists of uneven transverse control arms, while the rear suspension is made up of a rigid axle suspended by multi-link Salisbury components and a torque arm. There are anti-roll bars of various diameters at the front and rear, depending on the model. Four-wheel disc brakes are listed among standard equipment items, as is the Bosch ABS system. Each year the rack-and-pinion power steering keeps undergoing some ajustments geared to improve performance and its reduction ratio is better on the Z28 versions.

PROS
+ STYLE. The Camaro looks like an arrow in flight. Simply spectacular! It still makes heads turn even after all these years, especially the Z28, the SS and the Trans Am dressed in flashy-colored metal,

+ PERFORMANCES. With the new LS1 Corvette engine, acceleration time and pickup on the Z28-Tran Am models are pretty well the same as on the leader of the pack Chevrolet model car.

+ RIDE FEEL. Push the accelerator to the floor and the Z28 will fill you with its V8 surge and feline roar, a sensation that's really thrilling!

+VALUE. The price/performance ratio is still appealing to drivers who want to really feel alive at the wheel, especially those who talk about 0-60 mph take-off time from dawn till dusk.

+ HANDLING. Driving pleasure is directly proportional to road surface quality. The new stiffer frame helps keep the car right on track and cuts down on sway effect. So you can hit a pretty good lateral acceleration speed, albeit less sensational than that achieved in a Corvette, a model that benefits from a lower center of gravity and tires that have more grip.

+ INTERIOR DESIGN. The instrument panel was given a face-lift in 1997 and is now ergonomic and definitely less flashy and gawdy-looking. It looks swish, now that trim materials don't include that tacky plastic stuff that it sported not so long ago.

+ CONVERTIBLE MODEL. The device to remove the convertible roof is super efficient and the rear window is made of glass.

CONS
- SIZE. Is there still a market niche for the Camaro and the Firebird? It's so bulky and cumbersome and so very heavy and it's equipped with really out-of-date technology!

- TRACTION CONTROL. It is now optional on all models, and so accelerating on wet roads is not as solid and stable, which would make for safer street races...

- OUTWARD VIEW. Visibility sure wasn't a priority for the people who designed this vehicle. The instrument panel is very high and the seats swing low in this chariot so even the view out front isn't the greatest; lateral outward view is blocked by the high frame; towards the back, the thick B pillar and the sharply slanted rear window blot out the view.

- V6 ENGINE. With such a poor power to weight ratio, the V6 engine is more geared to quiet Sunday drives than to bold and brassy moves.

- V8 ENGINE. Not everyone can drive these cars! Its responses are almost brutal: with such a potentially high-performance engine and such a firm suspension, you're in for a bucking bronco ride on poor pavement.

-RIGIDITY. The convertibles lack structural stiffness. Frame torsion makes driving somewhat haphazard, so much so that a driver who guns it beyond his own capabilities... will be in a cold sweat!

- NOT TOO CONVENIENT. Given the size of this car, getting aboard is pretty tricky and involves a series of acrobatic moves even with those huge doors. Rear seats, storage space and trunk are so stingy they're something of a joke.

- TO BE IMPROVED UPON. The catalytic converter impinges on cabin space up front and it causes passenger discomfort due to a misshapen floor; the arduous speed shifter with the manual transmission; the convertible top protective cover that's a pain to use.

CONCLUSION
The mixed success of the Camaro and the Firebird clearly demonstrates that it's a vehicle from a time gone by. Mythical qualities aside, needs and expectations have changed. No doubt GM would have more success with a Camaro or a Firebird that could be an all-purpose hybrid with all-wheel drive and a fairly powerful engine. After all, even Porsche will soon have its very own utility vehicle!

Sports cars - $35,000

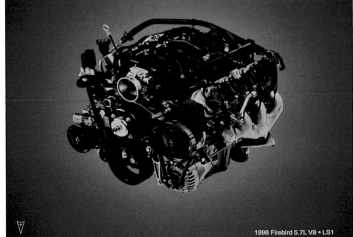

1998 Firebird 5.7L V8 • LS1

RATING	
GM F Series	
CONCEPT :	**62%**
Technology :	75
Safety :	90
Interior space :	35
Trunk volume :	40
Quality/fit/finish :	70
DRIVING :	**70%**
Cockpit :	80
Performance :	70
Handling :	70
Steering :	70
Braking :	60
ORIGINAL EQUIPMENT :	**78%**
Tires :	80
Headlights :	80
Wipers :	80
Rear defroster :	70
Radio :	80
COMFORT :	**58%**
Seats :	60
Suspension :	60
Sound level :	40
Conveniences :	50
Air conditioning :	80
BUDGET :	**50%**
Price :	45
Fuel economy :	40
Insurance :	40
Satisfaction :	75
Depreciation :	50
Overall rating :	**63.6%**

NEW FOR 2000

- 16- and 17-inch wheels.
- Child-safety seat anchors.
- Steering wheel-mounted radio controls.
- Monsoon sound system on the V6 convertible and Z28.
- Exterior Red and interior Ebony colors.

Compare
Performance,
Specifications, Prices,
and Classification
at the end of this chapter.

EQUIPMENT

CHEVROLET Camaro	cpe.	con.	cpe. Z28 Trans AM	con. Z28 Trans AM	cpe. Formula
PONTIAC Firebird					
Automatic transmission:	O	O	S	S	S
Cruise control:	O	O	S	S	S
Power steering:	S	S	S	S	S
Anti-lock brakes:	S	S	S	S	S
Traction control:	O	O	O	O	O
Air conditioning:	SM	SM	SM	SM	SM
Leather:	O	O	O	O	O
AM/FM/radio-cassette:	S	S	S	S	SCd
Power door locks:	O	S	O	S	S
Power windows:	O	S	O	S	S
Tilt steering:	S	S	S	S	S
Dual adjustable mirrors:	SM	SM	SM	SE	SE
Alloy wheels:	O	O	S	S	S
Anti-theft system:	S	S	S	S	S

Colors

Exterior: Black, Red, Teal, White, Gold, Blue, Green, Orange, Pewter, Ebony.

Interior: *Cloth:* Neutral, Dark Gray, Red.
Leather: White, Dark Gray, Neutral.

AT A GLANCE...

HISTORIC
Introduced in: 1967-1993.
Made in: Ste-Thérèse, Quebec, Canada.

DEMOGRAPHICS

Model	Men/Wom.	Age	Married	College	Income $
Camaro	82/18 %	46	50 %	35 %	56,000
Firebird	88/12 %	40	39 %	47 %	50,000

INDEX
Safety:	90 %	Satisfaction:	75 %
Depreciation:	50 %	Insurance:	$ 950 -1,000
Cost per mile:	$ 0.50	Number of dealers:	4,466

SALES

	Canada			USA		
Model	1997	1998	Result	1997	1998	Result
Camaro	1,554	1,168	- 24.8 %	55,973	47,577	- 15.0 %
Firebird	979	984	+ 0.5 %	32,524	31,692	- 2.6 %

MAINTENANCE REQUIRED BY WARRANTY
First revision:	Frequency:	Diagnostic plug:
3,000 miles	6,000 miles	Yes

Sports cars - $35,000

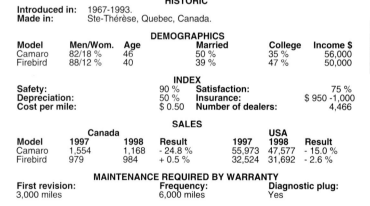

Weird

Honda is known as a manufacturer with a sporty bent and it offers more front-wheel drive coupes than most of its direct competitors. The Prelude, which should be its flagship model, has never enjoyed major success either because of its lack of personality or because of its high price, this year's model being a case in point. Logically, the S2000 roadster added to this model-year's lineup should serve as the basis for a rear-wheel coupe that could be a good replacement for the Prelude, even if it were sold at a higher price.

MODEL RANGE

The Honda Prelude is sold in two versions, base and Type SH, equipped with the same mechanical organs including a 2.2L engine with standard 5-speed manual transmission. Strangely enough, only the base model can receive an optional 4-speed automatic with sequential shifter. Original equipment items include disc brakes with antilock braking device and 16-inch wheels fitted with light alloy rims. Interior features include climate control, cruise control, tilt steering wheel, power locks, windows and mirrors, sunroof and theft-deterrent system. The Type SH version gets added leather-clad shifter knob and ATTS system, that is, Active Torque Transfer System.

TECHNICAL FEATURES

The most recent Prelude's body is longer and higher so as to provide more generous rear seat and trunk space. It's a steel unibody that's stiffer to provide crisper road handling, while really cutting down on noise, vibration and harshness. The new structure is 55% more torsion-resistant and 40% more flexion-resistant. Compared to the previous model, this has lowered the noise level by 3.5 decibels when travelling over rough pavement. To further keep noise interference down, the exhaust and intake systems have had a going over and wheel housings are covered with sandwich panels to reduce road roar. The new automatic transmission with sequential shifter, called "Sport-Shift", is controlled by a more powerful processor that allows you to engage the clutch in a linear fashion, so it's more progressive. The shifter is unique, for besides moving in parallel, it also shifts laterally so you can change gears manually without engaging the clutch. An indicator on the dashboard tells the driver what mode and gear have been selected. The Type SH model is equipped with ATTS. This system allows you to vary rotation speed and torque on the inside wheel when taking a curve, so there's no floating wheel effect and there's better control of unwanted straight directional pull.

PROS

+ PERFORMANCES. They have a bit more character than those on the former model and both versions are equipped with the same engine. Accelerations and pickup are super thanks to a state-of-the-art engine that only asks to be revved up and you really feel the second breath it gets with the VTEC beyond 5,000 rpm., and gas consumption is quite reassuring.

+ HANDLING. It's beyond a doubt this model's forte. The well-honed suspension really does its stuff since the Prelude goes into even the tightest curves with assurance, and powertrains provide good vehicle flow and sway and body waver are well under control.

+ DRIVING PLEASURE. It's great with such clean, cohesive demeanor due to smooth, direct and nicely assisted steering and the super-quick sequential shifter that lets you use engine power to full advantage up to fourth gear.

+ BRAKES. They're effective and easy to apply as required, so they're right-on and gradual. ABS works like a charm. Emergency stopping distances are within the average range.

+ CABIN DESIGN. The instrument panel on the current model is light years ahead of the previous one. It's logical, location of controls and dials respect good ergonomics, but it's pretty ordinary-looking, since the only available shade is black... Yet trim materials are a cut above now that plastic components and seat fabric are spiffy-looking.

+ CONVENIENCE FEATURES. The storage compartments inside the Prelude cabin are nicely located and they're a good size. The trunk is high, but it isn't too deep or wide, so it doesn't hold terribly much luggage especially since it connects with the cabin via a ski slot.

CONS

- PRICE. The Prelude is expensive and it doesn't resell as quickly or with as much profit as was the case at one time.

- STEERING. It gets light at times and seems to jerk around its circuit, a problem caused by the power steering pump.

- RIDE COMFORT. It doesn't jive with Sport since the Prelude doesn't really provide seating for four, the suspension is ruthless and noise interference is sometimes pretty pervasive.

- ACCESS. It's tricky boarding into the front seats with the narrow opening angle of the doors and the really slanted windshield, whereas getting to the rear seats is, yes, hazardous with the snugger leg and head room.

-QUALITY. Some accessories like the radio are shamefully deficient for such a swishy car that doesn't come cheap and headlamps and wipers are below par.

CONCLUSION

Even though it survived annihilation, the coupe's sales figures are falling behind on the different North American markets. It owes this in part to its price and odd appearance but also to its single-purpose character which does not drive buyers to spend so much for so little.

RATING	
HONDA Prelude	
CONCEPT :	**61%**
Technology :	85
Safety :	80
Interior space :	30
Trunk volume :	30
Quality/fit/finish :	80
DRIVING :	**72%**
Cockpit :	80
Performance :	70
Handling :	65
Steering :	80
Braking :	65
ORIGINAL EQUIPMENT :	**75%**
Tires :	80
Headlights :	80
Wipers :	65
Rear defroster :	70
Radio :	80
COMFORT :	**76%**
Seats :	85
Suspension :	70
Sound level :	70
Conveniences :	80
Air conditioning :	75
BUDGET :	**59%**
Price :	35
Fuel economy :	70
Insurance :	45
Satisfaction :	85
Depreciation :	60
Overall rating :	**68.6%**

NEW FOR 2000

• No major changes.

Compare
Performance,
Specifications, Prices,
and Classification
at the end of this chapter.

EQUIPMENT

HONDA Prelude	base	Type SH
Automatic transmission:	O	-
Cruise control:	S	S
Power steering:	S	S
Anti-lock brakes:	S	S
Traction control:	-	S
Air conditioning:	S	S
Leather:	-	S
AM/FM/radio-cassette:	SCd	SCd
Power door locks:	S	S
Power windows:	S	S
Tilt steering:	S	S
Dual adjustable mirrors:	SE	SE
Alloy wheels:	S	S
Anti-theft system:	S	S

Colors

Exterior: Black, Red, Blue, White.

Interior: Black.

AT A GLANCE...

HISTORIC
Introduced in: 1979-1997.
Made in: Sayama, Japan.

DEMOGRAPHICS

Model	Men/Wom.	Age	Married	College	Income $
Prelude	69/31 %	29	41 %	60 %	52,000

INDEX

Safety:	80 %	Satisfaction:	87 %
Depreciation:	38 %	Insurance:	$ 800-865
Cost per mile:	$ 0.50	Number of dealers:	1,001

SALES

	Canada				USA		
Model	1997	1998	Result		1997	1998	Result
Prelude	2,586	2,207	- 14.7 %		16,678	15,399	- 7.7 %

MAINTENANCE REQUIRED BY WARRANTY

First revision:	Frequency:	Diagnostic plug:
3,000 miles	3,000 miles	Yes

Sports cars - $35,000

Hungry

The Tiburon proved beyond all doubt that there was room on the market for a small sport coupe with energy and style. In spite of the the skepticism expressed by some industry experts, it succeeded in surpassing more experienced and more competent models unable to offer such a consistently good package. To sustain consumer interest, it has been rejuvenated and now has a more powerful engine. By maintaining its competitive price, Hyundai should manage to keep on attracting a young and enthusiastic clientele saddled with budget limitations.

MODEL RANGE

The Tiburon sports coupe is sold in two trim levels: a base model and an FX both equipped with a 2.0L engine. The base model's original equipment items include power steering, adjustable mirrors and steering wheel, power windows and a radio with tape deck. The FX gets added power locks, higher-caliber stereo sound system, light alloy wheels, rear spoiler (shark fin?) and rear wiper, rear-wheel disc brakes and fog lamps. Only the FX version can be equipped with the Touring options package, including four-channel ABS, variable assist steering and leather seats.

TECHNICAL FEATURES

The Tiburon is inspired by the Elantra platform. Its style derives from those exhibited based on the various designs for the HCD III concept car that Hyundai took on a world tour. The general public simply loved this car, so the automaker decided to build it. The steel monocoque body has sleek, flowing lines but it only has a fair to midling aerodynamic prowess with a drag coefficient of only 0.33. The four-wheel indepent suspension is made up of MacPherson struts up front and a dual-link setup at the rear along with gas-filled shocks. The base model is equipped with disc and drum brakes, wheras the FX benefits from four-wheel disc brakes, but the antilock braking system is sold as an extra. The 16-valve DOHC Beta engine was developed exclusively by Hyundai engineers. It's equipped with electronic fuel-injection, automatically adjusting hydraulic valve lifters, dual-port fuel injectors and an electronic distributorless ignition system. The 140-hp 2.0L provides all the muscle and torque required. As for the automatic gearbox, it's equipped with a new technological feature called electronic control feedback to improve gear selection.

PROS

+ **STYLING.** It's even more spectacular than it was on the first version. Almost cartoon-like, it copies the aggressive personality characteristic of the Firebird. No driver will go unnoticed behind the wheel of this car — it sends out a loud and clear message. The Tiburon is out to eat up the road and anything foolish enough to get in its way!

+ **DRIVING.** This car zips nimbly around, even with its front-wheel drive, and this is true for both versions. Engine and car response are lively and crisp, so you can take curves with ease and steering responds beautifully in this situation, so handling is taut and clean. The outward view is generous with the thin roof supports, high windshield and frameless windows.

+ **PERFORMANCES.** The 2.0L deserves to be called sporty but with some reservations, since figures obtained for accelerations and pickup are comparable to those of the Elantra. But it provides enough torque to give you a thrill, even with the automatic.

+ **HANDLING.** It's competent because of the well-honed suspension developed in association with Porsche and good-quality original tires.

+ **RIDE COMFORT.** It's pretty amazing for a vehicle of this type. The cabin is roomy up front and front seats provide excellent lateral support and noise interference is quite discreet at cruising speed.

+ **VALUE.** The price/equipment ratio is interesting, especially for the FX that's better and easier to resell as a used car.

+ **CABIN DESIGN.** It's pretty trim and looks a bit like the first Eagle Talon interior with its asymmetrical instrument panel and the white-on-black analog instruments that are easy to read.

+ **CABIN SPACE.** It's average for the category thanks to the longer wheelbase and wide wheel tracks. Yet front seat passengers have more breathing room than the poor folks in the rear seats that should be used only in a pinch, as is always the case on this type of vehicle.

+ **CONVENIENCE FEATURES.** This isn't a usual feature for this type of car, but it hasn't been overlooked since there are lots of handy storage spots here and there throughout the cabin and the modular trunk can hold an adequate amount of luggage.

CONS

- **ERGONOMICS.** The instrument panel isn't too great in this regard, for the main section curves inward rather than outward, so you have to lean forward to reach some controls such as the radio and air conditioning dials, that are in reverse order.

- **REAR SEATS.** They're more suitable for small children than for adults, for leg and head room are too snug and getting aboard is rather dangerous.

- **GLARE.** The instrument panel reflecting up into the windshield and the reflecting glass on the instruments are distracting and tiring on really sunny days.

CONCLUSION

The Tiburon is one of the bestsellers in its class, which is clear proof that a well designed, well built and fun-to-drive model still has its place in a world virtually monopolized by utility vehicles. Sized like a mini-Firebird, it seems to thumb its nose at GM, which never took the time to reevaluate the market - much to its present chagrin.

RATING	
HYUNDAI Tiburon	

CONCEPT :		**64%**
Technology :	80	
Safety :	70	
Interior space :	40	
Trunk volume :	55	
Quality/fit/finish :	75	

DRIVING :		**67%**
Cockpit :	80	
Performance :	60	
Handling :	60	
Steering :	80	
Braking :	55	

ORIGINAL EQUIPMENT :		**76%**
Tires :	80	
Headlights :	75	
Wipers :	75	
Rear defroster :	70	
Radio :	80	

COMFORT :		**73%**
Seats :	80	
Suspension :	70	
Sound level :	60	
Conveniences :	80	
Air conditioning :	75	

BUDGET :		**61%**
Price :	70	
Fuel economy :	75	
Insurance :	55	
Satisfaction :	75	
Depreciation :	30	

Overall rating :		**68.2%**

NEW FOR 2000

- Revamped body design, in a style similar to the Turbulence prototype unveiled at the last Seoul Auto Show.
- Standard 140-hp 2.0L engine on both versions.

Compare Performance, Specifications, Prices, and Classification at the end of this chapter.

EQUIPMENT

HYUNDAI Tiburon	base	FX
Automatic transmission:	O	O
Cruise control:	-	S
Power steering:	S	S
Anti-lock brakes:	-	O
Traction control:	-	-
Air conditioning:	O	O
Leather:	-	O
AM/FM/radio-cassette:	S	S
Power door locks:	-	S
Power windows:	S	S
Tilt steering:	S	S
Dual adjustable mirrors:	SM	SE
Alloy wheels:	O	S
Anti-theft system:	-	-

Colors

Exterior: Silver, Violet, Green, Red, White, Black.

Interior: Black.

AT A GLANCE...

HISTORIC

Introduced in:	1997.
Made in:	Ulsan, South Korea.

DEMOGRAPHICS

Model	Men/Wom.	Age	Married	College	Income $
Tiburon	60/40 %	34	37 %	48 %	30,000

INDEX

Safety:	70 %	Satisfaction:	77 %
Depreciation:	45 %	Insurance:	$ 650
Cost per mile:	$ 0.46	Number of dealers:	500

SALES

	Canada			USA		
Model	1997	1998	Result	1997	1998	Result
Tiburon	1,897	2,187	+ 15.3 %	9,391	8,530	- 9.2 %

MAINTENANCE REQUIRED BY WARRANTY

First revision:	Frequency:	Diagnostic plug:
4,000 miles	3 months / 4,000 miles	Yes

Sports cars - $35,000

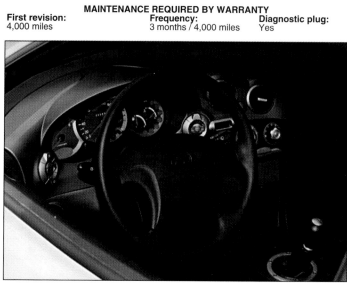

MAZDA

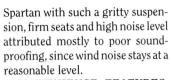

Stallion

Reintroducing the fashion for small roadsters, the Miata has created a genuine automotive industry phenomenon. The advent of a number of similar models has done nothing to hurt its success, mostly because the newcomers are higher priced and not as attractive. Last year's revamping has eliminated some of the problems found on the first version, with no apparent effect on its appeal.

MODEL RANGE

The Miata is a small two-seater roadster motivated by a 1.8L 4-cylinder engine linked to a standard 5-speed manual gearbox or optional 4-speed automatic. Original equipment items include power steering, power mirors, windows and door locks, aluminum rims and a radio receiver and Cd player. The "Leather" options package adds cruise control, Torsen differential, antilock braking system as well as a more sophisticated Bose sound system.

TECHNICAL FEATURES

The steel unibody has been reinforced so it's even sturdier than before. It includes a fully independent suspension, based on the MacPherson strut setup both front and rear, with gas-filled shocks and stabilizer bar for both axles.

Mazda has also improved the dual aluminum rail organization, a sort of subframe linking front and rear power trains that was used so brilliantly on the original model. The car is equipped with disc brakes, but an antilock braking device is still only available as an added option on the base model. The 1.8L DOHC 4-cylinder engine now develops 140 hp, giving an added edge to the weight/power ratio.

OUTSTANDING

++ STYLE. Such a classic body appeals to most people, but, like its predecessor, it lacks a certain make my day flavor. The first version was inspired by the Lotus Elan, but the second looks a lot like the Triumph Spitfire of the seventies.

++ DRIVING PLEASURE. The feeling is out of this world with such a lively, frisky engine, transmission, steering and suspension. You feel like you're melded to the machine. Controls are right where you want them and average-height drivers will find the cockpit made-to-measure.

PROS

+ PERFORMANCES. Accelerations and pickup are noticeably more powerful so you can really let loose with this brawnier engine. Yet it's a pity that a more exotic engine such as the 1.8L V6 that powered the former MX-3 coupe isn't offered with the Leather option package.

+ ROADHOLDING. It's still very competent thanks to a perfect weight distribution (50/50). The Miata takes even tight curves with perfect aplomb, it literally sticks to the road and wheel function is amazingly assured. Yet it's more genteel than it was, due to suspension modifications that makes for smoother travel, but of course, car path remains highly dependable.

+ CONTROLS. The gearbox is a real joy to use; gears are nicely calibrated and changing gears is quick and very precise and the small shifter that you control with a flick of the wrist is downright fun. The same goes for steering that now sports a tidy Momo steering wheel that's really neat. The nifty-design pedals lets you do the famous heel and toe of yore and the logical, ergonomic dashboard is an added plus.

+ CONVERTIBLE TOPS. They're really neat, waterproof and a breeze to install. The soft top can be folded down with one hand and the hard top lets you drive this beauty even in the winter, with the right tires. The hard top is also equipped with an electric defroster and good news for owners, the hard top on the former model fits perfectly on the new model...

+ BRAKES. They're easy to gauge, dig in when needed and are tough soldiers, achiveing trim, stable stops, thanks to effective ABS.

+ NICE FEATURES. The nicer convertible top that now includes a glass window and electric defroster, the wind deflector that does its stuff when the top is down and effective wipers and washers.

CONS

- LIMITED USE. Unless you live in Florida or California, the Miata can only mostly be used in warm weather, so you have to own another car for winter travel.

- RIDE COMFORT. It's downright spartan with such a gritty suspension, firm seats and high noise level attributed mostly to poor sound-proofing, since wind noise stays at a reasonable level.

- CONVENIENCE FEATURES. They're noticeably a cut above when it comes to trunk space, since the spare tire and battery are now lodged inside the trunk floor, but storage spots inside the snug cabin are stingy indeed.

- FUEL CONSUMPTION. It would be more economical if the car weighed less and if it were possible to drive the Miata in a cool, collected manner...

- SAFETY FEATURES. Mazda would have demonstrated a greater sense of responsibility if it had installed a roll bar, even as an extra, integrated into the body design.

- VISIBILITY. It's poor at rear quarterback with both convertible tops, since there are big lateral blind spots and exterior mirrors are too small and set too far back.

- DESIGN DETAILS. The interior is terribly basic and dreary with all that black and trim materials aren't too spiffy, such as the plastic stuff on the door trim that's very chintzy-looking. A bit of imagination wouldn't hurt, would it?

- POOR FEATURES. Weak headlights, ho-hum exhaust noise and poorly located cup-holders.

CONCLUSION

Everyone dreams of the day they'll find enough courage to buy a car of this kind. Just for the fun of it, just to leave everyday worries behind, just to have fun on the road!

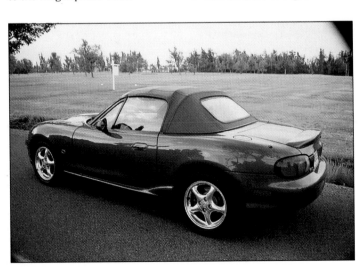

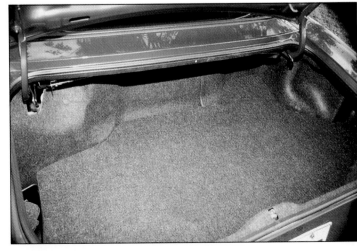

RATING
MAZDA Miata

CONCEPT :		**52%**
Technology :	80	
Safety :	70	
Interior space :	20	
Trunk volume :	10	
Quality/fit/finish :	80	
DRIVING :		**71%**
Cockpit :	80	
Performance :	60	
Handling :	75	
Steering :	80	
Braking :	60	
ORIGINAL EQUIPMENT :		**76%**
Tires :	80	
Headlights :	75	
Wipers :	70	
Rear defroster :	80	
Radio :	75	
COMFORT :		**53%**
Seats :	70	
Suspension :	60	
Sound level :	20	
Conveniences :	40	
Air conditioning :	75	
BUDGET :		**62%**
Price :	50	
Fuel economy :	75	
Insurance :	45	
Satisfaction :	85	
Depreciation :	55	
Overall rating :		**62.8%**

NEW FOR 2000

- Standard power sideview mirrors, windows and locks on all models.
- Withdrawal of the "Evolution Orange Mica" color.
- Pre-cabling for fog lights with the Leather options package.

Compare Performance, Specifications, Prices, and Classification at the end of this chapter.

EQUIPMENT

MAZDA Miata	base	Leather
Automatic transmission:	O	O
Cruise control:	O	S
Power steering:	S	S
Anti-lock brakes:	O	S
Traction control:	-	S
Air conditioning:	O	O
Leather:	O	S
AM/FM/radio-cassette:	SCd	SCd
Power door locks:	S	S
Power windows:	S	S
Tilt steering:	-	-
Dual adjustable mirrors:	SE	SE
Alloy wheels:	S	S
Anti-theft system:	-	-

Colors

Exterior: White, Black, Red, Blue, Silver, Green.

Interior: Cloth: Black. Leather: Tan.

AT A GLANCE...

HISTORIC

Introduced in: 1989.
Made in: Hofu, Japan.

DEMOGRAPHICS

Model	Men/Wom.	Age	Married	College	Income $
Miata	31/69 %	44	25 %	77 %	55,000

INDEX

Safety:	65 %	Satisfaction:	85 %
Depreciation:	40 %	Insurance:	$ 835
Cost per mile:	$ 0.48	Number of dealers:	871

SALES

	Canada			USA		
Model	1997	1998	Result	1997	1998	Result
Miata	594	1,047	+ 76.3 %	17,218	19,843	+ 15.2 %

MAINTENANCE REQUIRED BY WARRANTY

First revision	Frequency:	Diagnostic plug:
5,000 miles	5,000 miles	Yes

Calling...

Allegedly designed to attract a younger clientele group to the showrooms of the venerable Mercury make, all the Cougar has managed to do is draw in potential buyers interested in the former Probe model. It comes as no surprise that this model's sales figures haven't beaten any records, especially at a time when this kind of vehicle is far from the most popular on the market.

MODEL RANGE
The Cougar is a 3-door coupe. Its style is inspired by the "Edge Design" approach that blends curves and tight, sleek lines. The Cougar borrows the Contour/Mystique sedans' engines: the 2.0L DOHC Zetec 4-cylinder and 2.5L DOHC Duratec V6. The first comes with a 5-speed manual gearbox only, while the second can be linked up to an optional 4-speed automatic. Standard equipment includes, among other items, climate control, a remote powered rear door opener, 15-inch rims and anti-theft cut-off switch and alarm. The Cougar V6 model's equipment is a cut above — it includes items such as chrome tailpipe extensions.

TECHNICAL FEATURES
The Cougar is a direct spin-off of the Contour/Mystique/Mondeo platform but wheelbase and wheel track design are a bit different. Yet it shares almost 70% of the three sedans' components. Besides, the Cougar chassis is now 20% more rigid than that of the Contour! Its steel body is mounted on a unitized frame and yields an average drag coefficient of 0.32. The fully independent suspension is mounted on subframes via rubber insulator joints. Up front, it uses MacPherson struts, whereas the rear axles are suspended on four control arms. There are anti-roll bars both front and rear. Both models are equipped with disc and drum brakes. Disc brakes are available, but only as an extra, as are ABS and traction control.

PROS
+ LOOKS. This modern, daring coupe design is really different from typically easy-going, cushy Mercury products, usually geared to a more seasoned clientele. You can't not notice this car, it's both bold and beauteous, but younger folk like it more than sensible drivers. Exactly what Mercury had in mind...

+ REAR DOOR. It's light and doesn't lift too high up. It has a neat handle, so it's easy to close shut. There's also a removable luggage-covering shelf.

+ CONVENIENCE FEATURES. This is a sports car, but it's also versatile thanks to its modular trunk, since the 50/50 split-fold rear that can be lowered as needed.

+ RIDE COMFORT. Front seats are beautifully sculpted and they offer wonderful lateral and lumbar support. Front seat passengers have loads of leg room and the driver even has a footrest. Simply super!

+ HANDLING. Derived from the European Mondeo, the suspension is a great compromise between comfort and roadholding, so you can hit lateral speeds worthy of the most speedy and expensive cars out there. But on our test model, the front end was unstable and dealing with torque was a bit tricky on wet surfaces.

+ EXHAUST SYSTEM. Not all noise is unpleasant. For example, the Cougar's exhaust has a gutsy growl and you don't mind at all, but it's too bad performances aren't as impressive as all this sound and fury...

CONS
- STYLE. It's pretty unique, but it's overdone both inside and out and will tend to go out of fashion in no time. Some accessories are just gadgets, really, and seem a bit silly.

- PERFORMANCES. They're disappointing, compared to those of the former Ford Probe that was a heck of a lot more fun to drive. The 4-cylinder engine puts out more power, when motivated along, more so than the V6 that's a bore in comparison.

- STEERING. It's quite quick and nicely powered, but it just isn't crisp and clean enough when you feel like heading in another direction.

- EQUIPMENT. This sports coupe, bearing the muscular Mercury crest, can't really boast of rich equipment, since four-wheel disc brakes, rear wiper, cruise control and 16-inch tires mounted on alloy rims are all extras, each and every one.

- NOISE. With a rear hatch door, noise is always more pervasive than in a two or four-door vehicle. Our sound-level meter recorded noise levels inside the Cougar that were the highest among all cars we tested this year!

- REAR SEATS. Automakers say that rear seats on a coupe are never used. In that case, why install such minuscule seats, when a big trunk would be just as useful?

- VISIBILITY. With such a sharp, angular body design that requires a rather high rear end, backing up is tricky due to reduced rear outward view.

- STEERING WHEEL. You have a good grip, but it's so ridiculously huge and jars with the modern interior design. The Momo steering wheel installed as standard equipment on the latest Miata is proof that designers can come up with a nice blend of practical elegance and safety features, since it holds a latest-generation airbag as well.

- OPENING THE TRUNK. The remote control for the rear door opener is located in a rather strange spot, that is at floor level, near the hood lid switch. Why not have installed it inside the door instead, or on the instrument panel, where it would be more within reach?

- ACCESS. The convertible trunk is huge, but the opening is so bloody high that you could end up with a sore back from loading or unloading heavy luggage!

CONCLUSION
Although it may not have come along at the ideal time, to its credit the Cougar has the kind of styling that attracts attention. Unfortunately, its mechanical components fail to live up to the expectations of young buyers.

RATING
MERCURY Cougar

CONCEPT : 66%
Technology : 80
Safety : 80
Interior space : 35
Trunk volume : 60
Quality/fit/finish : 75

DRIVING : 64%
Cockpit : 75
Performance : 45
Handling : 65
Steering : 75
Braking : 60

ORIGINAL EQUIPMENT : 75%
Tires : 75
Headlights : 75
Wipers : 65
Rear defroster : 80
Radio : 80

COMFORT : 64%
Seats : 75
Suspension : 75
Sound level : 30
Conveniences : 60
Air conditioning : 80

BUDGET : 60%
Price : 70
Fuel economy : 70
Insurance : 60
Satisfaction : 50
Depreciation : 50

Overall rating : 65.8%

NEW FOR 2000
- A center console with two cupholders.
- Standard cigarette lighter.

Compare Performance, Specifications, Prices, and Classification at the end of this chapter.

EQUIPMENT

MERCURY Cougar	I-4	V-6
Automatic transmission:	-	O
Cruise control:	O	O
Power steering:	S	S
Anti-lock brakes:	O	O
Traction control:	-	O
Air conditioning:	SM	SM
Leather:	-	-
AM/FM/radio-cassette:	S	S
Power door locks:	S	S
Power windows:	S	S
Tilt steering:	S	S
Dual adjustable mirrors:	SEH	SEH
Alloy wheels:	S	S
Anti-theft system:	S	S

Colors
Exterior: Orange, Gold, Red, Green, Blue, Silver, Black, White.
Interior: Silk, Black, Brown.

AT A GLANCE...

HISTORIC
Introduced in: 1999.
Made in: Flat Rock, Michigan, USA.

DEMOGRAPHICS
Model	Men/Wom.	Age	Married	College	Income $
Cougar	58/42 %	36	26 %	69 %	45,000

INDEX
Safety: 80 % Satisfaction: 78 %
Depreciation: NA % Insurance: $ 565-675
Cost per mile: $ 0.46 Number of dealers: 5,200

SALES
Model	Canada 1997	1998	Result	USA 1997	1998	Result
Cougar	705	2,264	+ 221.1 %	30,516	38,216	+ 25.2 %

MAINTENANCE REQUIRED BY WARRANTY
First revision: 5,000 miles
Frequency: 6 months
Diagnostic plug: Yes

Sports cars - $35,000

TOYOTA

Celica

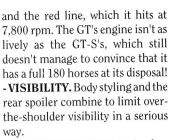

A Rogue

Usually, when a vehicle is revamped it's often bigger and heavier than the one it replaces. When it reinvented the Celica, Toyota showed an original approach and the newcomer is shorter and lighter than its predecessor. Considering the not very encouraging sales figures recorded for the Celica last year, the revision process could be considered as an act of faith on the part of Japan's leading automobile manufacturer.

MODEL RANGE

The latest Celica coupe is available in GT and GT-S versions, both powered by a 1.8L 4-cylinder engine derived from the Corolla's unit and equipped with a variable valve timing system. The standard transmission is a 5-speed (GT) or 4-speed (GT-S) manual or an optional automatic (with shifting controlled via steering wheel-mounted buttons on the GT-S). The GT model's standard equipment includes power steering, air conditioning, a radio and Cd player, ABS brakes, power locks, power windows and power sideview mirrors and alloy wheels. The GT-S adds ABS brakes, fog lights, cruise control, a more elaborate system with a windshield integrated antenna, a leather-wrapped steering wheel, a sunroof and a rear spoiler. Options include a theft deterrent system, an automatic transmission, leather trims and remote keyless entry.

TECHNICAL FEATURES

The Celica coupe has a steel unibody and offers good resistance to torsion and flexion. The fully independent suspension features MacPherson struts in the front and double arms and anti-roll bars in the rear. On the GT-S, standard equipment includes rack-and-pinion steering and four disc brakes with ABS.

PROS

+ STYLING. The Celica's lines are similar to those of the Mercury Cougar, but scaled down. The mix of rounded and elongated styling results in a rather exciting sculptural look. Head- and taillights are original and the overall effect is eye-catching without looking copied.

+ SIZING. More compact that the previous model, the Celica is easy to handle and its strong lines give it a dynamic personality that spells its charm.

+ DRIVEABILITY. It's enhanced by a steering wheel with a good grip, a responsive and precise steering system that keeps the Celica exactly on track and provides excellent feedback on road conditions, a light clutch pedal and precise shifting.

+ HANDLING. In spite of its front-wheel drive, the Celica is fun to use and very agile on winding roads, where its behavior is sure and predictable.

+ BRAKING. Power is easy to gauge, reliable and well-balanced. However, stopping distances could be shorter on a car described as a sports model and some wagons show more stopping efficiency.

+ COCKPIT. The driving position is good and visibility is satisfactory — the dashboard is airy, functional, ergonomic and attractive.

+ FUEL ECONOMY. Under normal circumstances with the 1.8L engine it stands at 24 mpg, which gives the Celica a cruising range of 300 miles.

+ COMFORT. Although firm the suspension capitalizes on a long wheelbase and sufficient travel and on most roads, never reacts brutally. Front seats fit like a glove and the noise level is reasonable at cruising speeds. The engine is louder as it climbs into the upper rpm range, which is perfectly normal for this type of vehicle.

+ PRACTICALITY. This sport coupe has a number of storage spaces and a reasonably sized trunk — split fold down seats provide extra cargo space when needed.

+ BONUS POINTS. For the chime that warns the driver that the vehicle is in reverse, preventing a number of false moves.

CONS

- PRICE. It costs a lot to experience the joys of driving a sports car and this phenomenon isn't peculiar to the Celica, whose price for the GT-S version is comparable to the price for a Cougar V6 or a Camaro Z28.

- PERFORMANCE. Like most modern engines, the 1.8L lacks torque in the lower rpm range and shows its power only between 4,000 rpm and the red line, which it hits at 7,800 rpm. The GT's engine isn't as lively as the GT-S's, which still doesn't manage to convince that it has a full 180 horses at its disposal!

- VISIBILITY. Body styling and the rear spoiler combine to limit over-the-shoulder visibility in a serious way.

- PASSENGER ROOM. As is often the case on this kind of vehicle, rear seats are cramped and with very limited headroom, are suited only for small children. The high belt line limits visibility and to make things even worse, the windows don't roll down all the way.

- EXHAUST. It's too quiet to be very impressive. Though it remained within legal limits, the previous model's system was more expressive.

- BAD MARKS. For a pedal design that hinders smooth heel-toe movement. For instruments with orange-colored displays that are hard to read. For adjustable front seats with no memory function and the fact that only the right-hand backrest can be moved forward to facilitate rear-seat access.

CONCLUSION

The new Celica is a welcome addition to the Toyota lineup, which had begun to show a serious lack of vehicles designed to be fun to drive. It's every bit as practical as it is economical, more than reason enough to explain its acquisition.

RATING TOYOTA Celica		
CONCEPT :		**64%**
Technology :	80	
Safety :	90	
Interior space :	30	
Trunk volume :	40	
Quality/fit/finish :	80	
DRIVING :		**73%**
Cockpit :	80	
Performance :	65	
Handling :	70	
Steering :	80	
Braking :	70	
ORIGINAL EQUIPMENT :		**75%**
Tires :	80	
Headlights :	80	
Wipers :	65	
Rear defroster :	75	
Radio :	80	
COMFORT :		**71%**
Seats :	80	
Suspension :	70	
Sound level :	50	
Conveniences :	75	
Air conditioning :	80	
BUDGET :		**61%**
Price :	35	
Fuel economy :	75	
Insurance :	50	
Satisfaction :	90	
Depreciation :	55	
Overall rating :		**68.8%**

New 2000 Model

NEW FOR 2000

• New model available in GT and GT-S versions equipped with a 1.8L engine derived from the Corolla's engine.

Compare Performance, Specifications, Prices, and Classification at the end of this chapter.

EQUIPMENT

TOYOTA Celica	GT	GT-S
Automatic transmission:	O	O
Cruise control:	O	S
Power steering:	S	S
Anti-lock brakes:	S	S
Traction control:	-	-
Air conditioning:	S	S
Leather:	-	O
AM/FM/radio-cassette:	SCd	SCd
Power door locks:	S	S
Power windows:	S	S
Tilt steering:	S	S
Dual adjustable mirrors:	SE	SE
Alloy wheels:	S	S
Anti-theft system:	O	O

Colors

Exterior: Blue, Black, Red, Silver, White.

Interior: Red, Blue, Amethyst.

AT A GLANCE...

HISTORIC

Introduced in:	1971, 1994, 2000.
Made in:	Tahara, Japan.

DEMOGRAPHICS

Model	Men/Wom.	Age	Married	College	Income $
Celica	38/62 %	45	44 %	62 %	115,000

INDEX

Safety:	80 %	Satisfaction:	88 %
Depreciation:	50 %	Insurance:	$ 735
Cost per mile:	$ 0.48	Number of dealers:	1 233

SALES

	Canada			USA		
Model	1997	1998	Result	1997	1998	Result
Celica	70	40	- 42.9 %	9,021	4,290	- 52.4 %

MAINTENANCE REQUIRED BY WARRANTY

First revision:	Frequency:	Diagnostic plug:
3,000 miles	3,000 miles	Yes

Sport - $35,000

SPORTS CARS under $ 35,000
PERFORMANCE

Model/ version	Type / timing valve / fuel system	Displacement cu in	Power hp @ rpm	Torque lb-ft @ rpm	Compres. ratio	Driving wheels / transmission	Final ratio	Acceler. 0-60 mph s	Standing 1/4 & 5/8 mile s		Passing 50-75 mph s	Braking 60-0 mph ft	Top speed mph	Lateral acceler. G	Noise level dBA	Fuel economy mpg City	Highway	Fuel type Octane
ACURA Integra																		
LS, GS	L4 1.8 DOHC-16-MPFI	112	139 @ 6300	122 @ 5200	9.2 :1	front - M5*	4.27	8.5	17.2	29.7	6.4	134	124	0.82	68	25	31	R 87
						front - A4	4.36	9.2	18.0	30.5	6.9	148	116	0.82	68	24	31	R 87
GS-R	L4 1.8 DOHC-16-MPFI	109	170 @ 7600	128 @ 6200	10.0 :1	front - M5	4.40	7.5	16.8	29.0	5.2	131	131	0.85	67	25	30	S 91
Type R	L4 1.8 DOHC-16-MPFI	109	195 @ 8000	130 @ 7500	10.6 :1	front - M5	4.40	6.7	16.2	28.5	4.8	134	137	0.90	70	24	31	S 91
CHEVROLET Camaro																		
base L36	V6* 3.8 OHV-12-SFI	231	200 @ 5200	225 @ 4000	9.4 :1	rear - M5*	3.23	8.6	15.8	29.7	6.2	131	115	0.85	68	20	33	R 87
						rear - A4	3.08	9.4	17.0	30.8	6.7	138	112	0.85	68	20	32	R 87
Z28 LS1	V8* 5.7 OHV-16-SFI	346	305 @ 5200	335 @ 4000	10.1 :1	rear - M6	3.42	5.3	14.0	25.4	3.7	125	143	0.87	72	17	29	S 91
						rear - A4*	2.73	5.8	14.5	26.0	4.0	131	137	0.87	72	17	26	S 91
Z28 SS	V8 5.7 OHV-16-SFI	346	320 @ 5200	340 @ 4400	10.1 :1	rear -M6	3.42	5.2	13.8	25.2	3.6	125	149	0.88	72	16	26	S 91
CHRYSLER Sebring - DODGE Avenger																		
base coupe	L4*2.0 DOHC-16-MPSFI	122	140 @ 6000	130 @ 4800	9.6 : 1	front - M5*	3.94	10.0	18.0	31.7	8.5	141	103	0.76	69	21	34	R 87
						front - A4	3.91	11.3	18.6	32.8	8.5	134	100	0.76	70	20	31	R 87
base conv.	L4*2.4 DOHC-16-MPSFI	148	150 @ 5200	167 @ 4000	9.4 : 1	front - A4	3.91	10.2	17.8	31.6	7.5	141	106	0.78	69	20	32	R 87
option	V6 2.5 SOHC-24-MPSFI	152156/163 @ 5000		170 @ 4400	9.0 : 1	front - A4	3.91	9.8	17.3	31.4	7.0	148	109	0.78	68	18	29	R 87
FORD Mustang																		
base	V6 3.8 OHV-12-SFI	232	190 @ 5250	220 @ 2750	9.36 :1	rear - M5*	3.27	7.8	16.2	28.8	6.3	131	106	0.80	67	19	31	R 87
						rear - A4	3.27	8.6	17.0	30.2	6.7	137	103	0.80	67	18	30	R 87
GT	V8 4.6 SOHC-16-SFI	281	260 @ 5250	302 @ 4000	9.1 :1	rea r- M5*	3.27	6.4	14.8	26.8	4.8	125	136	0.85	68	16	27	R 87
						rear - A4	3.27	7.2	15.2	27.5	5.6	131	132	0.85	68	16	26	R 87
Cobra	V8 4.6 DOHC-32-SEFI	281	320 @ 6000	317 @ 4750	9.85 :1	rear - M5	3.27	5.6	13.8			127	150	0.90				S 91
HONDA Prelude																		
base	L4* 2.2 DOHC-16-MPFI	131	195 @ 6600	156 @ 5250	10.0 :1	front - M5*	4.226	6.9	15.2	26.5	5.2	138	137	0.81	70	21	27	S 91
SH	L4* 2.2 DOHC-16-MPFI	131	200 @ 7000	156 @ 5250	10.0 :1	front - M5	4.226	7.1	15.1	26.0	5.1	138	137	0.81	70	20	26	S 91
						front - A4	4.785	8.5	16.6	29.5	6.0	134	131	0.81	70	20	29	S 91
HYUNDAI Tiburon																		
base	L4*2.0 DOHC-16-MPFI	121	140 @ 6000	133 @ 4800	10.3 :1	front - M5*	3.84	8.4	16.0	29.5	6.3	138	115	0.80	66-70	21	31	R 87
						front - A4	4.35	9.1	16.7	30.6	6.7	144	112	0.80	66-70	20	30	R 87
MAZDA Miata																		
base	L4* 1.8 DOHC-16-IEPM	112	140 @ 6500	119 @ 5000	9.5 :1	rear - M5*	4.30	7.8	16.1	28.4	5.8	144	124	0.88	72-78	21	31	R 87
						rear - A4	4.10	9.1	17.2	30.7	6.5	151	115	0.88	72-78	21	31	S 91
MERCURY Cougar																		
I-4	L4* 2.0 DOHC-16-MPSFI	122	125 @ 5500	130 @ 4000	9.6 :1	front - M5	3.82	10.5	17.8	32.0	7.4	131	109	0.80	67	24	28	R 87
V-6	V6 2.5 DOHC-24-MPSFI	155	170 @ 6250	165 @ 4250	9.7 :1	front - M5*	4.06	8.6	16.7	30.5	6.6	134	115	0.82	67	19	29	R 87
						front - A4	3.77	10.0	17.5	32.0	7.2	128	112	0.82	68	20	32	R 87
PONTIAC Firebird																		
base	V6* 3.8 OHV-12-SFI	231	200 @ 5200	225 @ 4000	9.4 :1	rear - M5*	3.23	8.6	15.8	29.7	6.2	131	115	0.85	68	18	31	R 87
						rear - A4	3.08	9.4	17.0	30.8	6.7	138	112	0.85	68	18	29	R 87
For./TA	V8* 5.7 OHV-16-SFI	346	305 @ 5200	335 @ 4000	10.1 :1	rear - M6	3.42	5.3	14.0	25.4	3.8	125	149	0.87	72	15	27	S 91
						rear - A4*	2.73	5.8	14.5	26.0	4.0	131	137	0.87	72	16	25	S 91
option	V8 5.7 OHV-16-SFI	346	320 @ 5200	345 @ 4400	10.1 :1	rear -M6	3.42	5.0	13.8	25.2	3.6	125	143	0.88	72	15	25	S 91
TOYOTA Celica																		
GT	L4 1.8-DOHC-16-MPSFI	108	140 @ 6400	125 @ 4200	10.0 :1	front - M5*	-									26	37	R 87
						front - A4	-									26	41	R 87
GT-S	L4 1.8-DOHC-16-MPSFI	108	180 @ 7600	130 @ 6800	11.5 :1	front - M6*	-	7.4	15.8	26.7	5.6	138	124	0.85	67-72	23	35	R 87
						front - A4	-									24	33	R 87

Sports cars - $35,000

SPORTS CARS under $ 35,000
SPECIFICATIONS

Model	Version Trim	Body/ Seats	Cabin volume cu ft	Trunk volume cu ft	Cd	Wheel base in	Lgth x Width x Hght in x inx in	Curb weight lb	Susp. ft/rr	Brake ft/rr	type	Steering ø turns ft number	Fuel tank gal	dimensions	Standard tires make	model	Standard powertrain	99 Price msrp $
ACURA		General warranty: 4 years / 50 000 miles: powertrain: 5 years / 60 000 miles; surface rust: 5 years/ unlimited.																
Integra	LS	3dr.cpe.4	77.1	13.3	0.32	101.1	172.4x67.3x52.6	2528	ih/ih	dc/dc	pwr.r&p.	34.8 2.98	13.2	195/60R14	Yokohama	Y-376	L4/1.8/M5	19,655
Integra	GS	3dr.cpe.4	76.2	13.3	0.32	101.1	172.4x67.3x52.6	2639	ih/ih	dc/ABS	pwr.r&p.	34.8 2.98	13.2	195/55R15	Michelin	XGT-V4	L4/1.8/M5	21,305
Integra	GS-R	3dr.cpe.4	76.2	13.3	0.32	101.1	172.4x67.3x52.6	2667	ih/ih	dc/ABS	pwr.r&p.	34.8 2.98	13.2	195/55R15	Michelin	XGT-V4	L4/1.8/M5	21,305
Integra	Type R	3dr.cpe..4	77.1	13.3	0.32	101.2	172.4x66.7x51.9	2583	ih/ih	dc/ABS	pwr.r&p.	34.8 2.98	13.2	195/55R15	Bridgestone	RE010	L4/1.8/M5	22,555
CHEVROLET		General warranty: 3 years / 36 000 miles; antipollution: 5 years / 50 000 miles; perforation corrosion: 6 years / 100 000 miles. Road assistance.																
Camaro	base	2dr.cpe. 2+2	82.1	12.9	0.32	101.1	193.5x74.1x51.3	3306	ih/rh	dc/ABS	pwr.r&p.	40.7 2.67	16.8	215/60R16	BF Goodrich	T/A	V6/3.8/M5	17,240
	base	2dr.con. 2+2	80.8	7.6	0.36	101.1	193.5x74.1x51.8	3500	ih/rh	dc/ABS	pwr.r&p.	40.7 2.67	16.8	215/60R16	BF Goodrich	T/A	V6/3.8/M5	22,740
	Z28- SS	2dr.cpe.2+2	82.1	12.9	0.32	101.1	193.5x74.1x51.3	3439	ih/rh	dc/ABS	pwr.r&p.	40.1 2.28	16.8	235/55R16	Goodyear	Eagle GS-C	V8/5.7/A4	21,485
	Z28	2dr.con. 2+2	80.8	7.6	0.36	101.1	193.5x74.1x51.8	3575	ih/rh	dc/ABS	pwr.r&p.	40.1 2.28	16.8	235/55R16	Goodyear	Eagle GS-C	V8/5.7/A4	28,465
CHRYSLER		General warranty: 3 years / 36 000 miles; surface rust: 3 years; perforation: 7 years / 100 000 miles; roadside assistance: 3 years /36 000 miles.																
Sebring	LX	2dr.cpe. 4	91.1	13.1	0.32	103.7	190.9x69.7x53.0	3154	ih/ih	dc/dr	pwr.r&p.	39.4 2.4	15.9	205/55R16	Michelin	XW4	L4/2.0/M5	17,875
Sebring	LXi	2dr.cpe. 4	91.1	13.1	0.32	103.7	190.9x69.7x53.0	3203	ih/ih	dc/dc	pwr.r&p.	40.7 2.35	15.9	215/50R17	Goodyear	Eagle GT	V6/2.5/A4	21,975
Sebring	JX	2dr.con. 4	89.1	11.3	0.36	106.0	192.6x70.1x54.8	3439	ih/ih	dc/dr	pwr.r&p.	40.0 2.8	15.9	205/65R15	Michelin	MX4	L4/2.4/A4	24,505
Sebring	JXi	2dr.con. 4	89.1	11.3	0.36	106.0	192.6x70.1x54.8	3443	ih/ih	dc/ABS	pwr.r&p.	40.0 2.8	15.9	215/55R16	Michelin	XGT4	V6/2.5/A4	24,820
DODGE		General warranty: 3 years / 36 000 miles; surface rust: 3 years; perforation: 7 years / 100 000 miles; roadside assistance: 3 years /36 000 miles.																
Avenger	base	2dr.cpe. 4	91.1	13.1	0.32	103.7	190.2x69.1x53.0	3137	ih/ih	dc/dr	pwr.r&p.	39.4 2.4	15.9	205/55R16	Michelin	XW4	L4/2.0/M5	16,120
	ES	2dr.cpe. 4	91.1	13.1	0.32	103.7	190.2x69.1x53.0	3172	ih/ih	dc/dc	pwr.r&p.	40.7 2.4	15.9	215/50R17	Goodyear	Eagle GT	L4/2.0/M5	18,395
FORD		General warranty, antipollution & battery: 3 years / 36 000 miles; corrosion perforation: 5 years / unlimited.																
Mustang	base	2dr.cpe.4	93.9	10.9	0.33	101.3	183.2x73.1x53.1	3069	ih/rh	dc/dc	pwr.r&p.	37.0 2.38	15.7	205/65R15	Goodyear	Eagle GA	V6/3.8/M5	16,995
Mustang	base	2dr.con.4	83.0	7.7	0.38	101.3	183.2x73.1x53.2	3210	ih/rh	dc/dc	pwr.r&p.	37.0 2.38	15.7	205/65R15	Goodyear	Eagle GA	V6/3.8/M5	21,690
Mustang	GT	2dr.cpe.4	93.9	10.9	0.36	101.3	183.2x73.1x53.3	3274	ih/rh	dc/ABS	pwr.r&p.	38.0 2.38	15.7	225/55R16	BF.Goodrich	-	V8/4.6/M5	21,400
Mustang	GT	2dr.con.4	83.0	7.7	0.38	101.3	183.2x73.1x53.3	3428	ih/rh	dc/ABS	pwr.r&p.	38.0 2.38	15.7	225/55R16	BF.Goodrich	-	V8/4.6/M5	25,490
Mustang	Cobra	2dr.cpe.4	83.0	7.7	0.38	101.3	183.5x73.1x53.2	3430	ih/rh	dc/ABS		37.9 2.5	15.7	245/45ZR17	BF.Goodrich	Comp T/A	V8/4.8/M5	-
			93.9	10.9	0.38	101.3	183.5x73.1x53.5	3565	ih/ih	dc/ABS		37.9 2.5	15.7					-
HONDA		General warranty: 3 years / 36 000 miles; powertrain: 5 years / 60 000 miles.																
Prelude	base	2dr.cpe. 4	78.3	8.7	NA	101.8	178.0x68.9x51.8	2954	ih/ih	dc/ABS	pwr.r&p.	36.1 2.8	15.9	205/50R16	Bridgestone	Potenza R 92	L4/2.2/M5	25,865
Prelude	Type SH	2dr.cpe. 4	78.3	8.7	NA	101.8	178.0x68.9x51.8	3042	ih/ih	dc/ABS	pwr.r&p.	37.4 2.7	15.9	205/50R16	Bridgestone	Potenza R 92	L4/2.2/M5	26,365
HYUNDAI		General warranty: 3years / 36 000 miles; powertrain: 5 years / 60 000 miles; corrosion perforation: 5 years / 60 000 miles; antipollution: 5 years / 36 000 miles.																
Tiburon	base	2dr.cpe. 2+2	80.0	12.8	0.33	97.4	170.9x68.1x51.3	2535	ih/ih	dc/dr	pwr.r&p.	34.1 2.8	14.5	195/60R14	Michelin	XGTV4	L4/2.0/M5	14,434
Tiburon	FX	2dr.cpe. 2+2	80.0	12.8	0.33	97.4	170.9x68.1x51.3	2586	ih/ih	dc/dc	pwr.r&p.	34.1 2.8	14.5	195/55R15	Michelin	XGTV4	L4/2.0/M5	15,734
MAZDA		General warranty: 3 years / 50 000 miles; powertrain: 5 years / 100 000 miles; corrosion: 5 years / unlimited.																
Miata	base	2dr.con.2	NA	15.1	0.37	89.2	155.3x66.0x48.4	2308	ih/ih	dc/dc	pwr.r&p.	30.2 2.7	12.7	185/60R14	Toyo	R22	L4/1.8/M5	20,545
Miata	leather	2dr.con.2	NA	15.1	0.37	89.2	155.3x66.0x48.4	2319	ih/ih	dc/ABS	pwr.r&p.	30.2 2.7	12.7	195/50R15	Michelin	Pilot SX	L4/1.8/M5	27,325
MERCURY		General warranty, antipollution & battery: 3 years / 36 000 miles; corrosion perforation: 5 years / unlimited.																
Cougar	I-4	3dr.cpe.2+2	84.2	14.5	0.32	106.4	185.0x69.6x52.2	2892	ih/ih	dc/dr	pwr.r&p.	37.0 3.28	15.5	205/60R15	Firestone	Firehawk GTA	L4/2.0/M5	16,790
Cougar	V-6	3dr.cpe.2+2	84.2	14.5	0.32	106.4	185.0x69.6x52.2	3005	ih/ih	dc/dr	pwr.r&p.	37.0 3.28	15.5	205/60R15	Firestone	Firehawk GTA	V6/2.5/M5	17,295
PONTIAC		General warranty: 3 years / 36 000 miles; antipollution: 5 years / 50 000 miles; perforation corrosion: 6 years / 100 000 miles. Roadside assistance.																
Firebird	base	2dr.cpe. 2+2	84.0	12.9	0.32	101.1	193.3x74.4x51.2	3322	ih/rh	dc/ABS	pwr.r&p.L	37.92.67	16.8	215/60R16	BFGoodrich	Comp T/A	V6/3.8/M5	18,785
Firebird	base	2dr.con. 2+2	80.6	7.6	0.36	101.1	193.3x74.4x51.8	3402	ih/rh	dc/ABS	pwr.r&p.R	40.62.67	16.8	215/60R16	BFGoodrich	Comp T/A	V6/3.8/M5	25,405
Firebird	Formula	2dr.cpe. 2+2	84.0	12.9	0.32	101.1	193.3x74.4x51.2	3340	ih/rh	dc/ABS	pwr.r&p.L	37.82.28	16.8	245/50ZR16	Goodyear	Eagle GS-D	V8/5.7/A4	23,685
Firebird	Trans Am	2dr.cpe. 2+2	84.0	12.9	0.32	101.1	193.7x74.4x51.8	3397	ih/rh	dc/ABS	pwr.r&p.	- 2.28	16.8	245/50ZR16	Goodyear	Eagle GS-D	V8/5.7/A4	26,795
Firebird	Trans Am	2dr.con. 2+2	80.6	7.6	0.36	101.1	193.7x74.4x51.8	3514	ih/rh	dc/ABS	pwr.r&p.R	40.12.28	16.8	245/50ZR16	Goodyear	Eagle GS-D	V8/5.7/A4	30,865
TOYOTA		General warranty: 3 years / 36 000 miles; powertrain 5 years / 60 000 miles; corrosion, perforation: 5 years / unlimited.																
Celica	GT	cpe.3 p.2+2	NA	NA	NA	102.4	170.4x68.3x51.4	2425	ih/ih	d/ABS	pwr.r&p.	NA NA	14.5	195/60R15	-	-	L4/1.8/M5	-
Celica	GT-S	cpe.3 p.2+2	NA	NA	NA	102.4	170.4x68.3x51.4	2500	ih/ih	d/ABS	pwr.r&p.	NA NA	14.5	205/55R16	Yokohama	AD VAN	L4/1.8/M6	34 825

Notes: 1) Tire makes and models are provided solely as an indication; they are subject to change without prior notice from the automobile manufacturers.
2) See the 2000 price list at the back of this edition.

Sports cars - $35,000

SPORT CARS under $ 35,000
CLASSIFICATION

		OUR CLASSIFICATION							YOUR CLASSIFICATION	
Rank	Models	Concept	Driving	Equipment	Comfort	Budget	Ratings	Rank	Models	98 Sales
1	**TOYOTA Celica**	64	73	75	71	61	**68.8 %**	1	**FORD Mustang**	144,732
2	ACURA Integra	64	70	74	71	64	68.6 %	2	CHRYSLER FG (cpe.)	51,342
2	HONDA Prelude	61	72	75	**76**	59	68.6 %	3	CHEVROLET Camaro	47,577
3	HYUNDAI Tiburon	64	67	76	73	61	68.2 %	4	MERCURY Cougar	38,216
4	CHRYSLER Sebring &							5	ACURA Integra	34,904
4	DODGE Avenger	**71**	60	69	68	**68**	67.2 %	6	CHRYSLER FG (con.)	33,584
5	FORD Mustang	61	**76**	73	65	57	66.4 %	7	PONTIAC Firebird	31,692
6	MERCURY Cougar	66	64	75	64	60	65.8 %	8	DODGE Avenger	24,084
7	CHEVROLET Camaro &							9	MAZDA Miata	19,843
7	PONTIAC Firebird	62	70	**78**	58	50	63.6 %	10	HONDA Prelude	15,399
8	MAZDA Miata	52	71	76	53	62	62.8 %	11	HYUNDAI Tiburon	8,530
								12	TOYOTA Celica	4,290

NOTES

Sport
$35,000

AUDI TT

BMW Z3

CHEVROLETCorvette

DODGE Viper

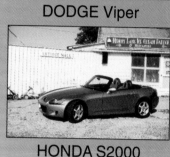

HONDA S2000

JAGUAR XK8

MERCEDES-BENZ CLK

MERCEDES-BENZ SLK

Comparative Test

SPORTS CARS
from 35 to $ 70,000

**See their performance, their specifications, their price
and their classification at the end of this chapter.**

VOLVO C70

PORSCHE Boxster-911

PLYMOUTH Prowler

Image Driven

An exceptional phenomenon in the automotive industry, Audi's TT roadster all but entered standard production exactly as it was conceived by stylists who designed it three years before. This proves how extraordinarily well targeted the prototype project really was and how strongly it captured the imagination of consumers when it was officially launched. It also proves that the Volkswagen group is ready and willing to take on market niches based mostly on a strong image.

MODEL RANGE

The TT coupe will first be imported in the USA with a FWD or quattro AWD animated by a 1.8L turbocharged engine developing 180 hp, mated to a 5-speed manual transmission. In Canada only the quattro will be available with the same engine. The convertible version will only be introduced on the market afterwards. It's a 2+2 coupe whose original equipment includes most of the current creature comforts such as automatic climate control, major power accessories and an 80-Watt radio and tape deck. For now, no automatic transmission is in the works, but Audi offers option packages like the performance package including Xenon headlamps and 17-inch wheels equipped with summer tires, the comfort package with heated seats and six-function onboard computer as well as the audio package consisting of a Bose sound system and 6-CD changer.

TECHNICAL FEATURES

Due to production costs, the TT's body is made entirely of steel that's galvanized on both sides, but the hood is made of aluminum. In spite of the big tires, large orifices and wide frontal surface, the maximum drag coefficient varies between 0.34 and 0.35. The front suspension is a MacPherson strut setup with A-arms mounted on an independent cradle. The FWD version has a rear tubular torsion axle, while the quattro rear suspension consists of dual transversal A-arms and a longitudinal trailing arm with gas-filled shocks and anti-roll bar in all cases. Diagonal double-circuit brakes are vented discs up font and full discs at the rear with a standard antilock braking-traction control device (FWD) with electronic power divider of pressure applied. Four-wheel disc brakes are paired up with an ABS 5.3 system including electronic control of pressure on rear wheels.

PROS

+ **STYLE.** It's been a long time since we've seen such a gorgeous model. It's startling at first, but you get used to the bulky, but graceful shape of this speedster that looks solid as a rock.

+ **SAFETY.** The TT coupe benefits from an extremely stiff body, so passengers can be assured good protection in the event of a collision, but it's also equipped with front and side-impact airbags.

+ **HANDLING.** The quattro version is the most impressive. It seems to be literally glued to the road without any maneuvers or adjustments.

+ **BRAKES.** They're easy to adjust, grip just when and how you want and they do so smoothly and progressively. We weren't able to take exact measurements, but "hard" stops were achieved quite quickly and linings hold up well on very serpentine stretches.

+ **RIDE COMFORT.** Even when the road surface goes awry, the TT is never actually uncomfortable, as is the case for scads of sports cars. The suspension isn't really too flexible, but it's well-adjusted and benefits from enough travel to take a bruising from the bumps, without jostling occupants.

+ **CABIN DESIGN.** It's gorgeous inside, since the approach is to imitate race car stylistics. The lovely, muted black instrument panel serves as a jewel case for the numerous circular shapes of cast-aluminum, such as the air vents, steering wheel rim, speed shifter, etc. You also find this polished metal on the pedals assembly and footrest.

+ **QUALITY.** No doubt about it, Audi is one of the best in the industry when it comes to quality. Engineering follows stringent standards, the design is methodically developed, assembly is meticulous and finish job is simply flawless.

+ **CONVENIENCE FEATURES.** For a sports coupe, the TT provides lots of storage spots such as a big glove compartment, door side-pocket netting, a sort of shelf above the passenger's feet and an open compartment on the transmission tunnel. The trunk isn't huge, but it has a regular shape and the rear seatbench back forms a platform when folded down, so you can store golf bags length-wise.

CONS

- **STEERING.** The system is no fun on the FWD. It springs this way and that and it isn't always easy keeping the front end on track when going into curves.

- **VISIBILITY.** It isn't ideal. You're seated low down, the body belt is high and roof supports are very thick. Exterior mirrors are generous, but they're located too far back, so you have to turn your head to peer into them.

- **PERFORMANCE.** Although the base engine provides reasonable power, it's really too bad that the 225 hp engine has been withdrawn — it made users feel like race-car drivers!

- **REAR SEATS.** As is always the case on this type of vehicle, they're next to useless and only suited to very small children.

- **CONSOLE.** It gobbles up a lot of space, especially the aluminum bar that forms a handle that you're always hitting your knee against.

- **ACCESS.** It's no picnic climbing aboard in the rear seats, since the front seats don't free up enough space and due to the very arched roof design.

- **TO BE IMPROVED UPON.** Remote-control switches to open the rear hatch door, gas tank filler hole cap and to deactivate the alarm system are hard to reach, hidden in a compartment at the extremity of the center console.

CONCLUSION

Still not amazingly popular, the TT roadster will soon be joined by a convertible. Besides its price, which compares with the cost of a Z3, S2000 and SLK, it offers the advantage of year-round driveability thanks to a very reliable quattro AWD system, perfect in poor weather.

RATING AUDI TT		
CONCEPT :		64%
Technology :	90	
Safety :	90	
Interior space :	30	
Trunk volume :	25	
Quality/fit/finish :	85	
DRIVING :		76%
Cockpit :	85	
Performance :	70	
Handling :	70	
Steering :	75	
Braking :	80	
ORIGINAL EQUIPMENT :		79%
Tires :	80	
Headlights :	80	
Wipers :	70	
Rear defroster :	80	
Radio :	85	
COMFORT :		67%
Seats :	80	
Suspension :	75	
Sound level :	40	
Conveniences :	60	
Air conditioning :	80	
BUDGET :		41%
Price :	0	
Fuel economy :	65	
Insurance :	40	
Satisfaction :	75	
Depreciation :	25	
Overall rating :		65.4%

NEW FOR 2000

• The only engine is the 180-hp 1.8L, available with FWD or quattro in the U.S. and, in Canada only in the quattro version.

Compare Performance, Specifications, Prices, and Classification at the end of this chapter.

EQUIPMENT

AUDI TT	1.8T FWD	1.8T quattro
Automatic transmission:	-	-
Cruise control:	S	S
Power steering:	S	S
Anti-lock brakes:	S	S
Traction control:	S	--
Air conditioning:	SA	SA
Leather:	s	S
AM/FM/radio-cassette:	S	S
Power door locks:	S	S
Power windows:	S	S
Tilt steering:	S	S
Dual adjustable mirrors:	SEH	SEH
Alloy wheels:	S	S
Anti-theft system:	S	S

Colors

Exterior: Black, Yellow, Red, Grey, Silver, Blue, Green.

Interior: Black, Grey, Denim blue .

AT A GLANCE...

HISTORIC
Introduced in: 2000.
Made in: Györ, Hongria.

DEMOGRAPHICS

Model	Men/Wom.	Age	Married	College	Income $
TT	NA				

INDEX

Safety:	90 %	Satisfaction:	NA %
Depreciation:	NA %	Insurance:	$ 1,000
Cost per mile:	$ 0.75	Number of dealers:	290

SALES

	Canada			USA		
Model	1997	1998	Result	1997	1998	Result
TT	Not on the market at that time.					

MAINTENANCE REQUIRED BY WARRANTY

First revision:	Frequency:	Diagnostic plug:
7,500 miles	7,500 miles	Yes

Sports cars $35-70,000

Surging

BMW was right on target when it decided to include a roadster in its 3 Series. The Z3 enjoyed staggering success and in the United States, it ranks second behind the Chevrolet Corvette. Its popularity is explained by the fact that it provides a variety of equipment and performance levels, which means that it fits a variety of budgets. Not particularly attractive, the coupe seems destined to less popularity; meanwhile the M5 is noticeably more exclusive in character.

MODEL RANGE

The Z3 is available in four versions: a special-order coupe and three roadsters: the base model equipped with the 323's 2.5L 6-cylinder engine, the 2.8 powered by the 328's 2.8L engine or the M animated by the M3 engine, with 5-speed manual transmission. Original equipment on the base model includes power steering, anti-lock braking system, power locks, windows and mirrors, radio-cassette player, light alloy rims and anti-roll bars that offer better passenger protection if ever the car flips over. The 2.8 and M are also fitted with power roof device, air conditioning, cruise control, traction control, leather trim, heated seats, CD changer and theft-deterrent system.

TECHNICAL FEATURES

The Z3 is built on the pared down 318i convertible platform. Models differ according to trim design and some exterior accessories or flared touches on the body. The body consists of a steel monocoque shell with some panels that are galvanized on both sides. Build is super solid and fairly light. The windshield frame acts as a roll bar up front and

there are also the very same self-deploying roll bars that equip the 3-Series convertibles. Suspensions are inspired by those of the latest M3 model. Up front there are MacPherson struts and arc-shaped lower arms, while there's a rear classic semi-trailing arm setup, with various-design coil springs, shock absorbers, anti-roll bars and links according to model. Four-wheel disc brakes are paired up with a standard ABS device. Traction control distributes torque to the wheel offering the best grip, according to accelerations and braking maneuvers.

PROS

+ STYLE. It's sleek yet it's a BMW beauty. Its design is a clever blend of modern and retro touches, a mix of current technical musts and traditional roadster attributes.

+ PERFORMANCES. The 2.8 and M versions are brawnier than the base model, but the L6 engine doesn't achieve the performances you get in a Miata, at least technically speaking. Accelerations and pickup range from normal to zoomy. The M model's 240-hp engine is so lively that you have to keep an eye on things if you don't want to get tracked down by radar... The best compromise is still the 2.8 model that's motivated by a smooth, slick engine that doesn't burn too much petrol.

+ DRIVING PLEASURE. It's just great with the low-slung driver's seat, exhaust roar and wind effect that makes you feel like you're in a road rocket. And the manual shifter is a real treat...

+ STEERING. It's nearly perfect. It's right-on precise, benefits from ideal assistance and reduction ratio and a short steer angle diameter really makes for clean moves.

+ HANDLING. Competent thanks to the sophisticated suspension and great-grip tires that perform like champions even on poor road surfaces. On slalom runs, the car exhibits agility and aplomb and handles curves beautifully, but watch your foot on the accelerator on damp roads, otherwise the rear end tends to slide even with traction control.

+ BRAKES. Easy to gauge, they achieve very short emergency stops and they're stable and tough as nails.

+ RIDE COMFORT. The suspension and seats are firm, but not unpleasant in the long run and the optional air deflector shunts wind nicely when the top is down.

+ CONVENIENCE FEATURES. They're pretty good, really. The trunk may be fairly small, but it holds two suitcases and a travel bag and the cabin includes enough storage spots.

CONS

- ROOFTOP. It's pretty basic, although this year it is lined, it doesn't hold up against the wet outdoors (above the side windows) and it's fitted with a plastic rear window, incredible when the one on the less pricey Miata is made of glass and includes an electric defroster. Lastly, the roof cover is hell to install and its design is pretty homespun, nothing like what you'd expect from a factory-made item.

- NOISE. Noise becomes a real pain on the highway because of the rooftop and body soundproofing is pretty thin.

- CONTROLS. Some switches are poorly located, like the power window switches on the center console and especially the steering column that isn't adjustable and doesn't budge one bloody bit.

- ROAD AUTONOMY. With a meager 13 gallon gas tank, the Z3 can cover 250 miles or less, which is pretty tight for highway hauls.

- QUALITY. Finish details and trim material texture are spiffier on the 2.8 and M than on the base model. The lower end model is a poor church mouse in comparison.

- TO BE IMPROVED UPON. Low beam headlights are less effective than high beam, poorly located battery that's hard to remove.

CONCLUSION

There's no reason why the Z3 shouldn't continue to ride its current wave. Although from the technical standpoint its various versions are impeccable, if it wants to keep consumers on side maybe BMW should see to its model's main drawbacks in the equipment area.

RATING
BMW Z3

CONCEPT :   **57%**
Technology :	85
Safety :	80
Interior space :	20
Trunk volume :	20
Quality/fit/finish :	80

DRIVING :   **82%**
Cockpit :	80
Performance :	75
Handling :	75
Steering :	90
Braking :	90

ORIGINAL EQUIPMENT :   **62%**
Tires :	85
Headlights :	75
Wipers :	70
Rear defroster :	0
Radio :	80

COMFORT :   **64%**
Seats :	80
Suspension :	60
Sound level :	50
Conveniences :	50
Air conditioning :	80

BUDGET :   **54%**
Price :	10
Fuel economy :	70
Insurance :	45
Satisfaction :	80
Depreciation :	65

Overall rating :   **63.8%**

NEW FOR 2000
- **Fully lined soft top.**
- **Passenger-detector air bags.**
- **225/50R16 tires and Cross Spoke wheels.**
- **Chrome-trimmed grille and headlights.**
- **Taillights and 3/4 panelling.**
- **Redesigned center console, CD player, analog clock.**

Compare
Performance,
Specifications, Prices,
and Classification
at the end of this chapter.

EQUIPMENT

BMW Z3	2.3	2.8	M
Automatic transmission:	O	O	-
Cruise control:	O	S	S
Power steering:	S	S	S
Anti-lock brakes:	S	S	S
Traction control:	O	S	S
Air conditioning:	O	S	S
Leather:	O	SH	SH
AM/FM/radio-cassette:	S	SCd	SCd
Power door locks:	S	S	S
Power windows:	S	S	S
Tilt steering:	-	-	-
Dual adjustable mirrors:	S	S	S
Alloy wheels:	S	S	S
Anti-theft system:	O	S	S

Colors
Exterior: Violet-Red, Red, Green, Black, White, Silver, Blue.

Interior: *Cloth:* Anthracite-black, Blue-black, Green-black. *Leatherette:* Black-Grey.
Leather: Black, Violet-black, Red-black, Green-beige, 2 tone beige.

AT A GLANCE...

HISTORIC
Introduced in:	1997.
Made in:	Spartanburg, South Carolina, USA.

DEMOGRAPHICS
Model	Men/Wom.	Age	Married	College	Income $
Z3	73/27 %	45	54 %	64 %	115,000

INDEX
Safety:	80 %	Satisfaction:	80 %
Depreciation:	45 %	Insurance:	$ 1,000
Cost per mile:	$ 0.80	Number of dealers:	350

SALES
	Canada			USA		
Model	1997	1998	Result	1997	1998	Result
Z3	NA			19,760	20,613	+ 4.3 %

MAINTENANCE REQUIRED BY WARRANTY
First revision:	Frequency:	Diagnostic plug:
15,000 miles	15,000 miles	Yes

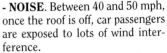

Newfound Success

Since it was revamped, the Corvette has enjoyed an incredible surge in popularity and its sales place it at the top of its class. While its main features remain unchanged, its underpinnings show marked improvement. A sturdier body has lead to a number of improvements in handling ease and comfort, two areas that were drawbacks in the previous model.

MODEL RANGE

The Chevrolet standard bearer is now available in three distinct versions: there's a coupe convertible equipped with a fixed panel, a classic convertible and the new "hardtop" coupe. Each model is animated by a 5.7L V8 that delivers 345 hp. This gutsy powerplant is paired up with a standard 4-speed automatic transmission. A 6-speed manual transmission is offered as an extra.

TECHNICAL FEATURES

The dashing body is made of composite polymer (fiberglass). The aerodynamic drag coefficient is only 0.29! The body is mounted on a surrounding chassis with tubular steel frame siderails. The chassis vibrates at 23 Hz when the roof is installed and at 21 Hz with the roof removed. The main chassis consists of components made of hydroformed galvanized steel. An aluminum cradle up front receives the main mechanical elements. The fully independent suspension uses, both front and rear, double unequal-length trailing control arms, transverse leaf springs made of composite materials and an anti-roll bar. The windshield is lodged in an aluminum structure that solidifies the instrument panel sector. A steel roll bar is built into the rear roof section. Steering, of magnetic design, is variable assist. Oversized disc brakes incorporate standard ABS and traction control. By integrating the manual transmission into the rear axle, along with the differential, an almost perfect weight distribution of 51.5/48.5% was achieved.

PROS

+ DRIVING FEEL. The engine never seems to be short of power surge and the low growl it lets out when it's coaxed is really thrilling!

+ BRAKES. Our braking measurements for the Corvette are among the best we've ever seen. You can stop the Corvette at 60 mph within 110 feet, when the average for the car industry is 140 feet.

+ PERFORMANCES. With a power to weight ratio of 9.4 lbs/hp, you're in for brawny accelerations and pick-up. The surge is simply spectacular and thanks to the nonslip differential, car path is straight-ahead perfect.

+ HANDLING. The stiff chassis and the Goodyear Eagle F1 tires that bite the Tarmac ensure remarkable handling on dry surfaces. Even on the "comfort" mode of the adaptive suspension, body sway is kept to a minimum. We hit almost 1 G in lateral acceleration, a record for a mass-produced car.

+RIDE COMFORT. Forget the old Corvette. The ride in the C5, blessed with "supple" or "average" adaptive suspension modes, is neither too rocky, nor too rough. You won't have to make an appointment with your chiropractor after each jaunt. But when you set the suspension to "sport" mode, expect a very firm, hard ride, especially on poor road surfaces!

+ FUEL ECONOMY. At the end of our road test, we calculated an average 19 mpg gas consumption, which seems almost reasonable given the circumstances...

+ CONVENIENCE FEATURES. You now have outside access to the trunk. It holds a fair amount, for example two suitcases, two totebags and the hardtop roof panel. This panel is so light, that one person can handle it like a charm.

+ OUTWARD VIEW. The coupe has lots of wide windows, so front visibility is super, compared to before. At the back, the rear window is very slanted and exterior mirrors sit too low, so there's room for improvement. But the rear window on the convertible is teeny tiny.

+ PRICE. Given the "PPP" (Price/Power/Performance) ratio, the Corvette is a pretty reasonable buy.

CONS

- FRONT END. It's loaded down with the engine, so it tends to do Olympic dives and needs to be put back on track. The rougher the road, the rougher the ride!

- SIZE. Parking manoeuvres in the 15 ft. Corvette are no picnic. Ironically, even aboard, space is skimpy. Hulky, tall folks will feel terribly cramped.

- ROAD CLEARANCE. The thin rubber flap located on the front bumper sits at 2 inches from the ground, so it gets scratched and scuffed up in no time!

- NOISE. Between 40 and 50 mph, once the roof is off, car passengers are exposed to lots of wind interference.

- A MISSING FEATURE. There's no indicator on the dashboard for the automatic transmission, so you don't know which gear you're in. As a result, you have to keep looking down to check it out.

- UNBELIEVABLE. This car is definitely not equipped with powerful enough headlights and should be fitted with halogen headlamps. On an other hand windshield wipers are awfully sluggish.

- PRACTICALITY. The glove compartment is too small and there's not a door side-pocket in sight. As for the console compartment, it holds next to nothing: you can stash two maps or a glasses case and that's about it!

VERY POOR FEATURES

-- STYLE. The rear body extremity is humungous and brutish-looking compared to the neat front end stylistic touches. The stylists seemed to have finished their task once they designed the front end!

CONCLUSION

The latest reincarnation of the Corvette is a resounding success. Its road ease and performance levels will steal away a considerable number of buyers usually attracted to more traditionally popular models.

RATING
CHEVROLET Corvette

CONCEPT : — 65%
Technology :	90
Safety :	90
Interior space :	15
Trunk volume :	50
Quality/fit/finish :	80

DRIVING : — 86%
Cockpit :	80
Performance :	85
Handling :	90
Steering :	75
Braking :	100

ORIGINAL EQUIPMENT : — 77%
Tires :	90
Headlights :	75
Wipers :	65
Rear defroster :	75
Radio :	80

COMFORT : — 55%
Seats :	80
Suspension :	60
Sound level :	20
Conveniences :	30
Air conditioning :	85

BUDGET : — 42%
Price :	0
Fuel economy :	40
Insurance :	35
Satisfaction :	80
Depreciation :	55

Overall rating : — **65.0%**

NEW FOR 2000
- Remote keyless entry.
- Torch Red interior trims.
- LEV-compliant engine.
- Yellow and Green exterior colors.
- Z51 suspension with bigger anti-roll bars.
- Aluminum alloy wheels.

Compare
Performance,
Specifications, Prices,
and Classification
at the end of this chapter.

EQUIPMENT

CHEVROLET Corvette	cpe.	ht	cabrio
Automatic transmission:	S	NA	S
Cruise control:	S	S	S
Power steering:	S	S	S
Anti-lock brakes:	S	S	S
Traction control:	S	S	S
Air conditioning:	SM	SM	SM
Leather:	S	S	S
AM/FM/radio-cassette:	S	S	S
Power door locks:	S	S	S
Power windows:	S	S	S
Tilt steering:	S	S	S
Dual adjustable mirrors:	SEH	SEH	SEH
Alloy wheels:	S	S	S
Anti-theft system:	S	S	S

Colors

Exterior: Black, White, Red, Pewter, Silver, Blue, Yellow, Green.

Interior: Black, Light Grey, Red, Oak.

AT A GLANCE...

HISTORIC
Introduced in: 1953, 1963, 1968, 1984, 1997.
Made in: Bowling Green, Kentucky, USA.

DEMOGRAPHICS
Model	Men/Wom.	Age	Married	College	Income $
Corvette	74/26 %	45	60 %	66 %	100,000

INDEX
Safety:	90 %	Satisfaction:	80 %
Depreciation:	40 %	Insurance:	$ 1,450
Cost per mile:	$ 0.90	Number of dealers:	4,466

SALES
	Canada			USA		
Model	1997	1998	Result	1997	1998	Result
Corvette	625	758	+ 21.3 %	22,724	29,208	+ 28.5 %

MAINTENANCE REQUIRED BY WARRANTY
First revision:	Frequency:	Diagnostic plug:
3,000 miles	6 months / 6,000 miles	Yes

Sports cars $35-70,000

A Class Of Its Own

At a time now long gone by, the team in charge of Chrysler decided to show just how dynamic the make was by building a small series of quintessentially North American standard production models. The Viper was the first concrete expression of this commitment and on a small scale, it tested unusual technical solutions destined to be applied to future models produced on the usual large scale.

MODEL RANGE

The Viper is an exotic car that's available as an RT/10 convertible or in a three-door GTS coupe. Both models are powered by an 8.0L V10 engine that develops a whopping 450 hp and is linked exclusively to a 6-speed manual gearbox. Original equipment on both versions is quite elaborate since it includes air conditioning, power windows, locks and mirrors, power steering and luxury items such as leather-clad seats and a sophisticated sound system. Yet we notice that there isn't any ABS-traction control system offered, even as an extra. We'd like to mention that two model year ago, the RT/10 traded its sliding lateral panels for power windows and was even furbished with real genuine door locks...

TECHNICAL FEATURES

The Viper has a rolled steel chassis reinforced with a tubular structure. The independent four-wheel suspension has some forged aluminum components and consists of an arrangement of unequal-length A-arms with adjustable spring-shock ensembles and stabilizer bar both front and rear. The car is equipped with power rack-and-pinion steering and huge vented disc brakes. Body panels are built of forced injection synthetic composite mate-rials. The frame around the windshield including the top of the instrument panel serves as a roll bar up front. This design was patented and really beefs up vehicle structure. The limited slip differential uses a disc system, but no automatic transmission is available. The pedal assembly is adjustable length-wise so an ideal pilot position can be achieved.

OUTSTANDING

++ GTS COUPE. This thrilling car is wonderfully like the Cobra Daytona that participated in the Le Mans 24-hour race in the golden days of yore. Its closed body design makes it practical for everyday use, even in poor weather, since visibility and trunk size are much better than these same features are on the conver-tible that really isn't as down-to-earth a car.

++ DRIVING PLEASURE. All that engine power really moves this baby and wheel response is as direct as it gets. So it's you against this amazing machine with the roaring rev of this V10 beauty in the background. With a car such as this, the sky is literally the limit. But under rainy skies, the driver will have to be a bit diplomatic if he or she wants to stay on the road.

PROS

+ LOOKS. The Viper isn't blessed with the Prowler's handsome flamboyance, but its giant, oversized nose sure evokes power to burn.

+ V10 ENGINE. It puts out awesome power and torque, so you're in for rocket accelerations and pickup and you take off in a thunderous roar. But you do need quite a bit of room to express yourself, so city driving is more frustrating than thrilling.

+ HANDLING. With such minimal sway, well-honed suspension and humungous tires, the Viper is literally riveted to the road and is in perfect balance, a rare feat, on dry roads. In the rain, it's a good idea to drive with an egg under your right foot, so to speak, and to be careful when accelerating on curves...

+ BRAKES. They're brawny brutes, easy to apply as needed and quite balanced even without ABS. The tires cost an arm and a leg, so it's wise to avoid wild stops.

+ COCKPIT. The adjustable pedal assembly is a real plus when it comes to driver comfort. You're also less distracted when changing gears.

+ SAFETY. Air bags, the hard top on the GTS coupe and the roll bar on the roadster ensure good passenger protection.

+ TECHNICAL FEATURES. When Chrysler built the Viper, it went all out and used state-of-the-art technology to match its engineering ambitions and at no time do you get the impression of being in a Kit-Car. The small inconveniences you run across are typical of this type of vehicle.

CONS

- BUDGET. You have to have money to burn in order to acquire, feed and maintain this fast car, not to mention the many small snags that come up when you're behind the wheel of such a vehicle...

- RIDE COMFORT. The bucket seats are well upholstered, but cabin space is snug and the suspension doesn't spare passengers on rough surfaces. Engine heat and noise are hard to take on long trips.

- CONVENIENCE FEATURES. There isn't much storage space inside the roadster cabin and the trunk is very small, so you'd better travel light (but a credit card is a must).

- MANEUVERABILITY. The Viper doesn't do a U-turn on a dime. It's crippled by a big steer angle diameter, hulky body and big tires. You need patience to be a Viper pilot.

VERY POOR FEATURES

- - OUTWARD VIEW. It's still the roadster's biggest handicap. The rear and side windows are very narrow and the roll bar creates a big blind spot at rear quarterback. Visibility is even worse when the top is up. Best not to have claustrophobic tendencies...

CONCLUSION

The Viper is an integral part of the American automotive mythology. It has no real direct competitor and reigns supreme as the most powerful product on this continent. Sold in minimal numbers, it has an excellent resale value that should attract many a collector.

Sports cars $25-70,000

RATING
DODGE Viper

CONCEPT :		61%
Technology :	90	
Safety :	90	
Interior space :	20	
Trunk volume :	30	
Quality/fit/finish :	75	

DRIVING :		88%
Cockpit :	80	
Performance :	100	
Handling :	100	
Steering :	80	
Braking :	80	

ORIGINAL EQUIPMENT :		76%
Tires :	90	
Headlights :	80	
Wipers :	60	
Rear defroster :	70	
Radio :	80	

COMFORT :		46%
Seats :	75	
Suspension :	50	
Sound level :	10	
Conveniences :	20	
Air conditioning :	75	

BUDGET :		41%
Price :	0	
Fuel economy :	20	
Insurance :	40	
Satisfaction :	85	
Depreciation :	60	

| **Overall rating :** | | **62.4%** |

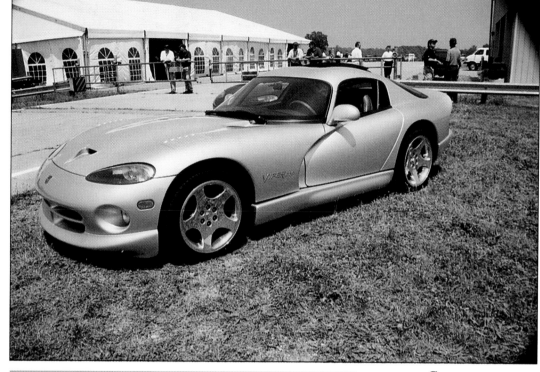

NEW FOR 2000

- Silver Gray exterior color.
- Child-safety seat anchors.
- ACR (American Club Racer) competition options group.
- Anti-pollution system to minimize pollutants when filling up.

Compare
Performance,
Specifications, Prices,
and Classification
at the end of this chapter.

EQUIPMENT

DODGE Viper	RT/10 convertible	GTS coupe
Automatic transmission:	-	-
Cruise control:	-	-
Power steering:	S	S
Anti-lock brakes:	-	-
Traction control:	-	-
Air conditioning:	S	S
Leather:	S	S
AM/FM/radio-cassette:	SCd	SCd
Power door locks:	S	S
Power windows:	S	S
Tilt steering:	S	S
Dual adjustable mirrors:	SE	SE
Alloy wheels:	S	S
Anti-theft system:	-	-

Colors

Exterior: Silver, Red, Black.

Interior: Grey & Black.

AT A GLANCE...

HISTORIC
Introduced in: 1992 (roadster 2 seats).
Made in: Conner Avenue, Detroit, Michigan, USA.

DEMOGRAPHICS

Model	Men/Wom.	Age	Married	College	Income $
Viper	94/6 %	54	57 %	58 %	100 000

INDEX

Safety:	90 %	Satisfaction:	86 %
Depreciation:	40 %	Insurance:	$ 1,459
Cost per mile:	$ 1.45	Number of dealers:	1887

SALES

	Canada				USA	
Model	1997	1998	Result	1997	1998	Result
Viper	101	79	- 21.8 %	1,458	1,248	- 14.4 %

MAINTENANCE REQUIRED BY WARRANTY

First revision:	Frequency:	Diagnostic plug:
5,000 miles	6 months	Yes

Sports cars
$35-70,000

Gadget

To mark its 50th anniversary and the beginning of the third millennium, the Honda firm has decided to produce a convertible, positioned somewhere between the Mazda Miata and the BMW Z3. From the first it takes its 4-cylinder engine, and from the second it borrows its price and high-level performance.

MODEL RANGE

The S2000 is available in only one version, powered by a 2.0-litre 4-cylinder engine with a 6-speed manual transmission. Its standard equipment includes a manually operated air conditioning system, a power soft top, a stereo sound system with a CD player, power doors, power sideview mirrors and power locks, cruise control, a theft deterrent system with an immobilizer, and leather upholstery.

TECHNICAL FEATURES

Inspired by the SSM prototype unveiled at the Tokyo Auto Show in 1995, the S2000 has a steel body. Its hybrid unitized design includes an X-shaped beam, providing the same resistance to flexion and torsion as a standard vehicle, without any excess weight. The fully independent suspension features double triangular arms in the front and multiarms in the rear. Both systems are distinctive because of the fact that their joints are positioned inside the wheel wells. The two systems are complemented by anti-roll bars and gas shock absorbers. Four disc brakes and ABS are standard. The rack-and-pinion steering system is assisted electrically, one of the first applications of a technology developed very recently. However, the heart and soul of the 2000 roadster is its engine. This 2.0-litre 4-cylinder unit is typically Honda, with a

with an output of 120-hp per litre and a nominal output of 240-hp and 153-lb.-ft. of torque. These numbers are reached in the very high range, between 6,000 and 9,000 rpm - red line numbers! In addition to the VTEC system, this model features a direct ignition system and a low-pressure exhaust system. The manual transmission has 6 close ratio gears and the differential is an anti-lock. One of the characteristics that best epitomizes the S2000 roadster is red: a button used to spark the engine once the key is in the ignition, just like on competition cars.

PROS

+ LOOKS. They're very exciting from some angles and a radical change from the stereotypes of the past. This model's smooth lines are interesting, as is the treatment given to roll bars positioned each side of the spoiler.

+ RIDE. The engine is eager to be pushed to the limit and sounds a lot like a race car's, the steering system is precise, the steering wheel has a very good grip and the gear shift lever is well designed - this car feels like a real racer.

+ QUALITY. Like all Honda products, the S2000 was developed, manufactured and finished with a great deal of care and attention to detail. Nothing is left to chance and a glance at any number of details shows high quality.

+ LAYOUT. The cockpit is a model of logic and ergonomics.

+ WIND. It's been tamed effectively by Honda engineers and channelled to ensure that it does nothing to spoil romantic weekend outings! Not much noise seeps inside even when crosswinds are strong and the small spoiler is effective, at least at reasonable speeds.

+ BONUS POINTS. For the sophisticated air conditioning system designed to work with the top down, and for bucket seats that mold well and provide good support.

CONS

- STYLING. It lacks strength and personality. Compared to its closest rivals such as the Z3, SLK or Boxster, it's dull and uninspired.

- ENGINE. Its power and torque are located at very high rpm and aren't very well suited to current driving conditions - drivers have to exceed posted speed limits to use it to the maximum, with the predictable consequences. On winding roads it's taxed to the limit, quickly becoming noisy and hard to control.

- CONVERTIBLE TOP. Its simplistic design is very disappointing and it's unacceptable that on a car sold at this price, it has no lining and no glass windshield or electric defroster. To make matters even worse, when the top is down positioning its cover is one of the most complex operations imaginable!

- PRACTICALITY. Compared to its

rivals, the S2000 is the least practical when it comes to daily use. No glovebox, no door pockets, only one cupholder and a minuscule center console. In the trunk the emergency wheel is almost completely flat and in a pinch, if you want to store a standard tire that's gone flat, you'll have to empty it. A fun prospect, wouldn't you agree!

- INSTRUMENTATION. The digital instrument cluster isn't the most attractive in the industry and doesn't look very sporty at all.

- STEERING WHEEL. It can't be adjusted in any direction, which for some drivers makes it hard to find the ideal driving position.

- VISIBILITY. All of Honda's scientific prowess couldn't manage to eliminate the blind spots resulting from the convertible top. A shame!

- FLAWS. Poor insulation that lets heat generated by the engine seep inside the passenger compartment — very annoying in the summer months. The starter, more unusual than practical . The minimal choice of exterior and interior colors, far from accommodating every taste.

CONCLUSION

In spite of everything there is to like about this model, it seems that Honda has wasted a lot of precious time with the S2000. Instead of trying to compete with BMW, Porsche and Mercedes-Benz with minimal arguments in its favor, maybe it should have focused its energy on developing a coupe-convertible like the del Sol, more realistic, more practical and more popular on all counts. Unfortunately, this looks a lot like a repetition of the NSX adventure.

Sports cars $35-70,000

RATING HONDA S2000		
CONCEPT :		56%
Technology :	85	
Safety :	90	
Interior space :	10	
Trunk volume :	10	
Quality/fit/finish :	85	
DRIVING :		77%
Cockpit :	75	
Performance :	80	
Handling :	70	
Steering :	80	
Braking :	80	
ORIGINAL EQUIPMENT :		62%
Tires :	85	
Headlights :	80	
Wipers :	65	
Rear defroster :	-	
Radio :	80	
COMFORT :		62%
Seats :	85	
Suspension :	75	
Sound level :	50	
Conveniences :	20	
Air conditioning :	80	
BUDGET :		55%
Price :	0	
Fuel economy :	70	
Insurance :	40	
Satisfaction :	90	
Depreciation :	75	
Overall rating :		**62.4%**

New 2000 Model

NEW FOR 2000

• New model commemorating the make's 50th anniversary and the third millennium.

Compare Performance, Specifications, Prices, and Classification at the end of this chapter.

EQUIPMENT

HONDA — **S2000**

Automatic transmission:	-
Cruise control:	S
Power steering:	S
Anti-lock brakes:	S
Traction control:	S
Air conditioning:	SM
Leather:	S
AM/FM/radio-cassette:	SCd
Power door locks:	S
Power windows:	S
Tilt steering:	-
Dual adjustable mirrors:	S
Alloy wheels:	S
Anti-theft system:	S

Colors

Exterior: Red, Charcoal.

Interior: Red, Black.

AT A GLANCE...

HISTORIC
Introduced in: 2000.
Made in: Japan.

DEMOGRAPHICS

Model	Men/Wom.	Age	Married	College	Income $
S2000	NA				

INDEX

Safety:	90 %	Satisfaction:	(Honda)	90 %
Depreciation:	NA %	Insurance:		$ 900
Cost per mile:	$ 0.75	Number of dealers:		1,000

SALES

	Canada			USA		
Model	1997	1998	Result	1997	1998	Result
S2000	Not on sale during this period.					

MAINTENANCE REQUIRED BY WARRANTY

First revision:	Frequency:	Diagnostic plug:
4,000 miles	4,000 miles	Yes

Sports cars $35-70,000

Reincarnation

There's no question that the celebrated British make has the knack of designing cars that dreams are made of. At a time when half of all automobile sales depend on consumer "feelings", Jaguars have a special place of their own on the sports and luxury car market because of the ambiance they create and because they make people want to own one. The XK models are no exception to the rule and in their own special way, they perpetuate the Coventry' builders world-renowned approach.

MODEL RANGE

The XK8's are offered as a 2-door, 2-passenger coupe and convertible in a single trim level, equipped with a 4L V8 engine associated with a five-speed automatic transmission with regular or sequential shifter. As to be expected for such expensive cars, equipment is very rich. It includes more particularly an antilock braking system and traction control.

TECHNICAL FEATURES

The steel monocoque body includes some galvanized panels. Aerodynamics are quite good, since the drag coefficient is 0.35 for the coupe and 0.36 for the convertible. The fully independent suspension consists of a double wishbone arrangement, mounted on an aluminum cradle and adjusted so as to offset front nosedive effect. The same system holds for the rear end, that controls rearing up on acceleration, and there's a stabilizer bar both front and rear. Disc brakes benefit from an ABS device and the P Zero tires were designed by Pirelli, specifically for these versions. The engine that motivates the XK8's is a V8, the first in the Coventry firm's history. This engine design isn't of Ford origin, but it still took advantage of project planning advice from the American giant. It's a 4.0L model

that develops 290 hp and 290 lb.ft of torque. The engine block and cylinder head are made of an aluminum alloy. The engine has DOHC distribution with four valves per cylinder. It's equipped with a device called "Variable Cam Phasing", that allows for varying camshaft timing, so as to obtain 80% maximum torque between 1,400 and 6,400 rpm. This mechanism, located at the camshafts' extremity, modifies when exactly the intake valves open, but not how long they remain so. The ZF 5-speed automatic transmission maximizes engine performances while maintaining low fuel consumption.

OUTSTANDING

++ SILHOUETTE. It's irresistibly like the legendary XK-E (E-TYPE) design. The car is a different size from the original, but the overall look is very zippy and stylistic touches are super sleek, maybe a bit too much so.

PROS

+ THE V8 ENGINE. It's the lion's heart of this model, it's responsive, zesty and creamy smooth, and yet it has a discreet and serene demeanor. It provides awesome performances, no mean feat since these vehicles aren't exactly featherweights, but the power to weight ratio is nice and comfortable.

+ DRIVING PLEASURE. It's terrific with such clean, right-on front and rear end directional flow due to the rigid structure, even on the convertible. Accurate steering and brakes make the pilot look like a champion.

+ QUALITY. It's better than it was, since assembly is more meticulous and the fit and finish job is very fine, but it's still not on a par with what you get on German or Japanese rivals. Leather seats have a typical, velvety Connolly feel, but the lovely scent is gone forever, a real pity. The convertible soft top is of impeccable construction, for it's lined and can be raised or lowered automatically.

+ HANDLING. It's by far superior to that of former XJS versions, since behavior is stable and easy to control in all situations. This is due to the stiff build and sophisticated suspension components.

+ STEERING. It's smooth, direct and crisp, so you can control car path with remarkable ease on the highway and on city streets where maneuvers are reasonably good.

CONS

- VEHICLE SIZE. The XK8 models are more at home on straight-ahead runs or on wide curves rather than on tight slalom runs, since hefty vehicle weight and imposing size hamper agility and cut down on driving scope that's not one bit sporty.

- BODY. It's a bit too stripped down, since it isn't dressed up in the usual Jaguar chrome finery on rims, mirrors, taillights and bumpers... Jaguar should take care of this sad state of affairs.

- COCKPIT. It's penalized by the seat design and somehow you don't feel that you're benefitting from much lateral or lumbar support. Toe and hip room are awfully snug and it's no fun getting aboard with the unusually wide door threshold.

-VISIBILITY. It's nowhere wonderful, due to the high frame belt, bulky windshield supports and the blind spot at rear quarterback caused by the convertible top, less obvious on the coupe, but both models are afflicted with a narrow, severely slanted rear window.

- INSTRUMENT PANEL. Like the exterior, it lacks stylistic accents with those thick, massive wood panels. Ergonomics aren't too great either, not with the inverted order climate control and sound system dials and the switches located at the right that are out of reach.

- REAR SEATS. They're totally useless due to terribly stingy head and leg room. It would have been clever to come up with a design that lets you store luggage by lowering the seatbench back to form a platform.

-TO BE IMPROVED UPON. No rear wiper on the coupe.

CONCLUSION

The XK8 models are the reincarnation of the legendary E-Type of the 60's. Despite their modern styling, they have all the charm and all the spirit of the former models, pivotal to their era. They need very little else to be perfect. A few less wood inlays inside and a bit more chrome outside and they would be well on their way to following tradition to the letter and winning over diehard purists.

Sports car $35-100,000

RATING		
JAGUAR XK8		
CONCEPT :		**68%**
Technology :	85	
Safety :	90	
Interior space :	40	
Trunk volume :	40	
Quality/fit/finish :	85	
DRIVING :		**77%**
Cockpit :	75	
Performance :	80	
Handling :	70	
Steering :	80	
Braking :	80	
ORIGINAL EQUIPMENT :		**77%**
Tires :	85	
Headlights :	80	
Wipers :	65	
Rear defroster :	75	
Radio :	80	
COMFORT :		**70%**
Seats :	80	
Suspension :	80	
Sound level :	50	
Conveniences :	60	
Air conditioning :	80	
BUDGET :		**45%**
Price :	0	
Fuel economy :	50	
Insurance :	30	
Satisfaction :	85	
Depreciation :	60	
Overall rating :		**67.4%**

NEW FOR 2000

- **Different 17-inch alloy wheels.**
- **Automatic windshield wipers.**
- **Cargo net.**
- **Child-safety seat anchors.**
- **Exterior colors: Platinum, Titanium.**

Compare
Performance,
Specifications, Prices,
and Classification
at the end of this chapter.

EQUIPMENT

JAGUAR XK8	coupe	convertible
Automatic transmission:	S	S
Cruise control:	S	S
Power steering:	S	S
Anti-lock brakes:	S	S
Traction control:	S	S
Air conditioning:	S	S
Leather:	S	S
AM/FM/radio-cassette:	SCd	SCd
Power door locks:	S	S
Power windows:	S	S
Tilt steering:	S	S
Dual adjustable mirrors:	S	S
Alloy wheels:	S	S
Anti-theft system:	S	S

Colors

Exterior: Green, Black, Beige, White, Red, Blue, Platinum, Titanium.

Interior: Black, White, Tan, Blue.

AT A GLANCE...

HISTORIC

Introduced in: 1997.
Made in: Browns Lane, Coventry, England.

DEMOGRAPHICS

Model	Men/Wom.	Age	Married	College	Income $
XK8	79/21 %	46	81 %	68 %	125,000

INDEX

Safety:	90 %	Satisfaction:	87 %
Depreciation:	40 %	Insurance:	$ 1,350
Cost per mile:	$ 1.15	Number of dealers:	130

SALES

	Canada			USA		
Model	1997	1998	Result	1997	1998	Result
XK8	356	292	- 18.0 %	6,915	5,861	- 15.2 %

MAINTENANCE REQUIRED BY WARRANTY

First revision:	Frequency:	Diagnostic plug:
4,000 miles	6,000 miles	Yes

Sports car
$35-100,000

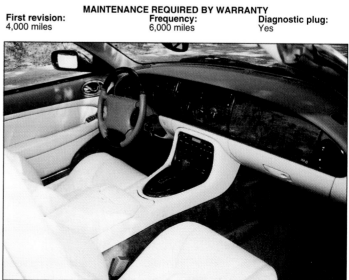

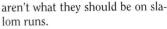

To introduce models exactly the same as those available from BMW, its direct competitor, the Stuttgart firm developed a coupe and a convertible from its base C-Class model. Not content with using a 3.2L V6 engine, these two models are now available with a V8, something unheard of in the enemy's camp.

MODEL RANGE

The CLK family includes a two-door coupe and convertibles offered in a base 320 version equipped with a 3.2L V6 paired up with a 5-speed automatic transmission or 430 animated by a 4.3L V8 that it shares with numerous other Mercedes models. Detailed standard equipment includes the full range of technical and comfort-related accessories now considered mandatory on vehicles in this class.

TECHNICAL FEATURES

Built on the C-Class platform, the CLK coupes and convertible have a unique body design. This neat, streamlined car has good aerodynamics, yielding a 0.31 drag coefficient. The headlamp design, similar to that of the E-Class, adds a special flavor to the ensemble and it really blends in nicely with the traditional grille, bringing a fresh new look to these models.

The steel unitized body is incredibly rugged, especially that of the convertible to which Mercedes brought some ingenious applications so that the body could adequately withstand torsion and flexion. The front suspension is made up of a double wishbone arrangement with geometry designed to improve stability, reduce rolling resistance and give longer life to tires as well as offset rear end lift and nosedive.

On the rear, there's the famous

Bull's-eye

multi-link trailing arm setup that's one of the finest and most lightweight systems in the world. Disc brakes are associated with a device that adapts response to driver style so as to offer optimum efficiency. The antilock braking system and traction control use the same electronic components to ensure vital vehicle stability that also benefits from an optional anti-skid system (ESP) that keeps the car on an even keel during extreme maneuvers like taking a curve or skidding on a slippery surface.

PROS

+ LOOKS. These vehicles are quite compact, but they're lovely, more at 3/4 front and in profile than at 3/4 rear where they look quite narrow.

+ PRICE. Considering their gorgeous looks, state-of-the-art technical assets, rich equipment and exquisite craftsmanship, the price for these two models seems very competitive.

+ SAFETY FEATURES. This car is equipped with four airbags, so it's ahead of other rival models when it comes to passive or active safety devices. Mercedes-Benz was the first carmaker to take this route even before such matters fell under government jurisdiction.

+ PERFORMANCES. They were pretty zippy with the 3.2L V6, but they've become out of this world exotic with the 4.3L V8 that brings

a whole new driving sensation to this car category.

+ DRIVING PLEASURE. These well-thought out cars are very competent and they're reassuring to drive. They're solid and cohesive, so they can be driven in a relaxed and layed-back manner and suddenly be unleashed in a whole series of curves where the driver will wonder if he or she has lost the magic touch...

+ TRUNK. It's really generous for this type of vehicle, especially since it can be extended by lowering the rear seatbench that's also fitted with a ski-size pass-through.

+ NICE FEATURES. The high tech climate control that has several settings, the super-effective windshield wiper-washer system and the rear fold-back headrests.

+ VERY CLEVER. "High tech" cupholders and the rain-sensitive sensor that adapts wiper speed to rain intensity.

CONS

- NOISE. It's strange that on such a technically sophisticated car, road noise should be so pervasive and the engine should let you know it's there whenever your toe touches the accelerator. It seems that German carmakers don't consider low noise level as being a comfort factor.

- STEERING. It suffers from a poor reduction ratio, so it adversely affects the spontaneous soar of sporty driving, and agility and precision

aren't what they should be on slalom runs.

- REAR SEATS. They've undergone a lot of modifications but they're still only useful in a pinch, for space is snug and upholstery is terribly hard on the backside.

- CONTROLS. Those located on the center console aren't too handy and the zigzag shifter can really get to you, especially since there's no shifter position indicator on the instrument panel.

- STABILITY. Several times during our road test, the CLK exhibited sensitivity to crosswinds and to road surface quality. In the latter case, it should be pointed out that it was equipped with good-quality snow tires, which can't really be considered to be a factor causing such uncivilized behavior.

- STORAGE COMPARTMENTS. The door side-pockets are neat, but the glove compartment and center console compartment are terribly tiny.

- UPKEEP. The purchase price and fuel consumption are relatively understandable, but upkeep bills seem a bit much at times, even if you can afford to dish out the cash.

- TO BE IMPROVED UPON. Power windows and the windshield wipers that are annoyingly slow and headlamps that aren't too impressive on low beam.

CONCLUSION

Sales statistics for the U.S. show that these models have hit a bull's-eye, proving once again that Mercedes-Benz was right on mark - even to the point of making consumers hope that the return of coupes and convertibles is part of a lasting strategy.

Sports cars $35-70,000

RATING
MERCEDES-BENZ CLK

CONCEPT :		69%
Technology :	90	
Safety :	90	
Interior space :	35	
Trunk volume :	40	
Quality/fit/finish :	90	

DRIVING :		74%
Cockpit :	80	
Performance :	80	
Handling :	70	
Steering :	80	
Braking :	60	

ORIGINAL EQUIPMENT :		78%
Tires :	80	
Headlights :	80	
Wipers :	60	
Rear defroster :	85	
Radio :	85	

COMFORT :		69%
Seats :	80	
Suspension :	80	
Sound level :	40	
Conveniences :	65	
Air conditioning :	80	

BUDGET :		51%
Price :	0	
Fuel economy :	55	
Insurance :	35	
Satisfaction :	90	
Depreciation :	75	

| Overall rating : | | 68.2% |

NEW FOR 2000
- ESP anti-skid system standard on all models.
- CLK 430 convertible equipped with a 275-hp V8 engine.
- Slight exterior design touch-ups.
- Instrument cluster layout.
- Steering wheel-mounted controls and Touch Shift gear shifting system.

Compare Performance, Specifications, Prices, and Classification at the end of this chapter.

EQUIPMENT

MERCEDES-BENZ CLK	coupe	convertible
Automatic transmission:	S	S
Cruise control:	S	S
Power steering:	S	S
Anti-lock brakes:	S	S
Traction control:	S	S
Air conditioning:	SA	SA
Leather:	S	S
AM/FM/radio-cassette:	SCd	SCd
Power door locks:	S	S
Power windows:	S	S
Tilt steering:	S	S
Dual adjustable mirrors:	SEH	SEH
Alloy wheels:	S	S
Anti-theft system:	S	S

Colors
Exterior: Black, White, Blue, Bordeaux, Red, Silver, Green.

Interior: Convertible : Black, Blue, Green. Coupe : Black, Oyster, Ash.

AT A GLANCE...

HISTORIC
Introduced in: coupe: 1998, convertible: 1999.
Made in: Sindelfingen, Germany.

DEMOGRAPHICS
Model	Men/Wom.	Age	Married	College	Income $
CLK	69/31 %	46	71 %	71 %	135,000

INDEX
Safety:	90 %	Satisfaction:	88 %
Depreciation:	25 %	Insurance:	$ 1,350
Cost per mile:	$ 1.10	Number of dealers:	380

SALES
	Canada			USA		
Model	1997	1998	Result	1997	1998	Result
CLK	NA			1,236	11,622	+ 840.3 %

MAINTENANCE REQUIRED BY WARRANTY
First revision:	Frequency:	Diagnostic plug:
3,000 miles	6,000 miles	Yes

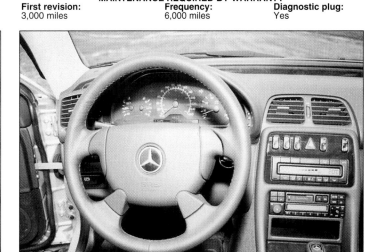

Limping

Intended to take on BMW's Z3, the SLK is incompetent and its sales stand at about the half-way point compared to its arch rival. In large part this explains its lack of sporty capabilities, regardless of its remarkable performance levels. In North America, even supercharged 4-cylinder engines don't make the ultimate grade and a 3.2L V6 would make the SLK more attractive.

MODEL RANGE

The SLK is a compact roadster whose folding hardtop automatically drops above the trunk on sunny days and lifts back into place if poor weather sets in. It's sold in a single model equipped with a 2.3L supercharged 4-cylinder engine associated with a 5-speed automatic or manual transmission. Original equipment is very extensive, which explains in part the stiff price. The SLK benefits from air conditioning, antilock braking system, leather seats, light alloy wheels, Bose high fidelity sound system, oodles of power accessories, theft-deterrent system and the only options are metallic exterior body paint, heated seats and cellular phone.

TECHNICAL FEATURES

The SLK convertible coupe is a from-scratch original, since it isn't inspired by any model already existing in the Mercedes lineup. Its steel monocoque build has remarkable aerodynamics for this type of vehicle, since it has an average 0.35 drag coefficient. To cut down on weight, a cast-magnesium partition separates the gas tank from the trunk. The fully independent suspension consists of a double wishbone arrangement up front including anti-dive geometry and a multilink setup at the rear with anti-lift geometry and stabilizer bar on both axles. The car is equipped with power rack-and-pinion steering and disc brakes paired up with a standard ABS device. The 185-hp engine is borrowed from the C-Class and gets a boost from the Roots supercharger equipped with an intercooler.

PROS

+ VERSATILITY. You can buy this handsome roadster at a pretty reasonable price and enjoy the benefits of both a zippy coupe and a convertible. The biggest bonus this combination has to offer is the hardtop, a solid, insulated and soundproofed design as well as windows that will dissuade thieves or vandals. Visibility is enhanced by the generous windows, even in the winter since the rear window is equipped with an electric defroster.

+ STYLE. This tiny car is elegant and has lots of panache. It has a nicely balanced shape and is stuffed with highly polished features. The cabin is lovely as well and has a neat retro look, just enough to set a warm, classic atmosphere.

+ HARDTOP. It folds down automatically and is an incredibly clever piece of engineering know-how and daring as eager onlookers will agree when they watch the roof being raised or lowered in the twinkle of an eye. It's waterproof and insulated so the car can be used year round. The top is activated automatically via a hydraulic pump that does its magic trick in a mere 25 seconds.

+ EFFECTIVE. Steering is clean and nicely assisted but it could be a bit more direct. Brakes are smooth and they're easy to apply.

+ PERFORMANCES. They're great with such vigorous accelerations and pickup, despite sluggish supercharger response time — its effects are only perceived at 3,000 rpm.

+ ROADHOLDING. The SLK stays really cool and level-headed. It's lively, maneuvers well and sticks to the road on most turns and it's stable and can't be flustered the least bit on straight runs.

+ SAFETY. It benefits from the robust car build that incorporates a folding roll bar, four airbags and 3-point pretensioner seatbelts.

+ QUALITY. This vehicle can boast of a super-neat design and enviable craftsmanship, perfectly in keeping with Mercedes-Benz standards. Its structure is quite rigid and is solidly put together, finish details are meticulously rendered and materials used are attractive and chosen to last.

+ NICE FEATURES. Nifty, efficient original accessories such as headlights, wipers, tires, air conditioning and defroster that equips the rear window.

CONS

- DRIVING. It's hard getting comfy behind the wheel because the steering column doesn't tilt. The engine is a poor match for this car and it needs the supercharger to really zoom. The 2.3L engine shakes and rattles like a regular, run of the mill model and unpleasant exhaust noise is a real disappointment. In this regard, the SLK is a total fiasco, for a small 6-cylinder engine would give it a lot more character and provide more torque and more impressive roar.

- TRUNK. It's small and hard to get to when the top is stored inside and there isn't a sliver of space behind the seats to store anything at all.

- VISIBILITY. It isn't perfect towards the rear since the headrests and wind deflector block the view in the main mirror and exterior mirrors are terribly smallish.

- NOISE LEVEL. On bad roads the less than sturdy body rattles and rolls and even at lower speeds wind seeps in through the windshield.

- CONVERTIBLE TOP. The complex power mechanism tends to break down and often needs to be adjusted.

- TO BE IMPROVED UPON. Some items like the tiny sun visors that are pretty useless and could not fold up in two.

CONCLUSION

The SLK's versatile body is unique in the automotive industry. Its main attraction, a hard convertible top, explains its fairly respectable sales figures. Though, it's a pity that it's saddled with an engine considered weak by North American standards.

RATING		
MERCEDES-BENZ SLK		
CONCEPT :		56%
Technology :	85	
Safety :	80	
Interior space :	20	
Trunk volume :	15	
Quality/fit/finish :	80	
DRIVING :		74%
Cockpit :	80	
Performance :	70	
Handling :	80	
Steering :	80	
Braking :	60	
ORIGINAL EQUIPMENT :		78%
Tires :	80	
Headlights :	80	
Wipers :	70	
Rear defroster :	80	
Radio :	80	
COMFORT :		69%
Seats :	80	
Suspension :	70	
Sound level :	40	
Conveniences :	75	
Air conditioning :	80	
BUDGET :		51%
Price :	0	
Fuel economy :	70	
Insurance :	45	
Satisfaction :	80	
Depreciation :	60	
Overall rating :		65.6%

NEW FOR 2000

- **Electric Green and Copper colors on design versions available as of Fall 1999.**
- **Free maintenance (United States).**

Compare Performance, Specifications, Prices, and Classification at the end of this chapter.

EQUIPMENT

MERCEDES-BENZ	SLK
Automatic transmission:	S
Cruise control:	S
Power steering:	S
Anti-lock brakes:	S
Traction control:	S
Air conditioning:	SA
Leather:	S
AM/FM/radio-cassette:	SCd
Power door locks:	S
Power windows:	S
Tilt steering:	S
Dual adjustable mirrors:	SEH
Alloy wheels:	S
Anti-theft system:	S

Colors

Exterior: Black, White, Blue, Red, Yellow, Silver, Green, Cooper.

Interior: Black, Blue, Oyster, Salsa.

AT A GLANCE...

HISTORIC

Introduced in: 1997.
Made in: Sindelfingen, Germany.

DEMOGRAPHICS

Model	Men/Wom.	Age	Married	College	Income $
SLK	66/34 %	50	68 %	61 %	115,000

INDEX

Safety:	80 %	Satisfaction:	85 %
Depreciation:	40 %	Insurance:	$ 1 000
Cost per mile:	$ 0.75	Number of dealers:	380

SALES

	Canada			USA		
Model	1997	1998	Result	1997	1998	Result
SLK	325	295	- 9.2 %	6,890	10,620	+ 54.1 %

MAINTENANCE REQUIRED BY WARRANTY

First revision:	Frequency:	Diagnostic plug:
3,000 miles	7,500 miles	Yes

The Prowler roadster is the perfect example of a car that serves no other purpose than to flatter its driver and only incidentally, its passenger. Not so bad considering that many a similar model can't do as much. Purely North American, it reminds baby boomers of the golden years that were the 1950s of their youth.

Fifties

MODEL RANGE

The Prowler roadster only comes in a single two-door convertible model animated by the latest 3.5L V6 and 4-speed automatic gearbox with "AutoStick" sequential shifter. The car looks rather simplistic in design, but it's loaded with standard equipment, well, at least you get the basics to be comfortable, such as air conditioning, CD player and power locks, windows and mirrors. But the spare tire and ABS-traction control system are unknown in this cohort, which is surprising when you think of the expensive low-profile tires that equip this car. How in the world could you drive to a garage without causing damage if you get a flat?...

TECHNICAL FEATURES

The body design hails back to the hot-rods of the fifties, but the car's features are at the cutting edge of automobile technology.

This rear-wheel drive roadster has a chassis and body made of aluminum panels that are glued and reveted together. Some components like the fenders are built of composite materials. There's really no point in going on and on about the drag coefficient of this beauteous body. In this case, it doesn't really matter, does it?

The four-wheel independent suspension is composed of transverse A-arms and rear axle supported by longitudinal, transverse and oblique control arms. Most of the elements are made of forged aluminum just like on race cars. The suspension is completed by stabilizer bars, coil springs and telescopic shocks. Brakes are four-wheel discs but are unfortunately deprived of any ABS or traction control system. Rack-and-pinion steering benefits from variable assist power.

OUTSTANDING

++ STYLE. This fabulous car is just irresistible and everyone is drawn by its magnetism. Of all the cars we've had the chance to try out, this one is way ahead when it comes to an innate power to attract attention. It's a great concept. The body design is exquisite right down to minor touches like the headlamps, bumpers and grille.

++ DRIVING PLEASURE. Getting behind the wheel of this vehicle is a rare thrill. The car responds beautifully. There are all kinds of great growls and squeals when you accelerate so you get quite an adrenalin rush. Besides, it is unusual nowadays to be able to drive a car whose wheels and front suspension are visible, which adds to the experience.

++ STEERING. It's almost perfect. It's smooth, precise and well powered without getting any negative feedback from the wheels.

PROS

+ TECHNICAL FEATURES. Chrysler wasn't cheap when it put this baby together. Aluminum chassis, body and suspension elements aren't exactly items that are commonly used in the automobile industry. The suspension geometry is inspired by that of race cars and the automatic transmission with sequential shifter are proof of same.

+ PRICE. You could say that it's almost reasonable, but fat chance of paying the suggested retail price when this car is worth so much nowadays because of the great demand. Gas consumption is pretty reasonable as well, it's about 20 mpg and maintenance costs are affordable since so many parts are borrowed from mass-produced cars.

+ PERFORMANCES. The Prowler doesn't exactly tear up the tarmac, but accelerations are vigorous and the noise it emits is a feast for the ears of car fanatics. Pickup isn't quite as dramatic, but this engine has enough juice to scare you a bit on serpentine roads.

+ QUALITY. For a limited edition car, the assembly and trim materials are very much like those of mass-produced cars, even better than similar attributes on the Viper.

+ THE LIGHT RETRO TOUCH. The old-style tachometer on the steering column and the other instrument gauges exude real retro charm...

CONS

- OUTWARD VIEW. It's very limited when the roof is up because of the high frame, high dashboard and teeny rear window.

- BRAKES. They don't benefit from ABS, so stops are pretty haphazard and take long stretches to achieve. The small wheels up front tend to lock up in no time, so stopping on a dime is out of the question.

- RIDE COMFORT. The ride isn't bad on smooth surfaces, but the Prowler really shakes up passengers on poor roads and the suspension is without pity. Finally, the lovely roar that thrilled you during the first 30 or so miles is no thrill at all on long jaunts.

- CONVENIENCE FEATURES. They're non-existent, for storage compartments and trunk are purely symbolic and the mini-trailer offered as an option for luggage is far from being a gadget.

- FLAWS. Access to headlight controls, poor quality anchors for the convertible top, body stiffness when travelling with the top down, doors that rattle. Windshield wipers are small and terribly lazy, forcing the driver to slow down when travelling in heavy rain.

CONCLUSION

A superb collector's item, the Plymouth Prowler can be used as a means of transportation provided its occupants are willing to travel with not much knowledge of their surroundings, even if heads do turn everywhere they drive by.

Sports car $35-100,000

RATING
PLYMOUTH Prowler

CONCEPT :		48%
Technology :	90	
Safety :	75	
Interior space :	0	
Trunk volume :	0	
Quality/fit/finish :	75	

DRIVING :		70%
Cockpit :	50	
Performance :	80	
Handling :	70	
Steering :	90	
Braking :	60	

ORIGINAL EQUIPMENT :		68%
Tires :	90	
Headlights :	75	
Wipers :	50	
Rear defroster :	50	
Radio :	75	

COMFORT :		40%
Seats :	80	
Suspension :	40	
Sound level :	0	
Conveniences :	10	
Air conditioning :	70	

BUDGET :		50%
Price :	0	
Fuel economy :	70	
Insurance :	30	
Satisfaction :	50	
Depreciation :	100	

| **Overall rating :** | | **55.2%** |

NEW FOR 2000
- Silver exterior color and black bumpers.
- Automatic rearview mirror showing compass, exterior temperature and onboard computer readings.
- Safety lock for the gear shift lever.
- Bigger fuel tank.

Compare Performance, Specifications, Prices, and Classification at the end of this chapter.

EQUIPMENT

PLYMOUTH Prowler	base
Automatic transmission:	S
Cruise control:	S
Power steering:	S
Anti-lock brakes:	-
Traction control:	-
Air conditioning:	SM
Leather:	S
AM/FM/radio-cassette:	SCd
Power door locks:	S
Power windows:	S
Tilt steering:	-
Dual adjustable mirrors:	SE
Alloy wheels:	S
Anti-theft system:	S

Colors

Exterior: Red, Black, Silver.

Interior: Pebble.

AT A GLANCE...

HISTORIC
Introduced in: 1997.
Made in: Conner Avenue Detroit, Michigan, USA.

DEMOGRAPHICS

Model	Men/Wom.	Age	Married	College	Income $
Prowler	95/5 %	45	65 %	45 %	100,000

INDEX

Safety:	80 %	Satisfaction:	78 %
Depreciation:	65 %	Insurance:	$ 1,300
Cost per mile:	$ 0.65	Number of dealers:	1822

SALES

	Canada			USA		
Model	1997	1998	Result	1997	1998	Result
Prowler	11	146	+ 1227.3 %	120	1,594	+ 1228.3%

MAINTENANCE REQUIRED BY WARRANTY

First revision:	Frequency:	Diagnostic plug:
5,000 miles	6 months / 6,000 miles	No

Sports cars $35-70,000

Porsche has found success once again. After many lean years, the Zuffenhausen builder has refurbished its lineup, adding a new model, the Boxster, and this time out genuinely revamping its flagship model, the 911. For the new millennium, Porsche has beefed up its model range. Now more powerful, the Boxster S and 911 are at the top.

MODEL RANGE

The Boxster roadster is now available in a base version equipped with a 2.7L horizontally opposed 6-cylinder engine or in an S version powered by a 252-hp 3.2L engine. The 911, already available as a 2- or 4-wheel drive Carrera, as a coupe or a convertible powered by a 3.4L engine and a 6-speed manual or 5-speed automatic Tiptronic transmission, now also comes as a 420-hp 3.6L Turbo. While sporty, these cars also offer elaborate equipment. There's nothing missing inside: air conditioning, leather trims and major power systems are all there!

TECHNICAL FEATURES

After a fifty-year tradition of a rear-engine setup, Porsche has introduced the platform shared by the Boxster and the 911 model, that includes a mid-engine arrangement. Aerodynamics are excellent, since the drag coefficient is 0.30. The steel monocoque body is galvanized on both sides and is mounted on a subframe for greater structural rigidity. Front and rear suspensions consist of a MacPherson design, namely struts with transversal and longitudinal control arms, supported by coil springs and anti-roll bar at both ends. Disc brakes are equipped with single-piece calipers fitted with four pistons, like those

Exotic

used on Formula 1 racecars, linked to a fifth-generation antilock braking system. Cars benefit from power rack-and-pinion steering.
The engines that equip these cars were developed specifically for them. It's a 6-cylinder with cylinders set in opposed rows to form an H shape, tailored to meet the needs of the respective models. They're crammed with high tech features such as transversal flow water-cooling that maintains the temperature constant around the cylinders and separate cooling for the cylinder head. Actuators located in the camshaft chains of command (a system patented by Porsche called Variocam) allow for variable intake valve opening time. The Tiptronic automatic transmission includes an electronic traction control device and a limited slip differential that stabilizes accelerations on slippery roads.

OUTSTANDING

++ STYLE. You have to admit that Porsche's are gorgeous cars with their smooth, polished lines. The 911 was redesigned but didn't loose an ounce of the charisma that buyers have loved over the years, while the Boxster roadster, derived from the same source, adds a touch of mischievous non-conformity.

PROS

+ PERFORMANCE. The engines on these two models are a sheer joy for speed lovers and from the Boxster

S to the 911 Turbo, they can reach top speeds of 185 mph (300 kph), going from 0 to 60 mph (0 to 100 kph) in approximately 4.5 seconds.
+ BRAKES. They're brawny, balanced, easy to apply and tough as nails, so they provide optimal safety. In the coming months, Porsche plans to introduce ceramic discs that should result in even more improvement.
+ HANDLING. It's in keeping with this carmaker's reputation. These cars handle beautifully, due to the mid-engine setup, excellent tire quality and highly honed suspensions.
+ SAFETY. Passenger protection is assured due to the generous collapsible section at the front end (which explains the big overhang), magnesium roll bars, reinforced windshield frame and the two front-impact and two side-impact airbags.
+ RIDE COMFORT. It's quite good, in spite of the snug cockpit that seats two comfortably and all the luxury accessories add to travel pleasure.
+ CONVERTIBLE TOP. Its power mechanism works like a charm and it's super rigid and waterproof. But the wind deflector is a must for travelling with the top down...

CONS

- PERFORMANCES. The 2.7L Boxster's output is disappointing, especially with the Tiptronic transmission, for performances aren't at

all exotic, since staid sedans (Regal or Intrigue) achieve the same acceleration and pickup figures, in spite of their more lowly origins...
- TRANSMISSION. The Tiptronic formula doesn't seem as solid as when it was first introduced, compared to others offered on the market. Dials located on the steering wheel are not really practical, for speeds shift on their own when the needle hits the red zone. Trying to change speeds on curve could lead to serious thumb sprains...
- QUALITY. Materials and finish in the passenger compartment fail to reach the same level as they did on previous models.
- CONVENIENCE FEATURES. As was to be expected, such an elitist car doesn't offer too many down-to-earth amenities. Door side-pockets replace the glove compartment and both trunks contain precious little.
- NOISE LEVEL. It's high at all times and gets tiring after a while. It's mostly made up of wind and exhaust noise.
- AUTONOMY. Depending on driving style, it will be limited by the restricted gas tank capacity and fuel consumption is pretty high with lows at around 16 miles per gallon.
- WARRANTY. It's one of the most restrictive in the industry, a lovely gesture that says reams about the carmaker's confidence in his product...

CONCLUSION

Porsche has a place all its own on the automotive market, where its history and legendary expertise are an integral part of the make's magnetism. The only problem is that current products don't always live up to the reputation built by previous models.

RATING
PORSCHE Boxster - 911

CONCEPT :   62%
Technology :	90
Safety :	90
Interior space :	20
Trunk volume :	30
Quality/fit/finish :	80

DRIVING :   83%
Cockpit :	80
Performance :	85
Handling :	80
Steering :	80
Braking :	90

ORIGINAL EQUIPMENT :   79%
Tires :	90
Headlights :	80
Wipers :	70
Rear defroster :	75
Radio :	80

COMFORT :   60%
Seats :	80
Suspension :	70
Sound level :	10
Conveniences :	60
Air conditioning :	80

BUDGET :   44%
Price :	0
Fuel economy :	65
Insurance :	35
Satisfaction :	85
Depreciation :	35

Overall rating :   65.6%

NEW FOR 2000

- The Turbo version of the 911, with a 420-hp output.
- The S version of the Boxster, with a 252-hp engine.

Compare Performance, Specifications, Prices, and Classification at the end of this chapter.

EQUIPMENT

PORSCHE	Boxster base	Boxster S	911 Car.2	911 Car.4	911 GT3	911 Turbo
Automatic transmission:	O	O	O	O	O	O
Cruise control:	S	S	S	S	S	S
Power steering:	S	S	S	S	S	S
Anti-lock brakes:	S	S	S	S	S	S
Traction control:	S	S	S	S	S	S
Air conditioning:	SA	SA	SA	SA	SA	SA
Leather:	S	S	S	S	S	S
AM/FM/radio-cassette:	SCd	SCd	SCd	SCd	SCd	SCd
Power door locks:	S	S	S	S	S	S
Power windows:	S	S	S	S	S	S
Tilt steering:	S	S	S	S	S	S
Dual adjustable mirrors:	SEH	SEH	SEH	SEH	SEH	SEH
Alloy wheels:	S	S	S	S	S	S
Anti-theft system:	S	S	S	S	S	S

Colors
Exterior: Grey, White, Red, Black, Blue, Yellow.

Interior: Grey, Black, Red, Green.

AT A GLANCE...

HISTORIC
Introduced in:	1997: Boxster, 1999: 911.
Made in:	Zuffenhausen, Stuttgart, Germany.

DEMOGRAPHICS
Model	Men/Wom.	Age	Married	College	Income $
Boxster	NA				
911	NA				

INDEX
Safety:	90 %	Satisfaction:	87 %
Depreciation:	35 %	Insurance:	$ 1,125-1,350
Cost per mile:	$ 0.77-1.05	Number of dealers:	210

SALES
Model	Canada 1997	1998	Result	USA 1997	1998	Result
Boxster	455	516	+ 13.4 %	6,888	9,678	+ 40.5 %
911	304	430	+ 41.4 %	5,851	7,561	+ 29.2 %

MAINTENANCE REQUIRED BY WARRANTY
First revision:	Frequency:	Diagnostic plug:
15,000 miles	15,000 miles	Yes

Sports car $35-100,000

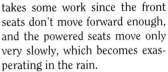
When it decided to add a coupe and a convertible to its 70 series, Volvo penetrated a market niche that Mercedes, BMW and Jaguar had tended to monopolize for a long time. While this automotive class doesn't generate as many sales as sedans and wagons, it projects a luxurious and sporty image that gives the Swedish builder access to the select club of prestige makes. And such a gain in status is vital to the continued success of its operations.

MODEL RANGE

The C70 is available as a 2-door coupe or convertible in a single trim, powered by a 2.4L 5-cylinder engine with 190 hp and 4-speed automatic transmisstion or by a 2.3-liter engine putting out 236 horses, with a standard 5-speed manual or optional 4-speed automatic transmission. Standard equipment includes cruise control, power steering, antilock brakes, air conditioning, two front and two side airbags, heated front seats, stereo, adjustable steering column, power windows, doors, etc., alloy wheels and an anti-theft system. The convertible top automatically tucks away.

TECHNICAL FEATURES

The C70 series steel unibody splits the weight 60/40. The rounder shape improves the drag coefficient to a remarkable 0.29 on the coupe and 0.34 on the convertible. The front suspension is outfitted with MacPherson struts, and the semi-independent rear axle, called "Delta-Link", a Volvo creation designed to control roll and flexibility, is assisted by an anti-roll bar. The four-wheel disc brakes are controlled by an anti-lock system, and a balancing system between front and rear evenly distributes braking force. The 236 hp engine is identical to the 5-cylinder turbo on the sedans and the sporty T-5 wagons.

OUTSTANDING

++STYLING. It is still traditional and very Volvo, but it exudes class. Several small touches bring Jaguar to mind, and the copper color on the coupe adds to the allure.

PROS

+SAFETY. A great deal of research was conducted to guarantee that the structural rigidity of these vehicles would match that of the sedans and wagons. The convertible required special attention because it is more susceptible to damage in the event of a crash, and has been reinforced in several key spots. The body includes two retractable roll bars that activate as soon as the car begins to turn over. Both vehicles also include two front and two side airbags as well as headrests on rear seats.

+INTERIOR SPACE. Seemingly compact, the body is comparable in size to the sedan, making the interior unusually large for this kind of car. The rear-seat passengers can be relatively comfortable in both the coupe and the convertible.

+PERFORMANCE. Once the Turbo reaches a good cruising speed, acceleration and passing are superb, worthy of Grand Touring cars.

+QUALITY. With these two cars, Volvo has reached a level of luxury never before seen by this manufacturer. The half-wood, half-leather steering wheel, as well as the fine leatherwork, is very "Jaguaresque".

+DRIVING. In spite of the power under the hoods of these cars, they are most enjoyable driven at normal speeds on Arizona back roads and in chic California area. At most, the 6-cylinder in the S80 would be better than the Turbo for this kind of American-style touring.

+REMARKABLE. The eight-speaker stereo system is of unusual quality and depth for vehicles of this price.

+WELL DESIGNED. The molded rubber sections around the windshield are refined and well-finished. The wind-breaking cover for unoccupied rear seats is efficient, even though some effort is required to put it on.

CONS

-THE TURBO. The slow response time ruins a bit of the fun, but is less bothersome under normal conditions.

-BRAKING. It was less impressive than on the sedans and wagons. Note that the vehicle that was made available to us was seriously mistreated by some of our less scrupulous colleagues.

-ACCESS. Getting to the rear seats takes some work since the front seats don't move forward enough, and the powered seats move only very slowly, which becomes exasperating in the rain.

-VISIBILITY. The height of the rear and the top of the convertible create large blind spots, which doesn't help when parking.

-STORAGE. There is a lack of storage space since both the glove box and the center console are quickly filled up and the side-door pockets are tiny.

-WORTH REVIEWING. The speaker in the middle of the dashbord looks a little out of place and a little odd, but this is the price you pay for such outstanding sound.

CONCLUSION

The C70 models are blue-blood automobiles and their elaborate content is available at a cost lower than the average for this category's traditional leaders.

Class

RATING
VOLVO C70

CONCEPT :   72%
Technology :   85
Safety :   90
Interior space :   60
Trunk volume :   45
Quality/fit/finish :   80

DRIVING :   76%
Cockpit :   80
Performance :   70
Handling :   70
Steering :   80
Braking :   80

ORIGINAL EQUIPMENT :   77%
Tires :   80
Headlights :   80
Wipers :   65
Rear defroster :   80
Radio :   80

COMFORT :   67%
Seats :   80
Suspension :   75
Sound level :   30
Conveniences :   70
Air conditioning :   80

BUDGET :   53%
Price :   0
Fuel economy :   70
Insurance :   40
Satisfaction :   90
Depreciation :   65

Overall rating :   69.0%

NEW FOR 2000

• Side air bags that have been extended to protect head, chest and shoulder.

Compare Performance, Specifications, Prices, and Classification at the end of this chapter.

EQUIPMENT

VOLVO C70	coupe	convertible
Automatic transmission:	O	O
Cruise control:	S	S
Power steering:	S	S
Anti-lock brakes:	S	S
Traction control:	S	S
Air conditioning:	S	S
Leather:	SH	SH
AM/FM/radio-cassette:	S	S
Power door locks:	S	S
Power windows:	S	S
Tilt steering:	S	S
Dual adjustable mirrors:	SEH	SEH
Alloy wheels:	S	S
Anti-theft system:	S	S

Colors
Exterior: Black, White, Red, Blue, Green, Silver, Graphite, Grey, Sand, Teal.

Interior: Blue, Taupe, Grey.

AT A GLANCE...

HISTORIC
Introduced in: 1992,1997.
Made in: Uddevalla, Sweden.

DEMOGRAPHICS

Model	Men/Wom.	Age	Married	College	Income $
C70	85/15 %	43	46 %	55 %	113,500

INDEX

Safety:	90 %	Satisfaction:	90 %
Depreciation:	35 %	Insurance:	$ 915
Cost per mile:	$ 0.75	Number of dealers:	405

SALES

Model	Canada 1997	1998	Result	USA 1997	1998	Result
C70	NA					

MAINTENANCE REQUIRED BY WARRANTY

First revision:	Frequency:	Diagnostic plug:
Tbo : 5,000 miles	Tbo : 5,000 miles	Yes

Sports cars $35-70,000

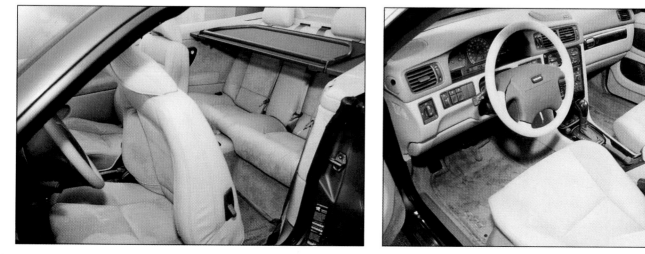

SPORTS CARS from 35 to $ 70,000
PERFORMANCE

Model/ version	Type / timing valve / fuel system	Displacement cu in	Power hp @ rpm	Torque lb-ft @ rpm	Compres. ratio	Driving wheels / transmission	Final ratio	Acceler. 0-60	Standing 1/4 & 5/8		Passing 50-75	Braking 60-0 ft	Top mph	Lateral G	Noise dBA	City	Highway	Octane
AUDI TT																		
TT FWD	L4T 1.8 DOHC-20-MPSFI	108	180 @ 5500	173 @ 1950	9.5 :1	front - M5	3.938	7.4*					129*			22	34	S 91
TT quattro	L4T 1.8 DOHC-20-MPSFI	108	180 @ 5500	173 @ 1950	9.5 :1	all - M5	3.938	8.0	16.2				129*			21	33	S 91
BMW Z3																		
2.3	L6 2.5 DOHC-24-EFI	152	170 @ 5500	181 @ 3500	10.5 :1	rear - M5*	3.15	8.0	15.7	27.0	6.8	121	128*	0.86	68-75	22	32	S 91
						rear - A4	4.27	8.9	16.5	28.4	7.0	125	128*	0.86	68-76	19	29	S 91
2.8	L6 2.8 DOHC-24-EFI	170	193 @ 5500	203 @ 3950	10.2 :1	rear - M5*	3.15	7.0	15.4	26.0	5.6	121	128*	0.87	67-74	19	27	S 91
						rear - A4	4.10	7.8	16.0	26.4	6.0	125	128*	0.87	67-74	18	27	S 91
M	L6 3.2 DOHC-24-EFI	192	240 @ 6000	236 @ 3800	10.5 :1	rear - M5*	3.23	6.6	15.0	25.2	4.8	121	137	0.88	68-75	20	30	S 91
CHEVROLET Corvette																		
Corvette	V8 5.7 OHV-16-SFI	346	345 @ 5600	350 @ 4400	10.1 :1	rear - A4*[1]	2.73	5.3	14.0	25.3	3.5	115	167	0.95	72-80	17	27	S 91
						rear - M6*[2]	3.42	5.0	13.8	24.8	3.2	108	170	0.95	72	18	29	S 91

[1] standard coupe, convertible.   [2] standard hardtop, option coupe and convertible.

Model/ version	Type / timing valve / fuel system	Displacement cu in	Power hp @ rpm	Torque lb-ft @ rpm	Compres. ratio	Driving wheels / transmission	Final ratio	Acceler. 0-60	Standing 1/4 & 5/8		Passing 50-75	Braking 60-0 ft	Top mph	Lateral G	Noise dBA	City	Highway	Octane
DODGE Viper																		
RT/10-GTS	V10 8.0 OHV-20-MPSFI	488	450 @ 5200	490 @ 3700	9.6:1	rear - M6	3.07	4.3	12.4	21.5	2.8	131	165	1.00	75	13	20	S 91
HONDA S2000																		
S2000	L4 2.0 DOHC-16-MPSFI	122	240 @ 8300	153 @ 7500	11.0 :1	rear - M6	4.10	6.6	14.7	26.1	4.6	128	145	0.85	67-74	20	27	S 91
JAGUAR XK8																		
coupe	V8 4.0 DOHC-32-EFI	244	290 @ 6100	290 @ 4250	10.75 :1	rear - A5*	3.06	6.7	15.0	28.0	4.4	125	152	0.85	64-72	17	25	S 91
convertible	V8 4.0 DOHC-32-EFI	244	290 @ 6100	290 @ 4250	10.75 :1	rear - A5*	3.06	7.0	15.2	28.4	4.6	131	149	0.85	64-72	17	25	S 91
MERCEDES-BENZ CLK																		
CLK 320	V6 3.2 SOHC-18-SFI	195	215 @ 5700	229 @ 3000	10.0 :1	rear - A5	3.07	7.3	15.5	26.4	5.2	125	131	0.83	66	20	30	S 91
CLK 430	V8 4.3 SOHC-24-SFI	260	275 @ 5750	295 @ 3000	10.0 :1	rear - A5	2.87	NA								14	27	S 91
MERCEDES-BENZ SLK																		
SLK 230	L4 C2.3 DOHC 16 SFI	140	185 @ 5300	200 @ 2500	8.8 :1	rear - A5	3.27	7.8	15.8	28.2	5.5	134	143	0.88	70	21	32	S 91
						rear - M5	3.46	NA								22	33	S 91
PLYMOUTH Prowler																		
Prowler	V6 3.5 SOHC-24-MPSFI	215	253 @ 6400	255 @ 3950	9.9 :1	rear - A4	3.89	7.0	14.3	26.0	4.6	151	124	0.85	78-82	19	27	S 92
PORSCHE Boxster - 911																		
Boxster	H6 2.7 DOHC- 24-SFI	164	220 @ 6400	192 @ 4750	11.0 :1	rear - M5*	3.56	7.0	14.8	27.0	4.8	115	146	0.91	70-75	18	27	S 92
						rear - A5	4.02	7.8	15.2	28.4	5.1	118	143	0.91	70-75	16	25	S 92
Boxster S	H6 3.2 DOHC- 24-SFI	194	252 @ 6250	225 @ 4500	11.0 :1	rear - M5*	3.44	6.1		26.6			150			15	29	S 92
						rear - A5	3.73	6.7		27.5			148			14	27	S 92
911 C2	H6 3.4 DOHC- 24-DFI	207	296 @ 6800	258 @ 4600	11.3 :1	rear - M6*	3.44	5.2	13.4	25.6	4.2	121	170	0.91	68.74	14	28	S 91
						rear - A5	3.45	6.0	14.0	26.0	4.3	125	168	0.91	68-74	13	26	S 91
911 C4	H6 3.4 DOHC- 24-DFI	207	296 @ 6800	258 @ 4600	11.3 :1	rear - M6*	3.44	5.2	13.6	25.8	4.2	122	170	0.91	68.74	14	28	S 91
						rear - A5	3.68	6.0	14.2	26.2	4.5	125	168	0.91	68-74	13	26	S 91
911 Turbo	H6 3.6 DOHC- 24-DFI	220	420 @ 6000	413 @ 4600	9.4 :1	rear - M6*	3.44	4.5	13.0	22.6	2.8	115	186	0.91	68.76	13	27	S 91
						rear - A5	2,89	5.2	14.0	24.2	4.2	121	182	0.91	68-76	12	25	S 91
VOLVO C70																		
C70	L5T 2.4 DOHC-20-MPSFI	149	190 @ 5100	199 @ 1600	9.0 :1	front - A4	NA											S 91
C70	L5T 2.3 DOHC-20-MPSFI	141	236 @ 5400	244 @ 2400	8.5 :1	front - A4	2.56	6.8	14.8	26.5	4.8	131	146	0.85	67-74	19	25	S 91
						front - M5*	4.00	NA								18	25	S 91

SPORTS CARS from 35 to $ 70,000
SPECIFICATIONS

Model	Version Trim	Body/Seats	Cabin volume cu ft	Trunk volume cu ft	Cd	Wheel base in	Lgth x Width x Hght in x inx in	Curb weight lb	Susp. ft/rr	Brake ft/rr type	Steering ø ft	turns number	Fuel tank gal	dimensions	Standard tires make	Standard tires model	Standard powertrain	99 Price msrp $
AUDI	General warranty: 3-years / 50,000 miles; perforation corrosion: 10-years; free maintenance: 3-years / 50,000 miles; roadside assistance: 3-years.																	
TT	1.8T FWD	2dr.cpe. 2+2	58.9	13.8	0.34	95.3	159.1x69.4x53.0	2656	ih/th	dc/ABS	pwr.r&p. 34.3	2.8	14.5	205/55R16	Michelin	Pilot SX	L4T/1.8/M5	-
TT	1.8T quattro	2dr.cpe. 2+2	58.9	10.8	0.34	95.6	159.1x69.4x53.0	2910	ih/ih	dc/ABS	pwr.r&p. 34.3	2.8	16.4	205/55R16	Michelin	Pilot SX	L4T/1.8/M5	-
BMW	General warranty : 4-years/ 50,000 miles; corrosion: 6-years / unlimited: antipollution: 8-years / 80,000 miles.																	
Z3	2.3	2dr.con. 2	NA	5.8	0.42	96.3	158.5x68.5x50.9	2689	ih/ih	dc/ABS	pwr.r&p. 32.8	3.0	13.5	225/50ZR16	Michelin	Pilot MXM	L6/2.3/M5	30,520
Z3	2.8	2dr.con. 2	NA	5.8	0.42	96.3	158.5x68.5x50.9	2778	ih/ih	dc/ABS	pwr.r&p. 32.8	3.0	13.5	225/50ZR16	Dunlop	SP 8000	L6/2.8/M5	36,770
Z3	M roadster	2dr.con. 2	NA	5.8	0.42	96.8	158.5x68.5x49.8	2976	ih/ih	dc/ABS	pwr.r&p. 34.1	3.0	13.5	ft225/45ZR17	Dunlop	SP 8000	L6/3.2/M5	40,270
Z3	M coupe	2dr.cpe. 2	NA	11.2	0.37	96.8	158.5x68.5x50.4	2976	ih/ih	dc/ABS	pwr.r&p. 34.1	3.0	13.5	rr245/40ZR17	Dunlop	SP 8000	L6/3.2/M5	-
CHEVROLET	General warranty: 3-years / 36,000 miles; antipollution: 5-years / 50,000 miles; perforation corrosion: 6-years / 100,000 miles. Roadside assistance.																	
Corvette	coupe	2dr.cpe.2	51.4	24.8	0.29	104.5	179.7x73.6x47.7	3245	il/il	dc/ABS	pwr.r&p. 40.0	2.32	20.0	fr.245/45ZR17	Goodyear	Eagle F1	V8/5.7/A4	38,777
Corvette	hardtop	2dr.cpe.2	51.8	13.3	0.29	104.5	179.7x73.6x47.7	3172	il/il	dc/ABS	pwr.r&p. 40.0	2.32	20.0		Goodyear	Eagle F1	V8/5.7/M6	39,265
Corvette	convertible	2dr.cpe.2	NA	13.9	0.32	104.5	179.7x73.6x47.8	3247	il/il	dc/ABS	pwr.r&p. 40.0	2.32	20.0	rr275/40ZR18	Goodyear	Eagle F1	V8/5.7/A4	45,675
DODGE	General warranty: 3-years / 36,000 miles; corrosion: 10-years; roadside assistance: 3-years / 36,000 miles.																	
Viper	RT/10	2dr.con. 2	NA	6.8	0.46	96.2	175.1x75.7x44.0	3439	ih/ih	dc/dc	pwr.r&p. 12.34	2.4	19.0	ft275/35ZR18	Michelin	Pilot MXX3	V10/8.0/M6	66,425
Viper	GTS	2dr.cpe. 2	NA	9.2	0.35	96.2	176.7x75.7x47.0	3458	ih/ih	dc/dc	pwr.r&p. 12.34	2.4	19.0	rr335/30ZR18	Michelin	Pilot MXX3	V10/8.0/M6	68,925
HONDA	General warranty: 3-years / 36,000 miles; powertrain: 5-years / 60,000 miles.																	
S2000	roadster	2dr.con. 2	48.3	5.4	NA	94.5	162.2x68.9x50.6	2810	ih/ih	dc/ABS	pwr.r&p. 10.8	NA	13.2	ft205/55VR16	Bridgestone	Potenza	L4/2.0/M6	
														rr225/50VR16	Bridgestone	Potenza		
JAGUAR	General warranty: 4-years / 50,000 miles; corrosion: 6-years / unlimited; antipollution : 4-years / 50,000 miles ; free maintenance: 2-years / 20,000 miles.																	
XK8	coupe	2dr.cpe.2+2	NA	11.1	0.35	101.9	187.4x72.0x50.5	3673	i/i	dc/ABS	pwr.r&p. 40.7	2.8	20.0	245/50ZR17	Pirelli	P Zero	V8/4.0/A5	66,630
XK8	convertible	2dr.con.2+2	NA	9.5	0.36	101.9	187.4x72.0x51.0	3867	i/i	dc/ABS	pwr.r&p. 40.7	2.8	20.0	245/50ZR17	Pirelli	P Zero	V8/4.0/A5	71,330
MERCEDES-BENZ CLK	General warranty: 4-years / 50,000 miles; corrosion perforation; 5-years / unlimited.																	
CLK	320	2dr.cpe.5	80.7	11.0	0.31	105.9	180.2x68.7x53.9	3212	ih/ih	dc/ABS	pwr.ball 35.1	3.2	16.4	205/55R16	MichelinEnergy	MXV4	V6/3.2/A5	41,195
CLK	320	2dr.con.4	75.7	9.6	0.32	105.9	180.2x68.7x54.3	3564	ih/ih	dc/ABS	pwr.ball 35.1	3.2	16.4	205/55R16	MichelinEnergy	MXV4	V6/3.2/A5	47,795
CLK	430	2dr.cpe.5	80.7	11.2	0.31	105.9	180.2x68.7x53.9	3322	ih/ih	dc/ABS	pwr.ball 35.1	3.2	16.4	ft225/45ZR17	Michelin	Pilot SX	V8/4.3/A5	48,495
CLK	430	2dr.con.4	75.7	9.6	0.32	105.9	180.2x68.7x54.3	3664	ih/ih	dc/ABS	pwr.ball 35.1	3.2	16.4	rr245/40ZR17	Michelin	Pilot SX	V8/4.3/A5	-
MERCEDES-BENZ SLK	General warranty: 4-years / 50,000 miles; corrosion perforation; 5-years / unlimited.																	
SLK	Kompressor	2dr.cpe. 2	-	3.6-9.5	0.35	94.5	157.3x67.5x50.7	3036	ih/ih	vd/ABS	pwr.ball 34.7	3.1	14.0	205/55R16	Dunlop	SP8080	L4C/2.3/A5	40.595
PLYMOUTH	General warranty: 3-years / 36,000 miles; surface rust: 3-years ; perforation: 7-years / 100,000 miles; roadside assistance: 3-years / 36,000 miles.																	
Prowler	convertible	2dr.con. 2	47.9	1.8	NA	113.3	165.3x76.5x50.9	2838	ih/ih	dc/dc	pwr.r&p. 38.4	3.1	12.0	ft225/45VR17	Goodyear	Eagle GS-D	V6/3.5/A4	40.000
														rr295/40VR20	Goodyear	Eagle GS-D		
PORSCHE	General warranty: 2-years / unlimited; antipollution : 2-years / 25,000 miles; surface rust-perforration 3-years-10-years / unlimited.																	
Boxster	base	2dr.con. 2	NA	9.2	0.31	95.1	169.8x70.1x50.8	2777	ih/ih	dc/ABS	pwr.r&p. 35.8	2.98	15.3	ft205/55ZR16	Bridgestone	S-02	H6/2.7/M5	41,765
Boxster	Tiptronic	2dr.con. 2	NA	9.2	0.31	95.1	169.8x70.1x50.8	2888	ih/ih	dc/ABS	pwr.r&p. 35.8	2.98	15.3	rr225/50ZR16	Bridgestone	S-02	H6/2.7/A5	-
Boxster	S	2dr.con. 2	NA	9.2	0.31	95.1	169.8x70.1x50.8	2855	ih/ih	dc/ABS	pwr.r&p. 35.8	2.98	15.3	205/55ZR17	Bridgestone	S-02	H6/3.2/M6	-
Boxster	S-Tiptronic	2dr.con. 2	NA	9.2	0.31	95.1	169.8x70.1x50.8	2943	ih/ih	dc/ABS	pwr.r&p. 35.8	2.98	15.3	rr255/40ZR17	Bridgestone	S-02	H6/3.2/A5	-
911	Carrera 2	2dr.cpe.2	NA	3.5	0.30	92.5	174.4x69.5x51.8	2910	ih/ih	dc/ABS	pwr.r&p. 34.8	3.0	16.9	ft205/50ZR17	Bridgestone	S-02	H6/3.4/M6	65,765
911	Carrera con.	2dr.con.2	NA	3.5	0.32	92.5	174.4x69.5x51.4	2910	ih/ih	dc/ABS	pwr.r&p. 34.8	3.0	16.9	rr255/40ZR17	Bridgestone	S-02	H6/3.4/A5	-
911	Carrera 4	2dr.cpe.2	NA	3.5	0.30	92.5	174.4x69.5x51.8	2910	ih/ih	dc/ABS	pwr.r&p. 34.8	3.0	16.9	as previous	Bridgestone	S-02	H6/3.4/M6	-
911	Turbo	2dr.cpe.2	NA	3.5	0.32	92.5	174.6x72.0x51.0	2910	ih/ih	dc/ABS	pwr.r&p. 34.8	3.0	16.9	ft225/40ZR18	Bridgestone	S-02	H6/3.6/M6	-
														rr295/30ZR18				
VOLVO	General warranty: 4-years / 50,000 miles; corrosion: 8-years / unlimited; antipollution: 5-years / 50,000 miles.																	
C70	Coupe	2dr.cpe. 4	-	14.2	0.29	104.9	185.7x71.6x55.5	3214	ih/sih	dc/ABS	pwr.r&p. 38.4	3.0	18.5	225/45ZR17	Michelin	Pilot SX	L5T/2.4/M5	39,970
C70	Convertible	2dr.con. 4	-	8.0	0.34	104.9	185.7x71.6x56.3	3631	ih/sih	dc/ABS	pwr.r&p. 38.4	3.0	18.5	205/55R16	Pirelli	P6000	L5T/2.4/M5	43,970

Sports car $35 to $70,000

Notes: 1) Tire makes and models are provided solely as an indication; they are subject to change without prior notice from the automobile manufacturers.

2) See the 2000 price list at the back of this edition.

SPORTS CARS from 35 to $ 70,000
CLASSIFICATION

OUR CLASSIFICATION

Rank	Models	Concept	Driving	Equipment	Comfort	Budget	Ratings
1	**VOLVO C70**	**72**	76	77	67	53	**69.0 %**
2	MERCEDES-BENZ CLK	69	74	78	69	51	68.2 %
3	JAGUAR XK8	68	77	77	**70**	45	67.4 %
4	PORSCHE Boxster-911	62	83	**79**	60	44	65.6 %
4	MERCEDES-BENZ SLK	56	74	78	69	51	65.6 %
5	AUDI TT	64	76	**79**	67	41	65.4 %
6	CHEVROLET Corvette	65	86	77	55	42	65.0 %
7	BMW Z3	57	82	62	64	54	63.8 %
8	DODGE Viper	61	**88**	76	46	41	62.4 %
9	HONDA S2000	56	77	62	62	**55**	62.4 %
10	PLYMOUTH Prowler	48	70	68	40	50	55.2 %

YOUR CLASSIFICATION

Rank	Model	98 Sales
1	**CHEVROLET Corvette**	**29,208**
2	BMW Z3	20,613
3	MERCEDES-BENZ CLK	11,622
4	MERCEDES-BENZ SLK	10,620
5	PORSCHE Boxster	9,678
6	PORSCHE	7.561
7	JAGUAR XK8	5,861
8	PLYMOUTH Prowler	1,594
9	DODGE Viper	1,248

Not classified:
AUDI TT
VOLVO C70
HONDA S2000

NOTES

CHRYSLER NS Series

FORD Windstar

GM M Series

GM U Series

HONDA Odyssey

MAZDA MPV

Comparative Test

MINI-VANS

See their performance, their specifications, their price and their classification at the end of this chapter.

TOYOTA Sienna

NISSAN Quest

Minivans

Exclusive

Chrysler minivans continue to dominate, shattering sales records throughout North America in spite of increasingly fierce and heavy competition. On the verge of a revamping, they still have a comfortable lead when it comes to technology and marketing and their closest rivals have no alternative other than cutting prices to gain a larger market share.

MODEL RANGE

The Caravan-Voyager (short version) are available in base, SE and LE trim levels and the Grand Caravan-Grand Voyager (long version) are sold in SE, LE and sporty ES. Chrysler offers the Town & Country in LX and LXi models in two wheelbase lengths. The short versions are equipped with the base 2.4L 4-cylinder engine, the SE versions with a 3.0L V6, the long versions are driven by a 3.3L V6 and the Town & Country and AWD vehicles, by a 3.8L engine that now develops 180 hp. The second sliding door on the driver's side is still only available as an extra, but even lower-end models have standard automatic transmission, power steering, ABS and now all passengers can benefit from headrests.

TECHNICAL FEATURES

The new models are longer and wider than before and fitted with bigger windows. The latest-generation Chrysler minivans are the most modern of the three most popular models sold. The steel unibody is much beefier and aerodynamic performance is near car-like. The front suspension includes a cast-aluminum crossmember that adds precision to the geometry and cuts down on vehicle weight and steer angle diameter. The rear suspension consists of a tubular rigid axle suspended by two single-leaf springs along with a torque bar to avoid rear end zizag effect. Disc and drum brakes paired up with ABS are standard equipment for all models. All-wheel drive model benefits from a transfer box and viscous coupling that distributes 10% of the power to the rear wheels when there's less adherence. Chrysler should dust off its power trains since they aren't as gutsy as those of the competition, even if power to weight ratios are still favorable.

PROS

+ ESTHETICS. The body design is appealing, functional and benefits from good aerodynamic efficiency. The monochrome paint finishes are just gorgeous (Town & Country and Sport), but some years there doesn't seem to offer much choice of color.

+ RIDE COMFORT. The ride is superb. The suspension is cushy, front seats provide effective support and noise and vibration are kept to a minimum even on the lower-end models.

+ CABIN SPACE. It's now 10% roomier for both body styles. There's more legroom, hip and shoulder room and the space between seats is wider and the doors are set lower.

+ HANDLING. A rigid aluminum crossmember has improved front end aim, so you can negotiate curves with ease, especially with the 16-inch tires that are highly recommended. The rear end is more civilized on poor pavement and roads and the vehicle stays on an even keel, in spite of the rather rustic design.

+ QUALITY. Engineering, assembly, fit and finish as well as trim materials have moved up a notch and the over-all look doesn't have "utility-vehicle" written all over it, not like before.

+ FUEL ECONOMY. The Chrysler V6 engines aren't the newest kids on the block, but they're among the most frugal when it comes to gas, since consumption is always below average for this type of displacement.

+ ACCESS. It's handier with the lowered door threshholds, the optional second sliding door and the outside handle on the rear hatch.

+ NICE FEATURES. The rear seat headrests that now come as standard equipment, the defroster that gets rid of ice build-up at the base of the windshield, wiper blades that keep on going even in extremely cold temperatures and the little wheels on the seatbenches that help shifting the seat benches around as needed.

CONS

- AUTOMATIC GEARBOX. The 4-speed electronically controlled gearbox offers practically no braking effect when downshifting, gear changes are sometimes iffy and the shifter isn't too reliable. A real pain.

- HEADLIGHTS. They're nowhere bright enough, a feature that's totally unacceptable and unworthy of the progressive Chrysler image. They're the worst around. Ridiculous.

- STORAGE COMPARTMENTS. They're downright skimpy. The glove compartment is tiny, the storage drawer under the seat is way out of reach and the storage bin is located way down on the console. There aren't any nice, big side-pockets on the doors and no storage shelves in the rear seat area (Kia came up with this item). We still miss the little storage tub under the dashboard on the old model that was so darn handy...

- INSTRUMENT PANEL. It looks great, but it isn't too practical or ergonomic, for some controls are hard to reach and the center console is way too low.

- SEATBENCHES. They're hard, seat and back cushions are short and they're horribly heavy and hard to handle. They aren't modular at all, so if you want to store stuff, you have to slip it under one of the seats...

- REAR HATCH DOOR. Hard to close because the hydraulic jacks are poorly balanced. Which means you have to make several attempts before you succeed.

- TO BE IMPROVED UPON. No step built into the rear bumper and coat hooks that can't hold a clothes hanger...

CONCLUSION

Opponents may be more and more competent, Chrysler still has a monopoly on North America's small minivan market. Due next year, the next generation should keep it in the lead even though the popularity for this kind of vehicle is bound to decline in the coming years.

RATING
CHRYSLER NS series

CONCEPT : 79%
Technology :	80
Safety :	80
Interior space :	90
Trunk volume :	65
Quality/fit/finish :	80

DRIVING : 59%
Cockpit :	75
Performance :	35
Handling :	40
Steering :	80
Braking :	65

ORIGINAL EQUIPMENT : 71%
Tires :	80
Headlights :	40
Wipers :	65
Rear defroster :	80
Radio :	90

COMFORT : 80%
Seats :	90
Suspension :	80
Sound level :	80
Conveniences :	70
Air conditioning :	80

BUDGET : 64%
Price :	50
Fuel economy :	75
Insurance :	60
Satisfaction :	85
Depreciation :	50

Overall rating : 70.6%

NEW FOR 2000

- AWD 3.8L engine compliant with California LEV standards.
- Stereo radio and cassette player standard on the Caravan-Grand Caravan.
- New exterior colors: Silver, Patriot Blue, Aquamarine, Green, Inferno Red.

Compare Performance, Specifications, Prices, and Classification at the end of this chapter.

EQUIPMENT

DODGE Caravan	base	SE	LE	ES	FWD	AWD
PLYMOUTH Voyager	base	SE			long	long
CHRYSLER Town & Country	reg	reg	reg	extd	SX	LXi/Ltd
Automatic transmission:	S	S	S	S	S	S
Cruise control:	O	S	S	S	S	S
Power steering:	S	S	S	S	S	S
Anti-lock brakes:	O	S	S	S	S	S
Traction control:	-	-	O	S	S	S
Air conditioning:	O	SM	SM	SA	SA	SA
Leather:	-	-	O	O	O	S
AM/FM/radio-cassette:	O	S	S	S	S	SCd
Power door locks:	O	O	S	S	S	S
Power windows:	O	O	S	S	S	S
Tilt steering:	O	S	S	S	S	S
Dual adjustable mirrors:	SM	SEH	SEH	SEH	SEH	SEH
Alloy wheels:	-	O	O	S	S	S
Anti-theft system:		O	O	O	O	O

Colors
Exterior: Grey, Green, Red, Amethyst, White, Teal, Cranberry, Blue, Champagne, Slate, Silver, Aquamarine.
Interior: Beige, Grey, Silver.

AT A GLANCE...

HISTORIC
Introduced in:	1984 (regular); 1987 (extended).
Made in:	Windsor, Ontario, Canada; St-Louis, Missouri, USA.

DEMOGRAPHICS
Model	Men/Wom.	Age	Married	College	Income $
Carav./Voy.	67/33 %	45	85 %	57 %	38,000
Gd Car./Voy.	70/30 %	45	94 %	49 %	46,500
T & Country	76/24 %	50	93 %	55 %	66,500

INDEX
Safety:	85 %	Satisfaction:	85 %
Depreciation:	48 %	Insurance:	$ 550-800
Cost per mile:	$ 0.55	Number of dealers:	1,822

SALES
	Canada			USA		
Model	1997	1998	Result	1997	1998	Result
Caravan	53,028	51,636	- 2.6 %	285,736	293,819	+ 2.8 %
T & Country	37,279	38,553	+ 3.4 %	76,653	71,981	- 6.1 %
Voyager	2,298	2,540	+ 10.5 %	156,056	156,971	+ 0.6 %

MAINTENANCE REQUIRED BY WARRANTY
First revision:	Frequency:	Diagnostic plug:
5,000 miles	6 months / 6,000 miles	Yes

Mid Size Cars

Huge

The Windstar is the most serious and most dangerous rival for Chrysler's minivans. A price-lowering policy has hoisted Ford to the midway point of sales levels established by the Caravan-Voyager. Ford is relying on a more powerful 3.8L engine and crash-test results to point out that the Windstar is stronger and safer than its alternatives. However, the claim is true only in part since the maximum towing capacity and 5-star rating are applicable only with the optional side airbags.

MODEL RANGE
The Windstar still comes in a single long-wheelbase model. The new model is almost the same size as before, but it's 0.4 inch shorter, 1.2 inches wider and sits 2.2 inches lower. The front overhang has been trimmed down as well. Ford offers four versions: 3.0L, LX, SE and SEL. Only the 3.0L version receives the 3.0L V6. The three other versions are animated by a 3.8L V6. All models are equipped with a 4-speed automatic transmission. There are umpteen equipment item variations, but all models are equipped with power steering, antilock braking system, rear wiper and a 7-passenger seating setup. The new driver's side sliding door isn't available on the 3.0L model; it's manually operated on the LS and SE, but has a power function on the SEL.

TECHNICAL FEATURES
The 2000 Windstar platform resembles that of the former Taurus. The steel monocoque body is very stiff, which explains high safety scores awarded by the NHTSA. Which also explains why the Windstar is more of a heavyweight than its rivals. The new body design hasn't affected aerodynamics any, since the drag coefficient is the same.
The independent front suspension consists of MacPherson struts, while the rear torsion axle acting as a stabilizer bar is fitted with coil springs. The Windstar is unique because of its very spacious interior and a floor height that's lower than average, to facilitate access. For 2000, the two engines aren't any more powerful, but torque is muscular. Steering system is power rack & pinion, and brakes are disc/drums with ABS braking system.

PROS
+ SAFETY FEATURES. Ford was bent on keeping Windstar's hard-earned five-star safety collision scores, which proves that the body is super-robust, even with the second sliding door opening. We also took note that side-impact airbags with head and chest protection assure front seat passenger protection.
+ ENGINE POWER. The 200-hp V6 now develops more torque, so it's ahead of the competition at GM and Chrysler (185-180 hp). It procures crisp acceleration and pickup surge, thanks to the favorable power to weight ratio.
+ CABIN SPACE. The really roomy interior can accomodate up to seven passengers and all their luggage. The cargo hold can be extended by removing the two rear seatbenches now equipped with wheels for easier manipulation (a Chrysler idea that was first introduced three years ago!)
+ RIDE COMFORT. The Windstar ride is comfy with such a well-honed suspension, thick, plush seats and effective sound dampening.

+ BRAKES. They're nice and gradual and have a lot of bite, no doubt they're the best in this vehicle category. Emergency stops are achieved in less than 135 ft, no mean feat even with ABS.
+ DRIVE FEEL. The ride is so cushy and civilized that you feel like you're at the wheel of a big sedan rather than inside an SUV.
+ ROBUST BUILD. The super-stiff chassis is a great basic asset for such a big vehicle, the fit and finish job is well rendered and trim material is quite nice.
+ NICE FEATURES. The parking brake lever located to the right of the driver's seat, handy rear radar detection device, good-design hatch door handle and intermittent rear wiper. Even the base model has a middle seatbench fitted with headrests!

CONS
- CHOICE. There isn't much engine, body format and cabin layout choices (it's not really modular), which is a handicap.
- FUEL CONSUMPTION. The 3.8L engine's fuel consumption is high and easily goes beyond the 14 mpg level when the vehicle is loaded to capacity.
- LOOKS. No doubt about it, Ford is having a hard time with its design team that can't seem to come up with a coherent approach for these vehicles, since they don't really have any recognizable family traits other than the famous oval grille...
- SWAY. The super-cushy suspension causes a heck of a lot of swish and sway, which causes serious understeer that the poor-quality tires can't offset.
- INSTRUMENT PANEL. It's been reworked but it still isn't too ergonomic. The main section is too low and its irregular shape doesn't make for good use of available space.
- SEATBENCHES. The middle and rear seatbenches are afflicted with short cushions and the rear one is hell to get to. They're heavy and hard to lug about. Too bad Ford is unaware of the Nissan track design that's so neat on the Quest/Villager duo. It makes the cabin so marvellously modular.
- CONVENIENCE FEATURES. Storage space is terribly sparce for a minivan. The glove compartment doesn't hold much and the console compartment is too low and hard to reach. At least this year, front doors are fitted with side-pockets on some trim levels!
- TO BE IMPROVED UPON. Off-center rear wiper that only sweeps a tiny section of the window...and not where you need it! The undue complexity of the sliding doors' automatic closing system can only bring additional related problems.

CONCLUSION
The Windstar is a huge vehicle whose heavy cockpit provides optimal protection for passengers, but at the cost of only mediocre performance levels. The model range is limited and the Mercury Villager from the same family fails to live up to reasonable expectations.

RATING
FORD Windstar

CONCEPT : 84%
Technology : 80
Safety : 100
Interior space : 85
Trunk volume : 80
Quality/fit/finish : 75

DRIVING : 61%
Cockpit : 80
Performance : 50
Handling : 35
Steering : 70
Braking : 70

ORIGINAL EQUIPMENT : 72%
Tires : 75
Headlights : 75
Wipers : 65
Rear defroster : 70
Radio : 75

COMFORT : 72%
Seats : 75
Suspension : 70
Sound level : 75
Conveniences : 60
Air conditioning : 80

BUDGET : 60%
Price : 50
Fuel economy : 50
Insurance : 60
Satisfaction : 85
Depreciation : 55

Overall rating : 69.8%

NEW FOR 2000

- Optional adjustable pedals.
- Video center to entertain kids.

Compare
Performance,
Specifications, Prices,
and Classification
at the end of this chapter.

EQUIPMENT

FORD Windstar	3.0L	LX	SE	SEL
Automatic transmission:	S	S	S	S
Cruise control:	O	S	S	S
Power steering:	O	S	S	S
Anti-lock brakes:	S	S	S	S
Traction control:	-	-	-	-
Air conditioning:	O	SM	SA	SA
Leather:	-	-	-	S
AM/FM/radio-cassette:	O	S	S	SCd
Power door locks:	-	S	S	S
Power windows:	-	S	S	S
Tilt steering:	-	S	S	S
Dual adjustable mirrors:	SM	SE	SEH	SEH
Alloy wheels:	O	O	S	S
Anti-theft system:	S	S	S	S

Colors

Exterior: Red, Blue, Gold, Green, Brown, White, Silver, White.

Interior: Blue, Graphite, Parchment.

AT A GLANCE...

HISTORIC
Introduced in: 1995-1999.
Made in: Oakville, Ontario, Canada.

DEMOGRAPHICS
Model	Men/Wom.	Age	Married	College	Income $
Windstar	75/25 %	45	90 %	47 %	50,000

INDEX
Safety:	100 %	Satisfaction:	85 %
Depreciation:	48 %	Insurance:	$ 600
Cost per mile:	$ 0.51	Number of dealers:	5 200

SALES
Model	Canada 1997	1998	Result	USA 1997	1998	Result
Windstar	52,114	48,300	- 7.3 %	205,356	190,173	-7.4 %

MAINTENANCE REQUIRED BY WARRANTY
First revision:	Frequency:	Diagnostic plug:
5,000 miles	6 months	Yes

Mid Size Cars

The Astro and the Safari are very popular in spite of the limitations linked with their technology, borrowed from the pickups from which they are very closely derived. Unlike front-wheel drive minivans, they can haul remarkably heavy loads thanks to a powerful 4.3L Vortec V6 engine.

Work Horses

MODEL RANGE

The Astro and Safari are available on one extended wheelbase in 4X2 or 4X4 version in three trim levels: base, LS and LT at Chevrolet as well as SLX, SLE and SLT at GMC. A 4.3L V6 engine powers these vans, linked to a 4-speed electronically controlled automatic transmission.

TECHNICAL FEATURES

The Astro and Safari are almost identical twins, except for a few minor variants. These minivans are pretty boxy-looking, yet they yield a drag coefficient of 0.38, which is pretty respectable given the considerable vehicle hulk. The steel monocoque body has an ancillary H-frame up front that adds to overall structural rigidity. The independent front suspension uses cross-struts on the 4X2 versions and torsion bars on the 4X4's. At the rear, the rigid axle suspension of Salisbury design is supported by dual leaf springs. The vehicle is equipped with variable assist recirculating ball steering. The front disc brakes and rear drum brakes are linked to standard ABS. It's too bad that these models have no traction control system to stabilize starts with light loads, especially on slippery road surfaces. These vans have a hauling capacity of 1765 pounds and a towing capacity of 5 500 lbs. This kind of prowess is often the reason behind the purchase, since there isn't

a single front-wheel drive minivan on the road that can boast of such brawn.

PROS

+ VERSATILITY. The Astro and the Safari have a dual personality: they can seat up to eight passengers, then be converted into work vehicles capable of hauling a heavy load or pulling a hefty trailer. Load volume is up to 170 cu.ft.

+ SIZE. The midsize body of these vans places them in a category midway between minivans and bulky delivery vans.

+ ENGINE. Interior and exterior design features are more nicely crafted than before and the instrument panel is more ergonomic.

+ COCKPIT. Broad windows, generous rearview mirrors and a big rear window (on models with triple-panel Dutch doors in the rear) provide excellent visibility in all directions. And the transmission shifter located behind the steering wheel is really handy. Lastly, the transmission downshifts quickly while shifting gears and offers good braking effect.

+ CONSOLE. The console near the engine hood is really neat and compensates for the missing glove compartment.

+ STEERING. The 4X2's maneuver better than the 4X4's due to a smaller turn angle diameter. The 4X4's however have more direct steering,

which makes for more quick moves.

+ NICE FEATURES. The triple-panel Dutch rear doors are very practical and they're fitted with a windshield wiper and electric defroster, features you don't get on conventional swing doors.

CONS

- SAFETY FEATURES. Collision tests run by the United States N.H.T.S.A. infer low-level passenger safety. These tests indicate that serious bodily harm could occur in some types of accidents.

- FUEL CONSUMPTION. We recorded one of the highest gas consumption levels in the minivan category. A V8 engine of low displacement would no doubt be a better choice and it would provide more torque.

- RELIABILITY. It hasn't improved much and fewer than 70% of owners indicate that they are satisfied with their purchase.

- BRAKES. Long stretching stopping distances on emergency stops, flimsy lining strength in intensive use and unpredictable brake pedal (the pedal is sometimes mushy) are real handicaps on these vehicles!

- STEERING. At low speeds, it's too sensitive, whereas for normal driving, it's sometimes too firm, and it's vague at the center. Definitely not a showpiece in the genre.

- HANDLING. This really depends mostly on tire quality. Besides, the

high-perched center of gravity on these vans requires some prudence, especially on tight curves. In winter conditions, it would be wise to equip these vehicles with good-quality wintertires so as to avoid some clumsy pas de deux.

- LACK OF SPACE. Rear seat passengers enjoy more leg room than the driver and front seat passenger, because the engine protrudes inside the cabin, as do the front wheel wells, so you end up with a far from flat floor. Besides, these rear-wheel drive vehicles come equipped with the usual drive gear, so the floor is very high and it's hard to climb aboard both up front and at the rear.

- TO BE IMPROVED UPON. The front door opening angle is too narrow. As well, the front seat adjustment controls are so inconveniently located that you have to open the door to use them!

- RIDE COMFORT. The rather rough and ready suspension isn't a friend of uneven road surfaces. The seat cushions are very short and stingy. And there sure is a lot of resounding noise at certain speeds. If you're looking for comfort, best to shop elsewhere!

- HANDICAP. These vans are so high that you can't park them in a regular garage or in an inside parking lot.

CONCLUSION

These minivans may not be as refined as their front-wheel drive rivals, but unlike them, they're real work horses and they welcome the challenge of hauling heavy loads.

Minivans

RATING
CHEVROLET-GMC Astro-Safari

CONCEPT : 72%
Technology :	70
Safety :	50
Interior space :	100
Trunk volume :	70
Quality/fit/finish :	70

DRIVING : 52%
Cockpit :	80
Performance :	35
Handling :	35
Steering :	75
Braking :	35

ORIGINAL EQUIPMENT : 63%
Tires :	70
Headlights :	70
Wipers :	60
Rear defroster :	40
Radio :	75

COMFORT : 69%
Seats :	75
Suspension :	70
Sound level :	50
Conveniences :	70
Air conditioning :	80

BUDGET : 54%
Price :	50
Fuel economy :	40
Insurance :	60
Satisfaction :	75
Depreciation :	45

Overall rating : 62.0%

NEW FOR 2000
- New door, headlight and seat belt chimes.
- Silver-colored wheel covers on the base model.
- Remote keyless entry, headlight warning function and battery protection.
- Improved Vortec engine, 27-gallon fuel tank, ABS brakes and improved exhaust system.

Compare Performance, Specifications, Prices, and Classification at the end of this chapter.

EQUIPMENT

CHEVROLET Astro GMC Safari	base SLX	LS SLE	LT SLT
Automatic transmission:	S	S	S
Cruise control:	O	S	S
Power steering:	S	S	S
Anti-lock brakes:	S	S	S
Traction control:	-	-	-
Air conditioning:	SM	SM	SM
Leather:	-	-	O
AM/FM/radio-cassette:	O	O	O
Power door locks:	O	S	O
Power windows:	O	S	S
Tilt steering:	O	S	S
Dual adjustable mirrors:	SM	SE	SE
Alloy wheels:	-	O	S
Anti-theft system:	S	S	S

Colors
Exterior: White, Silver, Lime, Grey, Blue, Black, Green, Copper, Red, Bronze.

Interior: Medium Grey, Blue, Red, Neutral.

AT A GLANCE...

HISTORIC
Introduced in: 1986.
Made in: Baltimore, Maryland, USA.

DEMOGRAPHICS
Model	Men/Wom.	Age	Married	College	Income $
Astro	77/23 %	45	87 %	30 %	36,000
Safari	80/20 %	45	93 %	32 %	36,000

INDEX
Safety:	50 %	Satisfaction:	75 %
Depreciation:	53 %	Insurance:	$ 825 -1,000
Cost per mile:	$ 0.51	Number of dealers:	4,466

SALES
	Canada			USA		
Model	1997	1998	Result	1997	1998	Result
Astro/Safari	29,205	20,092	- 31.2 %	147,177	126,898	- 13.7 %

MAINTENANCE REQUIRED BY WARRANTY
First revision:	Frequency:	Diagnostic plug:
3,000 miles	6,000 miles	Yes

Modular

These minivans are a good replacement for their predecessors. Although they're based on the same platform and use the same mechanical components, their body configuration is more practical and their size is similar to their Chrysler counterparts, a benchmark in this category. They're most remarkable for their modular passenger compartment and the fact that they come with only one powertrain choice.

MODEL RANGE

These minivans are available with a standard or extended wheelbase. All come with an optional left-side sliding door. At Chevrolet, 5 different trims are available: Value, Base, LS, LT and Warner Bros. The Silhouettes are uniquely long and available in GL, GS or Premiere versions, all with a standard four-door configuration. The Montana (known as the Trans Sport in Canada) is available in only one finish and trim. The automatic transmission, manually controlled air conditioning system, power steering and ABS brakes are all standard. Dual air bags and side air bags are also available at no extra charge.

TECHNICAL FEATURES

The Venture has a monocoque chassis clad in steel metal work that's galvanized on both sides, except for the roof panel. The engine hood is made of aluminum. The chassis rests on an H-subframe that adds to structural integrity. The independent front suspension consists of MacPherson struts and stabilizer bar. At the rear, the semi-independent suspension is made up of a torsion axle suspended by coil springs. The rear suspension also includes a stabilizer bar. A «Tourism» suspen-

sion adds pneumatic self-levelling devices. The 3.4L V6, a tried and tested engine, develops 185 hp and 210 lb.ft. of torque, which makes it the gutsiest original engine in the minivan market. It's mounted on an independent cradle affixed to the body via rubber components. The 4-speed electronically controlled automatic transmission sends power to the front wheels. Braking is taken care of via a disc/drum system and four-wheel ABS. Power steering is rack-and-pinion. Chevrolet offers four setups for the rear section of the vehicle: individual seats (the ultra-light 42 lb seats on last year's model), full or split seatbenches, or captain's chair seats. Depending on the type of seating, the Venture can accomodate six to eight passengers.

PROS

+ RIDE COMFORT. The Venture is a spoiler on the highway. Its silky smooth suspension, nicely crafted and cushy front seats and effective soundproofing prove that highway driving is its forte. As far as noise level goes, you only hear tire hum, depending on the condition of the road surface.

+ PERFORMANCES. The Venture needs about 11 seconds to climb to 60 mph and pickup is adequate for passing, at least with half a load. It isn't too gas-thirsty, since average consumption is about 22 mpg.

+ DRIVING PLEASURE. The automatic gearbox is, without a doubt, this minivan's strong suit. It shifts gears without a hitch and provides lots of braking effect when shifting from 3rd to 2nd gear.

+ HANDLING. In most cases, the vehicle stays nice and stable. You can go into tight curves with ease.

+ GREAT FEATURES. We really liked the remote-control for the sliding passenger-side door, all the spots to stash stuff, the rear bumper that doubles as a step and brisk wipers that clear a large section of the windshield.

CONS

- SEATS. Seat cushions are too low. Seats aren't as comfortable as they should be, especially the intermediate seatbench. Rear seats are hard and flat and headrests are pretty simplistic.

- FINISH DETAILS. The vehicles we tested didn't exhibit a top-notch engineering job. Wires, ducts and electrical harnesses (in the engine compartment) were hanging every which way because the supports had given out. In the winter, windshield wipers and climate control air vents located at the base of the windshield under the hood are forever freezing up, so they're nonfunctional. Lastly, the chassis on the extended model lacks rigidity, a conclusion we arrived at due to the racket coming from the frame when

on poor roads.

- BRAKING. The brake pedal is spongy and hard to gauge. Stopping distances are surprisingly long and are evidence of poor quality linings. The rudimentary ABS system fails to control wheel locking and makes it hard to keep these models on course.

- HEATING. Eventually it does manage to heat up the passenger compartment, but it takes a long, long time before occupants feel stop shivering.

- COMPLICATED. The control unit that oversees turn signal lights, windshield wipers and washer, cruise control and dimming of headlights (whew!) is tough to use. European counterparts of this minivan (Opel Sintra) have different controls that are a heck of a lot more user-friendly. What's all this talk about making the grade on the world market?

- SUSPENSION. On uneven pavement or roads, the suspension gets ornery when the front wheels get thrust power. There just isn't enough suspension travel.

- ACCESS. Set in way back, almost under the windshield and instrument panel, the engine isn't easy to get to when you want to do routine maintenance checkups.

- FINISH DETAILS. The interior trim isn't too nice, even on the luxury versions with such a bland palette and bargain basement plastic.

CONCLUSION

GM minivans are very competitive given their price, performance capabilities and sizing. Unfortunately, they still have a long way to go when it comes to quality, reliability and some design details.

Mid Size Cars

RATING
GM U Series

CONCEPT : 69%
Technology : 75
Safety : 50
Interior space : 80
Trunk volume : 70
Quality/fit/finish : 70

DRIVING : 52%
Cockpit : 75
Performance : 35
Handling : 45
Steering : 70
Braking : 35

ORIGINAL EQUIPMENT : 77%
Tires : 70
Headlights : 80
Wipers : 70
Rear defroster : 85
Radio : 80

COMFORT : 70%
Seats : 70
Suspension : 75
Sound level : 50
Conveniences : 75
Air conditioning : 80

BUDGET : 61%
Price : 50
Fuel economy : 65
Insurance : 70
Satisfaction : 70
Depreciation : 50

Overall rating : 65.8%

NEW FOR 2000
- Three-door models withdrawn.
- Grey or Neutral interior trims.
- Redesigned instrument cluster.
- Warner Bros. version from Chevrolet.
- Smoky Caramel Metallic color.
- Improved traction control system.

Compare
Performance,
Specifications, Prices,
and Classification
at the end of this chapter.

EQUIPMENT

CHEVROLET Venture / OLDSMOBILE Silhouette / PONTIAC Montana	base	LS	LT	GL	GS	GLS	base
Automatic transmission:	S	S	S	S	S	S	S
Cruise control:	O	S	S	S	S	S	O
Power steering:	S	S	S	S	S	S	S
Anti-lock brakes:	S	S	S	S	S	S	S
Traction control:	-	O	S	O	O	S	O
Air conditioning:	SM	SM	SM	SM	SM	SM	SM
Leather:	-	O	O	O	O	S	-
AM/FM/radio-cassette:	O	S	SCd	S	SCd	SCd	O
Power door locks:	O	S	S	S	S	S	O
Power windows:	O	S	S	S	S	S	O
Tilt steering:	S	S	S	S	S	S	S
Dual adjustable mirrors:	SE	SE	SE	SEH	SEH	SEH	SEH
Alloy wheels:	O	S	S	O	O	S	O
Anti-theft system:	S	S	S	S	S	S	S

Colors
Exterior: White, Green, Red, Sand, Silver, Blue, Teal.

Interior: Grey, Neutral, Brown, Teal.

AT A GLANCE...

HISTORIC
Introduced in: 1997.
Made in: Doraville, Georgia, USA.

DEMOGRAPHICS

Model	Men/Wom.	Age	Married	College	Income $
Venture	68/32 %	46	86 %	38 %	40,000
Silhouette	78/22 %	52	88 %	44 %	45,000
Trans Sport	74/26 %	45	86 %	40 %	22,000

INDEX
Safety: 50 % Satisfaction: 70 %
Depreciation: 50 % Insurance: $ 800
Cost per mile: $ 0.55 Number of dealers: 4,466

SALES

Model	Canada 1997	1998	Result	USA 1997	1998	Result
Venture		GM U Series		77,414	97,374	+ 25.8 %
Silhouette	32,852	39,822	+ 21.2 %	24,615	37,554	+ 52.6 %
Montana				51,961	59,048	+13.6 %

MAINTENANCE REQUIRED BY WARRANTY
First revision: 3,000 miles
Frequency: 6 months / 6,000 miles
Diagnostic plug: Yes

Minivans

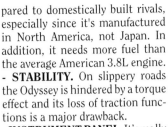
Misleading?

The grass is always greener, as the saying goes, but after a while things can begin to look different. That's exactly what seems to have happened to the Odyssey last year, though at the time based on prototype vehicles it seemed far ahead of the pack. After test driving a number of standard production models, opinions have changed and statistics are very revealing.

MODEL RANGE

The «big Odyssey» is a full-blown minivan, offered in a single 7-passenger, extended wheelbase model and equipped with two sliding doors. It's sold in LX and EX versions, both receiving the same mechanical components, namely a 3.5L V6 with electronically controlled 4-speed automatic transmission. Original equipment on the LX includes air conditioning, antilock braking system, power windows, locks and quarter windows, cruise control, tilt steering column, radio and tape deck and theft-deterrent system with engine shut-off function. The EX is equipped with added features, namely power sliding doors, traction control, power multi-ajustable driver's seat, stereo sound system including a CD player, keyless entry system, automatic climate control, 16-inch light alloy rims and power mirrors.

TECHNICAL FEATURES

The new Odyssey's steel unitized body comes with its most vulnerable panels galvanized. The body is based on a very rigid framework integrated into the platform. The frame itself includes four circles that form roof pillars and that reinforce the structure as a whole. There are no official figures on the drag coefficient, but the vehicle's flowing lines should yield pretty good aerodynamics. The suspension is fully independent, a rare feature for

a minivan. Up front, it consists of MacPherson struts with a cast-metal lower A-arm, while at the rear, there's a Honda-design double-wishbone arrangement. Vehicles are equipped with disc and drum brakes and standard antilock braking device that benefits from an electronic distribution control unit that lightens rear wheel pressure when approaching wheel lock threshold. The EX is the only model that can receive standard electronic traction control that's hooked up to ABS sensors.

PROS

+ CABIN SPACE. By opting for the big format, Honda has given the latest model minivan every possible chance of appealing to the greatest number of potential buyers. You can convert the cabin interior according to specific needs thanks to the removable individual seats and the rear seatbench that can fold down into the floor.

+ HANDLING. It derives from that of Honda car models and is enhanced by the reasonably low center of gravity that keeps the vehicle level on curves, especially with the wheel tracks that are the widest in the category. Vehicle sway is moderate and nicely under control, so the Odyssey takes all kinds of curves with aplomb.

+ PERFORMANCES. The 210-hp engine that powers the most recent Honda minivan puts it ahead of the Windstar when it comes to muscle. The Odyssey achieves brisk accel-

erations and goes from 0-60 mph in less than 11 seconds, which is remarkable for a vehicle animated by 3.5L V6 and weighing more than two tons with one passenger aboard...

+ EQUIPMENT. It' very generous, even on the LX, which explains why the Odyssey is in the upper echelon, in direct competition with American luxury versions.

+ QUALITY. It was a vital ingredient at every step of the way, in regard to engineering, assembly and finish details, since this new vehicle exhibited the same topnotch tolerances and standards as are found on Honda cars.

+ CONVENIENCE FEATURES. The Odyssey is super-versatile with its modular cabin. It's loaded with storage areas, such as the one located at the base of the console, the generous glove compartment, door side-pockets and the fold-up tray located between the front seats, borrowed from the CR-V.

+ MAGIC SEAT. What a super idea to have integrated this rear seatbench that equipped the original Odyssey. It folds down into the cargo hold floor. And when the seatbench is occupied, the base prevents luggage from shifting around.

+ NICE FEATURES. Neat details, such as the driver's footrest, a rare item on a minivan, as well as standard headrests for all passengers.

CONS

- COST. Like other Honda models, the Odyssey seems expensive com-

pared to domestically built rivals, especially since it's manufactured in North America, not Japan. In addition, it needs more fuel than the average American 3.8L engine.

- STABILITY. On slippery roads the Odyssey is hindered by a torque effect and its loss of traction functions is a major drawback.

- INSTRUMENT PANEL. It's really hulky and high. It blocks the frontward view in the front seats, which is contrary to current practice.

- POWER DOORS. This is quite a nice feature, but it's more of a gadget compared to how complex the doors are themselves.

- COMFORT. The ride isn't as velvet-smooth as in the Grand Caravan or the Windstar. The seats could be both softer and more contoured. Lastly, sound-proofing is so poor that at one point, the ride simply becomes unpleasant.

- CABIN DESIGN. It's rather blah and depending on color combinations, it's very run-of-the-mill, so you don't get the impression of being inside a luxury, top-of-the-line product, given the current price.

- SPARE TIRE. It isn't too handy, since it's hidden in a compartment located under the floor behind the driver's seat. But at least it stays nice and clean and it's out of sight...

- FLAWS. An emergency wheel that's hard to reach, positioned in a floor space behind the driver's seat, a rear windshield wiper that isn't intermittent, a rear hatch window that doesn't open, a small fuel tank that limits the vehicle's touring range.

CONCLUSION

Although well designed, the Odyssey is not as perfect as it seems at first glance and its high price attracts justifiably stronger criticism.

Minivans

Odyssey

HONDA

RATING HONDA Odyssey		
CONCEPT :		**79%**
Technology :	80	
Safety :	80	
Interior space :	90	
Trunk volume :	65	
Quality/fit/finish :	80	
DRIVING :		**59%**
Cockpit :	75	
Performance :	40	
Handling :	50	
Steering :	80	
Braking :	50	
ORIGINAL EQUIPMENT :		**74%**
Tires :	80	
Headlights :	75	
Wipers :	60	
Rear defroster :	80	
Radio :	75	
COMFORT :		**71%**
Seats :	75	
Suspension :	70	
Sound level :	50	
Conveniences :	80	
Air conditioning :	80	
BUDGET :		**58%**
Price :	35	
Fuel economy :	50	
Insurance :	50	
Satisfaction :	90	
Depreciation :	65	
Overall rating :		**68.2%**

NEW FOR 2000

• **Seat-belt anchoring points built into the seat design.**

Compare Performance, Specifications, Prices, and Classification at the end of this chapter.

EQUIPMENT

HONDA Odyssey	LX	EX
Automatic transmission:	S	S
Cruise control:	S	S
Power steering:	S	S
Anti-lock brakes:	S	S
Traction control:	-	S
Air conditioning:	SM	SA
Leather:	-	-
AM/FM/radio-cassette:	S	SCd
Power door locks:	S	S
Power windows:	S	S
Tilt steering:	S	S
Dual adjustable mirrors:	SE	SE
Alloy wheels:		S
Anti-theft system:	S	S

Colors

Exterior: Blue, Green, Beige, Silver.

Interior: Grey, Ivory, Green.

AT A GLANCE...

HISTORIC
Introduced in: 1999.
Made in: Alliston, Ontario, Canada.

DEMOGRAPHICS

Model	Men/Wom.	Age	Married	College	Income $
Odyssey	71/29 %	46	87 %	51 %	46,000

INDEX
Safety:	90 %	Satisfaction:	87 %
Depreciation:	35 %	Insurance:	$ 835
Cost per mile:	$ 0.49	Number of dealers:	1,001

SALES

Model	Canada 1997	1998	Result	USA 1997	1998	Result
Odyssey	2,004	4,124	+ 105.8 %	20,333	13,665	- 32.8 %

MAINTENANCE REQUIRED BY WARRANTY
First revision: 3,000 miles
Frequency: 3,000 miles
Diagnostic plug: Yes

Compact

Mazda finally decided to change its MPV minivan. And it's quite a change: from rear-wheel to front-wheel drive, from swing-out to sliding doors, from a 3.0L to a 2.5L engine. The revamping is one of the first examples of globalization under the Ford 2000 plan, featuring a differnt platform and a Ford engine derived from the Duratec.

MODEL RANGE

The latest MPV is a compact minivan featuring a short wheelbase. It's available in three finishes: DX, LX and ES, different from one another because of their equipment and presentation and all powered by the same 2.5L V6 engine and 4-speed automatic transmission. Basic equipment on the DX version includes power steering, an automatic transmission, air conditioning, and a steering wheel column and sideview mirrors that are manually adjustable. The LX adds the usual power systems, ABS brakes with a pressure limiter for rear tires and a theft deterrent system. The ES is the only model with leather upholstery, alloy wheels, a sophisticated sound system and a number of other attributes included to justify its high price.

TECHNICAL FEATURES

Built on the sole wheelbase typical of a Ford platform, the steel unibody results in a 20% weight gain. Developed in Japan, it was given a few design revisions in California. Its floor houses a chassis with thick siderails and nine cross-members that run along its entire length. In the front, the powertrain is installed on an independent frame. The front suspension features MacPherson struts and the rear uses a solid axle.

Both assemblies also include stabilizer bars and coil springs. The power steering varies assistance to match speed levels. Brakes are mixed and the ABS system is standard on the LX and ES versions. For the moment, no traction control or AWD systems are available.

PROS

+ PRICE. It's competitive, even compared to short wheelbase models from domestic builders; in fact, the base model can lay claim to being the least expense imported model.

+ STYLING. It's exciting and in keeping with the philosophy newly adopted by Mazda. It bears a certain resemblance to other recent models such as the Protegé, with the typical pointy front end echoed in the Japanese builder's logo itself.

+ PASSENGER ROOM. Designers have made optimal use of the new MPV's compact sizing. Seats are roomy and passengers don't feel cramped, as they do on the Quest-Villager models.

+ DASHBOARD. It's simple, functional and shaped to take up minimal space. Its ergonomic design is remarkable and all controls are within very easy reach.

+ CLEVER DETAILS. Mazda has borrowed a concept introduced by Honda and the MPV's rear bench seat folds into the floor; when the seat is in use, its fold-away space

can be used to store smaller items. Middle seats slide to the sides to form the kind of bench seat found on the Odyssey and they can be moved to the rear to nestle comfortably under the hatch.

+ RIDE. It's good thanks to the excellent steering wheel positioning, well-designed cockpit and good visibility.

+ BONUS POINTS. For seat belt buckles built into seat cushions. For a well-positioned hand brake, located immediately adjacent to the driver's seat. For power windows on the sliding doors, a rare feature in the minivan world, resulting excellent ventilation.

CONS

- ENGINE. The weight-power ratio stands at 21.6 lbs./hp, not the most favorable. The lack of torque is obvious early on and as soon as speeds begin to climb, the transmission has to downshift and the engine has to work hard. Acceleration and pick-up is barely adequate with only two passengers aboard imagine travelling with a whole family and a load of baggage!

- SEATS. They're terribly uncomfortable, their padding is very firm and they don't fit well enough to provide adequate support. In this day and age, it's unbelievable that such elementary amenities are still lacking.

- ACCESS. In spite of their width

front doors open only at a 45° angle and sliding doors aren't wide enough for heftier passengers; on the inside, space is limited and it isn't easy to move around from one seat to another.

- FUEL CONSUMPTION. Test drives generated an average of 17 mpg (14 l/100 km), the same level as a V6 with more than 3.0L to offer. So why didn't designers use a bigger and more economical engine, like the one found on GM's U-Series minivans for instance?

- BASE MODEL. Bucking the current trend, the MPV DX is a bare-bones model. It won't be easy to resell under the circumstances and as a result, the LX is the better choice.

- FLAWS. A high gear ratio, the impractical German-type gear shift lever, the fixed hatch window, the minimal number of storage spaces available to middle-seat passengers.

CONCLUSION

The latest MPV is more universal than the previous model. If it weren't for its marginal engine and awful seats, it would win our seal of approval. To its credit, for the most part it's well designed, well assembled and generally appealing.

Minivans

RATING	
MAZDA MPV	
CONCEPT :	**78%**
Technology :	80
Safety :	90
Interior space :	80
Trunk volume :	60
Quality/fit/finish :	80
DRIVING :	**62%**
Cockpit :	80
Performance :	40
Handling :	50
Steering :	80
Braking :	60
ORIGINAL EQUIPMENT :	**72%**
Tires :	80
Headlights :	80
Wipers :	60
Rear defroster :	60
Radio :	80
COMFORT :	**69%**
Seats :	60
Suspension :	75
Sound level :	50
Conveniences :	80
Air conditioning :	80
BUDGET :	**53%**
Price :	40
Fuel economy :	50
Insurance :	50
Satisfaction :	80
Depreciation :	45
Overall rating :	**66.8%**

New 2000 Model

NEW FOR 2000

- **The MPV has been totally revamped, now offering front-wheel drive, sliding rear doors and a 2.5L V6 engine.**

Compare Performance, Specifications, Prices, and Classification at the end of this chapter.

EQUIPMENT

MAZDA MPV	DX	LX	ES
Automatic transmission:	S	S	S
Cruise control:			
Power steering:	S	S	S
Anti-lock brakes:	-	S	S
Traction control:			
Air conditioning:	S	S	S
Leather:	-	-	S
AM/FM/radio-cassette:	SCd	SCd	SCd
Power door locks:	-	S	S
Power windows:	-	S	S
Tilt steering:	S	S	S
Dual adjustable mirrors:	SM	SEH	SEH
Alloy wheels:	O	O	S
Anti-theft system:	-	-	-

Colors

Exterior: Silver, Red, White, Sand, Black, Blue, Green.

Interior: Beige, Grey.

AT A GLANCE...

HISTORIC

Introduced in:	1988, 2000.
Made in:	Horoshima, Japan.

DEMOGRAPHICS

Model	Men/Wom.	Age	Married	College	Income $
MPV	74/26 %	42	84 %	58 %	50,000

INDEX

Safety:	90 %	Satisfaction:	80 %
Depreciation:	55 %	Insurance:	$ 635
Cost per mile:	$ 0.55	Number of dealers:	875

SALES

	Canada			USA		
Model	1997	1998	Result	1997	1998	Result
MPV	2,010	2,125	+ 5.7 %	15,599	12,425	- 20.3 %

MAINTENANCE REQUIRED BY WARRANTY

First revision:	Frequency:	Diagnostic plug:
5,000 miles	5,000 miles	Yes

Minivans

Flexible

Minivans with short wheelbases are increasingly unpopular. In recent years, they've grown so thin that the most recent models - such as the Honda Odyssey - exist only in an extended wheelbase version. The Villager, the shorter equivalent of the Windstar, has seen its sales plummet on the Canadian market, to the point that Ford has decided to withdraw it.

MODEL RANGE

The Villager/Quest duo was created by Nissan in the United States, yet these minivans are built by Ford at the Ohio plant. They're virtual clones that only differ as to cabin layout and exterior stylistic touches. Compared to former models, the new arrivals are 4.7 inches longer, 1.2 inches wider and the rear overhang has been extended by 3.2 inches, which has allowed for more leg room for middle seatbench passengers. The Villager comes in base, Estate and Sport versions and the Quest is sold in GXE, SE and GLE. They're powered by a 3.3L Nissan V6 that delivers 170 hp, that is 19 more hp than its predecessor, associated with a 4-speed automatic transmission.

TECHNICAL FEATURES

These newcomers still have the former Maxima platform. But the engine is the Pathfinder powerplant, with some refinements to better suit these vehicles. So it's imported from Japan and constitutes the only component hailing from outside the United States.

The independent front suspension is made up of MacPherson struts and the rear rigid axle is suspended by a new Hotchkiss single-leaf spring. A disc and drum brake duo equips all models, with optional antilock system for the Mercury versions and standard ABS for Nissan counterparts!

The Villager/Quest models are the only minivans boasting of a modular seat arrangement coined "Quest Trac". It consists of middle and rear seatbenches mounted on longitudinal tracks, so they can slide and be positioned as desired. This design offers 66 different cargo and seating area configurations, helps optimize use of all available space without having to remove the seats that are heavy. A great idea that unfortunately hasn't as yet been taken up by the competition.

PROS

+ CABIN DESIGN. These two minivans have pretty gorgeous cabins furbished with luxury accessories, so they're geared to appeal to buyers who want to replace their luxury car rather than to commercial delivery types!

+ MODULAR SEATS. The convenient Quest Trac seat design is still one of a kind. It's really surprising that not a single other automaker has borrowed this idea for their minivans, not even Ford for its Windstar!

+ RIDE COMFORT. The cushy suspension, thick seats and competent soundproofing make for fatigue-free long-distance trips.

+ PERFORMANCES. Thanks to the new 3.3L engine, accelerations and pickup are a cut above what they were with the former 3.0L model, so overall performances are now average, but of course, higher fuel consumption goes with the territory! At least now these vehicles can pull trailers weighing up to 3,500 lb. when using the proper hookup equipment.

+ ROADHANDLING. These vehicles handle nice and safely, in spite of the sway generated by the flexible suspension. The Quest SE is more competent with its stiffer suspensions, rear antiroll bar and 16-inch tires.

+ QUALITY. Here we have an exception that deserves mention: an American product assembled in Ohio is on a par with Japanese assembly standards. Which shows that a little cooperation can go a long way...

+ EQUIPMENT. The Quest is more richly equipped than the Mercury, since the latter has only optional antilock braking system and theft-deterrent system.

+ INSTRUMENT PANEL. It has a fresh, new look and looks really neat. It's ergonomic and well-organized, but some controls are still tricky to use.

+ NICE FEATURES. The shelf with holding net installed in the luggage compartment that lets you stack heavy items, front door side-pockets and rear window that opens.

CONS

- SAFETY FEATURES. Nissan still has some work ahead as far as safety goes. Even with the rigid frame, airbags, standard headrests for all passengers and standard ABS brake system for the Nissan models (optional on the Ford models!), these minivans have thus far only earned rather low scores when it comes to passenger protection.

-BRAKES. They aren't too powerful. They don't dig in when applied and don't hold up too well and without ABS, front wheels tend to lock at the drop of a hat in emergency situations.

-CABIN SPACE. Even with the new-design body, cabin space is insufficient for the 7-passenger layout, since remote rear occupants have to put up with cramped leg room. The narrow cabin interior makes it tough getting around inside. Lastly, it would be tricky stuffing seven passengers' luggage into the cargo hold!

-FRONT SUSPENSION. The front suspension is overloaded and tends to bottom out on bumpy surfaces, so you have to slow down to maintain a reasonable comfort level.

-STEERING. It's over-assisted and gets light and vague. The steer angle diameter is wide as well, which doesn't help maneuvering, not with the short wheelbase.

- COCKPIT. Tall drivers feel cramped and would appreciate being able to push the seat back more.

-TO BE IMPROVED UPON. The center console that's slung too low and you almost have to bend over to adjust the air conditioning controls.

CONCLUSION

Of all short wheelbase models, the Nissan Quest and its Villager counterpart at Mercury are those that have sold best to date, with the sole exception of the Caravan-Voyager. However, it seems that the trend is more and more favorable for extended wheelbase models, which don't cost much more and offer a maximum amount of space for passengers and baggage.

RATING
MERCURY Villager NISSAN Quest

CONCEPT :		**76%**
Technology :	80	
Safety :	80	
Interior space :	80	
Trunk volume :	60	
Quality/fit/finish :	80	
DRIVING :		**61%**
Cockpit :	80	
Performance :	40	
Handling :	50	
Steering :	75	
Braking :	60	
ORIGINAL EQUIPMENT :		**74%**
Tires :	80	
Headlights :	80	
Wipers :	65	
Rear defroster :	70	
Radio :	75	
COMFORT :		**70%**
Seats :	75	
Suspension :	75	
Sound level :	50	
Conveniences :	70	
Air conditioning :	80	
BUDGET :		**58%**
Price :	40	
Fuel economy :	50	
Insurance :	60	
Satisfaction :	85	
Depreciation :	55	
Overall rating :		**67.8%**

NEW FOR 2000

- **Nissan Quest: no changes.**
- **Mercury Villager: more elaborate standard equipment on the Sport and Estate versions.**

Compare
Performance,
Specifications, Prices,
and Classification
at the end of this chapter.

EQUIPMENT

NISSAN Quest MERCURY Villager	base	Sport	Estate	GXE	SE	GLE
Automatic transmission:	S	S	S	S	S	S
Cruise control:	S	S	S	O	S	S
Power steering:	S	S	S	S	S	S
Anti-lock brakes:	O	O	O	S	S	S
Traction control:	-	-	-	-	-	-
Air conditioning:	SM	SM	SM	SM	SM	SA
Leather:	-	O	S	O	O	S
AM/FM/radio-cassette:	S	S	S	S	S	SCd
Power door locks:	S	S	S	SM	S	S
Power windows:	S	S	S	S	S	S
Tilt steering:	S	S	S	S	S	S
Dual adjustable mirrors:	SE	SEH	SEH	SM	SEH	SEH
Alloy wheels:	O	S	S	-	S	S
Anti-theft system:	O	O	O	O	S	S

Colors

Exterior: Red, Blue, Green, Silver, Black, White, Grey, Gold.

Interior: Mink, Grey, Green.

AT A GLANCE...

HISTORIC
Introduced in: 1993.
Made in: Avon Lake, Ohio, USA.

DEMOGRAPHICS

Model	Men/Wom.	Age	Married	College	Income $
Quest	72/28 %	43	87 %	45 %	37,500
Villager	70/30 %	47	80 %	48 %	42,000

INDEX

Safety:	80 %	Satisfaction:	85 %
Depreciation:	46 %	Insurance:	$ 565
Cost per mile:	$ 0.55	Number of dealers:	5,200

SALES

	Canada			USA		
Model	1997	1998	Result	1997	1998	Result
Quest	3 189	1 972	- 38.2 %	46,858	30,466	- 35.0 %
Villager	3 417	2 199	- 35.6 %	55,168	38,495	- 30.2 %

MAINTENANCE REQUIRED BY WARRANTY

First revision:	Frequency:	Diagnostic plug:
5,000 miles	6 months/ 5,000 miles	Yes

Minivans

Livid

The Sienna failed to create the kind of excitement Toyota had anticipated for its mid-size model. Roomier than short wheelbase vehicles without the size and weight of extended wheelbase alternatives, it's capable of offering appreciable passenger comfort and considerable cargo space. As is often the case at Toyota, this minivan's styling is nothing particularly exciting and even died-in-the-wool fans of the make recognize that the leading Japanese manufacturer's designers could have done better.

MODEL RANGE

The Sienna is a 3 or 4-door compact minivan that seats 7. Size-wise, it sits between the Caravan and the Windstar. It's sold in CE, LE and XLE versions, the latter being an options package. Original equipment includes the automatic transmission, two airbags, manual air conditioning, four-wheel antilock braking, radio and tape deck, tilt steering wheel and intermittent-function wipers. The LE also receives power locks, windows and mirrors and cruise control. Other items are available as extras on the LE, such as leather trim seats, light alloy wheels, sunroof and theft-deterrent system.

TECHNICAL FEATURES

The Sienna is built on the Camry platform with some modifications to suit its design. Compared to the Previa that it replaced, its engine location is much more contemporary, since the V6 is set transversely between the front wheels. The steel unitized body with some galvanized panels includes two independent cradles that support the suspensions, of MacPherson strut design up front and torsion bars at the rear. Vehicles are equipped with disc and drum brakes and standard power rack-and-pinion steering as well as a tire pressure surveillance system. The 3.0L 24-valve DOHC V6 engine is the most muscular of this displacement, since it develops 194 hp, almost as much as the 3.8L on the Windstar...

PROS

+ RIDE COMFORT. It's due to the nicely adjusted suspensions that are neither too soft nor too stiff and the robust frame that's well sound-proofed.

+ PERFORMANCES. Benefitting from a very favorable power to weight ratio, the Sienna achieves accelerations and pickup comparable to those of a passenger car and performance figures prove it.

+ VALUE. For a reasonable price, the Sienna comes with a good array of equipment, even the entry-level CE that comes with a perfectly decent number of items.

+ CABIN SPACE. This aspect was well thought out, since there's more room for seven occupants in the Sienna than in the Villager, Caravan or Venture with short wheelbase, without having to deal with rigidity problems that afflict extended wheelbase models.

+ ROADABILITY. It's competent and balanced, demonstrating sure moves on straight roads and a reassuring, level demeanor on wide curves and turns, even when going at a good clip.

+ STEERING. It's quick, accurate and nicely powered, so it doesn't suffer from torque fallout on hard accelerations.

CONS

- STYLE. This vehicle design created by Toyota is very blah and looks too much like the Villager-Quest with a bigger rear overhang due to more generous cabin space. But we notice that the slide-rail for the sliding doors isn't as neatly integrated into the over-all design, as is the case on Chrysler or GM rivals. The Sienna doesn't have the unique traits that were the major asset of the Previa.

- CHOICE. You don't have much, since the Sienna comes in a single length, with a single wheelbase and this vehicle will only appeal to folks who like the tad more space that's available compared to the short wheelbase Caravan-Voyager-Quest-Venture-Montana models.

- SEATS. They're pretty awful. They're flat, so offer no hip or shoulder support and upholstery is pretty thin. Also, the rear seatbench is tough to get to and its dual-section design isn't as handy when you want to remove it, not like the former design on the defunct Previa.

- PARKING BRAKE. The foot pedal is one of the most awkward on the market and Toyota could have come up with something more innovative.

- VISIBILITY. It's truncated at rear quarterback due to the bulky C pillar and the narrow rear window, not to mention the rear seat headrests.

- SWISH & SWAY. On snaky roads, the overly flexible suspension generates so much sway that you have to slow down and the front end tends to nosedive on less than perfect road surfaces.

- MANEUVERABILITY. The steer angle diameter doesn't jive with the long wheelbase body design, so parking maneuvers are no joy.

- BRAKES. Those on the first models we tested were real wimps and simulated emergency stopping distances stretched out pretty far. But standard ABS helps keep vehicle path perfectly straight.

- TIRES. The Goodyear Affinity tires of our test vehicle didn't impress us too much, not with the poor gripping power they exhibited on dry roads and they groan at the least turning maneuver.

- CABIN DESIGN. The interior is very economy-line with the shiny finish on some plastic components that really looks cheap.

- TO BE IMPROVED UPON. Poor ergonomics on the instrument panel with the really low center console and some poorly located accessories, insufficient storage spots since only the front door side-pockets are of a suitable size.

CONCLUSION

For some time now, Toyota hasn't enjoyed the success it once had. The Sienna (like the RAV4 in another category) isn't a unanimous favorite and its sales trail far behind those of the category's leaders. Motorists and potential buyers may even begin to miss the previous model.

RATING
TOYOTA Sienna

CONCEPT :		76%
Technology :	80	
Safety :	75	
Interior space :	80	
Trunk volume :	65	
Quality/fit/finish :	80	

DRIVING :		59%
Cockpit :	75	
Performance :	45	
Handling :	50	
Steering :	80	
Braking :	45	

ORIGINAL EQUIPMENT :		72%
Tires :	70	
Headlights :	80	
Wipers :	60	
Rear defroster :	75	
Radio :	75	

COMFORT :		72%
Seats :	70	
Suspension :	80	
Sound level :	50	
Conveniences :	80	
Air conditioning :	80	

BUDGET :		62%
Price :	40	
Fuel economy :	60	
Insurance :	70	
Satisfaction :	85	
Depreciation :	55	

Overall rating :		68.2%

NEW FOR 2000

- Radio/cassette and compact disc player standard on all models.

Compare Performance, Specifications, Prices, and Classification at the end of this chapter.

EQUIPMENT

TOYOTA Sienna	CE	LE	XLE
Automatic transmission:	S	S	S
Cruise control:	O	S	S
Power steering:	S	S	S
Anti-lock brakes:	S	S	S
Traction control:	S	S	S
Air conditioning:	S	S	S
Leather:	-	O	O
AM/FM/radio-cassette:	SCd	SCd	SCd
Power door locks:	O	S	S
Power windows:	O	S	S
Tilt steering:	S	S	S
Dual adjustable mirrors:	S	SEH	SEH
Alloy wheels:	-	O	S
Anti-theft system:	O	O	S

Colors

Exterior: Black, Burgundy, Sable, Spruce, Green, Blue, Iris.

Interior: Grey, Oak.

AT A GLANCE...

HISTORIC

Introduced in: 1998.
Made in: Georgetown, Kentucky, USA.

DEMOGRAPHICS

Model	Men/Wom.	Age	Married	College	Income $
Sienna	73/27 %	45	92 %	61 %	53,000

INDEX

Safety:	75 %	Satisfaction:	87 %
Depreciation:	45 %	Insurance:	$ 565
Cost per mile:	$ 0.51	Number of dealers:	1,233

SALES

	Canada			USA		
Model	1997	1998	Result	1997	1998	Result
Sienna	4,037	15,138	+ 275.0 %	15,180	81,391	+ 436.2 %

MAINTENANCE REQUIRED BY WARRANTY

First revision:	Frequency:	Diagnostic plug:
3,000 miles	3,000 miles	Yes

Mid Size Cars

MINIVANS

PERFORMANCE

Model/ version	*ENGINES* Type / timing valve / fuel system	Displacement cu in	Power hp @ rpm	Torque lb-ft @ rpm	Compres. ratio	*TRANSMISSIONS* Driving wheels / transmission	Final ratio	Acceler. 0-60 mph s	Standing 1/4 mile s	Standing 5/7 mile s	*PERFORMANCE* Passing 50-75 mph s	Braking 60-0 mph m	Top speed mph	Lateral acceler. G	Noise level dBA	Fuel economy mpg City	Fuel economy mpg Highway	Fuel type Octane
CHEVROLET Astro - GMC Jimmy																		
4x2	V6 4.3 OHV-12-SFI	262	190 @ 4400	250 @ 2800	9.2 :1	rear - A4	3.73	10.5	17.9	32.3	7.8	158	106	0.67	68	16	22	R 87
4x4	V6 4.3 OHV-12-SFI	262	190 @ 4400	250 @ 2800	9.2 :1	rear/4 - A4	3.73	11.3	18.5	33.0	8.5	164	103	0.67	68	16	21	R 87
CHEVROLET Venture - OLDSMOBILE Silhouette - PONTIAC Montana																		
regular	V6 3.4 OHV-12-SFI	205	185 @ 5200	205 @ 4000	9.6 :1	front - A4	3.29	10.8	17.7	32.2	8.6	148	106	0.72	67	16	23	R 87
long	V6 3.4 OHV-12-SFI	205	185 @ 5200	205 @ 4000	9.6 :1	front - A4	3.29	11.5	18.4	33.5	9.2	171	103	0.71	68	16	23	R 87
CHRYSLER Town & Country - DODGE Caravan - PLYMOUTH Voyager																		
1)	L4 2.4 DOHC-16-MPSFI	148	150 @ 5200	167 @ 4000	9.4 :1	front - A3	3.19	-								21	28	R 87
2)	V6 3.0 SOHC-12-MPSFI	181	150 @ 5200	176 @ 4000	8.9 :1	front - A3/A4	3.19	11.5	18.6	34.8	9.7	148	103	0.70	68	19	26	R 87
3)	V6 3.3 OHV-12-MPSFI	201	158 @ 4850	203 @ 3250	8.9 :1	front - A4	3.62	11.3	18.2	32.8	8.3	131	106	0.70	68	18	26	R 87
4)	V6 3.8 OHV-12-MPSFI	231	180 @ 4400	240 @ 3200	9.6 :1	front - A4	3.45	10.5	17.8	32.0	7.6	137	109	0.70	67	17	26	R 87
5)	V6 3.8 OHV-12-MPSFI	231	180 @ 4400	240 @ 3200	9.6 :1	all - A4	3.45	11.0	18.3	32.7	8.2	157	103	0.70	67	16	25	R 87
1) std Car-Voy 2) std Gd Car-Voy & SE, Car-Voy SE, opt base 3) std Car-Gd Car LE,T&C SX & LX, opt all models 4) std T&C LXi, option Car LE- Gd Car LE-SE, T&C LX 5) standard AWD																		
FORD Windstar																		
3.0L	V6 3.0 OHV-12-MPSFI	182	150 @ 5000	186 @ 3750	9.3 :1	front-A4	-											
LX,SE,SEL	V6 3.8 OHV-12-MPSFI	232	200 @ 4900	240 @ 3600	9.3 :1	front-A4	3.37	9.4	16.9	30.6	6.8	128	109	0.67	68	17	24	R 87
HONDA Odyssey																		
LX, EX	V6 3.5 SOHC-24-MPSFI	212	210 @ 5200	229 @ 4300	9.4 :1	front - A4	3.91	9.2	17.0	31.0	6.8	138	118	0.75	68	19	25	R 87
MAZDA MPV																		
base	V6 2.5 DOHC-24-MPFI	152	170 @ 6250	165 @ 4250	9.7 :1	front - A4	4.37	10.8	18.4	32.8	8.4	148	112	0.75	68-70	18	24	R 87
NISSAN Quest																		
base	V6 3.3 SOHC12-MPSFI	200	170 @ 4800	200 @ 2800	8.9 :1	front - A4	3.86	10.6	17.8	32.6	8.0	148	112	0.75	67-71	16	26	R 87
TOYOTA Sienna																		
CE, LE	V6 3.0 DOHC-24-MPSFI	183	194 @ 5200	209 @ 4400	10.5 :1	front - A4	3.63	10.0	17.5	31.5	6.7	141	112	0.76	68	18	26	S91

SPECIFICATIONS

Model	Version Trim	Traction	Body/ Deats	Wheel base in	Lgth x Width x Hght in x inx in	Curb weight lb	Susp. ft/rr	Brake ft/rr	Steering type	Steering ø ft	Steering turns number	Fuel tank gal	Standard tires dimensions	Standard tires make	Standard tires model	Standard powertrain	99 Price msrp $
CHEVROLET - GMC	**General warranty: 3 years / 36 000 miles; antipollution: 5 years / 50 000 miles; perforation corrosion: 6 years / 100 000 miles. Road assistance.**																
Astro - Safari	base / SLX	4x2	4dr.van. 5/8	111.2	189.8x77.5x74.9	4195	ih/rl	dc/dr/ABS	pwr.ball	38.3	3.10	25.0	215/75R15	Uniroyal	Tiger Paw	V6/4.3/A4	**21,547**
Astro - Safari	LT / SLT	4x4	4dr.van. 5/8	111.2	189.8x77.5x74.9	-	ih/rt	dc/dr/ABS	pwr.ball	41.7	2.70	25.0	215/75R15	Uniroyal	Tiger Paw	V6/4.3/A4	**23,847**
CHEVROLET	**General warranty: 3 years / 36 000 miles; antipollution: 5 years / 50 000 miles; perforation corrosion: 6 years / 100 000 miles. Roadside assistance.**																
Venture	regular	4x2	4dr.van. 7	112.0	186.9x72.0x67.4	3699	ih/rh	dc/dr/ABS	pwr.r&p.	37.4	3.0	20.0	215/70R15	General	XP 2000 GT	V6/3.4/A4	**21,375**
Venture	long	4x2	4dr.van. 7	120.0	200.9x72.0x68.1	3838	ih/rh	dc/dr/ABS	pwr.r&p.	39.7	3.0	25.0	215/70R15	General	XP 2000 GT	V6/3.4/A4	**23,675**
CHRYSLER	**General warranty: 3 years / 36 000 miles; surface rust: 3 years ; perforation: 7 years / 100 000 miles; roadside assistance: 3 years / 36 000 miles.**																
Town & Country	SX	4x2	4dr.van.7	113.3	186.4x76.8x68.7	3957	ih/rl	dc/dr/ABS	pwr.r&p.	37.7	3.14	20.0	215/65R16	Michelin	MX4	V6/3.3/A4	**27,965**
Town & Country	LX/LXi AWD	4x4	4dr.van.7	119.3	199.7x76.8x68.7	4345	ih/rl	dc/dc/ABS	pwr.r&p.	39.4	3.14	20.0	215/65R16	Michelin	MX4	V6/3.8/A4	**36,720**
DODGE-PLYMOUTH	**General warranty: 3 years / 36 000 miles; surface rust: 3 years ; perforation: 7 years / 100 000 miles; roadside assistance: 3 years / 36 000 miles.**																
Caravan-Voyager	base	4x2	4dr.van. 5/7	113.3	186.3x76.8x68.5	3516	ih/rl	dc/dr	pwr.r&p.	37.7	3.14	20.0	205/75R14	Goodyear	Conquest	L4/2.4/A3	**18,585**
Caravan-Voyager	SE	4x2	4dr.van. 5/7	113.3	186.3x76.8x68.5	3708	ih/rl	dc/dr/ABS	pwr.r&p.	37.7	3.14	20.0	215/65R15	Goodyear	Conquest	V6/3.0/A4	**22,460**
Caravan	LE	4x2	4dr.van. 5/7	113.3	186.3x76.8x68.5	3966	ih/rl	dc/dr/ABS	pwr.r&p.	37.7	3.14	20.0	215/65R15	Goodyear	Conquest	V6/3.3/A4	**26,280**
Gd Caravan-Voyager	base	4x2	4dr.van. 7	119.3	199.6x76.8x68.5	3684	ih/rl	dc/dr/ABS	pwr.r&p.	39.4	3.14	20.0	215/70R15	Goodyear	Conquest	V6/3.0/A4	**21,720**
Gd Caravan-Voyager	SE	4x2	4dr.van. 7	119.3	199.6x76.8x68.5	3812	ih/rl	dc/dr/ABS	pwr.r&p.	39.4	3.14	20.0	215/70R15	Goodyear	Conquest	V6/3.0/A4	**23,445**
Gd Caravan	ES	4x2	4dr.van. 7	119.3	199.6x76.8x68.5	4050	ih/rl	dc/dr/ABS	pwr.r&p.	39.4	3.14	20.0	215/60R17	Goodyear	Conquest	V6/3.8/A4	**29,485**
FORD	**General warranty, antipollution & battery: 3 years / 36 000 miles; corrosion perforation: 5 years / unlimited.**																
Windstar	3.0	4x2	3dr.van. 7	120.7	200.9x76.6x66.1	NA	ih/srh	dc/dr/ABS	pwr.r&p.	40.7	2.8	26.0	205/70R15	Firestone	Affinity	V6/3.0/A4	**18,955**
Windstar	LX	4x2	4dr.van. 7	120.7	200.9x76.6x65.8	NA	ih/srh	dc/dr/ABS	pwr.r&p.	40.7	2.8	26.0	215/70R15	Firestone	Affinity	V6/3.8/A4	**24,240**
Windstar	SE	4x2	4dr.van. 7	120.7	200.9x76.6x65.8	NA	ih/srh	dc/dr/ABS	pwr.r&p.	40.7	2.8	26.0	215/70R15	Firestone	Affinity	V6/3.8/A4	**28,075**
Windstar	SEL	4x2	4dr.van. 7	120.7	200.9x76.6x65.8	NA	ih/srh	dc/dr/ABS	pwr.r&p.	40.7	2.8	26.0	225/60R16	Firestone	Affinity	V6/3.8/A4	**30,995**
HONDA	**General warranty: 3 years / 36 000 miles; powertrain: 5 years / 60 000 miles.**																
Odyssey	LX	4x2	4dr.van. 7	118.1	201.2x65.6x68.5	4211	ih/ih	dc/dr/ABS	pwr.r&p.	37.7	3.0	20.0	215/65R16	Goodyear	Conquest	V6/3.5/A4	**23,615**
Odyssey	EX	4x2	4dr.van. 7	118.1	201.2x65.6x68.5	4288	ih/ih	dc/dr/ABS	pwr.r&p.	37.7	3.0	20.0	215/65R16	Goodyear	Conquest	V6/3.5/A4	**26,215**
MAZDA	**General warranty: 3 years / 36 000 miles; powertrain: 5 years / 60 000 miles.**																
MPV	DX	4x2	4dr.van. 7	111.8	187.0x72.1x68.7	3657	ih/sih	dc/dr	pwr.r&p.	37.4	3.3	18.5	205/65R15	Yokohama	Radial 376	V6/2.5/A4	**19,995**
MPV	LX	4x2	4dr.van. 7	111.8	187.0x72.1x68.7	3662	ih/sih	dc/dr	pwr.r&p.	37.4	3.3	18.5	205/65R15	Yokohama	Radial 376	V6/2.5/A4	**22,050**
MPV	ES	4x2	4dr.van. 7	111.8	187.0x72.1x68.7	3662	ih/sih	dc/dr	pwr.r&p.	37.4	3.3	18.5	205/65R15	Yokohama	Radial 376	V6/2.5/A4	**25,550**
NISSAN	**General warranty, antipollution & battery: 3 years / 36 000 miles; corrosion perforation: 5 years / unlimited.**																
Quest	GXE	4x2	4dr.van. 7	112.2	194.8x74.9x67.3	-	ih/rl	dc/dr/ABS	pwr.r&p.	38.7	3.0	20.0	215/70R15	Goodyear	Eagle LS	V6/3.3/A4	**22,679**
Quest	SE	4x2	4dr.van. 7	112.2	194.8x74.9x67.3	-	ih/rl	dc/dr/ABS	pwr.r&p.	38.7	3.0	20.0	225/60R16	-	-	V6/3.3/A4	**24,419**
Quest	GLE	4x2	4dr.van. 7	112.2	194.8x74.9x67.3	-	ih/rl	dc/dr/ABS	pwr.r&p.	38.7	3.0	20.0	215/70R15	Goodyear	Eagle LS	V6/3.3/A4	**26,819**
OLDSMOBILE	**General warranty: 3 years / 36 000 miles; antipollution: 5 years / 50 000 miles; perforation corrosion: 6 years / 100 000 miles. Roadside assistance.**																
Silhouette short	GS	4x2	4dr.van. 7/8	112.0	187.4x72.2x67.4	3746	ih/rh	dc/dr/ABS	pwr.r&p.	37.4	3.0	20.0	205/70R15	BFGoodrich	Touring	V6/3.4/A4	**25,470**
Silhouette long	GLS	4x2	4dr.van. 7/8	120.0	201.4x72.2x68.1	3942	ih/rh	dc/dr/ABS	pwr.r&p.	39.7	3.0	25.0	215/70R15	BFGoodrich	Touring	V6/3.4/A4	**28,765**
PONTIAC	**General warranty: 3 years / 36 000 miles; antipollution: 5 years / 50 000 miles; perforation corrosion: 6 years / 100 000 miles. Roadside assistance.**																
Montana short	base	4x2	4dr.van. 7/8	112.0	187.2x72.7x67.4	3730	ih/rh	dc/dr/ABS	pwr.r&p.	37.4	3.0	20.0	215/70R15	General	XP2000GT	V6/3.4/A4	**21,905**
Montana long	base	4x2	4dr.van. 7/8	120.0	201.2x72.7x68.0	3942	ih/rh	dc/dr/ABS	pwr.r&p.	39.7	3.0	25.0	215/70R15	General	XP2000GT	V6/3.4/A4	**24,510**
TOYOTA	**General warranty: 3 years / 36 000 miles; powertrain 5 years / 60 000 miles; corrosion, perforation: 5 years / unlimited.**																
Sienna	CE	4x2	3dr.van. 7	114.2	193.5x73.4x67.3	3759	ih/sih	dc/dr/ABS	pwr.r&p.	40.0	2.9	20.9	205/70R15	Dunlop	SP 40	V6/3.0/A4	**21,928**
Sienna	LE	4x2	4dr.van. 7	114.2	193.5x73.4x67.3	3891	ih/sih	dc/dr/ABS	pwr.r&p.	40.0	2.9	20.9	205/70R15	Dunlop	SP 40	V6/3.0/A4	**24,858**
Sienna	XLE	4x2	4dr.van. 7	114.2	193.5x73.4x67.3	-	ih/sih	dc/dr/ABS	pwr.r&p.	40.0	2.9	20.9	205/70R15	Dunlop	SP 40	V6/3.0/A4	**26,994**

Notes: 1) Tire makes and models are provided solely as an indication; they are subject to change without prior notice from the automobile manufacturers.
2) See the 2000 price list at the back of this edition.

CLASSIFICATION

OUR CLASSIFICATION

Rank	Models	Concept	Driving	Equipment	Comfort	Budget	Ratings
1	**CHRYSLER NS Series**	79	59	71	**80**	**64**	**70.6 %**
2	FORD Windstar	**84**	61	72	72	60	69.8 %
3	TOYOTA Sienna	76	59	72	72	62	68.2 %
3	HONDA Odyssey	79	59	74	71	58	68.2 %
4	NISSAN Quest						
4	MERCURY Villager	76	61	74	70	58	67.8 %
5	MAZDA MPV	78	**62**	72	69	53	66.8 %
6	GM U Series	69	52	**77**	70	61	65.8 %
7	GM M Series	72	52	63	69	54	62.0 %

YOUR CLASSIFICATION

Rank	Models	98 Sales
1	**CHRYSLER NS**	**522,771**
2	GM U Series	193,976
3	FORD Windstar	190,173
4	GM M Series	126,898
5	TOYOTA Sienna	81,391
6	MERCURY Villager	38,495
7	NISSAN Quest	30,466
8	HONDA Odyssey	13,665
9	MAZDA MPV	12,425

Minivans

HONDA CR-V

JEEP Cherokee

JEEP TJ

KIA Sportage

NISSAN Xterra

SUZUKI Grand Vitara

TOYOTA RAV4

Comparative Test

COMPACT SPORT UTILITY VEHICLES

See their performance, their specifications, their price and their classification at the end of this chapter.

Compact SUVs

A Favorite

The CR-V is the bestselling sport utility vehicles of recent vintage. Still, in the U.S. it bows to the venerable Cherokee, whose sales have never been better. The CR-V sets itself apart from the pack with less radical styling, at the crossroads of several design approaches. It's one of the few vehicles equally popular among male and female buyers, though for very different reasons.

MODEL RANGE

The CR-V is a 4-door multi-purpose all-wheel drive vehicle offered in LX with manual transmission or EX with an automatic. Both models are powered by a 146-hp 2.0L 4-cylinder engine that's already been used on other Honda models. Original equipment is rich for both trim levels and includes in all cases: power steering, antilock braking system, cruise control, climate control and main power functions.

TECHNICAL FEATURES

The CR-V steel unitized body yields an unpublished drag coefficient. In spite of its rather high ground clearance (8.25 in.), this vehicle can't really be classified as having a genuine all-terrain temperament, since it isn't equipped with the transfer case that would give it a range of short gear ratios, nor with true-grit tires and protective plates to keep major organs out of harm's way are nowhere in sight.

The four-wheel independent suspension consists of a double wishbone setup with coil springs and stabilizer bars. Vehicles are equipped with power rack-and-pinion steering and disc and drum brakes linked to a standard ABS device. The all-wheel drive requires no intervention on the part of the driver. When road adherence is picture perfect, the front wheels do the work, but when things get slick, both powertrains are fitted with a

hydraulic pump that turns along with the wheels. As soon as wheel rotation speed fluctuates, the increased pressure deploys a multidisc clutch that distributes torque to rear wheels in a proportion that can vary between 100% up front and 0% at the rear to 50-50% on both extremities. This device acts, as the name indicates, in real time.

PROS

+ LOOKS. The CR-V doesn't look like an army vehicle and it attracts two very different kinds of buyers, both of which like to know that they can always go exactly where they want to go.

+ SIZE. The CR-V is unique because it constitutes the intelligent synthesis of features found on several vehicles. All-wheel drive allows for safe driving on all kinds of surfaces, seats are very straight and you can get around inside the cabin a bit as if you were inside a minivan. The vehicle has four swing doors as on a station wagon, it's easy to drive and handles like a regular car and boasts of car-like performances and safety features.

+ DRIVING PLEASURE. Driving this vehicle is straightforward and not the least bit complicated. Controls are smooth and right-on, visibility is super in all directions and the engine has enough pep to spice up the ride.

+ CONVENIENCE FEATURES. The CR-V is very versatile. You can climb aboard the cabin with no trouble at all and there are loads of handy storage spots. The fold-away

shelf located between the front seats, along with the picnic table that also serves as a floor in the luggage hold are indications of how innovative Honda stylists can be. The luggage compartment volume can easily be extended by lowering the 40/60 split-folding rear seat. The dual-section hatch door is easy to use and makes for easy cargo hold access.

+ ROADHOLDING. In spite of impressive wheel travel, roll and sway are well under control and wheels grip like champions when taking curves and the CR-V is very agile in such circumstances.

+ QUALITY. Body components look rather flimsy and some trim materials aren't too great, but assembly and finish are very clean and dependability seems to be on a level with other Honda vehicles, according to new owners.

+ PERFORMANCE. With a few extra horses the CR-V provides better acceleration and pick-up than the previous model and fuel economy is good, especially with the automatic transmission.

+ MANEUVERABILITY. The short steer angle diameter, reasonable reduction ratio and excellent visibility make getting around in the concrete jungle less of a task.

+ PRICE. It's reasonable considering the extensive equipment included. It's quite competitive in comparison with the 4-cylinder Cherokee to which you have to add a few options to arrive at an equivalent equipment level.

+ FUEL ECONOMY. The 2.0L engine yields a decent 20 lbs/hp power

to weight ratio and does an honest 20 mpg.

CONS

-STEERING. It's a bit over-assisted, but more important, response is springy which isn't always fun and coming back to center isn't automatic.

-BRAKES. They could be more effective, they don't dig in when applied and emergency stops are very long to achieve. But brakes are nice and gradual and very accurate and the vehicle stays right on course thanks to ABS that works like a Trojan to do the job right.

- NOISE LEVEL. It's pervasive no matter what, because of the cabin layout and lack of soundproofing that doesn't dampen engine and road noise as it should. Bodywork is light and the doors and hood sound hollow when you close them shut.

- LIMITATIONS. The CR-V isn't a true-grit all-terrain beast, but rather an «all-road» beauty. Poorly protected mechanical components discourage rambles in the wild, for only the gas tank has a protective plate.

-TO BE IMPROVED UPON. Some poorly located controls, shifter and hand brake that are both hassles to use, teeny tiny wheels and rear wiper that doesn't have an intermittent function.

CONCLUSION

There's no reason to think that things won't continue to go well for the CR-V. It's the first of a new race of versatile vehicles sure to swarm the market!

RATING
HONDA CR-V

CONCEPT :   **74%**
Technology :	85
Safety :	80
Interior space :	70
Trunk volume :	55
Quality/fit/finish :	80

DRIVING :   **58%**
Cockpit :	75
Performance :	50
Handling :	50
Steering :	75
Braking :	40

ORIGINAL EQUIPMENT :   **73%**
Tires :	80
Headlights :	85
Wipers :	70
Rear defroster :	70
Radio :	60

COMFORT :   **73%**
Seats :	75
Suspension :	80
Sound level :	40
Conveniences :	90
Air conditioning :	80

BUDGET :   **64%**
Price :	40
Fuel economy :	70
Insurance :	55
Satisfaction :	90
Depreciation :	65

Overall rating :   **68.4%**

NEW FOR 2000

• No changes.

Compare
Performance,
Specifications, Prices,
and Classification
at the end of this chapter.

EQUIPMENT

HONDA CR-V	LX	EX
Automatic transmission:	O	S
Cruise control:	S	S
Power steering:	S	S
Anti-lock brakes:	S	S
Traction control:	-	-
Air conditioning:	S	S
Leather:	-	-
AM/FM/radio-cassette:	O	SCd
Power door locks:	S	S
Power windows:	S	S
Tilt steering:	S	S
Dual adjustable mirrors:	S	S
Alloy wheels:	-	S
Anti-theft system:	-	-

Colors

Exterior: Black, Red, Silver, Green, Blue, Gold.

Interior: Grey.

AT A GLANCE...

HISTORIC
Introduced in: 1997.
Made in: Saima, Japon.

DEMOGRAPHICS
Model	Men/Wom.	Age	Married	College	Income $
CR-V	50/50 %	39	75 %	62 %	54,000

INDEX
Safety:	80 %	Satisfaction:	88 %
Depreciation:	45 %	Insurance:	$ 665
Cost per mile:	$ 0.50	Number of dealers:	1,001

SALES
	Canada				USA	
Model	1997	1998	Result	1997	1998	Result
CR-V	14,778	14,306	- 3.2 %	66,752	100,582	+ 50.7 %

MAINTENANCE REQUIRED BY WARRANTY
First revision:	Frequency:	Diagnostic plug:
3,000 miles	3,000 miles	Yes

Compact SUVs

Veteran

The Cherokee continues to sell in staggering quantities. In fact, it's so popular there's no question of replacing it - at least for the time being. It's so much a part of the automotive landscape that it's well on its way to becoming a classic, an enduring replica of itself. And with a revised engine that provides more power, it's even more thundering than ever before!

MODEL RANGE

The Cherokee is available in 3 or 5-door models, with either RWD or AWD in SE, Sport, Classic and Limited versions, the two latter replacing the Country. The SE version is animated by a 2.5L 4-cylinder engine, but the Sport, Classic and Limited receive a 4.0L in-line 6 engine. The manual gearbox comes standard and the 3 or 4-speed automatic is sold as an extra. Dual airbags are part of the original equipment but four-wheel ABS is still only an option.

TECHNICAL FEATURES

The Cherokee consists of a steel structure made up of an H-frame built into a steel unibody. Vehicle design isn't too refined when it comes to aerodynamics, since the drag coefficient sits at about 0.50. The rigid axle suspensions are equipped with longitudinal control arms, anti-roll bar as well as coil springs up front and leaf springs at the rear. Vehicles are equipped with disc and drum brakes, but the ABS system is only available as an extra. The 4X4's benefit from on-demand «Select-Trac» all-wheel drive, standard on the SE version, but from a full-time «Command-Trac» system that's part of the original equipment on other versions. Both engines that are starting to show their age are linked up with a standard manual transmission and an optional 3-speed (2.5L) or 4-speed automatic, the latter being stand-ard on the Classic and Limited versions.

PROS

+ STYLE. Handsome and familiar, it's a real classic and exudes a reassuring solid as a rock feeling.

+ SIZE. It's very compact, so you can go anywhere and this vehicle maneuvers beautifully. The 4.0L 6-cylinder engine gives it a unique top of the heap athletic status, so it makes light work of heavy loads.

+ OFF-ROAD CAPABILITIES. The Cherokee is a real acrobat. It can tackle off-road maneuvers with no trouble at all, due to wide entrance and exit angles, effective traction, reasonable weight and spare tire stored inside the cargo hold to optimize ground clearance.

+ SLICK MOVES. This vehicle is nice and compact, benefits from a short steer angle diameter and lively steering, though the latter suffers from a slightly poor reduction ratio, so it doesn't require much maneuvering space. Visibility is terrific in all directions due to large windows and relatively thin roof supports.

+ PERFORMANCES. They have more zip with the 6-cylinder engine since the power to weight ratio is more favorable than for the 4-cylinder.

+ MODEL CHOICE. The Cherokee is one of the few SUV's that comes in 2 body designs, 4 trim levels, equipped with RWD or AWD, 3 all-wheel drive transmission modes...

+ HANDLING. This vehicle has a high center of gravity, but it's amazingly confident for a vehicle of this type, sway is limited and the big tires let you take curves, even tighties, with a certain aplomb.

+ VALUE. The Cherokee is among the vehicles that have top resale value in the category, due to dependability and long-life components, at a more appealing price than for some of the competition.

+ CABIN LAYOUT. The new instrument panel is more convenient than before. It's more ergonomic with its main section that juts out, so main controls are within reach.

+ COCKPIT. It's been improved with the new steering column and the seat enfolds you more and is quite nicely upholstered.

+ QUALITY. It's been noticeably enhanced when it comes to finish job and trim materials and the vehicle looks generally less bare bone basic.

CONS

- RIDE COMFORT. It's far from perfect with those big tires and rigid axles that give occupants quite a shaking up and the seat and back cushions on the seatbench are too short. Wind whistling around the angular body and roaring engines create loud, pervasive noise.

+ FUEL CONSUMPTION. It doesn't reflect this vehicle's modest exterior dimensions, averaging 15 mpg.

- ACCESS. You have to go through a workout to board and unboard because of the narrow doors on the 4-door model and high ground clearance, so some folks will have to opt for the 2-door version that's equipped with add-on running boards.

- SAFETY FEATURES. They're penalized by missing standard rear seat headrests and chronically weak headlights.

-BRAKES. They're not too hot, emergency stops take longer than average to achieve and ABS isn't standard, so vehicle path is very unpredictable. The automatic transmission doesn't provide much braking effect.

- PERFORMANCES. The 2.5L engine is anemic, especially with the automatic gearbox when the air conditioner is on. With the manual, you have to often shift gears to maintain speeds.

-FUEL CONSUMPTION. It's poor with both engines that are God-awful old. They're very greedy, given the real power they can put out.

- TOWING CAPACITY. Even properly equiped, the Cherokee is unable to tow the 5000 lb as advertised by its manufacturer, without taking any serious risks or burning a ridiculous ammount of fuel.

- DESIGN. It's starting to get terribly outdated with its narrow, low clearance cabin, and the luggage compartment isn't huge and it holds the spare tire.

- TO BE IMPROVED UPON: Missing storage spots on the door panels and no footrest for the driver.

CONCLUSION

This veteran model is beginning to show the weight of a good number of years of service. While its purchase price is affordable, on a daily basis it's expensive and frustrating to use.

Compact SUVs

RATING
JEEP Cherokee

CONCEPT : 66%
Technology :	75
Safety :	70
Interior space :	60
Trunk volume :	50
Quality/fit/finish :	75

DRIVING : 54%
Cockpit :	75
Performance :	35
Handling :	40
Steering :	70
Braking :	50

ORIGINAL EQUIPMENT : 74%
Tires :	80
Headlights :	70
Wipers :	65
Rear defroster :	75
Radio :	80

COMFORT : 61%
Seats :	70
Suspension :	60
Sound level :	50
Conveniences :	50
Air conditioning :	75

BUDGET : 57%
Price :	50
Fuel economy :	55
Insurance :	50
Satisfaction :	80
Depreciation :	50

Overall rating : 62.4%

NEW FOR 2000
- Better headlamps on all models.
- Chrome design details on the Limited version, different graphic details and different alloy wheels.
- New exterior colors.

Compare Performance, Specifications, Prices, and Classification at the end of this chapter.

EQUIPMENT

JEEP Cherokee	SE 3dr.wgn. 4x2	Sport 3dr.wgn. 4x4	Classic 4dr.wgn. 4x4	Limited 4dr.wgn. 4x4
Automatic transmission:	O	O	S	S
Cruise control:	O	O	O	S
Power steering:	S	S	S	S
Anti-lock brakes:	O	O	O	O
Traction control:	O	O	O	O
Air conditioning:	O	O	O	O
Leather:	-	-	-	S
AM/FM/radio-cassette:	O	S	S	S
Power door locks:	-	O	O	S
Power windows:	-	O	O	S
Tilt steering:	O	O	O	S
Dual adjustable mirrors:	SM	SE	SE	SEH
Alloy wheels:	O	O	S	S
Anti-theft system:	O	O	O	O

Colors
Exterior: Red, Blue, Green, Grey, White, Black, Chili Pepper, Gold, Jade, Sand.

Interior: Camel, Pebble.

AT A GLANCE...

HISTORIC
Introduced in:	1984.
Made in:	Toledo, Ohio, USA.

DEMOGRAPHICS
Model	Men/Wom.	Age	Married	College	Income $
Cherokee	67/33 %	38	71 %	55 %	50,000

INDEX
Safety:	70 %	Satisfaction:	78 %
Depreciation:	48 %	Insurance:	$ 690
Cost per mile:	$ 0.55	Number of dealers:	1,029

SALES
	Canada			USA		
Model	1997	1998	Result	1997	1998	Result
Cherokee	6,905	7,863	+ 13.8 %	130,041	146,298	+ 12.5 %

MAINTENANCE REQUIRED BY WARRANTY
First revision:	Frequency:	Diagnostic plug:
7 500 miles	6 months	Yes

Compact SUVs

Replica

The TJ (Wrangler) is the ultimate version of a historic model designed during World War II to provide troops with better mobility. In civilian life, the Jeep was used for just about every purpose under the sun before becoming the recreational-type vehicle it is now.

MODEL RANGE

The Jeep Wrangler is sold in a soft top convertible SE model driven by a 2.5L 4-cylinder engine or Sport and Sahara powered by a 4.0L in-line 6 engine. The SE is rather poorly equipped, since it doesn't even receive power steering, radio or rear seatbench. All you get are dual airbags, a soft top and two half-doors with vinyl tops and a spare tire. You have to pick the Sport trim level to be equipped with power steering, AM/FM radio and rear seatbench, while the Sahara also gets radio and tape deck, adjustable steering column, intermittent wipers, more generous-size tires and gas tank as well as distinctive stylistic accents, including light alloy rims. In all cases, the automatic transmission, air conditioning, hard top, antilock braking system and cruise control are among items found on the long list of options.

TECHNICAL FEATURES

The Jeep Wrangler is made up of a steel body mounted on a steel frame that's been reworked so as to integrate the «Quadra Coil» coil spring suspension inherited from the former Grand Cherokee. Front and rear axles are still rigid, but they're maintained and directed by various longitudinal and transverse control arms and assisted by stabilizer bars. All models are equipped with disc and drum brakes and a rustic ABS system is available as an option only

on versions equipped with a six-cylinder engine. The engines are the venerable 4-cylinder and in-line 6-cylinder models that can be linked to an antique 3-speed automatic transmission that's sold as an extra.

PROS

+ **IN FASHION.** The Jeep is still the preferred vehicle of those who like being different and living on the edge. They like to project the image of being wild and wooly adventurous sorts...

+ **STYLE.** This vehicle's legendary look has not only been respected, but it's even sporting some items more akin to those on the original model.

+ **HANDLING.** Vehicle stability is more of a sure thing since it's been revised to receive Grand Cherokee suspension components.

+ **CAPABILITIES.** The Jeep shines on off-road maneuvers, since it can overcome all kinds of obstacles due to generous entrance and exit angles, very gutsy traction, high ground clearance and agility due to its trim size.

+ **INSTRUMENT PANEL.** It's straightforward and functional, well-suited to this type of vehicle, for gauges and controls are located according to good ergonomics.

+ **CLIMATE CONTROL.** It's finally works as it should, due to an efficient air vent system that nicely distributes warm or cool air

throughout the cabin interior.

+ **ACCESS.** It's lots less of a chore getting to the rear seats because of the cleverly designed front passenger seat that frees up lots of boarding space. Too bad the driver's seat isn't equipped with the same device.

+ **CONVENIENCE FEATURES.** Storage space includes a genuine glove compartment, small door side-pockets, a tub located on the dashboard and a cup-holder on the center console.

CONS

- **BRAKES.** The ones equipping our various test vehicles were dangerous on sudden stops, for wheel lock set in early on and in a disshevelled, unpredictable way, throwing the vehicle off balance and so stopping distances really stretched out, with or without ABS.

- **FUEL EFFICIENCY.** Both engines are behind the times in this department. The 4-cylinder is rough, noisy as heck and lacks both power and torque, even with the manual gearbox. The 6-cylinder engine has more get up and go, but it guzzles a lot of gas.

- **RIDE COMFORT.** It's only manageable on silky California highways, elsewhere the suspension kicks up a fuss. Then there's the constant ruckus of wind, engine and road noise to add to the torture.

- **STEERING.** It's quick and makes

for good moves, but it's over-assisted, so it's light as a feather and you really have to keep an eye on it, for it can throw the vehicle off-course.

- **CABIN SPACE.** It's cramped and terribly narrow. Front seat passengers get squished against the doors and the rear seatbench is, well, a seatbench.

- **CONVERTIBLE SOFT TOP.** It's nicely tailored, waterproof and less noisy than before, but it's a nightmare removing even the smallest section, so imagine what you have to deal with when you want to remove it completely...

- **SUSPENSIONS.** They're quite sophisticated (especially up front), so repairs would probably cost a fortune, even after a minor accident.

- **CARGO SPACE.** It's ridiculously small, can't accommodate much and is hard to access. Even a very minimum amount of baggage means condemning the rear bench seat and the fold-down process is a frustration in itself.

- **FLAWS.** Windshield wipers aren't efficient and can't keep up in poor weather conditions.

CONCLUSION

Despite regular revisions, the TJ's technical features remain terribly simplistic and outdated. However, it has good off-road capabilities and its lack of refinement doesn't seem to matter to consumers, since it continues to beat sales records.

Compact SUVs

RATING
JEEP Wrangler

CONCEPT :		54%
Technology :	75	
Safety :	80	
Interior space :	40	
Trunk volume :	0	
Quality/fit/finish :	75	

DRIVING :		45%
Cockpit :	75	
Performance :	30	
Handling :	45	
Steering :	60	
Braking :	15	

ORIGINAL EQUIPMENT :		56%
Tires :	75	
Headlights :	75	
Wipers :	55	
Rear defroster :	0	
Radio :	75	

COMFORT :		43%
Seats :	70	
Suspension :	30	
Sound level :	0	
Conveniences :	40	
Air conditioning :	75	

BUDGET :		55%
Price :	50	
Fuel economy :	40	
Insurance :	50	
Satisfaction :	80	
Depreciation :	55	

Overall rating :		50.6%

NEW FOR 2000
- LEV improvements to the 4.0L L6 engine.
- Improved 5-speed manual transmission.
- Radio and cassette player standard on the Sport version.
- New exterior colors.
- Child-safety seat anchors.
- Bigger fuel tank.

Compare
Performance,
Specifications, Prices,
and Classification
at the end of this chapter.

EQUIPMENT

JEEP Wrangler	SE	Sport	Sahara
Automatic transmission:	O	O	O
Cruise control:	O	O	O
Power steering:	S	S	S
Anti-lock brakes:	-	O	O
Traction control:	-	-	-
Air conditioning:	O	O	O
Leather:	-	-	-
AM/FM/radio-cassette:	O	S	S
Power door locks:	-	-	-
Power windows:	-	-	-
Tilt steering:	O	O	S
Dual adjustable mirrors:	SM	SM	SM
Alloy wheels:	O	O	S
Anti-theft system:	O	O	O

Colors

Exterior: Chili Pepper, Amethyst, Grey, Blue, Green, Sand.

Interior: Blue, Tan, Grey.

AT A GLANCE...

HISTORIC
Introduced in:	1987-1997.
Made in:	Toledo, Ohio,USA.

DEMOGRAPHICS
Model	Men/Wom.	Age	Married	College	Income $
Wrangler	61/39 %	32	50 %	49 %	55,000

INDEX
Safety:	70 %	Satisfaction:	77%
Depreciation:	50 %	Insurance:	$ 650
Cost per mile:	$ 0.55	Number of dealers:	1,029

SALES
Model	Canada 1997	1998	Result	USA 1997	1998	Result
Wrangler	6,153	6,093	- 1.0 %	81,956	83,861	+ 2.3 %

MAINTENANCE REQUIRED BY WARRANTY
First revision:	Frequency:	Diagnostic plug:
3,000 miles	6 months / 6,000 miles	Yes

Locomotive

After the Korean head office's bankruptcy and the takeover by Hyundai, Kia is continuing on its quest to conquer the world. Long after it entered the U.S. market, it has finally decided to take on Canada. In keeping with tradition, it's relying on two main models. In the automobile sector it has the Sephia, a mid-size car similar to the Toyota Corolla, and the Sportage, a sport utility which has fared quite well in the US.

MODEL RANGE

While Canadians who buy a Sportage have to be content with a 4-door extended cab version and nothing else, further South consumers can choose either a 4x2, short wheelbase or a 2-door convertible versions. All are powered by a modern 130-hp DOHC 4-cylinder engine with a 5-speed manual or 4-speed automatic transmission. Standard equipment on the AWD includes power windows, power locks and power sideview mirrors, a tilt steering wheel, alloy wheels, theft deterrent and air conditioning systems; ABS brakes and a radio/cassette player are optional.

TECHNICAL FEATURES

The steel body features five crossmembers. Its drag coefficient is unknown, but in spite of its rounded lines, given its height it is probable only average. The front suspension features double triangular arms, while the rear has a solid axle with four longitudinal arms and a Panhard bar. The assembly includes two antiroll bars and hydraulic shock absorbers. The Sportage offers a drum-disc brake combination, a power-assisted recirculating ball steering system and an optional ABS system.

PROS

+ PRICE. The Sportage is one of the least expensive vehicles in its class. Yet considering its capabilities and its satisfaction rating, it does better than a lot of other costlier and more reputed vehicles.

+ VERSATILITY. In the city or over hill and dale, the Sportage is perfectly at home and can take on any situation.

+ SIZE. The Sportage is well-proportioned, long enough to take on four passengers, but thanks to its turning radius, not too long to make city parking complicated.

+ LOOKS. This little sport utility vehicle is a looker and its rounded styling is a noticeable departure from the army tank looks typical of the category.

+ DESIGN. The exterior is more appealing than the inside, which looks very utilitarian on the base version. Our test drive model included seats with leather trims and fake wood inlays are available as an option.

+ HANDLING. Unless its driver is very inept, the Sportage is very consistent. It tends to take corners lying down, but at the speeds it travels at the tendency is nothing really dangerous. However, depending on the options package, tire quality varies and is an issue that needs addressing.

+ DRIVEABILITY. In spite of marginal engine power, this small sport ute is fun to drive. The steering system is precise and well assisted, the brake pedal is responsive, power is easy to gauge, and visibility is good in every direction.

+ OFF-ROAD TALENTS. A nice surprise: we took the Kia out into the wilds and regardless of its city-slicker tires, it got along just fine. Contrary to what we'd feared, its smooth suspension was no problem. However, heftier tires with more grip would be a definite plus.

+ COMFORT. It's surprising given that 4x4 models are usually stiff and tend to hop. The Kia's smooth suspension goes a long way in swallowing road defects. Although seats don't provide ideal support, they are generously padded. The noise level is very acceptable at cruising speeds and is annoying only during acceleration.

+ QUALITY. For a vehicle sold at this price, the Kia is surprisingly consistent. Its body is sturdy and the plastics it features look better than those found on some luxury sedans manufactured by American builders.

+ BONUS MARKS. For the adjustable front center armrest, the airbag designed to protect the driver's knees, good front and side visibility.

CONS

- PERFORMANCE. Levels are mediocre given the poor weight/power ratio. The small 2.0L 4-cylinder engine does all it can, but it has to be pushed. Hilly terrain makes this vehicle's limitations very obvious, especially if it's loaded to capacity.

- BRAKING. Efficiency is very average and the distance needed for panic stops is close to 164 ft. (50 m). However, power is easy to gauge and the car is easy to keep on course when braking.

- FRONT-END ASSEMBLY. Off-road it's easy to see that the excessively supple front-end is a negative - the vehicle jolts from one obstacle to another and is hard to steer.

- REAR SEATS. They can accommodate only two adults, space is limited and the bench seat is virtually a torture chamber.

- OVERSIGHTS. Mounted on the outside, the spare tire hurts rear visibility; the hatch is hard to open, front windshield wipers are painfully slow and the rear windshield's isn't intermittent. The remote fuel-door release is oddly positioned.

CONCLUSION

In all of the countries where Kia wants to establish a presence, the Sportage is the locomotive that can plough the way to decent sales levels. For the moment, it is by far the most attractive product in this market niche.

RATING	
KIA Sportage	
CONCEPT :	**68%**
Technology :	70
Safety :	75
Interior space :	70
Trunk volume :	50
Quality/fit/finish :	75
DRIVING :	**49%**
Cockpit :	75
Performance :	15
Handling :	30
Steering :	75
Braking :	50
ORIGINAL EQUIPMENT :	**69%**
Tires :	70
Headlights :	75
Wipers :	55
Rear defroster :	70
Radio :	75
COMFORT :	**68%**
Seats :	75
Suspension :	75
Sound level :	50
Conveniences :	70
Air conditioning :	70
BUDGET :	**66%**
Price :	70
Fuel economy :	65
Insurance :	70
Satisfaction :	75
Depreciation :	50
Overall rating :	**64.0%**

NEW FOR 2000

• **No major changes.**

Compare
Performance,
Specifications, Prices,
and Classification
at the end of this chapter.

EQUIPMENT

KIA Sportage	4WD
Automatic transmission:	O
Cruise control:	O
Power steering:	S
Anti-lock brakes:	O
Traction control:	O
Air conditioning:	O
Leather:	O
AM/FM/radio-cassette:	O
Power door locks:	S
Power windows:	S
Tilt steering:	S
Dual adjustable mirrors:	S
Alloy wheels:	S
Anti-theft system:	S

Colors

Exterior: White, Black, Red, Beige

Interior: Beige, Grey.

AT A GLANCE...

HISTORIC

Introduced in:	1994.
Made in:	South Korea.

DEMOGRAPHICS

Model	Men/Wom.	Age	Married	College	Income $
Sportage	75/25 %	35	75 %	55 %	45,000

INDEX

Safety:	75 %	Satisfaction:	75 %
Depreciation:	30 %	Insurance:	$ 550
Cost per mile:	0.48 $	Number of dealers:	115

SALES

	Canada			USA		
Model	1997	1998	Result	1997	1998	Result
Sportage	Not on sale during this period.			19,831	27,529	+ 38.8 %

MAINTENANCE REQUIRED BY WARRANTY

First revision:	Frequency:	Diagnostic plug:
3,000 miles	6,000 miles	Yes

Compact SUVs

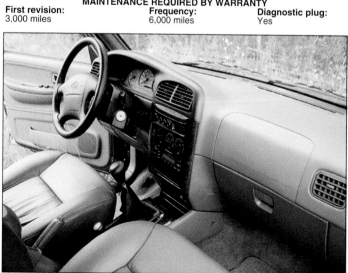

Lean And Mean

For some time now, manufacturers have been intent on making utility vehicles more and more luxurious and more and more comfortable. The process has gone so far, it's almost hard to remember what it's really like to drive a genuine 4x4. But here comes Nissan to bring us back to reality with its Xterra. With its "toolbox" design, this builder's new utility is clearly made of stronger stuff than most and it's more than ready to take on a challenge.

MODEL RANGE

Canadian buyers have only one model to decide on, a 3.3L V6 AWD with a manual or automatic transmission and a single equipment package; American consumers can choose from a wide range of models with rear-wheel or four-wheel drive, a 2.4L 4-cylinder or 3.3L V6 engine, and a manual or automatic transmission. Equipment goes from virtually nothing to virtually everything, it all depends on the trim. Though detailed information was unavailable at press time, we can only conclude that the pared down Canadian version leaves very little room for personalization.

TECHNICAL FEATURES

The Xterra is based on both the Pathfinder and the Frontier, sharing most of their mechanical components. Given its squared and rustic lines, its steel unibody is no marvel of aerodynamics. Supporting structures are made of extremely resistant Durasteel, ensuring optimal rigidity. The front suspension is composed of superimposed triangles and the rear assembly includes a solid axle with two leaf springs. On the Canadian market, the Xterra has a recirculating ball steering system and standard disc/drum antilock brakes.

PROS

+ **STYLING.** It's very original and creates a strong impression given unusual detailing like the raised roof, tube-shaped luggage rack and hatch-mounted first-aid kit.

+ **USEABLE SPACE.** Rear seats provide plenty of legroom. The cargo area is huge and the rear seat folds down for even more space.

+ **SIZING.** The Xterra is compact and designed for minimal overhang; its short turning radius results in good handling.

+ **PERFORMANCE.** Levels are decent given this midsize ute's weight: more than two tons when loaded to capacity. Acceleration is better than pick-up and overtaking vehicles on the open road calls for some caution.

+ **PRACTICALITY.** There are many storage spaces, mostly located in the front of the vehicle, including deep door pockets, a good-sized glovebox and a small but deep console.

+ **BONUS MARKS.** For the many assist grips, a feature not found very often, not even on the Range Rover.

CONS

- **SUSPENSION.** It couldn't be more rudimentary and does nothing to help occupants cope with bad roads, where it's plainly and simply uncomfortable. Luckily, well-padded seats help counter the problem.

- **HANDLING.** Since most sport utilities have automobile suspensions, drivers aren't used to slowing down considerably when merging into highways traffic. This doesn't hold true for the Xterra and because of its high center of gravity, it shows some instability unless you ease up on the gas.

- **FUEL CONSUMPTION.** Although not as high as it was on the old Pathfinders, this model isn't as economical as the CR-V, RAV4 and company, especially off-road.

- **BRAKING.** It's easy to gauge power when slowing down, but in emergencies stopping distances are longer than average.

- **LACK OF CHOICE.** The marketing approach chosen for the Canadian market is ridiculous. How can everybody go for the same prepackaged paraphernalia? Doesn't Nissan know that buyers come in a very wide variety of shapes, sizes and tastes? In contrast, in the U.S. the choice is almost too wide. How about a happy medium?

- **ACCESS.** It's easier to get into the front, where doors are long and open wider than they do in the rear, where they're very narrow. Loading baggage is difficult because of a high ground clearance. Luckily running boards are designed with functionality in mind.

- **HEADLIGHTS.** They aren't very efficient and their reach and brightness isn't enough in very rainy weather.

- **STEERING SYSTEM.** It has the disadvantage of being overassisted, making it light and imprecise at center. Although everything is fine off-road, on the highway the Xterra is overly sensitive to crosswinds, which can be a major inconvenience.

- **OVERSIGHTS.** There is no speed indicator with the automatic transmission and the Xterra has no vanity mirrors built into visors - typical Nissan cost-cutting. The radio is positioned very low, which forces drivers to take their eyes off the road when using its controls.

CONCLUSION

Although original and dynamic, the Xterra lacks refinement when it comes to comfort and handling, neither of which are up to current standards. Some people think that it's intended to take on the RAV4 and Honda CR-V, but it's only a Pathfinder in disguise, and far from economical to use.

XTerra NISSAN

RATING
NISSAN Xterra

CONCEPT : 73%
Technology : 75
Safety : 70
Interior space : 70
Trunk volume : 70
Quality/fit/finish : 80

DRIVING : 57%
Cockpit : 75
Performance : 35
Handling : 35
Steering : 80
Braking : 60

ORIGINAL EQUIPMENT : 72%
Tires : 75
Headlights : 75
Wipers : 60
Rear defroster : 75
Radio : 75

COMFORT : 70%
Seats : 75
Suspension : 60
Sound level : 70
Conveniences : 70
Air conditioning : 75

BUDGET : 52%
Price : 35
Fuel economy : 40
Insurance : 45
Satisfaction : 90
Depreciation : 50

Overall rating : 64.8%

New 2000 Model

NEW FOR 2000

• New model derived from the Pathfinder.

Compare Performance, Specifications, Prices, and Classification at the end of this chapter.

EQUIPMENT

NISSAN — Xterra

Automatic transmission: S
Cruise control: S
Power steering: S
Anti-lock brakes: S
Traction control: -
Air conditioning: S
Leather: -
AM/FM/radio-cassette: S
Power door locks: S
Power windows: S
Tilt steering: S
Dual adjustable mirrors: S
Alloy wheels: S
Anti-theft system: -

Colors

Exterior: Yellow, Silver.
Interior: Grey.

AT A GLANCE...

HISTORIC
Introduced in: 2000.
Made in: Kyushu (Japan).

DEMOGRAPHICS

Model	Men/Wom.	Age	Married	College	Income $
Xterra	NA				

INDEX
Safety: 80 %   Satisfaction: (Nissan) 88 %
Depreciation: 30 %   Insurance: $ 600
Cost per mile: $ 0.55   Number of dealers: 1,100

SALES

Model	Canada 1997	1998	Result	USA 1997	1998	Result
Xterra	Not on sale during this period.					

MAINTENANCE REQUIRED BY WARRANTY
First revision: 7,500 miles
Frequency: 7,500 miles
Diagnostic plug: Yes

Compact SUVs

Short-winded

Revamped only last year, these two vehicles are trying to catch up with their competitors, who've had time to reach the top of the sales hit parade. In spite of interesting innovations on the part of both builders' engineers, there's still a lot to do to bring them up to par with the Honda CR-V or Toyota RAV4, bench marks in this class.

MODEL RANGE

The Chevrolet Tracker is identical to the Suzuki Vitara and Grand Vitara that take after the Sidekick, except for a few finish details and equipment items. In Canada, the only model sold is equipped with all-wheel drive and comes in a 2-door convertible or 4-door station wagon in a single trim level. The convertible is driven by a 1.6L 4-cylinder engine and the station wagon gets a new 2.0L engine derived from the former 1.8L with a standard manual gearbox, as well as four-wheel ABS and power steering.

TECHNICAL FEATURES

The steel unibody is now mounted on a separate, much beefier chassis. Aerodynamic yield isn't as efficient as that of a small car, but it's been refined and is pretty impressive. The wheelbase lengths haven't changed, but the vehicle itself is longer and wider. The front suspension is independent and is made up of struts with upper A-arms and rigid axle supported by longitudinal control arms and reactive A-arm, whereas the rear axle is maintained by five trailing arms and suspended by coil springs. The transmission can only shift from rear-wheel to all-wheel drive on demand, by engaging the transfer box that activates the front wheels via shift-on-the-fly, but front wheel hubs kick in automatically. Steering is now powered and of rack-and-pinion design and the disc and drum brakes are linked to ABS.

PROS

+ LOOKS. These neat, compact utility vehicles are spiffy-looking and quite appealing with their more refined silhouette. As always, they're sure to please the customers, who are mostly ladies.

+ CABIN SPACE. Both models are roomier because they're longer and wider.

+ PRICE. Both models are sold at affordable prices, which explains why they aren't loaded with equipment. But it's nice to be able to buy a convertible or station wagon without wincing.

+ 2.0L ENGINE. It may not be as brawny as the V6 offered by Suzuki, but the new engine that animates the station wagon puts out adequate performances. Too bad they didn't give the same engine to the convertible that simply doesn't have much get up and go.

+ HANDLING. On the road we noticed that major improvements have been achieved in regard to roadability. It's a lot more competent with the more rigid platform and more accurate rack-and-pinion steering.

+ MANEUVERABILITY. The rack-and-pinion steering has cut down on the steer angle diameter for both vehicles, so they can squeeze into tight spots, both in the city and in the bush.

+ FINISH DETAILS. The cabin has a whole new look that's modern and functional; it feels more like a car than a SUV. We're sorry that some trim material still looks a bit cheap...

+ CONVENIENCE FEATURES. The Tracker's are very versatile. Well-planned storage compartments and the baggage compartment on the 4-door wagon can be extended by lowering the rear seat-bench. A nice touch: the rear door is a single swing panel, so luggage access is handier, but it's too bad the hinges are on the right, as is the case with the competition, since the vehicle is designed for export markets to countries where you drive on the left side of the road...

CONS

- STABILITY. It still really depends on the road surface, wind and tire grip for on poorly maintained roads, even experienced drivers will get some unpleasant surprises with the short wheelbase on the convertible.

- EFFICIENCY. The three engines used to power these vehicles are gas guzzlers, especially given their low displacement levels; they're barely strong enough to hoist these vehicles to decent performance levels.

- QUESTIONABLE. Off-the-road capabilities of these vehicles is even more dubious than on former models, because entrance and exit angles as well as ground clearance have been reduced and the original tires really aren't up to treks in the wild.

- DISCOMFORT. The ride is far from comfy with such a sensitive suspension that reacts badly to the least road flaw, seat upholstery is pretty hard and sound dampening is next to nil.

-BRAKES. They're still not up to par, yielding the same long stretches on sudden stops. But vehicle path is more predictable with standard ABS assistance.

-AUTOMATIC GEARBOX. It's rough and noisy with such a stop-and-start shifter and it siphons off a lot of juice from the engines, especially the 1.6L that doesn't amount to a hill of beans.

- NOISE LEVEL. It's high at all times and generated mostly from the engine, a result of poor front-end insulation.

- ACCESS. It's still a bit of a task getting to the rear seats inside the convertible because of lack of space and missing running boards.

-TO BE IMPROVED UPON. The very jittery suspension on the two-door soft top model, the near-stingy heater, cramped rear seats and inadequate baggage compartment,

CONCLUSION

Attractive bodies seek skilled engines to power two very thirsty vehicles.

RATING
CHEVROLET Tracker

CONCEPT : 60%
Technology :	80
Safety :	75
Interior space :	40
Trunk volume :	30
Quality/fit/finish :	75

DRIVING : 53%
Cockpit :	80
Performance :	25
Handling :	50
Steering :	75
Braking :	35

ORIGINAL EQUIPMENT : 75%
Tires :	80
Headlights :	75
Wipers :	80
Rear defroster :	70
Radio :	70

COMFORT : 61%
Seats :	75
Suspension :	60
Sound level :	25
Conveniences :	70
Air conditioning :	75

BUDGET : 63%
Price :	60
Fuel economy :	70
Insurance :	50
Satisfaction :	80
Depreciation :	55

Overall rating : 62.4%

NEW FOR 2000
• Exterior colors: **Dark Blue, Bright Blue, Metallic Copper Brown.**

Compare
Performance,
Specifications, Prices,
and Classification
at the end of this chapter.

EQUIPMENT

CHEVROLET Tracker	2dr.	4dr.
Automatic transmission:	O	O
Cruise control:	O	O
Power steering:	S	S
Anti-lock brakes:	O	O
Traction control:	-	-
Air conditioning:	O	O
Leather:	-	-
AM/FM/radio-cassette:	O	O
Power door locks:	-	O
Power windows:	-	O
Tilt steering:	O	O
Dual adjustable mirrors:	SM	SM
Alloy wheels:	O	O
Anti-theft system:	-	-

Colors
Exterior: White, Black, Silver, Green, Red, Violet, Blue.

Interior: Medium Grey.

AT A GLANCE...

HISTORIC
Introduced in:	1990, 1999.
Made in:	Ingersoll, Ontario, Canada.

DEMOGRAPHICS
Model	Men/Wom.	Age	Married	College	Income $
Tracker	45/55 %	39	56 %	33 %	33,500
Gd Vitara	59/41 %	44	57 %	39 %	30,000

INDEX
Safety:	80 %	Satisfaction:	80 %
Depreciation:	45 %	Insurance:	$ 725
Cost per mile:	$ 0.50	Number of dealers:	4,466

SALES
Model	Canada 1997	1998	Result	USA 1997	1998	Result
Tracker	2,746	2,453	- 10.7 %	33,354	20,296	- 39.1 %
Gd Vitara	4,167	3,922	- 5.9 %	-	5,910	-

MAINTENANCE REQUIRED BY WARRANTY
First revision:	Frequency:	Diagnostic plug:
3,000 miles	6,000 miles	Yes

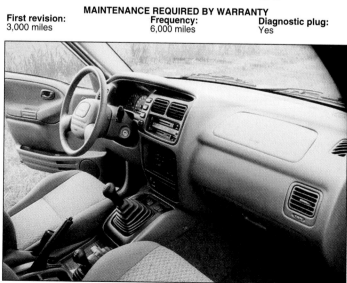

Compact SUVs

Toy Story

The RAV4 was easily outdistanced by the Honda CR-V on both the American and Canadian markets. So appealing to automotive experts when it was launched, the vehicle's toylike looks fell far short from convincing young families that it was a versatile and practical choice.

MODEL RANGE

The RAV4 is sold in a short-wheelbase two-door model or a longer four-door version both equipped with all-wheel drive. Both models share the same engine, namely a 2.0L 16-valve DOHC 4-cylinder paired up with a standard 5-speed manual transmission or an optional 4-speed automatic. The two-door model comes with fairly slim trimmings, since it only benefits from power steering, cruise control, radio and tape deck, manually adjusted exterior mirrors and light alloy rims. The 4-door is more lush, since it's equipped with added features such as antilock braking system, air conditioning, main power accessories and a theft-deterrent system.

TECHNICAL FEATURES

The RAV4's steel unibody includes some panels that are rustproofed and it gets special treatment since it's lighter-weight than a body mounted on a conventional frame and because it's fitted with appropriate reinforcements, it's sufficiently rigid. The four-wheel independent suspension consists of MacPherson struts up front and the rear axle is supported by lower L-arms that act as a torsion bar. Vehicles are equipped with power rack and pinion steering and disc and drum brakes with standard ABS on the 4-door. The full-time all-wheel

drive benefits from a main viscous-coupled non-slip differential that works automatically via a hydraulic system with the automatic gearbox and by pushing on a button located on the dashboard with the manual. The first gear ratio is fairly short on both gearboxes, eliminating the need for a high and low gear transfer case. The engine is a robust 4-valve per cylinder 2.0L DOHC with good muscle and torque.

PROS

+ PRICE. It seems more reasonable than when the vehicle was first introduced and considering the array of standard equipment, the RAV4 is a good buy, especially with its steady resale value...

+ PERFORMANCES. They're very much like those you get on a car thanks to the reasonable power to weight ratio, clever gear ratios on the transmission and the smooth, versatile engine that puts out good pickup power at low rpm, even with the automatic.

+ DESIGN. It looks full of vigor with its mischievous body stylistics and multicolored seat fabric that's a nice change from the run-of-the-mill grey you see on so many vehicles.

+ DRIVING PLEASURE. The driver benefits from nice and high seating, good straight-ahead and lateral visibility, logical instrument panel with easy to reach dials and controls.

+ HANDLING. It's reassuring, even on the short wheelbase model that behaves like a small car, but you have to take its high center of gravity into account when negotiating tight curves at high speeds. The RAV4 is nimble on slalom runs and it handles like a charm in the city.

+ RIDE COMFORT. The 4-door model is more comfy, since it benefits from a longer wheelbase and it's less jittery than the tiny 2-door model that plays leapfrog on poor roads.

+ QUALITY. It's totally in keeping with the top of the heap Toyota philosophy. Assembly is super solid, finish job and trim materials are topnotch and not at all cheap-looking.

+ CONVENIENCE FEATURES. In this regard, the RAV4 is a real charmer, for there are lots of storage spots for travellers. The glove compartment is really big, door side-pockets are a generous size and there are storage shelves on the main section of the instrument panel. The trunk is versatile and is really handy with the big swing rear hatch door and you have loads of luggage space as required, even on the two-door version, but of course, it isn't as roomy when the rear seat-bench is occupied.

CONS

- LIMITED PERFORMANCES. The RAV4 isn't a genuine all-terrain

cowboy, for it isn't equipped with studded tires and a true grit transfer case is sorely missed when tackling tough terrain that's full of major obstacles or when adherence is really iffy. Before trailing behind other 4X4's, you have to be aware of its limitations and you should bring along a winch fitted with a long cable.

- CABIN SPACE. The vehicle is narrow and you feel like you're crammed alongside your travelling companions for the body design is slimmer towards the top.

- ACCESS. Fairly stout people will have difficulty accessing the back seat on both versions. On the 2-door, space is limited and on the 4-door, the entrance is too narrow.

- RIDE COMFORT. This tiny Toyota isn't great for long trips, since the seats don't offer much support and suspension jitters get more on your nerves than for short runs or when you're driving to work. The 2-door model short wheelbase generates a rocking chair effect that's far from soothing on rough road surfaces.

- VISIBILITY. It's rather poor towards the rear due to the spare tire and headrests that get in the way.

- TO BE IMPROVED UPON. The rear hatch that opens the wrong way from the sidewalk, because in Japan, people drive on the left side of the road...

CONCLUSION

Fun to drive and to look at, the RAV4 is too expensive and not practical enough to be a hit. At least this time out, reason dominates passion.

RATING
TOYOTA RAV4

CONCEPT :		71%
Technology :	80	
Safety :	75	
Interior space :	50	
Trunk volume :	70	
Quality/fit/finish :	80	

DRIVING :		58%
Cockpit :	75	
Performance :	45	
Handling :	40	
Steering :	80	
Braking :	50	

ORIGINAL EQUIPMENT :		75%
Tires :	85	
Headlights :	75	
Wipers :	65	
Rear defroster :	70	
Radio :	80	

COMFORT :		71%
Seats :	80	
Suspension :	70	
Sound level :	50	
Conveniences :	80	
Air conditioning :	75	

BUDGET :		70%
Price :	55	
Fuel economy :	75	
Insurance :	55	
Satisfaction :	90	
Depreciation :	75	

Overall rating :	69.0%

NEW FOR 2000

• **Standard carpeting on all models.**

Compare Performance, Specifications, Prices, and Classification at the end of this chapter.

EQUIPMENT

TOYOTA RAV4 (4x4)	2dr.	4dr.
Automatic transmission:	O	O
Cruise control:	S	S
Power steering:	S	S
Anti-lock brakes:	O	S
Traction control:	-	-
Air conditioning:	O	S
Leather:	-	-
AM/FM/radio-cassette:	S	SCd
Power door locks:	O	S
Power windows:	O	S
Tilt steering:	O	S
Dual adjustable mirrors:	SM	SE
Alloy wheels:	S	S
Anti-theft system:	O	S

Colors
Exterior: Violet, Red, White, Sequoia, Black, Green, Saphire, Silver.

Interior: Grey.

AT A GLANCE...

HISTORIC
Introduced in: 1997.
Made in: Toyota City, Japan.

DEMOGRAPHICS

Model	Men/Wom.	Age	Married	College	Income $
RAV4	NA				

INDEX

Safety:	70 %	Satisfaction:	87 %
Depreciation:	25 %	Insurance:	$ 955
Cost per mile:	$ 0.45	Number of dealers:	1 233

SALES

	Canada			USA		
Model	1997	1998	Result	1997	1998	Result
RAV4	11 421	8 781	- 23.1 %	67 489	64 990	- 3.7 %

MAINTENANCE REQUIRED BY WARRANTY

First revision:	Frequency:	Diagnostic plug:
3 000 miles	3 000 miles	No

Compact SUVs

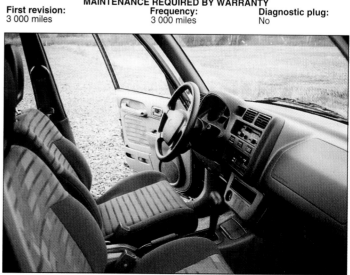

COMPACT SPORT UTILITY VEHICLES

PERFORMANCE

Model/version	Type / timing valve / fuel system	Displacement cu in	Power hp @ rpm	Torque lb-ft @ rpm	Compres. ratio	Driving wheels / transmission	Final ratio	Acceler. 0-60 mph s	Standing 1/4 mile s	Standing 5/8 mile s	Passing 50-75 mph s	Braking 60-0 mph ft	Top speed mph	Lateral acceler. G	Noise level dBA	Fuel economy mpg City	Fuel economy mpg Highway	Fuel type Octane
CHEVROLET Tracker - SUZUKI Vitara																		
2 dr. conv.	L4 1.6 SOHC-16-MPFI	97	97 @ 5200	103 @ 4000	9.5 :1	rear/4 - M5*	5.12	12.2	18.7	34.2	10.2	144	103	0.75	70	27	33	R 87
4 dr.Vitara	L4 2.0 DOHC-16-MPFI	122	127 @ 6000	134 @ 3000	9.7 :1	rear/4 - M5*	4.62	NA								27	29	R 87
						rear/4 - A4	4.87	NA								27	29	R 87
Gd Vitara	V6 2.5 DOHC-24-MPFI	152	155 @ 6500	160 @ 4000	9.5 :1	rear/4 - M5*	4.30	NA								23	29	R 87
						rear/4 - A4	4.87	NA								22	28	R 87
HONDA CR-V																		
LX	L4 2.0 DOHC-16 MPFI	120	146 @ 6200	133 @ 4500	9.6 :1	all - M5*	3.70	NA								18	29	R 87
EX	L4 2.0 DOHC-16 MPFI	120	146 @ 6200	133 @ 4500	9.6 :1	all - A4	3.10	11.0	17.7	32.0	7.6	138	97	0.75	69	18	28	R 87
JEEP Cherokee																		
1)	L4 2.5 OHV-8-MPSFI	150	125 @ 5400	150 @ 3250	9.2 :1	rear/4 - M5*	4.10	12.5	18.8	35.2	11.0	157	93	0.68	69	18	28	R 87
						rear/4 - A3	3.55	13.5	19.5	36.8	11.8	161	90	0.68	68	18	22	R 87
2)	L6 4.0 OHV-12-MPSFI	242	190 @ 4600	225 @ 3000	8.8 :1	rear/4 - M5*	3.07	9.0	16.6	30.5	7.0	167	112	0.70	69	18	22	R 87
						rear/4 - A4*	3.55	10.0	17.5	31.3	8.0	164	109	0.70	69	15	21	R 87
1) SE. 2) Sport, Classic, Limited, option SE.																		
JEEP Wrangler																		
1)	L4 2.5 OHV-8-MPSFI	150	120 @ 5400	140 @ 3500	9.2 :1	rear/4 - M5*	4.11	13.5	18.6	36.5	10.8	197	87	0.75	68-76	18	20	R 87
						rear/4 - A3	3.73	14.8	20.0	37.2	11.5	190	81	0.75	68-76	16	19	R 87
2)	L6 4.0 OHV-12-MPSFI	242	185 @ 4600	222 @ 2800	8.8 :1	rear/4 - M5*	3.07	10.5	17.3	32.5	8.1	157	103	0.75	68-78	16	22	R 87
						rear/4 - A3	3.07	11.2	18.8	34.0	9.9	167	100	0.75	68-78	15	20	R 87
1) SE. 2) Sport, Sahara, option SE.																		
KIA Sportage																		
Base, EX	L4 2.0 DOHC-16-MPSFI	122	130 @ 5500	127 @ 4000	9.2 :1	all - M5*	NA	13.0	18.5	34.2	12.1	164	100	0.70	68	20	23	R 87
						all - A4	NA									19	23	R 87
NISSAN Xterra																		
XE	V6 3.3 SOHC-12-MPSFI	199	170 @ 4800	200 @ 2800	8.9 :1	rear/4 - A4	4.36									15	20	R 87
						rear/4 - M5*	4.36											
TOYOTA																		
RAV4	L4 2.0 DOHC-16-MPSFI	122	127 @ 5400	132 @ 4600	9.5 :1	all - M5*	4.933	11.5	18.2	32.7	9.5	141	103	0.70	68	22	26	R 87
						all - A4	4.404	13.0	18.5	34.2	12.1	147	100	0.70	68	22	26	R 87

SPECIFICATIONS

Model	Version Trim	Traction	Body/Seats	Wheel base in	Lgth x Width x Hght in x in x in	Curb weight lb	Susp. ft/rr	Brake ft/rr	type	Steering ø ft	turns number	Fuel tank gal	dimensions	Standard tires make	model	Standard powertrain	99 Price msrp $
CHEVROLET-SUZUKI General warranty: 3-years / 50,000 miles. 24 hrs roadside assistance.																	
Tracker-Vitara JX, JLX	2 door	4x4	2dr.con.4	86.6	148.8x66.7x66.5	2717	ih/rh	dc/dr	pwr.ball	31.5	3.8	14.8	205/75R15	Bridgestone	Dueler H/T	L4/1.6/M5	15,719
Tracker-Vitara JX	4 door	4x4	4dr.wgn.5	97.6	159.8x66.7x66.5	2891	ih/rh	dc/dr	pwr.ball	34.8	3.8	17.4	215/65R16	Bridgestone	Dueler H/T	L4/2.0/M5	17,429
Grand Vitara	4 door	4x4	4dr.wgn.5	97.6	164.5x70.0x66.5	3196	ih/rh	dc/dr	pwr.ball	34.1	3.8	17.4	235/60R16	Bridgestone	Dueler H/T	V6/2.5/M5	19,429
HONDA General warranty: 3-years / 36,000 miles; powertrain: 5-years / 60,000 miles.																	
CR-V	LX	4x4	4dr.wgn.5	103.2	177.6x68.9x65.9	2943	ih/rh	dc/dr/ABS	pwr.r&p.	34.8	3.0	15.3	205/70R15	Bridgestone	Dueler H/T	L4/2.0/M5	19,365
CR-V	EX	4x4	4dr.wgn.5	103.2	177.6x68.9x65.9	2976	ih/rh	dc/dr/ABS	pwr.r&p.	34.8	3.0	15.3	205/70R15	Bridgestone	Dueler H/T	L4/2.0/A4	20,865
JEEP General warranty: 3-years / 36,000 miles; surface rust 1-year / 12,000 miles; perforation 7-years / 100,000 miles; roadside assistance 3-years / 36,000 miles.																	
Cherokee	SE	4X2	3dr.wgn.5	101.4	167.5x69.4x63.9	3018	rh/rl	dc/dr	pwr.ball	35.1	2.94	20.0	215/75R15	Goodyear Wrangler AP		L4/2.5/M5	16,575
Cherokee	Sport	4X2	5dr.wgn.5	101.4	167.5x69.4x63.9	3154	rh/rl	dc/dr	pwr.ball	35.1	2.94	20.0	225/75R15	Goodyear Wrangler RT/S		L6/4.0/M5	19,300
Cherokee	Classic/Limited	4X2	5dr.wgn.5	101.4	167.5x69.4x63.9	3194	rh/rl	dc/dr	pwr.ball	35.1	2.94	20.0	225/70R15	Goodyear Wrangler RT/S		L6/4.0/A4	21,680
Cherokee	SE	4X4	3dr.wgn.5	101.4	167.5x69.4x64.0	3179	rh/rl	dc/dr	pwr.ball	35.1	2.94	20.0	215/75R15	Goodyear Wrangler AP		L4/2.5/M5	18,090
Cherokee	Sport	4X4	5dr.wgn.5	101.4	167.5x69.4x64.0	3353	rh/rl	dc/dr	pwr.ball	35.1	2.94	20.0	225/75R15	Goodyear Wrangler RT/S		L6/4.0/M5	21,845
Cherokee	Classic/Limited	4X4	5dr.wgn.5	101.4	167.5x69.4x64.0	3395	rh/rl	dc/dr	pwr.ball	35.1	2.94	20.0	225/70R15	Goodyear Wrangler RT/S		L6/4.0/A4	23,195
Wrangler	SE	4x4	2dr.con.2	93.4	147.7x66.7x71.1	3318	rh/rl	dc/dr	pwr.ball	32.8	3.0	15.1	205/75R15	Goodyear Wrangler RT/S		L6/4.0/M5	14,870
Wrangler	Sport	4x4	2dr.con.4	93.4	147.7x66.7x71.1	3437	rh/rl	dc/dr	pwr.ball	32.8	3.0	15.1	215/75R15	Goodyear Wrangler RT/S		L6/4.0/M5	18,430
Wrangler	Sahara	4x4	2dr.con.4	93.4	147.7x66.7x71.1	3461	rh/rl	dc/dr	pwr.ball	32.8	3.0	19.0	225/75R15	Goodyear Wrangler GS-A		L6/4.0/M5	20,660
KIA General warranty: 3-years / 36,000 miles; powertrain 5-years / 60,000 miles; corrosion, perforation: 5-years / unlimited.																	
Sportage	base	4x4	2dr.con.4	104.2	162.5x68.1x65.0	3350	ih/ih	dc/dr	pwr.ball	NA	NA	15.8	205/75R15	-		L4/2.0/M5	14,945
Sportage	EX	4x4	5dr.wgn.5	104.2	162.5x68.1x65.0	3395	ih/ih	dc/dr	pwr.ball	NA	NA	15.8	205/75R15	-		L4/2.0/M5	19,045
NISSAN General warranty: 3-years / 50,000 miles; powertrain 6-years / 60,000 miles; corrosion, perforation & antipollution: 6-years / unlimited.																	
Xterra	XE	4x4	5dr.wgn.5	104.2	178.0x70.4x74.0	3963	ih/rl	dc/dr/ABS	pwr.ball	35.4	3.4	19.4	265/70R15	-		V6/3.3/M5	
TOYOTA General warranty: 3-years / 36,000 miles; powertrain 5-years / 60,000 miles; corrosion, perforation: 5-years / unlimited.																	
RAV4	2WD	4x2	2dr.wgn.4	86.6	147.6x66.7x64.8	2700	ih/ih	dc/dr	pwr.r&p.	33.5	2.7	15.3	215/70R16	Bridgestone Dueler H/T		L4/2.0/M5	16,148
RAV4	4WD	4x4	4dr.wgn.4	94.9	163.8x66.7x65.0	2844	ih/ih	dc/dr/ABS	pwr.r&p.	36.1	2.7	15.3	215/70R16	Bridgestone Dueler H/T		L4/2.0/M5	18,248

Notes: 1) Tire makes and models are provided solely as an indication; they are subject to change without prior notice from the automobile manufacturers.
2) See the 2000 price list at the back of this edition.

CLASSIFICATION

OUR CLASSIFICATION

Rank	Models	Concept	Driving	Equipment	Comfort	Budget	Ratings
1	**TOYOTA RAV4**	71	58	75	71	70	69.0 %
2	HONDA CR-V	74	58	73	73	64	68.4 %
3	NISSAN Xterra	73	57	72	70	52	64.8 %
4	KIA Sportage	68	49	69	68	66	64.0 %
5	JEEP Cherokee	66	54	74	61	57	62.4 %
5	CHEVROLET Tracker	60	53	75	61	63	62.4 %
6	JEEP Wrangler	54	45	56	43	55	50.6 %

YOUR CLASSIFICATION

Rank	Models	98 Sales
1	JEEP Cherokee	146,298
2	HONDA CR-V	100,582
3	JEEP Wrangler	83,861
4	TOYOTA RAV4	64,990
5	KIA Sportage	27,529
6	CHEVROLET Tracker	20,296
7	SUZUKI Grand Vitara	5,910

Not classified:
NISSAN Xterra

Compact SUVs

DODGE Durango

FORD Explorer

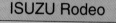
GM S-10 Series

ISUZU Rodeo

JEEP Grand Cherokee

LAND ROVER Discovery

LEXUS RX 300

Comparative Test

MID-SIZE SPORT UTILITY VEHICLES

See their performance, their specifications, their price and their classification at the end of this chapter.

TOYOTA 4Runner

NISSAN Pathfinder

MERCEDES-BENZ ML

Intermediate

The first Dodge sport utility vehicle since the Ramcharger, the Durango has achieved a degree of success, ranking just behind the Explorer in Canada and placing fourth in the United States. Derived from the Dakota pickup truck, given its midsize styling it's in a very special class, somewhere between average-size and big utes. It offers an interesting choice of powertrains that includes two strong V8. The Durango has a third bench seat and is designed to accommodate seven occupants.

MODEL RANGE

This midsize multipurpose all-terrain vehicle is available in a four-door wagon in SLT or SLT+ models, the latter being an option package. It's sold equipped with a standard 4.7L V8 engine that can be replaced by two optional V8 engines, either the 5.2L or the 5.9L LEV (low emission). The transmission can be either rear or all-wheel drive on demand thanks to a manual transfer case and 4-speed automatic transmission. Original equipment is quite rich, for it includes all the frills you find on this type of vehicle, except ABS and a theft-deterrent system. Pretty stingy when you check out the price...

TECHNICAL FEATURES

The Durango is a direct descendant of the Dakota pickup truck. It has the same chassis, main mechanical features and front end design including the same dashboard and controls. The steel unibody is mounted via twelve insulator components to a robust H-chassis integrating five crossmembers and providing high-level torsion rigidity. The chassis is painted with an electrostatic technique for better rust resistance. The front suspension on the rear-wheel versions consists of uneven-length control arms and a

MacPherson strut. This layout has enhanced the steer angle diameter, back to center positioning and stability on curves. The suspension on the all-wheel drive versions still includes torsion bars, whereas the rear suspension includes a more sophisticated rear axle supported by leaf springs for more ride comfort and more competent handling on all versions. RWD vehicles are equipped with rack-and-pinion steering, the AWD's are fitted with recirculating ball steering. Brakes are disc and drum, but they don't benefit from a standard ABS system.

PROS

+ **STYLE.** This vehicle has smashing looks. Its big bold, muscular form is appropriate for a utility vehicle. It sits high and looks ready to pounce and overcome any obstacle on its path. The over-all look is simple, even austere, which gives it a serious down-to-brass-tacks character that suits such a practical vehicle. A very unique design.
+ **CABIN SPACE.** The Durango is the only vehicle in its category to seat eight passengers inside a cabin that really doesn't look as spacious as that. The baggage compartment is no Scrooge either when it comes to space, since load capacity is 1 453 liters.
+ **STRENGTH.** Right off, Dodge equipped the Durango with a muscular V8 that works like a charm on the Dakota. With such a powerplant, it has a pretty awesome load

capacity and trailering prowess, and it's almost on a par with the Expedition since it can handle up to 7,300 lb.
+ **SIZE.** All that engine power motivating a compact SUV impresses just about everyone that's not quite up to tackling a Yukon, Expedition or Suburban. A short steer diameter and good reduction ratio ensure good maneuverability of this brute.
+ **TRACTION.** Whether you're pulling heavy loads with the RWD vehicle or carving a path through rough terrain in a 4X4, the Durango offers competent and balanced traction.
+ **SOLID AS A ROCK.** This is the first impression you get when you climb aboard this vehicle. You get a sense of the awesome vehicle weight and you know there's a lot of beef on the bone.
+ **INSTRUMENT PANEL.** It may not be one of the most splashy or lavish ones around, but at least it's logical and has a nice, let's-get-down-to-business look. But radio controls are located out of the driver's reach.
+ **SUSPENSION.** You could say this vehicle is somewhat rustic, especially at the rear, but it provides pretty amazing ride comfort compared to the roughing up you get in same brand minivans equipped with leaf springs that are radiocarbon dated...
+ **CLEVER TOUCHES.** The compartment located under the luggage floor pan can hide all kinds of stuff out of sight. And you can consider the seats as being modular,

given how easily you can fold down both seatbenches, either entirely or partially.

CONS

- **FUEL CONSUMPTION.** When it was first sold, this newcomer was available unit by unit and only with the 5.2L V8 engine that's a real gas glutton, the kind that easily throws back 12 mpg and even more on off-the-road treks...
- **BRAKES.** They don't kick in with much gusto and they're not too effective or balanced, since they're not linked up to any ABS system, which isn't too safe in emergencies. Brakes are hard to gauge as well, due to a rather spongy pedal.
- **SEATS.** They're terribly disappointing, they're quite flat up front and don't offer enough lateral support, and the seatbenches are thinly upholstered.
- **STEERING.** It lacks spontaneity on the 4X4, so driving is blurry. This is due in part to the big bouncy tires, but especially because of the recirculating ball steering. After all, the 4X2 has rack-and-pinion steering.
- **TECHNICAL FEATURES.** They're pretty simplistic, really, since there isn't a transmission system that can automatically transfer power to wheels adhering to the road surface. Most of the competitors benefit from this feature.

CONCLUSION

More utilitarian than most of its competitors, the Durango is positioned somewhere above the Grand Cherokee given its sizing and somewhere below it given its lack of luxury equipment. This is a vehicle made for professionals: it calls for a considerable budget, especially when it comes to fuel consumption.

Mid-Size SUVs

RATING
DODGE Durango

CONCEPT :		79%
Technology :	75	
Safety :	80	
Interior space :	80	
Trunk volume :	80	
Quality/fit/finish :	80	

DRIVING :		56%
Cockpit :	75	
Performance :	45	
Handling :	50	
Steering :	70	
Braking :	40	

ORIGINAL EQUIPMENT :		75%
Tires :	75	
Headlights :	75	
Wipers :	65	
Rear defroster :	80	
Radio :	80	

COMFORT :		74%
Seats :	75	
Suspension :	80	
Sound level :	55	
Conveniences :	80	
Air conditioning :	80	

BUDGET :		49%
Price :	20	
Fuel economy :	20	
Insurance :	50	
Satisfaction :	80	
Depreciation :	75	

Overall rating :		66.6%

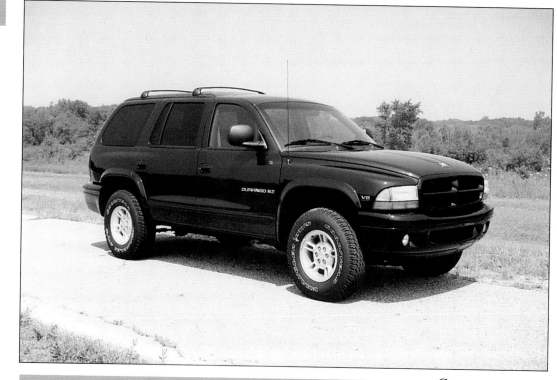

NEW FOR 2000
- **The Sport version with its two-color front-end.**
- **Optional factory-installed running boards.**
- **Five-spoke alloy wheels.**
- **Colors: Sierra Bronze and Aquamarine.**

Compare
Performance,
Specifications, Prices,
and Classification
at the end of this chapter.

EQUIPMENT

DODGE Durango	Sport	SLT
Automatic transmission:	S	S
Cruise control:	S	S
Power steering:	S	S
Anti-lock brakes:	S re.	S re.
Traction control:	-	-
Air conditioning:	S	S
Leather:	-	S
AM/FM/radio-cassette:	S	SCd
Power door locks:	S	S
Power windows:	S	S
Tilt steering:	S	S
Dual adjustable mirrors:	SE	SE
Alloy wheels:	S	S
Anti-theft system:	O	S

Colors

Exterior: Silver, Blue, Green, Red, White, Driftwood.

Interior: Pebble, Beige, Gray.

AT A GLANCE...

HISTORIC
Introduced in: 1998.
Made in: Newark, Delaware, USA.

DEMOGRAPHICS

Model	Men/Wom.	Age	Married	College	Income $
Durango	71/29 %	43	84 %	46 %	64,000

INDEX

Safety:	80 %	Satisfaction:	78 %
Depreciation:	25 %	Insurance:	$ 650
Cost per mile:	$ 0.57	Number of dealers:	1,887

SALES

	Canada			USA		
Model	1997	1998	Result	1997	1998	Result
Durango	269	7 576	+ 2716.4 %	20,263	156,923	+ 764.4 %

MAINTENANCE REQUIRED BY WARRANTY

First revision:	Frequency:	Diagnostic plug:
5,000 miles	6 months / 6,000 miles	Yes

The Conqueror

The Explorer is still the bestselling sport utility in North America, with close to half a million units snapped up. It's hard to pinpoint the reason for the craze. In any event, Ford's reputation in the sport ute market is solidly ensconced and it has always managed to point the way for its counterparts. In the United States, dealerships have an Explorer clone, the Mountaineer, not available in Canada.

MODEL RANGE

Ford offers a whole range of Explorer models: 2 and 4-door models, RWD and AWD vehicles as well as full-time all-wheel drive versions. There is now only a single 2-door version called Sport, but there are, in all, four 4-door versions sold: XL, XLT, Eddie Bauer and Limited. A standard 4.0L OHV V6 engine animates the Sport, XL and XLT models with either a 5-speed manual transmission or an optional 5-speed automatic (the latter comes standard on the XLT). A 4.0L SOHC V6 equips the Eddie Bauer and Limited models, but comes as an option on the other models.

The 5.0L Thunderbolt V8 powerplant can also equip the XLT, Eddie Bauer and Limited. Both engines are linked to a 5-speed automatic transmission.

TECHNICAL FEATURES

The Explorer's steel body is mounted on an H frame and bolted down via rubber insulator components. Aerodynamics have gone up a notch since the 1998 reworked design; now the drag coefficient is 0.41 due to a more rounded-out grille design. The front suspension is independent. It uses a combination of unequal-length control arms with torsion bars and the rigid rear axle is supported by leaf springs. The base model V6 develops 160 hp compared to 210 hp for the SOHC V6. The V8 that's been on the circuit for quite a while is well-liked for its impressive torque output. The electronically controlled all-wheel drive "Control Trac" system is regulated via a button located on the dashboard. It has an "Auto" mode that shifts power to the front wheels when rear wheels lose their grip. The 5-speed automatic transmission is a variant of the former 4-speed automatic, to which a fifth gear called "Swap Shift" has been added.

PROS

+ LOOKS. The Explorer is a winner and handsome looks have a lot to do with it, even if the newest touch up job wasn't everyone's cup of tea.

+ CHOICE. This is an important factor, since the wide model range lets all kinds of buyers find just the vehicle they need and can afford.

+ CABIN SPACE. The 4-door version is roomier due to a 9.8 inches longer wheelbase. Five occupants and all their effects can be nicely accomodated.

+ ENGINES. The mighty 210 hp 4.0L V6 and the 5.0L V8 really pump out the power, considering the Explorer's power to weight ratio. These engines have what it takes to pull pretty hefty loads.

+ ROADABILITY. The front suspension, first introduced in 1995, has enhanced vehicle competence and adds to steering precision.

+ CABIN LAYOUT. The owner of a luxury car will be right at home aboard an Eddie Bauer or Limited. Actually, their respective equipment is lush and includes lots of accessories geared to spoiling travellers.

+ RELIABILITY. The Explorer is known for its darn good dependability, a definite asset, as proven by J.D. Power studies and the high owner satisfaction rate. This trait gives it a real edge over the main competition.

+ RIDE COMFORT. The load-levelling air suspension sure adds to the already comfortable ride feel. It's now available on the XLT, Eddie Bauer and Limited versions. These vehicles are blessed with really cushy seats and superb soundproofing, so long-distance travellers will enjoy the ride.

+ INSTRUMENT PANEL. It's ergonomic, classy-looking and very user-friendly and the center console has loads of storage space.

+ CONVENIENCE FEATURES. The 4-door version offers more amenities. Access is easier, but there's also another neat feature, namely the rear door that's fitted with a hinged window that can be opened independently to stash stuff.

CONS

- BUDGET. This vehicle is a pricey purchase and is by no means cheap to run, since even insurance premiums are costly. What a sheer waste of money when you know that Explorer owners only use 30% of its potential!

- BASE V6 ENGINE. It's terribly sluggish. Accelerations and pickup are lazy, which can be downright dangerous when passing on the highway, for instance. We think the 210-hp SOHC V6 engine is a better choice.

- BRAKES. It isn't the greatest, not with those long stretches required to come to a full stop, even with four-wheel disc brakes. Brake pad resistance to intensive use is only fair to midling, but sudden stops are nice and straight, thanks to standard ABS.

- RWD MODELS. The base RWD model is far from cushy. Poor seat design, jumpy suspension and simplistic sound dampening don't make for what you'd call a pleasure trip.

- TO BE IMPROVED UPON: Low ground clearance on the lower-end models and tough rear seat access due to skimpy space on the 2-door model and due to narrow doors on the 4-door versions.

CONCLUSION

The Explorer is the most widely sold sport utility on the North American market. In part, it owes its staggering success to its sturdy construction and the many touchups Ford persists in making time and time again. However, from the strictly technical standpoint, some of its competitors show more refinement.

RATING
FORD Explorer - Mercury Mountaineer

CONCEPT :		77%
Technology :	80	
Safety :	90	
Interior space :	65	
Trunk volume :	75	
Quality/fit/finish :	75	

DRIVING :		55%
Cockpit :	75	
Performance :	60	
Handling :	40	
Steering :	70	
Braking :	30	

ORIGINAL EQUIPMENT :		77%
Tires :	75	
Headlights :	75	
Wipers :	70	
Rear defroster :	75	
Radio :	90	

COMFORT :		66%
Seats :	75	
Suspension :	75	
Sound level :	60	
Conveniences :	40	
Air conditioning :	80	

BUDGET :		53%
Price :	30	
Fuel economy :	40	
Insurance :	65	
Satisfaction :	80	
Depreciation :	50	

| **Overall rating :** | | **65.6%** |

NEW FOR 2000

- Heated front seats and leather upholstery (Limited).
- Soundproofing material to cut down on engine noise (Sport, XLT, Eddie Bauer and Limited).
- Roof-mounted console (XLT, Eddie Bauer and Limited).

Compare
Performance,
Specifications, Prices,
and Classification
at the end of this chapter.

EQUIPMENT

FORD Explorer	XL 4dr. 4x2	Sport 2dr. 4x4	XLT 4dr. 4x4	EB 4dr. AWD	Limited 4dr. AWD
Automatic transmission:	O	O	S	S	S
Cruise control:	O	O	S	S	S
Power steering:	S	S	S	S	S
Anti-lock brakes:	S	S	S	S	S
Traction control:	-	-	-	S	S
Air conditioning:	SM	SM	SM	SA	SA
Leather:	-	-	-	S	S
AM/FM/radio-cassette:	S	S	SCd	SCd	SCd
Power door locks:	O	S	S	S	S
Power windows:	O	S	S	S	S
Tilt steering:	O	O	S	S	S
Dual adjustable mirrors:	SM	SE	SE	SE	SEH
Alloy wheels:	-	S	S	S	S
Anti-theft system:	S	S	S	S	S

Colors

Exterior: Gold, Green, Orange, Brown, Red, Blue, Platinum, White, Black.

Interior: Medium graphite , Dark graphite, Brown.

AT A GLANCE...

HISTORIC
Introduced in: 1991 (Explorer), 1997 (Mountaineer).
Made in: Louisville, Kentucky & St-Louis, Missouri, USA.

DEMOGRAPHICS

Model	Men/Wom.	Age	Married	College	Income $
Explorer	71/29 %	43	75 %	53 %	53,000
Mountaineer	NA				

INDEX

Safety:	85 %	Satisfaction:	80 %
Depreciation:	50 %	Insurance:	$ 650
Cost per mile:	$ 0.55	Number of dealers:	5 200

SALES

	Canada			USA		
Model	1997	1998	Result	1997	1998	Result
Explorer	23,013	19,809	- 13.9 %	383,852	431,488	+ 12.4 %
Mountaineer	NA					

MAINTENANCE REQUIRED BY WARRANTY

First revision:	Frequency:	Diagnostic plug:
5 ,000 miles	6 months / 5,000 miles	Yes

Mid-Size SUVs

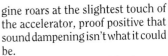

The vehicles in this series rank just behind the Explorer on the sales front. Because they're often less expensive than their main competitors, they're also very popular. They are derived from the S-10 and Sonoma pickups and in the latest revamping process, have been given a much more rigid body. All share the same features, geared to reflect the make's primary objectives, and their powertrains are all identical.

MODEL RANGE

GM offers the Blazer-Jimmy in either 2 or 4-door models, with either rear or all-wheel drive. The Envoy, on the other hand, is only sold in a 4-door 4X4 version. Chevrolet is offering three trim levels: base, LS and LT. At GMC, the equivalent versions are called: SL, SLS and SLT. The Envoy is a cream of the crop model exclusive to the GMC lineup. Generally speaking, these vehicles are richly equipped and goodies include standard automatic gearbox, climate control, cruise control, tilt steering wheel (except the lower end versions), four-wheel ABS and a PASS-Lock theft deterrent system.

TECHNICAL FEATURES

The central tube chassis is welded onto the body that's clad in dual-side galvanized sheet metal, except for the roof. "Insta-Trac" all-wheel drive that equips the 4X4's isn't in constant mesh, but can be activated by shift-on-the-fly. A new permanent «AutoTrac» system is available as an option for 2000 (standard on the Envoy). On the 4X4's, torque is distributed 35/65% to front and rear respectively. The independent front suspension consists of A-arms and cross-struts, with coil springs for the 4X2's and torsion bars for the 4X4's. At the rear, the rigid axle is suspended from semi-elliptic leaf springs. An anti-roll bar completes

Reliable?

each setup. There are three shock absorber modes: the first is geared to ride comfort with a negative effect on pulling force; the second is firmer, so it helps when hauling heavy trailers; the third is super firm and maximizes trailering capabilities. Since 1998, the vehicle is equipped with four-wheel disc brakes linked to standard ABS. But since 1998, the 4.3L V6 Vortec engine develops 15 hp less than the 4.0L V6 that drives the Explorer and GM doesn't offer a V8 model engine, unlike the competition.

PROS

+ PERFORMANCES. The V6 engine provides top-notch accelerations and pickup; in 4X2 mode, performances are akin to those of an average family sedan. On off-the-road maneuvres, the muscular torque is a welcome traveller.

+ RIDE COMFORT. Highway driving is very comfy, except with the reinforced suspension. Road irregularities are well disguised and the big tires act in quite a civilized manner.

+ HANDLING. With a tougher chassis and frame, road handling on these SUV's seems more reassured, especially on rough surfaces. But don't go thinking it's perfect.

+ BRAKES. The four-wheel brakes provide powerful and never-die braking. It cuts down on the stopping distances and ABS stabilizes vehicle path. But brakes are hard to apply, since the pedal is spongy.

+ QUALITY. In comparison with the

first Blazer models, the new generation is definitely better crafted. Even finish and trim materials seem plusher.

+ INTERESTING. Insta-Trac lets you engage the rear wheels while driving, at whatever speed. It's easy to apply, thanks to an electronically controlled transfer box.

+ DESIGN DETAILS. The interior is both elegant and ergonomic. Controls and accessories are generally conveniently located and easy to reach and the instrument panel has a neat lay-out.

+ SEATS. Nicely shaped seats provide quite a bit of lateral support and lots more lumbar support. The cockpit is easy to adjust to. The rear seatbench cushion is low-slung, but upholstery is cushy.

+ STORAGE COMPARTMENTS. The glove compartment isn't too roomy, but front and rear side-pockets on the upper end models make up for this stingy feature.

CONS

- FUEL CONSUMPTION. These vehicles are juggernauts (4 045 lbs) and the V6 displacement is pretty respectable, so gas consumption is always below 18 mpg.

- CABIN SPACE. Considering the hulk of these vehicles, cabin space is disappointing. Only four travellers can be comfortably seated, due to the really narrow body; a fifth passenger would only want to climb aboard in a pinch.

- SOUNDPROOFING. Road noise coming from the chassis and engine roars at the slightest touch of the accelerator, proof positive that sound dampening isn't what it could be.

- ACCESS. It's limited in the rear seats, whether it's a 2 or 4-door vehicle and rear seats are tough to get to due to a narrow door opening angle and poorly located handles.

- HATCHBACK. Some models come with a small hatch door linked to a swing door, a design combination that limits access to the luggage hold. The single-panel rear door with lifting rear window is more convenient. You can even stash away small parcels by simply raising the rear window.

- OUTWARD VIEW. It's awfully limited towards the rear. The 2-door versions are pretty crummy in this regard, yielding some major blind spots.

- TO BE IMPROVED UPON. Some controls are so bloody complicated that the engineers should go back to the drawing board, such as the shifter located to the left of the steering wheel and we noticed that some models aren't equipped with rear seat headrests.

CONCLUSION

The most common complaint among these vehicles' users is reliability. Problems are never major, but trips to the repair shop are a regular occurrence. This shows that the S-10 series needs better quality, something not yet found throughout this particular manufacturer's entire lineup.

RATING
CHEVROLET Blazer - GMC Jimmy

CONCEPT :		73%
Technology :	75	
Safety :	75	
Interior space :	65	
Trunk volume :	75	
Quality/fit/finish :	75	

DRIVING :		58%
Cockpit :	80	
Performance :	55	
Handling :	45	
Steering :	70	
Braking :	40	

ORIGINAL EQUIPMENT :		74%
Tires :	80	
Headlights :	80	
Wipers :	70	
Rear defroster :	60	
Radio :	80	

COMFORT :		67%
Seats :	75	
Suspension :	70	
Sound level :	50	
Conveniences :	60	
Air conditioning :	80	

BUDGET :		52%
Price :	45	
Fuel economy :	40	
Insurance :	50	
Satisfaction :	75	
Depreciation :	50	

Overall rating :		64.8%

NEW FOR 2000

- Improved Vortec V6 engine.
- Power lock differential (standard on 4x4s).

Compare
Performance,
Specifications, Prices,
and Classification
at the end of this chapter.

EQUIPMENT

CHEVROLET Blazer GMC Jimmy	base SL	LS SLS	ZR2 SLE	LT SLT	TrailBlazer
Automatic transmission:	S	S	S	S	S
Cruise control:	O	S	S	S	S
Power steering:	S	S	S	S	S
Anti-lock brakes:	S	S	S	S	S
Traction control:	-	-	-	-	-
Air conditioning:	SM	SM	SM	SA	SA
Leather:	-	-	-	S	S
AM/FM/radio-cassette:	O	S	S	S	SCd
Power door locks:	O	S	S	S	S
Power windows:	O	S	S	S	S
Tilt steering:	O	S	S	S	S
Dual adjustable mirrors:	SM	SE	SE	SE	SE
Alloy wheels:	O	S	S	S	S
Anti-theft system:	S	S	S	S	S

Colors
Exterior: White, Black Blue, Gold, Green, Red, Copper, Beige, Pewter.

Interior: Graphite, Medium Gray, Beige.

AT A GLANCE...

HISTORIC
Introduced in: 1983 (Blazer, S-10/Jimmy).
Made in: Moraine, OH, Linden NJ, USA.

DEMOGRAPHICS
Model	Men/Wom.	Age	Married	College	Income $
S Series	80/20 %	46	75 %	28 %	$39 000

INDEX
Safety:	75 %	Satisfaction:	75 %
Depreciation:	50 %	Insurance:	$ 710
Cost per mile:	$ 0.55	Number of dealers:	4,466

SALES
Model	Canada 1997	1998	Result	USA 1997	1998	Result
S Series	20,168	19,946	- 1.1 %	221,400	219,710	- 0.8%

MAINTENANCE REQUIRED BY WARRANTY
First revision: 3,000 miles
Frequency: 6 months / 6,000 miles
Diagnostic plug: Yes

Mid-Size SUVs

Overrated

Since its last revamping, the Rodeo has found the path to success once again. The two main reasons are its very appealing body styling and an engine that can provide more power than users found on previous models. But compared to some products from Japan and Europe, its underpinnings aren't as refined. And over the years, it has shed the inexpensive price tag so attractive when it first came onto the market.

MODEL RANGE

The latest Rodeo is sold as a 4-door station wagon in S and LS trim levels. The base model sold in the United States is a rear-wheel drive vehicle animated by a 2.2L in-line 4 engine with 5-speed manual gearbox. Both models sold in Canada are all-wheel drive vehicles powered by a 3.2L V6 with standard 5-speed manual gearbox on the S version and standard 4-speed automatic on the LS. The S version has pretty basic equipment, but it does include a radio-cassette player, whereas the LS is more richly equipped, since the only major option available is leather seat trim.

TECHNICAL FEATURES

The Rodeo's basic structure consists of a 6-crossmember steel H-frame to which the body is affixed. The vehicle has been pared down, so it's shorter, wider and more lightweight. The front suspension is made up of double transverse Y-shaped trailing arms with torsion and anti-roll bars, while the rear rigid axle is supported by five longitudinal control arms and suspended on coil springs. Standard protective plates cover the radiator, gas tank, crankcase and transfer case. Four-wheel disc brakes are linked to four-wheel ABS on all models. Weight has been reduced by 285 lb. due to modifications to the chassis, rear suspension and aluminum main drive shaft and due to more compact engines made up of aluminum and magnesium components as is the ABS control unit containing hydraulic and electronic controls. The new V6 engine pumps out more power and torque than its predecessors, thanks to its four valves per cylinder and its variable intake system that optimizes engine power no matter what the r.p.m. All-wheel drive remains «on demand», but it's activated by a button rather than a shifter and a hydraulic pressure system makes such an operation smooth below 60 mph.

PROS

+ LOOKS. It looks more compact and muscular than ever and exudes a solid, invincible feel that's the key to any SUV's success. The ribbed side stone deflectors and wider wheelhouses really suit the Rodeo.

+ CABIN SPACE. The cabin is a bit wider and accomodates four passengers who'll appreciate the nicely proportioned space.

+ ENGINE. The 3.2L V6 now finally has the wallop that was sorely lacking on the Rodeo. Accelerations and pickup are zippy on roads and on off-road maneuvers, more generous torque really helps you make tracks.

+ HANDLING. On good road surfaces, it benefits from the vehicle's structural rigidity and crisp steering.

+ COCKPIT. Driving is made easy due to the excellent driver's position who'll enjoy the nice blend created by the steering wheel, seat and pedals. And visibility all-round is super with the nice, big mirrors and instruments that are well-organized and easy to read.

+ OFF-THE-ROAD MANEUVERS. The Rodeo can really tackle rough terrain nicely due to its generous ground clearance, big entry and exit angles and its new rear suspension that keeps it more level and provides better grip on rough turf.

+ NICE FEATURES. The more traditional rear HATCH design that facilitates baggage compartment access, rear windows that lower all the way down and standard steel plates protecting powertrain components when driving on uneven terrain.

CONS

- PRICE. It's less competitive than before, since the LS version sells at prices comparable to top-of-the-line American rivals, once it gets all the trimmings, yet it doesn't fetch as good a resale price. Even the S version is stripped down to basics and is expensive considering what it has to offer.

-SUSPENSION. It's mushy and the vehicle slips at the least bump on the road, which really affects ride comfort and handling as soon as the going gets rough. It's the most controversial element on the Rodeo, for this wild and wooly suspension really jostles passengers and those big tires, soft shocks and wheelbase that's 4 inches shorter than on the Explorer don't help any either.

- STEERING. Assistance is more positive than before, but its high reduction ratio and wide steer angle cripple maneuverability.

- INSTRUMENT PANEL. Its design is pretty straightforward, yet some controls aren't located where you'd expect them to be, like the inverted radio and climate control dials and the switches located to the left of the steering wheel that are clean out of sight.

- ACCESS. Narrow doors don't open wide at all, so rear seat access is problematic with such skimpy space to wrestle into. Lastly, we'd like to see standard, conveniently located footrests and assist grips.

- THE S VERSION. Stingy equipment makes it hell to resell, especially since the better equipped LS doesn't cost much more.

- DISTRIBUTION. Dealerships are few and far between, which can complicate upkeep and needed repairs.

CONCLUSION

Never mind its magnetic looks, the Rodeo hasn't changed very much over the years and it offers minimal technology for a considerable asking price.

RATING		
ISUZU Rodeo		
CONCEPT :		**76%**
Technology :	80	
Safety :	75	
Interior space :	60	
Trunk volume :	90	
Quality/fit/finish :	75	
DRIVING :		**61%**
Cockpit :	80	
Performance :	55	
Handling :	45	
Steering :	70	
Braking :	55	
ORIGINAL EQUIPMENT :		**76%**
Tires :	80	
Headlights :	75	
Wipers :	75	
Rear defroster :	75	
Radio :	75	
COMFORT :		**64%**
Seats :	75	
Suspension :	65	
Sound level :	40	
Conveniences :	60	
Air conditioning :	80	
BUDGET :		**55%**
Price :	20	
Fuel economy :	50	
Insurance :	60	
Satisfaction :	80	
Depreciation :	65	
Overall rating :		**66.4%**

NEW FOR 2000

• Minor changes to front and rear bumper design.

Compare Performance, Specifications, Prices, and Classification at the end of this chapter.

EQUIPMENT

ISUZU Rodeo/Amigo	S	LS	LSE
Automatic transmission:	O	S	S
Cruise control:	O	S	S
Power steering:	S	S	S
Anti-lock brakes:	S	S	S
Traction control:	-	-	-
Air conditioning:	O	S	S
Leather:	-	O	S
AM/FM/radio-cassette:	S	SCd	SCd
Power door locks:	O	S	S
Power windows:	O	S	S
Tilt steering:	O	S	S
Dual adjustable mirrors:	SM	SEH	SEH
Alloy wheels:	O	S	S
Anti-theft system:	O	S	S

Colors

Exterior: Black, Silver, White, Green, Bordeaux.

Interior: Gray, Beige.

AT A GLANCE...

HISTORIC
Introduced in: 1991-1998.
Made in: Lafayette, Indiana, USA.

DEMOGRAPHICS

Model	Men/Wom.	Age	Married	College	Income $
Rodeo	75/25 %	46	74 %	50 %	$ 40 000

INDEX

Safety:	75 %	Satisfaction:	80 %
Depreciation:	28 % (1 year)	Insurance:	$ 850-975
Cost per mile:	$ 0.50	Number of dealers:	NA

SALES

Model	Canada 1997	1998	Result	USA 1997	1998	Result
Rodeo	358	1,248	+ 248.6 %	61,071	63,627	+ 4.2 %

MAINTENANCE REQUIRED BY WARRANTY

First revision:	Frequency:	Diagnostic plug:
3 000 miles	6 000 miles	No

Mid-Size SUVs

The Grand Cherokee was completely redesigned last year. It continues to enjoy unqualified success thanks to its unusual styling and a new V8 engine that provides remarkable performance capabilities. As a bonus, its handling has improved significantly, virtually matching all of the advantages offered by a luxury car.

MODEL RANGE

This SUV is sold as a four-door station wagon, with either RWD or AWD, in Laredo and Limited trim, equipped with the 4.0L inline 6 that powered the former model as standard equipment or with the latest 4.7L V8 linked to a new 4-speed automatic gearbox. The 4X4 versions offer several all-wheel drive devices including the latest "Quadra-Drive".

TECHNICAL FEATURES

The Grand Cherokee body is still a steel unibody, so overall height can be trimmed down, while maintaining generous ground clearance, which isn't the case for a body-on-frame formula. It's extremely rigid because it integrates a chassis frame to the lower body. Yet, even with its taut lines, aerodynamic yield isn't that of a car, but it's more efficient than on the former model. The recirculating ball steering system was created to provide more right-on precision than is possible with a rack-and-pinion arrangement and four-wheel disc brakes benefit from a standard antilock braking system. The new V8 engine is modular, that is, the 3.5L V6 gets two more cylinders. This engine is more muscular than the 5.2L engine that animated the former version, but torque isn't as gutsy, yet fuel consumption and

Cramped

pollutant emissions are lower. The new 4-speed automatic gearbox is quite unique since it applies overdrive as soon as you hit second gear and the «Quadra-Drive» full-time all-wheel drive benefits from viscous coupling power distribution and it comes as original equipment with the V8. Lastly, climate control uses an infrared sensor that adjusts cabin temperature to occupants' body temperature.

PROS

+ **STYLE.** The esthetic charm still works its magic, which is the secret behind this vehicle's appeal. The overall design is a dashing blend of refined luxury and rugged, make my day traits.

+ **SUSPENSION.** It's the latest Grand Cherokee's forte since it procures super-competent handling both on and off the road and offers ride comfort worthy of a regal, top of the heap sedan.

+ **VALUE.** Prices are pretty well what they were for the older models, yet original equipment is very extensive and incorporates a number of major, state-of-the-art technical features, so this vehicle is a real bargain and it doesn't depreciate as much as most of the competition out there.

+ **RIDE COMFORT.** Jeep engineers have once again demonstrated their cunning way of taming rigid axle suspensions so as to procure ride

comfort similar to that achieved by a MacPherson strut setup. There are neat-design, thickly cushioned seats both front and rear, soundproofing takes its task seriously and climate control provides nice, even temperatures.

+ **HANDLING.** This vehicle is extremely stable and neutral on all kinds of curves, with no center of gravity fallout and off-road capabilities are absolutely amazing.

+ **PERFORMANCES.** The new 4.7L V8 brings a whole new driving dimension to the latest Grand Cherokee. Power output, lively response and a clever transmission put it on a par with lots of cars when it comes to accelerations and pickup. Locomotion elements are responsive and quick on the draw and the turbine roars away at full tilt.

+ **BRAKES.** They grip like champions and are easy to apply, stops are achieved within short distances and with straight-ahead confidence and they're tough as nails.

+ **THE "QUADRA-DRIVE".** This feature is a perfect example of topnotch Jeep know-how when it comes to all-wheel drive, for this device automatically transfers available torque to the wheel or wheels with the best grip on things.

+ **NICE FEATURES:** How easily the cargo hold can be transformed, the big rear hatch and door handles, the window that opens on the hatch door, the rear fender that serves as a running board, storage bins that make up for the slim, trim glove compartment.

CONS

- **CABIN SPACE.** The Grand Cherokee has a shorter wheelbase than rivals, which makes for slicker off-road maneuvers, but cabin space is pretty snug and there isn't enough leg room for either front or rear seat passengers and rear doors are still awfully narrow, so getting aboard is a bit of a chore.

- **SAFETY FEATURES.** Strange that this vehicle doesn't come equipped with side-impact airbags, a definite must on such a high tech vehicle...

- **STORAGE SPACE.** There aren't many spots to store stuff up front and compartments are teeny tiny, they don't even exist in the rear and backseat travellers have to settle for two seat pockets and cup-holders.

- **APPEARANCE.** The plastic parts that make up the dashboard look just about as cheap as those on the latest LH Chrysler products.

- **INSTRUMENT PANEL.** It's terribly plain and dull-looking, gauges and instruments are hard to read and there's no indicator for the shifter position, an item that you find on even the lowliest Honda Civic...

CONCLUSION

In spite of good looks and a refined AWD transmission, the Grand Cherokee suffers the consequences of cramped sizing and a design concept that some potential buyers find just too special.

RATING
JEEP Grand Cherokee

CONCEPT :   **78%**
Technology :	85
Safety :	90
Interior space :	70
Trunk volume :	65
Quality/fit/finish :	80

DRIVING :   **70%**
Cockpit :	80
Performance :	60
Handling :	50
Steering :	80
Braking :	80

ORIGINAL EQUIPMENT :   **79%**
Tires :	80
Headlights :	80
Wipers :	80
Rear defroster :	75
Radio :	80

COMFORT :   **74%**
Seats :	80
Suspension :	80
Sound level :	60
Conveniences :	70
Air conditioning :	80

BUDGET :   **39%**
Price :	10
Fuel economy :	30
Insurance :	45
Satisfaction :	85
Depreciation :	25

Overall rating :   **68.0%**

NEW FOR 2000

- Dark Metallic Gray fillers on the Laredo.
- Chrome logos on the Laredo.
- New Limited badge.
- Two new exterior colors.

Compare Performance, Specifications, Prices, and Classification at the end of this chapter.

EQUIPMENT

JEEP Grand Cherokee

	Laredo 4x2	Limited 4x2	Laredo 4x4	Limited 4x4
Automatic transmission:	S	S	S	S
Cruise control:	S	S	S	S
Power steering:	S	S	S	S
Anti-lock brakes:	S	S	S	S
Traction control:	-	-	-	-
Air conditioning:	SM	SA	SM	SA
Leather:	O	S	O	S
AM/FM/radio-cassette:	S	SCd	S	SCd
Power door locks:	S	S	S	S
Power windows:	S	S	S	S
Tilt steering:	S	S	S	S
Dual adjustable mirrors:	SE	SEH	SE	SEH
Alloy wheels:	S	S	S	S
Anti-theft system:	O	S	O	S

Colors
Exterior: Black, Platinum, White, Champagne, Amethyst, Slate, Red, Blue, Sienna, Taupe.
Interior: Pebble, Camel, Taupe.

AT A GLANCE...

HISTORIC
Introduced in:	1993-1999.
Made in:	Jefferson North, Detroit, USA & Graz, Austria.

DEMOGRAPHICS
Model	Men/Wom.	Age	Married	College	Income $
Grand Cherokee	70/30 %	46	80 %	51 %	$ 55 500

INDEX
Safety:	80 %	Satisfaction:	85 %
Depreciation:	25 %	Insurance:	$ 975-1185
Cost per mile:	$ 0.51	Number of dealers:	1 029

SALES
	Canada			USA		
Model	1997	1998	Result	1997	1998	Result
Grand Cherokee	17,163	15,760	- 8.2 %	279,195	260,875	-6.6 %

MAINTENANCE REQUIRED BY WARRANTY
First revision:	Frequency:	Diagnostic plug:
3 000 miles	6 months / 6 000 miles	Yes

Mid-Size SUVs

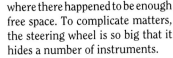

Rustic

Land Rover developed a more affordable version of its Ranger Rover: the Discovery. In all of the Camel rally races held around the world, it's easily recognizable because of its high-perched body.

MODEL RANGE

The Discovery is a 4-door vehicle available solely with a 4.0L V8 engine and a 4-speed automatic transmission. Its equipment is elaborate and luxurious, including remote keyless entry, power locks, power windows and power sideview mirrors, air conditioning, an Alpine sound system, cruise control and a full-size spare tire and alloy wheel.

TECHNICAL FEATURES

The Discovery is derived from the Range Rover and shares its sturdy six-crossmember chassis. Its body is made of steel and its most exposed panels are galvanized. Front and rear suspension feature a solid axle supported by longitudinal arms, Panhard and antiroll bars and variable air springs. Its four disc brakes are coupled with an antilock system to provide optimal off-road capabilities. The engine has a 188-hp output and the automatic transmission is controlled electronically. AWD is permanent and the traction control system limits tire slip by automatically applying brake pressure to the wheel with the least traction. The rear-end assembly includes automatic level control to ensure optimal steering consistency. To ensure full compatibility with the automatic transmission, the Discovery features a locking center differential.

PROS

+ DRIVEABILITY. In spite of its size the Discovery is fun to drive; it's easy to handle, controls are smooth and visibility is almost perfect from all angles.

+ VERSATILITY. The Discovery goes from the highway to uncharted territory with no hesitation. It's roomy cargo area can accommodate an extra bench seat or two auxiliary seats.

+ PERFORMANCE. Acceleration and pick-up are very good for a vehicle as heavy as this one and its weight explains its high fuel consumption.

+ CARGO SPACE. With the spare tire stored on the hatch, there's plenty of room for baggage.

+ QUALITY. Meticulous manufacturing and careful finish are both obvious and most materials are of excellent quality.

+ VISIBILITY. Thanks to large windows and the vehicle's height, it's excellent. The driving position is satisfactory as well.

+ BONUS MARKS. For the two sunroofs that make the passenger compartment bright and the two side-positioned storage spaces in the cargo area.

+ BRAKING. Power is progressive and easy to gauge, but given the vehicle's weight, stopping distances are long.

CONS

- PRICE. This pseudo sport utility is very expensive to buy, maintain and insure and its fuel consumption can easily reach 10 mpg.

- SUSPENSION. Its excessive stiffness jostles passengers and the steering system tends to lose precision. It reacts oddly to very bumpy roads and its unpredictable behavior forces drivers to stick to lower speeds in some circumstances.

- RELIABILITY. Owners continue to complain about questionable reliability, all the more so since dealerships are few and far between. No wonder seeing Land Rovers on flatbed trucks is nothing very surprising.

- PASSENGER ROOM. It's disappointing given the vehicle's size; rear seats are cramped and access is ridiculously hard.

- FLAWS. It's very strange that a vehicle sold at this price has so few assist grips; there is no dummy pedal for the driver.

- SEAT ADJUSTMENT. In the front, since the control is located between the center tunnel and the seat - an idea borrowed from the old Jaguar - it's almost impossible to make any adjustments in transit.

- HANDLING. The Discovery's turning radius is so long, this vehicle just doesn't corner. On winding roads it loses motor functions and on very rough off-road trajectories, it loses all agility.

- ERGONOMICS. The dashboard is very strangely laid out and some controls seem to be positioned where there happened to be enough free space. To complicate matters, the steering wheel is so big that it hides a number of instruments.

- FLAWS. Chimes that go off for no obvious reason and rattling noises that are inexplicable on a vehicle in this class; the lack of cupholders is unthinkable for North American motorists.

- TIRES. They provide good grip under most circumstances, but can't always be counted on when weather conditions are tougher.

CONCLUSION

As a vehicle that's already badly outdated, the Discovery doesn't have enough to convince potential buyers. A good Expedition can get the same job done with fewer problems along the way.

Mid-Size SUVs

RATING
LAND ROVER Discovery

CONCEPT :   86%
Technology :   85
Safety :   90
Interior space :   90
Trunk volume :   80
Quality/fit/finish :   85

DRIVING :   65%
Cockpit :   85
Performance :   50
Handling :   60
Steering :   80
Braking :   50

ORIGINAL EQUIPMENT :   78%
Tires :   85
Headlights :   80
Wipers :   65
Rear defroster :   75
Radio :   85

COMFORT :   75%
Seats :   80
Suspension :   80
Sound level :   60
Conveniences :   75
Air conditioning :   80

BUDGET :   26%
Price :   0
Fuel economy :   0
Insurance :   15
Satisfaction :   70
Depreciation :   45

Overall rating :   66.0%

NEW FOR 2000

- Body colors.
- Optional navigational system.

Compare Performance, Specifications, Prices, and Classification at the end of this chapter.

EQUIPMENT

LAND ROVER	Discovery
Automatic transmission:	S
Cruise control:	S
Power steering:	S
Anti-lock brakes:	S
Traction control:	S
Air conditioning:	SA
Leather:	S
AM/FM/radio-cassette:	SCd
Power door locks:	S
Power windows:	S
Tilt steering:	S
Dual adjustable mirrors:	S
Alloy wheels:	S
Anti-theft system:	S

Colors

Exterior: White, Silver, Marine, Red, Green, Black

Interior: Grey, Black, Tan.

AT A GLANCE...

HISTORIC
Introduced in: 1970 (2dr.); 1981 (4dr.)
Made in: Solihull, Angleterre.

DEMOGRAPHICS

Model	Men/Wom.	Age	Married	College	Income $
Discovery	-				

INDEX

Safety:	90 %	Satisfaction:	78 %
Depreciation:	45 %	Insurance:	$ 2 250
Cost per mile:	$ 1,15	Number of dealers:	2

SALES

Model	Canada 1997	1998	Result	USA 1997	1998	Result
Discovery	337	291	- 13.6%	NA		

MAINTENANCE REQUIRED BY WARRANTY

First revision:	Frequency:	Diagnostic plug:
3 000 miles	6 month / 6 000 miles	Yes

Mid-Size SUVs

City Slicker

When it came up with the RX 300, Lexus wanted to prove that it too could develop a 4x4 vehicle from one of the most popular sedans of the hour. Based on the Camry's platform and mechanical system, this model is designed to attract a clientele group looking for originality and reliability. It's the bestselling Lexus model and with reason: its versatility goes far beyond anything a sedan can offer.

MODEL RANGE

The RX 300 is a luxury all-purpose vehicle offered in a unique version powered by a single 3.0L multivalve V6 that develops 220 hp, linked to an electronically controlled four-speed automatic transmission. The U.S. model is sold with front-wheel or all-wheel drive. As is the case for all Lexus vehicles, original equipment is very rich, but this model can also be equipped with a rear spoiler, category II trailer hookup and roof rack with several adapters.

TECHNICAL FEATURES

The RX 300 is closely inspired by the ES 300 sedan and shares its platform consisting of a steel unitized body equipped with front and rear independent cradles supporting the drive shaft as well as transmission and suspension elements. The structure is super solid with a special view to achieving optimum handling and good resistance in the event of a collision. Exterior dimensions are a tad bigger than those of the Grand Cherokee and like the Mercedes-Benz M-Class, this vehicle is equipped with four airbags protecting front seat passengers, namely two frontal and two side-impact devices. The streamlined shape has good aerodynamic yield, since the drag coefficient is recorded at 0.36, better than that of the Mercedes with only a 0.39 Cx. Front and rear

suspensions are made up of specially designed MacPherson struts. The vehicle is equipped with four-wheel disc brakes assisted by a standard antilock braking device. The V6 is derived from the Lexus ES 300 engine. It hits 80% of its torque at 1,600 r.p.m., thanks to variable valve timing called VVTi. The all-wheel drive system is borrowed from the Celica All-Trac model that's sold in Asia and Europe. In normal situations, power is distributed 50/50 between front and rear wheels. A viscous-coupled main differential and a rear limited-slip Torsen differential redistribute juice to wheels benefitting from the best grip, when there's wheel slip.

PROS

+ PRICE. It's pretty down-to-earth, so it can compete with that of the Mercedes ML 320, its main rival.

+ STYLE. Its elegance makes you clean forget that the RX 300 is a 4X4, since its silhouette is more refined than that of an SUV, as is often the case on such a vehicle.

+ PERFORMANCES. It only takes about 9 seconds to accelerate from 0 to 60 mph and pickup is just as peppy due to a favorable power to weight ratio, which explains why fuel consumption is so efficient.

+ RIDE COMFORT. There's a pretty high ground clearance, but it's still no problem getting inside the front seats and no need to put your back out in the process. In the rear seat area, the seatbench is mounted on tracks, so it can be

pushed forward and its back cushion can recline, so together with those on the front seats, behold, you have a bed...

+ CONVENIENCE FEATURES. The cargo hold is nice and convenient and the seatbench can be folded down to obtain a perfectly flat floor. The console between the front seats holds all kinds of clever storage compartments. The 6-CD changer is housed inside the dashboard and the ventilation system is fitted with a particulate air filter that you only need to change ever three years, simply by hand and without any tool required, via the glove compartment.

+ QUALITY. It's simply great all-round, since assembly, finish job and choice of trim components are impeccable. But the leather seating and wood appliqués aren't exactly posh...

+ A NICE FEATURE: Amazingly bright headlamps.

CONS

-SUSPENSION. Insufficient travel and too much flexibility cripples off-road maneuvers, so the RX 300 is mostly an on-road or smooth terrain vehicle. On the road, the suspension causes lots of sway so, along with the hard, crummy-quality tires, you're in for some pretty awful surprises.

- BRAKES. We weren't convinced that they were effective, not with those ever so long stops, touchy application and we had to readjust vehicle path even with ABS.

- MANEUVERABILITY. Steering is quick and accurate, but it's over-assisted and suffers from too wide a steer angle diameter and poor visibility due to thick C and D pillars.

- NOISE LEVEL. There's more racket than you'd ever expect on a vehicle in this snobby class.

- ACCESS. It's awkward with those narrow doors and really slanting C pillar in the rear seat area.

-INSTRUMENT PANEL. Such an overdone, style-is-all design is out of date as soon as the vehicle comes off the assembly line. When it's not showing data from the GPS navigation system, the liquid crystal screen is indicating air ventilation and stereo settings, but readings are hard to see. Lastly, some touch screen controls are highly unusual.

- TO BE IMPROVED UPON. The low-slung seatbench, poorly located cup-holders for rear seat passengers (on the center console) and the sluggish sweep of wipers that often slip off the windshield surface.

CONCLUSION

The Lexus RX 300's only real handicap is the fact that when it encounters very rough roads, it doesn't do as well as its direct competitors. This isn't a real 4x4 model and has never claimed to be one either. In any case, most of its buyers prefer big city boulevards to snake-infested back roads.

RATING		
LEXUS RX 300		
CONCEPT :		**80%**
Technology :	85	
Safety :	90	
Interior space :	80	
Trunk volume :	60	
Quality/fit/finish :	85	
DRIVING :		**59%**
Cockpit :	70	
Performance :	50	
Handling :	40	
Steering :	70	
Braking :	65	
ORIGINAL EQUIPMENT :		**77%**
Tires :	70	
Headlights :	85	
Wipers :	75	
Rear defroster :	75	
Radio :	80	
COMFORT :		**71%**
Seats :	75	
Suspension :	75	
Sound level :	45	
Conveniences :	80	
Air conditioning :	80	
BUDGET :		**45%**
Price :	10	
Fuel economy :	60	
Insurance :	40	
Satisfaction :	90	
Depreciation :	25	
Overall rating :		**66.4%**

NEW FOR 2000

- Opalescent Mineral Green color.
- Optional rear spoiler.

Compare
Performance,
Specifications, Prices,
and Classification
at the end of this chapter.

EQUIPMENT

LEXUS RX 300	AWD
Automatic transmission:	S
Cruise control:	S
Power steering:	S
Anti-lock brakes:	S
Traction control:	S
Air conditioning:	SA
Leather:	O
AM/FM/radio-cassette:	S
Power door locks:	S
Power windows:	SA
Tilt steering:	S
Dual adjustable mirrors:	SEH
Alloy wheels:	S
Anti-theft system:	S

Colors

Exterior: Gold, Silver, Black, Red, Blue, Brown, Bronze.

Interior: Cloth: Ivory. Leather: Black, Ivory.

AT A GLANCE...

HISTORIC
Introduced in: 1999.
Made in: -

DEMOGRAPHICS

Model	Men/Wom.	Age	Married	College	Income $
RX 300	60/40 %	46	82 %	50%	$ 68 000

INDEX

Safety:	90 %	Satisfaction:	92 %
Depreciation:	47 %	Insurance:	$ 1 550
Cost per mile:	$ 0.58	Number of dealers:	170

SALES

Model	Canada 1997	1998	Result	USA 1997	1998	Result
RX 300	-	2,249	-	-	42,191	-

MAINTENANCE REQUIRED BY WARRANTY

First revision:	Frequency:	Diagnostic plug:
4 000 miles	4 000 miles	Yes

Mid-Size SUVs

Snob

When it arrived on the market, Mercedes' 4x4 created a huge fuss and proceeded to beat previous sales records. Although viewed more as an automobile than a utility vehicle, it doubles as both and can be used as either. The arrival of clearly sportier V8 engines has sparked new interest in the M-Class, never one to go unnoticed.

MODEL RANGE

The M-Class is a lineup of intermediate SUV's of the same format as the currently most popular models. This vehicle is available as a four-door station wagon with lifting rear hatch in Classique or Elegance trim, as a ML320 model equipped with a V6 or a V8-animated ML430. The Classique version is really loaded with nice items, including most of the usual comfort and luxury features. The Elegance model and the 430 also receive leather-trim seats and eight-way adjustable power front seats that are heated as well, a power sunroof, wood appliqués and Bose high-fidelity sound system. All 2000 models are equipped with a brake-assisted system and an ESP anti-skid device.

TECHNICAL FEATURES

When Mercedes was working on its star North American-bound product design, the carmaker adopted tried and true solutions. The M-Class is more like the Ford Explorer than the Grand Cherokee, build-wise, with its body mounted on a separate chassis, procuring maximum strength and stifling as much noise, vibration and shakes from the axles and powertrains as possible. The chassis is built of rust-proof steel and is equipped with a fully independent suspension, based on unequal-length control arms,

torsion bars and anti-roll bars. Rack-and-pinion steering is variable assist and four-wheel disc brakes are linked to a four-channel antilock braking system. The all-wheel drive system is neat, since it doesn't use locking differentials to maintain continuous wheel function. It takes up the 4ETS system already used on Mercedes all-wheel drive models, including an electronic system that controls individual wheel rotation via the ABS sensors and that distributes power depending on the best adherence by activating the differentials. On off-road maneuvers, you get a shorter axle ratio by touching a button located on the dashboard. When it comes to safety, Mercedes is way ahead of most of the competition, since it uses a safety cage around the cabin, front and side-impact airbags as well as tensioner front seat belts.

PROS

+ PRESTIGE. Why deprive yourself of showing off a Mercedes in your driveway for a price not terribly higher than what you'd have to dish out for an Explorer Limited?

+ PRICE. The Classique version is almost affordable and is comparable to the upper-crust "Limited" versions of American rivals, given the really rich array of equipment.

+ SAFETY. It's the best around both for passive protection with its four airbags and safety anti-roll cage

and for active protection, with such competent demeanor due to all those nice driving aids such as anti-skid control, ABS and traction control that put it in a class all its own.

+ DRIVING PLEASURE. All the driving enhancements put the M-Class way above the horde of rivals, for engine and transmission oomph and ease procure topnotch performances and pleasure. Such car-like traits are dramatically different from those of rivals of pickup ancestry.

+ STYLE. It's created a trend that Lexus cloned in no time flat, but its soft lines aren't any more efficient when it comes to aerodynamics since the drag coefficient is only 0.39.

+ SIZE. This intermediate vehicle is well suited to scads of North American buyers' needs. It's quite trim yet it offers lots of cabin and luggage storage space and the cargo hold is bigger than is the case for most of the competition.

+ RIDE COMFORT. It's simply remarkable, the suspension is a silky sophisticate, seats are super-comfy and noise is kept to a decent minimum at cruising speed.

+ NICE FEATURES: The bright headlights for safer travel, enough storage spots and the handy luggage cover.

CONS

- QUALITY. Some finish details don't jive with the German

carmaker's reputation and plastic components are pretty run of the mill. Our test vehicle squeaked and rattled quite a bit.

- STEERING. It suffers from a poor reduction ratio, so you have to reel it in on off-road rambles and when trying to park.

- REAR SEATBENCH. Hard to get to with those narrow doors and it isn't too useful with its really snug three-passenger capacity. To make matters worse, the seat removal device is so bloody complicated that even an engineer won't make it work at the first attempt.

- TO BE IMPROVED UPON. The weird control for cruise control, the awkward power window control that's located on the center console, the far from precise gas gauge, the CD player that's located in the cargo hold and that you can't get to when the hold is full of luggage. And we're still complaining because there's no shifter position indicator and no assist grips to help out when boarding.

CONCLUSION

The Mercedes 4x4 is phenomenally successfully mostly because of its price, which puts a fairly sophisticated vehicle in your driveway for a price barely higher than you'd pay for a full-size North American model.

RATING
MERCEDES-BENZ M-Class

CONCEPT :		78%
Technology :	85	
Safety :	90	
Interior space :	65	
Trunk volume :	70	
Quality/fit/finish :	80	

DRIVING :		69%
Cockpit :	80	
Performance :	60	
Handling :	50	
Steering :	80	
Braking :	75	

ORIGINAL EQUIPMENT :		79%
Tires :	80	
Headlights :	80	
Wipers :	75	
Rear defroster :	80	
Radio :	80	

COMFORT :		75%
Seats :	80	
Suspension :	75	
Sound level :	60	
Conveniences :	80	
Air conditioning :	80	

BUDGET :		49%
Price :	10	
Fuel economy :	50	
Insurance :	35	
Satisfaction :	80	
Depreciation :	70	

Overall rating :	70.0%

NEW FOR 2000

• The ML55 AMG model, with a 342-hp engine output.

Compare
Performance,
Specifications, Prices,
and Classification
at the end of this chapter.

EQUIPMENT

MERCEDES-BENZ	ML320 Classic	ML320 Elegance	ML430
Automatic transmission:			
Cruise control:	S	S	S
Power steering:	S	S	S
Anti-lock brakes:	S	S	S
Traction control:	S	S	S
Air conditioning:	S	S	S
Leather:	SM	SA	SA
AM/FM/radio-cassette:	-	S	S
Power door locks:	SCd	SCd	SCd
Power windows:	S	S	S
Tilt steering:	S	S	S
Dual adjustable mirrors:	S	S	S
Alloy wheels:	SEH	SEH	SEH
Anti-theft system:	S	S	S
	S	S	S

Colors

Exterior: Silver, Black, White, Ruby, Green, Emerald.

Interior: *Cloth:* Gray. *Leather:* Sand, Gray.

AT A GLANCE...

HISTORIC
Introduced in: 1998.
Made in: Tuscaloosa, Alabama, USA.

DEMOGRAPHICS

Model	Men/Wom.	Age	Married	College	Income $
ML320	65/35%	45	80%	52%	$ 60 000

INDEX

Safety:	90%	Satisfaction:	82 %
Depreciation:	30%	Insurance:	$ 1675
Cost per mile:	$ 0.55	Number of dealers:	380

SALES

	Canada			USA		
Model	1997	1998	Result	1997	1998	Result
ML320	459	3,030	+ 560.1 %	14,569	43,134	+ 196.0 %

MAINTENANCE REQUIRED BY WARRANTY

First revision:	Frequency:	Diagnostic plug:
3 000 miles	10 000 miles	Yes

Mid-Size SUVs

NISSAN-INFINITI

Pathfinder - QX4

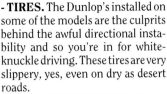

The Pathfinder was one of the first Japanese utility vehicles to enter the North American market, where not so long ago it symbolized the globetrotter spirit. Since then others have followed in its wake and it isn't alone anymore. To follow the current automotive trend, a deluxe clone was concocted: the Infiniti QX4, offering the distinction of a special suspension and an AWD system borrowed from the competition.

MODEL RANGE

The Pathfinder is a 4-door SUV with rear or all-wheel drive sold in XE and LE rear-wheel drive versions and XE, SE and LE all-wheel drive versions. All models are animated by the same 3.3L V6 engine paired up with a standard manual gearbox on the XE and SE and with a standard automatic on LE models. The base model XE is equipped with power steering, antilock braking, manual air conditioning, radio and tape deck and tilt steering column. The LE is loaded with all the posh amenities you could dream of enjoying on an upper-crust vehicle, all but the sunroof.

TECHNICAL FEATURES

The Pathfinder has a steel unibody integrated with an H-frame (monoframe), so as to achieve rock of Gibraltar flexion and torsion resistance. The only standard protective plate on these vehicles covers the gas tank. The fully independent suspension is made up of MacPherson struts up front and of a rigid axle guided by five control arms with coil springs and stabilizer bar at the rear extremity. Disc and drum brakes are hooked up to standard ABS on all versions. Vehicles are equipped with rack-and-pinion steering and a 3.3L V6 that delivers 168 hp. The all-wheel drive is "on demand". It includes two conventional differentials on front and rear axles, but the latter can be replaced by another viscous-coupled limited-slip differential. The transfer case can be engaged via shift-on-the-fly at speeds up to 50 mph and front hub lock is automatic.

Handicaped

PROS

+ OVERALL DESIGN. The Pathfinder has inherited some family traits from its predecessor, but it's now more like a car than a true blue utility vehicle.

+ SIZE. The Pathfinder is a superhancy vehicle that takes full advantage of its overall size to provide really roomy cabin space. Leg room is quite generous in the rear seat section and the luggage compartment is absolutely humungous, modular and easily accessible via the clever-design rear hatch. Climbing on board is a breeze with the comfortable ground clearance and several convenient assist grips.

+ HANDLING. The structure is much more rigid and this pays off when it comes to competent, crisp vehicle control. There isn't as much sway thanks to better calibrated springs and shocks. So this vehicle takes curves with aplomb, especially since the center of gravity isn't perched quite as high as in the past.

+ RIDE COMFORT. Passengers will appreciate the nicely proportioned cabin space, the less uncivilized suspension, neat-design seats and effective sound dampening.

+ STEERING. The rack-and-pinion system is direct, willing and easy to adjust, which yields good maneuverability, since the steer angle diameter is relatively short.

+ COCKPIT. Nothing fancy, but it has a good layout and the driver, sitting nice and high, enjoys good peripheral vision all round, now that the spare tire is stashed under the cargo hold floor. The dashboard is no-frills plain, which is an understatement, but at least it's more ergonomic than on the previous model.

+ QUALITY. Assembly is solid, finish touches are neat and materials are spiffy. Equipment is fairly extensive, even on the base model.

CONS

- SAFETY. The American highway bureau (NHTSA) didn't give a high score to this vehicle, given the serious passenger injuries that could occur in the event of a collision. But the sturdier frame has improved handling and ride comfort and brakes do benefit from a standard antilock braking device.

- ENGINE. The Pathfinder's V6 has never for one minute been the best choice for this type of vehicle, since torque is only fair to midling. Accelerations and pickup are far from brilliant with an engine that's always straining and catching its breath.

- BRAKES. They're smooth and easy to apply and achieve straight-on stops in emergency situations, even though there's a bit of wheel lock. But stopping distances are far too long, which could lead to a sad state of affairs.

- TIRES. The Dunlop's installed on some of the models are the culprits behind the awful directional instability and so you're in for white-knuckle driving. These tires are very slippery, yes, even on dry as desert roads.

- FUEL CONSUMPTION. It's far from efficient since fuel bills are always high, and let's face it, performances are rather blah. This engine would be better suited to a car than an SUV.

- TRANSMISSION. Gears are poorly spaced on both the manual and the automatic, so you can't really get the energy ooze out of the high-end torque characteristic of this engine.

- GROUND CLEARANCE. It's lower than before, which cripples some maneuvers on rough terrain and the vehicle has a tendency to bottom out with those 15-inch wheels. We regret that there are still no standard protective plates keeping the engine and transmission components out of harm's way.

- TO BE IMPROVED UPON. Seat upholstery that's terribly firm, poorly designed left footrest for the driver and some inconveniently located controls, such as those for the rear wiper.

CONCLUSION

These two vehicles suffer from an engine that is poorly suited to off-road use, lacking torque and power in the lower rpm range and constantly needing to be pushed to the limit, which explains their poor fuel economy.

Pathfinder - QX4   NISSAN-INFINITI

RATING
NISSAN Pathfinder

CONCEPT :   72%
Technology : 80
Safety : 60
Interior space : 70
Trunk volume : 70
Quality/fit/finish : 80

DRIVING :   57%
Cockpit : 75
Performance : 35
Handling : 35
Steering : 80
Braking : 60

ORIGINAL EQUIPMENT :   75%
Tires : 75
Headlights : 75
Wipers : 75
Rear defroster : 75
Radio : 75

COMFORT :   70%
Seats : 75
Suspension : 60
Sound level : 70
Conveniences : 70
Air conditioning : 75

BUDGET :   52%
Price : 35
Fuel economy : 40
Insurance : 45
Satisfaction : 90
Depreciation : 50

Overall rating :   65.2%

NEW FOR 2000

• No changes after a few cosmetic revisions for 1999.

Compare Performance, Specifications, Prices, and Classification at the end of this chapter.

EQUIPMENT

NISSAN Pathfinder	XE	SE	LE
Automatic transmission:	O	O	S
Cruise control:	-	S	S
Power steering:	S	S	S
Anti-lock brakes:	S	S	S
Traction control:	-	-	-
Air conditioning:	SM	SA	SA
Leather:	-	O	SC
AM/FM/radio-cassette:	SCd	SCd	SCd
Power door locks:	-	S	S
Power windows:	-	S	S
Tilt steering:	S	S	S
Dual adjustable mirrors:	SM	SEH	SEH
Alloy wheels:	O	S	S
Anti-theft system:	-	S	S

Colors
Exterior: Red, Blue, Chestnut, Beige, Green, Ebony, Gray, White.
Interior: Gray, Beige.

AT A GLANCE...

HISTORIC
Introduced in: 1986-1996.
Made in: Kyushu, Japan.

DEMOGRAPHICS

Model	Men/Wom.	Age	Married	College	Income $
Pathfinder	76/24 %	39	68 %	57 %	$ 49 000

INDEX
Safety: 60 %   Satisfaction: 92 %
Depreciation: 50 %   Insurance: $ 1065 -1 155
Cost per mile: $ 0.51   Number of dealers: 1 100

SALES

Model	Canada 1997	1998	Result	USA 1997	1998	Result
Pathfinder	9,204	8,720	- 5.3 %	73,365	68,003	- 7.3 %

MAINTENANCE REQUIRED BY WARRANTY
First revision: 7 500 miles
Frequency: 7 500 miles
Diagnostic plug: No

Mid-Size SUVs

TOYOTA

4Runner

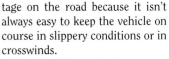

Exclusive

Derived from the Tacoma pickup, the 4Runner is the biggest sport utility vehicle sold by Toyota in Canada; in the United States, it has the Land Cruiser for company. Given it higher than average selling price and its very austere design features, this vehicle attracts a very specific clientele group: buyers who want to use it for work-related purposes and who know that it's nothing if not reliable.

MODEL RANGE

The 4Runner is only available in a single 4-door body style, in SR5, SR5 V6 and Limited trim. The base engine is a 3.4L V6 with 5-speed manual gearbox or 4-speed automatic. All-wheel drive is on demand, otherwise the 4Runner is a rear-wheel drive vehicle. The SR5 version is equipped with power steering, radio and tape deck, tilt steering wheel, manually adjustable mirrors and intermittent wipers. You have to go to the SR5 V6 if you want a standard V6. This model also receives cruise control, antilock braking, power locks and windows, heated exterior mirrors, air conditioning, light alloy wheels and CD player. The Limited version is equipped with all of the above, as well as an automatic transmission, leather-clad seats, theft-deterrent system and sunroof.

TECHNICAL FEATURES

The 4Runner isn't just a simple inheritor of the Tacoma pickup's genes, since it now only borrows its chassis, main suspension components and engines. It has its own unique body that's built of steel and mounted on an H-frame. The front suspension is a double wishbone setup and the rigid rear axle is suspended on coil springs and held in place by four longitudinal control arms. All models are equipped with disc and drum brakes and the SR5 V6 and Limited benefit from four-wheel antilock braking. On the Limited, you can go from RWD to AWD via shift-on-the-fly by simply pressing a button located on the dashboard.

PROS

+ STYLE. During the last face-lift, body stylistics got beefed up and the vehicle now has a more bulky, massive look and it also seems lower-slung on its wheels than before (optical illusion created by the running boards). This year again, its silhouette got a touch-up so it has an even more distinctive appearance.

+ CABIN SPACE. It's more generous with the longer wheelbase, so occupants can enjoy more leg room and access is easier with the lower floor threshold.

+ COCKPIT. The driver is comfy and benefits from better visibility than before.

+ REAR HATCH. It's definitely more convenient than the previous design, allowing easy access to the cargo hold that sits quite high off the ground.

+ QUALITY. Toyota's signature is written all over this vehicle. Construction craftsmanship is superb, fit and finish are super-tight and trim materials are lovelier in spite of a total lack of imagination when it comes to the over-all look.

+ OFF-ROAD MANEUVERS. Capabilities are excellent thanks to generous ground clearance and wide cornering and exit angles, even if the running boards sometimes get in the way when you're driving over really big mounds.

+ RIDE COMFORT. Front seats are now nicely shaped and cushion upholstery is plusher. Soundproofing is as effective as that of a car.

+ SATISFACTION. The high owner satisfaction rate indicates just how reliable this vehicle is and it keeps an excellent resale value, a rare fact on the used vehicle market.

CONS

- PRICE. It's steep, and it is a 4Runner after all, so we find the price unjustified for a vehicle that's more multi-purpose than a real SUV.

- HANDLING. Depending on the type of tire, it's not always a sure thing, due to the high center of gravity, flexible suspension that causes major wavering motion and big tires that sometimes bounce hard when you're not expecting it.

- FUEL CONSUMPTION. Such hefty vehicle weight translates into heavy fuel consumption comparable to that of rivals.

- STEERING. It's overly light due to over-assistance, which is an advantage on rough terrain since it reacts quickly, but it's a disadvantage on the road because it isn't always easy to keep the vehicle on course in slippery conditions or in crosswinds.

- MANUAL GEARBOX. It isn't a joy to use, since it doesn't jive with engine capabilities and clutch pedal travel is too long.

- RIDE COMFORT. It's never perfect with this type of vehicle that's jumpy and jittery due to the humungous tires that faithfully render road faults every mile of the way. Road and wind noise are constant and undesirable companions.

- ACCESS. Tall or bulky folks will have a tough time climbing up into the rear seats. Even with the lower floor threshold, the doors are narrow and the step is high.

CONCLUSION

The 4Runner's sturdiness and reliability have earned the trust of a considerable number of customers whose livelihood depends on their means of transportation. Its high cost is the price to pay for Toyota know-how when it comes to quality, but to its credit the 4Runner is fairly easy to resell given its renown and recognition.

4Runner

TOYOTA

RATING		
TOYOTA 4Runner		
CONCEPT :		**71%**
Technology :	80	
Safety :	60	
Interior space :	65	
Trunk volume :	70	
Quality/fit/finish :	80	
DRIVING :		**58%**
Cockpit :	80	
Performance :	35	
Handling :	50	
Steering :	75	
Braking :	50	
ORIGINAL EQUIPMENT :		**78%**
Tires :	75	
Headlights :	80	
Wipers :	80	
Rear defroster :	75	
Radio :	80	
COMFORT :		**70%**
Seats :	80	
Suspension :	65	
Sound level :	50	
Conveniences :	75	
Air conditioning :	80	
BUDGET :		**52%**
Price :	30	
Fuel economy :	45	
Insurance :	40	
Satisfaction :	85	
Depreciation :	60	
Overall rating :		**65.8%**

NEW FOR 2000

- 4-cylinder engines withdrawn.
- Optional leather trims on the SR5 models.
- Carpeting and radio/Cd player standard on all models.

Compare
Performance,
Specifications, Prices,
and Classification
at the end of this chapter.

EQUIPMENT

TOYOTA 4RUNNER	SR5	SR5 V6	LIMITED
Automatic transmission:	O	O	S
Cruise control:	O	S	S
Power steering:	S	S	S
Anti-lock brakes:	O	S	S
Traction control:	-	-	-
Air conditioning:	O	S	S
Leather:	O	O	S
AM/FM/radio-cassette:	S	SCd	SCd
Power door locks:	O	S	S
Power windows:	O	S	S
Tilt steering:	S	S	S
Dual adjustable mirrors:	SM	SEH	SEH
Alloy wheels:	-	S	S
Anti-theft system:	-	-	S

Colors

Exterior: White, Gray, Black, Teal, Blue, Blue steel, Silver, Jade.

Interior: *Cloth:* Gray, Oak.   *Leather:* Oak.

AT A GLANCE...

HISTORIC

Introduced in:	1985-1996.
Made in:	Tahara, Japan.

DEMOGRAPHICS

Model	Men/Wom.	Age	Married	College	Income $
4Runner	81/19 %	42	66 %	51 %	$ 40 000

INDEX

Safety:	60 %	Satisfaction:	85 %
Depreciation:	38 %	Insurance:	$ 1 285
Cost per mile:	$ 0.51	Number of dealers:	1 233

SALES

	Canada			USA		
Model	1997	1998	Result	1997	1998	Result
4Runner	7,546	7,116	- 5.7 %	128,496	118,484	- 7.8 %

MAINTENANCE REQUIRED BY WARRANTY

First revision:	Frequency:	Diagnostic plug:
3 000 miles	3 000 miles	No

Mid-Size SUVs

MID-SIZE SPORT UTILITY VEHICLES
PERFORMANCE

Model/ version	Type / timing valve / fuel system	Displacement cu in	Power hp @ rpm	Torque lb-ft @ rpm	Compres. ratio	Driving wheels / transmission	Final ratio	Acceler. 0-60 mph s	Standing 1/4 mile s	Standing 5/8 s	Passing 50-75 mph s	Braking 60-0 mph ft	Top speed mph	Lateral acceler. G	Noise level dBA	Fuel economy mpg City	Fuel economy mpg Highway	Fuel type Octane
CHEVROLET Blazer - GMC Jimmy - OLDSMOBILE Bravada																		
4x2	V6 4.3 OHV-12-SFI	262	190 @ 4400	250 @ 2800	9.2 :1	rear - M5	3.42	9.0	16.7	29.8	6.5	144	115	0.72	69	16	24	R 87
						rear - A4*	3.42	9.4	17.2	30.6	6.8	157	118	0.72	69	16	22	R 87
4x4	V6 4.3 OHV-12-SFI	262	190 @ 4400	250 @ 2800	9.2 :1	four - M5	3.42	9.6	17.2	30.4	7.0	148	109	0.72	69	15	21	R 87
						four - A4*	3.42	9.9	17.5	30.6	7.7	153	115	0.72	69	13	22	R 87
Bravada	V6 4.3 OHV-12-SFI	262	190 @ 4400	250 @ 2800	9.2 :1	rear/all -A4	3.70	10.7	17.8	30.6	7.7	154	112	0.72	69	15	20	R 87
DODGE Durango																		
4x2	V8 4.7 SOHC-16-MPSFI	287	235 @ 4800	295 @ 3200	9.3 :1	rear/ 4 - A4*	3.92	NA								-	-	R 87
	V8 5.2 OHV-16-MPSFI	318	230 @ 4400	300 @ 3200	9.1 :1	rear/ 4 - A4*	3.55	9.0	17.0	30.8	7.0	167	115	0.73	67	13	20	R 87
	V8 5.9 OHV-16-MPSFI	360	245 @ 4000	335 @ 3200	8.9 :1	rear/ 4 - A4	3.55	NA								12	17	R 87
4x4	V8 4.7 SOHC-16-MPSFI	287	235 @ 4800	295 @ 3200	9.3 :1	rear/ 4 - A4*	3.92	NA								-	-	R 87
	V8 5.2 OHV-16-MPSFI	318	230 @ 4400	300 @ 3200	9.1 :1	rear/ 4 - A4*	3.92	9.5	17.2	31.0	7.0	190	115	0.70	68	13	18	R 87
	V8 5.9 OHV-16-MPSFI	360	245 @ 4000	335 @ 3200	8.9 :1	rear/ 4 - A4*	3.92	NA								11	18	R 87
FORD Explorer - MERCURY Mountaineer																		
1)	V6 4.0 OHV-12-MPSFI	244	160 @ 4200	225 @ 2750	9.0 :1	rear/all - M5*	3.27	9.0	16.6	30.6	6.6	180	106	0.72	68	16	22	R 87
						rear/all - A5	3.27	NA										
2)	V6 4.0 SOHC-12-MPSFI	244	210 @ 5250	240 @ 3250	9.7 :1	rear/all - A5	3.55	8.5	16.4	29.5	6.1	187	109	0.73	68	16	22	R 87
3)	V8 5.0 OHV-16-MPSFI	302	215 @ 4200	288 @ 3300	9.0 :1	rear/all - A4	3.73	10.0	17.2	30.7	6.8	177	109	0.72	70	13	21	R 87

1) Std ExplorerXL, Sport 4X2, XLT.   2) Std Eddie Bauer, Limited & Mountaineer; opt. XL, Sport 4X2, XLT.   3) opt. Mountaineer, XLT, Eddie Bauer & Limited.

Model/ version	Type / timing valve / fuel system	Displacement cu in	Power hp @ rpm	Torque lb-ft @ rpm	Compres. ratio	Driving wheels / transmission	Final ratio	Acceler. 0-60 mph s	Standing 1/4 mile s	Standing 5/8 s	Passing 50-75 mph s	Braking 60-0 mph ft	Top speed mph	Lateral acceler. G	Noise level dBA	Fuel economy mpg City	Fuel economy mpg Highway	Fuel type Octane
ISUZU Rodeo																		
S/Amigo	L4 2.2 DOHC-24-MPFI	193	130 @ 5200	144 @ 4000	NA	rear/4 - M5												R 87
LS	V6 3.2 DOHC-24-MPFI	193	205 @ 5400	214 @ 3000	9.1 :1	rear/4 - A4	4.3	9.7	17.0	31.7	6.9	154	103	0.72	68-70	17	21	R 87
JEEP Grand Cherokee																		
base	L6 4.0 OHV-12-MPSFI	242	195 @ 4600	230 @ 3000	8.8 :1	rear/4 - A4	3.73	9.5	17.0	30.4	6.9	131	118	0.75	66-72	15	22	R 87
option	V8 4.7 SOHC-16-MPSFI	288	235 @ 4800	295 @ 3200	9.3 :1	rear/4 - A4	3.73	8.5	16.4	29.6	6.2	134	124	0.75	65-72	14	20	R 87
LAND ROVER Discovery																		
Series II	V8 4.0 OHV-16-MPSFI	240	188 @ 4750	250 @ 2600	9.35 :1	all - A4	3.54	NA								13	16	S 91
LEXUS RX 300																		
RX 300	V6 3.0 DOHC-24-MPSFI	183	220 @ 5800	222 @ 4400	10.5 :1	front - A4	3.080	9.5	16.6	30.2	6.5	131	112	0.71	66-72	18	21	R 87
RX 300	V6 3.0 DOHC-24-MPSFI	183	220 @ 5800	222 @ 4400	10.5 :1	all - A4	3.291	10.4	17.2	29.9	6.7	144	112	0.71	66-72	17	20	R 87
MERCEDES-BENZ M-Class																		
ML320	V6 3.2 SOHC-18-SFI	195	215 @ 5500	233 @ 3000	10.0 :1	all - A5	3.69	9.0	17.0	30.5	7.2	134	112*	0.75	65-70	16	20	S 91
ML430	V8 4.3 SOHC-24-SFI	260	268 @ 5500	288 @ 3000	10.0 :1	all - A5	3.46	8.0					112*			15	19	S 91
ML55 AMG	V8 5.5 SOHC-24-SFI	332	342 @ 5500	376 @ 3000	10.5 :1	all - A5	3.46	6.9					144			14	18	S 91
NISSAN Pathfinder - INFINITI QX4																		
base	V6* 3.3 SOHC-12-MPSFI	200	168 @ 4800	196 @ 2800	8.9 :1	rear/4 - M5*	4.636	10.3	17.3	31.4	7.0	154	103	0.68	64-70	15	19	R 87
QX4	V6* 3.3 SOHC-12-MPSFI	200	168 @ 4800	196 @ 2800	8.9 :1	rear/4 - A4	4.636	11.6	18.4	33.7	9.0	148	100	0.68	65-70	14	19	R 87
TOYOTA 4Runner																		
SR5 V6	V6* 3.4 DOHC-24-MPSFI	206	183 @ 4800	217 @ 3600	9.6 :1	rear/4 - M5*	3.91	10.0	17.2	31.1	7.0	141	103	0.75	68	16	19	R 87
Limited	V6* 3.4 DOHC-24-MPSFI	206	183 @ 4800	217 @ 3600	9.6 :1	rear/4 - A4*	3.91	11.5	18.3	32.8	8.2	148	100	0.75	68	17	20	R 87

MID-SIZE SPORT UTILITY VEHICLES
SPECIFICATIONS

Model	Version Trim	Traction	Body/ Deats	Wheel base in	Lgthx Width x Hght in x inx in	Curb weight lb	Susp. ft/rr	Brake ft/rr	type	Steering ø ft / turns number	Fuel tank gal	dimensions	Standard tires make	model	Standard powertrain	99 Price msrp $
CHEVROLET - GMC	General warranty: 3-years / 36,000 miles; antipollution: 5-years / 50,000 miles; perforation corrosion: 6-years / 100,000 miles. Road assistance.															
Blazer-Jimmy	base	4x2	2dr.wgn.4	100.5	176.8x67.8x64.9	3519	ih/rl	dc/ABS	pwr.ball	34.8 3.38	19.0		Michelin	XW4	V6/4.3/A4	18,995
Blazer-Jimmy	base	4x2	4dr.wgn.5	107.0	183.3x67.8x64.3	3673	ih/rl	dc/ABS	pwr.ball	36.6 3.38	18.0		Michelin	XW4	V6/4.3/A4	24,095
Blazer-Jimmy	base	4x4	2dr.wgn.4	100.5	176.8x67.8x64.5	3849	it/rl	dc/ABS	pwr.ball	35.2 2.97	19.0		Michelin	XW4	V6/4.3/A4	21,995
Blazer-Jimmy	base	4x4	4dr.wgn.5	107.0	183.3x67.8x64.2	4041	it/rl	dc/ABS	pwr.ball	39.5 2.97	18.0		Michelin	XW4	V6/4.3/A4	26,095
GMC	Envoy	4x4	4dr.wgn.5	107.0	183.3x67.8x64.2	4078	it/rl	dc/ABS	pwr.ball	39.5 2.97	18.0		Michelin	XW4	V6/4.3/A4	34,125
DODGE	General warranty: 3-years / 36,000 miles; surface rust: 3-years; perforation: 7-years / 100,000 miles; roadside assistance: 3-years /36,000 miles.															
Durango	SLT	4x2	4dr.wgn.5-6	115.9	193.3X71.5X71.0	4259	ih/rl	dc/dr/ABS	repwr.r&p.	39.03.15	25.0		235/75R15	Goodyear Wrangler RT/SV8/4.7/A4		26,580
Durango	SLT	4x2	4dr.wgn.5-6	115.9	193.3X71.5X71.0	4394	ih/rl	dc/dr/ABS	repwr.r&p.	39.03.15	25.0		235/75R15	Goodyear Wrangler RT/SV8/5.2/A4		-
Durango	SLT	4x4	4dr.wgn.5-7	115.9	193.3X71.5X72.9	4512	it/rl	dc/dr/ABS	repwr.ball	39.03.15	25.0		235/75R15	Goodyear Wrangler RT/SV8/4.7/A4		28,580
Durango	SLT	4x4	4dr.wgn.5-7	115.9	193.3X71.5X72.9	4656	it/rl	dc/dr/ABS	repwr.ball	39.03.15	25.0		235/75R15	Goodyear Wrangler RT/SV8/5.2/A4		-
Durango	SLT	4x4	4dr.wgn.5-7	115.9	193.3X71.5X72.9	4678	it/rl	dc/dr/ABS	repwr.ball	39.03.15	25.0		235/75R15	Goodyear Wrangler RT/SV8/5.9/A4		-
FORD	General warranty, antipollution & battery: 3-years / 36,000 miles; corrosion perforation: 5-years / unlimited.															
Explorer	Sport	4x2	2dr.wgn.4/5	101.7	180.8x70.2x67.1	3675	it/rl	dc/ABS	pwr.r&p.	34,7 3.5	17.5		235/75R15	Firestone Wilderness	V6/4.0/M5	20,590
Explorer	XL	4x2	5dr.wgn.4/5	111.5	190.7x70.2x67.1	3891	it/rl	dc/ABS	pwr.r&p.	37.3 3.5	21.0		225/70R15	Firestone Wilderness	V6/4.0/M5	22,500
Explorer	Eddie Bauer	4x4	5dr.wgn.4/5	111.5	190.7x70.2x67.5	4145	it/rl	dc/ABS	pwr.r&p.	37.3 3.5	21.0		255/70R16	Firestone Wilderness	V6/4.0/A5	33,950
Explorer	Limited	4x4	5dr.wgn.4/5	111.5	190.7x70.2x67.5	4244	it/rl	dc/ABS	pwr.r&p.	37.3 3.5	21.0		255/70R16	Firestone Wilderness	V6/4.0/A5	34,650
ISUZU	General warranty: 3-years / 36,000 miles; powertrain: 5-years / 60,000 miles ; perforation: 6-years / 100,000miles.															
Rodeo	S	4x4	4dr.wgn. 5	106.4	183.2x70.4x66.1	3853	ih/rh	dc/ABS	pwr.r&p.	38.4 3.64	21.1		235/75R15	Bridgestone Dueller 684	V6/3.2/M5	24,185
Rodeo	LS	4x4	4dr.wgn. 5	106.4	183.2x70.4x66.4	3929	ih/rh	dc/ABS	pwr.r&p.	38.4 3.64	21.1		245/70R16	Bridgestone Dueller 684	V6/3.2/A4	26,985
JEEP	General warranty: 3-years / 36,000 miles; surface rust 1-year / 12,000 miles; perforation 7-years / 100,000 miles; roadside assistance 3-years / 36,000 miles.															
Grand Cherokee	Laredo	4x2	4dr.wgn. 5	105.9	181.5x72.3x69.4	3739	rh/rh	dc/ABS	pwr.ball	36.4 2.94	20.6		225/75R16	Goodyear Wrangler ST	L6/4.0/A4	26,520
Grand Cherokee	Limited	4x2	4dr.wgn. 5	105.9	181.5x72.3x69.4	3814	rh/rh	dc/ABS	pwr.ball	36.4 2.94	20.6		245/70R16	Goodyear Eagle LS	V8/4.7/A4	32,285
Grand Cherokee	Laredo	4x4	4dr.wgn. 5	105.9	181.5x72.3x69.4	3915	rh/rh	dc/ABS	pwr.ball	36.4 2.94	20.6		225/75R16	Goodyear Wrangler ST	L6/4.0/A4	28,490
Grand Cherokee	Limited	4x4	4dr.wgn. 5	105.9	181.5x72.3x69.4	4050	rh/rh	dc/ABS	pwr.ball	36.4 2.94	20.6		245/70R16	Goodyear Eagle LS	V8/4.7/A4	34,715
LAND ROVER	General warranty: 4-years / 50,000 miles; corrosion perforation: 6-years / unlimited mileage & roadside assistance.															
Discovery	Series II	4x4	4dr.wgn. 5	100.0	185.2x74.4x76.4	4575	rh/rh	dc/ABS	pwr.worm	39.0 3.5	24.5		255/65HR16	-	V8/4.0/A4	34,775
LEXUS	General warranty: 4-years / 50,000 miles; powertrain: 6-years / 70,000 miles; corrosion perforation: 6-years / unlimited mileage & roadside assistance.															
RX 300	base	4x2	4dr.wgn. 5	103.0	180.1x71.5x65.7	3900	ih/ih	dc/ABS	pwr.r&p.	41.3 2.6	17.2		225/70R16	Goodyear Eagle LS	V6/3.0/A4	32,500
RX 300	base	4x4	4dr.wgn. 5	103.0	180.1x71.5x65.7	3693	ih/ih	dc/ABS	pwr.r&p.	41.3 2.6	17.2		225/70R16	Bridgestone Dueller HT	V6/3.0/A4	33,900
MERCEDES-BENZ	General warranty: 4-years / 50,000 miles with 24 hours road assistance.															
ML320	Classic	4x4	4dr.wgn. 5/7	111.0	180.6x72.2x69.9	4200	ih/ih	dc/ABS	pwr.r&p.	37.1 3.62	18.5		255/65R16	General Grabberst	V6/3.2/A5	35,545
ML320	Elegance	4x4	4dr.wgn. 5/7	111.0	180.6x72.2x69.9	4237	ih/ih	dc/ABS	pwr.r&p.	37.1 3.62	18.5		255/65R16	General Grabberst	V6/3.2/A5	-
ML430	430	4x4	4dr.wgn. 5/7	111.0	180.6x72.2x69.9	4431	ih/ih	dc/ABS	pwr.r&p.	37.1 3.62	18.5		275/55R17	General Grabberst	V8/4.3/A5	44,345
ML55	AMG	4x4	4dr.wgn. 5/7	111.0	180.6x72.2x69.9	4652	ih/ih	dc/ABS	pwr.r&p.	37.1 3.62	23.8		285/50R18	-	V8/5.5/A5	-
MERCURY	General warranty, antipollution & battery: 3-years / 36,000 miles; corrosion perforation: 5-years / unlimited.															
Mountaineer	Base	4x2	5dr.wgn.4/5	111.5	190.7x70.2x67.5	3929	it/rl	dc/ABS	pwr.r&p.	37.3 3.5	21.0		255/70R16	Firestone Wilderness	V6/4.0/A5	27,780
Mountaineer	XLT	4x4	5dr.wgn.4/5	111.5	190.7x70.2x67.5	4149	it/rl	dc/ABS	pwr.r&p.	37.3 3.5	21.0		255/70R16	Firestone Wilderness	V6/4.0/A5	29,780
NISSAN	General warranty: 3-years / 50,000 miles; powertrain: 6-years / 60,000 miles; perforation corrosion & antipollution: 6-years / unlimited.															
Pathfinder	XE	4x4	4dr.wgn.5	106.3	178.3x68.7x67.1	3975	ih/rh	dc/dr/ABS	pwr.r&p.	42.0 3.2	21.1		265/70R15	Bridgestone Dueller HT	V6/3.3/M5	26,669
Pathfinder	SE	4x4	4dr.wgn.5	106.3	178.3x68.7x67.1	4065	ih/rh	dc/dr/ABS	pwr.r&p.	42.0 3.2	21.1		265/70R15	Bridgestone Dueller HT	V6/3.3/M5	29,769
Pathfinder	LE	4x4	4dr.wgn.5	106.3	178.3x68.7x67.1	4034	ih/rh	dc/dr/ABS	pwr.r&p.	42.0 3.2	21.1		265/70R15	Bridgestone Dueller HT	V6/3.3/A4	33,469
OLDSMOBILE	General warranty: 3-years / 36,000 miles; antipollution: 5-years / 50,000 miles; perforation corrosion: 6-years / 100,000 miles. Roadside assistance.															
Bravada	base	4x4	4dr.wgn.5	107.0	183.7x67.8x63.2	4050	it/rl	dc/ABS	pwr.ball.	39.5 2.97	18.6		235/70R15	Uniroyal	-	V6/4.3/A4	31,668
TOYOTA	General warranty: 3-years / 36,000 miles; powertrain 5-years / 60,000 miles; corrosion, perforation: 5-years / unlimited.															
4Runner	SR5 V6	4x4	4dr.wgn. 5	105.3	178.7x68.1x69.3	3884	ih/rh	dc/dr/ABS	pwr.r&p.	37.4 3.5	15.4		265/70R16	Bridgestone Dueler H/T	V6/3.4/M5	27,028
4Runner	Limited	4x4	4dr.wgn. 5	105.3	178.7x70.9x69.3	3975	ih/rh	dc/dr/ABS	pwr.r&p.	37.4 3.5	15.4		265/70R16	Bridgestone Dueler H/T	V6/3.4/A4	36,228

Notes: 1) Tire makes and models are provided solely as an indication; they are subject to change without prior notice from the automobile manufacturers.
2) See the 2000 price list at the back of this edition.

Mid-Size SUVs

MID-SIZE SPORT UTILITY VEHICLES
CLASSIFICATION

OUR CLASSIFICATION

Rank	Models	Concept	Driving	Equipment	Comfort	Budget	Rating
1	**MERCEDES M-Class**	78	69	**79**	**75**	49	**70.0 %**
2	JEEP Grand Cherokee	78	**70**	**79**	74	39	68.0 %
3	INFINITI QX4	76	62	78	73	45	66.8 %
4	DODGE Durango	79	56	75	74	49	66.6 %
5	ISUZU Rodeo	76	61	76	64	**55**	66.4 %
5	LEXUS RX 300	**80**	59	77	71	45	66.4 %
6	TOYOTA 4Runner	71	58	78	70	52	65.8 %
7	FORD Explorer	77	55	77	66	53	65.6 %
8	MERCURY Mountaineer	72	57	75	70	52	65.2 %
8	NISSAN Pathfinder	72	57	75	70	52	65.2 %
9	GM Blazer-Jimmy	73	58	74	67	52	64.8 %
10	OLDS Bravada	73	57	74	67	52	64.6 %

YOUR CLASSIFICATION

Rank	Models	98 Sales
1	**FORD Explorer**	**431,488**
2	JEEP Grand Cherokee	260,875
3	CHEVROLET Blazer	219,710
4	DODGE Durango	156,923
5	TOYOTA 4Runner	118,484
6	GMC Jimmy	73,301
7	NISSAN Pathfinder	68,003
8	ISUZU Rodeo	63,627
9	MERCURY Mountaineer	47,595
10	MERCEDES M-Class	43,134
11	LEXUS RX 300	42,191
12	OLDS Bravada	30,202
13	INFINITI QX4	20,055

Not classified:
LAND ROVER Discovery (NA)

NOTES

Mid-Size
SUVs

Comparative Test

FULL-SIZE SPORT UTILITY VEHICLES

See their performance, their specifications, their price and their classification at the end of this chapter.

AMG Hummer

CHEVROLET-GMC

FORD-LINCOLN

ISUZU Trooper

LAND ROVER Range Rover

TOYOTA - LEXUS

Full-size SUVs

Extremist

When the Hummer took over from the Jeep in the ranks of the American army, there could be no doubt that sooner or later, the public would clambser for the right of using it too. Been there, done that - but as simplistic and affordable as the Jeep was, as elaborate and expensive the Hummer is. Selling at the same price as a big Mercedes, only fanatical sport utility buyers will venture onto this extreme terrain.

MODEL RANGE

The Hummer is an all-terrain vehicle that comes with either a soft or hardtop. This pickup truck comes in either a 2 or a 4-door cab model, with short or long wheelbase, whereas the station wagon is equipped with 5 doors.

The 6.5L Diesel V8 engine comes standard, linked to a General Motors 4-speed automatic and a high and low-torque transfer case. The optional 6.5L turbodiesel V8 delivers 195 hp. Standard equipment includes power steering, AM/FM radio and tape deck and intermittent-function wipers.

Other items are also available as extras: air conditioning, cruise control, ABS, power windows and locks and alloy wheels. Depending on your needs, you can also add on a 6-ton winch and a system that regulates tire pressure while travelling, either to compensate for a minor flat or to increase traction on rough terrain.

TECHNICAL FEATURES

The anodized aluminum body is assembled with rivets and Cybond glue and it's mounted on a robust rolled steel-section chassis. The engine is mounted above the longitudinal section so as to offer maximum ground clearance, while the front and rear differential supports are installed symmetrically at both extremities. The hood is made of polyester resin reinforced with fiberglass, whereas the doors are made of steel. The fully independent suspension consists of a double wishbone setup and braking is assured by four discs mounted on the differential extremities. The vehicle is equipped with full-time all-wheel drive as well as front and rear Torsen differentials. The tires are unique, for they can be driven in an off-center fashion via a whole series of reduction pinions, to free up the underside of the vehicle as much as possible. The huge tires can be fitted with optional interior tires made of solid rubber to provide greater mobility and reduce external tire damage in the event of a blow-out.

OUTSTANDING

++ OFF-ROAD CAPABILITIES. This vehicle is incredibly versatile, since it can climb 42-inch steps, drive around in 27 inches of water or mud and climb very steep hills. It's too big to maneuver nimbly in the bush, but on open terrain, it can get over just about any obstacle in its way, slowly but surely.

PROS

+ STYLE. This vehicle has a very military look, so it sure gets noticed in urban settings and its sheer hulk gives it center stage, so to speak. The rings up on the hood sure inspire lots of questions from onlookers who have trouble believing they're used when parachuting the vehicle. Its multi-purpose, massive shape isn't exactly graceful, but it's functional and you know it'll never go out of style...

+ VERSATILITY. It's amazing, since besides never going out of style, it can go just about anywhere. Besides American army uses, its mission is to get to really isolated spots, so it's an ideal vehicle for police forces, rescue teams of all ilks and electric power or telephone companies.

+ DRIVING. It's really easy to drive, so almost anyone can get behind the wheel of this beast. Vehicle demeanor is smooth and predictable and controls are stripped down to a basic minimum.

+ TRACTION. The full-time all-wheel drive makes it the ideal vehicle for hauling heavy loads or trailers.

+ QUALITY. This vehicle is built according to stringent military standards, which explains its awesome reliability and tough durability. The builder doesn't foresee reconditioning these vehicles for another 10 years, according to typical army practice...

CONS

- BUDGET. It costs a mint, due to strict building standards and top-notch quality and so not everyone can own one and gas bills are never cheap.

- VEHICLE SIZE. It's really very wide, so you have to drive it as though it were a tank when getting around in the city and forget about looking for a parking spot. Besides, visibility is problematic in just about every direction with both rooftops, since the roof supports are thick and there are big blind spots.

- PERFORMANCES. They're limited, since accelerations and pickup are very laborious, so you have to drive like a truck driver. Yet, on the highway, it can easily maintain a 75 mph cruising speed that scares compact cars to death...

- CONVENIENCE FEATURES. They're not too hot, since the cabin can only accomodate four passengers in "capsules" of space that are gobbled up by the enormous center console. At the rear, the cargo hold doesn't jive with the humungous dimensions of this beast. There aren't any storage spots and access to the cabin, engine and cargo hold is acrobatic, due to the high ground clearance and there are no standard running boards to make life easier.

CONCLUSION

The Hummer is one of the most extraordinary products on four wheels. It's the ultimate utility vehicle on the current market and its price matches its exclusive manufacturing features and performance capabilities. To appreciate it to the fullest possible extent, users had better know exactly what they've let themselves in for - otherwise it well might be a big and clumsy problem.

RATING
AMG Hummer

CONCEPT : — 81%
- Technology : 85
- Safety : 80
- Interior space : 80
- Trunk volume : 80
- Quality/fit/finish : 80

DRIVING : — 38%
- Cockpit : 75
- Performance : 0
- Handling : 30
- Steering : 70
- Braking : 15

ORIGINAL EQUIPMENT : — 62%
- Tires : 90
- Headlights : 80
- Wipers : 60
- Rear defroster : 0
- Radio : 80

COMFORT : — 50%
- Seats : 70
- Suspension : 50
- Sound level : 20
- Conveniences : 30
- Air conditioning : 80

BUDGET : — 43%
- Price : 0
- Fuel economy : 20
- Insurance : 50
- Satisfaction : 85
- Depreciation : 60

Overall rating : 54.8%

NEW FOR 2000

- No major changes.

Compare Performance, Specifications, Prices, and Classification at the end of this chapter.

EQUIPMENT

AM GENERAL Hummer	2dr. p-u.	4dr. sdn.	4dr. con.	4dr. wgn.
Automatic transmission:	S	S	S	S
Cruise control:	O	O	O	O
Power steering:	S	S	S	S
Anti-lock brakes:	O	O	O	O
Traction control:	O	O	O	O
Air conditioning:	S	S	S	S
Leather:	S	S	S	S
AM/FM/radio-cassette:	-	-	-	-
Power door locks:	S	S	S	S
Power windows:	S	S	S	S
Tilt steering:	S	S	S	S
Dual adjustable mirrors:	-	-	-	-
Alloy wheels:	S	S	S	S
Anti-theft system:	O	O	O	O

Colors
Exterior: Red, Black, Yellow, Metallic Silver, Green, White.

Interior: Tan, Gray, Black.

AT A GLANCE...

HISTORIC
- Introduced in: 1985.
- Made in: South Bend, Indiana, USA.

DEMOGRAPHICS

Model	Men/Wom.	Age	Married	College	Income $
Hummer	100/0 %	48	80 %	35 %	$ 110 000

INDEX
- Safety: 90 %
- Depreciation: 40 %
- Cost per mile: $ 1.00
- Satisfaction: 83 %
- Insurance: $ 1 175
- Number of dealers: 40

SALES

Model	Canada 1997	1998	Result	USA 1997	1998	Result
Hummer	NA					

MAINTENANCE REQUIRED BY WARRANTY
- First revision: 3 000 miles
- Frequency: 6 000 miles
- Diagnostic plug: No

When Ford introduced the Expedition and its more luxurious counterpart, the Lincoln Navigator, no one dreamed how these mastodons' sales would soar. The perfect evidence that in North American societies what's big is what's good, these vehicles simply followed in the footsteps left by GM's Suburban, the true precursor of this kind of vehicle.

Dinosaurs

MODEL RANGE

This big four-door wagon comes in RWD or AWD. It's sold in two trim levels, XLT and Eddie Bauer, and can accomodate from 5 to 8 passengers, depending on cabin layout. The standard engine is a 4.6L V8 paired up with a 4-speed automatic transmission. A 5.4L V8 powerplant is available as an option. The Expedition's original equipment is, in a nutshell, reasonable considering the going price. Ford has even added standard cruise control on the XLT, a feature it didn't benefit from in 1998. Illuminated running boards are listed among the options.

TECHNICAL FEATURES

Just as the Chevrolet Tahoe is inspired from the former C/K pickup, the Expedition is a «spin-off» from the F-150 pickup. It has the F-150 ladder chassis frame and front end design, right up to the B pillar. The steel unibody is mounted to the chassis via rubber insulator components. The front suspension is identical to that of the F-150 and uses a combination of unequal-length control arms fitted with coil springs on the RWD models and torsion bars on the AWD models. But the rear suspension is different since the rigid rear axle is supported by five control ams and suspended on coil springs. An air suspension with ground clearance control is sold as an extra on the AWD models. Four-wheel disc brakes benefit from all-wheel ABS. The driver can switch from RWD to AWD by touching a power switch located on the dash. There are various settings: RWD, AWD H, AWD L and Auto. The automatic mode sends power to the front wheels as soon as there's rear wheel slippage, without any interference from the driver.

PROS

+ STYLE. The Expedition has a bold and beautiful appearance. The neat, well-proportioned body design makes the vehicle seem trimmer than it actually is. From a distance, without a scale reference, it's easy to think you're looking at an Explorer, especially from the rear, since both vehicles have a similar rear end design.

+ CABIN SPACE. From five to eight passengers can climb aboard an Expedition. Naturally, luggage space becomes more limited depending on how many occupants there are, but let's say, you have a more than comfortable margin...

+ RIDE COMFORT. This SUV is super comfy. The rear end is less jumpy than that on its rivals that have bouncier leaf springs. The AWD version has a bit more firm demeanor, but it doesn't really affect comfort. Nice-design seats are really comfortable and sound damp-ening does the trick quite nicely.

+ MANEUVERABILITY. The Expedition has a steer angle diameter that's 3 ft less than the F-150, so it handles well. Ford engineers put a lot of thought into this, after hearing female buyers speak up and state how important this feature is.

+ HANDLING. The front suspension really keeps this beauty on track, even in crosswinds or on poorly kept-up roads.

+ REAR DOOR. It's a breeze to open or close with the well-adjusted door jacks and hinged window that provides access to the luggage hold without having to lift the hatch door.

+ STORAGE SPACE. There are lots of handy storage spots inside the Expedition. The center console and door side-pockets hold lots of stuff, which makes up for the small-ish glove compartment.

+ NICE FEATURES: We really liked the simple, easy-to-use control that engages wheel traction, now offering an automatic AWD mode. Also, we'd like to mention two neat options: illuminated running boards that provide safe boarding and the new adjustable pedal.

CONS

-BUDGET. It takes a lot of cash to buy and operate this vehicle, since average fuel consumption is about 13 mpg. In fact, only the insurance premium seems fairly reasonable in this budget bonanza of more or less expensive items.

- VEHICLE SIZE. The big, brawny Expedition isn't easy to maneuver on narrow downtown streets and parking in those tiny allotted spots is no picnic.

- PERFORMANCES. The 4.6L V8 feels wimpy, due to hefty vehicle weight. Accelerations and pickup are more of a chore and if you have a lot of people to take here and there or if you have to pull heavy loads, the 5.4L V8 is a better choice.

- FIT AND FINISH. Some finish details could be neater. For example, some of the plastic inserts in the inner door panels seem to fit rather poorly.

- ACCESS. Climbing aboard 4X4 versions is no easy matter, even with all the handles and such, since the vehicle sits so high. Which makes the optional runningboards a real must.

- THE THIRD SEATBENCH. Passengers who have to sit on the remote rear seatbench won't be any too comfy. It's tough getting there, the seatbench is less thickly upholstered than the middle seatbench and it's flat as a pancake.

- NO DIESEL? Ford should offer a diesel engine as an option for this big brute. It would increase sales in parts of the world where gas doesn't come cheap.

CONCLUSION

Given their capabilities, these vehicles aren't very expensive to operate as long as gas prices stay within a reasonable range - if not, these dinosaurs are the first to suffer at the hands of a whole new environment.

RATING
FORD Expedition

CONCEPT : 85%
Technology : 80
Safety : 75
Interior space : 100
Trunk volume : 90
Quality/fit/finish : 80

DRIVING : 53%
Cockpit : 80
Performance : 45
Handling : 35
Steering : 75
Braking : 30

ORIGINAL EQUIPMENT : 78%
Tires : 85
Headlights : 70
Wipers : 80
Rear defroster : 70
Radio : 85

COMFORT : 71%
Seats : 75
Suspension : 75
Sound level : 50
Conveniences : 75
Air conditioning : 80

BUDGET : 46%
Price : 0
Fuel economy : 20
Insurance : 70
Satisfaction : 80
Depreciation : 60

Overall rating : 66.6%

NEW FOR 2000

- New running boards on the Eddie Bauer version.
- New hidden radio antenna, heated sideview mirrors.
- Improved center console with cupholders.
- Optional side air bags.
- Optional navigation system.

Compare
Performance,
Specifications, Prices,
and Classification
at the end of this chapter.

EQUIPMENT

FORD Expedition	XLT 4x2 4dr.	XLT 4x4 4dr.	E.Bauer 4x2 4dr.	E.Bauer 4x4 4dr.
Automatic transmission:	S	S	S	S
Cruise control:	S	S	S	S
Power steering:	S	S	S	S
Anti-lock brakes:	S	S	S	S
Traction control:	-	-	-	-
Air conditioning:	SM	SM	SA	SA
Leather:	-	-	S	S
AM/FM/radio-cassette:	S	S	SCd	SCd
Power door locks:	S	S	S	S
Power windows:	S	S	S	S
Tilt steering:	S	S	S	S
Dual adjustable mirrors:	SE	SE	SE	SE
Alloy wheels:	O	O	S	S
Anti-theft system:	S	S	S	S

Colors

Exterior: Gold, Green, Red, Blue, Silver, White, Black.

Interior: Medium graphite, Dark graphite, Brown.

AT A GLANCE...

HISTORIC
Introduced in: 1997.
Made in: Wayne, Michigan, USA.

DEMOGRAPHICS

Model	Men/Wom.	Age	Married	College	Income $
Expedition	68/32%	42	72%	40 %	$ 55 000

INDEX
Safety: 75 %   Satisfaction: 78 %
Depreciation: 38 %   Insurance: $ 950
Cost per mile: $ 0.64   Number of dealers: 5 200

SALES

Model	Canada 1997	1998	Result	USA 1997	1998	Result
Expedition	7,977	6,660	- 16.5 %	225,703	214,524	- 4.5 %

MAINTENANCE REQUIRED BY WARRANTY
First revision: 5 000 miles
Frequency: 6 months / 5 000 miles
Diagnostic plug: Yes

Full-size SUVs

This year GM is revamping its sport utility vehicles, basing them on the make's pickups, which were revised last year. No big surprises in store: the front fascia is virtually unchanged and the mechanical system is exactly the same.

MODEL RANGE

GM now offers five variants of these big station wagons. The Tahoe, Yukon and Suburban remain unchanged. Besides the rather stripped-down-to-essentials base versions, Chevrolet offers three other trim levels for the Tahoe: LS, LT and Sport and two others for the Suburban: SL, SLE and SLT. Yet two new luxury models are now part of this already wide range of products: the GMC Yukon Denali and the Cadillac Escalade, the first mass-produced truck bearing the GM cream of the crop division crest. These two vehicles are lavishly furbished clones of the 4-door Tahoe-Yukon's. They share the same 5.7L 255-hp V8 gas engine. The Denali and Escalade are all-wheel drive vehicles and they're equipped with an AutoTrac transfer box with a 4X4 automatic mode. The Tahoe-Yukon and Suburban 4X4's come with a conventional transfer box with floor shifter, except on the LT and SLT equipped with standard AutoTrac. 4X2 Tahoe-Yukon and Suburban versions are also available, as well as 2-door versions. The last Tahoe-Yukon and Suburban can be equiped with Vortec V8 4800, 5300 and 6000. These vehicles are equipped with a 4-speed automatic transmission, variable assist power steering, dual air bags, ABS system and intermittent wipers. More elaborate models benefit from climate control, cruise control, power windows, tilt steering wheel, remote-control mirrors and alloy rims.

TECHNICAL FEATURES

These utility vehicles share the platform inspired by the former C/K pickup trucks. The Tahoe, Yukon, Denali and Escalade have a body 12 inches shorter than that of the Suburban. The galvanized steel body sits on a ladder chassis made up of side-frames and 5 crossmembers. They're very boxy-looking and the air displacement surface is huge, yielding a telltale drag coefficient of 0.45. The fully independent suspension consists of A-arms up front and, for the 4X2's, coil springs, while 4X4's are fitted with torsion bars. At the rear, the rigid rear axle is suspended from semi-elliptic leaf springs. There are front disc brakes and rear drum brakes, linked to ABS.

PROS

+ CABIN AND LUGGAGE SPACE. These vehicles are really spacious. The Tahoe can welcome six passengers aboard, and the Suburban, up to nine...not to mention their luggage!

+ PRICE. Some versions of these vehicles are offered at competitive prices compared to more modest vehicles like the Blazer, Grand Cherokee or Explorer.

+ PERFORMANCES. With 255 hp under the hood, the Yukon-Tahoe's achieve performances akin to those of big passenger car sedans. That's why GM created a model for police fleets, to replace the defunct Caprice.

+ HANDLING. It's much more precise than on previous generations thanks to a rigid chassis and improved suspension capabilities.

+ RIDE COMFORT. These big beauties are comfy on the highway at cruising speed, since the suspension is civilized in such circumstances and the noise level is acceptable.

+ DRIVING PLEASURE. These truck-like vehicles will appeal to true-blue truck fans, with their smooth controls and neat-design cabin interior. The dashboard isn't a model of ergonomics, but it holds a lot of instruments and storage compartments, not to mention the big compartment between the front seats that even includes a writing tablet!

+ CAPABILITIES. These utility vehicles can boast of impressive load and trailering capabilities (8 000 lbs), when equipped with hitching devices recommended by the automaker.

+ FINISH DETAILS. The upper-crust models have a tight, clean look and fit, but you have to check off a lot of items on the options list if you want to have a complete array of equipment.

+ OUTWARD VIEW. The driver sits nice and high, the frame belt is low and there are big mirrors, so over-all visibility is super.

+ HANDLING. These vehicles are safe, but they don't handle like a car, not with the high perched center of gravity and more sluggish personality.

CONS

- FUEL CONSUMPTION. The V8 engines are gas-guzzlers. Even the diesel engine can't seem to slake its thirst.

- MANEUVERABILITY. The imposing hulk of these vehicles and especially the wide steer angle are definite drawbacks in city streets.

- SEATS. Cushions are short and they don't provide much lateral support because they're terribly flat. With the leather trim seats on some models, there's even less support!

- DISCOMFORT. These vehicles can't hide their humble origins on poor road surfaces. The rear end slips and slides quite a bit and road noise from the frame builds up over the miles.

- TO BE IMPROVED UPON. The two side swing doors are standard equipment and really make luggage hold access easy, but they do block rearward view. But on the other hand, the optional rear door with swing panel isn't much better, since once it's open, it cuts you off from the luggage loading area. But it does provide better visibility.

CONCLUSION

At long last, these big GMs have fallen into step with their competitors. Their modern engines and much more rigid bodies make them a lot more roadworthy.

Seniors

RATING
CHEVROLET-GMC Tahoe-Yukon, Suburban

CONCEPT : 77%
Technology :	75
Safety :	75
Interior space :	85
Trunk volume :	75
Quality/fit/finish :	75

DRIVING : 57%
Cockpit :	80
Performance :	40
Handling :	40
Steering :	75
Braking :	50

ORIGINAL EQUIPMENT : 75%
Tires :	75
Headlights :	80
Wipers :	75
Rear defroster :	70
Radio :	75

COMFORT : 68%
Seats :	70
Suspension :	70
Sound level :	50
Conveniences :	70
Air conditioning :	80

BUDGET : 46%
Price :	20
Fuel economy :	20
Insurance :	55
Satisfaction :	80
Depreciation :	55

Overall rating : 64.6%

NEW FOR 2000

• Revamped vehicles based on the pickups introduced last year.

Compare Performance, Specifications, Prices, and Classification at the end of this chapter.

EQUIPMENT

CHEVROLET Tahoe GMC Yukon	base	LS SLE	LT SLT
Automatic transmission:	S	S	S
Cruise control:	O	S	S
Power steering:	S	S	S
Anti-lock brakes:	S	S	S
Traction control:	-	-	-
Air conditioning:	O	S	S
Leather:	-	-	S
AM/FM/radio-cassette:	O	S	SCd
Power door locks:	O	O	O
Power windows:	-	S	S
Tilt steering:	O	S	S
Dual adjustable mirrors:	SM	SE	SE
Alloy wheels:	O	S	S
Anti-theft system:	S	S	S

Colors

Exterior: Black, White, Red, Blue, Pewter, Copper, Green, Gray, Gold.

Interior: Neutral, Gray, Blue, Red.

AT A GLANCE...

HISTORIC
Introduced in:	1936 (Suburban); 1970 (Blazer); 1995 (Yukon, Tahoe).
Made in:	Arlington, Texas & Janesville, WI, USA; Silao, Mexico.

DEMOGRAPHICS
Model	Men/Wom.	Age	Married	College	Income $
Suburban	80/20 %	42	75 %	45 %	$ 60 000
Tahoe	60/40 %	38	61 %	30 %	$ 44 000
Yukon	85/15 %	43	66 %	44 %	$ 48 000

INDEX
Safety:	75 %	Satisfaction:	80 %
Depreciation:	45 %	Insurance:	$ 965
Cost per mile:	$ 0.65	Number of dealers:	4 466

SALES
	Canada			USA		
Model	1997	1998	Result	1997	1998	Result
Tahoe	NA			124,125	133,235	+ 7.3 %
Suburban	NA					

MAINTENANCE REQUIRED BY WARRANTY
First revision:	Frequency:	Diagnostic plug:
3,000 miles	6 months / 6,000 miles	No

Full-size SUVs

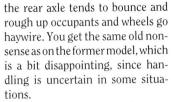

Out Of Touch

Although its sales have dropped to alarming depths, the Trooper is still on the market. Given the gap between standards prevalent on the North American and Japanese markets, it's smaller than most of the other competitors in this category. On our streets it looks puny, in Asia it looks huge. To boot, it's the only model of its type that doesn't come with a V8. The Trooper never recovered from the defamation campaign launched by some automotive industry experts who claimed that its instability was a danger factor.

MODEL RANGE

This big multi-purpose all-terrain vehicle is offered in a 5-door station wagon model with all-wheel drive on demand, in S, LS and Limited trim. All models are equipped with a standard updated 3.5L V6 engine linked to a standard manual transmission for the L and LS and four-speed automatic for the Limited. The Limited is blessed with rather unlimited equipment, the LS is richly equipped, but the lower-end S model has been really spruced up, since it now has all the main power accessories, aluminum rims, cruise control and a theft-deterrent system, all of which really add to its value.

TECHNICAL FEATURES

The steel unibody is mounted on a 7-crossmember H-frame. Aerodynamics aren't too great, not with its squarish front end and hefty tires. Standard steel protective plates keep the radiator, gas tank, crankcase and transfer case out of harm's way. The independent front suspension consists of transverse A-arms with torsion and stabilizer bar, whereas the rear rigid axle is rigged up to four trailing arms, torque arm, stabilizer bar and coil springs. A four-link navigational system controls wheel camber when torque is applied on accelerations and wheel travel has been increased both front and rear to provide for a smoother ride. Four-wheel disc brakes are assisted by a standard all-wheel ABS device. The new larger-displacement engine benefits from a variable intake system so as to maximize power and torque. A new full-time all-wheel drive equips the S version only, while the other two versions are equipped with an on-demand system, a feature that's the cat's meow for buyers. It can be engaged via shift-on-the-fly at whatever speed; this T.O.D. system distributes torque equally to front and rear wheels, so handling is really neutral and there's no oversteer or understeer effect, since it reacts to the accelerator pedal position and to the clean emission system valves.

PROS

+ STYLE. It's bold and forever young, no matter what the trend. It especially appeals to buyers who are hankering for a Range Rover, but don't have half the cash needed to purchase one. But this vehicle's technical features and performances are a far cry from what you get on a Rover.

+ RIDE COMFORT. It's velvety on highways and you almost feel like you're travelling in a big sedan with such a smooth suspension and nice-design, cushy seats.

+ EQUIPMENT. Last year's base model was very stripped down to basics, but now the S version is almost on a par with the LS, except for a few luxury items that aren't too vital.

+ VERSATILITY. The spacious cabin is as roomy as a minivan and can accomodate five passengers. The luggage compartment is generous and easy to get to thanks to unequal-width double swing doors.

+ COCKPIT. The driver sits nice and high, and can enjoy good straight-ahead and lateral view and the nicely organized dashboard has lots of instruments.

+ QUALITY. No doubt about it, this vehicle is well-built. Construction, finish details and trim components are spiffy, which can't be said about the rather bizarre overall design since some interior and exterior color shades may be splashy, but they aren't well-coordinated.

+ NICE FEATURES. The rear seat-bench can be removed like a charm and front seat armrests are ajustable.

CONS

- SUSPENSION. It's far too flexible, so you have to really watch it, since it creates a lot of sway and wishy washy behavior in crosswinds or on gouged-out surfaces where the rear axle tends to bounce and rough up occupants and wheels go haywire. You get the same old nonsense as on the former model, which is a bit disappointing, since handling is uncertain in some situations.

- BRAKES. They were tough on our test vehicle, but lacked oomph and were unstable on sudden stops that were hard to control with such a soft pedal.

- BUDGET. The Trooper isn't cheap to buy or operate, since fuel consumption rarely goes over 14 mpg: a V8 wouldn't be any greedier and would put out more juice and torque.

- ACCESS. It's always awkward boarding with those narrow doors that don't open wide and the high as blazes ground clearance. A running board isn't even available as an extra.

-NOISE. The engine isn't a quiet, genteel sort and wind gusts around the cabin as you accelerate, a sure sign of poor aerodynamics.

- VISIBILITY. It's hampered towards the rear because of the thick roof supports and the spare tire installed on the rear door exterior.

- TO BE IMPROVED UPON. crummy-performance headlights, wipers and climate control and really skimpy storage compartments for rear seat travellers.

CONCLUSION

Trapped in the amalgam of more or less huge vehicles, the Trooper looks scrawny and it doesn't fit into the same league as its rivals. But once its suspension problems are solved, it could be a serious candidate for buyers looking for a cost-efficient choice.

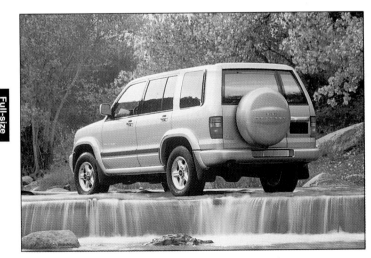

RATING		
ISUZU Trooper		
CONCEPT :		77%
Technology :	80	
Safety :	70	
Interior space :	65	
Trunk volume :	90	
Quality/fit/finish :	80	
DRIVING :		59%
Cockpit :	80	
Performance :	55	
Handling :	45	
Steering :	70	
Braking :	45	
ORIGINAL EQUIPMENT :		76%
Tires :	75	
Headlights :	80	
Wipers :	80	
Rear defroster :	70	
Radio :	75	
COMFORT :		66%
Seats :	75	
Suspension :	80	
Sound level :	35	
Conveniences :	65	
Air conditioning :	75	
BUDGET :		41%
Price :	0	
Fuel economy :	20	
Insurance :	50	
Satisfaction :	85	
Depreciation :	50	
Overall rating :		**63.9%**

NEW FOR 2000

• No details available at press time.

Compare
Performance,
Specifications, Prices,
and Classification
at the end of this chapter.

EQUIPMENT

ISUZU Trooper	S	LS	Limited
Automatic transmission:	O	O	S
Cruise control:	S	S	S
Power steering:	S	S	S
Anti-lock brakes:	S	S	S
Traction control:	S	S	S
Air conditioning:	S	S	S
Leather:	-	-	S
AM/FM/radio-cassette:	S	SCd	SCd
Power door locks:	S	S	S
Power windows:	S	S	S
Tilt steering:	S	S	S
Dual adjustable mirrors:	SEH	SEH	SEH
Alloy wheels:	S	S	S
Anti-theft system:	S	S	S

Colors

Exterior: White, Green, Silver, Red, Black, Blue.

Interior: Brown, Gray, Beige.

AT A GLANCE...

HISTORIC
Introduced in:	1981-1998.
Made in:	Fujisawa, Japon.

DEMOGRAPHICS
Model	Men/Wom.	Age	Married	College	Income $
Trooper	55/45 %	50	94 %	45 %	$ 60 000

INDEX
Safety:	70 %	Satisfaction:	85 %
Depreciation:	48 %	Insurance:	$ 1 050
Cost per mile:	$ 0.58	Number of dealers:	NA

SALES
Model	Canada 1997	1998	Result	USA 1997	1998	Result
Trooper	204	123	- 39.7 %	10,964	18,191	+ 65.9 %

MAINTENANCE REQUIRED BY WARRANTY
First revision:	Frequency:	Diagnostic plug:
3 000 miles	6 000 miles	Yes

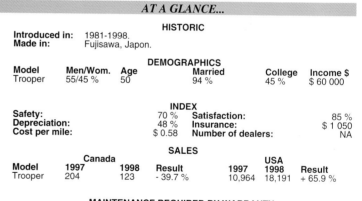

Full-size SUVs

Two-faced

It's safe to say that the Range Rover was the very first utility vehicle, at least in the sense the term is used today. In the 70s, it was the only vehicle in the world that could travel fast on the highway (in England) and turn off into fields whenever it wanted to. Its split personality spelt its success and made it popular throughout the world.

MODEL RANGE

The Range Rover is a 4-door sport utility available in two versions: the 4.0 SE and the 4.6 HSE. It's powered by a 4.0L or 4.6L V8, coupled with a 4-speed automatic transmission. Its equipment is every bit as detailed and luxurious as it would be on the best sedans manufactured in Britain and design details are ultra discreet and very tasteful.

TECHNICAL FEATURES

The Range Rover's body is supported by a a strong six-crossmember chassis. Its side panels are made of galvanized steel, while the roof, bumpers and doors are made of aluminum. Front and rear suspensions feature solid axles supported by cross arms with Panhard and antiroll bars and variable pneumatic shock absorbers.

Its V8 engines have an output of 188 and 222 horses respectively, and the automatic transmission is electronically controlled. Four-wheel drive is permanent and the traction control system limits tire slip by automatically applying brake pressure to the wheel with the least traction. The rear-end assembly includes automatic level control to ensure optimal steering consistency. To ensure full compatibility with the automatic transmission, the Range Rover features a locking center differential.

PROS

+ DRIVEABILITY. In spite of its size the Range Rover is fun to drive; it is easy to handle, controls are smooth and visibility is almost perfect from all angles.

+ VERSATILITY. Even if today's market includes a high number of vehicles that can go from paved ribbons of road to completely uncharted terrain, the Range Rover is the only sport utility that has both the grace of a Jaguar and the strength of a tractor. Its inside even features thick rubber mats designed specifically to keep it from getting dirty as it shifts from one role to the other.

+ PASSENGER ROOM. The passenger compartment is huge and can easily accommodate 5 occupants in luxury. However, it isn't easy to get inside and running boards would be a welcome addition, even when the adjustable suspension is positioned low.

+ HANDLING. In spite of its solid axle suspensions, the Range Rover offers good road stability thanks to automatic self-leveling. Its excellent tires hug the road and the steering system is precise.

+ PERFORMANCE. Acceleration and pick-up are very good for a vehicle as heavy as this one and its weight explains its high fuel consumption.

+ CARGO SPACE. With the spare tire stored under the floor, there's more than enough room for baggage and all manner of other sundry items.

+ LUXURY. Overall design is posh but not pretentious and replete with high-quality materials. Equipment is detailed and comparable to a limousine's.

+ QUALITY. The Range Rover is well-built and its finish is equally careful; most materials show excellent quality.

CONS

- PRICE. This pseudo sport utility is very expensive to buy, maintain and insure and its fuel consumption can easily reach 8 mpg.

- SUSPENSION. Its excessive smoothness leads to body roll that can be alarming at high speeds, when the steering system loses precision.

- RELIABILITY. Owners continue to complain about the Range Rover's questionable reliability, all the more so since dealerships are few and far between. No wonder it's not uncommon to see Range Rovers being carried away on flatbed trucks.

- FLAWS. It's very strange that a vehicle sold at this price has so few assist grips.

- HATCH. The cargo area hatch is not very practical and a different design would make it easier to reach items that have shifted in transit.

- GLOVEBOX. Although big, it isn't practical because the CD changer takes up too much room.

- CONSOLE. It's very wide, which limits the room available for front-seat passengers; meanwhile rear-seat occupants have plenty of room at their disposal.

- FLAWS. Chimes that go off with not much reason, rattling noises that are inexplicable on a vehicle in this class, dull leather trims that look like something borrowed from an economy-class Japanese vehicle.

CONCLUSION

Considering how much it costs to maintain this ultimate SUV, rare is the owner who will ever dare to venture off-road.

RATING
LAND ROVER Range Rover

CONCEPT :		86%
Technology :	85	
Safety :	90	
Interior space :	90	
Trunk volume :	80	
Quality/fit/finish :	85	

DRIVING :		65%
Cockpit :	85	
Performance :	50	
Handling :	60	
Steering :	80	
Braking :	50	

ORIGINAL EQUIPMENT :		78%
Tires :	85	
Headlights :	80	
Wipers :	65	
Rear defroster :	75	
Radio :	85	

COMFORT :		75%
Seats :	80	
Suspension :	80	
Sound level :	60	
Conveniences :	75	
Air conditioning :	80	

BUDGET :		26%
Price :	0	
Fuel economy :	0	
Insurance :	15	
Satisfaction :	70	
Depreciation :	45	

| **Overall rating :** | | **66.0%** |

NEW FOR 2000

• No major changes.

Compare
Performance,
Specifications, Prices,
and Classification
at the end of this chapter.

EQUIPMENT

LAND ROVER	Range Rover
Automatic transmission:	S
Cruise control:	S
Power steering:	S
Anti-lock brakes:	S
Traction control:	S
Air conditioning:	SA
Leather:	S
AM/FM/radio-cassette:	SCd
Power door locks:	S
Power windows:	S
Tilt steering:	S
Dual adjustable mirrors:	S
Alloy wheels:	S
Anti-theft system:	S

Colors

Exterior: White, Silver, Marine, Red, Green, Black.

Interior: Grey, Black, Tan.

AT A GLANCE...

HISTORIC
Introduced in: 1970 (2dr.); 1981 (4dr.).
Made in: Solihull, England.

DEMOGRAPHICS

Model	Men/Wom.	Age	Married	College	Income $
Range Rover					

INDEX

Safety:	90 %	Satisfaction:	78 %
Depreciation:	45 %	Insurance:	$ 1 500
Cost per mile:	$ 1.15	Number of dealers:	-

SALES

	Canada			USA		
Model	1997	1998	Result	1997	1998	Result
Range	337	291	- 13.6%	6,621	7,072	+ 6.8 %

MAINTENANCE REQUIRED BY WARRANTY

First revision:	Frequency:	Diagnostic plug:
3,000 miles	6 months / 6,000 miles	Yes

Full-size SUVs

Clones

These two vehicles are identical and like many others of the same generation they're the result of some kind of cloning process designed to develop a luxury model based on a utility vehicle. The only differences between the Land Cruiser and the LX 470 are interior design details and equipment levels. Considering their substantial price difference, it's easy to understand why manufacturers like this concept: it pays!

MODEL RANGE

The LX 470 only comes in a big four-door station wagon version in a single trim that has traded the old 6-cylinder engine for a 4.7L V8 with four-speed automatic transmission, full-time all-wheel drive and an adjustable hydropneumatic suspension. Other equipment items are quite extensive, since the only factory option is the sunroof. This vehicle has some distinctive stylistic traits such as grille, side guards, bulging wheelhouses, running boards, light alloy rims and roof rack.

TECHNICAL FEATURES

Just like its predecessor the LX 450, the 470 is based on the Land Cruiser platform. It consists of a shell chassis integrated with the steel body. For a vehicle with such a wide front surface, big tires and orifices, aerodynamic yield is remarkable since the drag coefficient is 0.40. The front suspension is now independent and uses A-arms and torsion bars, whereas the rigid rear axle is supported by four trailing arms. A hydropneumatic device provides three different ground clearance settings: high, normal and low. But as soon as vehicle speed goes beyond 19 mph, the suspension shifts back automatically to the normal setting. Another system controls shock absorber response depending on road conditions. The engine is now a DOHC 32-valve 4.7L V8 that develops 230 hp, linked to a 4-speed automatic transmission. All-wheel drive is full-time, benefitting from a viscous-coupled main differential that can be locked on demand so as to distribute available power to both front and rear wheels and there's a limited-slip differential at the rear. Four-wheel disc brakes have a servomechanism that's hydraulically activated and are associated with an ABS device. Lastly, a surprising feature on such a bulky vehicle, there's rack-and-pinion steering for clean, crisp precision.

PROS

+ PERFORMANCES. They literally blew us away, since this brute that weighs in at 5390 lbs. accelerates better than most lightweight, economy cars and passing on the highway is super-safe.

+ RIDE COMFORT. It's amazing and offers more of a lush limo feel rather than an SUV sensation, thanks to well-adjusted suspension travel that works like a charm over major off-road obstacles and is cool as a cucumber on the highway.

+ USEFUL SPACE. The cabin can accommodate 5 or even 8 passengers when the second optional seat-bench is installed in the cargo hold. There's lots of stretching space, even in the rear seats that are roomier than was the case on the 450. The rear hatch isn't the handiest around, but the luggage compartment is really huge when the third seatbench isn't installed.

+ DRIVING PLEASURE. It's more fun than you'd expect it to be. The cockpit is comparable to the mini-van arrangement, visibility is good and the dashboard layout is well-organized.

+ ACCESS. Boarding is more convenient with the running boards and nine cleverly located assist grips, but it's still a bit tough getting to the third seatbench.

+ HANDLING. It's pretty amazing with the well-adjusted suspension and full-time all-wheel drive. But this gentle giant isn't too quick on his feet and is rather awkward on tight curves or on slalom runs because of sheer hulk and pronounced sway. But it has a lot of vim and vitality and is steady as a rock.

+ QUALITY. Every last detail on this vehicle has been carefully attended to, be it design, build and finish job and the LX 470 is much less of a sport-utility vehicle per se than its predecessor.

CONS

-BUDGET. The LX 470 has many assets but it's sold at an appalling price that's much higher than that of its closest rivals. You can almost purchase two Expedition's for the same price... Not to mention the insurance premium that isn't cheap and fuel consumption that varies between 12 and 14 mpg, depending on needed juice...

- VEHICLE SIZE. The LX 470 isn't an ideal format for either city driving or for rambles in the underbrush, for this vehicle gets around in a lumbering sort of way and you have to be prudent when attempting delicate maneuvers.

- BRAKES. They didn't really satisfy us, since stopping distances stretch out pretty far, the stiff pedal is hard to gauge just right and even with the ABS device, you had to have your wits about you to keep this vehicle on the road during our test runs.

- STEERING. It's nicely powered, but a poor reduction ratio (3.8 tr) and wide turn angle diameter convert each move into a real chore and quick lane changes are dicey when it comes to keeping vehicle balance.

- TO BE IMPROVED UPON. Dull headlights that jar with other items on this superb vehicle and the inconvenient rear hatch door that could lift all in one piece and be powered, given the going price...

CONCLUSION

The Land Cruiser, available only in the U.S., and the Lexus LX 470 are very accomplished vehicles that are equally efficient on city streets, highways and off the beaten track. Each in their own right, their sturdiness and reliability make them very viable choices.

Full-size SUVs

RATING
LEXUS LX 470

CONCEPT : 84%
Technology :	80
Safety :	90
Interior space :	90
Trunk volume :	80
Quality/fit/finish :	80

DRIVING : 56%
Cockpit :	80
Performance :	50
Handling :	50
Steering :	80
Braking :	20

ORIGINAL EQUIPMENT : 76%
Tires :	80
Headlights :	70
Wipers :	75
Rear defroster :	75
Radio :	80

COMFORT : 76%
Seats :	80
Suspension :	75
Sound level :	70
Conveniences :	75
Air conditioning :	80

BUDGET : 43%
Price :	0
Fuel economy :	20
Insurance :	35
Satisfaction :	90
Depreciation :	70

Overall rating : 67.0%

NEW FOR 2000

• No major changes.

Compare
Performance,
Specifications, Prices,
and Classification
at the end of this chapter.

EQUIPMENT

LEXUS TOYOTA Land Cruiser	LX 470 base
Automatic transmission:	S
Cruise control:	S
Power steering:	S
Anti-lock brakes:	S
Traction control:	-
Air conditioning:	S
Leather:	S
AM/FM/radio-cassette:	SCd
Power door locks:	S
Power windows:	S
Tilt steering:	S
Dual adjustable mirrors:	S
Alloy wheels:	S
Anti-theft system:	S

Colors

Exterior: White, Black, Gold, Emerald, Beige, Mica, Green.

Interior: Taupe, Medium gray.

AT A GLANCE...

HISTORIC
Introduced in:	1998.
Made in:	Hino, Japan.

DEMOGRAPHICS
Model	Men/Wom.	Age	Married	College	Income $
Land Cruiser LX 470					

INDEX
Safety:	90 %	Satisfaction:	90 %
Depreciation:	40 %	Insurance:	$ 1 100
Cost per mile:	$ 1.10	Number of dealers:	170

SALES
Model	Canada 1997	1998	Result	USA 1997	1998	Result
Land Cruiser LX 450	NA NA			6,785	11,004	+ 62.2 %

MAINTENANCE REQUIRED BY WARRANTY
First revision:	Frequency:	Diagnostic plug:
4,000 miles	4,000 miles	Yes

FULL-SIZE SPORT UTILITY VEHICLES

PERFORMANCE

Model/version	Type / timing valve / fuel system	Displacement cu in	Power hp @ rpm	Torque lb-ft @ rpm	Compres. ratio	Driving wheels / transmission	Final ratio	Acceler. 0-60 mph s	Standing 1/4 & 5/8 mile s	Passing 50-75 mph s	Braking 60-0 mph ft	Top speed mph	Lateral acceler. G	Noise level dBA	City mpg	Highway mpg	Fuel type Octane
AMG Hummer																	
base	V8* 6.5D OHV-16-MI	396	170 @ 3400	290 @ 1700	21.5 :1	all-A4	2.72	20.5	22.0 42.0	NA	60	78	0.65	74	14	18	D
option	V8 6.5TD OHV-16-MI	396	195 @ 3400	430 @ 1800	21.5 :1	all-A4	2.72	18.5	21.0 39.0	NA	61	81	0.65	72	14	18	D
CADILLAC Escalade - CHEVROLET Tahoe- Suburban - GMC Yukon- Suburban																	
base	V8* 5.7 OHV-16-SFI	350	255 @ 4600	330 @ 2800	9.4 :1	four -A4	3.73	11.0	18.0 32.2	7.8	168	109	0.70	66	13.0	18.0	R 87
base	V8* 5.7 OHV-16-SFI	350	255 @ 4600	330 @ 2800	9.4 :1	rear/4 - A4*	3.42	9.3	16.8 30.5	6.6	151	109	0.68	68	13	18	R 87
option.Sub	V8TD 6.5 OHV-16-MI	395	180 @ 3400	360 @ 1800	19.5 :1	rear/4 - A4*	NA	13.5	19.2 36.0	10.8	170	93	0.66	71	15	22	D
option Sub.	V8 7.4 OHV-16-SFI	454	290 @ 4000	410 @ 3200	8.9 :1	rear/4 - A4*	NA	12.0	18.2 33.6	8.5	157	112	0.67	68	12	19	R 87
FORD Expedition - LINCOLN Navigator																	
base Exp.	V8*4.6 SOHC-16-SFI	281	240 @ 4750	293 @ 3500	9.0 :1	rear/4 - A4	3.31	11.5	18.5 33.4	9.0	148	106	0.70	68	14	21	R 87
option Exp.	V8 5.4 SOHC-16-SFI	330	260 @ 4500	345 @ 2300	9.0 :1	rear/4 - A4	3.31	11.0	18.0 32.8	8.0	157	109	0.70	68	13	19	R 87
base Nav.	V8 5.4 DOHC-32-MPSFI	330	300 @ 5000	335 @ 2750	9.5 :1	rear/4 - A4	3.31	9.8	16.8 30.8	7.0	157	112	0.62	68	12	17	R 87
						rear/4 - A4	3.73	10.5	17.6 31.5	7.8	177	109	0.62	68	11	17	R 87
ISUZU Trooper																	
base	V6* 3.5 DOHC-24-MPFI	213	215 @ 5400	230 @ 3000	9.1 :1	rear/4 - M5*	4.56	9.0	16.8 30.4	7.5	157	112	0.72	68-72	15	21	R 87
						rear/4 - A4	4.30	9.8	17.3 31.8	8.2	168	109	0.72	68-72	15	21	R 87
LAND ROVER																	
Range RoverV8 4.0	OHV-16-MPSFI	241	188 @ 4750	250 @ 2600	9.35 :1	all - A4	3.54	NA							13	16	S 91
Range RoverV8 4.6	OHV-16-MPSFI	277	222 @ 4750	300 @ 2600	9.35 :1	all - A4	3.54	NA							12	15	S 91
LEXUS LX 470																	
base	V8 4.7 DOHC-32-MPSFI	285	230 @ 4800	320 @ 3600	9.6 :1	all - A4	4.30	10.5	17.6 31.5	7.6	157	109	0.76	64-68	13	16	S 91
TOYOTA Land Cruiser																	
base	V8 4.7 DOHC-32-MPSFI	285	230 @ 4800	320 @ 3600	9.6 :1	all - A4	4.30	10.5	17.6 31.5	7.6	157	109	0.76	64-68	13	16	S 91

SPECIFICATIONS

Model	Version Trim	Traction	Body/ Deats	Wheel base in	Lgth x Width x Hght in x inx in	Curb weight lb	Susp. ft/rr	Brake ft/rr	type	Steering ø ft	turns number	Fuel tank gal	dimensions	Standard tires make	model	Standard powertrain	99 Price msrp $
AM GENERAL	General warranty: 3-years / 36,000 miles.																
Hummer	Hardtop	4x4	2dr.p-u.2	130.0	184.5x86.5x75.0	6391	ih/ih	dc/dc	pwr.ball	53.1	3.125+17		37x12.5R16.5	Goodyear	Wrangler MT	V8/6.5/A4	69,152
Hummer	Sedan	4x4	4dr.sdn.4	130.0	184.5x86.5x75.0	6790	ih/ih	dc/dc	pwr.ball	53.1	3.125+17		37x12.5R16.5	Goodyear	Wrangler MT	V8/6.5/A4	82,892
Hummer	Convertible	4x4	4dr.con.4	130.0	184.5x86.5x76.8	6640	ih/ih	dc/dc	pwr.ball	53.1	3.125+17		37x12.5R16.5	Goodyear	Wrangler MT	V8/6.5/A4	76,492
Hummer	Wagon	4x4	4dr.wgn.4	130.0	184.5x86.5x76.8	6980	ih/ih	dc/dc	pwr.ball	53.1	3.125+17		37x12.5R16.5	Goodyear	Wrangler MT	V8/6.5/A4	86,508
CADILLAC	General warranty: 4-years / 50,000 miles; antipollution: 5-years / 50,000 miles; perforation corrosion: 6-years / 100,000 miles. Roadside assistance.																
Escalade	base	4x4	4dr.wgn.6	117.5	201.2x77.0x74.3	5573	it/it	dc/dr/ABS	pwr.bal.	40.7	3.0	20	265/70R16	Firestone	Firehawk LS	V8/5.7/A4	46,525
CHEVROLET-GMC	General warranty: 3-years / 36,000 miles; antipollution: 5-years / 50,000 miles; perforation corrosion: 6-years / 100,000 miles. Roadside assistance.																
Tahoe-Yukon		4x2	2dr.wgn.5/6	111.5	188.0x77.1x70.8	4526	ih/rl	dc/dr/ABS	pwr.bal.	38.1	3.0	30.0	235/75R15	BF Goodrich	Long Trail	V8/5.7/A4	24,670
Tahoe-Yukon		4x4	2dr.wgn.5/6	111.5	188.0x77.1x71.4	4876	it/rl	dc/dr/ABS	pwr.bal.	39.0	3.0	30.0	245/75R15	BF Goodrich	Long Trail	V8/5.7/A4	27,270
Tahoe-Yukon		4x2	4dr.wgn.5/6	117.5	199.6x76.8x70.7	4420	ih/rl	dc/dr/ABS	pwr.bal.	39.8	3.0	30.0	235/75R16	BF Goodrich	Long Trail	V8/5.7/A4	30,470
Tahoe-Yukon		4x4	4dr.wgn.5/6	117.5	199.6x76.8x72.8	5332	it/rl	dc/dr/ABS	pwr.bal.	40.7	3.0	30.0	245/75R16	BF Goodrich	Long Trail	V8/5.7/A4	33,070
Suburban	C1500	4x2	4dr.wgn.6/9	131.5	219.5x76.7x72.5	4821	ih/rl	dc/dr/ABS	pwr.bal.	43.7	3.0	42.0	235/75R15	Uniroyal	Laredo	V8/5.7/A4	26,360
Suburban	K1500	4x4	4dr.wgn.6/9	131.5	219.5x76.7x72.4	5297	it/rl	dc/dr/ABS	pwr.bal.	44.7	3.0	42.0	245/75R16	Uniroyal	Laredo	V8/5.7/A4	28,960
FORD	General warranty, antipollution & battery: 3-years / 36,000 miles; corrosion perforation: 5-years / unlimited.																
Expedition	XLT	4x2	4dr.wgn.6	119.1	204.6x78.6x74.3	4848	ih/rh	dc/ABS	pwr.ball	40.4	3.3	26.0	255/70R16	Goodyear	Wrangler RT/S	V8/4.6/A4	29,995
Expedition	Eddie Bauer	4x2	4dr.wgn.6	119.1	204.6x78.6x74.3	-	ih/rh	dc/ABS	pwr.ball	40.4	3.3	26.0	255/70R16	Goodyear	Wrangler RT/S	V8/4.6/A4	35,865
Expedition	XLT	4x4	4dr.wgn.6	119.1	204.6x78.6x76.6	-	ih/rh	dc/ABS	pwr.ball	40.5	3.3	30.0	255/70R16	Goodyear	Wrangler RT/S	V8/4.6/A4	32,730
Expedition	Eddie Bauer	4x4	4dr.wgn.6	119.1	204.6x78.6x76.6	-	ih/rh	dc/ABS	pwr.ball	40.5	3.3	30.0	265/70R17	Goodyear	Wrangler RT/S	V8/4.6/A4	39,640
ISUZU	General warranty: 3-years / 36,000 miles; powertrain: 5-years / 60,000 miles ; perforation: 6-years / 100,000miles.																
Trooper	S	4x4	5dr.wgn.5	108.7	187.8x69.5x72.2	4389	it/rh	dc/ABS	pwr.ball	38.1	3.7	22.5	245/70R16	Bridgestone	Dueller 684	V6/3.5/M5	27,595
Trooper	LS	4x4	5dr.wgn.5	108.7	187.8x69.5x72.2	4398	it/rh	dc/ABS	pwr.ball	38.1	3.7	22.5	245/70R16	Bridgestone	Dueller 684	V6/3.5/M5	-
Trooper	Limited	4x4	5dr.wgn.5	108.7	187.8x69.5x72.2	4539	it/rh	dc/ABS	pwr.ball	38.1	3.7	22.5	245/70R16	Bridgestone	Dueller 684	V6/3.5/A4	-
LAND ROVER	General warranty: 4-years / 50,000 miles; corrosion perforation: 6-years / unlimited mileage.																
Range Rover	4.0 SE	4x4	5dr.wgn.5	108.1	185.5x74.4x71.6	4955	ra/ra	dc/ABS	pwr.ball	36.2	3.2	24.6	255/65HR16	-	-	V8/4.0/A4	58,625
Range Rover	4.6 HSE	4x4	5dr.wgn.5	108.1	185.5x74.4x71.6	4955	ra/ra	dc/ABS	pwr.ball	36.2	3.2	24.6	255/65HR16	-	-	V8/4.6/A4	66,625
LEXUS	General warranty: 4-years / 50,000 miles; powertrain: 6-years / 70,000 miles; corrosion perforation: 6-years / unlimited mileage & roadside assistance.																
LX 470	base	4X4	4dr.wgn.8	112.2	192.5x76.4x72.8	5401	it/rh	dc/ABS	pwr.r&p.	42.0	3.8	25.4	275/70R16	Michelin	LTX M/S	V8/4.7/A4	56,700
LINCOLN	General warranty: 4-years / 50,000 miles; corrosion perforation antipollution: 4-years / 50,000 miles.																
Navigator	base	4x2	4dr.wgn.7/8	119.0	204.8x79.9x75.2	NA	ih/ra	dc/ABS	pwr.ball	40.4	3.3	30.0	245/75R16	Continental	Contitrac AT	V8/5.4/A4	41,395
Navigator	base	4X4	4dr.wgn.7/8	119.0	204.8x79.9x76.7	5392	ih/ra	dc/ABS	pwr.ball	40.5	3.3	30.0	245/75R16	Continental	Contitrac AT	V8/5.4/A4	45,045
TOYOTA	General warranty: 4-years / 50,000 miles; powertrain: 6-years / 70,000 miles; corrosion perforation: 6-years / unlimited mileage & roadside assistance.																
Land Cruiser	base	4x4	4dr.wgn.7/8	112.2	192.5x76.4x72.8	5390	it/rh	dc/ABS	pwr.r&p.	39.7	3.8	25.4	275/70R16	Michelin	LTX M&S	V8/4.7/A4	47,038

Notes: 1) Tire makes and models are provided solely as an indication; they are subject to change without prior notice from the automobile manufacturers.
2) See the 2000 price list at the back of this edition.

CLASSEMENTS

OUR CLASSIFICATION

Rank	Models	Concept	Driving	Equipment	Comfort	Budget	Rating
1	**LEXUS LX 470**	84	56	76	**76**	43	**67.0 %**
2	FORD Expedition	85	53	78	71	**46**	66.6 %
2	LINCOLN Navigator	**86**	48	**80**	75	44	66.6 %
3	LAND ROVER Range	**86**	65	78	75	26	66.0 %
4	GM C/K Series	77	57	75	68	**46**	64.6 %
5	ISUZU Trooper	77	**59**	76	66	41	63.8 %
6	AMG Hummer	81	38	62	50	43	54.8 %

YOUR CLASSIFICATION

Rank	Models	98 Sales
1	**FORD Expedition**	214,524
2	CHEVROLET Tahoe	133,235
3	CHEVROLET Suburban	108,933
4	GMC Yukon	49,355
5	LINCOLN Navigator	43,859
6	ISUZU Trooper	18,191
7	LEXUS LX 470	11,004
8	LAND ROVER Range	7,072

Not classified:
AMG Hummer (NA)

Full-size SUVs

Comparative Test

COMPACT TRUCKS

See their performance, their specifications, their price and their classification at the end of this chapter.

DODGE Dakota

FORD Ranger

GM S-10 Series

NISSAN Frontier

TOYOTA Tacoma

Compact Trucks

Rigged Out

Chrysler has taken its competitors by surprise once again, introducing the latest version of the Dakota, a 4-door Quad Cab, ahead of schedule. Unveiled in Auto Shows throughout 1999, this model will be available for sale as of early 2000. Adding a midsize pickup to the lineup will boost sales, already on par with the international standards set for success. Roomier than its rivals but not really bigger, this pickup offers an unusual choice of engines, ranging up to a big V8 with more than 5.0L.

MODEL RANGE

The Dakota comes in either rear or four-wheel drive with regular or extended cabin, but it's still only fitted with two doors. Load capacity is 2,600 lb. and it can haul a trailer weighing up to 6,800 lb. Inside the extended cabin, there's a three-seater fold up seatbench facing frontwards. Trim levels are base, Sport and SLT for the regular cabin version, and base, Sport, Plus, SLT and SLT Plus for the Club Cab version. Standard equipment on all models includes power steering, rear-wheel ABS, radio, adjustable exterior mirrors and intermittent wipers.

TECHNICAL FEATURES

The steel unibody is mounted onto a robust steel H-frame chassis made up of five crossmembers boasting of tough torsion resistance. The chassis is painted via an electrostatic technique to improve rustproofing. The front suspension on the RWD models consists of unequal-length control arms and MacPherson strut. This helps reduce the steer angle diameter, control the tendency to spring back to center and improve stability on curves. The AWD models' suspension is still based on torsion bars, but at the rear the rigid axle supported by leaf springs has been modified so as to provide for smoother travel and better roadhandling. This revised rear axle suspension equips all models. Steering is rack-and-pinion on the RWD vehicles and recirculating ball on the AWD's; both types of steering are powered. Disc and drum brakes are associated with standard rear-wheel ABS. The base engine on the RWD version is a 2.5L 4-cylinder that only comes with a 5-speed manual gearbox, while the 3.9L V6 is standard on the Club Cab versions and the 5.2L V8 is optional for RWD and AWD pickups fitted with a standard 5-speed manual gearbox. For 2000, the 5.9L V8 engine is only available on the 4X2 R/T model.

PROS

+ STYLE. It's inspired by the Ram, but it's cleaner, crisper and the body is longer. What you have is a great-looking pickup that's raring to go. No wonder it's so popular.

+ VERSATILITY. The Dakota pickup truck is a great second vehicle, since it can tackle tasks when things have to get done and it can be a great companion when your're enjoying leisure activities. It can do all this due to a load capacity and trailering capabilities far superior to those of the average compact pickup, especially with a 5.2L V8 under the hood.

+ SIZE. You feel less cramped inside the Dakota cabin than when you climb aboard the main rivals. And don't forget that the extended cabin model truck can transport 4'X8' sheets of plywood without having to mount any special attachments.

+ V8 ENGINES. They pump out the power and torque it takes to really move this pickup and they provide exceptional load capacity and traction for this category.

+ CABIN SPACE. The Club Cab is equipped with a full-width seatbench facing the front that can accomodate three passengers more comfortably than the auxiliary seats on the competition or else it can hold quite a bit of luggage.

+ RIDE COMFORT. It's above average thanks to finely adjusted suspensions, thicker seat cushions and super soundproofing for a utility vehicle.

+ HANDLING. It's noticeably better with more precise directional prowess at the front end and the bigger-diameter tires keep things a lot more stable.

+ QUALITY. Compared to before, it's much more obvious. You get a nice solid feel both inside and out. The cabin interior is more carefully crafted and trim materials and touches really look great.

+ STEERING. It's more accurate on the RWD models since shorter steer angle diameters sure help make the moves you want. But the steering on the AWD versions isn't too responsive or precise at center and sometimes it seems to be dead or on hold.

CONS

- BRAKES. Stopping distances stretch out, a telltale sign of ineffective brakes. Brakes don't dig in when applied either. Besides, four-wheel ABS would really make for more stability, something this vehicle doesn't have much of in wet weather or when the box is empty...

- ACCESS. The Club Cab doesn't have the rear half-doors that make the competition shine and so climbing aboard or stashing stuff in the rear seat is a bit of a task.

- FUEL CONSUMPTION. It's never frugal with the V6 and much less so with the V8 engines. On the 4X4, it can easily go as low as 12 mpg when on rough terrain... An optional Diesel or natural gas engine would be attractive to some owners.

- SAFETY. Rear seat passengers don't benefit from headrests, so they tend to knock their skulls against the rear window whenever the driver's toe touches the accelerator.

- FINISH DETAILS. The cabin design isn't at all like the flamboyant body style. Such a dull, dreary look isn't the fruit of a lively imagination, especially the instrument panel that's very bare-bones basic.

CONCLUSION

Down to the very last letter, Dakota has followed the principles that have always meant success for this make. It has strong styling, a model range providing something for every taste, a wide choice of powertrains, and equipment that motorists' dreams are made of - a combination that have put this truck in a position envied by all.

RATING
DODGE Dakota

CONCEPT :   62%
- Technology :   80
- Safety :   75
- Interior space :   40
- Trunk volume :   40
- Quality/fit/finish :   75

DRIVING :   57%
- Cockpit :   70
- Performance :   40
- Handling :   55
- Steering :   70
- Braking :   50

ORIGINAL EQUIPMENT :   61%
- Tires :   80
- Headlights :   75
- Wipers :   70
- Rear defroster :   0
- Radio :   80

COMFORT :   71%
- Seats :   75
- Suspension :   70
- Sound level :   60
- Conveniences :   70
- Air conditioning :   80

BUDGET :   60%
- Price :   65
- Fuel economy :   30
- Insurance :   70
- Satisfaction :   80
- Depreciation :   55

Overall rating :   62.2%

NEW FOR 2000

- 8-foot cab model withdrawn.
- Quad Cab (4-door) scheduled for January 2000.
- New colors: Dark Red, Bronze Pearl, Amber, Patriot Blue.

Compare
Performance,
Specifications, Prices,
and Classification
at the end of this chapter.

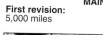

EQUIPMENT

DAKOTA regular cab.	Base 4x2 long	Sport 4x2 long	SLT 4x2 Base	Club Cab 4x2 Sport	Club Cab 4x4 SLT	4x4 SLT +
Automatic transmission:	O	O	O	O	O	O
Cruise control:	-	O	O	-	O	O
Power steering:	S	S	S	S	S	S
Anti-lock brakes:	S	S	S	S	S	S
Traction control:	-	-	-	-	-	-
Air conditioning:	O	O	S	O	S	S
Leather:	-	-	-	-	-	-
AM/FM/radio-cassette:	S	S	S	S	S	S
Power door locks:	-	O	O	-	O	S
Power windows:	-	O	O	-	O	S
Tilt steering:	O	O	S	O	O	S
Dual adjustable mirrors:	SM	SM	SM	SM	SM	SM
Alloy wheels:	-	S	S	-	S	S
Anti-theft system:	-	O	O	-	O	S

Colors
Exterior: Black, White, Amethyst, Green, Red, Blue, Driftwood, Yellow.

Interior: Pebble, Grey.

AT A GLANCE...

HISTORIC
- Introduced in: 1986, 1987 model.
- Made in: Dodge City, (Warren, Michigan)

DEMOGRAPHICS

Model	Men/Wom.	Age	Married	College	Income $
Dakota 4x2	94/ 6 %	53	83 %	23 %	$ 34,000
Dakota 4x4	89/11 %	46	70 %	25 %	$ 32,000

INDEX
- Safety: 75 %   Satisfaction: 80 %
- Depreciation: 45 %   Insurance: $ 835
- Cost per mile: $ 0.45   Number of dealers: 1,887

SALES

Model	Canada 1997	1998	Result	USA 1997	1998	Result
Dakota	10 898	14 286	+31.1 %	131,961	152,629	+15.7 %

MAINTENANCE REQUIRED BY WARRANTY
- First revision: 5,000 miles
- Frequency: 6 months
- Diagnostic plug: Yes

Compact Trucks

Rough And Ready

Following the example set by the F-Series pickup, the Ranger has captured the lion's share of sales in both the U.S. and Canada. Meanwhile, Mazda's B-Series - identical except for a few design details - has improved its score as well. The biggest sales go to the V6 engine and manual transmission, which has led Mazda to eliminate this particular combination. These trucks are renowned for their extraordinary sturdiness and resistance, making them models that can always be described as rough and ready.

MODEL RANGE

The Ranger comes in regular cabin and short or long box or in the extended SuperCab model with short box. The SuperCab cabin is now equipped with two rear doors that open opposite to the front doors, when these are open. There are two trim levels available: XL and XLT, with Flareside and Styleside boxes and RWD or AWD. Rear-wheel drive versions are fitted with a standard 2.5L 4-cylinder engine or with an optional 3.0L or 4.0L V6. All-wheel drive models are animated by a standard 3.0L V6. The 5-speed manual transmission comes standard on all models. An optional 4-speed automatic can be linked to the 3.0L V6 and a 5-speed automatic can be paired up with the 4.0L V6.

TECHNICAL FEATURES

These utility vehicles have a steel body set on a seven-crossmember H frame (eight for the SuperCab) via rubber insulator units. The front suspension is like that of the F-150, consisting of unequal-length control arms linked to coil springs on RWD models and torsion bars on the AWD models. The rear rigid axle is supported by very conventional leaf springs. Vehicles benefit from rack-and-pinion steering and disc and drum brakes associated with standard rear-wheel ABS or optional four-wheel ABS. On the 4X4's, front wheels get the go-ahead via a power switch located on the dashboard. This simplistic system doesn't include a main differential and can only be engaged on slippery road surfaces and at low speeds, otherwise it really deteriorates.

PROS

+ **RELIABILITY.** The owner satisfaction rate confirms this vehicle's dependability and tried-and-true technical features. The Ranger is known for its super-solid build and clean finish job that really add to its appeal and value.

+ **ON THE ROAD.** The front suspension is now less sensitive to road faults and provides competent moves and contributes to right-on steering.

+ **MANUAL GEARBOX.** It's easy to use with its smooth, accurate gears. And pedal travel and effort are well-calibrated.

+ **V6 ENGINES.** They have terrific load hauling and trailering capabilities, so they're the best choice for these utility vehicles.

+ **EXTENDED CABIN.** The 2000 extended cabin versions are equipped with a second rear door and you can cancel the original auxiliary seats if you so wish on the SuperCab versions.

+ **NICE FEATURES.** Windshield wipers that sweep a large span at a good clip, so visibility is good even in driving rain and bucket seats or 60/40 split-folding seatbench that offer good support.

CONS

- **PERFORMANCES.** The 2.5L 4-cylinder engine is fine for light tasks, but it delivers more sluggish accelerations and pickup and burns more gas with a full load and the air conditioner on. The V6 engines lack gusto at low rpm, they're far from smooth and they're real gas guzzlers. As is the case for Dodge, Ford should consider equipping the Ranger with a small V8, so as to satisfy buyers looking for power and torque in a vehicle without having to purchase an F-150.

- **RIDE COMFORT.** These pickups are out to get the job done, not pamper passengers. With an empty load, the suspension is jumpy and bounces constantly and you have to be pretty tough to take the rough ride as soon as the road surface gets the least bumpy.

- **BRAKES.** They're not impressive on the RWD models, since brakes only benefit from rear-wheel ABS and they're not too great, especially with a full load.

- **HANDLING.** Getting around on wet or damp surfaces is a hassle. The base model is equipped with a pretty flexible suspension and undersize tires, whereas the AWD models have the opposite handicap: their suspension is too hard and tires are too big.

- **STEERING.** Vehicles are equipped with rack-and-pinion steering, but it suffers from a poor reduction ratio and it's springy as heck, so it's no picnic. And the wide steer angle diameter really cripples maneuverability.

- **ALL-WHEEL DRIVE.** It's a far-from-perfect simplistic system that isn't too versatile and can only really be used on slippery roads, which limits vehicle use and safety features.

- **FUEL CONSUMPTION.** The V6's burn a lot of gas, especially for rough all-terrain use.

- **NO V8 AVAILABLE.** If the Ranger were powered by a V8 engine, it would be more versatile and could handle loads like a champion and benefit from gutsier traction, desirable traits on all-purpose vehicles, Naturally, there's the Dodge Dakota...

- **POOR FEATURE.** The base model seatbench is rather rudimentary. It provides no lateral or lumbar support. Why do you have to put yourself through such an ordeal?

CONCLUSION

The attractive price of basic versions and the reputation for sturdiness that Ford models have built goes a long way in explaining why consumers love these two models so very much. It's an old marketing credo: the better they are, the more people buy them - and vice versa.

RATING
FORD Ranger

CONCEPT : 60%
Technology :	80
Safety :	70
Interior space :	40
Trunk volume :	35
Quality/fit/finish :	75

DRIVING : 51%
Cockpit :	70
Performance :	30
Handling :	40
Steering :	75
Braking :	40

ORIGINAL EQUIPMENT : 54%
Tires :	70
Headlights :	80
Wipers :	70
Rear defroster :	0
Radio :	50

COMFORT : 56%
Seats :	65
Suspension :	50
Sound level :	50
Conveniences :	40
Air conditioning :	75

BUDGET : 62%
Price :	60
Fuel economy :	60
Insurance :	65
Satisfaction :	75
Depreciation :	50

Overall rating : 56.6%

NEW FOR 2000

Ranger: • Standard fog lights on the XLT, standard 15-inch wheels on the 4x2 XL.
B-Series: • 2.5L 4-cylinder engine withdrawn, 4 doors standard on all extended cab versions, standard 15-inch wheels.

Compare Performance, Specifications, Prices, and Classification at the end of this chapter.

EQUIPMENT

FORD Ranger MAZDA B-Series	XL base 4x2	XL SE 4x2	XLT X 4x4	XLT SE 4x4
Automatic transmission:	O	O	O	O
Cruise control:	O	O	O	O
Power steering:	S	S	S	S
Anti-lock brakes:	Sre.	Sre.	Sre.	Sre.
Traction control:	-	-	-	-
Air conditioning:	O	O	O	O
Leather:	-	-	-	-
AM/FM/radio-cassette:	O	O	S	S
Power door locks:	-	O	O	O
Power windows:	-	O	O	O
Tilt steering:	-	O	O	O
Dual adjustable mirrors:	SM	SM	SM	SE
Alloy wheels:	-	S	-	S
Anti-theft system:	-	-	-	-

Colors
Exterior: Black, White, Red, Scarlet, Platinum, Green, Gold.
Interior: Medium graphite , Brown.

AT A GLANCE...

HISTORIC
Introduced in: 1983
Made in: Louisville, Kentucky, Twin Cities, Minnesota, Edison, New Jersey, USA.

DEMOGRAPHICS
Model	Men/Wom.	Age	Married	College	Income $
Ranger	89/11 %	44	57 %	32 %	30,000
B Series	88/12%	40	70 %	36 %	35,000

INDEX
Safety:	75 %	Satisfaction:	75 %
Depreciation:	47 %	Insurance:	$ 635
Cost per mile:	$ 0.47	Number of dealers: (Ford)	5,200

SALES
Model	Canada 1997	1998	Result	USA 1997	1998	Result
Ranger	11,150	8,415	- 26.9 %	298,796	328,136	+ 9.8 %
B Series	3,990	3,722	- 5.3 %	37,697	41,620	+ 10.4 %

MAINTENANCE REQUIRED BY WARRANTY
First revision:	Frequency:	Diagnostic plug:
5,000 miles	6 months/ 5,000 miles	Yes

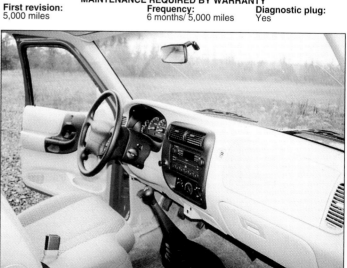

Compact Trucks

Lagging

In spite of the many efforts made by General Motors, its utilities can't catch up to Ford models, who've pranced around at the top of the sales hit parade in the U.S. for close to 20 years. The fate of its full-size trucks is exactly the same as the one suffered by its compact S-10 and Sonoma models. Still, to their credit the latter have an excellent and strong Vortec V6 whose characteristics are a decided advantage.

MODEL RANGE
The S-10 and Sonoma are almost identical twins. They're available in 4X2 and 4X4 versions, with regular or extended cabin, a long, short or «Sportside» box with running boards. Chevrolet and GMC offer them in three trim levels: base, LS and SS/ZR2 for the first vehicle; SL, SLS and SLE for the second. The 4X2 models are driven by a 2.2L 120-hp 4-cylinder base model engine; the 4X4's are powered by the 4.3L 180-hp Vortec V6. There are other engine models available, including a 190-hp powerplant for the 4X4's and another that develops 175 hp for the 4X2's. These pickup trucks aren't particularly loaded with equipment. The 4X2's are equipped with standard power steering, four-wheel ABS and intermittent wipers. The 4X4's also get four-wheel disc brakes.

TECHNICAL FEATURES
The body is made of steel that's galvanized on both sides, except for the roof panel and front frame panel. It rests on a ladder chassis with 5 crossmembers. The «InstaTrac» transfer box isn't in permanent mode, but it can be engaged via shift-on-the-fly. Engine torque is thus distributed at 35% to front wheels and at 65% to rear wheels. The independent front suspension consists of coil springs for the 4X2 models and torsion bars for the 4X4's. At the back, the rigid rear axle is supported by leaf springs. The 4X2 versions are equipped with disc and drum brakes, while the 4X4's benefit from four-wheel disc brakes. Moreover, recirculating ball steering has a variable assist system.

PROS
+ CHOICE. The wide variety of vehicles and trim levels is sure to meet each and every buyer's needs.

+ V6 ENGINE. The V6 engine packs more of a wallop than its counterparts that power rival brands. Accelerations and pickup are car-like.

+ RIDE COMFORT. Thanks to a well-honed suspension, even with an empty box, this pickup truck provides a pleasant ride. Even the 4X4 suspension is less nervous and jittery, yes, even with those big tires. Inside, you're in for a treat with those thickly upholstered, hip-hugger bucket seats. And soundproofing is quite adequate. The extended cabin seats two adults and two children in the rear fold-up auxiliary seats.

+ HANDLING. The rigid chassis and frame provide competent roadability on smooth pavement. But things get out of line quickly, so you have to keep taking your foot off the accelerator, especially on the 4X4 versions equipped with a firmer suspension and more generous tires.

+ CONVENIENT. The «InstaTrac» system automatically distributes available power to wheels with the best grip, which is a boon on difficult, uneven turf.

+ QUALITY. Compared with models in former years, over-all quality has climbed up a few notches. Build quality seems more consistent, finish details are rendered more carefully and trim materials are on the up and up.

+ THE 3RD DOOR! The third door on the driver's side is listed among original equipment items on extended cabin models. It sure helps boarding and loading stuff inside.

+ PRICE. These vehicles are sold at tempting prices. Yet original equipment is often limited.

+ STYLE. The S-10 and Sonoma pickup trucks are quite elegant; the sport and 4X4 versions attract quite a bit of attention, especially the Sportside models with their rear flare fenders.

CONS
-FUEL CONSUMPTION. The V6 engines aren't very economical to run because of their hefty displacement and weight (3 638 lbs). If fuel consumption is an issue or a priority for you, the 4-cylinder engine would maybe better suit your needs. But don't forget that this engine was designed for light tasks.

- NOISE LEVEL. The 4-cylinder models don't have appropriate sound dampening. Occupants are exposed to an unpleasant (and forever unfinished) symphony made up of road noise and squeals and such from the engine, when speeding up.

- QUALITY. These utilities' manufacturing quality and finish aren't up to the standards set by the industry's newest arrivals and some materials give them a down-market look.

- GROUND CLEARANCE. The S-10/Sonoma 4X4's are more limited on off-road maneuvers, more so than some rivals. In some cases, ground clearance is barely 8 inches.

-BRAKES. Braking isn't nice and gradual and it's only average on sudden stops. Luckily, ABS compensates by achieving greater vehicle stability. Besides, brake linings seem to hold up better than on former models.

- SEATS. Base models with regular cabin offer a pretty uncomfortable seat to occupants; they get no lateral or lumbar support when aboard this vehicle. As for the auxiliary seats, think of them as emergency tools. You don't always need them, but they're nice to have on hand when you're in a pinch.

-CONVENIENCE FEATURES. Vehicles are equipped with a very tiny glove compartment and only the more expensive members of the lineup have the right to door side-pockets and console compartment.

- TO BE IMPROVED UPON. GM should rethink a few accessories, such as the multifunction shifter to the left of the steering wheel that holds far too many controls.

CONCLUSION
They may be strong, but GM's compact pickups look down-market and aren't as well finished as their rivals. They put the "utilitarian" back into their utility designation, even on versions intended to attract an automobile clientele looking for versatility.

RATING
CHEVROLET S-10 - GMC-Sonoma

CONCEPT : 61%
- Technology : 75
- Safety : 60
- Interior space : 60
- Trunk volume : 40
- Quality/fit/finish : 70

DRIVING : 54%
- Cockpit : 80
- Performance : 45
- Handling : 40
- Steering : 75
- Braking : 30

ORIGINAL EQUIPMENT : 57%
- Tires : 70
- Headlights : 75
- Wipers : 70
- Rear defroster : -
- Radio : 70

COMFORT : 62%
- Seats : 65
- Suspension : 70
- Sound level : 45
- Conveniences : 50
- Air conditioning : 80

BUDGET : 52%
- Price : 45
- Fuel economy : 40
- Insurance : 45
- Satisfaction : 75
- Depreciation : 55

Overall rating : 57.2%

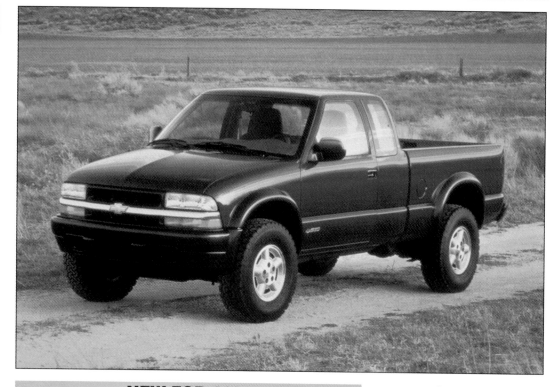

NEW FOR 2000

- An extended cab now available on the base version.
- Improvements to the 4.3L Vortec V6, manual transmission and ABS system.
- The Space Blue metallic color.

Compare Performance, Specifications, Prices, and Classification at the end of this chapter.

EQUIPMENT

CHEVROLET S-10-Series GMC Sonoma	base SL	LS SLS	Xtreme SLS	ZR2
Automatic transmission:				
Cruise control:	O	O	O	O
Power steering:	-	O	O	O
Anti-lock brakes:	S	S	S	S
Traction control:	S	S	S	S
Air conditioning:	-	-	-	-
Leather:	O	O	O	O
AM/FM/radio-cassette:	-	-	-	-
Power door locks:	O	O	O	O
Power windows:	O	O	O	S
Tilt steering:	O	O	O	S
Dual adjustable mirrors:	O	O	S	S
Alloy wheels:	-	O	S	S
Anti-theft system:	-	O	S	O
	S	S	S	S

Colors

Exterior: White, Onyx, Black, Blue, Green, Red, Copper, Silver, Gold.

Interior: Medium Grey, Graphite, Beige.

AT A GLANCE...

HISTORIC
Introduced in: 1982, 1994.
Made in: Linden NJ, Shreveport, LO, USA.

DEMOGRAPHICS

Model	Men/Wom.	Age	Married	College	Income $
S-10 Sonoma	88/12 %	44	59 %	28 %	$ 35,000

INDEX

Safety:	90 %	Satisfaction:	75 %
Depreciation:	45 %	Insurance:	$ 600
Cost per mile:	$ 0.44	Number of dealers:	4,466

SALES

Model	Canada 1997	1998	Result	USA 1997	1998	Result
S-10	8,513	7,490	- 12.0 %	192,314	228,093	+ 18.6 %
Sonoma	-			41,714	54,819	+ 31.4 %

MAINTENANCE REQUIRED BY WARRANTY

First revision:	Frequency:	Diagnostic plug:
3,000 miles	6 months / 10,000 miles	Yes

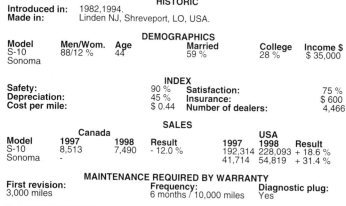

Exciting

Just when everyone thought that Japan's second leading builder was running out of steam, it began to show its newfound energy by introducing original models. The 4-door Crew Cab version took a long time to get here, but here it is at last! Users can now designate "clean" and "dirty" zones, using the same vehicle for business and pleasure. Since its revamping two years ago, the Frontier has established an image that's more exciting than anything found among its rivals. Let's hope that Nissan will reap the benefits.

MODEL RANGE

Frontier pickups are available in regular or extended frame, regular cabin or King Cab, with rear or all-wheel drive, in XE and SE trim levels. The single engine model offered is the 2.4L 4-cylinder paired up with a 5-speed manual gearbox or an optional 4-speed automatic. In 1999, the King Cab all-wheel drive will be equipped with a 3.3L V6 developing 170 hp and 200 lb.ft of torque. Engine, transmission and gas tank on the 4X4 versions are protected by standard metallic plates.

TECHNICAL FEATURES

This compact Nissan pickup consists of a steel unibody and double-sided frame are mounted on an H-frame made up of five crossmembers.

The independent front suspension consists of torsion and stabilizer bar on both the 4X2 and 4X4 versions, and the rear rigid axle is supported by conventional leaf springs. Disc and drum brakes are linked to rear-wheel ABS on the 4X2 models and all-wheel ABS on the 4X4 models, with front wheels that engage automatically. It's been refined, it's more muscular and benefits from more torque, and it's more efficient

as well, with reduced internal friction and thus, less noise, shakes and rattles.) All-wheel drive is on demand but it can be engaged when driving at less than 25 mph, providing equal wheel function on both axles and it only comes with a manual gearbox.

The V6 engine with bigger 3.3L displacement, that only represents 18% of sales is once again available, but not on all models, which is a bit of a bugbear, for the 4-cylinder engines are real wimps on the 4X4's and they consume a lot of fuel.

PROS

+ CHOICE. The Frontier lineup has been extended with the arrival of the new V6 engine and one more choice of versions. The Crew Cab version is something new: a hybrid between a 4-door automobile and a truck whose separate box can be used for any number of purposes.

+ RIDE COMFORT. It's pretty cushy since this vehicle feels more like a car than an SUV, due to the really competent front suspension that takes care of those mean streaks on the road and the rear axle doesn't bounce you to kingdom come with an empty box. The split seatbench and bucket seats are reasonably comfy and they're not too firm. Noise is kept within a comfortable range as well.

+ PERFORMANCES. The 4-cylinder engine finally has some get up and go and provides good torque at low r.p.m. for better fuel economy. But it's better suited to a RWD trans-

mission and it's equally competent with either the manual or the automatic. The V6 offers more energy ooze, so it's more fun to put through its paces, at least on good-quality roads.

+ HANDLING. It's stable even on the base versions, but it would be a good idea to weigh down the rear end a bit when driving with an empty box in slippery conditions.

+ KING CAB. It's a definite ace in the hand for Nissan, since it's bigger than its Toyota counterpart. Two children can be seated behind the seat when needed or you can stash stuff back there.

+ COCKPIT. It's straightforward, but nicely set up, so the driver sits more comfortably inside the King Cab equipped with its individual seats that are more like the seating you get in a car. Outward view is super in all directions and the short, competent shifter on the manual gearbox is neat, as is the shifter for the automatic, located under the steering wheel.

+ CONVENIENCE FEATURES. This aspect is more obvious now that there are long, divided door side-pockets, a good-size glove compartment and notches in the box that let you divide it into sections with wooden panels and it's roomy since you can transport 4X8-ft. sheets of material.

+ QUALITY. Build is tough, the finish job is neat and tight and materials used are spiffy, as is the cabin itself, much more so than in the past.

CONS

- 4-CYLINDER ENGINE. It just doesn't have what it takes to really move the King Cab 4X4 over rough terrain, for torque output is too limited and gas consumption soars sky-high.

- BRAKES. They could be be brawnier and tougher, since stops are long and resistance to overheating is mediocre. But the antilock braking system keeps the vehicle straight on course.

- MANEUVERABILITY. The King Cab 4X4's agility is really crippled by the big steer angle diameter.

- SENSITIVITY. Crosswinds really affect demeanor for all models, but especially the King Cab 4X4.

- SEATBENCH. The original one on the base models is awfully uncomfortable, since it offers no lateral or lumbar support whatsoever.

-TO BE IMPROVED UPON: Poor-quality tires, paint and fabrics and owners complain about how hard it is to find some replacement parts and how expensive they are.

CONCLUSION

Nissan has shaken off the doldrums and intends to shake up the market by introducing new ideas. As a result of its looks and the fact that its versions have been carefully developed for North American markets, there's no question that its compact Frontier pickup is the most popular of all foreign makes.

RATING	
NISSAN Frontier	

CONCEPT :		**59%**
Technology :	75	
Safety :	70	
Interior space :	50	
Trunk volume :	25	
Quality/fit/finish :	75	

DRIVING :		**54%**
Cockpit :	75	
Performance :	35	
Handling :	40	
Steering :	75	
Braking :	45	

ORIGINAL EQUIPMENT :		**56%**
Tires :	70	
Headlights :	70	
Wipers :	70	
Rear defroster :	0	
Radio :	70	

COMFORT :		**67%**
Seats :	70	
Suspension :	70	
Sound level :	60	
Conveniences :	60	
Air conditioning :	75	

BUDGET :		**66%**
Price :	60	
Fuel economy :	75	
Insurance :	60	
Satisfaction :	85	
Depreciation :	50	

Overall rating :	**60.4%**

NEW FOR 2000

- New 4-door Crew Cab body available in 4x4 or 4x2 versions powered by a 3.3L V6 engine.
- "Desert Runner" King Cab version powered by a 3.3L V6.

Compare
Performance,
Specifications, Prices,
and Classification
at the end of this chapter.

EQUIPMENT

NISSAN Frontier Cab	XE std. 4x2	XE std. 4x4	XE K.Cab 4x2	SE K.Cab 4x4
Automatic transmission:	O	O	O	O
Cruise control:	O	O	O	S
Power steering:	Sre.	S	Sre.	S
Anti-lock brakes:	S	S	S	S
Traction control:	-	O	-	S
Air conditioning:	-	O	O	S
Leather:	-	-	-	-
AM/FM/radio-cassette:	O	O	O	SCd
Power door locks:	-	-	-	S
Power windows:	-	-	-	S
Tilt steering:	O	O	O	S
Dual adjustable mirrors:	SM	SM	SM	SE
Alloy wheels:	O	O	S	S
Anti-theft system:	-	-	-	S

Colors

Exterior: Red, Bronze, Blue, Green, Ebony, White, Beige, Sandstone.

Interior: Grey, Beige.

AT A GLANCE...

HISTORIC
Introduced in: 1965-1998.
Made in: Smyrna, Tennessee, USA.

DEMOGRAPHICS

Model	Men/Wom.	Age	Married	College	Income $
Frontier	88/12%	43	69%	33%	$ 36,000

INDEX

Safety:	75 %	Satisfaction:	85 %
Depreciation:	50 %	Insurance:	$ 600
Cost per mile:	$ 0.45	Number of dealers:	1,100

SALES

	Canada			USA		
Model	1997	1998	Result	1997	1998	Result
Frontier	2,271	1,739	- 30.1 %	121,861	91,629	- 24.8 %

MAINTENANCE REQUIRED BY WARRANTY

First revision:	Frequency:	Diagnostic plug:
7,500 miles	7,500 miles	Yes

Compact Trucks

Quiet

Like other products of the same Japanese make, the Tacoma compact pickup offers nothing particularly original except for super durability. Besides its price - hefty, of course - nothing sets it apart from its counterparts. Luckily it proves to be a good investment and can be resold quickly and at a good price, as witnessed by the fact that it's hard to find on the used vehicle market.

MODEL RANGE

The Tacoma pickup is sold in RWD or AWD models equipped with 4 or 6-cylinder engines linked to a standard manual gearbox or an optional automatic. They're available in base, Xtracab or SR5 trim levels. Body styles include regular cabin or extended (Xtracab) with regular, extended or cabin chassis. The base model Tacoma is equipped with power steering and dual airbags. The Xtracab gets added tilt steering wheel and intermittent wipers and the SR5 benefits from cruise control, antilock braking, radio and tape deck and light alloy wheels. All other items are included on the list of options.

TECHNICAL FEATURES

This pickup truck is built on a steel five-crossmember H-frame on which the cabin is mounted. The front suspension consists of a double wishbone setup and stabilizer bar and steering is rack-and-pinion. The rigid rear axle is supported by two leaf springs. Trucks are equipped with disc and drum brakes but four-wheel ABS is available as an extra for all models. ABS works differently on the all-wheel drive vehicles, since it's regulated by a deceleration detector. The engine, transfer case and gas tank on the 4X4's are covered with standard metallic protective plates. The Tacoma is powered by either a 142-hp 2.4L or 150 hp 4-cylinder engine or a 3.4L V6 that delivers 190 hp. All-wheel drive models are equipped with a system that allows you to shift from RWD to AWD via shift-on-the-fly at any speed, by simply pushing a button located on the transfer case lever. Safety-wise, the frame and cabin have been reinforced to guarantee better structural integrity, doors are fitted with side-impact beams and vehicles are equipped with dual airbags, height-adjustable shoulder belts up front and the windshield washer reservoir can hold 4.5 liters of cleaner fluid. The more spacious extended cabin is equipped with auxiliary seats facing frontwards that can be folded down flat to free up the cargo area. A fold-up shelf with two cup-holders allows for enough room to install a child's seat and is a unique asset in this category.

PROS

+ REPUTATION. Toyota pickup trucks are known for their reliability and impressive durability, which explains in part their hefty price, but these vehicles also fetch a higher than average resale price and recent models are as rare as hen's teeth on the used vehicle market.

+ QUALITY. This aspect is at the very foundation of Toyota's reputation. These trucks are robust and exhibit fine fit and finish details. The over-all effect and trim materials used are topnotch.

+ PERFORMANCES. The 2.7L 4-cylinder and 3.4L V6 pump out the power and have a nice and safe level of energy on reserve if needed and accelerations and pickup are brisk.

+ HANDLING. Some RWD models behave like cars as long as the box has a bit of ballast to assure good rear wheel function.

+ CAPABILITIES. Off-road prowess on the AWD models is a cut above what the competition can muster, thanks to generous ground clearance and wide, fine-tuned entrance and exit angles.

+ FUEL EFFICIENCY. The 2.4L 4-cylinder engine is very frugal, but it's more suited to light tasks.

+ RIDE COMFORT. The Xtracab cabin is quite roomy and passengers will be more comfy in the individual seats that are nicely contoured and offer good lateral and lumbar support. But the original seatbench is another kettle of fish.

CONS

- SAFETY. The NHSTA gave low marks to these vehicles on collision tests, so occupants may be vulnerable to serious injury in the event of an accident.

- PRICE. Typical of Toyota products, Tacoma's are often more pricey than rivals with an equivalent equipment level. Luckily, their low depreciation compensates for this snag.

- TORQUE. It's lacking at low rpm, as is the case with all V6 engines that also get awfully thirsty when tackling heavy jobs or travelling over rough turf.

- BRAKES. They're not up to snuff and stopping distances in emergency situations are long and vehicle path is pretty iffy without ABS.

- CHOICE. It's more restricted than for American carmakers in regard to body style, engines and model range.

- REAR SEATS. Access is acrobatic on the Xtracab and these seats aren't too useful because they face frontwards and so there's precious little toe room.

- ROADHOLDING. The 4X4's aren't too competent on curves, due to the high-perched center of gravity and the Xtracab's are clumsy because of the wide steer angle diameter.

CONCLUSION

The Tacoma compact pickup is more of an efficient work tool than a viable second vehicle alternative for families. In spite of its qualities, it remains a utility with average passenger room and comfort and the extended cab version is the only choice that provides more elaborate equipment. Lastly, its price is off-putting for potential buyers looking for an affordable choice.

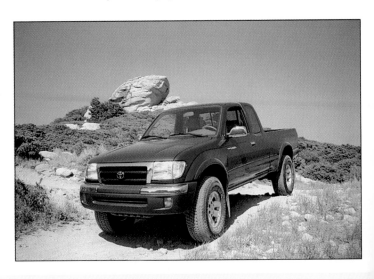

RATING
TOYOTA Tacoma

CONCEPT :   60%
Technology :	80
Safety :	50
Interior space :	30
Trunk volume :	60
Quality/fit/finish :	80

DRIVING :   56%
Cockpit :	80
Performance :	50
Handling :	30
Steering :	70
Braking :	50

ORIGINAL EQUIPMENT :   59%
Tires :	75
Headlights :	80
Wipers :	70
Rear defroster :	0
Radio :	70

COMFORT :   60%
Seats :	70
Suspension :	60
Sound level :	50
Conveniences :	40
Air conditioning :	80

BUDGET :   63%
Price :	60
Fuel economy :	65
Insurance :	50
Satisfaction :	85
Depreciation :	55

Overall rating :   59.6%

NEW FOR 2000

• **Carpeting and radio/CD player standard on all models.**

Compare
Performance,
Specifications, Prices,
and Classification
at the end of this chapter.

EQUIPMENT

TOYOTA Tacoma	Reg 2WD	Xtra 2WD	Xtra V6Ltd 4WD	V6 4WD
Automatic transmission:	O	O	O	O
Cruise control:	-	S	O	S
Power steering:	S	S	S	S
Anti-lock brakes:	-	O	O	S
Traction control:	-	-	-	-
Air conditioning:	O	O	O	S
Leather:	-	-	-	-
AM/FM/radio-cassette:	SCd	SCd	SCd	SCd
Power door locks:	-	-	-	S
Power windows:	-	-	-	S
Tilt steering:	O	O	S	S
Dual adjustable mirrors:	-	-	-	SE
Alloy wheels:	-	O	O	S
Anti-theft system:	-	-	-	-

Colors
Exterior: White, Black, Red, Jade, Seaweed, Blue, Crimson.

Interior: Grey, Oak.

AT A GLANCE...

HISTORIC
Introduced in:	1995.
Made in:	Tahara+Hino, Japan; Fremont-California, Georgetown-Kentucky, USA.

DEMOGRAPHICS
Model	Men/Wom.	Age	Married	College	Income $
Tacoma	89/11 %	35	69 %	42 %	$ 40,000

INDEX
Safety:	50 %	Satisfaction:	83 %
Depreciation:	46 %	Insurance:	$ 645
Cost per mile:	$ 0.55	Number of dealers:	1,233

SALES
	Canada			USA		
Model	1997	1998	Result	1997	1998	Result
Tacoma	2,627	3,103	+ 18.1 %	148,870	152,701	+ 4.7 %

MAINTENANCE REQUIRED BY WARRANTY
First revision:	Frequency:	Diagnostic plug:
3,000 miles	3,000 miles	No

Compact Trucks

COMPACT TRUCKS

PERFORMANCE

Model/ version	ENGINES Type / timing valve / fuel system	Displacement cu in	Power hp @ rpm	Torque lb-ft @ rpm	Compres. ratio	TRANSMISSIONS Driving wheels / transmission	Final ratio	PERFORMANCE Acceler. 0-60 mph s	Standing 1/4 mile s	Standing 5/8 mile s	Passing 50-75 mph s	Braking 60-0 mph ft	Top speed mph	Lateral acceler. G	Noise level dBA	Fuel economy mpg City	Fuel economy mpg Highway	Fuel type Octane
CHEVROLET S-10 - GMC Sonoma																		
4x2*	L4 2.2 OHV-8-SFI	134	120 @ 5000	140 @ 3600	9.0 :1	rear-M5*	2.73	12.5	18.5	35.7	10.7	148	91	0.75	70	22	32	R 87
						rear-A4	4.11	13.7	19.2	36.4	11.2	154	87	0.75	71	19	27	R 87
4x2 option	V6 4.3 OHV-12-SFI	262	175 @ 4400	240 @ 2800	9.2 :1	rear-M5*	3.42	8.0	15.8	28.2	5.8	148	103	0.77	69	16	24	R 87
			180 @ 4400	245 @ 2800	9.2 :1	rear-A4	3.42	8.5	16.4	29.5	6.0	144	109	0.77	69	16	22	R 87
4x4	V6 4.3 OHV-12-SFI	262	180 @ 4400	245 @ 2800	9.2 :1	rear/4-M5*	3.42	9.2	16.8	30.6	6.5	157	100	0.77	69	15	21	R 87
			190 @ 4400	250 @ 2800	9.2 :1	rear/4-A4	3.42	9.5	17.2	30.8	6.7	151	106	0.78	69	16	22	R 87
DODGE Dakota																		
1)	L4* 2.5 OHV-8-MPSFI	150	120 @ 5200	145 @ 3250	9.2 :1	rear - M5*	3.92	13.6	19.0	37.0	14.2	154	103	0.75	68	18	26	R 87
2)	V6* 3.9 OHV-12-MPSFI	238	175 @ 4800	225 @ 3200	9.1 :1	rear/ 4 - M5*	3.21	11.8	18.7	35.0	12.0	164	100	0.77	68	14	23	R 87
						rear/ 4 - A4	3.55	12.6	19.3	35.8	11.5	167	93	0.77	68	14	22	R 87
3)	V8 5.2 OHV-16-MPSFI	318	230 @ 4400	300 @ 3200	9.1 :1	rear/ 4 - A4	3.55	8.0	15.7	27.2	5.7	148	112	0.78	67	13	18	R 87
4)	V8 5.9 OHV-16-MPSFI	360	250 @ 4400	345 @ 3200	8.9 :1	rear - A4*	3.92	7.5	15.5	26.8	5.4	144	118	0.83	69	12	18	R 87
1) * 4x2	2) * 4x4, option 4X2	3) option	4X2, 4x4	4) R/T 4X2														
FORD Ranger - MAZDA B Series																		
4x2	L4* 2.5 SOHC-8-MPSFI	153	119 @ 5000	146 @ 3000	9.4 :1	rear - M5*	3.73	12.0	18.7	33.8	9.8	138	97	0.69	70	21	28	R 87
						rear - A4	4.10	12.8	18.8	34.2	10.5	148	93	0.69	69	20	26	R 87
4x4	V6* 3.0 OHV-12-MPSFI	182	150 @ 5000	185 @ 3750	9.1 :1	rear/4- M5*	3.73	11.0	18.3	32.2	8.7	151	100	0.71	68	16	24	R 87
						rear/4 - A4	3.73	12.2	18.8	33.8	9.8	157	97	0.71	68	16	24	R 87
option	V6 4.0 OHV-12-MPSFI	245	160 @ 4250	225 @ 3000	9.0 :1	rear/4- M5	3.55	9.5	17.2	31.4	7.5	157	106	0.73	68	18	22	R 87
						rear/4- A5	3.73	10.8	17.7	32.0	8.0	164	103	0.73	68	16	22	R 87
NISSAN Frontier																		
4x2	L4*2.4 SOHC-16-MPSFI	145	143 @ 5200	154 @ 4000	9.2 :1	rear - M5*	3.54	12.5	18.8	35.5	9.5	164	97	NA	68	21	27	R 87
						rear - A4	3.70	13.8	19.5	37.0	11.0	167	100	NA	68	18	25	R 87
4x4 XE	L4*2.4 SOHC-16-MPSFI	145	143 @ 5200	154 @ 4000	9.2 :1	rear/all-M5*	3.88	NA										
4x4 KC	V6 3.3 SOHC-12-MPSFI	200	170 @ 4800	200 @ 2800	8.9 :1	rear/all-M5	4.37	NA										
						rear/all-A4	4.37	NA										
TOYOTA Tacoma																		
1)	L4* 2.4 DOHC-16-MPSFI	149	142 @ 5000	160 @ 4000	9.5 :1	rear - M5*	3.416	NA								22	28	R 87
						rear - A4	3.583	NA								21	26	R 87
2)	L4* 2.7 DOHC-16-MPSFI	164	150 @ 4800	177 @ 4000	9.5 :1	rear/4 - M5*	3.615	12.5	19.0	36.5	10.8	151	100	0.75	68	17	23	R 87
3)	V6* 3.4 DOHC-24-MPSFI	206	190 @ 4800	220 @ 3600	9.6 :1	rear/4 - M5*	3.909	11.8	18.5	34.7	8.8	151	106	0.75	68	16	20	R 87
						rear/4 - A4	4.100	13.0	19.5	35.8	10,0	157	103	0.75	68	16	20	R 87

1) Tacoma 4X2. 2) Tacoma 4x4 Xtracab. 3)Tacoma V6

SPECIFICATIONS

Model	Version Trim	Traction	Body/ Seats	Wheel base in	Lgth x Width x Hght in x in x in	Curb weight lb	Susp. ft/rr	Brake ft/rr	Steering type	Steering ø ft	Steering turns number	Fuel tank gal	Standard tires dimensions	Standard tires make	Standard tires model	Standard powertrain	99 Price msrp $
CHEVROLET-GMC	**General warranty: 3-years / 36,000 miles; antipollution: 5-years / 50,000 miles; perforation corrosion: 6-years / 100,000 miles. Roadside assistance.**																
S-10-Sonoma short bed		4x2	2dr.p-u.2/3	108.3	190.1x67.9x62.0	3031	ih/rl	dc/dr/ABS	pwr.bal.	34.8	2.75	19.0	205/75R15	Uniroyal	Tiger Paw	L4/2.2/M5	**12,710**
S-10-Sonoma long bed		4x2	2dr.p-u.2/3	117.9	206.1x67.9x62.9	3102	ih/rl	dc/dr/ABS	pwr.bal.	36.7	2.75	19.0	205/75R15	Uniroyal	Tiger Paw	L4/2.2/M5	**13,374**
S-10-Sonoma extd cab		4x2	2dr.p-u.4/5	122.9	204.7x67.9x62.7	3240	ih/rl	dc/dr/ABS	pwr.bal.	41.7	2.75	19.0	205/75R15	Uniroyal	Tiger Paw	V6/4.3/M5	**15,942**
S-10-Sonoma short bed		4x4	2dr.p-u.2/3	108.3	190.1x67.9x63.4	3564	ih/rl	dc/ABS	pwr.bal.	34.8	2.75	19.0	205/75R15	Uniroyal	Tiger Paw	L4/2.2/M5	**17,253**
S-10-Sonoma long bed		4x4	2dr.p-u.2/3	117.9	206.1x67.9x64.4	3653	ih/rl	dc/ABS	pwr.bal.	36.7	2.75	19.0	205/75R15	Uniroyal	Tiger Paw	L4/2.2/M5	**17,585**
S-10-Sonoma extd cab		4x4	2dr.p-u.4/5	122.9	204.7x67.9x63.4	3757	ih/rl	dc/ABS	pwr.bal.	41.7	2.75	19.0	205/75R15	Uniroyal	Tiger Paw	V6/4.3/M5	**20,344**
DODGE	**General warranty: 3-years / 36,000 miles; surface rust: 3-years; perforation: 7-years / 100,000 miles; roadside assistance: 3-years /36,000 miles.**																
Dakota	reg.	4x2	2dr.p-u.2	111.9	195.8x71.5x65.6	3353	ih/rl	dc/dr/ABS*	pwr.r&p.	36.1	2.86	15.0	215/75R15	Goodyear	Wrangler ST	L4/2.5/M5	**13,870**
Dakota	long	4x2	2dr.p-u.2	123.9	215.2x71.5x65.3	3571	ih/rl	dc/dr/ABS*	pwr.r&p.	39.4	2.86	15.0	215/75R15	Goodyear	Invicta GL	V6/3.9/M5	**14,330**
Dakota	Club Cab	4x2	2dr.p-u.5	131.0	214.8x71.5x65.6	3876	ih/rl	dc/dr/ABS*	pwr.r&p.	41.3	2.86	15.0	235/75R15	Goodyear	Invicta GL	V6/3.9/M5	**17,065**
Dakota	reg.	4x4	2dr.p-u.2	112.0	195.8x71.5x67.9	3807	ih/rl	dc/dr/ABS*	pwr.ball	35.7	3.83	15.0	215/75R15	Goodyear	Wrangler RT/S	V6/3.9/M5	**17,350**
Dakota	Club Cab	4x4	2dr.p-u.5	131.0	214.8x71.5x68.5	4030	ih/rl	dc/dr/ABS*	pwr.ball	41.0	3.83	15.0	235/75R15	Goodyear	Wrangler RT/S	V8/5.2/M5	**20,275**
* ABS on rear wheels																	
FORD	**General warranty, antipollution & battery: 3-years / 36,000 miles; corrosion perforation: 5-years / unlimited.**																
Ranger	short XL	4x2	2dr.p-u.2	111.6	187.5x69.4x64.9	2961	ih/rl	dc/dr/ABS*	pwr.r&p.	-	-	16.5	205/75R14	Firestone	Radial ATX	L4/2.5/M5	**12,295**
Ranger	long XL	4x2	2dr.p-u.2	117.5	200.7x69.4x64.9	3366	ih/rl	dc/dr/ABS*	pwr.r&p.	-	-	20.0	205/75R14	Firestone	Radial ATX	L4/2.5/M5	**12,765**
Ranger	SprCab XL	4x2	2dr.p-u.3	125.7	202.9x69.4x64.8	3236	ih/rl	dc/dr/ABS*	pwr.r&p.	-	-	20.0	205/75R14	Firestone	Radial ATX	L4/2.5/M5	**15,750**
Ranger	short XL	4x4	2dr.p-u.2	111.6	188.7x70.3x64.9	3329	ih/rl	dc/dr/ABS	pwr.r&p.	-	-	16.5	215/75R15	Firestone	Wilderness HT	V6/3.0/M5	**16,175**
Ranger	long XL	4x4	2dr.p-u.2	117.5	199.5x70.3x64.9	3366	ih/rl	dc/dr/ABS	pwr.r&p.	-	-	20.0	215/75R15	Firestone	Wilderness HT	V6/3.0/M5	**16,645**
Ranger	SuperCab XL	4x4	2dr.p-u.3	125.9	201.7x70.3x64.8	3646	ih/rl	dc/dr/ABS	pwr.r&p.	-	-	20.0	215/75R15	Firestone	Wilderness HT	V6/3.0/M5	**17,785**
* on rear wheels.																	
MAZDA	**General warranty, antipollution & battery: 3-years / 36,000 miles; corrosion perforation: 5-years / unlimited.**																
B Series	short SX	4x2	2dr.p-u.2	111.6	187.5x69.4x64.9	3024	ih/rl	dc/dr/ABS*	pwr.r&p.	36.4	3.5	16.4	205/70R14	Firestone	Wilderness	L4/2.5/M5	**11,855**
B Series	CabPlus SE	4x2	2dr.p-u.2+2	125.7	202.9x69.4x64.9	3205	ih/rl	dc/dr/ABS*	pwr.r&p.	41.3	3.5	19.5	225/70R15	Firestone	Wilderness	V6/3.0/M5	**16,910**
B Series	short SX	4x4	2dr.p-u.2	111.6	187.7x70.3x64.7	3441	it/rl	dc/dr/ABS*	pwr.r&p.	37.4	3.5	16.4	215/75R15	Firestone	Wilderness	V6/3.0/M5	**18,170**
B Series	CabPlus SE	4x4	2dr.p-u.2+2	125.9	201.7x70.3x64.7	3602	it/rl	dc/dr/ABS*	pwr.r&p.	41.3	3.5	19.5	235/75R15	Firestone	Wilderness	V6/3.0/M5	**19,825**
* on rear wheels.																	
NISSAN	**General warranty: 3-years / 50,000 miles; powertrain: 6-years / 60,000 miles; perforation corrosion & antipollution: 6-years / unlimited.**																
Frontier	XE	4x2	2dr.p-u.2	104.3	184.3x66.5x62.8	3031	ih/rl	dc/dr/ABS	re.pwr.ball	33.5	3.8	15.9	215/65R15	Firestone	Wilderness	L4/2.4/M5	**12,010**
Frontier	XE KC	4x2	2dr.p-u.2+2	116.1	196.1x66.5x62.6	3172	ih/rl	dc/dr/ABS	re.pwr.ball	36.7	3.8	15.9	215/65R15	Firestone	Wilderness	L4/2.4/M5	**14,010**
Frontier	SE KC	4x2	2dr.p-u.2+2	104.3	184.3x66.5x62.6	3238	ih/rl	dc/dr/ABS	re.pwr.ball	36.7	3.8	15.9	215/65R15	BF Goodrich	-	L4/2.4/M5	**15,510**
Frontier	XE	4x4	2dr.p-u.2	104.3	184.3x66.5x66.1	3554	ih/rl	dc/dr/ABS	pwr.ball	35.4	3.8	15.9	235/75R15	Firestone	Wilderness	L4/2.4/M5	**16,510**
Frontier	XE-V6 KC	4x4	2dr.p-u.2+2	116.1	196.1x66.5x65.9	3700	ih/rl	dc/dr/ABS	pwr.ball	NA	3.8	19.3	235/75R15	Firestone	Wilderness	V6/3,3/M5	**18,810**
Frontier	SE-V6 KC	4x4	2dr.p-u.2+2	116.1	196.1x66.5x65.9	3726	ih/rl	dc/dr/ABS	pwr.ball	NA	3.8	19.3	265/70R15	BF Goodrich	-	V6/3.3/M5	**20,710**
TOYOTA	**General warranty: 3-years / 36,000 miles; powertrain 5-years / 60,000 miles; corrosion, perforation: 5-years / unlimited.**																
Tacoma	Reg	4x2	2dr.p-u.3	103.3	184.5x66.5x61.8	2579	ih/rl	dc/dr	pwr.r&p.	35.4	3.7	15.1	195/75R14	Dunlop		L4/2.4/M5	**13,118**
Tacoma	Xtra	4x2	2dr.p-u.5	121.9	203.1x66.5x62.2	2760	ih/rl	dc/dr	pwr.r&p.	41.3	3.4	15.1	215/70R14	Firestone		L4/2.4/M5	**15,288**
Tacoma	Xtra	4x4	2dr.p-u.5	121.9	203.1x66.5x67.7	3360	ih/rl	dc/dr	pwr.r&p.	40.0	3.5	18.0	225/75R15	Dunlop		L4/2.7/M5	**19,458**
Tacoma	SR5 V6	4x4	2dr.p-u.4	121.9	203.1x66.5x68.8	3430	ih/rl	dc/drABS	pwr.r&p.	40.0	3.5	18.0	31x10.5R15	Goodyear	Wrangler GSA	V6/3.4/M5	**20,548**

Notes: 1) Tire makes and models are provided solely as an indication; they are subject to change without prior notice from the automobile manufacturers.
2) See the 2000 price list at the back of this edition.

CLASSIFICATION

OUR CLASSIFICATION

Rank	Models	Concept	Driving	Equipment	Comfort	Budget	Ratings
1	**DODGE Dakota**	**62**	**57**	**61**	**71**	60	**62.2 %**
2	NISSAN Frontier	59	54	56	67	**66**	60.4 %
3	TOYOTA Tacoma	60	56	59	60	63	59.6 %
4	GM S-10 Series	61	54	57	62	52	57.2 %
5	MAZDA B Series -						
5	FORD Ranger	60	51	54	56	62	56.6 %

YOUR CLASSIFICATION

Rank	Models	98 Sales
1	**FORD Ranger**	**328,136**
2	CHEVROLET S-10	228,093
3	TOYOTA Tacoma	152,701
4	DODGE Dakota	152,629
5	NISSAN Frontier	91,629
6	GMC Sonoma	54,819
7	MAZDA B Series	41,620

Comparative Test

TRUCKS

See their performance, their specifications, their price
and their classification at the end of this chapter.

DODGE Ram

FORD F-150

GM C/K Series

TOYOTA Tundra

Trucks

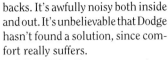
Warrior

In all of Dodge's history, no other pickup has sold as well as the Ram. There's no question, using a design concept to make it look like a truck that became world famous in the Second World War was a brilliant idea. Ingenious styling brought it solidly into the here and now, making it a modern, attractive and highly personalized product and giving it an edge that it still hasn't lost.

MODEL RANGE

Ram pickups are offered in 1500, 2500 and 3500 versions with rear or all-wheel drive, equipped with short or long boxes and cabins. The extended cabin called Club Cab can now be equipped, as an option package coined Quad Cab with four doors, that is, two rear doors allowing for easier boarding and loading. The 3.9L V6 base engine drives the 1500, a 5.2L and 5.9L V8 engine animate the 2500 and 3500, to which can be added a Cummins turbocharged diesel engine and an 8.0L V10 powerplant. Standard transmission is a 5-speed manual or a 4-speed automatic as an extra. Original equipment is rather stingy on the lower-end model that's a lowly workhorse, whereas the SLT can practically compete with genuine luxury vehicles.

TECHNICAL FEATURES

The Ram has a steel H-frame chassis consisting of five crossmembers and numerous reinforcements as to procure optimum rigidity. The side-frames on the front part of the chassis are welded and at the rear they're riveted for easier maintenance. The nicely rounded body design yields an acceptable aerodynamic efficiency for a vehicle of this type. It's mounted onto the chassis

via rubber insulators so as to reduce noise and vibration.

The independent front suspension consists of an asymmetrical double wishbone system on the 4X2 1500 and 2500 and rigid axle maintained by multiple bars on the 4X2 3500 and the 4X4's. The rear suspension is made up of a rigid axle and leaf springs. All models are equipped with disc and drum brakes and standard rear-wheel ABS, but all-wheel ABS is available as an extra.

OUTSTANDING

+ STYLE. Very manly, so to speak, which has no doubt affected a lot of buyers' choice, for it's modern, yet a tad retro, reminiscent of the famous Dodge trucks that participated in the Second World War. It's pretty hard not recognizing this pickup that was the ancestor of the Dakota and Durango.

PROS

+ RIDE COMFORT. It's one of the Ram's top assets for the suspension response is smooth, more obviously so on the 4X2's than on the 4X4's, always more nervous. Seats offer more support than before and soundproofing is almost car-like.

+ SOLIDITY. This pickup inspires confidence due to its extremely robust build. Some techniques used in chassis construction and cabin mounts have since been borrowed by the competition.

+ CHOICE. Besides the really wide range of model choice, depending on aspects that define each version, there's a remarkable choice of engines. With a range going from a V6 to a V10, including two V8's and a turbocharged Diesel, power and torque can be ordered à la carte.

+ VALUE. The Ram is a good investment either for work or leisure purposes. Rivals have caught up on the technical level, but this vehicle has a charm all its own that gives it an amazing resale value.

+ QUAD CAB. The four-door extended cab can seat up to six people quite comfortably. Or the rear section can be converted into a pretty roomy luggage hold, even though the layout isn't as clever as on the Ford F-150.

+ INSTRUMENT PANEL. It has a serious, well organized look. It's logical and ergonomic.

+ NICE FEATURE. The center part of the front seatbench has a fold-down armrest that can double as a desk...

CONS

- FUEL CONSUMPTION. You have to plan for a big gas budget, for the Ram (like its counterparts) doesn't run on water. The V8 engines does 12 to 14 mpg, so you're forever filling up.

-NOISE. The Diesel engine produces a lot of muscular power and torque, but it does have its draw-

backs. It's awfully noisy both inside and out. It's unbelievable that Dodge hasn't found a solution, since comfort really suffers.

- BRAKES. Emergency stops stretch out a heck of a long way and brakes don't have much bite when applied. The soft pedal doesn't make for precise braking. Brakes can dig in too much on sudden stops, causing some unpleasant surprises on wet roads and without ABS.

- MANEUVERABILITY. It could be better on the extended cab and Club Cab versions due to the huge steer angle diameter and it takes a lot of elbow grease to make a simple U-turn.

- ACCESS. Not too great on the 4X4's due to high ground clearance. Dodge should be able to come up with an original way of integrating a running board or step that wouldn't be affected by body-travel on rough terrain...

- BAGGAGE COMPARTMENT. Usually carmakers aren't shy about stealing ideas from the competition. What's Dodge waiting for? Why not give the rear seatbench in the Club Cab a fold-up feature as bright as the one designed by Ford for its F-150?

CONCLUSION

The Ram still has the wind in its sails, not only because of its powerful personality but also because of its many qualities, including a Diesel Cummins engine, a marvel of efficiency and performance. The hardest task ahead will be keeping this model young while protecting all of its many already acquired attributes.

RATING
DODGE Ram 1500

CONCEPT : 70%
Technology : 80
Safety : 70
Interior space : 60
Trunk volume : 65
Quality/fit/finish : 75

DRIVING : 55%
Cockpit : 75
Performance : 50
Handling : 35
Steering : 75
Braking : 40

ORIGINAL EQUIPMENT : 62%
Tires : 75
Headlights : 75
Wipers : 80
Rear defroster : 0
Radio : 80

COMFORT : 68%
Seats : 80
Suspension : 50
Sound level : 60
Conveniences : 70
Air conditioning : 80

BUDGET : 55%
Price : 50
Fuel economy : 30
Insurance : 60
Satisfaction : 80
Depreciation : 55

Overall rating : 62.0%

NEW FOR 2000

- 1500 and 2500 Club Cab models withdrawn.
- Dark Red, Bronze and Patriot Blue colors.

Compare
Performance,
Specifications, Prices,
and Classification
at the end of this chapter.

EQUIPMENT

DODGE Ram 1500 4x2	WS reg	ST extd	SLT Club Cab
Automatic transmission:	O	O	O
Cruise control:	O	O	S
Power steering:	S	S	S
Anti-lock brakes:	re.S	S	S
Traction control:	-	-	-
Air conditioning:	O	O	O
Leather:	-	-	O
AM/FM/radio-cassette:	O	S	S
Power door locks:	-	O	S
Power windows:	-	-	S
Tilt steering:	O	O	S
Dual adjustable mirrors:	SM	SM	SE
Alloy wheels:	-	O	S
Anti-theft system:	-	-	O

Colors
Exterior: Red, Driftwood brown, Green, Blue, Black, White.
Interior: Grey, Beige, Pebble.

AT A GLANCE...
HISTORIC
Introduced in: 1994.
Made in: Dodge City (Warren, Michigan), St-Louis, Missouri, USA. Largo Alberto & Saltillo, Mexico (Club Cab).

DEMOGRAPHICS
Model	Men/Wom.	Age	Married	College	Income $
Ram	92/8 %	48	81 %	19 %	$ 35 000

INDEX
Safety: 70 % Satisfaction: 80 %
Depreciation: 45 % Insurance: $ 950
Cost per mile: $ 0.62 Number of dealers: 1887

SALES
Model	Canada 1997	1998	Result	USA 1997	1998	Result
Ram	30,823	34,171	+ 10.9 %	350,257	410,130	+ 17.1 %

MAINTENANCE REQUIRED BY WARRANTY
First revision: 5,000 miles Frequency: 6 months Diagnostic plug: Yes

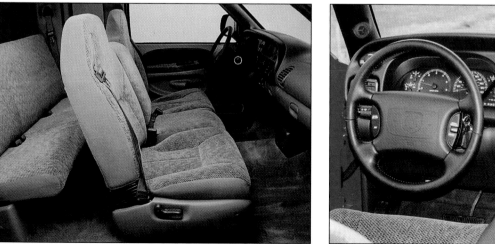

Champion

Ford's F-Series pickups are the uncontested sales champions in North America. With a phenomenal 835,000 units sold in 1998, they've shattered every single previous record. In fact, Ford now sells twice as many utility vehicles as it does ordinary automobiles. This phenomenon is characteristic of our times, when a vehicle has to play a wide range of different roles before consumers really go for it.

MODEL RANGE

By mixing and matching various elements vital to the F-150's character, we come up with about a hundred different versions, depending on rear or four-wheel drive, one of the six various wheelbase lengths, a Styleside or Flareside box and a regular or extended SuperCab. SuperCab versions have two rear doors that open opposite to the front doors and only when the latter are open. These additional doors free up a huge opening and provide super access to the rear seatbench, either for climbing aboard or for storing luggage on the platform created by the folded down bench. The F-150 comes in four equipment levels: "Work", XL, XLT and Lariat. Three Triton engines are listed in the catalogue: the 4.2L V6 that comes standard on the Work, XL and XLT versions; the 4.6L V8 that equips the Lariat but can be ordered as an extra on the other models; last of all, an optional 5.4L V8 than can equip all models. The Work, XL and XLT models come with a standard 5-speed manual gearbox or an optional 4-speed automatic. But the Lariat is equipped with a standard automatic gearbox. Again for 2000, Ford is also offering

a dual fuel V8 engine that can run on natural gas. All engines sport a device that prevents overheating, so the engine can keep running temporarily even if out of coolant.

TECHNICAL FEATURES

The F-150's steel body is set on a steel H frame consisting of 8 crossmembers. It's mounted onto the frame via rubber insulator pads that absorb secondary vibrations and other nonsense. Aerodynamics are quite good, due to the sleek front end, yielding a fairly low 0.37 drag coefficent. The front suspension is like that of the Expedition, that is, it consists of MacPherson struts and unequal-length control arms linked to coil springs on the RWD models and torsion bars on the AWD models. The rear rigid axle is supported by leaf springs. Vehicles are equipped with disc and drum brakes, with standard rear-wheel ABS. A four-wheel ABS system is listed among the options.

OUTSTANDING

++ OVERALL DESIGN. This super solid vehicle can go just about anywhere and do just about anything. Yet it's blessed with an elegant body design and provides real cabin comfort, so it's the ideal vehicle for everyday use.

PROS

+ SOLID BUILD. Brand name fanatics state the F-150's robust build

and reliability as the main reasons for their purchase. Yet the high owner satisfaction rate seems to contradict data on the still high problem rate per 100 vehicles.

+ MODEL CHOICE. With such a panoply of models, each and every customer can find what he or she is looking for.

+ LOOKS. The F-150 is a real looker with such classy, well-proportioned stylistic lines that don't make it seem any less robust and muscular. Actually, the rounded edges make the vehicle look smaller than it is.

+ RIDE COMFORT. For a heavy-duty vehicle, the ride is pretty darn comfy. Longer wheelbase models are equipped with a less jittery suspension. On the other hand, the AWD models with a short, high chassis do rough up passengers on bumpy roads.

+ REAR DOORS. The standard two rear doors on the SuperCab versions make a dramatic difference when it comes to convenience.

+ THE FEEL AT THE WHEEL. The independent front suspension has elimated wavering in crosswinds and on rutted roads, something that took the fun out of driving former F-150 pickup models.

+ STORAGE COMPARTMENTS. Upper-end models have more storage spots than do the lowly base models. The center armrest compartment can hold all the stuff that tends to hang around and make the

cabin look messy.

+ ENGINE EFFICIENCY. Engines are pretty efficient. They're smooth and gutsy. Even the V6's performances are a pleasant surprise. But these vehicles are heavyweights, so you can't really say they're fuel-efficient.

+ NICE FEATURES. The shifter that lets you go from RWD to AWD is really neat, as is the automatic AWD function that only kicks in when needed.

CONS

- BUDGET. These vehicles cost an arm and a leg. Purchase price and gas bills aren't within everyone's budget.

- FUEL CONSUMPTION. None of these conventional gas engines is fuel-frugal and unfortunately Ford doesn't offer a diesel as an alternative.

- ACCESS. You literally "climb" aboard the F-150 4X4 and even all those handles and assist grips don't compensate for the high floor threshold. Running boards look pretty essential as a purchase.

- STEERING. Steering is light and you have to have your wits about you when parking the really long models, no thanks to the big steer angle diameter.

CONCLUSION

For more than 20 years Ford has been the automotive industry's utility vehicle expert and other models such as the Explorer or the Ranger are so unbelievably popular they easily leave competitors in their dust. You have to wonder just how far the craze will go!

RATING
FORD F-150

CONCEPT :   75%
- Technology :   80
- Safety :   90
- Interior space :   75
- Trunk volume :   50
- Quality/fit/finish :   80

DRIVING :   56%
- Cockpit :   80
- Performance :   40
- Handling :   35
- Steering :   75
- Braking :   50

ORIGINAL EQUIPMENT :   79%
- Tires :   85
- Headlights :   75
- Wipers :   80
- Rear defroster :   70
- Radio :   85

COMFORT :   64%
- Seats :   70
- Suspension :   60
- Sound level :   50
- Conveniences :   60
- Air conditioning :   80

BUDGET :   52%
- Price :   40
- Fuel economy :   30
- Insurance :   60
- Satisfaction :   80
- Depreciation :   50

Overall rating :   65.2%

NEW FOR 2000

- Introduced in Detroit in 1999, the Super Crew version will give the F-150 four real doors.

Compare
Performance,
Specifications, Prices,
and Classification
at the end of this chapter.

EQUIPMENT

FORD F-150	Work 4x2	XL 4x2	XLT 4x4	Lariat 4x4
Automatic transmission:	O	O	O	O
Cruise control:	O	O	S	S
Power steering:	S	S	S	S
Anti-lock brakes:	S	S	S	S
Traction control:	-	-	-	-
Air conditioning:	-	-	SM	SM
Leather:	-	-	-	S
AM/FM/radio-cassette:	O	O	S	SCd
Power door locks:	-	-	S	S
Power windows:	-	-	S	S
Tilt steering:	O	O	S	S
Dual adjustable mirrors:	SM	SM	SE	SE
Alloy wheels:	O	O	S	S
Anti-theft system:	-	-	-	-

Colors

Exterior: Gold, Red, Blue, Green, Teal, Black, Silver, White.

Interior: Medium graphite, Brown, Blue, Dark graphite.

AT A GLANCE...

HISTORIC
Introduced in: 1996 (F-150), 1997 (F-250).
Made in: Kansas City, Missouri; Wayne, Michigan; Norfolk, Virginia; Louisville, Kentucky, USA. Oakville, Ontario, Canada.

DEMOGRAPHICS

Model	Men/Wom.	Age	Married	College	Income $
F-150 4x2	94/6 %	43	74 %	16 %	$ 35,000
F-150 4x4	94/6 %	39	60 %	25 %	$ 40 000

INDEX

Safety:	90 %	Satisfaction:	70 %
Depreciation:	50 %	Insurance:	$ 975
Cost per mile:	$ 0.55	Number of dealers:	5,200

SALES

Model	Canada 1997	1998	Result	USA 1997	1998	Result
F Series	80,950	74,859	- 7.5 %	746,111	836,629	+ 12.1 %

MAINTENANCE REQUIRED BY WARRANTY

First revision:	Frequency:	Diagnostic plug:
5,000 miles	6 months / 5,000 miles	Yes

Trucks

Refined

General Motors decided to revamp its pickups last year. It was about time: rivals were beginning to capitalize on their lead to consolidate sales levels. Although Ford is still ahead, GM is on its heels and it may well be that the latest Silverado-Sierra will give it the edge it needs to pull into first place.

MODEL RANGE

Chevrolet-GMC pickup trucks are technically identical and only differ according to some stylistic details and equipment items. There are lots of models divided up into two main families of 1/2 and 3/4-ton load capacity vehicles: the 4X2's (C 1500-2500) or 4X4's (K 1500-2500) with regular box and cabin or extended cabin in 2 or 3-door versions, with shortened box and flared side fenders called Sportside and short or long box with straight sides called Fleetside, with single or double rear wheels. Besides the 4.3L V6 and the 6.5L V8 turbocharged diesel identical to former models, you can choose between three new V8 engines: 4.8L, 5.3L and 6.0L. The Chevrolet Silverado's are sold in base, LS and LT trim levels and the GMC Sierra comes in SL, SLE and SLT models. Standard equipment on all these vehicles includes power steering and four-wheel disc brakes paired up to ABS.

TECHNICAL FEATURES

These pickup trucks are built on a galvanized steel H-frame including 9 cross-members. It's built in three sections; the front section is of hydroformed construction. The main section is U-shaped and is available in 4 lengths so as to be able to accommodate two wheelbase lengths and two cabin sizes. In fact, this new approach provides 65%

more structural integrity than was the case with the former chassis, yet it's 27% lighter. The rear end common to all models was designed to dramatically reduce the number of hookup links needed on former trailer hitches. The independent front suspension is made up of a double wishbone and added torsion bars on the 4X4's, while at the rear, the rigid rear axle is supported by leaf springs. Four-wheel disc brakes and ABS are standard equipment, as is the new rack-and-pinion steering on rear-wheel drive models with a half-ton load capacity. The body design has been completely renewed, it's wider and more spacious all round, more so than is the case for most of the competition and the third door now comes standard on the extended cabin. Lateral panels on the Sportside box are of composite material, so they're rust-proof and dent and scratch-proof. Seats and dashboard have really come a long way as far as ergonomics go and the climate control system is more effective and powerful.

PROS

+ HANDLING. The new super-solid chassis, along with the enhanced suspension have dramatically improved roadholding on the latest generation GM pickup trucks. This adds up to crisper follow-through and more stability so you can easily negociate all kinds of curves.

+ BRAKES. Four-wheel disc brakes with ABS, new-design linings, improved coolant system and balanced pressure application on rear wheels have really cut down on stopping distances by up to 30%.

+ QUALITY. It's better all-round, in terms of technical features, build, materials and finish details, so as to offer a product comparable if not superior to the competition.

+ PERFORMANCES. These pickup trucks can now receive the most powerful V8 engines in their class, so accelerations are a lot zoomier than before.

+ FINISH DETAILS. The cabin interior isn't really too different from what it was last year, but it's more refined and rounded out in the automobile sense of the term, with notably new thin-lens headlights. Inside the cabin, everything looks less like a utility vehicle, even on the lower end models fitted with more attractive-looking seats.

+ CONVENIENCE FEATURES. The cabin is roomier and is crammed with storage spots (the number varies with the trim level) and a running board step on the passenger side to facilitate boarding.

+ DRIVING PLEASURE. It's smoother than before, you feel more like you're at the wheel of a car, especially inside the half-ton load capacity models. Steering is silkier and more precise, brakes are easier to apply and the suspension be-

haves in a much more gentle fashion, since it benefits from beefier chassis rigidity. To all this, add excellent visibility offered by big, wide windows, nicely-sized mirrors and more powerful headlights.

+ RIDE COMFORT. The more flexible suspension, nicely shaped seats and more effective soundproofing have really added to cabin comfort, but it's more obvious inside the rear-wheel drive long-wheelbase models.

+ LOAD AND TRAILERING. Both have improved due to the more rigid chassis, roomier boxes, a whole range of new more powerful engines as well as more effective trailer hitch systems more suited to owners' needs.

CONS

- FUEL CONSUMPTION. It gets sky-high with the V8 gas engines and forces you to consider buying the turbocharged diesel engine if you're on the road a lot.

- MANEUVERABILITY. These bulky utility vehicles are tricky to put through certain maneuvers, which takes getting used to.

- RIDE COMFORT. In the short-wheelbase or 4X4's, the ride gets pretty bumpy as soon as the pavement goes awry and the turbocharged diesel engine makes the optional added sound dampening a must if you really want to be comfortable.

CONCLUSION

The C/K pickups are on the same level as their competitors. It remains to be seen if they can move ahead of them when the next 1999 sales statistics are compiled.

RATING
CHEVROLET Silverado-GMC Sierra

CONCEPT : **72%**
Technology :	80
Safety :	90
Interior space :	60
Trunk volume :	50
Quality/fit/finish :	80

DRIVING : **56%**
Cockpit :	80
Performance :	40
Handling :	40
Steering :	80
Braking :	40

ORIGINAL EQUIPMENT : **61%**
Tires :	75
Headlights :	80
Wipers :	80
Rear defroster :	-
Radio :	80

COMFORT : **70%**
Seats :	75
Suspension :	65
Sound level :	55
Conveniences :	75
Air conditioning :	80

BUDGET : **56%**
Price :	50
Fuel economy :	30
Insurance :	70
Satisfaction :	80
Depreciation :	50

Overall rating : **63.0%**

NEW FOR 2000

• **Emerald Green color to replace the former Prairie Green.**

Compare
Performance,
Specifications, Prices,
and Classification
at the end of this chapter.

EQUIPMENT

CHEVROLET Silverado	base	LS	LT
GMC Sierra	LS	SLE	SLT
	O	O	S
Automatic transmission:	O	O	S
Cruise control:	S	S	S
Power steering:	S	S	S
Anti-lock brakes:	-	-	-
Traction control:	O	S	S
Air conditioning:	-	O	S
Leather:	O	SCd	SCd
AM/FM/radio-cassette:	-	S	S
Power door locks:	-	S	S
Power windows:	S	S	S
Tilt steering:	SM	SE	SE
Dual adjustable mirrors:	O	S	S
Alloy wheels:	S	S	S
Anti-theft system:			

Colors

Exterior: Green, Grey, Gold, Red, Copper, Blue, Pewter, Black, White.

Interior: Neutral, Blue, Grey, Red.

AT A GLANCE...

HISTORIC
Introduced in:	1936-1992.
Made in:	Fort Wayne, Indiana, Pontiac, Michigan, USA. Oshawa, Ont., Canada.

DEMOGRAPHICS
Model	Men/Wom.	Age	Married	College	Income $
Silverado	96/4 %	49	65 %	15 %	$ 33,000
Sierra	96/4 %	47	61 %	18 %	$ 32,000

INDEX
Safety:	90 %	Satisfaction:	82 %
Depreciation:	50 %	Insurance:	$ 650
Cost per mile:	$ 0.58	Number of dealers:	4,466

SALES
	Canada			USA		
Model	1997	1998	Result	1997	1998	Result
C/K	86,214	84,641	- 1.8 %	552,990	555,990	+ 0.5 %

MAINTENANCE REQUIRED BY WARRANTY
First revision:	Frequency:	Diagnostic plug:
3,000 miles	6 months / 10,000 miles	Yes

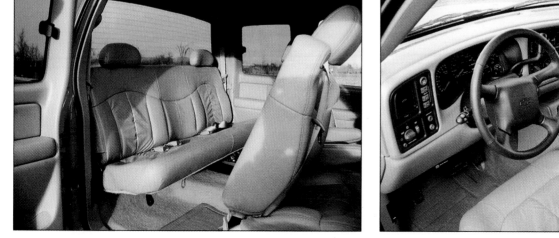

Trucks

After testing the market for a few years with the 6-cylinder engine T100 - far from able to take on the products offered by the three leading American builders - Toyota has taken the final step needed to tackle its rivals head on, bringing its V8 Tundra into the fray.

Vengeful

MODEL RANGE

The Tundra is available with rear-wheel or all-wheel drive and a regular cab or an extended "Access Cab", powered by either a 3.4L V6 or a 4.7L V8, with a 5-speed manual or optional 4-speed automatic transmission. New finishes have been dubbed the DLX And SR5. The first includes minimal equipment: power steering and a radio/cassette player. The SR5 adds an electronic 2-speed transfer case, cruise control, a split folding rear seat, halogen headlamps and a wide range of small design details more or less important to the average consumer. The Tundra also comes with three different options packages designed to help owners bring its equipment and presentation level in line with even the luxury car class.

TECHNICAL FEATURES

The Tundra is classically built, based on a steel chassis with five crossmembers to support the cab. The rear suspension features leaf springs and the front includes double superimposed triangles and a stabilizer bar. The Tundra is equipped with a rack-and-pinion steering system. Brakes are mixed, and the four-wheel antilock system is standard on some but optional on other models. It works differently on four-wheel drives, where it also has a deceleration detector. The engine, transfer case and fuel tank on 4x4 versions are protected by standard metal plates. Regardless of the speed level, AWD models can be shifted into all-wheel drive using a dashboard button. Safety features include a reinforced chassis and cab for more sturdiness, crash-resistant doors, standard dual airbags and a passenger-side airbag deactivating system. The extended cab model has 4 doors, including 2 rear suicide-type doors, a bench seat with two headrests, and a collapsible center armrest.

PROS

+ REPUTATION. The Toyota name is well-respected when it comes to reliability and durability. GM, Ford and Chrysler already know that they'll have to enhance the quality of their models now that the Tundra has come along and that consumers will make the inevitable comparisons.

+ QUALITY. It's obvious wherever you look; construction, finish and presentation have all improved and materials look less utilitarian.

+ TECHNOLOGY. The V8 engine is one of the most advanced of its generation. It's derived from the unit used to power the Lexus and as a result, is quiet and generates almost no vibration.

+ PERFORMANCE. Although the V6 makes this model behave a lot like the former T100, with the V8 acceleration and pick-up are significantly stronger and when driving without a heavy load and on wet roads, drivers would be well-advised to use the gas pedal wisely.

+ STYLING. Midway between the F-150 and the Dodge Ram, this truck is very American. Aggressive but not exaggerated, it exudes quiet power but isn't intended to be provocative.

+ COMFORT. For a utility vehicle the rear-wheel drive Tundra has a relatively smooth ride, a fairly low noise level at cruising speeds. Its comfy seats provide adequate support, even on the DLX version, but unfortunately they sport vinyl trims.

+ DRIVEABILITY. V8 engines are known for their smoothness and quietness, but the Tundra's is one of the silkiest found on a utility. On rear-wheel drive versions the steering system is precise and results in handling ease that is very satisfactory for a vehicle of this size.

+ PRACTICALITY. Although not as spectacular as GM's or Ford's, the dashboard is practical and ergonomic with its slightly overhanging center console putting radio and air conditioning controls within very easy reach. The simply designed center armrest makes it easy for occupants to slide from left to right inside the passenger compartment.

+ BONUS MARKS. For large storage spaces including a big glovebox, a dummy pedal for the driver's convenience, and a double 12-volt socket.

CONS

- PRICE. Toyota will soon find out if the clientele group specific to the pickup market is ready to pay more for superior quality. The experiment wasn't conclusive with the T100, hindered by its V6 engine. The Tundra has more arguments in its favor to win over a larger crowd of potential buyers.

- V6 ENGINE. It suffers from comparison with the V8 and its lack of torque in the lower rpm range seems to be more obvious than it was on the old T100. Fuel consumption levels climb quickly during intense or off-road use.

- BRAKING. On test drive vehicles emergency stopping distances were long and without an antilock system, the vehicle was hard to keep on course.

- TRAJECTORIES. A high ground clearance makes it harder to corner on 4x4 versions and handling ease is penalized by a long turning radius.

CONCLUSION

Now Toyota can compete on the North American market on equal footing with the big domestic builders. It may not totally upset the established order, but it will force manufacturers to look at quality as a crucial component in marketing strategies. And if that's all the Tundra ever accomplishes, the idea will have been worthwhile.

RATING
TOYOTA Tundra

CONCEPT :   **71%**
Technology :	80
Safety :	80
Interior space :	55
Trunk volume :	60
Quality/fit/finish :	80

DRIVING :   **64%**
Cockpit :	80
Performance :	60
Handling :	50
Steering :	80
Braking :	50

ORIGINAL EQUIPMENT :   **61%**
Tires :	75
Headlights :	80
Wipers :	70
Rear defroster :	0
Radio :	80

COMFORT :   **69%**
Seats :	75
Suspension :	60
Sound level :	60
Conveniences :	70
Air conditioning :	80

BUDGET :   **60%**
Price :	30
Fuel economy :	50
Insurance :	50
Satisfaction :	90
Depreciation :	80

Overall rating :   **65.0%**

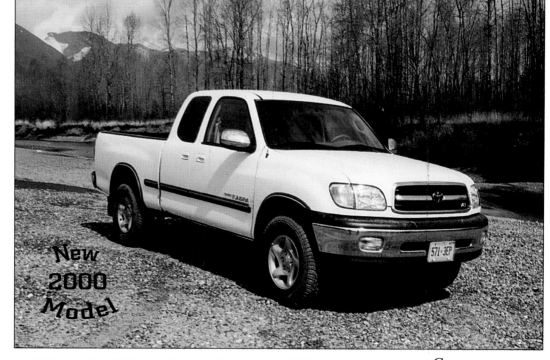

New 2000 Model

NEW FOR 2000

• A revamping of the former T100, now available with a powerful 4.7L V8.

Compare Performance, Specifications, Prices, and Classification at the end of this chapter.

EQUIPMENT

TOYOTA Tundra	DLX	SR5
Automatic transmission:	O	O
Cruise control:	-	S
Power steering:	S	S
Anti-lock brakes:	O	O
Traction control:	-	-
Air conditioning:	-	-
Leather:		O
AM/FM/radio-cassette:	S	SCd
Power door locks:	-	S
Power windows:	-	S
Tilt steering:	-	S
Dual adjustable mirrors:	SM	SE
Alloy wheels:	-	S
Anti-theft system:		

Colors
Exterior: White, Grey, Black, Red, Jade.

Interior: Grey, Oak.

AT A GLANCE...

HISTORIC
Introduced in:	2000.
Made in:	Indiana, USA.

DEMOGRAPHICS
Model	Men/Wom.	Age	Married	College	Income $
Tundra	NA				

INDEX
Safety:	80 %	Satisfaction:	90 %
Depreciation:	20 %	Insurance:	$ 675
Cost per mile:	$ 0.50	Number of dealers:	1,233

SALES
	Canada			USA		
Model	1997	1998	Result	1997	1998	Result
T100	118	48	- 59.3 %	28,381	7,959	- 72.0 %

MAINTENANCE REQUIRED BY WARRANTY
First revision:	Frequency:	Diagnostic plug:
4,000 miles	4,000 miles	Yes

TRUCKS

PERFORMANCE

Model/ version	Type / timing valve / fuel system	Displacement cu in	Power hp @ rpm	Torque lb-ft @ rpm	Compres. ratio	Driving wheels / transmission	Final ratio	Acceler. 0-60 mph s	Standing 1/4 & 5/8 mile s		Passing 50-75 mph s	Braking 60-0 ft	Top speed mph	Lateral acceler. G	Noise level dBA	Fuel economy mpg City	Highway	Fuel type Octane
CHEVROLET Silverado - GMC Sierra																		
base	V6 4.3 OHV-12-SFI	262	200 @ 4600	260 @ 2800	9.4 :1	rear - M5	3.08	11.7	18.0	33.0	7.6	183	90	0.63	68	16	22	R 87
options	V8 4.8 OHV-16-SFI	293	270 @ 5200	285 @ 4000	9.5 :1	rear/4 - M5	3.42	NA										R 87
	V8 5.3 OHV-16-SFI	325	285 @ 5200	325 @ 4000	9.5 :1	rear/4 - A4	3.42	NA										R 87
	V8 6.0 OHV-16-SFI	364	300 @ 4800	355 @ 4000	9.4 :1	rear/4 - M5	4.10	NA										R 87
	V8 TD 6.5 OHV-16-MI	394	215 @ 3400	440 @ 1800	19.5 :1	rear/4 - M5	3.73	NA										D
DODGE Ram																		
1500 4x2	V6* 3.9 OHV-12-MPSFI	238	175 @ 4800	230 @ 3200	9.1 :1	rear - M5*	3.21	12.0	18.6	33.2	8.4	157	100	0.71	68	14	22	R 87
1500 4X4	V8* 5.2 OHV-16-MPSFI	318	230 @ 4400	300 @ 3200	9.1 :1	rear - M5*	3.55	11.5	18.2	32.6	8.0	194	106	0.74	67	12	20	R 87
1500	V8* 5.9 OHV-16-MPSFI	360	245 @ 4000	335 @ 3200	8.9 :1	rear - M5*	3.54	9.0	16.5	31.5	6.5	184	103	0.75	67	12	20	R 87
option	L6DT 5.9 OHV-24-MI	359	235 @ 2700	460 @ 1600	17.5 :1	rear - M5*	3.54	14.0	19.5	33.0	12.0	174	93	0.72	72	16	23	D
option	V10 8.0 OHV-20-MPSFI	488	310 @ 4000	450 @ 2800	8.6 :1	rear/4 - M5*	3.54	8.5	16.6	30.4	6.5	184	109	0.73	69	10	14	R 87
FORD F Series																		
base	V6* 4.2 OHV-12-MPSFI	256	205 @ 4750	250 @ 3000	9.3 :1	rear/4 - M5	3.08	12.0	18.3	33.7	9.8	154	100	0.68	68	14	21	R 87
						rear/4 - A4	3.31	13.0	18.8	34.8	10.6	161	97	0.68	68	16	22	R 87
option	V8 4.6 SOHC-16-MPSFI	281	220 @ 4500	290 @ 3250	9.0 :1	rear/4 - M5	3.08	11.0	17.5	33.2	8.0	151	103	0.68	68	14	20	R 87
						rear/4 - A4	3.08	11.7	18.1	33.4	8.5	157	100	0.68	68	14	21	R 87
option	V8 5.4 SOHC-16-MPSFI	330	260 @ 4500	345 @ 2300	9.0 :1	rear/4 - A4	3.08	10.0	17.2	32.4	7.4	157	106	0.68	68	13	20	R 87
TOYOTA Tundra																		
base	V6 3.4 DOHC-24-SFI	206	190 @ 4800	220 @ 3600	9.6 :1	rear/4 - A4	-											
option	V8 4.7 DOHC-32-SFI	284	245 @ 4800	315 @ 3400	9.6 :1	rear/4 - A4	-											

SPECIFICATIONS

Model	Version Trim	Traction	Body/ Deats	Wheel base in	Lgth x Width x Hght in x inx in	Curb weight lb	Susp. ft/rr	Brake ft/rr type	Steering ø ft	turns number	Fuel tank gal	dimensions	Standard tires make	model	Standard powertrain	99 Price msrp $
CHEVROLET / GMC		*General warranty: 3-years / 36,000 miles; antipollution: 5-years / 50,000 miles; perforation corrosion: 6-years / 100,000 miles. Road assistance.*														
Silverado-Sierra reg.cab.short bed		4x2	2dr.p-u.3	119.0	203.1x78.5x71.2	3920	ih/rl	dc/ABS	pwr.r&p. 43.6	3.04	26.0		235/75R16	Uniroyal	Tiger Paw	V6/4.3/M5	15,995
Silverado-Sierra reg.cab.long bed		4x2	2dr.p-u.3	133.0	222.0x78.5x71.0	4032	ih/rl	dc/ABS	pwr.r&p. 40.4	3.04	34.0		235/75R16	Uniroyal	Tiger Paw	V6/4.3/M5	20,240
Silverado-Sierra long cab short bed.		4x2	2dr.p-u.3/5	143.5	227.6X78.5x71.2	4235	ih/rl	dc/ABS	pwr.r&p. 46.6	3.04	26.0		235/75R16	Uniroyal	Tiger Paw	V6/4.3/M5	16,295
Silverado-Sierra long cab & bed		4x2	2dr.p-u.3/5	157.5	246.5x78.5x70.8	4442	ih/rl	dc/ABS	pwr.r&p. 50.5	3.04	34.0		235/75R16	-		V6/4.3/M5	21,135
Silverado-Sierra reg.cab.short bed		4x4	2dr.p-u.3	119.0	203.3x78.5x73.8	4248	it/rl	dc/ABS	pwr.ball 43.6	2.88	26.0		245/75R16	GoodyearWrangler RT/SV6/4.3/M5			20,110
Silverado-Sierra reg.cab.long bed		4x4	2dr.p-u.3	133.0	222.2x78.5x73.8	4365	it/rl	dc/ABS	pwr.ball 44.6	2.88	34.0		245/75R16	GoodyearWrangler RT/SV6/4.3/M5			20,410
Silverado-Sierra long cab short bed.		4x4	2dr.p-u.3/5	143.5	227.6x78.5x73.8	4621	it/rl	dc/ABS	pwr.ball 47.2	2.88	26.0		245/75R16	GoodyearWrangler RT/SV6/4.3/M5			22,860
Silverado-Sierra long cab & bed		4x4	2dr.p-u.3/5	157.5	246.7x78.5x73.8	4749	it/rl	dc/ABS	pwr.ball 51.2	2.88	34.0		245/75R16	-		V6/4.3/M5	23,755
DODGE Ram		*General warranty: 3-years / 36,000 miles; surface rust: 3-years ; perforation: 7-years / 100,000 miles; roadside assistance: 3-years / 36,000 miles.*														
1500	Reg. cab. short bed	4x2	2dr.p-u.3	118.7	204.2x79.4x71.9	4224	ih/rldc/dr/ABS*	pwr.ball 40.9	3.2	25.9		225/75R16	GoodyearWrangler APc V6/3.9/M5			15,435
1500	Reg. cab. extd bed	4x2	2dr.p-u.3	134.7	224.1x79.4x72.1	4334	ih/rldc/dr/ABS*	pwr.ball 45.7	3.9	34.9		245/75R16	Michelin	LTX	V6/3.9/M5	15,705
1500	Cab/Quad extd bed	4x2	4dr.p-u.6	154.7	244.1x79.3x72.8	4665	ih/rldc/dr/ABS*	pwr.ball 52.4	3.9	34.9		215785R16	Michelin	LTX	V8/5.2/M5	20,910
1500	Reg. cab. short bed	4x4	2dr.p-u.3	118.7	204.2x79.4x74.7	4672	rt/rldc/dr/ABS*	pwr.ball 40.9	3.0	25.9		225/75R16	GoodyearWrangler APc V8/5.2/M5			20,770
1500	Reg. cab. extd bed	4x4	2dr.p-u.3	134.7	224.1x79.4x75.1	4746	rt/rldc/dr/ABS*	pwr.ball 45.6	3.7	34.9		245/75R16	Michelin	LTX	V8/5.2/M5	21,110
1500	Cab/Quad extd bed	4x4	4dr.p-u.6	154.7	244.1x79.3x77.2	5020	rt/rldc/dr/ABS*	pwr.ball 52.4	3.7	34.9		215785R16	Michelin	LTX	V8/5.2/M5	24,220

* ABS on rear wheels.

FORD		*General warranty, antipollution & battery: 3-years / 36,000 miles; corrosion perforation: 5-years / unlimited.*														
F-150	Reg. cab.short bed.Work	4x2	2dr.p-u.3	119.9	202.2x78.4x72.4	3849	ih/rldc/dr/ABS*	pwr.ball 40.5	3.3	25.0		235/70R16	Firestone	Wilderness	V6/4.2/M5	15,795
F-150	Reg. cab. extd bed Work	4x2	2dr.p-u.5	138.5	220.8x78.4x72.6	4235	ih/rldc/dr/ABS*	pwr.ball 40.4	3.3	25.0		235/70R16	Firestone	Wilderness	V6/4.2/M5	16,085
F-150	Sup.Cab.short bedt.XL	4x2	2dr.p-u.3	138.5	220.8x78.4x72.6	4045	ih/rldc/dr/ABS*	pwr.ball 45.9	3.3	25.0		235/70R16	Firestone	Wilderness	V6/4.2/M5	19,545
F-150	Sup.Cab.extd. bed XLT	4x2	2dr.p-u.3	157.1	239.4x78.4x72.4	4200	ih/rldc/dr/ABS*	pwr.ball 51.3	3.3	30.0		235/70R16	Firestone	Wilderness	V6/4.2/M5	22,740
F-150	Reg.cab.short bed. Work	4x4	2dr.p-u.3	120.2	203.7x79.5x72.1	3959	it/rl dc/dr/ABS	pwr.ball 45.9	3.3	24.5		235/70R16	GoodyearWrangler RT/SV6/4.2/M5			19,015
F-150	Reg. cab. extd. bed. Work	4x4	2dr.p-u.5	138.8	222.3x79.5x72.1	4339	it/rl dc/dr/ABS	pwr.ball 45.8	3.3	25.0		235/70R16	GoodyearWrangler RT/SV6/4.2/M5			19,305
F-150	Sup.Cab.short bedt.XL	4x4	2dr.p-u.5	138.8	222.3x79.5x75.3	4478	it/rl dc/dr/ABS	pwr.ball 45.8	3.3	25.0		235/70R16	GoodyearWrangler RT/SV6/4.2/M5			22,210
F-150	Sup.Cab.extd. bed. XLT	4x4	2dr.p-u.5	157.4	240.9x79.5x75.1	4605	it/rl dc/dr/ABS	pwr.ball 51.2	3.3	30.0		235/70R16	GoodyearWrangler RT/SV6/4.2/M5			26,705

* ABS on rear wheels.

TOYOTA		*General warranty: 3-years / 36,000 miles; powertrain 5-years / 60,000 miles; corrosion, perforation: 5-years / unlimited.*														
Tundra	Reg. cab.	4x2	2dr.p-u.3	128.3	196.8x75.2x70.9	3861	ih/rl	dc/dr	pwr.r&p.	- 3.4	26.4		245/70R16	-		V6/3.4/A4	-
Tundra	Access cab.	4x2	4dr.p-u.5	128.3	217.5x75.2x71.1	4298	ih/rl	dc/dr/ABS	pwr.r&p.	- 3.4	26.4		245/70R16	-		V8/4.7/A4	-
Tundra	Reg. cab.	4x4	2dr.p-u.3	128.3	196.8x75.2x70.9	4104	ih/rl	dc/dr	pwr.r&p.	- 3.4	26.4		245/70R16	-		V6/3.4/A4	-
Tundra	Access cab.	4x4	4dr.p-u.5	128.3	217.5x75.2x71.1	4398	ih/rl	dc/dr/ABS	pwr.r&p.	- 3.4	26.4		245/70R16	-		V6/3.4/A4	-
Tundra	Access cab.	4x4	4dr.p-u.5	128.3	217.5x75.2x71.1	4541	ih/rl	dc/dr/ABS	pwr.r&p.	- 3.4	26.4		245/70R16	-		V8/4.7/A4	-

Notes: 1) Tire makes and models are provided solely as an indication; they are subject to change without prior notice from the automobile manufacturers.
2) See the 2000 price list at the back of this edition.

CLASSIFICATION

OUR CLASSIFICATION

Rank	Models	Concept	Driving	Equipment	Comfort	Budget	Ratings
1	**TOYOTA Tundra**	71	**64**	61	69	**60**	**65.0 %**
2	FORD F-150	**75**	56	**76**	64	52	64.6 %
3	GM C/K Series	72	56	61	**70**	56	63.0 %
4	DODGE Ram	71	55	59	68	55	61.6 %

YOUR CLASSIFICATION

Rank	Models	98 Sales
1	FORD F Series	836,629
2	GM C/K Series	555,990
3	DODGE Ram	410,130
4	TOYOTA T100 (Tundra)	7,959

Trucks

Page	Brand	Model		$ Canada	$ USA
	Acura	CL	4 cyl	30 900	$ 23,100
	Acura	CL	6 cyl	35 000	$ 26,150
170	Acura	EL	SE	19 800	
	Acura	EL	Sport	21 600	
	Acura	EL	Premium	22 800	
254	Acura	Integra	RS	21 800	
	Acura	Integra	GS	26 000	$ 20,850
	Acura	Integra	GS-R	27 800	$ 22,100
	Acura	Integra	Type-R	30 800	
	Acura	Integra	LS		$ 20,000
	Acura	NSX	man ou aut	140 000	$ 88,000
210	Acura	RL	3.5L	55 000	$ 41,900
178	Acura	TL	3.2L	35 000	$ 27,950
366	Acura	SLX	base		$ 36,300
360	AM General	XLC2	2 p TDi	101 500	$ 68,362
	AM General	HMC0	4 p TDi	111 500	$ 75,702
	AM General	HMC4	4 p TDi	120 700	$ 82,042
	AM General	HMCS	4 p TDi	126 250	$ 85,718
	Aston-Martin	DB7	3.2L	175 000	
	Aston-Martin	DB7 volante	3.2L	185 000	
180	Audi	A4	1.8L T man	32 700	$ 23,790
	Audi	A4	1.8L T man quattro	35 450	$ 23,790
	Audi	A4	2.8L man	38 800	$ 28,390
	Audi	A4	2.8L quattro man	41 550	$ 28,390
212	Audi	A6	2.8L	48 880	$ 33,750
	Audi	A6	2.8L quattro	51 630	$ 33,750
	Audi	A6	2.7T	57 000	$ 39,600
	Audi	A6	4.2	70 000	$ 57,000
	Audi	A6	2.8L quattro	53 295	
242	Audi	A8	4.2L	90 450	$ 57,445
276	Audi	TT	4RM	nd	$ 30,500
	Bentley	Azure		500 000	
	Bentley	Continental	-R	440 000	
	Bentley	Continental	-T	450 000	
278	BMW	Série 3	318 Ti	27 800	$ 23,200
	BMW	Série 3	318 iS	34 300	
	BMW	Série 3	323 Ci	38 900	$ 28,700
	BMW	Série 3	328 Ci	46 900	$ 33,200
	BMW	Série 3	M3	62 900	$ 39,700
	BMW	Série 3	323i	34 900	$ 26,990
	BMW	Série 3	328i	44 900	$ 33,990
	BMW	Série 3	318 iC	44 900	
	BMW	Série 3	323 iC	49 900	$ 34,700
	BMW	Série 3	328 iC	58 900	$ 41,700
214	BMW	Série 5	528I	57 200	$ 38,900
	BMW	Série 5	528iT	59 150	$ 40,700
	BMW	Série 5	540 i ber	72 900	$ 53,900
	BMW	Série 5	540i fam	74 850	$ 53,485
244	BMW	Série 7	740 i	89 900	$ 62,400
	BMW	Série 7	740i LA	93 900	$ 66,400
	BMW	Série 7	750 i LA	137 900	$ 92,100
278	BMW	Z3	2.3	43 900	$ 29,950
	BMW	Z3	2.8	52 900	$ 36,200
	BMW	Z3	roadster M 3.2	61 900	$ 41,800
	BMW	Z3	roadster coupé	61 900	$ 41,800
146	Buick	Century 2000	Custom	25 440	$ 19,602
	Buick	Century 2000	Limited	26 009	$ 21,737
158	Buick	Le Sabre 2000	Custom	30 465	$ 23,235
	Buick	Le Sabre 2000	Limited	35 725	$ 27,340
216	Buick	Park Ave. 2000	base	41 850	$ 31,730
	Buick	Park Ave. 2000	Ultra	48 310	$ 36,800
146	Buick	Regal 2000	LS	27 695	$ 22,220
	Buick	Regal 2000	GS	30 989	$ 25,065
184	Cadillac	Catera 2000		42 310	$ 34,180
218	Cadillac	DeVille 2000	base	49 710	$ 39,500
	Cadillac	DeVille 2000	DHS	54 815	$ 44,700
	Cadillac	DeVille 2000	DTS	57 490	$ 44,700
220	Cadillac	Eldorado 2000	sport	53 230	$ 39,335
	Cadillac	Eldorado 2000	touring	56 925	$ 43,695
364	Cadillac	Escalade	base	63 055	$ 46,255
220	Cadillac	Seville 2000	SLS	59 970	$ 43,880
	Cadillac	Seville 2000	STS	63 775	$ 48,480
306	Chevrolet	Astro	cargo 2RM	23 290	$ 20,040
	Chevrolet	Astro	cargo 4RM	26 290	$ 22,440
	Chevrolet	Astro	base	23 839	$ 21,387
	Chevrolet	Astro	LS	27 025	$ 22,198
	Chevrolet	Astro	LT	30 925	$ 24,419
	Chevrolet	Astro	base 4RM	27 025	$ 22,940
	Chevrolet	Astro	LS 4RM	30 025	$ 24,419
	Chevrolet	Astro	LT 4RM	33 925	$ 25,940
340	Chevrolet	Blazer	base	26 895	$ 16,800
	Chevrolet	Blazer	LS	29 425	$ 18,970
	Chevrolet	Blazer	base	30 510	$ 19,270
	Chevrolet	Blazer	LS	34 200	$ 24,200
	Chevrolet	Blazer	LT (cuir)	37 450	$ 26,270
	Chevrolet	Blazer	base 4RM	28 750	$ 18,270
	Chevrolet	Blazer	LS 4RM	31 750	$ 19,870
	Chevrolet	Blazer	base 4RM	32 800	
	Chevrolet	Blazer	LS 4RM	36 485	$ 26,740
	Chevrolet	Blazer	LT 4RM	39 735	$ 28,470
	Chevrolet	Blazer	Trailblazer 4RM	41 645	$ 31,470
260	Chevrolet	Camaro 2000	base	25 890	$ 16,840
	Chevrolet	Camaro 2000	déc	32 915	$ 24,140
	Chevrolet	Camaro 2000	Z28	31 455	$ 21,265
	Chevrolet	Camaro 2000	déc Z28	38 095	$ 28,635
78	Chevrolet	Cavalier	base	15 365	$ 13,065
	Chevrolet	Cavalier	ber base	15 515	$ 13,165
	Chevrolet	Cavalier	ber LS	18 575	$ 14,710
	Chevrolet	Cavalier	Z24	20 035	$ 16,270
	Chevrolet	Cavalier	déc Z24	26 450	$ 19,735
280	Chevrolet	Corvette 2000	hardtop	51 665	$ 38,320
	Chevrolet	Corvette 2000		56 430	$ 38,895
	Chevrolet	Corvette 2000		63 410	$ 45,320
	Chevrolet	Express G 10	cargo	25 330	$ 20,310
	Chevrolet	Express G 10	standard	29 155	$ 22,760
	Chevrolet	Express G 10	LS	31 975	
160	Chevrolet	Impala	base		$ 18,790
	Chevrolet	Impala	LS		$ 22,635
	Chevrolet	Lumina	. base	23 074	$ 18,705
	Chevrolet	Lumina	. LS	23 749	
	Chevrolet	Lumina	LTZ	25 270	
	Chevrolet	Lumina	LTZ 3.8L	25 965	
108	Chevrolet	Malibu 2000	base	21 920	$ 16,460
	Chevrolet	Malibu 2000	LS	24 740	$ 17,467
66	Chevrolet	Metro	1.0	10 690	$ 9,185
	Chevrolet	Metro	1.3	11 350	$ 10,035
	Chevrolet	Metro		11 680	$ 10,610
100	Chevrolet	Prizm	base		$ 13,816
	Chevrolet	Prizm	LSi		$ 15,842
	Chevrolet	Monte Carlo 2000 LS		24 915	$ 19,290
	Chevrolet	Monte Carlo 2000 SS		26 345	$ 21,735
390	Chevrolet	Silverado cab. rég 2RM 4.3 V6		21 735	$ 15,355
	Chevrolet	Silverado cab. all 2RM 4.3 V6		25 060	$ 19,729
	Chevrolet	Silverado cab. rég 4RM 4.3 V6		25 235	$ 18,470
	Chevrolet	Silverado cab. all 4RM 4.8 V8		29 335	$ 23,524
	Chevrolet	Silverado cab. rég LS 2RM 4.3 V6		25 535	$ 19,601
	Chevrolet	Silverado cab. all LS 2RM 4.3 V6		28 860	$ 22,351
	Chevrolet	Silverado cab. rég LS 4RM 4.3 V6		29 035	$ 23,224
	Chevrolet	Silverado cab. allLS 4RM 4.8 V8		33 135	$ 26,146
	Chevrolet	Silverado cab. allLS 4RM 5.3 V8		34 045	$ 27,690
	Chevrolet	Silverado cab. All LT 2RM 4.8 V8		34 955	$ 28,110
	Chevrolet	Silverado cab. All LT 4RM 4.8 V8		38 600	$ 31,320
	Chevrolet	Silverado cab. All LT 4RM 5.3V8		39 510	$ 32,715
378	Chevrolet	S-10 cab.rég base		16 310	$ 12,590
	Chevrolet	S-10c ab.rég LS17 355		$ 13,612	
	Chevrolet	S-10 cab.rég xtreme		20 235	$ 13,590
	Chevrolet	S-10 cab.rég xtreme LS		21 205	$ 13,612
	Chevrolet	S-10 cab.rég base 4RM V6		21 270	$ 16,824
	Chevrolet	S-10 cab.rég LS 4 RM V6		22 755	$ 18,016
	Chevrolet	S-10 cab.all LS 19 140		$ 14,789	
	Chevrolet	S-10 cab.all. xtreme LS		22 625	$ 15,913
	Chevrolet	S-10 cab.all. LS 4RM V6		23 985	$ 18,847
364	Chevrolet/GMC	Suburban	1500 1/2	34 620	$ 25,575
	Chevrolet/GMC	Suburban	2500 3/4	35 720	$ 27,359
	Chevrolet/GMC	Suburban	1500 LS 1/2	41 570	$ 32,320
	Chevrolet/GMC	Suburban	2500 LS 3/4	42 540	$ 33,240
	Chevrolet/GMC	Suburban	1500 LT 1/2	45 525	$ 34,655
	Chevrolet/GMC	Suburban	2500 LT 3/4	46 095	$ 35,355
	Chevrolet/GMC	Suburban	1500 1/2t 4RM	37 620	$ 28,375
	Chevrolet/GMC	Suburban	2500 3/4 4RM	38 720	$ 29,959
	Chevrolet/GMC	Suburban	1500 1/2 LS 4 RM	44 570	
	Chevrolet/GMC	Suburban	2500 LS 3/4 4RM	45 540	
	Chevrolet/GMC	Suburban	1500 1/2 LT 4 RM	48 125	
	Chevrolet/GMC	Suburban	2500 3/4 4RM	49 095	
364	Chevrolet	Tahoe	base	34 395	$ 25,494
	Chevrolet	Tahoe	LT	35 755	
	Chevrolet	Tahoe	LT 4RM	50 360	$ 38 894
320	Chevrolet	Tracker	1.6 L	19 400	$ 13,925
	Chevrolet	Tracker	2.0L	21 310	$ 15,025
	Chevrolet	Tracker	base	20 615	$ 16,250
	Chevrolet	Tracker	base aut	21 850	
308	Chevrolet	Venture	cargo	25 115	$ 21,750
	Chevrolet	Venture	base	24 725	$ 20,450
	Chevrolet	Venture	base	25 900	$ 22,350
	Chevrolet	Venture	LS	28 680	$ 25,350
	Chevrolet	Venture	all.	27 030	$ 23,195
	Chevrolet	Venture	LS all.	29 810	
186	Chrysler	300M 2000	base	39 150	$ 29,085

2000 INDEX & PRICES

Page	Brand	Model		$ Canada	$ USA
110	Chrysler	Cirrus 2000	LX	22 180	
	Chrysler	Cirrus 2000	LXi	24 840	$ 19,935
162	Chrysler	Concorde 2000	base 2.7	27 635	$ 21,990
	Chrysler	Concorde 2000	LXi 3.2	32 355	$ 26,235
162	Chrysler	Intrepid 2000	base	25 060	$ 20,390
	Chrysler	Intrepid 2000	ES	29 425	$ 22,085
186	Chrysler	LHS 2000	base	41 450	$ 28,090
256	Chrysler	Sebring 2000	LX	23 380	$ 19,765
256	Chrysler	Sebring 2000	LXi	28 675	$ 22,100
	Chrysler	Sebring 2000	JX	32 335	$ 24,245
	Chrysler	Sebring 2000	JXi	34 960	$ 26,560
	Chrysler	Sebring 2000	JXi Ltd	35 230	
302	Chrysler	Town & Country 2000	LXi	41 260	$ 28,360
	Chrysler	Town & Country 2000	Limited	43 540	$ 34,625
	Chrysler	Town & Country 2000	Limited 4RM	46 760	$ 36,640
68	Daewoo	Lanos	S	12 495	$ 8,999
	Daewoo	Lanos	SX	15 295	$ 10,600
	Daewoo	Lanos	S	12 995	$ 9,699
	Daewoo	Lanos	SX	15 795	$ 10,900
112	Deawoo	Leganza	SE	-	$ 14,696
	Deawoo	Leganza	SX	20 295	$ 16,991
	Deawoo	Leganza	CDX	23 995	$ 18,911
82	Daewoo	Nubira	SX	16 295	$ 12,506
	Daewoo	Nubira	CDX	17 995	$ 13,810
	Daewoo	Nubira	SX	16 995	$ 13,106
	Daewoo	Nubira	CDX	18 995	$ 15,210
302	Dodge	Caravan	base 3.0	24 230	$ 18,685
	Dodge	Caravan	base 3.3	24 775	
	Dodge	Caravan	SE 3.3	27 445	$ 23,085
	Dodge	Caravan	SE 3.8	27 520	
	Dodge	Caravan	SE sport	29 450	
	Dodge	Caravan	LE	32 730	
	Dodge	Gd Caravan	base 3.0	25 890	$ 21 790
	Dodge	Gd Caravan	SE 3.3	28 255	
	Dodge	Gd Caravan	SE 3.8	28 330	$ 23,040
	Dodge	Gd Caravan	SE sport	30 260	$ 23,340
	Dodge	Gd Caravan	LE	33 745	$ 27,195
	Dodge	Gd Caravan	ES	36 120	$ 29,405
	Dodge	Gd Caravan	SE	34 765	$ 24,080
	Dodge	Gd Caravan	LE 4 RM	37 390	$ 30,370
	Dodge	Gd Caravan	ES 4 RM	39 610	$ 32,010
	Dodge	Dakota cab rég base 2.5L		17 585	$ 13,555
	Dodge	Dakota cab rég SLT 3.9 L		21 460	$ 13,820
	Dodge	Dakota cab rég SLT plus 3.9 L		22 425	
	Dodge	Dakota cab rég base 3.9L 4 RM		22 295	$ 17,030
	Dodge	Dakota cab. rég Magnum 5.2L 4 RM		24 000	
	Dodge	Dakota cab. rég sport 3.9 L 4 RM		23 910	
	Dodge	Dakota cab rég sport plus 5.2 L 4 RM		26 590	
	Dodge	Dakota cab rég SLT 3.9 L 4 RM		25 675	$ 18,030
	Dodge	Dakota cab rég SLT plus 3.9 L 4 RM		27 095	
	Dodge	Dakota cab all base 2.5L		20 950	$ 16,750
	Dodge	Dakota cab. all sport 2.5 L		21 075	
	Dodge	Dakota cab all sport plus 5.2 L		24 150	
	Dodge	Dakota cab all sport R/T 5.9 L		25 980	
	Dodge	Dakota cab all SLT 3.9 L		23 990	$ 17,750
	Dodge	Dakota cab all SLT plus 3.9 L		25 005	
	Dodge	Dakota cab all base 3.9L 4 RM		25 235	
	Dodge	Dakota cab. all sport 3.9 L 4 RM		25 630	
	Dodge	Dakota cab all sport plus 5.2 L 4 RM		28 250	
	Dodge	Dakotacab all SLT 3.9 L 4 RM		27 685	$ 19,955
	Dodge	DakotA cab all SLT plus 3.9 L 4 RM		29 105	
	Dodge	Dakota cab all SLT plus 5.2 L 4 RM		29 390	
336	Dodge	Durango	SLT 3.9L	36 030	$ 27,975
	Dodge	Durango	SLT 5.2L	36 705	$ 28,195
	Dodge	Durango	SLT 5.9L	37 215	$ 28,395
	Dodge	Durango	SLT plus 5.2L	39 255	
	Dodge	Durango	SLT plus 5.9L	39 765	
	Dodge	Durango	SLT 3.9L 4RM	37 395	$ 26, 895
	Dodge	Durango	SLT 5.2L 4RM	38 070	
	Dodge	Durango	SLT 5.9L 4RM	38 580	
	Dodge	Durango	SLT plus 5.2L 4RM	41 165	$ 32,795
	Dodge	Durango	SLT plus 5.9L 4RM	41 675	
	Dodge	Ram 1500	cab reg WS 3.9L	20 345	$ 14,895
	Dodge	Ram 1500	cab reg ST 3.9L	22 575	$ 16,960
386	Dodge	Ram 1500	club cab ST 5.2 L	26 255	
	Dodge	Ram 1500	quad cab ST 5.2L	27 245	
	Dodge	Ram 1500 cab reg ST 4 RM 5.2L		26 960	
	Dodge	Ram 1500 club cab ST 4RM 5.2L		29 790	
	Dodge	Ram 1500 quad cab ST 4RM 5.2L		30 780	
	Dodge	Ram 1500	cab rég SLT 5.2L	26 500	
	Dodge	Ram 1500	club cab SLT 5.2L	29 505	
	Dodge	Ram 1500	quad cab SLT 5.2L	30 495	$ 23,850
282	Dodge	Viper	R/T 10	93 255	$ 67,225
	Dodge	Viper	GTS	97 025	$ 69,725
	Ferrari	f-360	Modena		
	Ferrari	F-550	Maranello	295 000	

Page	Brand	Model		$ Canada	$ USA
	Ferrari	456	GT	315 750	
	Ferrari	456	GTA	321 800	
	Ferrari	F-355	spider	192 000	
114	Ford	Contour	LX	17 595	
	Ford	Contour	SE	19 695	$ 16,845
	Ford	Contour	SE V6	20 845	
	Ford	Contour	SVT	28 195	$ 22,715
164	Ford	Crown Victoria	base	31 895	$ 22,005
	Ford	Crown Victoria	LX	34 195	$ 24,120
	Ford	Excursion	5.4 XLT		$ 33,460
	Ford	Excursion	6.8 XLT		$ 36,775
338	Ford	Explorer	sport	28 995	$ 19,270
	Ford	Explorer	XL	29 895	
	Ford	Explorer	XLS	33 030	$ 23,290
	Ford	Explorer	XLT	36 395	$ 27,195
	Ford	Explorer	Eddie Bauer	41 795	$ 31,740
	Ford	Explorer	Limited	42 895	$ 31,995
	Ford	Explorer	sport 4RM	29 995	$ 23,070
	Ford	Explorer	XL 4RM	31 795	
	Ford	Explorer	XLS 4RM	34 930	$ 25,170
	Ford	Explorer	XLT 4RM	38 695	$ 29,150
	Ford	Explorer	XLT 4RM V8	40 095	
	Ford	Explorer	Eddie Bauer 4RM	44 295	$ 33,705
	Ford	Explorer	Eddie Bauer 4RM V8	45 195	$ 33,955
	Ford	Explorer	Limited 4RM	45 595	
	Ford	Explorer	Limited 4RM V8	46 595	$ 35,155
84	Ford	Focus	. base	14 895	$ 12,125
	Ford	Focus		17 595	$ 13,565
	Ford	Focus		15 595	$ 11,865
258	Ford	Mustang		20 995	$ 16,520
	Ford	Mustang	GT	27 995	$ 21,015
	Ford	Mustang	Cobra	36 995	$ 27,605
	Ford	Mustang		24 995	$ 21,370
	Ford	Mustang	GT	31 995	$ 25,270
	Ford	Mustang	Cobra	40 995	$ 31,605
148	Ford	Taurus	LX	24 495	$ 17,695
	Ford	Taurus	SE	25 595	$ 18,745
	Ford	Taurus	SE confort	26 495	$ 20,895
	Ford	Taurus	SE fam.	26 495	$ 19,900
	Ford	Taurus	SE confort fam.	27 695	
	Ford	Econoline	cargo base	24 295	
	Ford	Econoline	cargo RV	24 295	
	Ford	Econoline	Club XL	28 195	$ 22,445
	Ford	Econoline	Club XLT	31 595	$ 25,550
362	Ford	Expedition	XLT	41 195	
	Ford	Expedition	XLT 5.4	42 097	
	Ford	Expedition	Eddie Bauer	51 295	
376	Ford	Ranger cab rég XL 3.0L		15 595	$ 12,315
	Ford	Ranger cab rég XL Sport 3.0L		16 595	
	Ford	Ranger cab rég XLT 3.0L		18 495	$ 13,920
	Ford	Ranger cab rég Sport XLT 3.0L		18 995	
	Ford	Ranger cab rég XL 3.0L 4RM		20 895	$ 16,195
	Ford	Ranger cab rég XL Sport 3.0L 4RM		20 895	
	Ford	Ranger cab rég XLT 3.0L 4RM		22 995	$ 18,310
	Ford	Ranger cab rég Sport XLT 3.0L 4RM		23 495	
	Ford	Ranger super cab XL 3.0L		18 995	$ 15,300
	Ford	Ranger super cab XL Sport 3.0L		19 595	
	Ford	Ranger super cab XLT 3.0L		20 795	$ 16,020
	Ford	Ranger super cab Sport XLT 3.0L		21 295	
	Ford	Ranger super cab XL 3.0L 4RM		23 495	$ 17,355
	Ford	Ranger super cab XL Sport 3.0L 4RM		24 095	
	Ford	Rangersuper cab XLT 3.0L 4RM		24 895	
	Ford	Ranger super cab Sport XLT 3.0L 4RM		25 395	$ 19,435
388	Ford	Série F cab. rég base		20 695	$ 15,540
	Ford	Série F super cab. base		24 095	$ 18,840
	Ford	Série F cab. rég base 4RM		24 495	$ 19,040
	Ford	Série F cab. rég base 4RM 5.4L		27 358	
	Ford	Série F super cab. base 4RM 4.6L		27 995	
	Ford	Série F cab rég XL		21 495	$ 16,520
	Ford	Série F super cab. XL		25 495	$ 18,905
	Ford	Série F cab rég XL 4RM		25 895	$ 19,860
	Ford	Série F super cab. base 4RM 4.6L		29 695	$ 21,570
	Ford	Série F cab. rég XLT		25 895	$ 19,205
	Ford	Série F super cab. XLT		28 795	
	Ford	Série F cab. rég XLT 4RM		29 795	$ 22,620
	Ford	Série F super cab. XLT 4RM 4.6L		33 595	
	Ford	Série F cab. rég Lariat		33 195	$ 22,775
	Ford	Série F super cab. Lariat		37 395	$ 25,165
	Ford	Série F SVT Lighting		39 995	$ 29,355
304	Ford	Windstar	cargo	22 495	
	Ford	Windstar	base	24 295	$ 21,315
	Ford	Windstar	LX	28 195	$ 23,965
	Ford	Windstar	SE	31 795	$ 27,615
	Ford	Windstar	SEL	36 195	$ 30,515
	GMC	Yukon	Denali	58 565	

2000 INDEX & PRICES

Page	Brand	Model		$ Canada	$ USA
132	Honda	Accord	LX	23 800	$18,390
	Honda	Accord	EX	26 800	$20,700
	Honda	Accord	EX V6	31 000	$24,300
	Honda	Accord	DX	22 000	$15,200
	Honda	Accord	LX	24 300	$18,590
	Honda	Accord	EX cuir	27 500	$22,050
	Honda	Accord	EX V6 cuir	31 000	$22,850
86	Honda	Civic	hayon CX	14 200	$10,650
	Honda	Civic	hayon DX	15 200	$12,580
	Honda	Civic	coupé DX	16 200	
	Honda	Civic	coupé DX-G	17 700	
	Honda	Civic	coupé Si	18 800	$17,445
	Honda	Civic	coupé Si-G	20 300	
	Honda	Civic	berline LX	16 000	$14,830
	Honda	Civic	berline LX-G	17 500	
	Honda	Civic	berline EX	17 400	$16,730
	Honda	Civic	berline EX-G	18 900	
322	Honda	CR-V	LX	26 000	$18,950
	Honda	CR-V	EX	27 800	$21,250
310	Honda	Odyssey	LX	30 600	$23,200
	Honda	Odyssey	EX	33 600	$25,800
	Honda	Passport	2WD EX		$26,500
	Honda	Passport	2WD LX		$23,850
	Honda	Passport	4WD LX		$25,450
262	Honda	Prelude	base	27 800	$23,450
	Honda	Prelude	Type SH	31 800	$25,950
70	Hyundai	Accent	L	11 565	$8,999
	Hyundai	Accent	GSi	13 495	
	Hyundai	Accent	GL	12 995	$9,899
88	Hyundai	Elantra	GL	14 595	$11,499
	Hyundai	Elantra	GLS	17 695	$11,799
	Hyundai	Elantra	familiale GL	15 595	$12,399
	Hyundai	Elantra	familiale GLS	18 845	$12,499
134	Hyundai	Sonata	GL	19 495	$15,499
	Hyundai	Sonata	GLS	23 595	$17,499
264	Hyundai	Tiburon	base	17 895	$13,999
	Hyundai	Tiburon	FX	19 895	$14,899
	Hyundai	Tiburon	SE	20 895	
172	Infiniti	G20	Touring	29 950	$20,995
	Infiniti	G20	Luxury	32 950	$22,495
188	Infiniti	I30	de Luxe	39 700	$28,900
	Infiniti	I30	Touring	41 500	$32,200
222	Infiniti	Q45	touring	71 000	$49,900
	Infiniti	QX4	base	46 000	$33,550
	Isuzu	Amigo	2WD		$15,810
	Isuzu	Amigo	2WD V6		$18,330
	Isuzu	Amigo	4WD V6		$19,470
	Isuzu	Hombre	S	13 995	$11,545
	Isuzu	Hombre	XS allongé	16 995	$15,200
	Isuzu	Hombre	XS allongé 4RM V6	26 995	$20,075
342	Isuzu	Rodeo	S	29 660	$24,540
	Isuzu	Rodeo	LS	33 300	$27,490
	Isuzu	Rodeo	LSE	38 990	$30,150
	Isuzu	Oasis	base		$25,600
366	Isuzu	Trooper	S	32 975	$28,650
	Isuzu	Trooper	LS	37 995	
	Isuzu	Trooper	Limited	41 995	
	Isuzu	Vehi Cross			$28,900
246	Jaguar	XJ8	base	79 600	$55,200
	Jaguar	XJ8	Vanden Plas	90 600	$64,300
	Jaguar	XJ8	XJR	94 400	$68,450
	Jaguar	XK8	coupé	91 900	$65,750
	Jaguar	XK8	déc	99 900	$70 450
224	Jaguar	Type-S	V6 3.0L	59 950	$42,500
	Jaguar	Type-S	V8 4.0L	69 950	$48,000
90	Kia	Sephia	base	12 995	$9,995
	Kia	Sephia	LS	14 945	$10,995
328	Kia	Sportage	base	20 995	$14,795
	Kia	Sportage	base 4WD		$16,295
	Kia	Sportage	EX	23 595	$17,395
	Kia	Sportage	EX		$18,595
324	Jeep	Cherokee	SE	22 460	$16,445
	Jeep	Cherokee	SE	24 845	$17,485
	Jeep	Cherokee	Sport 4.0L	24 485	$18,870
	Jeep	Cherokee	Classic 4.0L	28 880	$21,370
	Jeep	Cherokee	Limited 4.0L	31 280	$23,090
324	Jeep	Cherokee	SE 4RM	24 680	$17,960
	Jeep	Cherokee	SE 4RM	26 210	$18,995
	Jeep	Cherokee	Sport 4.0L 4RM	26 705	$19,205
	Jeep	Cherokee	Sport 4.0L 4RM	28 240	
	Jeep	Cherokee	Classic 4.0L 4RM	30 245	$22,885
	Jeep	Cherokee	Limited 4.0L 4RM	33 285	$25,210
344	Jeep	Grand Cherokee Laredo		36 295	$26,570
	Jeep	Grand Cherokee Limited		43 300	$31,915
	Jeep	Grand Cherokee Laredo 4RM		37 195	$28,540
	Jeep	Grand Cherokee Limited 4RM		44 805	$34,345
	Jeep	Grand Cherokee Laredo V8 4RM		38 625	
	Jeep	Grand Cherokee Limited V8 4RM		46 235	
326	Jeep	TJ	SE	19 205	$14,460
	Jeep	TJ	Sport	22 310	$18,460
	Jeep	TJ	Sahara	25 305	$20,390
	Lamborghini	Diablo	VT	355 000	
	Lamborghini	Diablo	RoadsterVT	404 000	
	Lamborghini	Diablo	SV	379 000	
346	Land Rover	Discovery	SD	42 155	
	Land Rover	Discovery	LE	49 105	
	Land Rover	Discovery	LSE	54 105	
	Land Rover	Discovery II	5 pass	46 900	$34,150
	Land Rover	Discovery II	7 pass	49 900	
368	Land Rover	Range Rover	4.0 SE	84 000	$58,000
	Land Rover	Range Rover	4.6 HSE	96 000	$66,000
190	Lexus	ES300	base	44 235	$31,405
226	Lexus	GS300	base	59 220	$37,605
	Lexus	GS400	base	67 360	$46,005
248	Lexus	LS400	base	78 690	$53,805
370	Lexus	LX470	base	84 095	$59,005
348	Lexus	RX300	base	46 460	$32,505
	Lexus	SC300	base		$43,405
	Lexus	SC400	base		$55,905
228	Lincoln	Continental	base	52 795	$38,880
362	Lincoln	Navigator	base	63 795	$42,100$
			4WD	45,800	
230	Lincoln	Town Car	Executive	51 195	$38,630
	Lincoln	Town Car	Signature	52 595	$40,630
	Lincoln	Town Car	Cartier	54 495	$43,130
116	Mazda	626	DX	20 140	
	Mazda	626	LX	22 575	$18,245
	Mazda	626	LX V6	25 060	$19,445
	Mazda	626	ES V6	29 215	$22,445
194	Mazda	Millenia	2.3	39 595	$29,995
376	Mazda	Série-B	2500 SX cab. Courte	15 615	$11,495
	Mazda	Série-B	2500 SX cab. all	18 860	$15,995
	Mazda	Série-B	3000 SX cab. Courte	16 040	$11,890
	Mazda	Série-B	3000 Cab plus SX	18 395	
	Mazda	Série-B	3000 Cab plus SE	19 850	$16,465
	Mazda	Série-B	3000 cab courte 4RM	20 320	
	Mazda	Série-B	4000 Cab plus SX	19 735	
	Mazda	Série-B	4000 Cab plus SE	20 645	$16,865
	Mazda	Série-B	4000 Cab plus SE-Plus	24 265	
	Mazda	Série-B	4000 Cab all. SE	20 645	
	Mazda	Série-B	4000 Cab all. SE-Plus	24 265	$20,630
	Mazda	Série-B	4000 Cab Plus. SX 4 RM	24 075	$19,830
	Mazda	Série-B	4000 Cab Plus. SE 4 RM	24 975	$20,930
	Mazda	Série-B	4000 Cab Plus. SE Plus 4 RM	27 560	
	Mazda	Série-B	4000 Cab all. SE 4 RM	24 975	
312	Mazda	MPV	DX	24 555	$19,995
	Mazda	MPV	LX	28 455	$22,050
	Mazda	MPV	LX-Sport	30 255	
	Mazda	MPV	ES	33 080	$25,550
266	Mazda	Miata	base	26 025	$21,245
	Mazda	Miata	10th	35 650	
92	Mazda	Protegé	DX	14 970	$11,970
	Mazda	Protegé	SE	15 615	$13,245
	Mazda	Protegé	LX	17 295	$15,040
196	Mercedes-Benz	Classe C	230 Classic	37 950	
	Mercedes-Benz	Classe C	230 Kompressor	37 950	$31,200
	Mercedes-Benz	Classe C	230 Elegance	43 850	
	Mercedes-Benz	Classe C	230 Sport	45 650	
	Mercedes-Benz	Classe C	280	49 950	$35,600
	Mercedes-Benz	Classe C	280 sport	51 750	
	Mercedes-Benz	Classe C	C43	75 700	$53,000
288	Mercedes-Benz	CLK	320	57 750	$40,600

2000 INDEX & PRICES

Page	Brand	Model		$ Canada	$ USA
	Mercedes-Benz	CLK	320	67 750	$ 47,200
	Mercedes-Benz	CLK	430	68 750	$ 47,900
232	Mercedes-Benz	Classe E	300 TD	59 950	$ 42,400
	Mercedes-Benz	Classe E	320	66 750	$ 47,200
	Mercedes-Benz	Classe E	320 4-Matic	70 450	$ 48,990
	Mercedes-Benz	Classe E	320	67 500	$ 47,200
	Mercedes-Benz	Classe E	320 4-Matic	71 500	$ 49,900
	Mercedes-Benz	Classe E	430	74 250	$ 51,300
	Mercedes-Benz	Classe E	E55	98 900	$ 69,100
350	Mercedes-Benz	Classe M	320 Classic	47 550	$ 34,950
	Mercedes-Benz	Classe M	320 Elégance	53 500	
	Mercedes-Benz	Classe M	430	59 950	$ 43,750
	Mercedes-Benz	Classe M	ML55	octobre	
250	Mercedes-Benz	Classe S	430 short	92 500	
	Mercedes-Benz	Classe S	430 all	98 500	$ 69,700
	Mercedes-Benz	Classe S	500	112 850	$ 77,850
	Mercedes-Benz	Classe SL	500	115 900	$ 81,100
	Mercedes-Benz	Classe SL	600	165 750	$ 126,900
	Mercedes-Benz	CL	500		$ 91,900
	Mercedes-Benz	CL	600		$ 137,300
268	Mercury	Cougar	base	19 995	$ 16,445
	Mercury	Cougar	V6	21 895	$ 16,945
164	Mercury	Grand Marquis	GS	33 695	$ 22,415
	Mercury	Grand Marquis	LS	35 195	$ 24,415
114	Mercury	Mystique	GS	17 995	$ 16,145
	Mercury	Mystique	LS	20 095	$ 17,445
	Mercury	Mystique	LS V6	21 245	
148	Mercury	Sable	GS	24 595	$ 18,845
	Mercury	Sable	LS	25 295	$ 19,945
	Mercury	Sable	LS premium	27 395	$ 21,245
	Mercury	Sable	LS	25 795	$ 20,645
	Mercury	Sable	LS premium	27 895	$ 22,345
314	Mercury	Villager	base		$ 22,415
	Mercury	Villager	sport		$ 25,415
	Mitsubishi	Eclipse	GS man		$ 19,047
	Mitsubishi	Eclipse	GT man		$ 20,187
	Mitsubishi	Eclipse	RS man		$ 16,697
118	Mitsubishi	Galant	DE		$ 13,357
	Mitsubishi	Galant	ES		$ 18,257
	Mitsubishi	Galant	ES V6		$ 20,157
	Mitsubishi	Galant	GTZ		$ 23,757
	Mitsubishi	Galant	LS V6		$ 23,657
120	Nissan	Altima	XE	19 898	$ 14,990
	Nissan	Altima	GXE	21 998	$ 17,190
	Nissan	Altima	SE	25 398	$ 18,490
	Nissan	Altima	GLE	27 998	$ 19,990
380	Nissan	Frontier	King Cab XE 4 cyl	19 998	$ 13,540
	Nissan	Frontier	King Cab XE 6 cyl	22 998	
	Nissan	Frontier	Crew Cab XE	24 998	$ 17,290
	Nissan	Frontier	Crew Cab SE	27 698	$ 18,590
	Nissan	Frontier	King Cab XE 6 cyl 4RM	23 998	$ 18,340
	Nissan	Frontier	Crew Cab XE 4RM	27 998	$ 19,890
	Nissan	Frontier	Crew Cab SE 4 RM	30 798	$ 21,190
	Nissan	Frontier	Desert Runner		$ 17,890
136	Nissan	Maxima	GXE	28 590	$ 21,049
	Nissan	Maxima	SE	34 000	$ 23,649
	Nissan	Maxima	GLE	34 900	$ 26,249
94	Nissan	Sentra	XE	15 398	$ 11,799
	Nissan	Sentra	GXE	17 898	$ 14,199
	Nissan	Sentra	SE	21 998	$ 15,199
352	Nissan	Pathfinder	XE	33 298	$ 27,149
	Nissan	Pathfinder	SE	36 298	$ 30,249
	Nissan	Pathfinder	LE	41 498	$ 31,199
314	Nissan	Quest	GXE	27 798	$ 22,159
	Nissan	Quest	SE	32 498	$ 23,899
	Nissan	Quest	GLE	35 998	$ 26,299
330	Nissan	Xterra	4 cyl		$ 17,349
	Nissan	Xterra	2RM V6		$ 22,549
	Nissan	Xterra	4RM V6		$ 24,549
122	Oldsmobile	Alero	GX	20 995	$ 15,675
	Oldsmobile	Alero	GL	23 295	$ 17,650
	Oldsmobile	Alero	GLS	26 920	$ 21,635
	Oldsmobile	Alero	GX	20 995	$ 15,675
	Oldsmobile	Alero	GL	23 295	$ 17,650
	Oldsmobile	Alero	GLX	26 920	$ 21,365
200	Oldsmobile	Aurora	base	46 190	$ 36,229
150	Oldsmobile	Intrigue	GX 3.5L	27 994	$ 22,090
	Oldsmobile	Intrigue	GL 3.5L	29 574	$ 23,720
	Oldsmobile	Intrigue	GLS 3.5L	31 839	$ 25,720
308	Oldsmobile	Silhouette	GS	30 140	
	Oldsmobile	Silhouette	GL all.	30 160	$ 24,950
	Oldsmobile	Silhouette	GLS all	34 490	$ 28,640
	Oldsmobile	Silhouette	Premium	38 680	$ 31,550
302	Plymouth	Voyager	base	24 230	$ 18,865
	Plymouth	Voyager	SE	27 445	$ 23,085
	Plymouth	Voyager	SE Expresso	29 385	$ 24,680
	Plymouth	Voyager	LE	32 730	
	Plymouth	Grand Voyager	base	25 890	$ 21,690
	Plymouth	Grand Voyager	SE	28 255	$ 24,080
	Plymouth	Grand Voyager	SE Expresso	30 195	
	Plymouth	Grand Voyager	LE	33 745	
	Plymouth	Grand Voyager	SE 4RM	34 765	
	Plymouth	Grand Voyager	LE 4RM	37 390	
292	Plymouth	Prowler	base	55 000	$ 42,700
166	Pontiac	Bonneville	SE	30 740	$ 23,680
	Pontiac	Bonneville	SLE	35 685	$ 27,380
	Pontiac	Bonneville	SSEi	41 995	$ 31,635
260	Pontiac	Firebird	base V6	24 865	$ 18,490
	Pontiac	Firebird	base V6	33 265	$ 25,110
	Pontiac	Firebird	Formula	30 430	$ 23,530
	Pontiac	Firebird	Formula Ram Air	34 525	
	Pontiac	Firebird	Trans Am	34 750	$ 26,630
	Pontiac	Firebird	Trans Am Ram Air	38 845	
	Pontiac	Firebird	Trans Am	40 320	$ 30,700
	Pontiac	Firebird	Trans Am Ram Air	44 415	
124	Pontiac	Grand Am	SE	21 795	$ 15,920
	Pontiac	Grand Am	GT	26 020	$ 19,550
	Pontiac	Grand Am	SE	21 795	$ 16,220
	Pontiac	Grand Am	GT	26 020	$ 19,850
152	Pontiac	Grand Prix	GT	27 489	$ 21,395
	Pontiac	Grand Prix	GTP	30 970	$ 24,160
	Pontiac	Grand Prix	SE 3.1	25 399	
	Pontiac	Grand Prix	SE 3.8	26 524	$ 19,815
	Pontiac	Grand Prix	GT	27 489	$ 21,545
	Pontiac	Grand Prix	GTP	30 970	$ 24,310
78	Pontiac	Sunfire	SE	16 165	$ 13,910
	Pontiac	Sunfire	GT	20 605	$ 16,210
	Pontiac	Sunfire	SE 2.2L	16 135	$ 14,010
	Pontiac	Sunfire	SE 2.4L	22 105	
	Pontiac	Sunfire	GT	27 790	
	Pontiac	Sunfire	GT	-	$ 21,610
308	Pontiac	Transport	base	25 130	$ 19,895
	Pontiac	Transport	base	27 465	$ 22,325
	Pontiac	Transport	all.	28 595	
	Pontiac	Transport	Montana	28 565	$ 23,225
	Pontiac	Transport	Montana all.	30 905	
294	Porsche	911	Carrera	95 200	$ 65,030
	Porsche	911 Carrera Tiptronic		100 030	$ 68,450
	Porsche	911	Carrera 4	103 200	$ 70,480
	Porsche	911 Carrera 4 Tiptronic		108 030	$ 73,900
	Porsche	911	Carrera déc	109 000	$ 74,460
	Porsche	911 Carrera déc tiptronic		113 830	$ 77,880
	Porsche	911	Carrera 4 déc	117 000	$ 79,920
	Porsche	911 Carrera 4 déc tiptronic		121 830	$ 83,340
294	Porsche	Boxster	base	58 400	$ 41,000
	Porsche	Boxster	tiptronic	62 938	
	Rolls-Royce	Silver dawn		315 000	
	Rolls-Royce	Silver spur		355 000	
	Rolls-Royce	Spur		385 000	
	Rolls-Royce	Limousine		405 000	
202	Saab	9-3	base	33 800	$ 25,900
	Saab	9-3	base	33 200	$ 26,400
	Saab	9-3	SE	39 350	$ 31,700
	Saab	9-3		50 650	$ 39,450
	Saab	9-3	SE	57 750	$ 42,995
	Saab	9-3	Viggen		$ 37,750
234	Saab	9-5	base 4 cyl	40 200	$ 31,025
	Saab	9-5	base 6 cyl	40 200	$ 31,025
	Saab	9-5	SE	50 850	$ 34,225
	Saab	9-5	Aero	53 300	
	Saab	9-5	wgn V6	48 900	$ 36,900
96	Saturn	SC1		15 493	$ 12,535
	Saturn	SC1		16 618	
	Saturn	SC2		18 768	
	Saturn	SC2		20 848	$ 15,145
	Saturn	SL		13 488	$ 10,685
	Saturn	SL1		14 398	$ 12,345
	Saturn	SL2		17 183	$ 12,895
	Saturn	SW1		16 118	
	Saturn	SW2		20 348	$ 14,290
138	Saturn	LS	base	20 075	$ 15,010
	Saturn	LS1	base	22 440	$ 16,750
	Saturn	LS2	base	26 940	$ 20,135
	Saturn	LW1	base	25 220	$ 18,835

2000 INDEX & PRICES

Page	Brand	Model		$ Canada	$ USA
	Saturn	LW2	base	28 630	$ 21,360
	Subaru	Forester	L	26 695	$ 20,095
	Subaru	Forester	S	30 795	$ 22,595
	Subaru	Forester	Limited	33 195	
	Subaru	Impreza	RS	26 395	$ 19,295
	Subaru	Impreza	TS	21 995	
	Subaru	Impreza	Sport brighton	17 795	$ 16,295
	Subaru	Impreza	Sport Outback	24 995	$ 18,095
	Subaru	Legacy	Brighton wgn		$ 18,395
	Subaru	Legacy	Outback wgn		$ 25,895
	Subaru	Legacy	GT wgn		$ 23,695
	Subaru	Legacy	GT sdn		$ 22,795
	Subaru	Legacy	LTD sdn		$ 24,295
	Subaru	Legacy	L sdn		$ 19,195
98	Suzuki	Esteem	GL	13 995	$ 12,199
	Suzuki	Esteem	GLX	17 195	$ 13,299
	Suzuki	Esteem	wgn. GL	14 695	$ 12,699
	Suzuki	Esteem	wgn. GLX	18 495	$ 13,799
66	Suzuki	Swift	DLX	11 595	$ 9,099
320	Suzuki	Vitara	JA	17 795	$ 13,499
	Suzuki	Vitara	JX	19 995	$ 15,299
	Suzuki	Vitara	JX	22 295	$ 16,999
	Suzuki	Vitara	JX Deluxe	19 995	$ 17,999
	Suzuki	Grand Vitara	JX	23 495	$ 18,999
	Suzuki	Grand Vitara	JLX	26 495	$ 19,999
154	Toyota	Avalon	XL	35 895	$ 25,538
	Toyota	Avalon	XLS	42 805	$ 28,708
140	Toyota	Camry	CE	21 760	$ 17,418
	Toyota	Camry	CE V6	28 435	
	Toyota	Camry	LE	27 150	$ 20,288
	Toyota	Camry	XLE	31 425	$ 23,968
	Toyota	Solara	SE	26 245	$ 18,938
	Toyota	Solara	SE V6	29 815	$ 21,468
	Toyota	Solara	SLE	33 800	$ 26,098
270	Toyota	Celica	GT man	23 980	$ 21,240
	Toyota	Celica	GT aut	24 980	$ 22,240
	Toyota	Celica	GTS man	31 675	
	Toyota	Celica	GTS aut	32 545	
100	Toyota	Corolla	Base	15 180	$ 12,418
	Toyota	Corolla	CE	16 790	$ 13,108
	Toyota	Corolla	LE	20 155	$ 15,068
74	Toyota	Echo	man	13 835	-
	Toyota	Echo	aut.	14 835	-
	Toyota	Echo	man	14 175	-
	Toyota	Echo	aut	15 175	-
322	Toyota	RAV4		22 150	$ 16,668
	Toyota	RAV4	base	23 550	
	Toyota	RAV4	base	23 975	$ 18,078
316	Toyota	Sienna	cargo	24 830	
	Toyota	Sienna	CE	26 020	$ 21,608
	Toyota	Sienna	CE	27 200	$ 22,498
	Toyota	Sienna	LE	30 240	$ 24,538
	Toyota	Sienna	XLE	35 405	$ 26,574
354	Toyota	4Runner	base	-	$ 21,938
	Toyota	4Runner	SR5	30 800	$ 25,958
	Toyota	4Runner	SR5 V6	36 035	$ 28,008
	Toyota	4Runner	Limited	47 270	$ 36,468
382	Toyota	Tacoma	cab.reg	16 505	$ 11,428
	Toyota	Tacoma	xtracab	19 605	$ 13,978
	Toyota	Tacoma	xtracab 4RM	25 855	$ 17,748
	Toyota	Tacoma	xtracab 4RM V6	29 512	$ 19,738
	Toyota	Tacoma	xtracab SR5 4RM V6	35 465	$ 25,178
392	Toyota	Tundra	V6 man SR5 access cab		$ 20,175
	Toyota	Tundra	V6 man SR5 4 RM acc cab		$ 23,375
	Toyota	Tundra	V8 2 RM access cab		$ 24,495
	Toyota	Tundra	V8 4 RM access cab		$ 27,830
	Toyota	Tundra	Cab. reg V6		$ 15,835
	Toyota	Tundra	Cab. reg V6 SR5		$ 21,095
	Toyota	Tundra	Cab. reg V8 SR5		$ 22,710
	Toyota	Tundra	Pre-Runner V6 auto		$ 17,868
	Volkswagen	EuroVan	GLS	45 050	$ 31,300
	Volkswagen	EuroVan	MV	47 320	$ 32,800
126	Volkswagen	Golf	GL	18 950	$ 14,900
	Volkswagen	Golf	GL TDi	20 800	$ 16,195
	Volkswagen	Golf	GLS	21 800	$ 16,350
	Volkswagen	Golf	GLS TDi	23 300	$17,400
	Volkswagen	Golf	Gti GLS	23 950	$ 17,675
	Volkswagen	Golf	GTI GLX	29 800	$ 22,620
	Volkswagen	Golf	cabrio GL	29 100	
	Volkswagen	Golf	cabrio GL S	33 650	
	Volkswagen	Jetta	GL	20 990	$ 16,700

Page	Brand	Model		$ Canada	$ USA
126	Volkswagen	Jetta	GL TDi	22 850	$ 17,995
	Volkswagen	Jetta	GLS	23 100	$ 17,650
	Volkswagen	Jetta	GLS TDi	24 600	$ 18,700
	Volkswagen	Jetta	GLS VR6	25 990	$ 19,950
	Volkswagen	Jetta	GLX VR6	31 650	$ 24,110
102	Volkswagen	New Beetle	GL	21 500	$ 15,900
	Volkswagen	New Beetle	GLS	22 300	$ 16,850
	Volkswagen	New Beetle	GLS TDi	23 800	$ 17,900
	Volkswagen	New Beetle	1.8T	25 350	$ 19,000
	Volkswagen	New Beetle	GLX Turbo	28 050	$ 21,075
142	Volkswagen	Passat	GLS	29 100	$ 21,200
	Volkswagen	Passat	GLS V6	32 750	$ 23,800
	Volkswagen	Passat	GLX	38 300	$ 28,150
	Volkswagen	Passat	GLS wgn	29 900	
296	Volvo	C70	LT	49 995	$ 34,000
	Volvo	C70	HT	54 695	$ 43,500
	Volvo	C70	LT	58 995	$ 39,000
	Volvo	C70	HT	63 695	$ 45,500
236	Volvo	S80	2.9	49 995	$ 36,000
	Volvo	S80	T-6	55 995	$ 40,500
204	Volvo	S70	base	34 995	$ 27,500
	Volvo	S70	base STD	36 595	
	Volvo	S70	GLT Turbo	41 995	$ 31,700
	Volvo	S70	T5 Turbo	43 995	$ 33,300
	Volvo	V70	base	36 295	$ 28,800
	Volvo	V70	base STD	37 895	
	Volvo	V70	GLT turbo	43 295	$ 33,000
	Volvo	V70	T5 turbo	45 295	
	Volvo	V70	Turbo	45 495	$ 33,600
	Volvo	V70	Turbo-R	55 595	$ 41,000
	Volvo	V70	XC	48 365	$ 36,100